The Priority of John

John A. T. Robinson

THE PRIORITY OF JOHN

Edited by J. F. Coakley

SCM PRESS LTD

British Library Cataloguing in Publication Data

Robinson, John A. T.
The priority of John.
1. Bible. N. T. John——Chronology
I. Title II. Coakley, J. E.
226'.5066 BS2615.2

ISBN 0-334-02273-8

334 02273 8

First published 1985
by SCM Press Ltd
26–30 Tottenham Road, London N1

Photoset by The Spartan Press Ltd, Lymington
and printed in Great Britain by
The Camelot Press Ltd
Southampton

Contents

Editor's Note

John Robinson had produced a complete draft of the eight chapters of *The Priority of John* not long before his final illness was diagnosed in June 1983. At that point he had intended to break off and write the text of the Bampton Lectures for 1984 which would form a shorter and less technical exposition of the same thesis, and then to return to the final making-ready of the larger book. Judging however that he might not be able to carry out this latter task himself, he asked me in that case to see the typescript through to its publication, with the help and counsel of Professor C. F. D. Moule. (His introduction to this book dates from about this moment, and does not quite correspond to the turn of events.) When a little later he prevailed on Professor Moule to prepare and deliver the Lectures themselves in his place, he felt freed to give his remaining time to unfinished matters not directly connected with the present work.

The manuscript behind this book thus lacked the author's final touches. That these touches would have included fresh observations and arguments is clear from a mass of references and notes on slips marked 'check' or 'for incorporation' which he passed on to me and invited me to follow up. In the end however I thought it improper, as well as impracticable, to add to the book in trying to imitate the use he would himself have made of them. At the same time, Dr Robinson intended to make some abridgements, especially in the interests of streamlining the very full documentation in the footnotes and the occasional excursive or pace-slowing remarks in the text. Again he invited me to carry out this job, but since the publishers kindly applied no pressure in this direction it seemed better in general to leave the text and notes as they stood so that nothing that Dr Robinson thought it worth recording should be lost. What minor improvements and corrections I or Professor Moule have ventured to make have been at points where we felt so certain that he would have concurred that square brackets or the like would have been pedantic. Perhaps to the detriment of the analogy with the Fourth Gospel drawn by Dr Robinson in his Introduction, some roughness of liaison among the chapters has been repaired by eliminating duplications and adding cross-references.

I am glad to thank Mr Robert Esdaile for sharing in the editor's task by preparing the indices. It has also been a pleasure to have the support and help of Mr Stephen Robinson, especially in proof-reading.

J. F. COAKLEY

Introduction

It is a great honour to be appointed Bampton Lecturer. Yet I confess that I let my name go forward partly as a theological joke. For I discovered that almost exactly 200 years ago the lectures were given by George Croft,[1] Vicar of Arncliffe, the village of (now) some 60 souls in the Yorkshire Dales in which I live; and I thought this might be something of a local record. I fear they reveal no great original scholarship or depth of divinity. In fact they were precisely what in form they still are: eight university sermons from the pulpit of St Mary's, Oxford.

No doubt the lecturer-preacher was not then so conscious of the restriction of sermon-length to which the twentieth century has become accustomed and the exigencies of the modern liturgical round into which they have to be slotted. But today the invitation presents an almost impossible double exercise. One is expected by tradition to produce something of a *magnum opus* and at the same time to confine it to eight gobbets of half-an-hour plus, and even this hardly provides enough material for the commercial publication upon which the stipend depends! Various lecturers have met the problem in various ways, by expansion or contraction. But my intention is to produce two books, one heavy one (this) for the scholars and another popular version of more general appeal. For as Sir Edwyn Hoskyns said, 'Whatever the Fourth Gospel may be, it is not a text-book of metaphysics. Primarily it is the text-book of the parish priest and the inspiration of the straightforward layman.'[2] In that version I can skip most of the references to the on-going altercations between academics which make the other indigestible and also dated. In fact if I had the courage of my convictions, I would omit even from this all secondary references,[3] as my mentor C. H. Dodd was almost bold enough to do in

[1]*Eight Sermons Preached before the University of Oxford, in the Year 1786*, Oxford 1786. Their theme was 'a Vindication of the Church of England against the objections of the principal Sects' (3).

[2]E. C. Hoskyns and F. N. Davey, *The Fourth Gospel*, 1940, 6.

[3]For a courageous example of this, see R. Banks, *Paul's Idea of Community*, Exeter 1980.

his last, and what I still regard as his greatest, academic book, *Historical Tradition in the Fourth Gospel*,[4] which originally formed the first of the series of Sarum Lectures financed every other year from the same Bampton foundation. But the rest of us cannot presume to emulate that eminence. And especially when one is taking one's stand against the stream of critical orthodoxy, as I was in my *Redating the New Testament*,[5] one is bound to show that one has at least taken account of trends one rejects. The fashions and the follies of Johannine scholarship have perhaps swung to greater extremes than in most areas of New Testament study.[6] But even when one dissents from the assumptions, judgments or methods one can learn from them and has a duty to oppose presumptions with something else than other presumptions.

From my host of distinguished predecessors as Bampton Lecturers I would allude here to three others.

The first is the last set of lectures which chose St John as its subject, those of 1890, published under the title of *Modern Criticism Considered in Relation to the Fourth Gospel* by H. W. Watkins.[7] For the seed was sown for them by one of my heroes on this as on other subjects, Bishop J. B. Lightfoot,[8] during his last illness. Lightfoot subsequently wrote to Watkins saying: 'I have read your scheme, and entirely

[4]1963.

[5]1976. It is interesting that C. K. Barrett, whose great commentary, *The Gospel According to St John*, [1]1955; [2]1978, strikes me as the epitome of the critical orthodoxy from which I find myself departing, feels equally conscious of standing against the tide of much recent scholarship. He writes:

> To some of the most popular opinions I do not subscribe. I do not believe that Q holds the key to John; I do not believe that it is a Palestinian work aimed at Diaspora Judaism; I do not believe that it is possible to isolate sources, unless perhaps we should describe Mark as a source; I do not believe that John intended to supply us with historically verifiable information regarding the life and teaching of Jesus, and that historical traditions of great worth can be disentangled from his interpretative comments ([2]viii).

It is interesting that he makes virtually no reference to Dodd's *Historical Tradition* in his introduction.

[6]For successive surveys one can try H. W. Watkins, *Modern Criticism Considered in Relation to the Fourth Gospel*, London and New York 1890; B. W. Bacon, *The Fourth Gospel in Research and Debate*, New Haven and London [1]1910; [2]1918; W. F. Howard, *The Fourth Gospel in Recent Criticism and Interpretation*, 1931; [2](revised by C. K. Barrett) 1955; and R. Kysar, *The Fourth Evangelist and his Gospel: An Examination of Contemporary Scholarship*, 1975.

[7]For the details see the previous note.

[8]Cf. my *Joseph Barber Lightfoot*, Durham Cathedral Lecture, 1981, especially 16–19.

approve of it. No subject could be more useful at the present day.'[9] Lightfoot himself had lectured on John at Cambridge[10] before Westcott returned as Regius Professor in 1870, and nearly 200 pages of three other pieces of his on the Gospel were reproduced posthumously in his *Biblical Essays*[11] – and have been ignored by commentators ever since. In allowing the first of these, 'Internal Evidence for the Authenticity and Genuineness of St John's Gospel', given originally as a public lecture in 1871, to be reissued shortly before (or, in the event, after) his death[12] he said that he had withheld its publication previously because he had hoped to do more justice to it, but now, because it was rumoured that he was dissatisfied with it, he decided to have it printed 'in exactly the same form' to make it clear that eighteen years later he had nothing to withdraw.[13] He remained firm to the end on what he called the 'authenticity' and historicity of John, closing still with this 'brief confession of faith' which is the more significant coming from one who occupied most of his academic life commenting on Paul and the Apostolic Fathers: 'I believe from my heart that the truth which this Gospel more especially enshrines – the truth that Jesus Christ is the very Word Incarnate, the manifestation of the Father to all mankind – is the one lesson which, duly apprehended, will do more than all our feeble efforts to purify and elevate human life here by imparting to it hope and light and strength, the one study which alone can fitly prepare us for a joyful immortality hereafter.'[14]

Watkins was Archdeacon of Durham and had the nickname of him 'that leadeth Joseph like a sheep' (Ps. 80.1) – though it is hard to believe that the Bishop allowed anyone to lead him by the nose. Watkins was a

[9] *Modern Criticism*, viii.

[10] The manuscript of his notes is in the Durham Cathedral Library.

[11] London and New York 1893, 1–198. I have manuscript lecture-notes from my father of the last two in the form delivered at Cambridge in 1873, which contain additional material to the 1867–8 version that was printed in *Biblical Essays*.

[12] *The Expositor*, 4th Series, I, Jan.–Mar. 1890, 1–21, 81–92, 176–88.

[13] *Biblical Essays*, 3f.

[14] *Ibid.*, 43f. It is also reproduced as the summary of Lightfoot's faith in the sole, very inadequate, biography of him edited by G. R. Eden and F. C. Macdonald, *Lightfoot of Durham*, Cambridge and New York 1932, which also included this comment by A. C. Headlam: 'I think that on almost every main point which Lightfoot discussed, his judgment has prevailed. The one exception is the Johannine literature, and there our judgment must still be uncertain. The world of scholars is not prepared to accept the genuineness of the Fourth Gospel in the way that it accepts the genuineness of the Ignatian Epistles, but what will be the final verdict, I don't think any of us is quite prepared to say' (139). Headlam himself did not shift from his own conservative opinion.

fulsome – excessively fulsome – admirer,[15] and his work, unlike his master's, is spoilt by too blatant an apologetic interest.[16] Nevertheless it is an impressively learned survey (albeit with a strongly conservative bias) of all Continental and British criticism of the Gospel to date; and it is the more remarkable because of the extraordinary speed with which it was prepared (and he sent off his manuscript to the publishers the day after the last lecture) and the fact that, as well as running the Diocese as Archdeacon in the interregnum, his own chair was that of Hebrew!

The second series of Bampton Lectures to which I would allude is also the most neglected. These were those for 1913 by George Edmundson, *The Church in Rome in the First Century*,[17] which were evidently completely swamped by the First World War and as far as I can discover were never reviewed in any theological, historical or classical journal. By a piece of good fortune I discovered them in the course of preparing my *Redating the New Testament* and sought to resurrect and rehabilitate his rather notable contribution.[18] And it so happens that he gave his Bamptons at exactly the same age as I – sixty-four.

The third is a series, on which I shall be drawing several times, by my friend Geoffrey Lampe, *God as Spirit*.[19] Not only did I find myself in greater theological affinity with him than most of my other Cambridge colleagues, but, as later emerged, he gave the Lectures under the threat of the same fell disease from which I am suffering and he showed us if anyone did how a Christian should face death.[20]

Finally, I cannot end without thanking once again my incredibly long-suffering secretary, Stella Haughton, and also Trinity College, Cambridge, for granting me sabbatical and sickness leave. I wish too to thank, among many others, my former pupil J. F. Coakley of Lancaster

[15]Cf. *Modern Criticism and the Fourth Gospel*, 163–5, 350–3. He also wrote the anonymous memoir of Lightfoot published in *The Quarterly Review* 176, 1893, 73–105, and subsequently reprinted with a preface by Westcott, *Bishop Lightfoot*, London 1894.

[16]Cf. A. von Harnack's judgment on Lightfoot: 'There has never been an apologist who was less of an advocate than Lightfoot. . . . He has never defended a tradition for the tradition's sake.'

[17]London 1913.

[18]Cf. especially my biographical footnote on him in *Redating the New Testament*, 349.

[19]Oxford 1977; reissued London 1983.

[20]Cf. especially his moving Mere's Commemoration Sermon on 'Preparation for Death', which I was privileged to hear, reprinted in his *Explorations in Theology*, London 1981, 130–37, and in *G. W. H. Lampe, Christian, Scholar, Churchman: A Memoir by Friends*, ed. C. F. D. Moule, London 1982, 137–44.

University for checking endless unrewarding details with his usual cheerful and meticulous precision and Charlie Moule, my dear friend and predecessor as Dean of Clare, for overseeing the work of editing. Jean Cunningham undertook in her retirement the copy-editing of the book, and I should echo the tribute in Edward Schillebeeckx' book *Christ*, 'Those theologians whose books go through her hands are the most fortunate in the world.'[21]

It has been the fate of many books on John to be left unfinished,[22] for its interpretation naturally forms the crowning of a lifetime. I have myself been intending to write a book on the Fourth Gospel since the 'fifties, before I broke off (reluctantly) to be Bishop of Woolwich, though I am grateful now that I did not produce it prematurely at that time. It means however that I shall be compelled to refer to and often recapitulate material directly or indirectly related to the Johannine literature which I have written over the years (some of it indeed while I was bishop).

Many scholars in fact, if not most now, think that the author of the Gospel himself never lived to finish it and have seen the work as the product of numerous hands and redactors. As will become clear,[23] I prefer to believe that the ancient testimony of the church is correct that John wrote it 'while still in the body' and that its roughnesses, self-corrections and failures of connection, real or imagined, are the result of its *not* having been smoothly or finally edited. If so I am in good company. At any rate who could wish for a better last testimony from his friends than that 'his witness is true' (John 21.24)? In other words, he got it right – historically and theologically.

[21] *Christ*, ET 1980, 6.

[22] E.g., among recent commentaries, those by Scott Holland, E. C. Hoskyns, R. H. Lightfoot and J. N. Sanders.

[23] Chapter I, below.

Abbreviations

AASOR	*Annual of the American Schools of Oriental Research*, New Haven, Conn.
ATANT	Abhandlungen zur Theologie des Alten und Neuen Testaments, Zürich
AV	Authorized Version of the Bible
BA	*Biblical Archaeologist*, New Haven, Conn., Ann Arbor, Mich.
BASOR	*Bulletin of the American Schools of Oriental Research*, New Haven, Conn.
BETL	Bibliotheca Ephemeridum Theologicarum Lovaniensium, Louvain
Bibl	*Biblica*, Rome
BJ	Josephus, *Bellum Judaicum*
BJRL	*Bulletin of the John Rylands Library*, Manchester
BZNW	Beihefte zur *Zeitschrift für die neutestamentliche Wissenschaft*, Berlin
CBQ	*Catholic Biblical Quarterly*, Washington, D.C.
Compendia	*Compendia rerum Judaicarum ad Novum Testamentum: The Jewish People in the First Century, Historical Geography, Political History, Social, Cultural and Religious Life and Institutions*, ed. S. Safrai and M. Stern with D. Flusser and W.C. van Unnik, I.1-2, Assen 1974, 1976.
EKK	Evangelische-Katholischer Kommentar zum Neuen Testament, Zürich
ET	English translation
Évangile	M. de Jonge, ed., *L'Évangile de Jean*, BETL 44, 1977
FRLANT	Forschungen zur Religion und Literatur des Alten und Neuen Testaments, Göttingen
HE	Eusebius, *Historia Ecclesiastica*
HTR	*Harvard Theological Review*, Cambridge, Mass.
HUCA	*Hebrew Union College Annual*, Cincinnati

ICC	International Critical Commentary, Edinburgh and New York
IDB	*Interpreter's Dictionary of the Bible*, New York and Nashville
JBL	*Journal of Biblical Literature*, Philadelphia et al.
JJS	*Journal of Jewish Studies*, London
JQR	*Jewish Quarterly Review*, London
JR	*Journal of Religion*, Chicago
JRS	*Journal of Roman Studies*, London
JTS	*Journal of Theological Studies*, Oxford
KNT	Kommentar zum Neuen Testament, Leipzig
LCL	Loeb Classical Library, London and New York
LXX	Septuagint version of the Old Testament
NEB	New English Bible
NF	Neue Folge
NovT	*Novum Testamentum*, Leiden
*NovT*Suppl	Supplements to *Novum Testamentum*
n.s.	new series
NTApoc	*New Testament Apocrypha*, ed. E. Hennecke and W. Schneemelcher, ET, 2 vols., London and Philadelphia 1963–5, reprinted 1973–4
NTS	*New Testament Studies*, Cambridge
P	Papyrus
PEQ	*Palestine Exploration Quarterly*, London
PG	J.-P. Migne, ed., Patrologia Graeca, Paris 1844ff.
RB	*Revue Biblique*, Paris
RHR	*Revue de l'Histoire des Religions*
RSR	*Recherches de Science Religieuse*, Paris
RSV	Revised Standard Version of the Bible
RV	Revised Version of the Bible
SBLDS	Society of Biblical Literature Dissertation Series
SBLMS	Society of Biblical Literature Monograph Series
SBT	Studies in Biblical Theology, London and Naperville
SNTSMS	Society for New Testament Studies Monograph Series
StEv	*Studia Evangelica* (published in TU), Berlin
TDNT	G. Kittel and G. Friedrich, edd., *Theological Dictionary of the New Testament*, ET Grand Rapids, Mich. 1964–76
TEV	Today's English Version of the Bible
TLZ	*Theologische Literaturzeitung*, Leipzig

TU	Texte und Untersuchungen zur Geschichte der altchristlichen Literatur, Berlin
Twelve NTS	J. A. T. Robinson, *Twelve New Testament Studies* (see Bibliography)
Twelve More NTS	J. A. T. Robinson, *Twelve More New Testament Studies* (see Bibliography)
TZ	*Theologische Zeitschrift*, Basel
VC	*Vigiliae Christianae*, Leiden
WUNT	*Wissenschaftliche Untersuchungen zum Neuen Testament*, Tübingen
ZNW	*Zeitschrift für die neutestamentliche Wissenschaft*, Berlin
ZST	*Zeitschrift für systematische Theologie*, Gütersloh
ZTK	*Zeitschrift für Theologie und Kirche*, Tübingen

I

The Presumption of Priority

1. *A Change of Presumption*

In 1957 C. H. Dodd began a paper to the Cambridge Theological Society with the words: 'The presumption of literary dependence of John on the Synoptists no longer holds.' That was a factual statement, though it involved a bold and I believe percipient judgment on the contemporary state of Johannine studies, which has since been fully vindicated. It meant that the presumption had been reversed: as a result of a shift in scholarly opinion, the burden of proof had moved; one could no longer start by taking dependence for granted until proved otherwise.

I should like to begin by analysing the implications of such a statement, first in regard to the word 'presumption' and then in regard to 'dependence'.

A presumption sounds presumptuous, but it can be a purely neutral statement of the state of play or the rules of the game. It may be based on an impartial assessment of scientific opinion. For instance, one can now safely start from the presumption that the earth is round or that evolution and relativity are in the broadest sense 'true'. Or it may rest on a deliberately agreed axiom, e.g., that a man is to be presumed innocent until proved guilty, rather than the other way round. The presumption that he is innocent is to be distinguished from the prejudice that he is innocent (you may be strongly biased in his favour *against* the weight of the evidence) or the prejudgment that he is innocent (which would foreclose the conclusion, not the starting-point). A presumption again is to be distinguished from a presupposition. It will embody a number of presuppositions, but a presumption is a working hypothesis that these presuppositions may be accepted until proved otherwise. A presumption is a useful and indeed a necessary tool of investigation, whether for the policeman or the professor. It is presumptuous or dangerous only when more is claimed for it (e.g., that you need not even consider alternatives), or when it is unexamined. The presumption of John's dependence on or independence of the Synoptists is a time-saving and potentially illuminating working hypothesis, opening up other questions, as long as it itself is open to being modified or dropped. Yet which of these two presumptions is taken as a starting-point, and therefore what questions are seen as relevant, will obviously put the so-called 'facts' in a very different light. Presumptions can have a binding or a blinding effect on what one is able to 'see' in a situation or in the data before one. A change in presumption may be needed before one can recognize a solution.

Let me take a trivial example. In its Christmas chess competition of 1981 *The Guardian* set a problem with the challenge 'Beat Bobby Fischer', who had failed to crack it. It was a question of mating a king trapped in a corner. The 'obvious' presumption was that one began by moving the pieces towards the king and closing in upon it. But in fact it could be solved only by the improbable alternative of moving the king out of the corner into the open board where the pieces were. It was a question not so much of chess skill as of 'lateral thinking'. Until one changed one's initial presumption, no progress could be made – though then of course one still had to find the right combination of moves.

In this instance there was a correct and an incorrect presumption. Usually in real life it is not so clear, though the difference of presumption may lead to equally divergent results. Thus, within the field of New Testament scholarship, as the American scholar John Knox once said to me, it makes a considerable difference whether one regularly approaches a saying of Jesus with the question, Is there any reason why he should not have said this? or Is there any reason why he should? Since there is often no decisive evidence to the contrary, the answer you get will be determined by the question you ask. Scholars of equal repute will look at the same evidence from very different angles. Thus Jeremias formulated the 'principle of method' that 'in the synoptic tradition it is the inauthenticity and not the authenticity of the sayings of Jesus that must be demonstrated'[1] – though by prefacing it with the words 'in the synoptic tradition' he implied (though never stated) the opposite presumption in the case of the Johannine.

[1] *New Testament Theology* I, ET 1971, 37.

Bultmann, on the other hand, analysed the same material with the same tools in his *History of the Synoptic Tradition*[2] on the assumption that a saying must be attributed to the early Christian communities, who after all composed the Gospels, *unless* it could be shown otherwise. So, notoriously, the message of Jesus occupied but the first thirty-odd pages of his two-volume *Theology of the New Testament*,[3] whereas for Jeremias it filled the whole of the first (and, alas, only) volume. Neither presumption is in itself more scientific than the other – though it is often silently presupposed that the presumption of inauthenticity is more 'critical', thus implying an identification of criticism with scepticism – an equation common in the popular mind.[4] Yet there can be uncritical scepticism as much as uncritical conservatism.

But now let me pass to the implications of 'dependence' in the statement from which we started. The literary dependence of John on the Synoptists presupposes four assumptions: (1) that the Synoptic Gospels (or at least one or two of them) already existed; (2) that John knew them; (3) that he used them; and (4) that he depended upon them, at least in part, for his material. The presumption that John's dependence on the Synoptists no longer holds means that these four things can no longer be *assumed*. It does not mean denying them outright, except, in some degree, the last. It means proceeding on the hypothesis that they need not be taken into account as formative factors. One begins elsewhere. *A posteriori* they may still turn out to be true, but *a priori* they cannot be included in the reckoning.

I should like to test out a similar exercise on the priority of John. The presumption of scholars over the past one hundred and fifty years has been the posteriority of John. About the last scholar of repute to make the presumption of the priority of John was Schleiermacher,[5] and he did this on the perfectly rational ground that, as the only Gospel to come as he believed from the inner circle of the Twelve or directly from an apostle, it must be regarded as nearest to source. He also thought that it was written before the others reached their present form and does not relate to them, though he agreed that they shared common oral traditions. But since then even those who have regarded the author

[2] ET [2]1968.

[3] ET, 2 vols., New York and London 1952–5.

[4] And not so popular. It is presumed, for instance, throughout Don Cupitt's *The World to Come*, London 1982.

[5] *Einleitung ins neue Testament*, in *Sämtliche Werke* I, viii, Berlin 1845 (delivered as lectures in 1831–2), 315–44; c.f. *The Life of Jesus*, ET Philadelphia 1975, 393.

as John son of Zebedee have accepted the posteriority of John, in the sense that the picture of Jesus in the first three Gospels is primary, that supplied by what has regularly come to be styled 'the Fourth Gospel'[6] having to be fitted into that of the Synoptists historically or theologically or both, whether as supplement, corrective or interpretation. The presuppositions of this view have been that (1) the Synoptic Gospels already existed; (2) John knew them; (3) he wrote, consciously or unconsciously, in reaction to them; and (4) his portrait is to be seen and judged by us in their light. A shift in this presumption does not again mean a positive *denial* of these things – though it will challenge the adequacy especially of the last as a principle of interpretation. It merely asks that these things, if true, be established *a posteriori*, not fed into the calculation from the start.

On the other side, the presumption of the priority of John, at any rate as I am using the phrase, does not mean assuming that John was the first of the Gospels in time: it may or it may not have been. I am now persuaded in fact that *all* the Gospels were coming into being over a period more or less simultaneously, and at different stages their traditions and their redaction could well show signs of mutual influence – as well as, of course, between the Synoptists, of common written sources. But the priority of John does not depend on which Gospel was actually begun or finished first. Nor does it deny that John knew and presupposed traditions that he did not use. In fact he goes out of his way to say that there are many other things which he could have included but has not (John 20.30; cf. 21.25). At all sorts of points (the baptism of Jesus and the institution of the eucharist are obvious examples) he is clearly assuming awareness of what he does not choose to narrate. Indeed he is evidently presupposing, like Peter as reported at Caesarea, basic knowledge of the Christian facts and message: 'I need not tell you what happened lately over all the land of the Jews, starting from Galilee after the baptism proclaimed by John. You know about Jesus of Nazareth. . . . ' (Acts 10.37f.). Yet in his presentation the Gospel writer need no more be reacting to other presentations or looking over his shoulder at them than was Peter. Indeed it has been

[6]I drew attention in 'The New Look on the Fourth Gospel', reprinted in my *Twelve NTS*, 94–106, to some rather wicked words of the Old Testament scholar James Montgomery in his little book *The Origin of the Gospel According to St John*, Philadelphia 1923, 3 n.1: 'I may have academically "declassed" myself by using the name "Gospel of St John" in the title. . . . I frankly think that "Fourth Gospel" is a scholastic affectation. Why not the First, Second, and Third Gospels? Are we any surer of their authors? Any tyro knows that Deuteronomy is not "the Second Giving of the Law", but are we obliged to make constant profession of our critical attainments by calling that

correctly, I think, observed that 'it never appears as though the writer were consciously changing the synoptic version, even when the changes are considerable. It draws no attention to them; it never marks a correction.'[7] As far as the others were concerned, he could be the first in the field – neither supplementing, correcting nor interpreting them, nor they him.[8] As far as *our* assessment is concerned, the priority of John means that we begin with what he has to tell us on its own merits and ask how the others fit, historically and theologically, into that, are illumined by it, and in turn illumine it. For we *shall* assume that they and John are speaking of the same person and events and have much light to throw on each other. What we shall *not* assume is that John has to be slotted into the Synoptic picture. On the contrary, we shall ask what is to be learned by making the opposite presumption.

I cannot, like Dodd, say that the presumption of the posteriority of John 'no longer holds'. The case for even *considering* 'the priority of John' (which to most will no doubt sound a paradoxical and provocative title) has to be argued. The grounds for regarding it as a reasonable exercise will emerge as we go along. Now I am simply concerned with what would be involved in accepting, with all critical discrimination, a 'procedural' priority of John. As I have said, it does not necessarily mean the temporal priority of John, though I should be inclined to think that the writing that went into the Fourth Gospel may well have begun earlier *and* gone on later than in the case of the others. Nor, of course, does it imply the posteriority of the Synoptists in the sense that they are reacting to, or are to be judged by reference to, John. Procedural priority is compatible with complete openness on both these issues. What it does mean is beginning with John and asking how his picture, however near to source (and my answer would be: very near, yet also in its fullness the outcome of profound theological maturity), sheds original, and not merely reflected, light on everything else. But I would want to insist that this does not mean treating this light in isolation. For any illumination it has to give is as part of a

---

document the Fifth Book of Pseudo-Moses?' Cf. A. J. B. Higgins, *The Historicity of the Fourth Gospel*, 1960, ch. 3, 'Is John the "Fourth" Gospel?'.

[7] R. A. Edwards, *The Gospel According to John*, 1954, 130.

[8] H. E. Edwards, *The Disciple Who Wrote These Things*, 1953 (no relation of the previous Edwards, though a similar popular pastoral book – but much better – at almost the same time), rightly observed that these theories are not incompatible. The 'supplementary theory' in particular can embrace anything. 'Its upholders can account for all that the Evangelist has to say in three ways. If the author of our Gospel says what they [the other Gospels] say, he is quoting them; if what he says is out of harmony with

constellation. It is a sun, and a major sun, shining in its own light – yet not on its own. 'Is John also among the Synoptists?' is a question that I ventured to raise, and answer in the affirmative, many years ago.[9] Content and style apart, it is only in one formal relationship, namely, that of *literary* interdependence, which does not now loom as large as it once did in scholarly perspective, that he is to be set apart from the others. In many more respects he stands decisively on the side of the other evangelists rather than, say, of Paul or the author to the Hebrews, with whom the critics have often placed him.

Yet what illumination is to be got from giving priority to the light from that source? This can be discovered only by seeing what happens if one does allow this presumption. For until we are prepared to do so, some questions are not seriously entertained: they are ruled out, or smiled out, as naive, simplistic and uncritical. Particularly in the case of the Fourth Gospel, where the brief for the defence, as it were, has been left so much in the hands of one particular school, it has too quickly been *assumed* that the only motivation for taking these questions seriously can be a conservative or harmonistic one, which it has been fairly easy for scholars, though not others, to dismiss. Yet this itself is a quite uncritical assumption, and has led in my judgment to a less than open-ended approach to the evidence, both external and internal. It is healthy that it should now be being exposed for what it is by the fact that some of those working most closely with the new data from Palestinian,[10] Coptic and Hellenistic circles are now asking the same questions from a very different perspective.

Personally too I would claim not to come at them with any doctrinally conservative interest, as I hope that some of my other writings may show. It is simply that on historical grounds I find that they will not lie down or go away. In fact I am aware that I am but raising again some of the disturbing questions that a former Regius Professor at Oxford, Henry Scott Holland, asked in the first of the two

their statements, he is correcting them; if he tells us anything that is not to be found in their pages, he is supplementing them. In fact this theory will account, not only for all that the Fourth Evangelist has written; it would account equally well for anything he *might have* written' (111).

[9] In my essay 'The Place of the Fourth Gospel' in P. Gardner-Smith, ed., *The Roads Converge*, 1963, 49–74.

[10] E.g., F. M. Cross, *The Ancient Library of Qumran and Modern Biblical Studies*, New York and London 1958, 161f.: 'Some have suggested that John may be regarded no longer as the latest and most evolved of the Gospels, but the most primitive, and that the formative locus of its tradition was Jerusalem before its destruction'. Cf. J. H. Charlesworth, ed., *John and Qumran*, 1972, *passim* and especially W. H. Brownlee, 'Whence the Gospel according to John?', 166–94.

Introductions to his unwritten commentary more than sixty years ago,[11] whose opening pages Sir Edwyn Hoskyns asserted to be 'the best introduction in English to the study of the Fourth Gospel'.[12] He contended that often it is only when the Synoptists are read in the light of John that they become intelligible to themselves. In particular in all sorts of subtle ways the Synoptic picture is saying to us of Jesus in Jerusalem: He has been here before. Even in the Synoptists the centre of gravity of the Galilean ministry lies outside itself:

> He is only in Galilee at all, because He is under menace in Jerusalem. His dominating purpose is to plan His return to the fatal city, where His death is already a foregone conclusion. He goes to Jerusalem as One who has already made His offer, and whose death has been morally decreed.[13]

Scott Holland acknowledges at this point a study of John which has been totally forgotten, *The Gospel of the Rejection*[14] by Wilfred Richmond, his junior at Oxford and subsequently his editor. He shows John as presenting, as it were, the Jerusalem negative of the Galilean photograph, which alone explains how it developed as it did and why things had to turn out the way they did. We are so used to holding the Synoptic and Johannine pictures together that we forget the shock if we only had the positive and then suddenly held in our hands the negative. So *that's* what explains it! It would be like the effect of the first

[11] *The Fourth Gospel*, published posthumously as the second part of *The Philosophy of Faith and the Fourth Gospel*, 1920, especially 128–34 (adumbrated in Introduction II, written earlier, 153f.). It was republished separately in 1923.

[12] E. C. Hoskyns and F. N. Davey, *The Fourth Gospel*, 41. Cf. J. Armitage Robinson, *The Historical Character of St John's Gospel*, ²1929, 93: 'These two essays will be found to offer the most important contribution of recent times to the discussion of the Johannine authorship.' A Cambridge man may perhaps be permitted to draw attention also to the earlier article on 'The Historical Value of the Fourth Gospel' by A. E. Brooke in the volume of *Cambridge Biblical Essays*, ed. H. B. Swete, Cambridge and New York 1909, of which W. F. Howard was to write 'Probably this discriminating essay did as much as any other English contribution to check the tendency to abandon the historical element in both narrative and discourse (*The Fourth Gospel in Recent Criticism*, 1931, 28f.). Also from Cambridge: E. H. Askwith, *The Historical Value of the Fourth Gospel*, 1910, and V. H. Stanton, *The Gospels as Historical Documents*, 1903–20; III, *The Fourth Gospel*. That whole generation – between 1900 and 1920 – which thought of itself as the *epigoni* after Lightfoot, Westcott and Hort, seems to me to merit reappraisal and rediscovery. Of course their perspective is different from ours, as ours will be from that of two generations hence. But it is necessary to go beneath the changes of fashion which make things look superficially so dated.

[13] *Philosophy of Faith and the Fourth Gospel*, 133.

[14] London 1906.

photograph of the Turin Shroud in 1898, when the photographic negative turned out to be positive and revealed what was really there on the cloth all the time.

This presupposes that John is presenting us with a record, or what he calls a testimony, that is fundamentally independent of the others, goes back, through whatever stages of composition, to source and not simply to sources, and is at any rate *a* first written statement of the gospel, of primal rather than secondary significance.

Yet can one argue with critical responsibility or credibility for the 'priority' of John in this sense? Schleiermacher stood after all but on the threshold of the application of historical criticism to the Bible, although he had Lessing behind him,[15] and no one could take his judgment on these matters very seriously today. Not even those conservative English scholars whose critical responsibility one cannot dismiss, even if one does not follow their conclusions, argued for the priority of John. Men like Lightfoot and Westcott, Armitage Robinson and Headlam, who remained convinced of apostolic authorship to their dying day,[16] all assumed the posteriority of John, and Scott

[15]Lessing's position may be summed up in the following propositions from his 'New Hypothesis concerning the Evangelists regarded as merely Human Historians', translated in H. Chadwick, ed., *Lessing's Theological Writings*, London and Toronto 1956, 65–81:

> 'The opinion that John intended to write a mere supplement to the other three Gospels is certainly unfounded. One need only read him to receive quite another impression' (para. 52).
>
> 'That John did not know the other three Gospels at all is both unprovable and incredible' (para. 53).
>
> 'Rather, just because he had read the other three . . . and because he saw the effect of these Gospels, he found himself impelled to write his Gospel' (para. 54).
>
> 'If therefore [because the other Gospels gave no idea or a wrong idea of the Godhead of Christ] Christianity was not to die down again and to disappear among the Jews as a mere Jewish sect, and if it was to endure among the Gentiles as a separate, independent religion, John must come forward and write his Gospel' (para. 62).
>
> 'We accordingly have only two Gospels, Matthew and John, the Gospel of the flesh and the Gospel of the spirit' (para. 64).

Though he regarded Matthew as *the* first Gospel, Lessing nevertheless saw John as a prime witness to the truth about Jesus, in no way derivative from or dependent on the others.

[16]On Lightfoot, see Introduction, p. xi above. Westcott, who had earlier produced his commentary on the English text of the Gospel for *The Speaker's Commentary*, London 1880, was working on the Greek text to the end. It was published by his son, with his father's later notes but without substantial change, as *The Gospel according to St John*, 1908. J. Armitage Robinson republished his little book on *The Historical Character of St John's Gospel*, [1]1908, [2]1929, shortly before his death, reproducing in its preface (7–11) a still earlier lecture at Cambridge in 1901 from *The Study of the*

Holland believed that John was deliberately complementing the Synoptic record: 'He assumes that his readers are perfectly familiar with it, down to the smallest detail.'[17] To contend therefore that John was not writing against their background but (even if they existed and even if he knew them, *as is entirely possible*) was a primary source in whose light they too can be viewed may seem a quixotic enterprise verging on the irresponsible.[18] Yet I would claim to put it forward on historical critical grounds as an entirely scientific hypothesis that can account for the facts more satisfactorily than the opposite presumption that John's evidence is purely derivative or at best corrective.

Yet I wish to be careful not to seem to claim too much. I am *not* seeking to prove everyone else wrong or to argue that this is the only tenable position. I am attempting something much more modest – to try out a hypothesis, to explore what happens if one reverses the prevailing presumption that John is not a primary source. Like any hypothesis it can be tested – let alone established – only *a posteriori*, by adopting it and then seeing whether it yields a more adequate explanation of the data and opens up new and fruitful lines of enquiry. That must be the task of the main body of the book, as we look again in this perspective at the chronology of the ministry and the story, teaching and person of Jesus.

But first there is some obligation to show that it is an inherently

---

Gospels, London 1902, 126ff., with the comment: 'After the interval of twenty-seven years I have no desire to speak otherwise today.' A. C. Headlam, in *The Fourth Gospel as History*, 1948, returned after his retirement to convictions that had remained with him since his early association with W. Sanday, who had written *The Authorship and Historical Character of the Fourth Gospel* in 1872. But Sanday did shift his opinion later.

[17] *The Fourth Gospel*, 127. Cf. Sanday, *The Criticism of the Fourth Gospel*, 1905, 143: 'The Evangelist had the Synoptic Gospels before him; and, where he differs from them, he does so deliberately. Either his intention is to correct them, or at least he deliberately goes his own way.' Hoskyns equally presupposed that John and his readers knew the Synoptic tradition intimately and that John's aim was to enable them to read it truly. 'That the author of the Fourth Gospel had the three synoptic gospels before him when he composed his gospel is most improbable, for his relation to them is not that of an editor. But that he was familiar with the synoptic material, and even with its form, is certain' (*Fourth Gospel*, 87; cf. 67–92).

[18] One modern writer who argues, implicitly, for the priority of John is H. E. Edwards in *The Disciple Who Wrote These Things*. He believes that the Gospel was composed independently of the Synoptists and indeed before them (for he accepts the traditional later datings for the others), being written in the mid-60s as an instrument of evangelism in the Gentile city of Pella in the Decapolis, whence Christians had escaped from Jerusalem prior to the Jewish war. His topographical arguments seem to me groundless and indeed he spoils his book by tailing off into fantasy. But it contains a number of suggestive observations which I shall quote from time to time.

reasonable option which one may undertake to explore with critical responsibility. There are plenty of crazy hypotheses around which could work, or at any rate are difficult to disprove, but which need not be taken seriously scientifically. The line between craziness and sanity is indeed not always easy to draw, and on the fringes of medicine or science or any field of scholarship one must always beware of the tendency of the critical establishment to close ranks against anything that disturbs its fundamental presuppositions. An example of this could be Rupert Sheldrake's book *A New Science of Life*,[19] which offers a new and radical theory of 'formative causation' in biology. It may turn out to be wrong, like the hypothesis of 'continuous creation' in cosmology (Sir Fred Hoyle notwithstanding). But at least he is claiming to offer a hypothesis that is grounded in observed data, testable by further experiment, capable of disproof – therefore potentially scientific.

In the literary and historical field criteria are not so clear-cut. But if a hypothesis is to be open to serious consideration as a starter (whether it is a finisher can only be judged by its fruits), two preliminaries are necessary. It needs to be shown, in the case of John,

(1) negatively, that the cluster of presuppositions that have led to the accepted presumption of posteriority are not self-evidently true but are themselves highly questionable and require re-examination; and

(2) positively, that the presuppositions behind the alternative presumption are perfectly reasonable, that there are grounds, alike in place and time and personal continuity, for supposing that the Johannine tradition *could well* go back to source, and that this can no longer be ruled out as a 'moral impossibility' (I take the phrase from C. K. Barrett).

The latter task will occupy us in the next chapter. The remainder of this one will be given to the former, that is, to questioning the presuppositions on which the presumption of the posteriority of John has rested.

2. *The Long Shadow of Dependence*

The first, and most fundamental, is one we have already mentioned, namely, the dependence of John on the Synoptic Gospels. As Dodd said, this can certainly no longer be taken for granted. In fact there has been no more dramatic swing of the critical pendulum in recent New

[19] London 1981.

Testament studies than at this point.[20] When Barrett first produced his commentary in 1955,[21] one of the two great English-speaking commentaries on the Gospel in our generation,[22] to which I constantly find myself returning for reliable information, it represented, I felt even then, the last of the 'old look', presupposing, as most scholars then did, John's dependence, certainly on Mark, probably on Luke and possibly on Matthew.[23] By the time he produced the second, revised edition in 1978[24] he was very much in a minority in this position, sticking to his guns but aware that he was on the defensive. Of course counter-attacks have been made[25] and there will continue to be fluctuations on this front as on every other. But the *presumption* has undoubtedly shifted,[26] and the case for literary dependence has now to be argued against the odds. Dodd believed that the turn of the tide, in England at least,[27] was marked by P. Gardner-Smith's *St John and the Synoptic*

[20]It is comparable to another to which I drew attention in my *Redating the New Testament*, 1976, 224f., the dramatic shift at the end of the last century in the consensus among New Testament, but not classical, scholars on the dating of the book of Revelation from the 60s to the 90s of the first century AD.

[21]*The Gospel According to St John*, 1955.

[22]The other is that by R. E. Brown, *The Gospel According to John*, 1966–70.

[23]For a classic statement of this case, cf. B. H. Streeter, *The Four Gospels: a Study of Origins*, London and New York 1924, ch. 14. He played down any Matthaean contacts and tried to explain them away like the 'minor agreements' between Matthew and Luke. But cf. Hoskyns and Davey, *Fourth Gospel*, 81–5, and C. H. Dodd, *The Johannine Epistles*, 1946, xxxix–xlii. But none of the points of contact add up to literary dependence. Edwards, *The Disciple Who Wrote These Things*, 107f., makes the valid observation that if John was being written for the first time towards the end of the first century we should have expected him to show dependence on the Synoptic Gospels (or the Synoptic tradition) in precisely the reverse order: Matthew, then Luke, and Mark hardly at all. He quotes figures for Clement, Ignatius, Polycarp and the Epistle of Barnabas. Those for the Didache are even more striking.

[24]Cf. his earlier article, 'John and the Synoptic Gospels', *ExpT* 85, 1973–4, 228–33.

[25]Cf. J. Blinzler, *Johannes und die Synoptiker. Ein Forschungsbericht* (Stuttgarter Bibelstudien 5), Stuttgart 1965; F. Neirynck, 'John and the Synoptics', in M. de Jonge, ed., *L'Évangile de Jean*, 1977 (cited henceforth as *Évangile*), 73–106, and *Jean et les Synoptiques: examen critique de l'exégèse de M.-É. Boismard*, Leuven 1979.

[26]In a survey article, 'Johannine Christianity: Some Reflections on its Character and Delineation', *NTS* 21, 1975, 222–48, D. Moody Smith speaks in this connection of 'a very significant direction of scholarship, whether or not it deserves to be called a consensus' (227).

[27]For the same development on the Continent, cf. E. Haenchen, 'Johanneische Probleme' *ZTK* 56, 1959, 19–22; reprinted in his *Gott und Mensch*, Tübingen 1965, 78–81; and the references in Neirynck, 'John and the Synoptics', 72f. B. Noack, *Zur johanneischen Tradition*, Copenhagen 1954, argued for a common oral rather than literary tradition and convinced Bultmann ('Zur Johanneischen Tradition'; *TLZ* 60, 1955, 521.)

Gospels,[28] 'a book', he said, 'which crystallized the doubts of many, and has exerted an influence out of proportion to its size'.[29] He made this observation in the introduction to his own great work, *Historical Tradition in the Fourth Gospel*,[30] which was a massive demonstration of the greater probability that the Johannine material rested on tradition independent of and often more primitive than that of the Synoptic Gospels. At point after point he showed the inherent unlikelihood that John would have extracted and combined from the *different* Synoptic Gospels the features required to explain his own version, notably, for example, of the anointing of Jesus (John 12.1–8; Matt. 26.6–13; Mark 14.3–9; Luke 7.36–50),[31] but also of the feeding of the multitude, the cleansing of the temple, the entry into Jerusalem, the arrest and trial, and the sayings of Jesus common to John and the Synoptists.[32] Time and again an independent stream of oral tradition looks the more probable explanation. This is also the case with features that John does *not* include, e.g., as Dodd pointed out, the darkness at the crucifixion, the rending of the temple veil and the confession by the

[28] 1938. It ended with the words: 'If the view should gain ground that the Fourth Gospel, whatever its authorship and date, is an independent work, then a new chapter will have opened in the criticism of the Gospels and the study of Christian origins' (97).

[29] Cf. A. M. Hunter, *According to John*, 1968, 14: 'In 1938 Gardner-Smith's was a lone voice protesting Johannine independence: in 1968 his view may almost be said to represent "critical orthodoxy"'; also the survey and bibliography in S. Temple, *The Core of the Fourth Gospel*, London and Oxford 1975, 9–14.

[30] Published 1963 (here p. 8), but given in substance as the Sarum Lectures at Oxford in 1954–5.

[31] *Historical Tradition*, 162–73.

[32] H. E. Edwards (*The Disciple Who Wrote These Things*, 96f.) reproduces a list of the isolated sayings, statements and phrases with Synoptic parallels from Stanton, who used them as evidence of John's dependence on Mark in particular. He points out that 'each of them is given in the Fourth Gospel *in a different context* from that assigned to them in the Synoptic Gospels.' The list runs:

(1) The name given to Simon (John 1.40–42; cf. Mark 3.16; Matt. 16.18)
(2) The demand for a sign (John 6.30–32; cf. Mark 8.11f.)
(3) 'The Twelve' (John 6.67, 70; cf. Mark 3.16)
(4) Judas, the victim of Satanic inspiration (John 13.2, 27; cf. Luke 22.3)
(5) The use of spittle in healing a blind man (John 9.6f.; cf. Mark 8.22–26)
(6) 'A prophet has no honour' (John 4.44; cf. Mark 6.4)
(7) Isa. 6.9f. (spiritual blindness); (John 12.39f.; cf. Mark 4.12)
(8) 'He who loves his life' (John 12.25; cf. Mark 8.35)
(9) 'He who receives whom I send' (John 13.20; cf. Matt. 10.40, Mark 9.37)
(10) 'The servant is not greater than his master' (John 13.16; cf. Luke 6.40).

I have corrected the references in a few instances. He could have added others, e.g. 'Father save me from this hour' in 12.27 (cf. Mark 14.35f.).

centurion of Jesus as Son of God, all of which, if John had been following Mark, would have suited his symbolism splendidly. One could instance also the absence from John of the 'I am' or ἐγώ εἰμι on Jesus' lips at the climax of the trial before the high priest in Mark 14.62 or at the moment of reunion in the upper room in Luke 24.39. But there is no need to go over the ground again in detail. Many of the points Dodd made will come out in our subsequent treatment of the same passages. But Gardner-Smith's principle of method stands repeating:

> It is not a scientific proceeding to form a conclusion on one half of the evidence, and then to force the other half into agreement with it. The passages in which there are correspondences between St John and the Synoptists do not stand alone and should not be considered by themselves; indeed they form a small minority among the far more numerous passages in which the discrepancies are many and glaring.[33]

At least we may say at this point that the major presupposition of the posteriority of John, his dependence on the Synoptists, has taken such a battering that an alternative hypothesis is certainly not at this point precluded. Indeed it is urgently called for.

Yet Dodd, though he denied John's literary dependence on the Synoptic Gospels, believed that he relied on other tradition to which he stood in an external and second-hand relation. He speaks of it as material that 'came into his hands' in the form of 'information received', which he then 'took over', 'made use of' and 'worked upon'. It is a curiously passive relationship – though twice it is suggested that the evangelist 'sought for information'. But, however he acquired it, the presupposition is that he was 'incorporating material which, at a distance of place and time, he did not fully understand'.[34]

If we ask how it came down to him, Dodd is not very forthcoming:

> That some parts of it may have been written down by way of *aide-mémoire* is always possible, and such written sources may have intervened between strictly oral tradition and our Fourth Gospel. If so, I am not concerned with them.[35]

But there is a credibility gap here. Dodd never explains how this oral tradition was transmitted in such remarkably pristine condition over so wide a gap of space and time as he envisages (from an early circle of

[33] *St John and the Synoptic Gospels*, 92.
[34] For the detailed references see my summary in *Redating*, 263f.
[35] *Historical Tradition*, 424.

Judaean disciples to an Ephesian elder in the 90s of the first century). To that gap we shall return in the next chapter, but for now we may note that Dodd's analysis does not *depend* on the assumption of a purely external relationship of the evangelist to his tradition:

> If the balance of probability should appear to be on the side of authorship by John son of Zebedee,[36] much of what is written in the following pages would require some modification, but I do not think it would all fall to the ground. The material ascribed here to tradition would turn out to be the apostle's own reminiscences; but even so, it would be obvious that they had been cast at one stage into the mould of the corporate tradition of the Church – as why should they not be, if the apostle was actively immersed in just that ministry of preaching, teaching and liturgy which *ex hypothesi* gave form to the substance of the Church's memories of its Founder?[37]

To that issue too we must come back. One can only remark at this point that the evangelist gives no *impression* of being dependent on tradition to which he stood in a second-hand relation and which he did not always know what to make of. On the contrary, as P. H. Menoud put it, it is as if he is saying to us with sovereign freedom from beginning to end: 'La tradition, c'est moi!'[38] So the presumption, if found reasonable on its own merits, that he went back to source and not to sources cannot simply be ruled out as impossible or improbable.

Once the Synoptic Gospels are eliminated, Dodd saw no grounds for positing other written sources behind the Gospel of John. Indeed the external evidence for such sources is nil. A Synoptic sayings-source, such as Q must have been if it existed, is not, as is often asserted, purely hypothetical. Papias refers to the collection of *logia* (almost certainly sayings) associated with the name of Matthew,[39] and the Gospel of Thomas has now provided an example of just such a form.[40] There is nothing comparable for the suggested sources of John. But that of course has not inhibited scholars from positing them on internal

[36]Or, one might add, any first-hand witness.

[37]*Historical Tradition*, 17. Cf. the wide-ranging essay by D. A. Carson, 'Historical Tradition in the Fourth Gospel: After Dodd What?' in R. T. France and D. Wenham, edd., *Gospel Pespectives* II, Sheffield 1981, 83–145. He also quotes this passage and suggests that it would make more difference to Dodd's method, if not his conclusions, than he himself acknowledged (130).

[38]*L'Évangile de Jean d'après les recherches récentes*, Neuchâtel and Paris [2]1947, 77.

[39]Eusebius, *HE* 3.39.16.

[40]Cf. J. M. Robinson, '*LOGOI SOPHŌN*: On the Gattung of Q' in J. M. Robinson and H. Koester, edd., *Trajectories through Early Christianity*, 1971, 71–113.

grounds. Most notably Rudolf Bultmann[41] argued for two major sources (apart from a passion story); a revelatory-sayings source (*Offenbarungsreden-Quelle*) for the discourses and a signs-source (*Sēmeia-Quelle*) for the narrative. The former has commanded little credence,[42] but the latter has fared better[43] and has been elaborated by R. T. Fortna[44] into a *Grundschrift* for the whole Gospel narrative. One cannot but be impressed by the thoroughness with which the exercise is carried through – and I shall draw on insights that emerge from it. Similarly Dodd earlier confessed himself impressed by the attempts to rearrange the order of the Gospel: 'I have examined several of these rearrangements, and cannot sufficiently admire the patience and endless ingenuity which have gone to their making.'[45] Nevertheless he was still more impressed by their subjectiveness and by the lack of almost any agreed conclusions; and I would concur with Barrett's sane judgment:

> I take it that if the gospel makes sense as it stands it can generally be assumed that this is the sense it was intended to make. That it may seem to me to make better sense when rearranged I do not regard as adequate reason for abandoning an order which undoubtedly runs back into the second century – the order, indeed, in which the book was *published*.[46]

The fever for juggling with the order of John has now abated, and even

[41] *Das Evangelium des Johannnes*, Göttingen 1941; ET *The Gospel of John: a Commentary*, 1971. Cf. D. M. Smith, 'The Sources of the Gospel of John', *NTS* 10, 1963–4, 336–51; and *The Composition and Order of the Fourth Gospel: Bultmann's Literary Theory*, 1965.

[42] Cf. the history of this area of scholarship in Robinson and Koester, *Trajectories*, 52f., and the trenchant criticisms of B. Lindars, *Behind the Fourth Gospel*, 1971, 20–6.

[43] Cf. Robinson and Koester, *Trajectories*, 53–5 and 235–52. But cf. Barrett, 'Symbolism' in his *Essays on John*, 1982, 76: 'These simple observations seem to me to make nonsense of the theory that John used a special source consisting of miracles, describing them by the term σημεῖον, and giving them a special evaluation – which, as some hold, John proceeded to correct'; cf. *John*, 77.

[44] *The Gospel of Signs: A Reconstruction of the Narrative Source Underlying the Fourth Gospel*, 1970. Cf. J. Becker, 'Wunder und Christologie: zum literarkritischen und christologischen Problem der Wunder im Johannesevangelium', *NTS* 16, 1969–70, 130–48; W. Nicol, *The Sēmeia in the Fourth Gospel: Tradition and Redaction*, *NovT* Suppl 32, Leiden 1972; and, earlier, W. Wilkens, *Die Entstehungsgeschichte des vierten Evangeliums*, Zollikon 1958. The works of Fortna and Nicol are analysed by E. Ruckstuhl under the title 'The Signs Source Today' which forms the second part of his article 'Johannine Language and Style: The Question of their Unity', in *Évangile*, 129–47.

[45] *The Interpretation of the Fourth Gospel*, 1953, 289.

[46] *John*, 22; cf. Dodd, *Interpretation*, 290.

the most tempting transposition of chapters 5 and 6[47] is rejected by most recent studies.[48] Similarly the attempt to isolate a source from its subsequent editorial treatment, after the first stage of removing the obvious features of distinctively Johannine comment, symbolism and theology, becomes a highly subjective exercise. Fortna's analysis is inevitably interspersed with frequent examples of 'may', 'probably' and 'apparently' (with 'obviously' and 'clearly' thrown in to lend an air of confidence, but in effect provoking corresponding suspicion). Moreover the fact that words like 'conjectural', 'artificial' and 'arbitrary' are constantly hurled at opposing judgments, e.g. those of Bultmann, is scarcely reassuring.[49] The most charitable verdict is perhaps one that Fortna himself has passed on another, yet more elaborate and complex, analysis of Johannine sources (into two Johns, plus a pre-John and a post-John) by M.–É. Boismard and A. Lamouille:[50] 'I am not persuaded that such a multi-stage theory can be verified . . . all the while admitting that it is probably equally incapable of falsification.'[51]

The real question concerns the criteria used for distinguishing source material. Fortna readily admits that 'ideological' and 'stylistic' tests, i.e. the distinctive themes, tendencies, vocabulary or syntax of the evangelist, are of limited value or validity. He places almost all the weight on the 'contextual' test, concentrating on the many *aporiai*,[52] or

[47]Cf. below, ch. V, p. 195.

[48]Not, interestingly, by Aileen Guilding, *The Fourth Gospel and Jewish Worship: A Study of the Relation of St John's Gospel to the Ancient Jewish Lectionary System*, Oxford and New York 1960, 45f. I would judge it one of the many subjectivities of this study that its reconstructed lectionary cycle rests on this transposition, for which there is no manuscript or other ancient evidence.

[49]Thus, on the stories of the miraculous draft of fishes in Luke 5 and John 21, Fortna writes (*Gospel of Signs*, 97f.): 'Bultmann holds that in the tradition the Easter element was predominant and that it is Luke who has artificially inserted it into the Galilean ministry of Jesus. . . . From the foregoing, however, it appears that the story is basically a miracle like any other during Jesus's life-time and that it is John who has made it into an Easter story.' Who is to say which is right? Both would seem to me about equally arbitrary. Kümmel, *Introduction to the NT*, [2]1975, 213, comments: 'Fortna's arguments for the sequence of the seven miracles in the source can only be characterized as purely subjective.'

[50]*Synopse des Quatre Évangiles en français* III: *L'Évangile de Jean*, Paris 1977. Its position is summarized in English by Brown in *The Community of the Beloved Disciple*, 1979, 178f.

[51]'The Relation of Narrative and Discourse in the Fourth Gospel: An Approach to the Question', a paper prepared for the Fourth Gospel Seminar of the Society for New Testament Studies at Durham, August 1979.

[52]The term goes back to Eduard Schwartz, 'Aporien im vierten Evangelium', *Nachrichten der Göttinger Gesellschaft der Wissenschaften*, 1907, 342–72; 1908, 115–88, 497–560.

'perplexities', in the Johannine narrative – the breaks, *non sequiturs*, inconsistencies, corrections, repetitions, and other signs of less than smooth writing. These are the points where he says the sutures are to be spotted between the different layers of material – whether it be a redactor at work on the Johannine matter or John adapting a pre-Johannine source. That there are such roughnesses and disconnections in the Gospel is not to be questioned, though the eye of the critic for 'contradictions' where the ordinary reader has for centuries observed none often makes one wonder whether they are being read in rather than read out.[53] Moreover some at least of the self-corrections appear to be a deliberate part of the author's method, e.g.: 'If I testify on my own behalf, that testimony does not hold good' (5.31) and 'My testimony is valid, even though I do bear witness about myself' (8.14); and within a single verse, 'I pass judgment on no man, but if I do judge my judgment is valid because it is not I alone who judge' (8.16; cf. 11.25f.).[54] And Westcott pointed out[55] that many of the parenthetic statements are part of the limitations of John's style. Because of his inability to handle subordinate clauses they are not 'wrought into the texture of the narrative' but added in a disconnected manner.

But more than this is required to establish different 'hands' or 'sources'. Otherwise all they tell us is that this is not the 'seamless robe' that D. F. Strauss styled it.[56] They indicate that the Gospel has not been written at a single 'go' but put together, as many books are, from material spoken or written in the first instance for different occasions (a number of the editorial notes being for the purposes of adaptation)[57] and that it still contains duplications, retractions and rough edges which have not been smoothed out. If I or anyone else were to leave a manuscript in this state – as many commentators on John have done –

[53]Cf. Lindars, *Behind the Fourth Gospel*, 17, of other supposed 'inconsistencies'; 'Most of these can safely be set aside as the product of an over-subtle criticism discovering distinctions where none exist'; and Kümmel, *Introduction to the NT*, 210: the 'insoluble *aporiai* . . . are difficulties only if one applies to the text a completely inappropriate standard of logic and narrative sequence.'

[54]So Wayne Meeks, 'The Man from Heaven in Johannine Sectarianism', *JBL* 91, 1972, 48: 'There are a number of examples not only of double entendre which are progressively clarified by repetition and modification, but also of self-contradiction that are manifestly deliberate.'

[55]*John* I, civ.

[56]*Vorrede zu den Gesprächen von Ulrich von Hutten*, Gesammelte Schriften VII, Bonn [3]1877, 555f., quoted in full by Howard, *Fourth Gospel in Recent Criticism*, 297.

[57]Cf. H. E. Edwards, *The Disciple Who Wrote These Things*, 63f. for suggested instances.

the natural conclusion would be that it had not been finally edited, *not* that a series of redactors had been at work on it or that someone else's *Vorlage* underlay it. In fact this was Harnack's assessment of the Gospel of John towards the end of a long life: 'When more closely examined the work exhibits manifold irregularities which show that it still required a final revision'.[58] And a layman who quoted this in a lively and down-to- earth book on the Gospel said of its non sequiturs, 'So far from being due to the clumsiness of an editor they are due to the total absence of any editor at all.'[59] Indeed at the end of the day on any hypothesis one is left with the question why the Gospel still emerges as an unpolished work.

What is required to establish different hands, whether of redactor or source, is a difference of style or mind-set. That there are parts of the Gospel material which show a relatively thinner spread of distinctively Johannine characteristics (and also of 'Aramaisms',[60] though this aspect surprisingly is not touched on by Fortna) and that there are marginal differences of usage between the body of the Gospel and the Epilogue of chapter 21 (played down by Fortna) and somewhat more substantial ones between the Gospel and the Epistles (which is irrelevant to Gospel *sources*) is not to be denied, and must be taken into account when discussing the question of authorship.[61] But the overwhelming impression, borne out by a number of detailed studies,[62] is of the massive unity and consistency of the Johannine style. If it does not make source-analysis impossible, it makes it extremely precarious. Wayne Meeks sums up the situation well when he says:

> The major literary problem of John is its combination of remarkable stylistic unity and thematic coherence with glaringly bad transitions

[58]A. von Harnack, 'Zum Johannesevangelium', *Erforschtes und Erlebtes*, Giessen 1923, 42. That the manuscript was left in an unfinished state has also been suggested as the most probable hypothesis by D. M. Smith, *Composition and Order*, 239.

[59]A. H. N. Green-Armytage, *John Who Saw: a Layman's Essay on the Authorship of the Fourth Gospel*, London 1952, 143.

[60]CF. T. W. Manson, 'The Fourth Gospel' in *Studies in the Gospels and Epistles*, ed. M. Black, 1962, 115–17; A. J. B. Higgins, 'The Words of Jesus according to St. John', *BJRL* 49, 1966–7, 363–86, especially 372–7.

[61]Bultmann also believes I John to have used a source, as well as to have been subjected to an ecclesiastical redactor; but he makes no attempt to justify this conclusion on grounds of style.

[62]Cf. especially E. Schweizer, *Ego Eimi*, 1939, [2]1965; Menoud, *L'Évangile de Jean*, 12–26; E. Ruckstuhl, *Die literarische Einheit des Johannesevangeliums*, Freiburg 1951, and, basically reaffirming his earlier views, 'Johannine Language and Style', *Évangile*, 129–47, especially the conclusion on p. 145.

> between episodes at many points. The countless displacement, source, and redaction theories that litter the graveyards of Johannine research are voluble testimony to this difficulty.[63]

Indeed I have long found myself in agreement with the dictum of the American Johannine scholar Pierson Parker: 'It looks as though, if the author of the fourth Gospel used documentary sources, he wrote them all himself.'[64]

This difficulty would seem to dog all attempts to sort out non-Johannine or pre-Johannine sources, though another writer, H. M. Teeple,[65] claims to see in the internal variations of vocabulary and syntax within the *distinctive* Johannine style the evidence for (four) separate hands. This he does by the simple, but circular, process of assigning the seemingly synonymous words used in the Gospel, e.g. for 'seeing', 'sending', 'going', 'loving', 'from God', etc. to different strands and then employing these as criteria for reconstructing the source. The suggestion that a single author might deliberately employ stylistic variation[66] (or mean something subtly different, say by μετὰ τοῦτο, after this, and μετὰ ταῦτα, after these things) is dismissed as 'facile' or attributed to 'bias'[67] rather than 'objectivity' or 'scientific

[63]Meeks, 'Man from Heaven', 48. On the presence in John of supposedly divergent understandings, say, of eschatology or of spirit or flesh on which others have laid emphasis, Howard issues a salutary warning: 'It should be remembered that, if there is one book in the New Testament about whose unity of style there can be no question, it is the Epistle to the Hebrews. But in that book we find side by side, without any apparent sense of incongruity, the Judaic conception of the two ages, and the Platonic conception of the two worlds, the real and the phenomenal. In seeking to understand the inconsistencies of thought that are sometimes discernible in this Gospel we should not forget that it may represent a long growth in the writer's mind, that the sections may have been written at considerable intervals, under varying influences and in different moods' (*Fourth Gospel in Recent Criticism*, 101).

[64]'Two Editions of John', *JBL* 75, 1956, 304. He tells me that, thanks to my quotation of it, this is the remark for which he is now famous!

[65]*The Literary Origin of the Gospel of John*, Evanston, Ill. 1974.

[66]Cf. Howard, *Fourth Gospel in Recent Criticism*, 106f., 278f; E. D. Freed, 'Variations in the Language and Thought of John', *ZNW* 55, 1964, 167–97; L. Morris, 'Variation – A Feature of the Johannine Style', *Studies in the Fourth Gospel*, 1969, 293–319. Bultmann observes exactly the same penchant for stylistic variation in what he believes to be the separate author of I John (*The Johannine Epistles*, ET 1973, 31, 85).

[67]Cf. *Literary Origin*, 117: 'I once accepted the creative ability of the author as a possible cause of the literary structure of the gospel; as a result of the present study I now reject completely that facile explanation'; and p. 250 of the 'bias' controlling past theories of the literary origin of the Gospel of John: 'Such efforts were not genuine research. They were only dishonest apologetics masquerading as scholarship.' May he be forgiven!

scholarship'. In fact it is the subjectivity of criteria and above all the dismissive judgments on other practitioners that shakes one's confidence in these competing solutions. Thus Teeple writes off as 'sheer speculation'[68] the perfectly reasonable view advocated by Barrett and Brown in their commentaries or subsequently by Culpepper[69] that 'a group of teachers or disciples were instrumental in producing the Gospel'; while of his own attempt to apply strictly linguistic tests Lindars says that it 'only succeeds in demonstrating that the method is valueless, as the results do not even begin to be plausible'.[70]

Lindars himself, who is highly critical of Fortna's attempts to reconstruct what he calls 'the hypothetical (and I think chimerical) Signs Source', representing, he believes, but a 'pale ghost of John's theology',[71] argues that the evangelist constructs his 'homilies' out of 'units of tradition which came to John in the form of short collections or independent pieces, which he has used selectively and often adapted drastically'.[72] Again this is an entirely plausible hypothesis. Yet when for example he actually comes to analyse the long account of the raising of Lazarus (John 11.1–44)[73] one's confidence in putting one's finger on the sources evaporates. He says that, in addition to the story of Martha and Mary (Luke 10.38–42) and *possibly* the parable of Dives and Lazarus (Luke 16.19–31, of which he admits that the fourth evangelist 'shows no knowledge at all') we must 'assume' that 'John also had at his disposal a non-Synoptic story of the raising to life of a dead man'. Nevertheless he has to concede that 'apart from one detail (ἐνεβριμήσατο) it is impossible to recover any of it at all'. This word, expressing Jesus' intense grief (11.33, 38), we are told 'undoubtedly comes from the source, though it may well have implied a different emotion there'.[74] But he admits that the ground for saying this is simply that John's use of it is 'unusual' and that 'there is really nothing of the underlying story left apart from this word'. For the rest he has 'covered it up completely'. This seems to me a *reductio ad absurdum* of Johannine source-criticism and bears out the conclusion of Robert Kysar's not unsympathetic but searching survey that it is 'somewhat in

[68] *Literary Origin*, 28.

[69] R. A. Culpepper, *The Johannine School*, 1975.

[70] 'Traditions behind the Fourth Gospel' in *Evangile*, 108f.

[71] *Behind the Fourth Gospel*, 78f. For his detailed, and I think valid, criticisms, cf. 28–42.

[72] Ibid., 61.

[73] Ibid., 55–9.

[74] On this word, and the possibility of (mis)translation from the Aramaic, cf. Barrett's excellent comments in *John*, 398–400.

shambles'.[75]

Faced with such a handful of dust, I would agree with the comments of W. H. Brownlee on Fortna's 'source' which, he says,

> is sometimes so dull that it sounds more like an abstract [which after all is what it is], than an original composition: A more valid goal, it seems to me, is the recovery of a proto- Johannine narrative, which (since it is by the same author as much else) it will never be possible to separate completely from other Johannine contributions.[76]

Yet a recent attempt to do this and isolate an original and *very* primitive Aramaic 'core'[77] is equally arbitrary and has failed to win serious scholarly support.

In any case this exercise is irrelevant to the question of whether John represents a witness that goes back to source. That his material has been developed over a period in various stages is beyond dispute – though whether we can recover or isolate them is another matter. There is every reason to suppose, as Eusebius said long ago,[78] that the Gospel of John was put together out of 'unwritten preaching' material, composed for apologetic, catechetical and liturgical purposes, and may well have gone through different editions and redactions (whether by one hand or more). But this is entirely compatible with the hypothesis he was his own tradition, and stood in an internal rather than external relation to it.

The opposite presumption that he depended on sources, of whatever kind, would appear quite unproven. Just as Dodd regarded it (in the matter of the Gospel's order) 'to be the duty of an interpreter at least to see what can be done with the document as it has come down to us before attempting to improve upon it',[79] so I would urge that it is not

[75] *The Fourth Evangelist and his Gospel: An Examination of Contemporary Scholarship*, Minneapolis, Minnesota 1975, 24. Cf. 13–37, where he also takes into account the theories of R. Schnackenburg, *The Gospel according to St John* I, ET 1968, 44–58; J. Becker, 'Wunder und Christologie'; and W. Nicol, *Sēmeia* (see n. 44 above).

[76] Charlesworth, ed., *John and Qumran*, 181.

[77] Sydney Temple, *The Core of the Fourth Gospel*. For *his* treatment of the Lazarus story, 183–93 (in which there was no raising at all!); cf. below, ch. VI, p. 220. He terminates the 'core' at 20.10, thus (arbitrarily) cutting out all resurrection appearances. He also stretches credibility by assuming that it was lost for the best part of 50 years until it was found and re-edited (in virtually indistinguishable style) by a Christian leader who stood in a completely external relationship to it.

[78] *HE* 3.24.7.

[79] *Interpretation*, 290.

uncritical to begin by assuming that John is not using bits and pieces of other people's material (whether written or oral) but is writing, with whatever breaks in continuity, his own story from his own store. Sometimes in what have been designated 'Synoptic-type' stories, where Eduard Schweizer observed that the Johannine stylistic characteristics were relatively thin,[80] and in the passion narrative, he tells it comparatively 'straight'. At other times, especially, as we shall observe, in the sayings material,[81] his distinctive theological viewpoint has already been more fully assimilated. But it would be a mistake to assume that more factual accounts on which he has imposed less of his interpretation are not for that reason just as much his.

Divergence from or similarity to the Synoptic 'type' is an irrelevant criterion for assessing John, except on the presumption of Johannine posteriority. Yet what might be called 'the long shadow of dependence' is visible even in the work of those (like Dodd and Brown, Fortna and Lindars) who have abandoned the theory of literary dependence of John on the Synoptists. An alpha is consciously or unconsciously assigned to Johannine material which coincides or concurs with the Synoptists, a beta to that which is parallel or compatible, and a gamma to that which disagrees with them. Fortna, for example, uses the phrase 'distinctively non-synoptic' as a controlling category of discrimination. And there is constantly the hidden assumption that John starts in a minority of one to three, though the number of times that he has against him three of the Synoptic *sources* (Mark, Q, M or L) as opposed to three Synoptic *Gospels* is very few.

We rightly do not do this exercise the other way round and assess the Synoptic material by the degree to which it is 'distinctively non-Johannine'.[82] So, it is I believe unwarrantable to concede historical value to features in John, whether of content or order, because of their

[80]He noted (*Ego Eimi*, 100) the wedding at Cana (2.1–10), the cleansing of the temple (2.13–19), the healing of the court-official's son (4.46–53), the anointing at Bethany (12.1–8) and the triumphal entry (12.12–15) – apart, of course, from the clearly non-Johannine *pericope* of the woman taken in adultery (7.53–8.11).

[81]Cf. below, ch. VII, pp. 296-300, 322-5.

[82]The Q *logion* of Matt. 11.27 = Luke 10.22 ('No one knows the Son except the Father', etc.) ought to be no exception, and to mark it down because it sounds 'Johannine' is quite irrational. Cf. O. Cullmann, *The Christology of the New Testament*, ET [2]1963, 287: 'I see no reason to deny that Jesus spoke the words of Matt. 11.27 simply because of their close resemblance to a favourite theme of John.' On this *logion* see further below, chs. VII, pp. 315f., and VIII, pp. 359f.

Dodd observed that 'a severe concentration on the Synoptic record, to the exclusion of the Johannine contribution' (which he held 'leads to an impoverished, a one-sided,

approximation to the Synoptists and still more to deny it on the grounds of their divergence. Examples of such features might be the Johannine dating of the crucifixion or placing of the cleansing of the temple, where John is opposed in any case by only one of the Synoptic strands (the Markan, or 'triple' tradition). Each case requires to be argued on its own merits;[83] yet we shall encounter numerous instances where it is tacitly assumed that 'traditional', or 'pre-Johannine', and therefore more reliable, material is to be detected and gauged by this criterion. This does not mean that the test of 'multiple attestation', of how many *independent* sources witness to a feature in the story or teaching of Jesus, is not a valuable tool. Indeed John's independence of the Synoptists, if established on other grounds, can add significantly to the instances – to take a minor example, what he tells us about Joseph of Arimathea compared with Matthew, Mark and Luke. But that is no ground for saying that his information on Joseph derives from common, pre-Johannine tradition and is therefore superior to what he tells us about Nicodemus, of whom the Synoptists say nothing.

3. *Sources and Source*

This has introduced the question of historicity, which of course is different from that of establishing sources. Indeed Fortna abjures it as a confusing factor, choosing at the outset to 'leave aside all questions of historicity in isolating the pre-Johannine stratum in the gospel, since so much Johannine research has been distorted by the failure to insist that such a concern has its legitimate place only after the literary task is complete'.[84] In fact he regards Dodd as culpable in this respect. Yet the question of historicity, though independent, is certainly not irrelevant to the question of whether John goes back to source rather than

---

and finally an incredible view of the facts – I mean of the *facts*, as part of history'), 'proved to carry with it (as might have been expected) the rejection of elements in the Synoptics themselves which seemed to critics reminiscent of the Fourth Gospel: a notable *circulus in probando' (Interpretation*, 446).

[83]For a strong statement of this case, cf. T. W. Manson, 'The Fourth Gospel' in *Studies in the Gospels and Epistles*, 117f., ending with the words: 'But if John is right on a matter of capital importance such as this is [the nature of the Last Supper and the dating of the crucifixion], he has *eo ipso* established an indisputable claim to a full and unprejudiced hearing on every other point; and his evidence must be seriously considered as possible independent confirmation, where it agrees with the Synoptic tradition, and as a possible alternative where it does not.'

[84]*Gospel of Signs*, 226.

sources. The historicity of Nicodemus, for instance, is a case in point. The name is far better vouched for – whichever Nicodemus it may have been[85] – than that of the otherwise unknown Joseph of Arimathea, despite the fact that John is the only Christian source to mention him. The interrelation of tradition and event is more complex than the simple schema that one can ask the relation to event only 'after the literary task is complete'.

Indeed this relationship brings out another of the questionable presuppositions behind the presumption of John's posteriority. I am prepared to argue from the presumption, until proved otherwise, that the event, whether it be something that happened or that someone said, creates the tradition rather than the tradition the event. This may sound obvious, and can hardly be said to be unreasonable or uncritical. Yet time and again one senses in scholarly discussion, if not the reverse assumption, at least that the form of the question is: What source or tradition must John have been using, whether Synoptic or non-Synoptic, oral or written, for his work to have come out as it is? The question never even seems to be raised whether it may not be what it is because it has been shaped by the event itself.

For example, as is well known, there is a considerable degree of common order in the middle section of the story of Jesus as represented in Mark 6 and pars., and John 6, where a withdrawal to the wilderness, a feeding of the crowds, a journey across the lake, a walking on the water and a discourse about bread follow each other in different forms in both traditions. Moreover, there is also a parallel sequence in Mark 8, with different features being shared by the different accounts. This of course has been one of the strongest planks in the argument for John's literary dependence on the Synoptists. Yet, as Fortna rightly remarks,

> The verbal relationship between the two feeding stories in Mark 6 and 8 is in every way analogous to that between John's story and any of the synoptic versions, yet obviously no one suggests that Mark 6 is literarily dependent on Mark 8 or *vice versa*; rather the relationship between them is held to lie somewhere behind the extant texts.[86]

So far so good. But the inference he draws is that the proper emphasis in recent scholarship on the Johannine *tradition*,[87] 'confused though it

[85]See below, ch. VI, pp. 283–7.

[86]*Gospel of Signs*, 63.

[87]He cites the work of Noack, Wilkens, Dodd, Schnackenburg and Brown. Cf. especially B. Noack, *Zur johanneischen Tradition*.

is at times with considerations of historical reliability', should point to the conclusion that 'between such a (more or less fluid) tradition and the extant gospel lies a literary stage which only source criticism can uncover'. Yet this is a *non sequitur*. The question is never seriously considered whether the measure of agreement and disagreement between the accounts is not better to be explained by confused and divergent memories of a series of *events*, which actually happened in that order, in those places, at that time of the year, in those numbers, etc. Similarly Barrett quotes in favour of John's literary dependence on the Synoptists Gardner-Smith's 'rather lame comment' to account for the common sequence of the desert feeding and the walking on the lake: 'They go well together, and were no doubt associated in oral tradition. . . . this was a very good place to insert the miracle [of the walking]'.[88] It does not seem to occur to either of them that the explanation might be that the events happened in that order rather than that they were put together afterwards, by whatever process.

This is after all the presumption we make with regard to similar but differing press-reports, difficult as it may sometimes be to reconstruct precisely what was done or said behind the vagaries of the reporting. We assume that the accounts relate to the events, in however garbled a form, rather than to each other – unless otherwise indicated. Reasons for thinking otherwise are that, from their wording or selection of detail, they are evidently dependent on a common agency report or, more rarely, that there is deliberate literary plagiarism of one journalist by another. If the reporting of an incident or comment claims to be 'exclusive' and much the same is found in another paper, the natural inference is that the tag is wrong, that they *both* have access to and are describing the same event, not that one reporter has cribbed his material from the other. Perhaps I may repeat a few lines from a light-hearted comment I have used before from the layman I mentioned earlier:

> There is a world – I do not say a world in which all scholars live but one at any rate into which all of them sometimes stray, and which some of them seem permanently to inhabit – which is not the world in which I live. In my world, if *The Times* and *The Telegraph* both tell one story in somewhat different terms, nobody concludes that one of them must have copied the other, nor that the variations in the

[88] *St John and the Synoptic Gospels*, 33 (cf. 89 n.1); quoted, in part, by Barrett, *John*, 45.

> story have some esoteric significance. But in that world of which I am speaking this would be taken for granted. There, no story is ever derived from facts but always from somebody else's version of the same story.[89]

Of course, especially with historical evidence that is not contemporary, the most careful sifting and collation of accounts is necessary (and we shall return to this when considering in detail the sequence referred to from the watershed of the ministry of Jesus).[90] But the presumption is surely justified that an underlying event has at some point controlled the reports rather than simply the reports each other. And divergences in the accounts (such as those, for instance, in the Gospel descriptions of the empty tomb – the degree of darkness, the number of women, what they saw or did, and so on) will not suggest that the event did not take place. Indeed they may authenticate it more cogently than a suspiciously agreed story. Nor will they naturally be presumed to be evidence that each writer is redacting a common source rather than reacting to a common event. This presumption may of course be made uncritically, and more may be going on than meets the eye. But that *it* is made rather than the opposite is not in itself uncritical.

The presumption of whether a common event or a common source lies behind the tradition will affect many kinds of judgments that are made on the Gospel material. For instance, are Martha and Mary, with their closely similar characterization, mentioned by John and Luke because they were using each other or some underlying source, or because in real life they were 'there' – there being Bethany in John but not in Luke? And the same applies to the anointing (or perhaps, as Brown thinks, anointings) and to a great many details in the passion narrative, both in their similarities and in their divergences. Thus in common with many, perhaps now most, scholars I believe that there are basically three *independent* traditions of the trial and death of Jesus, the Markan, the Lukan and the Johannine, and that each goes

[89]Green-Armytage, *John Who Saw*, 12. For the continuation of this splendidly irreverent quotation, cf. my *Redating*, 356. The comment on the esoteric significance in the details would seem to me to apply to the engaging but in my judgment excessively literary incursion into Gospel criticism by another layman, Frank Kermode, *The Genesis of Secrecy*, Cambridge, Mass. and London 1979, and to the brand of New Testament scholarship on which he relies. He writes, 'The Gospels sound like history, and that they do so is the consequence of an extraordinary rhetorical feat' (113)! He also speaks of 'a lingering obsession with historicity, a wish to go on thinking of the gospel narrative as a map of truth' (130).

[90]See below, ch. V, pp. 190–201.

back, directly or indirectly, to source. Which at any point is nearer, or 'truer', must be judged on its own merits by historical and not *simply* by literary criteria.

Closely bound up with this is the question of harmonization, of the piecing together of the different traditions in their relation, again, to source rather than to sources. Harmonization has got a bad name; and clearly there can be quite uncritical harmonization. Yet if one is dealing with several genuinely independent accounts, each going back, however accurately or inaccurately, to the event, then it is legitimate to ask how they can be correlated and combined.

Two examples will come up for detailed discussion later, one at the beginning of Jesus' public life, the other at its end. That Jesus was 'from Nazareth' (whatever his place of *birth*) is universally agreed amongst our sources – despite the fact that, as A. E. Harvey points out in his Bampton Lectures,[91] the very existence of the place at the time was not attested outside the New Testament until an inscription was discovered in 1961, and despite the fact also that Matthew sees in the name some very dubious fulfilment of prophecy (2.23): no one supposes that the interpretation has created the event rather than *vice versa*. But that Jesus did not *live* at Nazareth during the period of the ministry but at Capernaum is stated by Matthew, again as fulfilment of prophecy (4.13–16), implied by Mark (2.1; 6.1) and Luke (4.16, 31), and is, I believe, to be inferred from John (2.12). This I suggest is legitimate harmonization, using one independent stream of tradition to support and confirm another, and from it other inferences may then be drawn. If this were merely a matter of one literary source building upon another it would be a house of cards. But if the facts were thus, the different facets of them may emerge in the different traditions – though this does not of course mean that they can all be reconciled.[92] Similarly, from the end of Jesus' life, one can correlate the names and number of the women at the cross in the different Gospels, and, as we shall see, draw some interesting conclusions. As long as one recognizes that the argument is hypothetical, it may nevertheless be a hypothesis that helps to explain other diverse and apparently unrelated phenomena. The dangers are obvious; but the exercise is not necessarily uncritical, *if*

[91] *Jesus and the Constraints of History*, 1982, 3.

[92] It would, for example, seem impossible to harmonize Luke's account (2.4, 39) that Jesus' parents lived in Nazareth before his birth with Matthew's (2.22f.) that they settled there only later – though one could always appeal to the argument from silence that Matthew says nothing about where they lived earlier or why Joseph came to be in Bethlehem.

there is some reason to believe that there is independent contact with the events. What is uncritical is to allow a methodological presumption to discount such contact *a priori*.

4. *Some Redaction-critical Assumptions*

Finally, in analysing presuppositions that would make the whole enterprise upon which we are engaged appear naive, especially in certain circles of academic fashion currently strong in Germany and America, I should like to put a question-mark against some assumptions behind the pursuit of redaction criticism *when followed uncritically*. Redaction criticism, in contrast with form criticism from which it grew, is, entirely properly, concerned with what the final shaper of the Gospel material, the evangelist, had in mind in arranging, selecting or slanting it as he did. But, as currently understood, this is implicitly defined as a 'redactor' working on 'sources'. So in order to get anywhere or have anything on which to operate, it is necessary to start by analysing out the sources. In the case of Matthew and Luke this is relatively simple, but in the case of John (or Mark) it is much more difficult. *Yet the method requires it*. As Lindars says, 'The reconstruction of the Signs Source is due to the impetus generated by the current interest in redaction criticism.'[93] And Fortna is quite explicit in the opening words of his Preface:

> This study is occasioned by the recent emergence of *Redaktionsgeschichte* as a method of gospel research. If, as that discipline proposes, an evangelist's purpose and meaning are to be investigated by examining his redaction of the sources available to him, it is obviously necessary to identify as objectively and distinctly as possible the exact form of a *Vorlage*.[94]

In other words, the discipline demands the sources, or it has nothing to get its teeth into. It is but a short step to saying that it creates the sources. Moreover its appetite grows by what it feeds on, and its teeth grind exceeding small. By the time that a Bultmann or a Fortna has finished with the Gospel of John it is a thing of shreds and patches[95] –

[93] *Behind the Fourth Gospel*, 28.

[94] *Gospel of Signs*, ix.

[95] One has only to contemplate the *disjecta membra* to which Bultmann (*John*, 218–22) reduces John 6.27–58. One feels that the scraps of verses and half-verses must have been lying scattered over the study floor and that the redactor or redactors collected them up with as much sympathetic understanding as a college bedmaker. But, worry not, the Professor has sorted that out and restored them to an intelligible order, viz. vv.

even though, as Lindars says, the latter reassembles the pieces into a single underlying source or *Grundschrift* with more confidence than the evidence would seem to warrant.[96]

Furthermore, redaction criticism, like form criticism, asks entirely legitimate and very fruitful questions about what the Gospels tell us of the history and conditions of the churches that created them and for whom they were written. A good example of this in the area of Johannine study is J. L. Martyn's *History and Theology in the Fourth Gospel*,[97] in which the Gospel of John is analysed from the point of view of the needs it met in the exigencies and crises of the Johannine community. Like much else in this discipline, this is a highly subjective exercise.[98] You have first to create and date your community and then imaginatively reconstruct the story of its life by reading back material out of the Gospel and Epistles. I shall later[99] have some fairly stringent criticism to make of the supposition from which he starts, namely, of the community reeling under the impact of the synagogue-ban following the Council of Jamnia in the 80s and 90s. But as long as one accepts the hypothetical nature of the approach, it can yield illuminating results. But if one is not careful it can lead one into the *non sequitur* that the more the Gospel tells us about the Johannine

---

27, 34, 35, 30–33, 47–51a, 41–46, 36–40 (with 28f. a detached fragment and 51b–58 an interpretation of the ecclesiastical redactor). Or cf. the order of the Good Shepherd discourse in John 10 on p. 300. Meeks' comment is in place when he speaks of Bultmann's 'obsessive attempt to discover a *rational* sequence in the Johannine discourses and narratives by the incredibly complex rearrangement-hypotheses in his commentary' ('Man from Heaven', 47). Or cf. Kümmel, *Introduction to the NT*, 210f., referring to S. Mendner, 'Nikodemus', *JBL* 77, 1958, 293–323: 'If the conversation with Nicodemus recounted in John 3 originally stood between 7.45–52a and 8.13f., and included only 3.13a, 7b, 9f., 12b, 13a, 31a, 32a, 33, 34a, 35, then Streeter's warning (*The Four Gospels*, 377) concerning the older source theories must be raised for the literary critics who propound such theories: "If the sources have undergone anything like the amount of amplification, excision, rearrangement and adaptation which the theory postulates, then the critic's pretence that he can unravel the process is grotesque. As well hope to start with a string of sausages and reconstruct the pig."'

[96]So too J. M. Robinson, who is otherwise sympathetic: *Trajectories*, 249.

[97]1968.

[98]Cf. the survey in Brown, *Community*, 171–82, of 'Recent Reconstructions of Johannine Community History'. There is as much disagreement as agreement among the practitioners. See too, subsequently, Carson, 'Historical Tradition in the Fourth Gospel' in France and Wenham, edd., *Gospel Perspectives* II, 109–12, who makes the wider comment with which I find myself in much sympathy: 'Extremely complex and detailed literary and critical theories are usually much less plausible than is often thought; yet somehow, unfortunately, they convey a general impression of convincing coherence even after detail after detail has been demonstrated to be implausible' (108).

[99]See below, ch. II, pp. 72–81.

community the less it tells us about Jesus. Thus, from the title of Martyn's book, the unwary reader might reasonably suppose that he was going to be treated to a discussion of the relation between historicity and theology in the Fourth Gospel, as for instance, classically, by Hoskyns in his commentary.[100] But it soon becomes clear that Martyn has no concern for the historicity of the Gospel in the usual sense,[101] but only for the history of the Johannine community and its theology; and for this he is commended in Norman Perrin's introduction to the method, *What is Redaction Criticism?*[102] History becomes redefined as the history of traditions. As James M. Robinson explicitly says,

> The category 'history' really refers 'in the New Testament' to the transmission of traditions about Jesus into varying historical situations that influenced them and were influenced by them. . . . The investigation of the 'historical Jesus' will be primarily in terms of the history of the transmission of traditions about Jesus.[103]

The history of Jesus is thus reduced to the history of the church's understanding of him.

But such a reduction is quite unwarranted. According to what questions one puts to a book of the New Testament, it can tell a great deal *both* about the church *and* about Jesus (a classic demonstration of this was Jeremias' study of the parables),[104] and the Fourth Gospel is no exception. But if you look only for one and ignore the other, then

[100] *The Fourth Gospel*, especially xxi–xlviii, 56–92, 119–26.

[101] He admits there is a residual element of the '*einmalig*', of what took place 'once upon a time', but the Gospel cannot be used as evidence for it. But if one wants to see what happens when all historical controls are severed, one should go to J. Bowman, *The Fourth Gospel and the Jews: A Study in R. Akiba, Esther and the Gospel of John*, Pittsburgh Theological Monograph Series 8, Pittsburgh, 1975, which presents the Fourth Gospel as the Christian answer at the end of the first century to the recently canonized book of Esther, on whose plot it is modelled!

[102] Philadelphia 1969, London 1970, 84. Commenting on another book Perrin writes: 'A strange book in that the author combines redaction criticism with the assumption "that Mark believes that the incidents he uses actually happened"!' (83; exclamation his).

[103] Robinson and Koester, *Trajectories*, 28, 29. It is interesting that Robinson's survey of 'the growing edge of Johannine research' in 'The Johannine Trajectory', 232–68, contains no reference to Dodd's work or to the problem of historicity. Cf. Koester in the same volume, 160: 'The determination of the *Sitz im Leben* must not be identified with the determination of the place, time, and situation in which Jesus said or did one thing or another'. Yet he stresses that the issue is 'the degree to which the earthly Jesus was the criterion of the church's proclamation and faith'. In other words, the Jesus of history was *part* of the Christ of faith. But if so, then questions of historicity are not indifferent or illegitimate.

[104] *The Parables of Jesus*, ET London and New York ²1963.

that is what you will find. And a study can be so slanted that this is the effect. I would say that this is what has tended to happen in Raymond Brown's *Community of the Beloved Disciple*, compared with the more balanced perspective of his commentary on the Gospel. Thus the proper names of the Gospel like Philip, Andrew or Thomas, become evidence primarily for 'the communities represented by the Twelve' in relation to 'the community of the Beloved Disciple', and so on.[105] Yet I believe that it is equally simplistic to assume that stories or sayings in the Gospel simply (or as near as makes no difference) tell us about the Johannine community as it is to assume that they simply tell us about Jesus. But the former is regarded as a sophisticated and critical viewpoint, the latter as naive and uncritical. In fact both represent monocular vision and partial perspectives.

The long shadow is to be seen here of Liberal Protestant scholarship, perpetuated in the presuppositions of the form- and redaction-critics, that there is a great gulf fixed between the Jesus of history and the Christ of faith, an either-or between event and interpretation, fact and symbolism – or 'myth' as Strauss[106] was disastrously to call it. He regarded the Fourth Gospel as almost wholly myth, and therefore *not* history, simply because it is, unquestionably, highly theological. This led in the next generation to the presupposition, almost the dogma, that the Gospels are *not* biographies, which in the modern sense clearly they are not, though, as Martin Hengel has insisted,[107] they do not differ *toto caelo* from other *Lives* in the ancient world nor, in particular, from the histories and story-cycles of the Old Testament. With that presupposition went the assumption that the Gospel writers (and John above all) were indifferent to questions of chronology or topography[108] and could not legitimately be used to provide the

[105] *Community*, 81–8. (Cf. more extremely Martyn, 'Glimpses into the History of the Johannine Community' in his *The Gospel of John in Christian History*, New York 1979, 103 n. 164: 'The possibility that the Beloved Disciple was an historical person who played a role in the early period cannot be pursued in the present book.' Brown chides him for this on p. 174 of his book.) The best support for Brown's position is to be found in the case of Peter. It 'cannot be accidental' that the beloved disciple is consistently mentioned together with Peter (13.23–6, 18.15–16, 20.2–10, 21.7, 20–3), and in terms which savour of 'one-upmanship'. That such constructions may reflect tension between communities associated with the two figures cannot be ruled out. See however below, ch. II, p. 51 n. 81.

[106] D. F. Strauss, *Life of Christ*, ET London 1846.

[107] *Acts and the History of Earliest Christianity*, ET London and Philadelphia 1979, 3–34.

[108] Cf. even Dodd's comment, quoted below, ch. III, p. 132 n. 27, that 'banal' remarks upon the time of year 'did not find a place in the gospel tradition' (*Historical Tradition*, 394).

answers to our (misplaced) interest in these matters. Or at any rate any information of this kind was so buried beneath the redactional process, which was only concerned with such details for non-historical reasons, as now to be irrecoverable.

But these *are* assumptions, and I believe can be shown to be unwarranted assumptions. I am convinced that the early Christian preaching both knew and cared much about the Jesus of history, and took that knowledge and care for granted in its audiences. Peter began his speech at Caesarea quoted earlier, 'I need not tell you what happened lately over all the land of the Jews. . . . You know about Jesus of Nazareth' (Acts 10.37f.; cf. 2.22 of the things 'which God did through him in your midst, as you yourselves know'); and Paul said of King Agrippa, 'I do not believe that he can be unaware of any of these facts, for this has been no hole-and-corner business' (Acts 26.26). Indeed Jesus himself is made to say in the Fourth Gospel, 'I have spoken openly to all the world . . . I have said nothing in secret. Ask my hearers what I told them; they know what I said' (John 18.20f.). In that knowledge the first Christians deliberately wrote Gospels to commend the faith that they proclaimed about Christ by appeal to what Jesus himself said and did and was. John, I am persuaded, was no exception to this. On the contrary he was, I believe, its supreme exemplification, presenting the gospel of the *Word* made *flesh* (1.14), with equal stress on both terms, no less concerned for the history because of the glory he saw in it, but rather reverencing it the more as the indispensable locus of the revelation. As Bultmann finely comments on 1.14,

> The δόξα is not to be seen *alongside* the σάρξ, nor *through* the σάρξ as through a window; it is to be seen in the σάρξ, and nowhere else. If man wishes to see the δόξα, then it is on the σάρξ that he must concentrate his attention.[109]

I believe that the seriousness with which this implies that John took history comes out in a greater respect for historicity than Bultmann himself, or Barrett[110] was prepared to acknowledge. The reverence for history in general cannot ignore the minute particular. Rather, like

[109] *John*, 63.

[110] Cf. his *John*, 98: 'John insisted upon the history of Jesus and upon interpreting it in terms of God. This is not an affirmation of the historical accuracy of John's account; the Fourth Gospel in fact adds little to our knowledge of the historical Jesus.' But I would agree that this can only be decided *a posteriori*, not *a priori* from his high doctrine of history.

Blake, John is prepared to see 'a world in a grain of sand' and 'eternity in an hour'. His is a cosmic, not an acosmic, mysticism.[111]

5. *A First Gospel*

I shall be contending that there is no either-or between recognizing John as the *omega* of the New Testament witness, the end-term, or an end-term, of its theological reflection, and also as its *alpha*, standing as close as any to the source from which it sprang. His theology does not, I believe, take us further from the history but leads us more deeply into it. And I shall often be echoing the lines from Browning's 'A Death in the Desert', which William Temple called 'the most penetrating interpretation of St John that exists in the English language':[112]

> What first were guessed as points, I now knew stars,
> And named them in the Gospel I have writ.[113]

He is concerned, I suggest, to present the *truth* of the history. It is not the whole truth. But that it is a primal vision, a first, though not necessarily the first, statement of the gospel in writing, from source and not from sources, I should wish strongly to insist, and hope to show to be critically well-grounded.

In fact I should be prepared to argue for the priority of John in much the same sense as I would now argue for the priority of Mark.[114] I would not accord Mark any absolute priority over Matthew or Luke (or necessarily say that his Gospel was the first to be finished), nor would I wish to claim that material from their shared written tradition is always to be found in its more original state in his Gospel: for at points it is he who seems to have developed it furthest. Yet I do not

[111]Hoskyns and Davey would enthusiastically agree, yet it is notoriously difficult to pin them down to straight (which I would insist does not mean bare or non-theological) historical statements. This is particularly true of Davey's Introductory Essay (*Fourth Gospel*, xxi–xlviii). But they are absolutely right in seeing John as setting up a barricade against any 'disentangling of history and interpretation' (123). John Marsh also correctly insists that all the evangelists are concerned with 'history as "what goes on" in "what takes place"' (*St John*, Pelican Gospel Commentaries, Harmondsworth 1968, 118 and Introduction, *passim*), but the theological interpretation so dominates that matters of chronology and topography are freely subordinated to it.

[112]From the time of his early essay in *Foundations* (ed. B. H. Streeter, London and New York 1912), 216, to his *Readings in St John's Gospel*, London [2]1945, xvii.

[113]From *Dramatis Personae*, 1864. Browning presupposed a more naive view of apostolic authorship than I, or indeed Temple, would allow.

[114]Cf. my exploratory article, 'The Parable of the Wicked Husbandmen: A Test of Synoptic Relationships', *Twelve More NTS*, 12–34.

believe that he stands in a literary dependence on the other two – as they, almost certainly, do on him. His was a first attempt to tell the story of Jesus – very possibly related to source through the preaching of Peter, as Papias[115] and Clement[116] said. John's was another, as near or perhaps nearer to source, and in its beginnings at least, as near in time.[117] But all this must await investigation.

I am not saying that John 'invented' the Gospel form – though I am pretty certain that Mark[118] did not; according to the tradition[119] he is a 'follower' if anyone is. In fact I doubt any diffusionist schema, that there can have been only one originator who was then copied in turn by everyone else.[120] Rather I believe that form inevitably followed function, from the moment that Christians first felt impelled to tell about Jesus. What Peter in the Acts summary (10.37) calls, curiously but expressively, *τὸ γενόμενον ῥῆμα* (the Christian 'thing'), or Paul (I Cor. 15.1) and Mark (1.1) *τὸ εὐαγγέλιον* (the gospel), or John (I John 1.5; 3.11) *ἡ ἀγγελία* (the message), could not but come out in what Luke (1.1) describes as 'many *διηγήσεις*', or accounts. Who first 'put it in hand to draw up' such written statements is of no greater significance than when Paul speaks of its oral presentation. 'Whether it be I or they' (I Cor. 15.11), is unimportant: what is important is that it should be first-hand.[121] This Paul is able to claim spiritually, though not historically (Gal. 1.11f.; I Cor. 15.3). The author to the Hebrews can say only that he heard it from those who heard the Lord, though he

[115]Eusebius, *HE* 3.39.15; cf. 5.8.3.

[116]Eusebius, *HE* 2.15.1f.; 6.14.6f.; Clement, *Adumbr.* on I Peter 5.13; and the letter edited by Morton Smith, *Clement of Alexandria and a Secret Gospel of Mark*, Cambridge, Mass. 1973, 446.

[117]Koester in *Trajectories*, 151, refers in passing to 'our oldest written gospels: the Gospel of Mark and the Gospel of John'; and in 1938 Gardner-Smith, *Saint John and the Synoptic Gospels*, 95, had said, 'We might tentatively suggest that Mark and John were almost contemporaries.'

[118]Contrast the *a priori* statement by W. Schmithals to present Bultmann's position in the introduction to the ET of his *John*, 6: 'Since Mark created the literary type of Gospel, to which John's writing also belongs, a direct or indirect acquaintance with the Gospel of Mark must surely be accepted.'

[119]Cf. the passages from Eusebius just cited.

[120]J. M. Robinson in *Trajectories*, 266–8, suggests a common form behind both Mark and John, which merely pushes the question back into the unknown.

[121]Cf. B. Gerhardsson, *Memory and Manuscript: Oral Tradition and Written Transmission in Rabbinic Judaism and Early Christianity* (Acta Seminarii Neotestamentici Upsaliensis XXII), Lund 1961, 283: 'The message was presented as an eyewitness account. In the first phase the object was to produce witnesses; in the second, to find witnesses to what the witnesses had said. . . . The information of the sources, that the Apostles presented their preaching and teaching in the form of an eyewitness

claims it was confirmed to him by the direct witness of God and the Spirit (Heb. 2.3f.). Peter claims, for himself and the other disciples, the status of direct eyewitnesses both before and after the resurrection and a commission (παραγγελία) from Jesus (Acts 10.39–42; cf. I Peter 5.1). John also claims to be among those who had heard and seen with his own eyes and handled the word of life (I John 1.1) and that the ἀγγελία he preached to his converts he had 'heard from him' (I John 1.5; cf. John 14.24; contrast the otherwise exactly parallel statement of Paul in I Cor. 15.1). Yet of all these John is the only one to have written a Gospel, and, if one accepts common authorship, or at any rate a tight common circle, the only New Testament figure to have written both a Gospel and Epistles (and the fact that there are no Synoptic counterparts to the Johannine Epistles merits perhaps more reflection that it has received). Moreover I am convinced that he knows the difference between the two – caring to observe and preserve, unlike many of his critics, the distinction of perspective proper to each.[122] Indeed no evangelist so clearly notes the difference between what the disciples understood at the time and what they came to see later through the Spirit (2.21f.; 7.39; 12.16, 33; 16.12–15, 25; 18.9; 21.19, 23; cf. Luke 24.6–8, 44–49). His witness, therefore, alike to the history and the theology, is, I believe, to be accorded a status of *primus inter pares*. It is not the truth (ἡ ἀλήθεια): for him only Christ (John 1.17; 8.32, [cf. 8.36]; 14.6) and the Spirit (I John 5.6) are that. But it is, as he affirms (John 19.35) and as his community acknowledges (John 21.24; III John 12), true (ἀληθής). I suggest that they were right.

At any rate this is the claim that I am persuaded it is worth while to take very seriously and to submit to rigorous critical investigation.

---

account, is definitely not a concession to *secondary* rationalistic and apologetic needs. These needs were there from the beginning. In the milieu in which the early Christian message was first delivered, there must have been a reaction which called for credentials and proof.'

[122]Cf. B. Gerhardsson, *The Origins of the Gospel Traditions*, ET 1979: 'Not even John, whose desire to permit Jesus' divine splendor to shine through in his words and deeds has strongly influenced the style of the Fourth Gospel, writes simply about the present for the present. He is conscious of a chronological, spatial, and factual distance between himself and Jesus' activity in Galilee and Judea' (44); 'The early Christians preserved the memory of a distinct segment of past history and feel their dependence on it' (46).

II

From Sources to Source

1. *A Shift in Perspective*

In the previous chapter we noted how questionable were some of the presuppositions which lay behind the presumption of current critical orthodoxy of the posteriority of John. This was necessary in order to show that there is even a case for entertaining an alternative presumption. The prevailing one cannot be taken for granted as beyond need of rethinking.

Nevertheless, the remoteness of John from source, making it look highly unlikely that it should be a first Gospel, has rested on a good deal of apparently powerful evidence suggesting that the contrary case carries with it the burden of proof. So before we can profitably explore the hypothesis of John's priority and see what happens if it is adopted, there is the further preliminary task of showing that it is an inherently reasonable one and well grounded in the available evidence.

Let it be said at once that the posteriority of John has appeared until recently entirely probable, if not 'obvious'. So let us begin by setting out how it has looked, under three headings, before going on to consider what has come to change the picture.

1. In *space*, the Gospel of John has seemed to belong to 'another world', both geographically and conceptually. It has been located in Ephesus or Alexandria, or some other centre of Philonic Judaism, oriental Gnosticism or what Dodd called 'the higher religion of Hellenism'. It has been seen, in B. W. Bacon's title, as *The Gospel of the Hellenists*,[1] in which, to quote E. F. Scott, a leading interpreter of this school, 'the Messianic idea is replaced by that of the Logos'[2] (though a

[1]Ed. C. H. Kraeling, New York, 1933.
[2]*The Fourth Gospel, its Purpose and Theology*, Edinburgh [2]1908, 6.

mere glance at the concordance will show how fallacious is that particular judgment).[3] It appears to be miles away from the simplicities of Galilean fisherfolk or even from Palestinian Judaism prior to the Jewish war of AD 66–70. That world was a closed book for the writer of the Fourth Gospel.

2. This leads to its distance in *time*. It has seemed to belong to another century, quite literally. Admittedly the dating has been coming down fairly constantly from the extremes to which it was pushed – to *c.* AD 170 – by F. C. Baur and the Tübingen school. It could not be put any later because Irenaeus mentioned it in *c.*180 – though certainly not as if it were a recent production. But a decisive factor in bringing the date down was the discovery of a fragment of the Gospel itself (P^{52}) which reached Egypt in time to be copied not much later than the first quarter of the second century. So the date has settled down *c.* 90–100 among conservatives and radicals alike. But that still puts it effectively beyond the literary life-time of an eyewitness, except a nonagenarian, or any controllable memory of the events. It cannot seriously be seen as a primary record, whatever early traditions it may incorporate.

3. In *person*, in consequence, it becomes, to quote two recent judgments, 'most implausible (nay impossible) that the Fourth Gospel was written by an eyewitness of the ministry of Jesus'[4] and a 'moral certainty' that it was not the work of John the son of Zebedee.[5] The 'beloved disciple' (if he was a real person and not simply an ideal figure) lies now buried irretrievably beneath the history and theology of the Johannine community. The language and thought-forms too are far removed from the competence of a Galilean fisherman.

Such has been the dominant critical assessment of the Gospel for more than a century. Is there any reason to shift, and if so what has made the difference?

It is not easy to put one's finger on anything decisive. In 1957 I gave a paper to a conference at Oxford, which I called, somewhat boldly at the time, 'The New Look on the Fourth Gospel'.[6] In it I said that I detected what were no more than straws in the wind – but they all seemed to be blowing in the same direction. Everything that has

[3]The Logos never recurs (as a title) outside the Prologue, whereas John uses 'the Christ' or 'Christ' 19 times, more frequently than Matthew (16 or 17) and as much as Mark (7) and Luke (12) put together.

[4]Brown, *Community*, 178.

[5]Barrett, *John*, 132.

[6]Published among the proceedings of the Conference on 'The Four Gospels in 1957' in K. Aland, ed., *StEv* I, TU 73, 1959, 338–50; reprinted in my *Twelve NTS*, 1962, 94–106.

happened since has confirmed me in my judgment.[7]

If one had to name one factor, the most powerful would be the effect of the discovery of the Dead Sea Scrolls in 1947. But these were neither a sufficient nor indeed a necessary cause. For isolated voices had pleaded before that for a consideration of what E. R. Goodenough called in the title of an article 'John a Primitive Gospel'.[8] And with the new evidence from Qumran came that from the discovery about the same time of the Coptic Gnostic library at Nag Hammadi in Upper Egypt,[9] which by intensifying research into Gnosticism has given a new impetus to controversy over the nature and dating of the Gnostic evidence and in particular over the whole thesis of a pre-Christian Gnosticism propounded by Bultmann and the History of Religions school.[10] The Jewish roots of Gnosticism have also become much clearer and have shown up the inadequacy of Harnack's designation of it as 'the acute Hellenization of Christianity'.[11] Its links with Jewish wisdom-speculation, apocalyptic and mysticism have provoked a growing body of literature.[12] Concurrently, there has been a major critical reassessment, associated with the name of J. Neusner and other Jewish and Christian scholars, of the use and dating of the Rabbinic material.[13] All this has been in the context of a reconsideration of the wider relationship between Judaism and Hellenism,[14] of the meaningfulness of any hard distinction between Hellenistic Judaism and

[7]'The New Look' was made the point of departure of A. M. Hunter's *According to John*, 14–16.

[8]*JBL* 64, 1945, 145–82. Other examples of early dating are listed in my *Redating*, 307f.

[9]The texts are collected and translated in J. M. Robinson, ed., *The Nag Hammadi Library in English*, Leiden and New York 1977.

[10]Cf. E. Yamauchi, *Pre-Christian Gnosticism*, Grand Rapids and London 1973; and a substantial body of other literature, conveniently summarized in J. D. G. Dunn, *Christology in the Making*, 1980, 305f.

[11]Cf. R. M. Grant, *Gnosticism and Early Christianity*, New York and London 1959; R. McL. Wilson, *The Gnostic Problem*, London 1958, 172–255; *Gnosis and the New Testament*, Oxford and Philadelphia 1968; G. W. MacRae, 'The Jewish Background of the Gnostic Sophia Myth', *NovT* 12, 1970, 86–101; Kümmel, *Introduction to the NT*, 224 (bibliography), and E. P. Sanders, ed., *Jewish and Christian Self-Definition* II, 1981, esp. ch. 11.

[12]Cf. below, ch. VII, p. 314 n. 44.

[13]See, summarily, the collections edited by Neusner, *The Study of Ancient Judaism*, I (Mishnah, Midrash, Siddur), II (The Palestinian and Babylonian Talmuds, New York 1981); and by his pupil W. S. Green, *Approaches to Ancient Judaism: Theory and Practice*, Scholars Press, I, 1978, II, 1980, III, 1981. An application to New Testament study is E. P. Sanders, *Paul and Palestinian Judaism*, London and Philadelphia 1977.

[14]M. Hengel, *Judaism and Hellenism*, ET London and Philadelphia 1974; and earlier V. Tcherikover, *Hellenistic Civilization and the Jews*, ET Philadelphia 1959.

Palestinian Judaism,[15] and of the question of how much Greek was spoken in Palestine in the first century, at every level, especially in Galilee and Jerusalem.[16] All this is fundamental to the placing of the Fourth Gospel.[17] As E. Schillebeeckx has put it,

> *Palestinian* Judaism (and Christianity) was more Hellenistic and more syncretistic than had earlier been supposed, and yet it was truly Jewish. To denounce the Gospel of John as a strange 'Hellenistic' cuckoo in the nest is an obsolete historical view.[18]

And R. Kysar concludes his exhaustive survey of recent scholarship on the evangelist and his setting with the words,

> If the preceding overview is at all accurate, one clue is crystal clear, namely, that contemporary research favours a Palestinian, Old Testament, Jewish setting for the thought of the Gospel.[19]

It was the Qumran evidence that acted as the 'loosener' and which

[15]One of Hengel's summary sections (103–6) is entitled 'The Judaism of Palestine as "Hellenistic Judaism".' Cf. also M. Smith, 'Palestinian Judaism in the First Century' in M. Davis, ed., *Israel: Its Role in Civilization*, New York 1956, 67–81; I. H. Marshall, 'Palestinian and Hellenistic Christianity: Some Critical Comments', *NTS* 19, 1972–3, 271–87; W. A. Meeks, '"Am I a Jew?" – Johannine Christianity and Judaism' in J. Neusner, ed., *Christianity, Judaism and other Greco-Roman Cults*, I, Leiden 1975, 163–86. Already Israel Abrahams had predicted in 'Rabbinic Aids to Exegesis', in H. B. Swete, ed., *Cambridge Biblical Essays*, 183: 'The supposition that Hellenistic and Pharisaic Judaisms were opposed forces will, I am convinced, not survive fuller research.'

[16]Cf. especially J. N. Sevenster, *Do you know Greek? How much Greek could the first Jewish Christians have known?*, *NovT* Suppl. 19, Leiden 1968; and the literature listed in my *Redating*, 133 n. 46. To this should be added E. Schürer, *The History of the Jewish People in the Age of Jesus Christ*, rev. ET, II, 1979, 52–80; S. Freyne, *Galilee from Alexander the Great to Hadrian, 323 B.C.E. to 135 C.E.*, Wilmington, Del. and Notre Dame, Ind., 1980, esp. 138–45 and notes; G. Mussies, 'Greek in Palestine and the Diaspora' in *Compendia* II.2, 1040–65 and the bibliography there contained; and, especially for the later period, S. Lieberman, *Hellenism in Jewish Palestine*, New York 1950, [2]1962; 'How much Greek in Jewish Palestine?' in A. Altmann, ed., *Biblical and other Studies*, Cambridge, Mass., 1963, 123–41; reprinted in his *Texts and Studies*, New York 1974, 216–34 (these in addition to his earlier *Greek in Jewish Palestine*, New York [1]1942, [2]1965).

[17]Cf. the perceptive assessment of the change in prospect by S. C. Neill, *The Interpretation of the New Testament 1861–1961*, Oxford and New York 1964, ch. 8, 'Salvation is of the Jews', especially 306–24.

[18]*Christ: the Christian Experience in the Modern World*, ET 1980, 320. William Temple no doubt meant the same thing when he wrote, 'The Gospel is through and through Palestinian. The notion that it is in any sense Hellenistic is contrary to its whole tenour' (*Readings in St John's Gospel*, xix). But we should now recognize that to insist that it is Palestinian is not to deny that it is *also* Hellenistic.

[19]*The Fourth Evangelist and His Gospel*, 144.

first made scholars realize that the Gospel of John *need* not be so Hellenistic or so late, and therefore so remote in space or time from the person and events it purported to record. For here in the heart of southern Palestine in the period before the Jewish war from one of the most conservative and xenophobic sections of Judaism was to be found what Bo Reicke early designated very percipiently as 'pre-Gnostic' thought-forms[20] with striking affinities with the Johannine writings.[21] It was not so much that there were closer verbal parallels than had been found before – there were not.[22] What was most significant was the emergence of the same qualified ethical and eschatological dualism, expressed in terms of light and darkness, truth and error, which was very different from the Gnosticizing metaphysical dualism, in which spirit is good, matter evil or unreal.[23]

One of the unhappier, but understandable, judgments that Dodd made as an old man was to underestimate the significance of the Qumran parallels, endorsing the judgment of F. C. Grant that they represented 'only "more of the same"'.[24] What he missed was that for the first time we had a body of thought which in fundamental, and not merely verbal, theological affinity, could represent a probable back

[20]'Traces of Gnosticism in the Dead Sea Scrolls', *NTS* 1, 1955, 137–41.

[21]Cf. among other studies especially K. G. Kuhn, 'Die in Palästina gefundenen hebräischen Texte and das Neue Testament', *ZTK* 47, 1950, 192–211, esp. 209f.; F.–M. Braun 'L'arrière-fond judaïque du quatrième évangile et la Communauté de l'Alliance' *RB* 62, 1955, 5–44; R. E. Brown, 'The Qumran Scrolls and the Johannine Gospel and Epistles' in K. Stendahl, ed., *The Scrolls and the New Testament*, 1957, 183–207, reprinted in his *New Testament Essays*, 1965, 102–31; Charlesworth, ed., *John and Qumran*, (especially the articles by Charlesworth, 'A Critical Comparison of the Dualism in 1QS 3.13–4.26 and the "Dualism" Contained in the Gospel of John', 76–106; G. Quispel, 'Qumran, John and Jewish Christianity', 137–55; M.–É. Boismard, 'The First Epistle of John and the Writings of Qumran', 156–65; W. H. Brownlee, 'Whence the Gospel According to John?', 166–94; and the full bibliography); also A. M. Hunter, *According to John*, 27–33; L. Morris, 'The Dead Sea Scrolls and St John's Gospel', in his *Studies in the Fourth Gospel*, 321–58.

[22]Though there are some striking similarities; cf. e.g., with John 1.2, 'By his knowledge everything has been brought into being, and everything that is, he established by his purpose, and apart from him nothing is done' (1QS 11.11). We also find common phrases like 'doing the truth', 'the spirit of truth', 'sons of light', 'witnesses to the truth', 'spring of living waters', etc.

[23]Of this dualism Brown writes: 'In no other literature do we have so close a terminological and ideological parallel to Johannine usage. Can such peculiar similarities between the two trains of thought (which were in existence in the same small region of the world at the same period of time) be coincidental?' (*NT Essays*, 120). Cf. the summary discussion in Kysar, *The Fourth Evangelist and his Gospel*, 131–7, coming to the same conclusion.

[24]Grant, *The Gospels, their Origin and Growth*, New York 1957, London 1959, 175f.; Dodd, *Historical Tradition*, 15.

ground and not simply a possible environment for the distinctive categories of the Johannine literature at an early date and on Palestinian soil. This is not to claim that there was any direct influence or connection, though we shall be taking note of possible contacts through the movement of John the Baptist[25] and perhaps nearer home in Jerusalem itself.[26] But the relationship is very different from the many other possible (or near impossible)[27] backgrounds which have been canvassed for John's thought.

This point can be made by running through, very briefly, the five backgrounds (apart from the highly important 'setting in early Christianity') which Dodd discussed in his *Interpretation of the Fourth Gospel*.[28]

1. *The Hermetic literature*, or 'higher religion of Hellenism', may indeed by very relevant to the reception of the Gospel in the Greek-speaking world to which it came and which later it influenced. For, as Dodd says, 'they found that it fitted into the context of Greek philosophy in which they had been trained'. But the Hermetica represent a fusion of Platonism, Stoicism and oriental thought in Egypt of the second and third centuries. Dodd postulates that 'the type of religious thought they represent can be traced to an earlier period'. Yet this is simply a presumption, and there is no evidence of direct influence of this body of thought in time or place on the writing of the Fourth Gospel.

2. *Hellenistic Judaism*: Philo of Alexandria. Philo, who died *c.* AD 50, is certainly a possible background in time.[29] Yet it becomes more and more doubtful if there was any specific influence from Alexandria. It is much more likely that Philo and John shared a common background in the Jewish Wisdom literature,[30] to which Philo gave an

[25]Below, ch. IV, pp. 173–9.

[26]Below, pp. 66f.

[27]E.g., J. E. Bruns, *The Christian Buddhism of St John*, New York 1971, who thinks there was direct influence of Buddhist teaching, via trade contacts with India. But the most far-fetched suggestion I have come across is that the newly discovered Ebla tablets in northern Syria (from *c.* 2500 BC!) could be an important new 'background' (M. Dahood, 'Ebla, Genesis and John', *The Christian Century*, April 15, 1981).

[28]1953, 10–130.

[29]Ironically Barrett, *The Gospel of John and Judaism*, 1975, 63, complains that Philo is *too* early! But this is because he places the Gospel of John 50 years later. For the same reason he questions whether in first-century Judaism, 'what applied to the time of Jesus applied equally to the time of John': 'the one lies more than a generation before AD 70 and the other almost a generation after' (64).

[30]For the evident connections here with John, cf. E. M. Sidebottom, *The Christ of the Fourth Gospel*, 1961, Appendix B, 203–7; Brown, *John* I, cxxii–cxxv, and Appendix II, 519–24.

allegorical and philosophical twist entirely absent from John. Brown accepts F.–M. Braun's summary that 'if Philo had never existed the Fourth Gospel would most probably not have been any different from what it is'.[31]

3. *Rabbinic Judaism.* Here there are very relevant connections at many points and the deep rooting of John in the world of rabbinic Judaism has been brought out by many studies, notably by Strack-Billerbeck,[32] Odeberg[33] and Schlatter[34] and more recently especially with reference to the midrashic tradition by such writers as Peder Borgen[35] and Wayne Meeks.[36] Yet the process of setting John in this context is always one of reading *back* from much later evidence in the Mishnah and the Talmud and the Midrashim. All one can be sure of is that John stands within a continuing Jewish tradition and is often our earliest witness to it.[37] There is little if anything that antedates John –

[31] *Jean le Théologien*, I: *Jean le Théologien et son Évangile dans l'Église ancienne*, 1959, 298; cited, Brown, *John* I, lviii. Similar estimates are made by T. W. Manson, *On Paul and John*, 1963, 149; B. Lindars, *The Gospel of John*, 1972, 40, 'There is really no connection with Philo's thought, which must be counted out of the influences on the Fourth Gospel'; H. Conzelmann, *An Outline of the Theology of the New Testament*, ET London and New York 1969, 330; and after a full discussion, Dunn, *Christology in the Making*, 1980, 220–8. Cf. already F. J. A. Hort, in a letter to E. Abbott, 5 August 1879, on influences of Philo on John: 'though I rather assumed their existence till I read Philo for myself, I now much doubt their existence' (A. Hort, *Life and Letters of F. J. A. Hort*, London 1896, II, 278); and Westcott, *John* I, xxxiv–ix. W. A. Meeks however makes the balanced comment: 'I do not, of course, pretend that Philo has had any direct influence upon the author of the Fourth Gospel'; nevertheless 'Philo constitutes a fixed point of inestimable value in every study of first-century Judaism and Christianity, not only because of the volume of his extant writings, but because he can be located precisely in place, time, and social class', adding 'If only we knew with comparable certainty one-tenth as much about the Gospel's author and the setting of his community as we know about Philo and the Alexandrian Jews, then our task would be much simpler' ('The Divine Agent and his Counterfeit in Philo and the Fourth Gospel' in E. S. Fiorenza, ed., *Aspects of Religious Propaganda in Judaism and Early Christianity*, Notre Dame, Ind., 1976, 43–67; quotations 44 and 60).

[32] H. L. Strack and P. Billerbeck, *Kommentar zum Neuen Testament aus Talmud und Midrasch*, Munich 1922–8, II, 302–853.

[33] H. Odeberg, *The Fourth Gospel Interpreted in its Relation to Contemporaneous Religious Currents in Palestine and the Hellenistic–Oriental World*, 1929.

[34] A. Schlatter, *Die Sprache und Heimat des vierten Evangelisten*, Gütersloh 1902; *Das Evangelium nach Johannes*, Stuttgart [4]1928; *Der Evangelist Johannes*, Stuttgart 1930, [2]1948.

[35] Especially *Bread from Heaven: An Exegetical Study of the Concept of Manna in the Gospel of John and the Writings of Philo*, *NovT* Suppl 10, 1965.

[36] *The Prophet-King: Moses Traditions and the Johannine Christology*, *NovT* Suppl 14, 1967, ch. 4.

[37] Thus, I. Abrahams, *Studies in Pharisaism and the Gospels*, I, 1917, 135, observes that John 7.22f., in that it recognizes the precedence of circumcision on the

or anything here that affords a background for his *distinctive* categories.

4. *Gnosticism*. The new Gnostic books have reinforced the belief that Gnosticism as an 'ism', as a *Weltanschauung* or system of salvation, is a second- and third-century phenomenon, though 'gnosticizing' ways of thought were certainly rife in Jewish and Christian circles of the first century. So far from John having drawn his motifs from a pre-Christian Gnosticism, with its own 'Redeemer-myth', it is much more a case of the gnosticizing of Christian motifs; and in this John was indeed seized on by the Gnostics,[38] as the first commentaries by Heracleon and other Valentinians show[39] and the earlier evidence of the Johannine Epistles clearly foreshadows. But John himself, unlike Paul who turned the language of his gnosticizing opponents against them, seems deliberately to have avoided it.[40] As a background, rather than a later and highly ambiguous environment,

---

eighth day over the sabbath law, is 'another instance of the Fourth Gospel's close acquaintance with Hebraic traditions', though our evidence of course is later (cf. M. *Shab*. 18.3; 19.2–5; *Ned*. 3.11). On 7.23 Dodd, *Historical Tradition*, 332, also quotes the judgment of Rabbi Eliezer, 'If circumcision, which affects only one of a man's bodily members, repels [i.e. takes precedence over] the Sabbath, how much more does that apply to *his entire body*?' (*Mek*. on Exod. 31.13). Abrahams also cites 7.27, 'When the Messiah appears no one is to know where he comes from', an idea which appears to be reflected in Justin, *Dial*. 8 and 110. Similarly G. Vermes, *Jesus the Jew*, London 1973, New York 1974, 55, notes: 'Strangely enough, the clearest echo of the antagonism between Galileans and Judaeans reported in the rabbinic writings is to be found in the Fourth Gospel in the New Testament', adding, 'This late work offers seemingly reliable evidence that attitudes definitely attested in the late first and second centuries AD are traceable to the age of Jesus.' He says the same of John's statements about 'the people of the land' (7.49; cf. 9.34), which even Martyn, who regards the Gospel as anything but a source-book for the Jesus of history, says 'stand proudly among the most accurate statements of Jewish thought in the whole New Testament' (*History and Theology in the Fourth Gospel*, 93). On the later legal ruling implied in the argument of John 8.33–41 cf. Jeremias, *Jerusalem in the Time of Jesus*, ET 1969, 351. The belief in 8.56 that Abraham was given a vision of the messianic age may be the same that reappears in II Esd. 3.13f., where he is shown by God how the world would end, and *Gen. R*. 44.22 where Rabbi Aqiba holds that the world to come was also revealed to him.

[38]Cf. Hippolytus, *Ref*. 5–7; Irenaeus, *Adv. haer*. 3.11.7. What is probably an early stage in this process is now to be seen in the Valentinian *Gospel of Truth*. Cf. Barrett, 'The Theological Vocabulary of the Fourth Gospel and the Gospel of Truth' in W. Klassen and G. F. Snyder, edd., *Current Issues in New Testament Interpretation: Studies in Honor of Otto A. Piper*, New York and London 1962, 210–13; reproduced in his *Essays on John*, 50–64.

[39]Cf. J. N. Sanders, *The Fourth Gospel and the Early Church*, 1943, ch. 3; and E. H. Pagels, *The Johannine Gospel in Gnostic Exegesis: Heracleon's Commentary on John*, SBLMS 17, New York and Nashville 1973.

[40]See below, ch. VII, pp. 327–9.

Gnosticism is increasingly coming to be seen as of very doubtful relevance.

5. *Mandaism.* This evidence, on which Bultmann sought to build so much, is the latest of all. The Mandaean canon cannot be dated before the early Islamic period (*c.* AD 700). Anything before that is, as Dodd says, pure inference and speculation. The notion that it goes back to the time of John the Baptist and that the Fourth Gospel takes over and answers productions of this Baptist sect seems less and less likely[41] (not least in the light of the Dead Sea Scrolls, which, as we shall see,[42] throw a good deal more light on the Baptist material in the Gospel of John). As a background for the Fourth Gospel the Mandaean material is now generally rejected.[43] Yet the fact that Bultmann, who broke the mould within which both the conservative and liberal estimates of John worked, was able to argue that the Logos-hymn of the Prologue came from an Aramaic, Palestinian and pre-Johannine source, and thus that whatever the date of the present Gospel 'one must reckon with the idea that Johannine Christianity represents an older type than does synoptic Christianity',[44] shows again how wary one must be of seeing the Fourth Gospel simply as Hellenistic and late. Indeed in the light of the Dead Sea Scrolls, W. Michaelis has gone so far as to write: 'It may now be said that the Palestinian character of the Gospel of John has become so clear that attempts to promote another provenance should really cease.'[45]

[41]Cf. e.g., K. Rudolph, *Die Mandäer*, I Prolegomena, Göttingen 1960, 80.

[42]See below, ch. IV, pp. 173–9.

[43]Thus G. D. Kilpatrick, summarizing 'The Religious Background of the Fourth Gospel' in F. L. Cross, ed., *Studies in the Fourth Gospel*, Oxford 1957, 43, says: 'We can discard the *Hermetica* along with the Mandaean texts and other evidences of Gnosticism. They constitute no significant part of the background of the Gospel, they do not provide the key to its interpretation.' But Kümmel, *Introduction to the NT*, 223, wishes to insist that 'the Mandaean writings are late, deformed witnesses for a Jewish Gnosticism which formed on the edge of Judaism and which is to be assumed as the intellectual background of John.'

[44]'Die Bedeutung der neuerschlossenen mandäischen und manichäischen Quellen für das Verständnis des Johannesevangeliums', *ZNW* 24, 1925, 100–46, specifically 142–5; reprinted in *Exegetica*, Tübingen 1967, 55–104, specifically 100–3.

[45]*Einleitung in das Neue Testament*, Berne 1961, 123; quoted and translated in Barrett, *The Gospel of John and Judaism*, 8. Cf. S. S. Smalley in D. A. Hagner and M. J. Harris, edd., *Pauline Studies: Essays Presented to Professor F. F. Bruce on his 70th Birthday*, Exeter and Grand Rapids, Mich., 1980, 105 n. 72: 'In these days of the "new look" on John, it is interesting to recall the comment on the Fourth Gospel by Charles Gore, originally written in 1922: "I am not without hopes that the essentially Palestinian, not Hellenistic, origin and character of the Gospel, and its high value as an historical witness both to the events of our Lord's life and to His teaching may soon come to be regarded as an 'assured result' of critical enquiry"' (C. Gore, *The Reconstruction of Belief*, London ²1926, 403 n. 1).

But the most that this shift has shown is that the Gospel *need* not be so Hellenistic or so late as was formerly supposed. It has certainly made the presumption of Johannine posteriority look a good deal shakier. But more is required to show that the opposite presumption is reasonable and well-grounded. For this it is necessary to try to demonstrate that the Johannine tradition *could well* go back 'to source', that is, to Jesus himself (though of course one can never *prove* that it does so) and to trace its connections with 'the beginning'.

With this aim in view we may look again at the three links, in space, time and person, from which we started in discussing its remoteness.

2. *The Link in Space*

What are the geographical connections of the Johannine writings? There is no place of address even in the Epistles – in notable contrast with those of Paul. I John does not even contain a proper name, except that of Cain, which is not much help in placing it. In the Fourth Gospel there is nothing to indicate where it was written – any more than there is in any of the others. But when John and his Gospel are referred to in the ancient world it is always in association with Ephesus. Irenaeus says that John published his Gospel there.[46] Justin Martyr says that he lived there,[47] a statement confirmed by Irenaeus on the authority of Polycarp,[48] who was bishop of Smyrna in the same area and claimed to have known John.[49] Polycrates, who was bishop at Ephesus at the end of the second century and a repository of Asian traditions, speaks of John's death there.[50] And similar accounts are preserved by Clement of Alexandria[51] and Origen.[52] The apocryphal Acts of John in Greek, which surprisingly do not mention the composition of the Gospel,[53]

[46]*Adv. haer.* 3.1.2; quoted, Eusebius, *HE* 5.8.4.

[47]*Dial.* 81.4.

[48]*Adv. haer.* 3.3.4; quoted, Eusebius, *HE* 3.28.6; 4.14.6.

[49]Irenaeus, *Ad Florinum*, quoted, Eusebius, *HE* 5.20.5f.

[50]In his letter to Victor, bishop of Rome; quoted, Eusebius *HE* 5.24.3; cf. 5.24.1–7 for the credentials that he claimed.

[51]*Quis dives salvetur?* 42.1–15; quoted, Eusebius, *HE* 3.23.5–19.

[52]In the third volume of his *Comm. in Gen.*; quoted, Eusebius, *HE* 3.1.1.

[53]But the work certainly implies the Gospel teaching; e.g., 'This Cross of Light is sometimes called Logos by me for your sakes, sometimes mind, sometimes Jesus, sometimes Christ, sometimes a door, sometimes a way, sometimes bread, sometimes seed, sometimes resurrection, sometimes Son, sometimes Father, sometimes Spirit, sometimes life, sometimes truth, sometimes faith, sometimes grace' (98; *NTApoc* II, 233). It is a thoroughly docetic production and says that John could not speak or write of what he had seen and heard (87, 93). But it would be unwarranted to infer from this that the author denied that he wrote a Gospel.

record the ministry of John in Ephesus *passim* and are attributed to Leucius Charinus from that area. Even the Syriac *History of John, the Son of Zebedee*,[54] which is non-docetic but highly thaumaturgical and an otherwise quite eccentric tradition, says that John came to Ephesus as a young man, ministered and wrote his Gospel there, still relatively early.

In the ancient tradition of the church there is simply no alternative to Ephesus as the place of writing. Alexandria has been canvassed,[55] on account of its supposed connections with Philonic Judaism. But this is purely hypothetical and falls down on the fact that it is surely inconceivable that, had there been any association of this Gospel with Alexandria, Clement and Origen, who prized it above all, would have made nothing of it. The only Gospel connected in ancient tradition with Alexandria is that of Mark, and that of course well after it was written – and in Rome.[56]

Moreover there are other pointers to Ephesus as the place of writing, apart from the external tradition. The Book of Revelation, addressed to the churches of the Ephesus area, clearly presupposes acquaintance with Christianity in the Johannine idiom, however doubtful common authorship must be. The false teachers attacked in I and II John evidently reflect a form of gnosticizing Judaism,[57] of which there are other signs in the same area (Colossians *passim*; I Tim. 1.3f.; 6.20; Rev. 2.9, 24; 3.9). I John 5.6 appears to counter the view that the divine Christ came upon the human Jesus at his baptism but left him before his crucifixion, a view later to be associated with Cerinthus,[58] whose encounter with John in Ephesus is attested on the authority of Polycarp.[59] Finally, the docetic-type heresy attacked in the Johannine Epistles (I John 4.2; II John 7) is even more strongly assailed later by Ignatius in the same area (*Smyrn.* 1–3).[60]

[54]Ed. W. Wright, *Apocryphal Acts of the Apostles*, Cambridge 1871, II, 3–60. It does not occur in any of the collections of New Testament apocrypha known to me. For quotations from it, cf. my *Redating*, 258f.

[55]E.g., by Sanders, *Fourth Gospel in the Early Church*, 39–43; B. P. W. Stather Hunt, *Some Johannine Problems*, London 1958, 97–123; and more recently and surprisingly Brownlee in *John and Qumran*, 189–91. Cf. H. C. Snape, 'The Fourth Gospel, Ephesus, and Alexandria', *HTR* 47, 1954, 1–14.

[56]Eusebius, *HE* 2.16.1; 2.24; and the (probably authentic) letter of Clement himself in Morton Smith, *Clement of Alexandria and a Secret Gospel of Mark*, 446–53.

[57]See below, ch. VII, pp. 327–9, and VIII, p. 346.

[58]Irenaeus, *Adv. haer.* 1.26.1.

[59]Irenaeus, *Adv. haer.* 3.3.4; quoted, Eusebius, *HE* 3.28.6; 4.14.6.

[60]One could also instance the influence of the Gospel on Melito of Sardis in the mid-second century.

I have given the evidence for the Ephesian location of John and his Gospel in some detail because, however much one tradition may be building on another,[61] this is a case where the external evidence is uncontested and is supported by whatever indications there are from the internal. There are of course other divergences in the same tradition, about *when* the Gospel was written, and above all there is confusion over *which* John is being talked about, the writer of the Gospel or the Apocalypse, if these were not the same person. That there were two tombs at Ephesus associated with John is stated by Dionysius of Alexandria[62] and is entirely possible. But that there were *no* Johns at Ephesus and that the entire tradition connecting it with the Gospel is groundless would seem quite improbable. It is worth emphasizing this, because it is merely uncritical to dismiss ancient tradition without due cause.

We may therefore with reasonable confidence provisionally locate the Epistles of John and at least the Prologue and Epilogue of the Gospel, which I have argued were written after them,[63] in the Ephesus area. Moreover I think one can say the same for the main body of the Gospel as we have it, which, I have argued,[64] presupposes an evangelistic purpose, directly or indirectly,[65] in the Greek-speaking *diaspora* of Judaism (cf. especially John 7.35, 'Will he go to the Dispersion among the Greeks, and teach the Greeks?'). But the Epistles clearly indicate that the message did not start there. They refer their readers back to what they heard 'at the beginning' of the mission

[61]It clearly does *not*, as Brownlee says, *John and Qumran*, 188f., all 'depend upon an alleged claim of Papias to have known the apostle himself during his residence at Ephesus (Eusebius, *HE* 5.20.4–8)'. This passage in fact refers to Polycarp. Eusebius himself denies that Papias met the apostle John (3.39.2–7) but does not question the Ephesian connection.

[62]*De prom.*, quoted, Eusebius, *HE* 3.39.6, 7.25.16. Actually, as Nolloth (*The Fourth Evangelist: his Place in the Development of Religious Thought*, London 1925, 63) points out, the word he uses, μνήματα, could mean no more than 'memorials' to John (cf. Jerome, *Vir. ill.* 9, 'duas memorias'), and so not imply two Johns as Dionysius and Eusebius wish.

[63]'The Relation of the Prologue to the Gospel of John', *Twelve More NTS*, 65–76.

[64]'The Destination and Purpose of St John's Gospel', *Twelve NTS*, 107–25; also 'The Destination and Purpose of the Johannine Epistles', ibid., 126–38.

[65]I should be perfectly happy to say that they were written for the Christian community in the service of its mission among Jews. In any case what became material for conversion no doubt started life as material for edification (cf. H. E. Edwards, *The Disciple Who Wrote These Things*, 55). Yet I still think that the difference of aim in John 20.31 ('that you may believe that Jesus is the Christ the Son of God and may have life in his name'; cf. 19.35 'that you too may believe') and I John 5.13 ('to you who believe in the name of the Son of God that you may know that you have eternal life') is decisive.

(I John 2.7, 24; 3.11; II John 6). Moreover this message claims to go back to 'the beginning' of the gospel and to Christ himself (I John 1.5; II John 5).[66] So the Ephesian Gospel is asserted to have a Palestinian origin.

How it 'travelled' is wrapped in oblivion. The early echoes (though no more) of the Gospel in Ignatius of Antioch[67] and the Odes of Solomon,[68] as well as more generally its Palestinian, Syrian or Transjordanian *Heimat*,[69] might suggest a route via Syria. Indeed a number of scholars have argued for a Syrian locale of the Gospel on such a basis.[70] But this must all remain very uncertain.[71]

More relevant is the Palestinian scene from which it comes. Of what geographical setting does the Gospel speak? In a recent article on

[66]Cf. the transition in II John 5f.: 'I am recalling the [command] *we* have had before *us* from the beginning. . . . This is the command which was given *you* from the beginning, to be *your* rule of life.'

[67]E.g., *Eph.* 6.1; *Magn.* 7.1; 8.2; and especially *Philad.* 7.1. Cf. further C. Maurer, *Ignatius von Antiochen und das Johannesevangelium*, Zürich 1949, 30–99. Barrett, 'Jews and Judaizers in the Epistles of Ignatius', reprinted in his *Essays on John*, 132–58, thinks them so slight as to be 'the sort of thing Ignatius might have picked up in his transit through Asia, if, as tradition asserts, this was the home of the Johannine literature' (152). For what it is worth, Theophilus of Antioch was later the first orthodox commentator on the Gospel.

[68]E.g., 6.11f.; 7.6; 10.5; 11.19; 12.7, 12; 16.19; 33.4; 41.11–15. For a fuller list cf. Charlesworth, 'The Odes of Solomon and the Gospel of John', *CBQ* 35, 1973, 298–322, who concludes that 'both reflect the same milieu, probably somewhere in Western Syria, and both were probably composed in the same community' (320). The latter judgment would seem to require more substantiation.

[69]Cf. the articles by Charlesworth, 'Qumran, John and the Odes of Solomon', and Quispel, 'Qumran, John and Jewish Christianity', in *John and Qumran*, 107–55; O. Cullmann, *The Johannine Circle*, ET 1976; Schillebeeckx, *Christ*, 305–432; and earlier C. F. Burney, *The Aramaic Origin of the Fourth Gospel*, Oxford 1922, and Bultmann, *Exegetica*, 100–3 (see n. 44 above), who said 'If the Gospel of John arose in Syria, as I believe, then the question about continuity would thereby find a more precise answer.'

[70]Already Sanday had written in *The Criticism of the Fourth Gospel*, 199: 'I have long thought that it would facilitate our reconstruction of the history of early Christian thought, if we could assume an anticipatory stage of Johannean teaching, localized somewhere in Syria, before the Apostle reached his final home at Ephesus. This would account more easily than any other hypothesis for the traces of this kind of teaching in the *Didache*, and in Ignatius, as well as in some of the earliest Gnostic systems.' But he wisely goes on: 'We cannot verify anything. We have no materials for this purpose. We can only deal a little with probabilities.' Similarly, Manson, *Studies in the Gospels and Epistles*, 119–21; Kümmel, *Introduction to the NT*, 247.

[71]A route further east is suggested by the Syriac *History of John* (see n. 54), which states that Ephesus was the first city to receive the gospel of Christ after Edessa, in N. Mesopotamia. But this curious statement apparently depends on the legend, itself probably baseless, about Edessa in Eusebius, *HE* 1.13.

'Johannine Geography'[72] C. H. H. Scobie has said that the phrase may indicate three things. It can tell us (1) what symbolic or theological significance the names of towns or areas have for the evangelist himself; (2) what light they throw on the locations of the Johannine community; and (3) what information they give us about the historical ministry of Jesus. He urges that all three levels have to be kept in mind.

At the first level, however, he agrees that there is no consistent 'theological geography' in the Gospel (in the way that R. H. Lightfoot argued, for example, that Galilee always stands for acceptance, Judaea for rejection) according to which the itineraries of the ministry would be determined by typological rather than topographical considerations.[73] This is not of course to say that John does not see symbolic significance in place-names as in everything else (just as Matthew does in Nazareth and Capernaum [2.23; 4.13–16] without thereby being supposed to have invented them for theological reasons), though the only time he specifically calls attention to such significance is in 9.7, of Siloam, which again he certainly did not create for the purpose. There is no doubt too that the saying about a prophet having no honour in his own country (4.44) acquires a more profound significance in the light of 1.11: John designates Judaea as his 'own land' (τὰ ἴδια) *to* which he came and where they did not receive him, in contrast to Galilee, the land *from* which he came (7.40–52) and where they did receive him (4.45).[74] Yet, as Scobie recognizes, there is really no case for saying that

[72] *Studies in Religion/Sciences Religieuses* 11, 1982, 77–84.

[73] *Locality and Doctrine in the Gospels*, London and New York 1938, 144–6. On this question see further D. M. Mollat, 'Remarques sur le vocabulaire spatial du quatrième évangile', in Aland, ed., *StEv* I, TU 73, 1959, 321–8; W. A. Meeks, 'Galilee and Judaea in the Fourth Gospel', *JBL* 85, 1966, 159–69; R. Fortna, 'Theological Use of Locale in the Fourth Gospel', in M. Shepherd and E. C. Hobbs, edd., *Gospel Studies in Honor of Sherman Elbridge Johnson (Anglican Theological Review*, Supplementary Series 3), 1974, 58–95; and W. D. Davies, *The Gospel and the Land*, 1974, 321–31, who concludes: 'Only by a *tour de force* can Judaea be made a symbol of the rejection, and Galilee and Samaria a symbol of the acceptance of the gospel. . . . To ascribe to John a developed geographical symbolism would be to run counter to his concentration on the Word made flesh in a Person' in whom there is a supersession of localized holy places (329).

[74] So Lightfoot, *Locality and Doctrine*, 144 (though in *St John's Gospel: a Commentary*, ed. C. F. Evans, Oxford and New York 1956, 35f., he interprets 4.44 to mean that Jesus' *Heimat* is neither in Judaea nor in Galilee but in heaven). Yet even this apparently highly-charged distinction is not so far removed from the matter-of-fact way Matthew distinguishes between Capernaum, the place where Jesus lived (τὴν ἰδίαν πόλιν, 9.1 [par. Mark 2.1]; cf. 4.13), and Nazareth, his place of origin (τὴν πατρίδα αὐτοῦ, 13.54; cf. Luke 4.16, 'where he was brought up').

place-names in John are there primarily for their symbolic or theological significance: usually there is nothing to suggest that any ulterior meaning is intended. As Dodd said,

> All attempts that have been made to extract a profound symbolical meaning out of the names of Sychar, the city of Ephraim, Bethany beyond Jordan, Aenon by Salim, of Cana and Tiberias, or again of Kedron, Bethesda (or Bethzatha), and Gabbatha, are hopelessly fanciful; and there is no reason to suppose that a fictitious topography would in any way assist the appeal of the gospel to an Ephesian public.[75]

But the second level, what they tell us about the Johannine communities, is for Scobie of prime importance.[76] Again this is not to be denied or despised. That there is a particular concentration of distinctive Johannine place-names in Samaria, Judaea, and in particular Jerusalem is obviously significant for the nature and locale of the earliest Johannine mission, and we shall be making full use of what this may tell us. But again it is possible to allow the valid insights of form criticism and redaction criticism to run away with one and to get things out of proportion.[77] This happens, for instance, when it is assumed that the mention of such towns as those just listed by Dodd *must* mean that there were Johannine churches in these places and that *that* is why they appear in the Gospel. Thus, by way of example, Scobie contends that the references to Cana and Bethsaida suggest 'the existence there of Johannine communities, jealously preserving their own traditions and regarding Capernaum as a rival', which is said in this Gospel to be 'played down in a remarkable way'. Yet this is simply not true. Two visits are made by Jesus to Cana, none to Bethsaida (compared with two in Mark), while Capernaum is actually mentioned more times in John than in any other Gospel! The rivalry is said to derive from the fact that Capernaum was the centre of a Petrine community, because excavations there have revealed a house-church over the site of what is supposed to have been Peter's house.[78] But this identification is quite

[75] *Interpretation*, 452f.

[76] He draws at this point on a largely forgotten book by K. Kundsin (a Latvian pupil of Bultmann's), *Topologische Überlieferungsstoffe im Johannesevangelium*, Göttingen 1925, who viewed the Johannine topography as evidence of subsequent Christian settlements.

[77] G. Dalman, *Sacred Sites and Ways*, ET London and New York 1935, 11–13, took Bultmann to task for this a long time ago.

[78] Cf. V. Corbo, *The House of St. Peter at Capharnaum*, ET Jerusalem 1969; V. Corbo, S. Loffreda, A. Spijkerman and E. Testa, *Cafernao*, I–IV, Pubblicazioni Dello

uncertain and it could just as easily, if not more probably, have been Jesus' own house which was thus revered.[79] In fact I shall argue that Peter, Jesus and the Zebedee family all lived in Capernaum, and in any case any rivalry between Peter and John and their communities[80] is in my judgment largely read into the Gospel rather than out of it.[81]

Above all the method becomes dangerous when it is assumed that the reason why the places receive mention is for what they tell us of the Johannine communities and *not* for any reliable information about the historical Jesus – though no doubt the fact that he went there may have been a factor in creating the communities in the first place. This is the same either-or that we met in the last chapter, and because he embraces this disjunction, what remains on the third level of Scobie's 'Johannine geography' is much reduced. Very little, to use his metaphor, gets through the second 'sieve'. Yet this is a matter of presupposition rather than of evidence. It is a question, as he says, whether the communities created the geographical traditions, or the traditions created the communities. If we make the opposite presupposition to his we shall, he admits, get a very different picture.

> Do we assume a gospel is historical unless proven otherwise, or do we assume it to be the product of a community/editor unless proven historical? What criteria can be applied to help to determine historicity? Without firm criteria the debate seems doomed to go round in circles for ever.[82]

Studium Publicum Franciscanum 19, Jerusalem 1972–5; and, more popularly, S. Loffreda, *A Visit to Capharnaum*, Jerusalem 1977.

[79]B. Pixner, to whom I shall be referring below (pp. 62f.), agrees with me. Of the 131 inscriptions (of which interestingly no less than 110 are in Greek and ten in Aramaic) the name of Peter only occurs in two. There are others to 'Jesus', 'Christ', 'the Lord', 'the Most High' and 'God'.

[80]Cf. e.g., Brown, *Community*, 84.

[81]There is no hint of antagonism between Peter and the beloved disciple in the passages where they appear together (see ch. I above, p. 31 n. 105). Indeed Peter is a good deal more 'put down' in the Gospel of Mark than of John: contrast e.g. Mark 8.32f. and John 6.66b–71; Mark 14.71f. and John 18.27. Cf. Schnackenburg, 'On the Origin of the Fourth Gospel' in D. G. Miller, ed., *Jesus and Man's Hope*, Pittsburgh 1970, I, 240: 'Why is this disciple, whom Jesus loved in such a signal way, associated . . . with Simon Peter? Not out of rivalry, let alone out of opposition!'; Schillebeeckx, *Christ*, 319: 'There is no question of opposition to Peter, as some interpreters claim.' He sees 'a *certain* tension' between the Johannine circle and 'the twelve'. But then, like Cullmann, he does not believe the beloved disciple was one of the Twelve. This will be discussed below, pp. 108f.

[82]From a personal letter, 9 November 1982.

I shall go on to suggest that the sheer facticity and detail and in many cases verifiability of the evidence *without any apparent theological or community interest* suggests that the presumption of historicity until proved otherwise is a thoroughly reasonable starting-point. But before we go on to make and test this presumption, it is worth remarking that if what he calls the 'wealth of geographical and topographical references' *are* primarily evidences of the distribution of Johannine communities, then it shows us a church with extraordinarily widespread Palestinian connections. And the later the Gospel is put the more enduring these must be presumed to be. This is a very different picture from that of a form of Hellenistic Christianity that had lost, if it had ever had, any links with the native soil of the Christian movement.

Yet let us look more carefully at this wealth of geographical and topographical references. Scobie's own summary is as good as any for conveying its sheer quantity:

> Some of the locations are also mentioned in the Synoptics: Galilee, the Sea of Galilee, Bethsaida, Capernaum, Nazareth, Samaria, Judaea, Bethany near Jerusalem, the Temple, the Temple Treasury, the house of the Last Supper, the court of the High Priest, the Praetorium, Golgotha, Jesus' tomb. But a surprising number are peculiar to John: Cana, Tiberias, Sychar, Joseph's field, Jacob's well, Mount Gerizim, Aenon near Salim, Bethany beyond Jordan, the house of Mary, Martha, and Lazarus, the place of Jesus' meeting with Martha, the tomb of Lazarus, Ephraim, the Pool of Bethesda, the Pool of Siloam, Solomon's Portico, the Wadi Kidron, the garden where Jesus was arrested, the door of the High Priest's court, the Pavement/Gabbatha, the garden in which Jesus' tomb was located.

The abundance and precision of detail is impressive, especially when contrasted, say, with the Gospel of Luke, whose author, when as in Acts he knows the ground, is remarkably precise – and accurate. But in his Gospel, especially in dealing with Galilee, with which he was evidently unfamiliar, and when he is on his own in the long central section 9.51–18.14,[83] he is extraordinarily vague and unspecific. Where he does not know, he generalizes. This contrast will come out time and again as we proceed, but it may be illustrated by the treatment of the tradition common to Luke and John about Martha and Mary. In Luke (10.38–42) it is introduced with the words, 'While they were on their way Jesus came to a village.' We are given no idea of its name or

[83]For details see below, ch. VI, pp. 212–16.

location, or why or when he went there, except that since the incident is set near the beginning of his final journey to Jerusalem we should assume that it was closer to Galilee than to the capital. On the other hand, in John (11.1–12.11) we are told its name, Bethany, its precise location, fifteen stades, or just under two miles, from Jerusalem, why Jesus went there on two separate occasions, from where (the other Bethany beyond Jordan and Ephraim) and, the second time, the exact day, six days before Passover, to which, as we shall see, it is possible to give a precise calendar dating. It is hard to believe that such detail is put in purely for symbolic purposes or that it does not rest upon genuine memory.

Furthermore, recent archaeological studies have tended to reinforce the belief that in Johannine topography we are in touch with a tradition which knew Palestine intimately.[84] Bruce E. Schein, who for many years has walked students from the Lutheran church in Jerusalem over every inch of the terrain, has written a book (albeit imaginative at times) to show that the author of the material must have known the land like the back of his hand;[85] and my own inevitably more hasty investigation of Johannine sites has led me in very much the same direction – even if not always to the same conclusions.

The details must come out in the discussion of the chronology and itinerary of the ministry of Jesus. But since the evidence of archaeology can also be abused, to jump too hastily to the conclusion that the Gospel of John is 'true', I would mention at this stage two examples, often fastened on, which I believe require more critical scrutiny.

The first is the location of the Praetorium and therefore of the Pavement, or *Λιθόστρωτον* in 19.13. We shall discuss this on its own

[84]Cf. W. F. Albright, *The Archaeology of Palestine*, Harmondsworth [3]1956, 242–9; 'Recent Discoveries in Palestine and the Gospel of St John' in W. D. Davies and D. Daube, edd., *The Background of the New Testament and its Eschatology*, Cambridge 1956, 153–71; R. D. Potter, 'Topography and Archaeology in the Fourth Gospel' in *StEv* I, TU 73, 1959, 329–37; reprinted in *The Gospels Reconsidered*, Oxford 1960, 90–8 (properly criticized at points by Barrett, *The Gospel of John and Judaism*, 36–8); J. Finegan, *The Archaeology of the New Testament*, Princeton, 1969; Davies, *The Gospel and the Land*, 288–335; as well as other more local studies referred to subsequently in context.

[85]*Following the Way: The Setting of John's Gospel*, Minneapolis 1980. Cf. earlier Westcott, *John* I, xxi: 'He moves about in a country which he knows'; and Scott Holland, *The Fourth Gospel*, 147–52, for the incidental character of so many of the details: 'There is no straining at unnatural exactitude, no conscious aim at work' (149f.). Streeter admitted John's 'first-hand knowledge of the topography of Palestine, and especially of the city of Jerusalem' but then unconvincingly explained it as 'a conscientious attempt by the author to piece together scattered bits of information picked up in Jerusalem' on pilgrimage (*Four Gospels*, 418f.).

merits in chapter VI.[86] But there is an understandable, if dangerous, temptation to allow preference to a large area of Roman paving which has been excavated near the site of the Antonia fortress and to use it as a visual demonstration of John's accuracy. As A. M. Hunter puts it, 'A pavement which you can see and walk on – with each stone of it more than a yard square and a foot thick – is vastly more convincing than any hypothetical courtyard.'[87] Unfortunately P. Benoit has shown, to my mind conclusively, not only that the Praetorium, on historical and literary grounds, is far more likely to have been in Herod's palace at the other end of the city but that the paving near the Antonia is to be dated, on archaeological grounds, from the time of Hadrian in the second century. This is *not* to say that John does not know what he is talking about, only that the *Λιθόστρωτον* or extensive raised pavement on which Herod's palace, like his temple, in all probability stood was utterly destroyed in the events of AD 70. The confirmation cannot be so direct or visual.

The other example is the Pool of Bethesda (5.1–9), which requires more detailed discussion.[88] Since the publication of Jeremias' monograph on its 'rediscovery'[89] it has been assumed that the colonnades round the four sides of the twin pools and one down the dividing rock-partition (4 + 1 = 5)[90] have 'vindicated' the Johannine description of its five porticoes, lost to view since the last days of the siege of Jerusalem. Unfortunately the entire theory is a construct of the imagination.

None of the hundred and more columns which Vincent[91] had

[86]Below, pp. 267f, where all the references are given.

[87]*According to John*, 52.

[88]The discrepancy of judgments that can be made on Johannine sites is nicely illustrated by two comments on this incident which Davies juxtaposes in *The Gospel and the Land*, 306 n. 33: 'The indications both of time and space are extremely vague . . ., evidently John was not interested in them' (Barrett, *John*, 249), and 'The factual details found in the introduction . . . are very accurate. They betray a knowledge of Jerusalem that militates against a late, or non-Palestinian origin' (Brown, *John* I, 209). Yet both of them accept the reconstruction of Jeremias which I shall show to be untenable!

[89]*Die Wiederentdeckung von Bethesda*, Göttingen 1949: ET of 2nd ed., *The Rediscovery of Bethesda*, Louisville, Ky., 1966.

[90]This explanation appears to go back to Origen (J. Wilkinson, *Jerusalem as Jesus Knew it*, 1978, 102); but there is no reason to suppose that he had seen anything (J. Murphy-O'Connor, *The Holy Land: An Archaeological Guide from the Earliest Times to 1700*, Oxford and New York 1980, 23). Indeed, as we shall see, he could not have, as there was no such thing to see. In A. E. Harvey, *A Companion to the New Testament*, Oxford and Cambridge 1979, 324, the explanation is ascribed to Cyril of Jerusalem.

[91]F.-M. Abel and L.-H. Vincent, *Jérusalem Nouvelle* II, Paris 1926, 669–72.

beautifully drawn round the sides of the pools were found *in situ* (as Jeremias admits) and in fact they are relics of the Byzantine church built over and to the east of the southern pool (they have crosses on them!). Nor is there any suggestion that the enormous basins, covering in all over 5,000 square metres and very deep[92] were used for anything but reservoirs for supplying water to the temple area of the city, at least until the construction of the still larger 'Pool of Israel' (*birket Israel*)[93] by Herod the Great on the northern flank of his temple pediment. Indeed they may even have been superseded by it in Jesus' time.[94] They would in any case have been highly unsuitable for a healing sanctuary, quite apart from the contamination of the water (especially for ritual purposes in the Temple); and paralytics if 'thrown' (βάλῃ) or even 'put' in (5.7) would have been in imminent danger of drowning. No healing properties, as far as I know, have ever been associated with static water-tanks, but always with springs or wells. Moreover, Jeremias' implausible explanation of the periodic 'troubling' of the water (5.7), by the emptying of one basin into the other through the system of canals that carried the water away, is now rendered quite impossible by the subsequent discovery[95] that the two pools were not even connected, the conduit from the northern and much older one, from the time of the monarchy (probably 'the upper pool' of Isa. 7.3; 36.2; II Kings 18.17),[96] passing beneath the level of the southern, from the Hasmonaean period (probably that constructed by Simon, son of Onias [220–195 BC], of whom Ecclus. 50.3 says 'In his day they dug the reservoir, a cistern as broad as the sea').

In fact the whole concentration on the twin pools is misplaced. They merely give the geographical location. The text and translation of John 5.2 are notoriously uncertain, but *probably* the NEB is right, with

[92]The southern pool has sides of 45m., 50m., 65m. and 47m., and a maximum depth of 14m. I take the figures from the monograph discussed below, A. Duprez, *Jésus et les dieux guerisseurs à propos de Jean 5*, Cahiers de la *Revue Biblique* 12, Paris 1970, 34. But they must be regarded as approximate in the present state of excavation.

[93]Measuring 109.8m. by 38–40m., with a depth of 24.4m. (Duprez, 35f.), and exceeding in volume both the Bethesda basins.

[94]So Duprez. Wilkinson, 'Ancient Jerusalem: Its Water Supply and Population', *PEQ* 106, 1974, 44f., believes that they were all in use together. But the Bethesda pools must have been abandoned by the time of the building in them of the foundations of the Byzantine church.

[95]Marie-Joseph Pierre and Jourdain-Marie Rousée, 'Sainte-Marie de la Probatique: état et orientation des recherches', *Proche-orient chrétien* 31, 1981, 23–42.

[96]From the context this must have been on the north of the city. Cf. also 'the old pool' of Isa. 22.11, contrasted with 'the lower pool' (Siloam) of 22.9. 'The King's (Hezekiah's?) pool' of Neh. 2.14 and the pool of Siloam (3.15) are evidently the same.

Barrett and Brown, in rendering it: 'Now at the Sheep-Pool in Jerusalem there is a place with five colonnades (or porches, στοαί). Its name in the language of the Jews is Bethesda'.[97] This last is primarily an indication of the area of the city which Josephus calls Bezetha,[98] or Neapolis (New Town). It was a relatively new quarter of Jerusalem in Jesus' time, built on a hill outside the northern wall opposite the Antonia and separated from it by a deep fosse to strengthen its fortifications.[99] In Aramaic the name was probably Bethzatha[100] but the Hebrew form Bethesda,[101] supported now by the copper scroll from Qumran (3Q15)[102] and adopted by Jeremias, could be interpreted to allude to the nearby 'house of mercy' or healing-sanctuary.

The excavation of this, which formed the foundation of A. Duprez's thesis,[103] has decisively altered the situation. For immediately to the east of the pools has been uncovered a site which at its lower level, dating from the middle of the second century BC to AD 70, contained a number of small grottoes with steps leading down to them, together with some rectangular stone basins presumably for washing, and at a higher level (third and fourth centuries AD, the time of Jerusalem as the Roman city of Aelia Capitolina) clear evidence from relics of votive offerings of a healing-sanctuary dedicated to Asclepius/Serapis, which was subsequently 'sanctified' no doubt by the building of the Byzantine church in the fifth century. Yet, despite Duprez, who is followed by Davies and Mackowski, there is no real evidence that this was a *pagan* sanctuary prior to 70 (though I would not doubt that it *could* have been, for Jerusalem was already a very 'mixed' city). Nor is there any hint in the text of John 5 that the significance of Jesus' action lay in his association with such a 'gravely unorthodox'[104] spot (it was not the man's 'orthodoxy' that was questioned but his breach of the sabbath

[97]The alternative is 'There is by the Sheep-Gate a pool' (RV and Nestle-Aland text). The Sheep-Gate is mentioned in Neh. 3.1, 32; 12.39 and was no doubt in the northern wall of the city. But there is no convention for omitting 'gate', nor was it taken in this way by any ancient commentator on John 5.2 (Jeremias, *Rediscovery*, 9).

[98]*BJ* 2.328, 530; 5.149, 151, 246, with variant readings.

[99]Josephus, *BJ* 5.149–51.

[100]Supported by ℵ, 33 and Eusebius, *Onomasticon* 58.

[101]A, C, Θ, fam. 1, 13, etc. P[66] and [75], B, W, etc. have 'Bethsaida' (or variants of it), but this almost certainly represents a confusion with the town of that name (1.44).

[102]Reading, apparently, *beth 'eshdathayin*, a dual form, which, as Barrett says (*John*, 252f.), could mean 'house of the two springs', presumably a reference to the twin pools.

[103]*Jésus et les dieux guérisseurs* (n. 92 above). Cf. Davies, *The Gospel and the Land*, 310–3; and the illustrated description in R. M. Mackowski, *Jerusalem, City of Jesus*, 1980, 79–83.

[104]Wilkinson, *Jerusalem as Jesus Knew it*, 102–4.

law; 5.10). Yet the evidence of the grottoes and basins, combined with its later use, clearly suggests its continuity as a place of healing (going perhaps right back to Canaanite times). And this is borne out by the statement of John 5.3 that 'in these *στοαί* there lay a crowd of sick people, blind, lame and paralysed'.[105] What was built over the entrances to the shallow grottoes and just how many there were cannot now be determined: there is no neat confirmation. But the description is entirely plausible, especially since the steps down are narrow and would not accommodate more than one patient with his bearers: it could be too late if the water had meanwhile receded.[106]

But what of the 'troubling' of the waters? It is a weakness of Duprez's case that he needs to argue that v.4 ('for from time to time an angel came down into the pool and stirred up the water. The first to plunge in after this disturbance recovered from whatever disease had afflicted him'), which is missing from the best manuscripts[107] and contains many non-Johannine features, is part of the original text. He interprets it to mean that a priest of the pagan sanctuary, seen as an 'angel', stirred it by hand behind the scenes! On the contrary, it is evidently a scribal gloss to seek to explain the phenomenon.

The most likely explanation is that we are dealing here with an intermittent siphon spring of the type still to be seen in the nearby Gihon spring on the west side of the Kidron valley, which (via Hezekiah's tunnel) supplies the Pool of Siloam. Such a spring works on rather the same principle as a self-flushing lavatory cistern. When the subterranean basin fills up its contents get siphoned off. The same quantity of water is therefore always discharged, though the intervals vary with the time that it takes to be replenished. In the case of the Gihon[108] the 'gush' (*giḥa*) lasts about forty minutes with a break of six to eight hours according to season. But figures would vary with the size of the basin and of the springs that fed it, and these could dry up for long stretches. If, as we shall argue,[109] Jesus' visit was at the Feast of Tabernacles, which marked the end of the dry season and part of whose purpose was to pray for rain, the springs would have been at

[105] A class of people specifically excluded from the temple ritual (Lev. 21.18; II Sam. 5.8). That Jesus took the opposite attitude to them is independently confirmed by Matt. 21.14.

[106] Not that only the 'first' got healed. That is part of the glossed explanation in 5.4 (see below).

[107] $P^{66, 75}$, ℵ, B, C*, W, etc.

[108] Cf. R. Amiran, in Y. Yadin, ed., *Jerusalem Revealed*, New Haven and London 1976, 75–8.

[109] Below, ch. III, pp. 138f.

their lowest and the delays therefore at their longest.

Though the limestone caves are present which are required for the hydrological conditions, there are today no active springs in the Bethesda area. This, I found, made the locals sceptical of the explanation. Yet interestingly Josephus speaks of just such intermittent springs in this very district in the final stages of the siege of Jerusalem. It is June 70 and he is with Titus' army addressing his fellow-countrymen within the city to dissuade them from further resistance against hopeless odds. By then the 'New Town' (Bezetha) had already been fought over and had changed hands, but Titus once again controlled it and had razed it to the ground (*BJ* 5.331–47), the 'five porticoes' doubtless included. So it is this area 'before the town' on the north side in front of the Antonia that is specifically in mind. This is what he says:

> As for Titus, the very springs flow more copiously for him which had erstwhile dried up for you. For before his coming,[110] as you know, Siloam and all the springs outside (or 'in front of', πρό) the town were failing, insomuch that water was sold by the *amphora*; whereas now they flow so freely for your enemies as to suffice not only for themselves and their beasts but even for gardens.[111]

Since the springs would be expected to diminish rather than increase at that time of year, he calls it a miracle or portent (τέρας), and therefore a sign that even God was against them.

I thought I had discovered this parallel but then found it had already been noted in this same connection by John Lightfoot in his *Horae Hebraicae et Talmudicae* in the seventeenth century! But I have not observed it in commentaries since. In any case it vindicates the possibility at least that the Bethesda grottoes were fed by such intermittent underground streams,[112] whose mysterious qualities (apart from any mineral properties) could easily have led to their

[110] 1 May, AD 70 (*BJ* 5.567).

[111] *BJ* 5.409f.; trans. H. St. J. Thackeray, LCL 1928. For gardens on this side of the city, cf. 'the garden gate' in the 'second' wall enclosing the northern district (*BJ* 5.146) and John 19.41.

[112] And no doubt the big pools as well. It is difficult to believe that these vast reservoirs, let alone the Strouthion Pool (176 by 46 ft.) supplying the Antonia (*BJ* 5.467) and still functioning today, the Pool of Israel and the so-called Pool of St Mary's Bath outside the north-east wall, could all have been filled by surface water from so small a catchment area. The watershed of impervious rock in Jerusalem is further west than the surface watershed (the Mount of Olives), thus causing more water to collect in the St Anne valley than would appear on the surface. I am grateful to personal conversations in Jerusalem for this information.

popular association with healing power and to the shrine which the archaeologists have uncovered. So John's account is impressively confirmed, even though again it is not possible to verify the porticos by sight.

This incident is characteristic of the Gospel's concentration on the ministry of Jesus in Jerusalem and its environs – though certainly not to the exclusion of that in Galilee (2.1–12; 4.43–54; 6.1–7.1),[113] Samaria (4.4–42) and Peraea (10.40–42). The proportion, so markedly different from the Synoptists, is an indication of what must have been of special interest to the earliest Johannine community. We cannot therefore be wrong to infer that the focusing upon the signs and teaching of Jesus in and around the capital and the controversies they provoked among the Jewish establishment provides a clue to the nature and locale of this community and its mission. This is borne out by the fact that when Paul came up for the council of Jerusalem, probably in 48, he met John there, engaged on work among the Jews (Gal. 2.9). The Gospel of John alone speaks of the Jews who responded to or believed on Jesus in Jerusalem (2.23; 7.40–52; 8.30; 9.35–38; 10.21; 11.45, 48; 12.11–19, 42–45) and of the presence of his 'disciples' there (7.3), though the Synoptists evidently presuppose it (Mark 11.3 and pars.; 14.13–16 and pars.). To repeat Scott Holland's question,[114] 'How did Joseph of Arimathea arrive at his belief?' (Matt. 27.57; Mark 15.43; Luke 23.50f.; John 19.38) – unless Jesus exercised the kind of ministry to which John testifies when he says that 'even among the rulers (the ἄρχοντες, or members of the Council) many believed on him, but would not acknowledge him on account of the Pharisees' (12.42). This would point to the kind of mission upon which the Johannine circle was particularly engaged, that is, among the members of the Jewish leadership ('the Jews' *par excellence* of this Gospel), and those repudiated by them – epitomized in the figures of Nicodemus (3.1–12; 7.50–52; 19.39), the crippled man (5.1–15) and the blind beggar (9.1–41).[115]

[113]Cf. the astonishing remark of Kümmel, *Introduction to the NT*, 245: 'In John all interest in Galilee is lacking.'

[114]*Fourth Gospel*, p. 131.

[115]Such a view was expressed by Hugo Delff, *Das vierte Evangelium*, Husum 1890, viiif. (quoted by H. W. Watkins, *Modern Criticism Considered in its Relation to the Fourth Gospel*, 294f.). He thought that the work was a product of Judaism while Jerusalem was still standing and that its specific purpose was the conversion not of the heathen or even of the Jews in general but of the class to which the writer belonged, namely the rulers and chief priests. The author, he held, was a person named John of

But can we say more of the nature and locale of this ministry? I believe that we may, on two counts.

Notable among those who are drawn to Jesus in Jerusalem are the 'Greeks', whose appearance is the signal that 'the hour has come for the Son of Man to be glorified' (12.20–24). I have argued,[116] and remain convinced, that these Ἕλληνες are Greek-speaking Jews or proselytes, who have come up to worship at the feast,[117] not Gentiles (τὰ ἔθνη are never mentioned in the Gospel or Epistles of John)[118] and mark the first-fruits of the ingathering of the Diaspora, 'the scattered children of God' (11.52), the other sheep of the flock (10.16),[119] for whom above all this Gospel is written. They are the same as 'the Dispersion among the Greeks' in 7.35, to whom Jesus will go, not literally as the Jews suppose, but through the message of the Gospel. Unfortunately it is impossible to be certain of this interpretation and exegetes are divided,[120] since 'the Greeks' in 7.35 could mean the Gentiles *among whom* the Jews are dispersed,[121] and in 12.20 the pilgrims up for worship *could* be Gentile 'God-fearers',[122] though the great mass of pilgrims would be Jews from the Diaspora.[123] But in addition to the *a priori* likelihood in John (where Pilate and his soldiers are the only Gentiles to be introduced even on the wings, in notable contrast with

---

Jerusalem, of high-priestly rank, who became a disciple of Jesus and after 70 went to Ephesus to become the 'presbyter John'!

[116]'The Destination and Purpose of St John's Gospel', *Twelve NTS*, 116f.

[117]So Bengel, who speaks of them as 'the Jews outside Palestine'.

[118]In III John 6f. ἐθνικός is used in the typically Jewish contemptuous sense of 'the heathen' with the same *contrast* with the community of faith as in Matt. 18.17.

[119]Martyn, 'Glimpses into the History of the Johannine Community', in *Évangile*, 172f., argues that the reading συναγαγεῖν (rather than simply ἀγαγεῖν) in P^{66} is to be accepted and makes it even more certain that the reference in 10.16 is to the ingathering of other Jews. But he still takes 'the Greeks' to refer to Gentiles (174).

[120]Thus the articles in *TDNT*, on διασπορά (K. L. Schmidt, II, 101f.) and Ἕλλην (H. Windisch, II, 509f.) favour opposite sides. H. B. Kossen, 'Who were the Greeks of John 12.20?' in *Studies in John: Presented to Dr J. N. Sevenster*, *NovT*Suppl 24, Leiden 1970, 97–110, in the end comes down on the side of Gentiles on contextual grounds (only), because, as he thinks, it reflects the expulsion of Christians from the synagogue; but see below, pp. 72–81.

[121]But Bultmann (*John*, 309), supported by Barrett (*John*, 325), is surely wrong in quoting Judith 5.19 in favour of διασπορά itself meaning 'the place in which the dispersed are found'. It must mean 'from their dispersion wherever it may be'.

[122]Cf. Schürer, *History* II, 309–13, 'Gentile Participation in Worship at Jerusalem'. They could bring or send sacrifices, but not eat them (Josephus, *BJ* 6.427f., *Ant.* 3.318f.; M. *Shek.* 7.6; b. *Pes.* 3b), and they would not have been allowed into the sanctuary (Acts 21.28f.). It is possible that 'all that fear the Lord', as distinguished from the house of Israel, in the *hallel* Psalms 118.2–4 and 135.19f. may refer to 'God-fearers'.

[123]Cf. e.g. Philo, *Spec. leg.* 1.69.

the Synoptists) I would adduce two further arguments.

The word προσκυνέω, worship, which for John has a deep significance (4.19–24), is used twice elsewhere in the New Testament of pilgrims to the feasts: Paul in Acts 24.11 and the Ethiopian eunuch in Acts 8.27 (God-fearers are attracted in Acts by the synagogue rather than the temple). We cannot of course be sure of the latter's standing, but one may say with confidence that Luke at any rate did not see him as a Gentile. In the pattern he is tracing of the expansion of Christianity, Acts 8 marks the incorporation by water and the Spirit of those who under the old covenant were disqualified from membership of the people of God, either because they were Samaritans (8.4–25) or eunuchs (8.26–39; cf. Deut. 23.1). It is made quite clear that the rubicon of admitting Gentiles, with the great debate that that entailed, is not crossed until Cornelius in 10.1–11.18.

The second point is the significance of a passage which I had not noticed before (and I have never seen remarked on) in the famous *Testimonium Flavianum* to Jesus in Josephus, *Ant.* 18.63. It is generally agreed that in our Greek text this passage has been subject to Christian interpolation and rewriting, but there is no real ground for rejecting it out of hand.[124] In it the statement is made, which there is no reason to ascribe to a Christian hand, that 'He won over many Jews and many of the Greeks (literally, of the Hellenic element: τοῦ Ἑλληνικοῦ)'. K. H. Rengstorf, the editor of the Josephus Concordance, agrees with me that this is unlikely to mean Gentiles, among whom there is otherwise no tradition of any significant mission on Jesus' part (and Matt. 10.6; 15.24 would militate against any Christian interpolation),[125] but that it refers to the Greek-speaking section of the Jews of Palestine whom Acts calls 'the Hellenists'. No other Gospel gives a hint

[124]For the latest and very judicious assessment, cf. L. H. Feldman, 'The *Testimonium Flavianum*: the State of the Question' in R. F. Berkey and S. A. Edwards, edd., *Christological Perspectives: Essays in Honor of Harvey K. McArthur*, New York 1982, 179–99. Feldman accepts that it is original to Josephus, very possibly modified by Eusebius, and does not question the authenticity of the words here cited from it. So too Schürer, *History* I, 428–41.

[125]H. St J. Thackeray, *Josephus, the Man and the Historian*, New York 1929, reissued 1967, in the course of a careful analysis of the *Testimonium* (136–49) agrees that 'the statement about the Greeks would be impossible for a Christian, who would know that his Master's missionary activity was confined to "the lost sheep of the house of Israel"' (146). He is compelled to take it as an anachronistic reference on Josephus' part to the Gentile mission (though Josephus clearly distinguishes Jesus' activity from that of 'the tribe of Christians'). But he agrees that τὸ Ἑλληνικόν is 'thoroughly Josephan' and refers to *BJ* 2.268 (where in the context of ethnic disturbances at Caesarea it clearly refers to Gentiles).

of such a ministry; but John may well reflect an interest in it.[126] The disciples who he says acted as intermediaries for 'the Greeks' are those with the Greek names of Andrew and Philip who came from the Hellenized city of Bethsaida-Julias (12.21f.; 1.44),[127] which had been made into a city by Philip the Tetrarch.[128] And Nicodemus, with his

[126]I see no reason with Cullmann in *The Johannine Circle* to suppose that these mean Hellenizers, or Graecophiles, or were on the fringe of Judaism, sitting light to the Law and the temple (those who opposed Stephen were very strongly attached to both of these: Acts 6.13f.), and John is certainly dealing with a Judaism firmly centred in the cultus. Nor is there any reason to suppose that all Greek–speaking Palestinian *Christians* were associated with Stephen and his circle, with whom Cullmann connects the beloved disciple (as does Schillebeeckx, *Christ*, 317–20): Barnabas, John Mark and Silas were not, all of whom spoke Greek. The links of the Johannine tradition are not with those round Stephen, like Philip the evangelist (who may well have supplied Luke with his material for Acts 8 and 10; cf. Acts 21.8), but with Philip the apostle and Andrew from Greek-speaking Galilee. In any case if the Johannine circle was connected with Stephen why was John left unmolested in Jerusalem when the persecution occasioned by the death of Stephen scattered the others (Acts 8.1, 14–17)?

[127]Cf. Dalman, *Sacred Sites*, 165: 'Anyone brought up in Bethsaida would not only have understood Greek, but would have been polished by intercourse with foreigners and have had some Greek culture.' Cf. his *Jesus-Jeshua*, ET London and New York 1929, 1–7. He also takes the 'Greeks' of John 12.20 to be Greek-speaking Jews, and Andrew and Philip to be genuinely Greek names, as opposed to Graecized names like Jesus (Jeshua).

[128]Cf. Josephus, *Ant.* 18.28: 'He also raised the village [Mark 8.23, 26] of Bethsaida on Lake Gennesaritis to the status of a city [Luke 9.10; John 1.44] by adding residents and strengthening the fortifications. He named it after Julia, the emperor's daughter.' He also died there and was buried in 'the tomb that he had himself erected before he died and there was a costly funeral' (18.108). John is technically wrong in describing it as being 'of Galilee' in 12.21. It was in Lower Gaulanitis (*BJ* 2.168). Yet the two were not clearly distinguished. It was only a political boundary during the reign of Herod Antipas, the two being previously and subsequently united (cf. Schlatter, *Der Evangelist Johannes*, 267). Judas 'the Galilean' (*Ant.* 18.23, etc.; cf. Acts 5.37) was actually 'a Gaulanite' (*Ant.* 18.3), and Ptolemy in his *Geography* (5.16.4) regards Bethsaida as belonging to Galilee. It was on the east side of the Jordan a little above where the river enters the lake (*BJ* 3.515). In New Testament times the town was on the lakeside (Mark 6.45). But the mouth of the river has silted up (as already observed by W. Sanday, *Sacred Sites of the Gospels*, Oxford 1903, 41), and the tel (et-Tell) now rises from the alluvial plain a mile or two from the shore. (According to Josephus, *BJ* 3.506, the lake was about 16 miles long, whereas it is now about 12½ miles. But his figures are notoriously unreliable.) The only excavation done there has been by the Syrian troops digging trenches in the 1967 war and throwing up plenty of shards. But the site appears to be beyond dispute, and Fr Bargil Pixner and I sat on top of it among the barbed wire ('Follow the cow-pats and you won't hit a mine!') tracing the scene of the battle personally described by Josephus in *Vita* 399–406 (the site of Sulla's camp and the location of the ambush are clearly identifiable). More interesting still was following the line of what (in Crusader times) was later to be called the *Via Maris*, some 20 ft. wide, across the shoulder of the ridge opposite, with its fine Roman paving (probably from after Jesus' time) only just beneath the grass. At one point the road almost doubles in

Graecized name,[129] is represented as engaging in a dialogue with Jesus that turns on the double meaning of ἄνωθεν (3.3f.) which only works in Greek. This cannot of course be used to demonstrate that Jesus actually conversed with him in Greek (though that is entirely possible)[130] but it may well indicate the milieu of the Johannine mission. If Paul 'talked and debated (συνεζήτει) with the Greek-speaking Jews', moving freely amongst them in Jerusalem after his conversion (Acts 9.28f.) and meeting their implacable hostility – they twice tried to murder him (9.29; 21.27–36), as well as stoning Stephen (6.8–7.59) – it could well explain the bitterness and the hounding (ζήτησις) of Jesus that runs through the Gospel, as well as the special hatred which the Johannine community must expect from the Jews (especially 15.18–25; 16.1–4): there is no reference to Gentile persecution, as in the corresponding Synoptic passages (Mark 13.9 and pars.; Matt. 10.18). The Gospel of John is both very Jewish and very Greek; and this setting may be an important part of the explanation.

But can one be more specific not merely about the nature but the locale of the Johannine mission in Jerusalem? Very tentatively, I suggest that one can.

Without prejudging the identity of the unnamed disciple in John 18.15f. or his identification with the disciple whom Jesus loved (whoever *he* was), it is clear that the Johannine circle had contacts with the high-priestly household. Whatever being 'γνωστός to', and perhaps still more 'a γνωστός of', the high priest may imply (and it certainly means more than a casual acquaintance),[131] there is no doubt that the

---

width. This is where, Pixner is convinced, the caravans drew up for the receipt of custom as they entered the territory of Herod Antipas, before the road forked for Capernaum and Chorazim. There is also at this point a paved side-street with piles of rubble, which has to be the remains of the τελώνιον where Levi and many 'tax-gatherers' worked and which Jesus passed as he went out along by the sea (Mark 2.13–15) from Capernaum (cf. Matt. 9.9). It certainly merits excavating. If coins cannot be found here, they will not be found anywhere! The line of the road is not located here on Avi-Yonah's map of Roman roads in Palestine (*Compendia* I. 1, 100) nor is it marked as paved.

[129]For his identification with Nakdimon ben Gurion, cf. below, ch. VI, pp. 283–7.

[130]So N. Turner, *Grammatical Insights into the New Testament*, Edinburgh 1965, 182. The aristocratic establishment could well have preferred outside church to speak the civilized language of Hellenism rather than the people's Aramaic. In worship of course Hebrew would have been the language. But already under Herod the Great Greek was the official language of the court, the Sanhedrin and the army (M. Stern, *Compendia* I. 1,256; cf. 248). Certainly the Roman trial, and any conversation of Jesus with Pilate, would have been conducted in Greek; and there is no hint in any of the Gospels of an interpreter being necessary.

[131]Cf. Luke 2.44; 23.49; and Dodd, *Historical Tradition*, 86f.

community had its connections below stairs if not above. John alone mentions the name of the high priest's servant, Malchus (18.10), which could suggest that he was familiar to his church (like Alexander and Rufus, the sons of Simon of Cyrene, to Mark's church in Rome [?]; Mark 15.21; cf. Rom. 16.13). The disciple is able to gain entry for Peter to the high priest's palace through knowing the girl on the door (18.16), and later one of the high priest's servants (whom John alone among the evangelists clearly distinguishes from the temple constables; 18.18) is known to be a relative of the one whose ear Peter cut off (18.26).

The beloved disciple also had a house in Jerusalem to which the mother of Jesus was taken (19.27).[132] Now it is noteworthy that all the early church traditions, for what they are worth,[133] locate the primitive Christian quarter in Jerusalem in the Mount Sion area in the south-west corner of the old city.[134] They include the scene of the last supper (the Cenacle), which is regularly identified with the upper room of Pentecost (Acts 1.14) and, rightly or wrongly, with the house of John Mark's mother (Acts 12.12), the seat of James the Lord's brother, the death-place of Mary (the Dormition), and the house where, according to Epiphanius of Salamis, James and the two sons of Zebedee and Mary the mother of Jesus kept one household (πολιτεία).[135] He also reports that when the Emperor Hadrian visited Jerusalem before the second Jewish revolt of 132–5 he

> found the city completely leveled to the ground and God's temple treaded down, except for a few houses and the church of God, which was quite small. To it the disciples returned after the Savior's ascension from the Mount of Olives. They went up to the Upper Room, for it had been built there – that is, in the part of the city called Sion, which part was exempted from destruction, as also were some of the dwellings around Sion and seven synagogues, the only ones which existed in Sion, like monks' cells. One of these survived until the time of Bishop Maximos [335–49] and King Constantine. It was

[132]See below, ch. VI, p. 288 n. 256.

[133]Often of course they are purely legendary – e.g. the rubbish in Epiphanius Monachus, *Vita B. Virginis;* PG 120.208f.

[134]Cf. B. Bagatti, *The Church from the Circumcision*, Jerusalem 1971, 116–22; D. Baldi, *Enchiridion locorum sanctorum*, Jerusalem ²1955, nos. 728–87; B. Pixner, 'Sion III, "Nea Sion": topographische und geschichtliche Untersuchung des Sitzes der Urkirche und seiner Bewohner', *Das Heilige Land* 111, 1979, 3–13; Wilkinson, *Jerusalem*, 164-71; Mackowski, *Jerusalem*, 139–47.

[135]*Haer.* 78.13; PG 42.720.

like a tent in a vineyard, to quote the Scriptures [Isa. 1.8].[136]

The Bordeaux Pilgrim confirms this in her visit of 333;[137] and in 348 Cyril of Jerusalem, bishop of the city at the time, speaks of 'the upper church of the apostles', recalling the site of Pentecost.[138] This church and the surviving synagogue were probably the same building,[139] since all Jews had been expelled from the city after the Bar-Cochba revolt in 135. Moreover it is likely that the building now known as 'David's Tomb', in the same complex as the Cenacle,[140] was originally a synagogue,[141] and judging from the graffiti a Christian one; and it has been persuasively argued[142] that it is the same first-century Jewish-Christian synagogue which, starting as a house-church, was to become the foundation of the fourth-century Byzantine basilica, Hagia Sion, 'the mother of all the churches'. At any rate there is no competing tradition for the location of the earliest Christian quarter.

It is also beyond reasonable doubt that the high priest's establishment was in the Mount Zion area,[143] whether, as has traditionally been supposed, on the site of St Peter in Gallicantu or further north in the present-day Armenian quarter.[144]

[136] *De mens. et pond.* 14; PG 43. 260f.; translation from Mackowski, *Jerusalem*, 143. Cf. J. E. Dean, *Epiphanius' Treatise on Weights and Measures: the Syriac Version*, Chicago and Cambridge 1935, p. 30.

[137] Wilkinson, *Egerias's Travels*, London 1971, 57f.

[138] *Cat.* 16.4; PG 33.924A. Earlier (*c.* 315) Eusebius had said that the gospel spread through Christ and his apostles to all the nations from Mount Zion, where Jesus stayed a long time and taught his disciples many things (*Dem. Ev.* 1.4; PG 22.44B).

[139] Epiphanius (*Haer.* 30.18; PG 41.436) says that the Jewish Christians continued to call their churches synagogues (cf. James 2.2).

[140] Cf. the reference in Peter's Pentecost speech to David's tomb being 'in our midst (ἐν ἡμῖν)' (Acts 2.29). Bagatti, *The Church from the Gentiles in Palestine*, Jerusalem 1971, 26, suggests that this text led to the identification of David's tomb with the spot. Historically of course it was the other side of the city, in the old 'city of David' (I Kings 2.10).

[141] J. Pinkerfield, 'David's Tomb: Notes on the History of the Building', Hebrew University Department of Archaeology, Louis Rabbinowitz Fund for the Exploration of Ancient Synagogues, *Bulletin* III, Jerusalem 1960, 41–3; cf. the correction noted in Mackowski, *Jerusalem*, 195 n. 16.

[142] Bagatti, *Church from the Circumcision*, 118–22; Mackowski, *Jerusalem*, 145–7, quoting further investigation by Pixner; cf. earlier Sanday, *Sacred Sites*, 80–7.

[143] Josephus, *BJ* 2.426, merely helps us to locate it in the Upper City, though not as high as Herod's palace (2.429). Cf. the Bordeaux Pilgrim, 'Climbing Sion from there you can see the place where the house of Caiaphas used to stand' (Wilkinson, *Egeria's Travels*, 157). Cyril, *Cat.* 13.38 (PG, 33.817), also speaks of the site as a desolation.

[144] Cf. M. Broshi, 'Excavations in the House of Caiaphas, Mount Zion' in Yadin, ed., *Jerusalem Revealed*, 57f. This is supported by Benoit and by Wilkinson, *Jerusalem*, 133–6,

But there is yet a third factor which could throw intriguing light on the connections of the Johannine community. This is the possibility raised in a monograph by Pixner called *An Essene Quarter on Mount Zion?*[145] In it he argues, I think persuasively, on literary and archaelogical grounds for an Essene enclave in New Testament times in the extreme south-west corner of the city. A gate in the old city-wall at this point, re-excavated since his article, corresponds with what Josephus (*BJ* 5.145) calls 'the gate of the Essenes', and there is evidence of a separate water-supply, latrines, cisterns and ritual baths with divided steps like those at Qumran, separating those going down impure and coming up clean.[146] None of this proves that it was an Essene quarter, despite fascinating connections with the Temple[147] and Copper Scrolls, though it fits their strict regimen very well. That there were Essenes in the capital, as in the other towns and villages of Judaea 'grouped', as Philo puts it, 'in great societies of many members',[148] is not only inherently likely but apparently presupposed by their attitude towards the temple:

> They send their votive offerings to the temple, but perform their sacrifices employing a different ritual of purification. For this reason they are barred from those precincts of the temple that are frequented by all the people and perform their rites by themselves (*Ant.* 18.19; cf. CD 11.17–21).[149]

I forbear to draw some of the connections Pixner does between the Essenes and the character (and calendar) of the early Christian community in Jerusalem. But simply with regard to the Johannine circle, his thesis could go some way to explain its links both with the high-priestly establishment, the Mount Zion area and the thought-

144, 166. Pixner doubts if the high priest could have afforded to be so lax over the 'graven images' of birds revealed in two of the frescoes and prefers the traditional site.

[145]Franciscan Press, Jerusalem, 1976; reprinted from *Studia Hierosolymitana* 1, 1976, 245–83. He is supported by Mackowski.

[146]This was not distinctive of the Essenes; cf. the reference to the same practice in the Gospel fragment, POxy. 840, in Jeremias, *The Unknown Sayings of Jesus*, ET London [2]1964, 47–60 (cited by Pixner, *Essene Quarter*, 271 n. 54).

[147]Cols. 45–7. Cf. J. Milgrom, *BA* 41, 1978, 105–20, especially 117; comparing Josephus, *BJ* 1.147–9; 5.145.

[148]*Hypothetica* 11.1; cf. Josephus, *BJ* 2.124; and in their own writings CD 12.19, 23.

[149]Also CD 12.1f., 'No man shall lie with a woman in the City of the Sanctuary, to defile the City of the Sanctuary with their uncleanness', and 11QPs[a] (the 'Apostrophe to Zion', reproduced in full by Pixner, *Essene Quarter*, 267f.); G. Vermes, *The Dead Sea Scrolls: Qumran in Perspective*, London 1977, Philadelphia 1981, 97, 105–9.

forms brought to light by the Qumran literature (though these last could also have come in via the Baptist movement and the disciples entering the following of Jesus in 1.35–40).

Nothing turns on any of this, but it may reinforce the conviction, borne out by the apparent authenticity of the topographical evidence, that the Johannine tradition does indeed reach back in space to the very heart of the earliest Christian community in Jerusalem and to the ministry of Jesus which brought it into existence. Yet this is but the first strand in the threefold cord which I believe can be traced between the rich maturity of John's theology and what Paul calls 'the beginning of the gospel' (Phil. 4.15).

3. *The Link in Time*

Our concern here is not with the absolute dating of the Fourth Gospel. That I have tried to establish in the chapter on the Gospel and Epistles of John in my *Redating the New Testament*,[150] and to it I shall inevitably be having to refer. Here we are concerned rather with the charge that it is so remote in time from the situation it describes that it could not credibly in any sense be a first Gospel. Is it not *par excellence* a presentation of 'the distant scene', as both conservatives and radical critics have, uniquely, at this point agreed?

Let us start with the basis of this unwonted concurrence. For the radicals it is because any lines of connection with the beginning are so attenuated and indirect as to afford little or no ground for first-hand contact. For the conservatives it is because they have accepted the tradition that the Gospel was written by the apostle John in extreme old age at the close of the first century AD. Yet it is worth looking more closely at this tradition. For, unlike those of place (Ephesus) and person (John) which are virtually unanimous (however confused the latter is by the question of *which* John), that of time is far less firmly grounded. That John wrote his Gospel (at whatever date) after the other three is common to ancient tradition[151] – though the reasons given for this,

[150]Ch. IX (254–311). I argued for the following rough stages in the history of the Johannine tradition:

30–50 Shaping of the Gospel material in dialogue with Palestinian Judaism
50–55 Preaching in the Ephesus area and the first edition of the Gospel
60–65 The Epistles, responding to the challenge of false teachers
65+ Second edition of the Gospel with Prologue and Epilogue.

[151]Irenaeus, *Adv. haer.* 3.1.1; Clement, quoted by Eusebius, *HE* 6.14.7; and Eusebius himself, *HE* 3.24.7.

that his purpose was to complement them by giving the 'spiritual' as opposed to the 'bodily' facts (Clement) or to supplement them by additional material at the beginning of the ministry (Eusebius), are no more than guesses unsubstantiated by modern critical study. The other fact attested by the tradition is that John *lived* to a great age, into the reign of Trajan (AD 98–117),[152] and Jerome sets his death in the year 98.[153] But that he *wrote* as a very old man is an inference that appears only late and is accompanied by statements which show that it is clearly secondary and unreliable.[154] Indeed for what they are worth, which is not much, other traditions indicate the contrary. Thus, the Muratorian canon, probably from the end of the second century and about contemporary with Irenaeus, describes John as urged to write when still surrounded by his fellow-disciples, including Andrew, who, Eusebius says, went to Scythia after 70.[155] The later Syriac *History of John*, though preserving the tradition that the Gospels were composed in the canonical order and that John lived to the age of one hundred and twenty, also says that he hesitated to write his Gospel lest they should say 'he is a youth' but was prevailed upon to do so by Peter and Paul (who, it agrees, were killed by Nero), visiting him in Ephesus prior to going on to see James in Jerusalem (i.e., before James' death in 62). Yet the picture of John looking back through the mists of time upon the events of his youth is perpetuated almost without question in conservative circles,[156] and, as we shall see, is reflected in the assumption by the other side read into the interpretation of John 21.23, 'that that disciple would not die'. The only evidence we have of what John could manage in extreme old age was his constant repetition of 'Little children, love one another'.[157] That he could have written the Epistles, let alone the Gospel, as an octo- or nonagenarian stretches belief.

But as always the external tradition is only as strong as the internal, and it is this that must decide the placing of the Gospel in time. The assumption again is that all the symptoms suggest that it is late. Yet if we

[152]Irenaeus, *Adv. haer.* 2.22.5; 3.3.4; quoted, Eusebius, *HE* 3.23.3f.

[153]*Vir. ill.* 9, 'the 68th year after our Lord's passion'.

[154]For the details, see my *Redating*, 257f.

[155]*HE* 3.1.1.

[156]E.g., Armitage Robinson, *Study of the Gospels*, 151–7; Scott Holland, *Fourth Gospel*, 127, 143, 174; C. F. Nolloth, *The Fourth Evangelist*; R. A. Edwards, *The Gospel According to St John*, who in this respect differed completely from his namesake H. E. Edwards. Westcott dated the Gospel to 'the last decennium of the first century, and even to the close of it' (*John* I, lxxxii) with the Epistles by the same author later still.

[157]Jerome, *In Gal.* III. 6, on Gal. 6.10.

run through the stock indicators of the 'silver age' in the late apostolic or sub-apostolic period, this is by no means as obvious as one might think.

Among the signs usually held to characterize the sub-apostolic age is a defensive obsession with the structure of the church's ministry and 'sound doctrine'. The Epilogue of the Gospel does indeed reveal a concern for the feeding of the flock (John 21.15–17) in much the same terms as Paul's speech to the elders of Miletus in Acts 20.28f. or I Peter 5.2–4 (neither of which I believe was composed after the mid–60s), but none for ministerial titles (there is none apart from 'the Elder' of II and III John 1) or apostolic succession (in III John 9f. Diotrephes has to be disowned for loving pre-eminence, though that is hardly simply a second-generation sin). Equally, the only possible emphasis on sound doctrine, on adherence to 'the Faith' rather than a concern for faith, is in II John 9, where in face of false teachers the local church is urged to 'stand by the doctrine of the Christ'; but it is doubtful whether διδαχή here means any more than the 'teaching' of Jesus (as in John 7.16f.; 18.19; and I John 2.27) or indeed is any more secondary than the original 'pattern of teaching' into which Paul says the Romans had been initiated (Rom. 6.17; cf. 16.17).

The notable absence of any reference to Jewish–Gentile controversy within the church, or indeed of any reference to the Gentiles, whether as a group or as individuals,[158] paralleled in the New Testament only by the Epistle of James, suggests that the Gospel is either very early, or very late when this issue is supposed to have died down. Yet it did not die down from the area of Jerusalem, as far as our evidence goes, until well after the last possible date for the Gospel, the final expulsion of the Jewish Christians with the rest of their race, by Hadrian in 135, when Jerusalem had its first Gentile bishop.[159] It is always an astonishment to me that it can be argued that the Epistle to the Ephesians is late (and non-Pauline) because it reflects the final resolution of the antagonism between Jews and Gentiles in the church: the stress which has to be laid

[158]The only exceptions are Pilate and his soldiers. The βασιλικός or court-official in 4.46–53 is not a centurion, nor is his faith commended as a Gentile, as in the parallel Synoptic story. He is presumably a Herodian and the kind of person described in Luke 8.3 in the figure of Chuza, a financial or political officer of Herod's administration. He could well indeed have been this very person, since we are told that his whole household became believers and Chuza's wife Joanna was among the women of substance who kept the movement supplied. At any rate we know of no other convert during the ministry from this social circle. The name Chuza occurs in Nabataean and Syrian inscriptions, and Herod the Great had a Nabataean bodyguard, Corinthus (Josephus, *BJ* 1.576f.; *Ant.* 17.55–7). Malchus was also a Nabataean name.

[159]For the long and sorry history of relations, cf. Bagatti's two books, *The Church from the Gentiles in Palestine* and *The Church from the Circumcision*.

upon the breaking down of the middle wall of partition and on preserving the unity of the one body suggests otherwise. Certainly in the Pastoral Epistles (e.g. Titus 1.10f.), whenever they are to be dated, 'those of the circumcision' are still giving plenty of trouble within the community. In John however circumcision is never mentioned as an issue within the church, only in relation to its precedence within Judaism over the sabbath law (7.22f.). Nor is the place of the law for Christians ever discussed, an issue which certainly did not go away.[160] *Νόμος* never even occurs in the Johannine Epistles and sin is unequivocally equated with 'lawlessness' (I John 3.4) in a thoroughly Jewish manner.[161]

Again, in John there is even less than in the Synoptists that can be taken as reference to the fall of Jerusalem after the event. Indeed the presumption is that it is still standing as the evangelist himself describes it in the three present tenses of 5.2 (though nothing can be built upon them): 'There is in Jerusalem a place which is called in the language of the Jews Bethesda, having five porches.' The only forecast is that the Romans would come and destroy the city and its holy place *if* the Jewish authorities left Jesus at large (11.48) – in fact an unfulfilled prophecy, for they did not and the Romans still came. The threat that the sanctuary would be destroyed is referred by John to the events of 30 (2.19–21), not to those of 70 (contrast Mark 13.2 and pars.). The relations of the Jews to the Romans remain obsequious and collaborationist to the end (19.12–15), with no reflection at all of the revolt of 66. There is no hint of state persecution, which hit the church with Nero in 65, only of bitter Jewish harassment. Certainly in the Epistles there is evidence of gnosticizing heresy, but this is no more advanced or elaborate (indeed less) than what we find in the same area in the Epistle to the Colossians, which if it is Pauline, as I am convinced it is, cannot be later than the early 60s or late 50s, and I would say is earlier.

Again, what reference there is to the Parousia, in John 21.23, is not to an event of the indefinite future but, if I interpret it aright,[162] to an

[160]For the recognition of this, cf. Martyn, *History and Theology in the Fourth Gospel*, 46 n. 77: 'It is a remarkable fact that the Gentile mission seems to play no part in the Fourth Gospel *as an issue*. Jewish opposition to John's church is never presented as the result of the church's inclusion of non-Jews. Nor is the Torah as the way of salvation the kind of issue it was in Paul's experience.'

[161]For the Jewishness of these Epistles, despite what is said to the contrary (e.g., by Meeks, 'Am I a Jew?' in Neusner, ed., *Christianity, Judaism and Other Greco-Roman Cults* I, 182, and Brown, *Community*, 96), cf. my 'Destination and Purpose of the Johannine Epistles', *Twelve NTS*, 126–38.

[162]For the argument cf. *Redating*, 279–82.

imminent expectation. It was being supposed that the beloved disciple would not die precisely because the end was thought to be so near (not because he was so old; Peter is the one who is to 'grow old'). After the death of the other 'pillars' (Gal. 2.9), James the Lord's brother in 62, Peter and Paul in 65+, John alone (if that is who he is) was seen to 'remain' (i.e., stay on to await the Parousia, as in Phil. 1.25). Thus, the coming could not now be long delayed if Jesus' supposed promise was still to find fulfilment that it must occur before the passing of that apostolic generation (Mark 9.1;[163] 13.30). To be sure, the evangelist here (21.20–22) corrects this expectation. But such a correction fits best, I believe, into the period shortly after the crucifixion of Peter (21.18f.),[164] with which it is closely connected.[165] There is no reason to suppose the misunderstanding waited another generation to be corrected. So the Epilogue (which no one would deny was the latest part of the Gospel and, I believe, with the Prologue, post-dates the Epistles) need not, I would argue, be dated much after 65. For this Brown criticizes me by saying, 'It is bad method to date a final composition on the presence of some early elements; a work cannot be dated earlier than its latest elements'.[166] But this last is precisely what I do. It is simply that I see no reason for dating the latest element anything like as late as he does.

Yet so far we have merely pointed to some stock indications of lateness which, perhaps surprisingly, are *not* to be found in John. But

[163]For a possible link between a misunderstanding of Mark 9.1 and the expectation of John 21.23, cf. my *Jesus and His Coming*, 1957, 90f.

[164]For the 'stretching out of the hands' meaning this, cf. *Did.* 16.6, the 'sign of the stretching out' (corresponding to the 'sign of the Son of man' in Matt. 24.30), and *Ep. Barn.* 12.4, where the stretching out of Moses' arms is seen as a type of cross. For other references to pagan and Christian sources, cf. Bernard, *John* II, 708–10. It is curious however that he makes no reference to the Odes of Solomon on which he wrote a commentary. Cf. 27.1–3, 'I extended my hands and hallowed my Lord, for the expansion of my hands is his sign. And my extension is the upright cross'; and 42.1f., 'I extended my hands and approached my Lord, for the expansion of my hands is his sign. And my extension is the common cross, that was lifted up on the way of the Righteous One'; tr. Charlesworth, *The Odes of Solomon*, Oxford 1973, [2]Missoula, Mont., 1977. Oddly Charlesworth too makes no reference to John 21.18.

[165]M. de Jonge, 'The Beloved Disciple and the Date of the Gospel of John' in E. Best and R. McL. Wilson, edd., *Text and Interpretation: Studies in the New Testament for Matthew Black*, Cambridge 1979, 99–114, says that I 'rightly object to the use of 21.20–25 as an argument in favour of a late dating of the Gospel', but dismisses my early dating with the words 'all this is very ingenious but hardly capable of proof' (110f.). Yet he produces no real arguments against it and in the end leaves the question open, which means exactly where it was.

[166]*Community*, 22; cf. 96.

the argument from silence cannot be conclusive; and there are two positive factors, one specific, the other more general, which are constantly cited to show that the Gospel belongs to the period when relations between Christianity and Judaism had reached a degree of distance and alienation entirely foreign to the situation of Jesus or of the pre–70 Palestinian scene.

First, there is the assumption that the three occurrences in this Gospel of the unique term ἀποσυνάγωγος (9.22; 12.42 and 16.2) reflect a formal exclusion of Christians from the synagogue with the introduction about AD 85–90 of the twelfth of the Eighteen Benedictions, the *birkat ha-minim*, the benediction against 'the heretics', and must therefore be dated after that. This decree is held to be quite different from previous acts of internal discipline or local expulsion and represents a watershed in Christian–Jewish relations, after which things were never to be the same again. In J. L. Martyn's words,

> Steps had to be taken to make it unmistakable that synagogue and church were formally separate and that any Jew who made the messianic confession would have to pay the price of absolute severance from the synagogue.[167]

Or, as F. J. Moloney restates it in an article written since my book and in answer to its thesis,

> It was the point of no return for the Christians: they had to declare themselves, and thus lose all contact with Judaism. This is no simple banning from the synagogue, but a complete expulsion from the heritage of Israel.[168]

[167]*History and Theology in the Fourth Gospel*, 46f. Martyn's book is generally regarded as having established the connection between the *birkat ha-minim* and the Johannine texts. But he himself is refreshingly modest. He has written subsequently, 'Glimpses into the History of the Johannine Community', in *Évangile*, 150f.: 'It would be a valuable practice for the historian to rise each morning saying to himself three times slowly and with emphasis "I do not know". . . . The number of points in the history of the Johannine community about which we may be virtually certain is relatively small, and we need to be clear about that.' But he goes on: 'One of these relatively secure points is surely the highly probable correspondence' here under review. For reasons given below I would wish to extend his scepticism.

[168]'The Fourth Gospel's Presentation of Jesus as "the Christ" and J. A. T. Robinson's *Redating*', *Downside Review* 95, 1977, 239–53 (241), reproduced with variations in the journal of the Fellowship for Biblical Studies: Teachers' Group, Strathcona, Victoria, Australia, *Emeth* 11.1, 1982, 25–35. See also since my book, but not in response to it, F. Manns, 'L'Évangile de Jean, réponse chrétienne aux decisions de Jabne', *Liber Annuus* 30, 1980, Studium Biblicum Franciscanum, Jerusalem, 47–92. It ranges a good deal wider than the issue here under discussion.

But the evidence he adduces for this is simply reproduced from the standard commentaries,[169] which have a habit of taking in each other's washing. It is really necessary to go back to source and look again at the primary evidence.

There are two (and only two) pieces of this that require to be considered. The first is the sole statement[170] which dates any of the material to the period concerned, that of Rabbi Gamaliel II. It is a *baraita*, an additional tradition belonging to the time of the Mishnah, to be found in the Babylonian Talmud:

> Our rabbis taught: Simeon Ha-Faqoli [the cotton dealer] ordered the Eighteen Benedictions before Rabban Gamaliel in Yavneh. Rabban Gamaliel said to the sages: Is there no one who knows how to compose a benediction against the *minim*? Samuel Ha-Qatan [the small] stood up and composed it. Another year [while serving as precentor], he [Samuel] forgot it and tried to recall it for two or three hours, yet they did not remove him.[171]

As Lawrence Schiffman says in the indispensable volume in the series *Jewish and Christian Self-Definition* that is devoted to this whole area,

> The specific function of the benediction was to ensure that those who were *minim* [and we will leave for the moment who these were] would not serve as precentors in the synagogue. . . . It cannot be overemphasized that while the benediction against the *minim* sought to exclude Jewish Christians from active participation in the synagogue service, it in no way implied explusion from the Jewish people.[172]

It was concerned with who was competent to lead the service, and Samuel the Small's regrettable amnesia (which hardly suggests that a fixed formula was in regular use at the time)[173] was overlooked because

[169]In their later books both Barrett, *The Gospel of John and Judaism*, 47f., and Brown, *Community*, 22, merely refer to what they said before and assume the same dating. Barrett talks without argument of 'the Johannine period' as corresponding to post-Jamnian Judaism. The same applies *a fortiori* to Bowman, *The Fourth Gospel and the Jews*, where it is simply equated with the period of Rabbi Aqiba.

[170]In the Australian version of his article, *Emeth* 11.1, 27, Moloney uses the word 'universally'. It is only the universality of repetition.

[171]B. *Ber.* 28b–29a, quoted from L. H. Schiffman, 'At the Crossroads: Tannaitic Perspectives on the Jewish–Christian Schism' in Sanders, ed., *Self-Definition* II, 150, who annotates and justifies the text followed (350).

[172]Ibid., 152.

[173]For the great variation in the blessings generally at this stage, cf. Safrai, 'The Synagogue', *Compendia* I.2, 922–6.

he could be assumed to be orthodox since he had composed it and would not wish to curse himself. It was not laying down a general ban on attendance or throwing anyone out such as the blind beggar. Moloney's imaginative reconstruction bears little relation to reality:

> Everyone attending the synagogue had to pray this prayer loudly, and thus it became a sort of shibboleth. Anyone who failed to call it out could easily be identified as a follower of Jesus, the Christ, and was turned out of the synagogue.[174]

But the most that members of the congregation needed to do was to say 'Amen'.[175]

Then there is the matter of the text of the Benediction and its interpretation. It is generally accepted that the earliest available version must be that which came to light in the Cairo Genizah fragments, now in the Cambridge University Library, first published by Solomon Schechter in 1898,[176] though this of course is a mediaeval document and cannot guarantee the text further back. It runs as follows:

> For the apostates let there be no hope. And let the arrogant government be speedily uprooted in our days. Let the *noṣrim* and the *minim* be destroyed in a moment. And let them be blotted out of the Book of Life and not be inscribed together with the righteous. Blessed art thou, O Lord, who humblest the arrogant.

The first question is what relation this text bears to the version composed in the time of Gamaliel II, and how the key terms *noṣrim* and *minim* are to be interpreted. This has been subjected to careful examination by another Jewish contributor to the same volume, Reuven Kimelman.[177] Here I can only summarize his conclusion,

[174]Jesus as "the Christ"', 241.

[175]Cf. M. *Ber*. 8.8: 'They may answer "Amen" after an Israelite who says a Benediction, but not after a Samaritan until they have heard the whole Benediction'; also T. *Sukk*. 4.6. For the *Tefillah* or *Shemoneh Esreh* (the Eighteen Benedictions) specifically, cf. M.*Ber*. 5.3f. where it is made clear that one individual speaks at a time and others may reply 'Amen'. The same evidently applied to 'blessings' in Christian worship (I Cor. 14.16, 27).

[176]*JQR*, 10, 1898, 657, 659. I quote the translation in R. Kimelman's article, '*Birkat ha-minim* and the Lack of Evidence for an anti-Christian Jewish Prayer in Late Antiquity', in *Self-Definition* II, 226–44. For an updated bibliography on the issues generated by the text he refers to P. Schäfer, *Studien zur Geschichte und Theologie des rabbinischen Judentums*, Leiden 1978, p. 53 n. 3.

[177]In an otherwise damning review of the volume J. Neusner writes of Kimelman 'His paper is persuasive and a solid and important contribution to its topic. Indeed I am inclined to think that, on his topic, it is definitive' (*The Second Century* 2, 1982, 247).

shared by other contributors,[178] that *noṣrim* is a later addition. It only occurs in the Geniza version, where

> the opening word is *noṣrim*, not *minim*. If *noṣrim* were present *ab initio* the talmudic nomenclature would likely have been *birkat ha-noṣrim*. Second, if the term were part of the statutory liturgy from the first century onwards, the term *noṣrim* should have become a common term in rabbinic literature. In fact *noṣrim* does not appear in tannaitic literature [and rarely later]. . . . Thus internal rabbinic evidence makes it highly unlikely that *noṣrim* was part of the original *birkat ha-minim*.[179]

He goes on to argue that of the references by Justin Martyr[180] to Jews cursing Christ or Christians only one mentions it in the context of synagogue *prayers* (*Dial.* 137) and that is said to be '*after* your prayers'; whereas if it were an allusion to the *birkat ha-minim* it would be in the middle of the statutory prayers.[181] In the fourth century with Epiphanius (*c.*315–403) and Jerome (*c.*340–420) there is specific reference to the cursing of Christians 'three times a day' (which must indicate the statutory Blessings) 'under the name Nazoraeans', but he contends that both writers are referring, explicitly or implicitly, to the contemporary sect of the Nazoraeans, who 'want to be both Jews and Christians', and whom they both disown as Christians.[182] That there was a general or earlier ban on Christians *as such* he denies. In fact

> . . . there is abundant evidence from patristic sources that Christians were frequenting the synagogues quite often. Indeed there is far-flung evidence that it was the church leadership that strove to keep

[178]Cf. Schiffman, 'At the Crossroads', 152; Urbach, 'Self-Isolation or Self-Affirmation in Judaism in the First Three Centuries: Theory and Practice', *Self-Definition* II, 288. J. Jocz, *The Jewish People*, 336 n. 257, also does not accept *noṣrim* as part of the original text, nor does Schürer, *History* II, 462f.

[179]*Self-Definition* II, 233f. In the Babylonian recension not even the *minim* appear, only 'slanderers', 'all who do wickedness', 'enemies' and 'the insolent'. Cf. Schürer, *History* II, 455–63.

[180]*Dial.* 16, 47, 93, 95f., 108, 123, 133, 137.

[181]The same point was made long ago by Schürer, *Geschichte des jüdischen Volkes im Zeitalter Jesus Christi*, Leipzig [4]1901, II, 543f. (cf. ET [2]II, 462f.) and G. Hoennicke, *Das Judenchristentum im ersten und zweiten Jahrhundert*, Berlin 1908, 387f.; both cited by W. Horbury, 'The Benediction of the *Minim* and Early Jewish–Christian Controversy', *JTS*, n.s. 33, 1982, 19–61 (21).

[182]*Self-Definition*, II, 236–8. Whether Epiphanius and Jerome were right in this is another matter. Cf. Horbury, 'Benediction', 24–8, who points out that Tertullian had already said that the Jews call Christians Nazarenes (*Adv. Marc.* 4.8.1).

Christians away from the synagogue and not the Jews who were excluding them. Such protest from the church Fathers demonstrates the receptivity of the synagogue to Christians. This situation is highly unlikely if the synagogue liturgy contained a daily curse against Christians.[183]

But he is probably minimizing the evidence, and another contributor to the same volume, Alan F. Segal, makes the point that

> Kimelman has emphasized the fact that the rabbis did not explicitly curse the Christians by name in the service. He has not shown that the *birkat ha-minim* was not taken by the Christians and Jews alike to have included Christians.[184]

In a masterly and learned survey of the whole issue William Horbury concludes that while Justin's evidence is to be trusted for the general attitude of charge and counter-charge between Jews and Christians from New Testament times onwards,[185] the formulation of the Twelfth Benediction

> was not decisive on its own in the separation of church and synagogue, but it gave solemn liturgical expression to a separation effected in the second half of the first century.[186]

In any case with whatever difference of emphasis, all the contributors to the symposium on Self-Definition who refer to it, as well as Horbury, would concur with Kimelman's conclusion that

> *birkat ha-minim* does not reflect a watershed in the history of the relationship between Jews and Christians in the first centuries of our era. Apparently there was never a single edict which caused the so-called irreparable separation between Judaism and Christianity. The separation was rather the result of a long process dependent upon

[183] *Self-Definition* II, 239, and for the evidence, 239f.; also J. H. Charlesworth, 'Christian and Jewish Self-Definition in the Light of Christian Additions to Apocryphal Writings', ibid., 27–55 and especially 311 n. 12.

[184] 'Ruler of This World: Attitudes about Mediator Figures and the Importance of Sociology for Self-Definition', ibid., 245–68 (409 n. 57).

[185] He commends G. W. H. Lampe, 'Church Discipline and the Interpretation of the Epistles to the Corinthians' in W. R. Farmer, C. F. D. Moule and R. R. Niebuhr, edd., *Christian History and Interpretation: Studies Presented to John Knox*, Cambridge and New York 1967, 358–60; and '"Grievous Wolves" (Acts 20.29)' in B. Lindars and S. S. Smalley, edd., *Christ and Spirit in the New Testament: Studies in Honour of C. F. D. Moule*, Cambridge 1973, 253–68.

[186] 'Benediction of the *Minim*', 61.

local situations and ultimately upon the political power of the church.[187]

But what of the *minim*? This term primarily refers to sectarian Jews,[188] among whom the sect or αἵρεσις of Christians[189] would undoubtedly be classed. But all the rabbinic evidence suggests that deviationism was assessed on grounds of *halakah*, practice or discipline, rather than doctrine. Indeed another contributor, E. E. Urbach, says that

> There is no evidence to show that people were excommunicated on the ground of harbouring non-orthodox beliefs. . . . While to Christians heresy mainly implied doctrinal dissent, in Judaism doctrinal dissent did not make a Jew into a heretic, a *min*.[190]

So much for the point upon which Moloney lays great stress[191] that the distinctive ground of separation mentioned in John was *christological*, which indeed it was, and *therefore* could only have reference to the decisive expulsion, datable to the *birkat ha-minim*.

So, to return to the point from which we began, what does all this tell us about the date of the Fourth Gospel? The answer that emerges from the most rigorous re-examination of the evidence by Jewish and Christian scholars is, Nothing. Horbury's carefully argued conclusion is that the Johannine passages have little direct relevance to the *birkat ha-minim*.

> Their complaint is of exclusion, rather than cursing. The Jamnian benediction, consistent as it is with such a result, hardly suffices to bring it about; incidental exclusion of heretical prayer-leaders, even if they are accompanied by other members of the congregation, falls short of the Johannine grievance.
> The Jamnian ordinance belongs to . . . more systematized opposition of the late first century, and probably reinforces an earlier exclusion attested in John,[192] although uncertainties of dating leave

[187] *Self-Definition* II, 244. This was confirmed for me by conversations in Jerusalem.

[188] Ibid., 228–32.

[189] Cf. Acts 24.5, 14; 28.22. It is the same word used to describe the 'parties' of the Sadducees and Pharisees (Acts 5.17; 15.5; 26.5; Josephus, *BJ* 2.119, 124, 162).

[190] 'Self-Isolation or Self-Affirmation', *Self-Definition* II, 269–98 (290, 292).

[191] 'Jesus as "the Christ"', 243–5.

[192] Cf. Brownlee in Charlesworth, ed., *John and Qumran*, 182f.: 'John 12.42 must describe the earlier situation which called forth this "benediction". . . . The evidence of the rabbinic malediction introduced about AD 85 points rather to an earlier and not to a later date for the Fourth Gospel'; and J. Painter, *John, Witness and Theologian*, London

open the possibility that these two measures may be contemporaneous.[193]

What is certain is that the Benediction gives no *ground* for the dating of John, and I know from discussion that Horbury agrees with me in this, as does Henry Chadwick.

Again, Kimelman says:

> John makes no reference to the prayers of the Jews nor to any curse and this is not helpful for establishing any part of the formulation of *birkat ha-minim*.

And he adds in a note:

> If a Palestinian milieu is necessary to explain John's use of terms, then a more likely candidate is Qumran, which seems to have had a parallel in the expulsion from the community (cf. 1QS 6.24–7.25; 8.16f., 22f.).[194] This parallel becomes more cogent in the light of the views of numerous scholars who have correlated Qumran material with the background of an early edition of John.[195]

Finally, Segal says:

> I see no certain evidence that synagogues opposing the Christian community in John were yet fully rabbinic. . . . It does not seem necessary to conclude that the opposition reported by the Johannine community is more formal than the kind of opposition reported by Paul or Luke/Acts. . . . It is probably better to describe the Jewish reaction as 'ostracism' rather than 'excommunication'.[196]

Indeed this seems to me strongly borne out by the little-observed fact that in John 12.42 it is members of the *Council* who fear being made ἀποσυνάγωγοι. This is not because anyone is threatening to cut them off from Judaism but because the Pharisees who have power with the

---

1975, 13: 'Because John shows no awareness of a formal test, it would seem that the formulation of the Gospel took place before AD 85.'

[193]'Benediction of the *Minim*', 52, 60. Cf. the reservation of Meeks, 'Man from Heaven', 55 n. 40: 'I doubt whether the separation can be identified specifically with the *Birkat ha-Minim* promulgated at Yavneh, and whether that decree itself can be dated so precisely.'

[194]Cf. also 1QS 5.18 and CD 9.23. For the severity of the penalty cf. Josephus, *BJ* 2.143f. on the Essenes. Cf. earlier Ezra 10.8 and M. *Taan*. 3.8, quoting a saying of R. Simeon b. Shetah (*c*. 80 BC).

[195]*Self-Definition* II, 235; 397 n. 59.

[196]Ibid., 410 n. 59; 257; 258.

people can see that they are effectively ostracized, boycotted from the fellowship of the religious community, which in such a tight unity of religion and life meant much more than being excluded from worship. What they have to fear is not expulsion but losing face with the people (v. 43).

This is precisely the conclusion that I reached in my *Redating*.[197] If there were any *other* reason to suppose that John was composed between 90 and 100, then it is possible, though only possible (since by then the Johannine community would have had no Palestinian setting, which is where the only evidence comes from),[198] that his references might carry some secondary allusion to the Benediction. But this is no ground for dating it in that period, any more than the supposed reference to Bar Cochba in John 5.43 as the one who 'comes in his own name' is ground for dating it, as was once done,[199] to 132–40.

But what of the fact, of which Moloney makes much, that John alone uses the word ἀποσυνάγωγος? Does not this suggest that he is talking about something in a class of its own? That the word is unique not only in the New Testament but (to our knowledge) in all Greek literature does not itself indicate that it is a specific or technical term.[200] Indeed the very fact that it has 'no precise parallel in rabbinic terminology'[201] suggests that it did not correspond to any established category. By itself it simply means 'put out of the synagogue', 'excluded from the meeting', and in 9.34f. it is paraphrased with ἐκβάλλειν, to 'throw out',

[197] 272–4. So too D. R. A. Hare, *The Theme of Jewish Persecution of Christians in the Gospel according to St Matthew*, Cambridge 1967, 48–56, whom I quoted. Cf. also A. E. Harvey, *Jesus on Trial*, 1976, 89, who argues that John 9.22 need not be an anachronism at all, and Carson, 'Historical Tradition in the Fourth Gospel' in France and Wenham, edd., *Gospel Perspectives* II, 123–5.

[198] This is one of the objections to the highly imaginative projection of the evidence on to a Greek-speaking city in Alexandria or Asia Minor that forms the starting-point of Martyn's reconstruction in *History and Theology in the Fourth Gospel*. There is no reason with him (32f.) to suppose that the 'agreement' of the Jews in John 9.22 represents a formal decree of universal application. The only other uses of συντίθημι (not συνεπιτίθημι, as incorrectly in my *Redating*, 274) in the New Testament (Luke 22.5; Acts 13.20) do not support this. And when John wishes to indicate a formal decree of the Council he makes it clear (11.47, 53, 57).

[199] E.g., P. W. Schmiedel, *The Johannine Writings*, ET London 1908, 200f.

[200] Indeed Martyn himself says 'The term itself . . . does not seem to carry any fearsome denotation, other than the natural concern any Jew might feel at being away from the fellowship of his synagogue' (*History and Theology*, 23). He compares it with ἀπόδημος, away from home.

[201] Kimelman, quoting W. Schrage, συναγωγή, in *TDNT* VII, 848. Moloney, 'Jesus as "the Christ"', 243, upbraids me for failing to cite this fact, but I suggest that it points in the opposite direction.

which is used, quite unspecifically, of Jesus himself (Luke 4.29), Stephen (Acts 7.58) and Paul (Acts 13.50). I would still maintain (and Segal agrees) that the warning of John 16.2, 'They will ban you from the synagogue', says no more than that of Luke 6.22, 'How blest are you when men hate you, when they outlaw (or separate, ἀφορίσωσιν)[202] you and insult you and ban (ἐκβάλωσιν) your very name as infamous.'[203] Now each of these advance notices by Jesus doubtless reflects the subsequent experience of the Johannine and Lukan communities. This is not in any way to be denied, though whether they are evidence *only* of this experience and *not* for the teaching of Jesus himself is another matter. But the excessive claims of contemporary redaction criticism come through again in the comments that Moloney appends to the final sentence of his article in the Australian version, with which, apart from the last clause, I would fully concur.

> The greatness of the Johannine community, as seen in its Gospel, lies in its capacity to take traditional terms and work through them towards a new meaning and a new depth as it faced the critically new situations in the life of a developing Christian church in Asia Minor, in the late 90s of the first century AD.[204]

But to it he adds the note:

> This is the exciting direction which is being taken by Johannine scholarship. It would be a closed door to anyone who opts for a pre-AD 70 dating.

Yet it would be a wide-open door on an earlier period. Indeed the forewarnings of John 15.18–16.4[205] and 16.32f. (to the extent that the last refers beyond the passion) could well echo and help to bear out a number of otherwise unsupported references to events in the earliest history of the church. These could include the putting to death of

[202]This is the same word used of Paul's voluntary separation of himself and his disciples from the synagogue of Ephesus in Acts 19.9. But it is made clear that he was compelled to it by Jewish abuse of 'the Way'.

[203]I would quote again Dodd, *Historical Tradition*, 410: 'The prospect of such exclusion was before Christians of Jewish origin early enough, at least, to have entered into the common tradition behind both Luke and John.'

[204]*Emeth* 11.1, 33.

[205]Cf. Lindars, 'The Persecution of Christians in John 15.18 – 16.4a' in W. Horbury and B. McNeil, edd., *Suffering and Martyrdom in the New Testament: Studies presented to G. M. Styler*, Cambridge 1981, 48–69.

Christians *in Jerusalem* by Paul (Acts 26.9–11);[206] the 'violent persecution' of the church in Jerusalem (Acts 8.1) the threat to Paul's life and his enforced departure after preaching in the city (Acts 9.28–30; 22.18; 26.20; Rom. 15.19); the scattering of Christians over the country districts of Judaea and Samaria (Acts 8.1); the sufferings of the churches in Judaea at the hands of their fellow-countrymen (I Thess. 2.14); the execution of James the brother of John in Jerusalem (Acts 12.1f.); not to mention the harassment and expulsion of Christian missionaries by 'the Jews' in Asia Minor and Greece (I Thess. 2.14–16; II Cor. 11.24–6; Acts 13.45–50; 14.2–6, 19f.; 17.5–9, 13; 18.6f., 12–17). All of these events took place in the 30s, 40s and early 50s, and none of the predictions in the main body of John's Gospel (in contrast with 21.18f.) need reflect anything later than that.[207]

Having now dealt at somewhat tedious length (for it is so constantly being reiterated) with the first and specific factor which is said to set John in the 90s of the first century, let us now look more briefly at the general one, namely, that his use of 'the Jews' and comparable phrases shows him to be writing at a far distance both of time and ethos.[208] He is said to be an outsider to the world of which he speaks. 'The Jews', it is maintained, are regularly referred to in antagonistic terms as a group quite alien to the community to which the author belongs. Moreover, says Barrett:

> The same impression is conveyed by references to the law as something from which both Jesus and the evangelist dissociate themselves:
>
> 10.34 Is it not written in your law. . . ?
>
> 15.25 It is to fulfil the word that is written in their law, 'They hated me without a cause.'
>
> 19.7 The Jews answered him, 'We have a law, and by that law he ought to die, because he made himself the Son of God.'

[206]Horbury, 'Benediction of the *Minim*', 53, draws attention to the wording in this passage where 'Saul's opposition to "the name of Jesus the Nazarene" is thought to have meant that "in all the synagogues . . . I compelled them to blaspheme"', and, linking it with the 'one who says "A curse on Jesus"' in I Cor. 12.3, suggests that the blaspheming and anathematizing of Christ by Jews mentioned by Justin (*Dial.* 35, 47, 137; *Apol.* 1.31) could go back to the very earliest times.

[207]Cf. Goodenough, who was an expert in this field if anyone was, in 'John a Primitive Gospel', *JBL* 64 1945, 147: 'These references to "Jews" might have been written during, or any time after, the Pauline persecution' (i.e., Paul's persecution of Christians in Jerusalem and beyond within three years of the crucifixion; Acts 26.9–11).

[208]Cf. e.g. Brown, *John* I, lxx–lxxiii.

> Such passages could have been written only by someone who was consciously standing outside Judaism. Of course, he may once have been a Jew.[209]

His last reference in fact is a bad example, since 'the Jews' are clearly here being distinguished from Pilate and the Romans, not from Jesus and Christians. The others too are intelligible as *ad hominem* arguments, as 'the law you take your stand on'[210] (8.17; 10.34) or 'they think they are living by' (15.25), just as 'you search the scriptures' and yet do not recognize the one to whom they witness (5.39f.). In the same way Matthew, the most Jewish of the Synoptists, speaks of 'the Jews' in a similarly external manner (28.15) and of 'their synagogues' (10.17) and 'your synagogues' (23.34) in equally polemical contexts. So too Matt. 17.27, relating to the very issue of Christian 'self-definition' over against the Jews in the crucial matter of the temple-tax urges payment, 'as we do not want to cause difficulty for these people (αὐτούς)'. This clearly presupposes a distancing of the two communities into 'them' and 'us', though nothing like the alienation of the separated religions, each with its own covenant, such as is evidenced in the post–70 *Epistle of Barnabas*. Indeed Matthew is seeking to *avert* a break and this passage strongly bears out the other indications that, as I have argued,[211] his Gospel reflects the uneasy co-existence of the 50s and early 60s rather than the situation after 70, when the temple was no more and the half-shekel tax was no longer the internal Jewish affair here presupposed but a levy imposed by the Romans for the upkeep of the temple of Jupiter Capitolinus in Rome. Of course Matthew's community was also strenuously engaged on the other front of the Gentile mission, as John's apparently was not, with the additional tensions which it created. But in other respects the Jewish-Christian milieu which they presuppose would appear to be not so very different. If Matthew's Gospel could have been written by a scribe 'discipled' to the kingdom of Heaven (13.52 – we find the same verb used of Joseph of Arimathea in 27.57), so John's could have come from a community which had arisen out of and was in internal dispute with the synagogue.

Yet what of the terrible objectivity and externality of his references

[209] *Gospel of John and Judaism*, 70.

[210] In his unpublished lectures on John at Cambridge, Lightfoot interpreted it as 'the law behind which you are always shielding yourselves, which you are always using as a weapon against me'. The 'distance' is polemical rather than racial or temporal.

[211] *Redating*, 102–7.

to the Jews? First, it is worth making the point that this is fundamentally no different, not only from Matthew where 'the Jews' are still perpetuating the rumour that the disciples stole the body of Jesus (28.15; cf. Justin, *Dial.* 38, 108), but from Paul, that Hebrew of the Hebrews (Phil. 3.5; cf. I Cor. 9.20). For *he* certainly is not writing after the supposedly 'unbridgeable gulf'. Indeed in his earliest epistle he speaks of 'the Jews' with the same objectivity and a personal animosity never quite paralleled in John:

> You have fared like the congregations in Judaea, God's people in Christ Jesus. You have been treated by your countrymen as they are treated by the Jews, who killed the Lord Jesus and the prophets and drove us out, the Jews who are heedless of God's will and enemies of their fellow-men, hindering us from speaking to the Gentiles to lead them to salvation.[212] All this time they have been making up the full measure of their guilt, and now retribution has overtaken them for good and all (I Thess. 2.14–16; cf. II Cor. 11.24, 26).

This passage is particularly interesting because already by the year 50 Paul is distinguishing 'the Jews' from Christians *in Judaea*.[213]

This raises the whole perplexing question of the definition of Ἰουδαῖος, which is no easier today than it was then. Even more than most such generic terms, like 'English' (is it linguistic or territorial or racial, when is it equivalent to 'British', etc.?), 'Jewish' covers a wide range of meanings and is determined largely according to context by that with which it is contrasted.[214] One of the most obvious

[212]Moloney, 'Jesus as "the Christ"', 244, says it is 'significant' that I do not quote this last clause, as indicating an 'all-important' difference from John. Of course the occasion of the rift in John was different, since, unlike Paul (Gal. 2.9), he was not engaged in the Gentile mission; but the heart of Paul's contention with the Jews and Judaizing Christians was just as 'christological' (I Cor. 1.22–4; Phil. 1.17f.; 3.2–11, 18; Acts 18.5f.).

[213]It is notable that it is never once referred to by Martyn.

[214]Cf. the comprehensive survey by Malcolm Lowe, 'Who were the Ἰουδαῖοι?', *NovT* 18, 1976, 101–30. He notes the shades of meaning in the word 'French': 'If we consider the word "French" in modern usage, then in the strictest sense a Frenchman is someone of French descent who lives in France, is a French citizen and speaks French. But we may also call someone "French" in a weaker sense if he is only some of these things (French Canadians, naturalized Frenchmen, children who happened to be born to tourists in France, Bretons). We also commonly speak of "the French" to mean the French *government* or its representatives (when they sign an agreement with "the Russians"), or the French *authorities* (when "the French" put a tourist on trial for a motoring offence)' (107). All these shifts of meaning and more are observable in the use of 'the Jews.' Unfortunately Lowe does not seem to me sufficiently to take his own advice not 'to force one of these meanings upon every occurrence of the word' (101). He properly stresses the geographical sense, 'Judaean', but minimizes the

contrasts, between Jew and Gentile, by which it is largely determined in Paul and Acts, as in Jewish literature generally, is in fact notably absent from John. As we have seen, there is no reference to the ἔθνη (ἔθνος in the singular refers to the Jewish nation: 11.48–52; 18.35) and the only use of ἐθνικός (III John 7) is typically Jewish and distinguishes 'heathen' from believers (as in Matt. 5.47; 6.7; 18.17). The sole example of the Jew-Gentile contrast is Pilate's highly significant question in John 18.35, 'Am I a Jew?' For apart from him the world of the Gospel is purely Jewish. Jesus' own Jewishness is never in doubt (4.9; 18.35); and he identifies himself with the Jews as 'we' over against the Samaritans (4.22). For this Gospel, it is '*from* the Jews that salvation comes' (4.22) – though that salvation is *for* the whole world. There is nothing nationalist, let alone racialist, about it. It is the most universalistic of all the Gospels (1.9, 29; 3.17; 12.32): the right to become children of God is for all who believe (1.12), exactly as for Paul (Rom. 3.22). Yet the message is specifically directed to the Jews, and the underlying question throughout is also one of Paul's, 'Who is the true Jew?' (Rom. 2.28). The answer for both is the Jew who accepts Jesus as his Messiah, who believes in him as the crown of all that Judaism stands for: the *shekinah* (John 1.14), the temple (2.21), the manna (6.32–5), the water (7.38), the light (8.12), the shepherd (10.14), the king (12.15), the vine (15.1). Being a Christian and being a true Jew are one and the same.[215]

Why then the antagonism? Because 'the Jews', or the great majority of them (for those who accept Jesus are also Jews: 2.23; 8.31; 11. 45; 12.11), do not believe. Who are these? In the mass of instances, the Jerusalem leadership, and especially the temple hierarchy. Typical is 7.15, where 'the Jews' reflect the 'establishment' attitude to the untrained and therefore unqualified rabbi. At times the line between leaders and led is blurred (e.g., 12.9, 'a great crowd of the Jews', or 18.20, 'all the Jews', and several times in ch. 11), but the usual contrast is with 'the crowd', the *plebs* (ὁ ὄχλος, used sixteen times of the city proletariat), or the ordinary inhabitants of Jerusalem (7.25, where the 'they' that they refer to are 'the Jews'; cf. 5.18). But in all cases except two 'the Jews' are Judaeans, as opposed to Galileans (or Greeks, who we have argued are also in this Gospel Jews), and these two instances

---

religious – in the laudable, but doubtful, interests of Jewish–Christian dialogue, in which he is engaged at the Van Leer Foundation in Jerusalem. In general Schillebeeckx, *Christ*, 335f. and 872f. n. 36, follows Lowe. Cf. also G. J. Cuming, 'The Jews in the Fourth Gospel', *ExpT* 60, 1948–9, 290–2; but again he is too sweeping.

[215]Cf. Paul's remarkable statement in Phil. 3.3, '*We* are the circumcision.'

may not in fact be exceptions. For in 6.41 and 52 'the Jews' in the synagogue at Capernaum, again distinguished from the 'crowd' (6.22, 24) with whom hitherto the dialogue has been conducted, with misunderstanding but without rancour,[216] could well be representatives of the establishment who had come down from Jerusalem to Galilee (even though they claim familiarity with his parents, 6.42), since Mark also mentions them at this same point in the ministry (7.1), as well as earlier in 3.22[217]. In fact οἱ Ἰουδαῖοι in John refers not only to the Jews of Palestine as opposed to the Diaspora (cf. the *contrast* in 7.35 between 'the Jews' and 'the Dispersion') but preeminently to the Jews of Judaea.[218] At a number of points Ἰουδαῖος has a primarily geographical reference, as in the adjective 'the Judaean countryside' in 3.22.[219] Thus in 7.1 'Jesus went about in Galilee; he would not go about in Judaea because the Jews (or Judaeans) sought to kill him'; or in 11.7 he says 'Let us go back to Judaea [from Peraea]. But his disciples retorted, "It is not long since the Judaeans were wanting to stone you"' (cf. also 11.54, where what is usually translated 'among the Jews' [RSV] must mean 'among the Judaeans' [NEB, 'in Judaea']).

This usage is in no way peculiar to John. Thus Josephus states in *Ant.*

[216]The dialogue falls into three sections: with the crowd (24–40), the Jews (41–58), and the disciples (60–71). I see no reason with Bultmann and others to posit the interpolation of a redactor in 51–58. Cf. Meeks' judgment ('Man from Heaven', 58): 'The literary unity of vv. 27–58 seems to me assured, whatever theological self-contradictions it may contain.' Brown's more plausible thesis (*John* I, 287–91) that it is Johannine material transferred from an institution discourse at the last supper still has to explain why teaching given to the disciples becomes transferred to the enemies of Jesus – the reverse of the tendency well documented by Jeremias in *The Parables of Jesus*.

[217]Cf. Luke 5.17, 'Pharisees and teachers of the law, who had come from every village of Galilee and from Judaea and Jerusalem, were sitting round' (following the Nestle text and NEB margin). But this is a typically generalizing Lukan note on which little can be rested (cf. Luke 4.44 compared with Mark 1.39).

[218]When John wants an overall or neutral term, geographically or religiously, he uses 'Israel' (1.31, 50; 3.10; 12.13) or 'Israelite' (1.48), as do Matthew (2.19–22, distinguishing Israel from Judaea, and 10.5f.) and Paul (Rom. 9.4, 6; 11.26; II Cor. 11.22; Gal. 6.16; Eph. 2.12). It is to be noted (cf. Lowe, 'Who were the Ἰουδαῖοι?' 118f.) that in all the Gospels it is Pilate and his soldiers who style Jesus 'King of the Jews' (note especially John 18.33–35), probably meaning 'king of Judaea' (like Herod the Great in Matt. 2.2) and 'supposing Jesus to be a Judaean upstart trying to seize power in his procurate'. Jews always call him 'king of Israel', whether in praise or scorn (Matt. 27.42; Mark 15.32; John 1.49; 12.13). Geographically Philo and Josephus equally distinguish between Judaea proper and Palestina (M. Stern, 'The Province of Judaea', *Compendia* I. 1, 346 n. 1).

[219]For this use of 'Judaea' in contrast to Jerusalem, cf. Mark 1.5; Matt. 3.5.

17.254 that many Galileans, Idumaeans and people from Jericho and Peraea had come to Jerusalem for Pentecost, where they were joined by 'a multitude from Judaea itself', literally 'of the Judaeans themselves' (*αὐτῶν Ἰουδαίων*). But then shortly afterwards (17.258) he calls them all 'Jews' in contrast with the Romans. One gets the same equivocation in Acts, which in 2.5 speaks of 'devout Jews [in contrast with Gentiles] from every nation under heaven', and then in 2.14 refers to 'Fellow Jews, and all you who live in Jerusalem', the latter being the Judaeans (cf. 2.9) as opposed to the non-Palestinian (but still Jewish) residents.

In fact 'Jews' is a word that takes its colour almost entirely from what it is contrasted with: Gentiles, Galileans, non-Palestinians, Greek-speakers,[220] Samaritans, Baptists[221] or Christians. It can indeed be used for 'Jewish Christians' (and is properly so rendered by the NEB in Gal. 2.13–15), but the differentiation of 'Jews' from 'Christians' is beginning to make itself felt as early as I Thess. 2.14. It is difficult sometimes to decide whether in John references to Jewish customs are primarily there to mark them off from Christian (certainly 2.6, and perhaps 19.42), Palestinian (perhaps 19.40) or Galilean (2.13; 5.1; 6.4; 7.2; 11.55). It would be foolish to rule out that the references to the feasts and customs of 'the Jews' may be there as explanatory notes for any Gentile readers, though I am not persuaded that this affects the main thrust of the destination and purpose of the Gospel. But it is noticeable that in every case except one (6.4), the phrase 'of the Jews' may be added to the name of the festivals to explain why it was necessary for Jesus to go to Judaea. This is especially true of 7.1–3: 'He wished to avoid Judaea because the Judaeans wanted to kill him. But the Judaean Feast of Tabernacles was at hand.'[222] The only feast *not* so designated is Dedication in 10.22, when Jesus is already in Judaea or Peraea. There the festival is said to be 'in Jerusalem', to tell the reader how he comes to be walking where he is (10.23).

Of course there is also a highly polemical tone to many of the references to 'the Jews' – and never more than in the internecine

[220]Cf. again Josephus, *Ant.* 18.63, where 'Jews' are contrasted with 'the Hellenic element' in much the same way, I believe, as 'Hebrews' and 'Hellenists' in Acts 6.1 or 'the Jews' and 'the Greeks' in John 12.11 and 20.

[221]John 3.25. But the text is uncertain. 'A Jew' is better supported than 'the Jews' (a fairly obvious correction). But I believe there is much to be said for the conjecture 'Jesus'. Cf. below, ch. IV, p. 171 n. 37.

[222]In 6.4 it may be put in to explain that Jesus was not in Jerusalem but in Galilee.

dispute of 8.31–59, where Jesus is imputed to be a bastard and a Samaritan[223] and his opponents sons not of Abraham but of the Devil. Yet neither side is denying the other's Jewishness, only their faithfulness to it. Again the contrast in 20.19, where the disciples are behind locked doors 'for fear of the Jews' could suggest a polarization with 'Christians' (as in Matt. 28.15), were it not that exactly the same phrase is used in 7.13; 9.22 and 19.38 of the relation between the authorities and their own people. None of these antagonisms need imply that the evangelist stands at any great distance of time or space. There is not, I believe, a trace of anti-Semitism, i.e., of *racial* anti-Jewishness in the Gospel.[224] For, to cite two complementary judgments, 'the Fourth Gospel is most anti-Jewish just at the points it is most Jewish' and 'where the gospel is being most anti-Jewish, it is relying heavily on Jewish traditions'.[225]

Yet the charge is constantly made that, even if John does not stand outside Judaism, he is so remote from the period he is treating that he uses 'the Jews' as a blanket term to cover his ignorance of the differences and divisions in pre–70 Palestinian Judaism, such as are still preserved in the Synoptists.[226] This I believe to be quite untrue, and the justification for saying so will, I trust, emerge in subsequent discussion of the story of Jesus, not least the passion narrative. Of course 'the Jews' is used as a general shorthand term for what today we should call 'the establishment'. But this does not mean that John was not well aware of the divisions and tensions within it – and between it and the rest. In fact he provides, I believe, as vivid and accurate a picture of the scene as any other first-century writer, Jewish or Christian – though of course from a Christian point of view.[227] The fact that he does not mention the Sadducees, who disappeared from

[223]For this as a Jewish term of abuse, cf. b. *Sot.* 22a; quoted, Jeremias, *Jerusalem*, 354.

[224]Cf. Brownlee, 'Whence the Gospel of John?' in Charlesworth, ed., *John and Qumran*, 183: 'In view of all these considerations, it is a misinterpretation of this Gospel to charge it with anti-Semitism.'

[225]Meeks, 'Am I a Jew?' in Neusner, ed., *Christianity, Judaism and Other Greco-Roman Cults* I, 172, and Segal in *Self-Definition* II, 247. Cf. Barrett, *Fourth Gospel and Judaism*, 71f.; Schillebeeckx, *The Christ*, 337; and earlier Sanday, *Authorship and Historical Character of the Fourth Gospel*, 189f., 213.

[226]Typically, Bultmann, *John*, 86f.

[227]Cf. M. de. Jonge, 'Jewish Expectations about the "Messiah" according to the Fourth Gospel', *NTS* 19, 1972–3, 246–70, especially 246–63; R. Schnackenburg, 'Die Messiasfrage im Johannesevangelium' in J. Blinzler et al., edd., *Neutestamentliche Aufsätze (Festschrift für J. Schmidt)*, Regensburg 1963, 240–64.

power after 70, or the scribes, who certainly did not, must not be taken to imply his ignorance of the earlier period. As a matter of fact, Mark and Luke only mention the Sadducees once each – in the question they put to Jesus in Mark 12.18 and pars. Matthew alone, with his ecclesiastical interest, expands on them (eight times). John knows very well that they and not the Pharisees dominated the Sanhedrin, though he shows himself conscious that while the former have the authority the latter have the power with the people (12.42) – which is exactly in line with what Jewish sources say of the Sadducees.[228] 'The rulers', i.e. members of the Council, are as a group distinguished from 'the Pharisees' (7.48; 12.42),[229] although he is quite aware that distinguished individual Pharisees sat on the Council (3.1; 7.50),[230] just as Josephus, describing the Sanhedrin, combines 'the chief priests and the most notable of the Pharisees' (*BJ* 2.411). In John too it is not in their party but in their judicial capacity as 'chief priests' that the Sadducees play an indispensable part in the story. As in all the Gospels, the Pharisees are the source and instigators of the *religious* opposition (cf. 4.1; 7.32; 8.13; 11.46; 12.19, 42). Yet for this to be translated into *judicial* action they have, however reluctantly, to make common cause with the chief priests, who once the plans to remove Jesus are under way increasingly assume control. Indeed in none of the Gospels are the Pharisees even mentioned in the trial narrative.[231] John is completely in line here. *Per contra* the only time before that that the chief priests

[228]In 1.24 the persons 'sent from the Pharisees' are not to be *equated* with 'the deputation of priests and Levites' in 1.19, as in the RSV's translation 'they had been sent from the Pharisees' (who would have had no power to send them): the οἱ is clearly no part of the true text. The Pharisees accompanied them rather than sent them. Incidentally, as Israel Abrahams observed (*Studies in Pharisaism and the Gospels* II, 1924, 37f.), John somewhat surprisingly is the only Gospel writer to mention the basic division between the priests and the Levites (apart from the parable of the good Samaritan).

[229]Cf. Josephus, *Ant.* 18.17: 'For whenever they assume some office, though they submit unwillingly and perforce, yet submit they do to the formulas of the Pharisees, since otherwise the masses would not tolerate them' (cf. 13.298; *BJ* 2.166); and b. *Yoma* 19b, 'My son, although we are Sadducees, we are afraid of the Pharisees.'

[230]John represents Nicodemus as occupying very much the same position as Gamaliel in Acts 5.34. Both are Pharisees, members of the Sanhedrin and famous teachers (like Gamaliel's son after him: Josephus, *Vita* 190f.). Martyn, *History and Theology in the Fourth Gospel*, 155–7, draws attention to the interesting parallels, but it is merely fanciful to suppose that they are elaborations of the same tradition.

[231]In Matt. 27.62 they emerge again, in company with the chief priests, on the day after the crucifixion to ask Pilate for the guard.

appear, or the constables of the court whom they alone can command, is (in company with the Pharisees) for the judicial purpose of arranging or effecting his arrest (John 7.32, 45; 11.47–57; 12.10). There is a clear awareness here of functional differences.[232]

Often of course 'the Jews' are generally 'the authorities', but when they alternate with 'the Pharisees' it may again be possible to detect a distinction of roles. Thus, in the healing of the blind man in ch. 9, it is 'the Pharisees' who object to the healing on religious grounds, because it breaks the sabbath law:[233] as a sinner this fellow cannot be a man of God (vv. 13–17). But in vv. 18–34 it is 'the Jews' who interrogate him (just as they do the cripple in 5.10–15). They represent the hierarchy, and their interest is whether he really has been healed. Is this a certifiable cure? For ascertaining this is their job (cf. Mark 1.44, 'Show yourself to the priest: . . . that will certify the cure'). But even when the medical facts are apparently beyond dispute they try to make him disavow the ground of healing; and when he still will not, they lay him under the ban which they alone have the power to serve. In vv. 40f. 'the Pharisees' are again introduced, but here once more the issue is the moral and religious one of whether they, who claim to be the very pillars of light and law, are blind, the charge regularly brought against them in Matthew (15.14; 23.16f., 24). They represent, as it were, the leaders of the Festival of Light or the Moral Majority rather

[232]Cf. already Brooke, 'The Historical Value of the Fourth Gospel' in Swete, ed., *Cambridge Biblical Essays*, 317f.

[233]Harvey, *Constraints of History*, 37f., discusses whether Jesus' actions on the sabbath were actually illegal under the regulations later codified in the Mishnah. He writes: 'According to John's gospel they were. Two episodes are recorded in that gospel: in one Jesus makes a paste and anoints the blind man's eyes (9.1–7), in the other he commands (and so takes responsibility for) the patient to carry his bed (5.1–9). Both of these actions were clearly illegal (M. *Shab*. 10.1–5; 7.2), and the evangelist explicitly records that they gave rise to attempts to bring Jesus to court (5.16; 9.16). In the synoptic gospels on the other hand the situation is quite different. In every case of sabbath healing Jesus does no more than speak certain words or at most touch the sufferer. He does nothing which could be regarded as a transgression of any known regulation. Nevertheless the gospels regard these episodes as being highly provocative to the Pharisees.' Indeed they specially accuse him in the matter of the plucking of corn on the sabbath of abetting something which is 'forbidden' (Mark 2.24 and pars). But he continues: 'We have therefore to decide whether the synoptics or the Fourth Gospel are more likely to be correct. Given the anxiety of the latter to represent Jesus' activity as constantly precipitating the threat of legal action, it is reasonable to prefer the synoptic account.' I suggest that this is pure prejudice in favour of Synoptic priority. It is John who explains the situation which the Synoptics describe. If the evidence were the other way round, no one would question where the preference should be given.

than the church authorities. The subtle difference of roles is not, I suggest, accidental.[234]

Barrett's remark at this point in his commentary, that 'John speaks indiscriminately of "the Jews" and "the Pharisees", probably with no clear knowledge of conditions in Palestine before AD 70',[235] needs therefore to be challenged. On the contrary, I believe that John's instinctive feel for the period, as for the terrain, before the Palestinian scene changed beyond recall, is impressive. That he knew the social, political and religious conditions, not only of the earliest years of Christianity in Jerusalem before his community left for Asia Minor (probably soon after the Council in 48),[236] but also of the ministry of Jesus himself, must be left to come out in what follows. But that the Johannine preaching material, however much adapted to its subsequent Diaspora destination, was first hammered out in the sort of disputes with the leadership of metropolitan Judaism that dominate the Gospel I cannot doubt. Nor can I believe that it *merely* reflects that community's history; I believe it really goes back (as it specifically claims) to the words and works of Jesus by which it was created and sustained.

That it represents also a profound reflection upon them is not of course in any way to be denied. But the argument from development, that it takes, fifty, sixty, a hundred years for such a degree of maturation, is I believe almost wholly subjective. Once the relevance of the *birkat ha-minim* has been discounted, then, as far as I can see, there is no positive reason for choosing for the composition of the Gospel AD 90–100 (the closing years of the reign of Domitian, which have been argued for the date of the Apocalypse – I believe wrongly – because of

[234]Westcott put the same difference in his own way: 'The Pharisees are moved by the symptoms of religious disorder: the high-priests (Sadducees) by the prospect of ecclesiastical danger' (*John* I, xviii). Dodd, *Historical Tradition*, 264f., while failing to observe the distinction in ch. 9 (making '"the Pharisees" act as an ecclesiastical court, with power to excommunicate' (9.34), which, as he says, 'does not appear to be historical'), notes the same difference in 1.19–25 'between the questions asked by the priests and Levites and the question asked by the Pharisees. The official deputation, as such, is content with obtaining from the Baptist a disavowal of any dangerous pretensions; its Pharisaic members (or the Pharisaic deputation) wish to probe more deeply into the theoretical basis of his baptism. There is nothing here inconsistent with what we know of conditions at the time.' He notes that Mark makes the same distinction between the official members of the Sanhedrin who challenge Jesus' authority (11.27) and the Pharisees (2.16–18; 7.5) who question the way of life he teaches.

[235]*John*, 360.

[236]See n. 150 above.

their supposed *state* persecution of the church). That decade is arrived at in fact purely by a process of elimination[237] – that (a) the Gospel depends on Luke, which was written in the 80s (neither of which statements I believe to be true), and (b) it cannot from the papyrus fragment discovered be much later than 100.

Wider comparison with other Christian development (theological, ethical and organizational) depends of course on the dating of other books of the New Testament and the sub-apostolic age. That is why I was driven to re-investigate the chronology of all the first-century Christian literature and also to conclude how precarious is the argument from development to dating, from christology to chronology.[238] But I would end this section with two fairly indisputable parallels for dating, one Christian and the other pagan.

The closest equivalent to the Johannine pre-existence christology, the nature of whose distinctiveness we must consider in the final chapter, is to be found in the later Pauline letters to the Philippians and Colossians (which I dated in the spring and summer of 58, but which cannot be very much later), and in the Epistle to the Hebrews (which I placed about 67). As Barrett concedes, without drawing the chronological inference, 'It must be allowed that the Pauline Christology of Col. 1.15–19 and the Johannine Christology of 1.1–18 could have been independently drawn out from similar materials in similar controversial circumstances',[239] and, one might add, in the same geographical area. So the end-term of Johannine theological reflection, represented by the prologue to the Gospel, cannot therefore be said to be wildly out of line if it is dated to about 65. That still allows for thirty-five years of reflection and development, but *also* for a direct link with the earliest days of Christianity. For, as we have seen,

[237]Cf. Kümmel, *Introduction to the NT*, 246, whose five-line statement on the date of John I quoted in *Redating*, 261.

[238]Cf. *Redating*, especially 344f.; also Gardner-Smith, *St John and the Synoptic Gospels*, 93–6; Hengel, 'Christologie and neutestamentliche Chronologie' in H. Baltensweiler and B. Reicke, edd., *Neues Testament und Geschichte: Oscar Cullmann zum 70. Geburtstag*, Zürich and Tübingen 1972, 43–67. Also for non-christological aspects of the relation between 'date and doctrine' in John, Paul and Hebrews, cf. H. E. Edwards, *The Disciple Who Wrote These Things*, 141–51.

[239]*John*, 56. Cf. Streeter, *Four Gospels*, 457: 'The question we have to ask is, how many years of further theological development must be allowed to a Church which already possessed Colossians, Ephesians and Philippians, to reach the point when it could make this reply? And the answer is a conditional one – five hundred years in a community that could produce no single mind above the commonplace; five years if a man of genius should arise so soon. The category of development, in the slow, patient, biological sense of that term, does not apply in cases of this sort. The Logos doctrine is

both Paul (I Cor. 15.1–3) and the writer to the Hebrews (2.3f.) claim to go back to those who heard it from the Lord,[240] if not, like John, to the Lord himself (I John 1.1–3, 5; cf. II John 5). Thus the 'omega' of the most advanced development in Christian theology need not be severed in time from the 'alpha', the 'beginning of the gospel'. Perhaps one may once again quote a conclusion from Kysar's exhaustive survey:

> The independence of the johannine form of Christian life and thought may mean that the so-called 'high christology' of the gospel is not so much an indication of the lateness of the gospel as it is of its peculiarity. It would appear that johannine Christianity articulated a 'high christology' early and in isolation from other developing forms of views of Christ. In other words, the old evolutionary schemes of Christian thought are undermined in an absolute way.[241]

The other parallel, from ancient classical literature, points to the same conclusion. I have previously used the analogy,[242] which Dodd and others have drawn, between the material for the historical Jesus and the material for the historical Socrates. Xenophon's *Memorabilia* and Plato's *Dialogues* correspond, one can say very broadly, to the approaches respectively of the Synoptists and the Fourth Gospel. The latter in each case presupposes a very considerable degree of recasting and transposition in the mind of the philosopher or the evangelist. Yet the point that I failed to observe, and which I have never seen made by any others who draw the parallel, is the implication for chronology. Plato's *Apology*, which corresponds to the Johannine trial narrative, was written probably within two or three years of Socrates' death in 399 BC and the *Phaedo*, which has striking analogies with the Last Discourses, within twenty or thirty years. Thus the distances in time would not be at all dissimilar. Indeed I become more and more persuaded that 'the trial narrative' as a genre of literature is regularly

---

consistent with almost any date for the Gospel.' He was arguing in favour of a date for John as *early* as 90–95!

[240] If, as I argued, Hebrews was written by Barnabas, then 2.3f. echoes rather remarkably the pristine period in Jerusalem described in Acts 4 and 5. But nothing depends on this.

[241] *The Fourth Evangelist and His Gospel*, 275.

[242] *Redating*, 271, 357.

produced when the need for it is first felt – to set straight the record of what really happened and of what the defendant really said and stood for. This was as true of Plato's *Apology* as of still more instant productions these days like *The Trial of Steve Biko* or *The Trial of Beyers Naude*, or even *The Trial of Lady Chatterley*. The believers in the cause do not wait forty to sixty years to supply such apologetic material, though it may indeed generate the demand for later editions and other versions (such as the demonstrably secondary *Apology* of Xenophon, which refers in §1 to the accounts of others) and perhaps expansions into 'Lives' that lead up to it.[243]

Finally, Plato's *Apology* was produced by a man who was present at the trial (*Apol.* 33b) (while Xenophon depended on another's report: *Apol.* 2), even if on his own admission he was absent through sickness on the last night which the *Phaedo* records (*Phaedo* 59a). Though he was Socrates' most mature interpreter, he was also among his most intimate younger disciples.[244] But that leads into the third and last strand we must consider, the connection in person.

4. *The Link in Person*

At the beginning it will be well to define the limits of our present concern. It is not primarily to answer the perennial question of who wrote the Fourth Gospel, any more than it was to say precisely where it was written or to date it for its own sake. It is to ask whether there is sufficient evidence for continuity in person, as well as in place and time, to claim that the Johannine tradition may be traced back to the beginning, that there is a real link between the omega and the alpha, and whether therefore it is a reasonable exercise to presume that John, *as well as* being the most mature piece of writing in the New Testament, could be *a* first Gospel.

For this it is not necessary to be able to demonstrate who the author was. In this respect there is a difference from the older conservative approach, for which 'authenticity and genuineness', to use J. B.

[243]Thus there is a considerable overlap between the last chapter of Xenophon's *Memorabilia* (4.8) and the opening of his *Apology*, suggesting that one grew out of the other, though which way round it is impossible to be sure. He also starts the *Memorabilia* from the trial of Socrates (1.1.1f.) before making the transition to his life (1.1.3).

[244]According to Diogenes Laertius (*Vitae*, 3.6) he was 20 when he became a pupil of Socrates and about 28 when Socrates died.

Lightfoot's terms[245] (and his generation was preoccupied with these, over against the fiction or forgery wished upon St John, as they saw it, by the radical Continental critics),[246] turned on apostolicity. This comes out very clearly in Scott Holland's treatment, for whom it was a question of apostolic authorship or nothing: 'Either the book was written by the Apostle, or we are totally unable to account for its existence.'[247] The question of who the author was is still fascinating, and important, and we shall be seeking to answer the question in the light of the evidence, external and internal, at the end. But at the beginning I would wish to insist that everything does not turn on it – nor, obviously, shall we ever reach proof or certainty.

The element of attestation by eyewitnesses is certainly important – as Luke, who was not one, testifies in the preface to his Gospel. The tradition was handed down to 'us', he says, through those who were 'from the beginning eyewitnesses and servants of the Gospel' (1.2). Yet it is noticeable that recent studies which stress John's Palestinian background,[248] while reaffirming the element of first-hand witness, have detached this from apostolic authorship or even apostolic origin. 'The beloved disciple' on whose testimony it is based tends to become an 'unknown Jerusalem disciple'. And the question of who ultimately the evangelist was becomes secondary.

To these issues we shall return. But at this stage I must enter a demurrer against the astonishing remark in the introduction to Bultmann's commentary that

> The Gospel itself makes no claim to have been written by an eyewitness. And in no way does it give occasion to presume that an eyewitness lies behind it, rather it completely contradicts such an assumption.[249]

[245]Cf. the three masterly presentations of the internal and the external evidence for 'the Authenticity and Genuineness of St John's Gospel', published posthumously in his *Biblical Essays*, 1–198. Lightfoot makes it plain that the basis of his concern is doctrinal: 'The genuineness of St John's Gospel is the centre of the position of those who uphold the historical truth of the record of our Lord Jesus Christ given us in the New Testament. Hence the attacks of the opponents of revealed religion are concentrated upon it' (48). He specifies them as Rationalists who deny the miraculous and Unitarians who deny 'the distinctive character of Christian doctrine'.

[246]The same is true of Sanday's *Authorship and Historical Character of the Fourth Gospel*, 1872; but it has almost disappeared in his subsequent *The Criticism of the Fourth Gospel*, 1905 – yet with a corresponding loss of sharpness.

[247]*The Fourth Gospel*, 196–201 (199).

[248]E.g., those by Sydney Temple, Cullmann, Schillebeeckx and Brown (in his *Community of the Beloved Disciple*).

[249]*John*, 11f. The introduction was written for the ET by W. Schmithals to present Bultmann's position. For Bultmann himself cf. 483f. He admits that the redactor saw the evangelist as an eyewitness, but considers this view incredible.

If that was said of the Third Gospel one could understand it, but of the Fourth it seems quite incredible. For the first sentence is expressly contradicted by the claim of 21.24:

> It is this same disciple [namely, 'the one whom Jesus loved . . . who at supper had leaned back close to him' (21.20)] who attests what has here been written. It is in fact he who wrote it, and we know that his testimony is true.

And the second is contradicted by 19.35, whether the evangelist is referring to himself or another:

> This is vouched for by an eyewitness, whose evidence is to be trusted. He knows that he speaks the truth, so that you too may believe.

Whether these claims are correct is another matter. But that they are made, and intended to be taken seriously, would seem beyond dispute.[250]

One would also like to know the ground of the 'certainty' claimed by Schillebeeckx when he writes, 'Certainly no one who had known the historical Jesus was still alive in the Johannine community.'[251] For on the face of it it is in contradiction to the implication of the present tense in 21.24, 'It is this same disciple, who *attests* what has here been written . . ., and *we* know that his testimony is true', and to the claim of I John 1.1: 'We have heard it; we have seen it with our own eyes; we have looked upon it, and felt it with our own hands' (cf. 1.2f., 5). One has at least got to account for these statements and explain why they should be made if they are so demonstrably false. Bultmann is reduced to saying that the 'we' here are 'the eschatological contemporaries of Jesus',[252] whatever that may mean, simply because he dates the Epistle

[250]The other passage which is quoted, 'he came to dwell among us, and we saw his glory' (1.14), does not necessarily imply eyewitness attestation; but if, as I have argued ('Relation of the Prologue to the Gospel', *Twelve More NTS*, 65–76), it is modelled on I John 1.1, the ἐθεασάμεθα there clearly refers to physical vision. Westcott argued that 'the Apostolic *we* [of v. 14] is distinguished from the Christian *we all* [of v. 16]' (*John*, I, liii n. 3). There is also the implicit stress on which the main body of the Gospel *ends* in the often-overlooked phrase 'There are many other signs that Jesus performed *in the face of his disciples*, which are not recorded in this book' (20.30). It is the only time John uses ἐνώπιον.

[251]*Christ*, 382.

[252]*The Johannine Epistles*, 10.

at a point when eye- and ear-witnesses could no longer be around. It is hardly for him to call Rudolf Schnackenburg's attempt to count pupils and representatives of John the son of Zebedee among 'the circle of "apostolic" witnesses'[253] 'a counsel of despair'.[254]

But just as the question of continuity in person is not to be equated with that of apostolic authorship or origin and does not turn on it, so it does not depend upon establishing an identity of hand throughout the Gospel, or between the main body of the Gospel and the Epilogue, or between the Gospel and the Epistles. This issue must be assessed on its own merits. But whether John is a first Gospel, of which one may presume priority rather than posteriority, does not hang on the result of that enquiry, on which again there will never be final agreement. The 'we' of the Johannine community which underlies the writings (John 1.14; 21.24; I John 1.1–3, 5; II John 5; etc.)[255] was clearly a tight circle and its continuity of witness would be perfectly compatible with several hands having been at work (and clearly there is a difference at any rate between the 'we' of 21.24 and the 'I' of 21.25), if that is where the probability pointed. A presumption, as I said at the beginning, does not imply prejudgment: the ends must be entirely open.

What the presumption of priority does imply is that the author (whoever may have penned what) is, as I put it, internal to his tradition. That is to say, he does not stand, as Dodd still presupposed, in an external relationship to material that came down to him to which he was an outsider. For that assumes that the Gospel is not a primary witness, however much it may incorporate such witness. The assertion of continuity in person presupposes that in some sense 'la tradition, c'est moi' (or 'c'est nous'). And that, as Menoud said,[256] is at any rate not an unreasonable *impression* left upon the reader of the Fourth Gospel. Whether it can be sustained remains to be tested.

But there is yet a further implication of continuity in person that requires to be emphasized before we turn to the evidence. This is to challenge one of the most powerful assumptions which form criticism took over from the study of folklore and the origins of 'saga'. For the discipline began with the centuries-long span of the Pentateuchal stories and comparable literature stretching back into the nameless

[253] *Die Johannesbriefe*, [4]1970, 57.

[254] *Johannine Epistles*, 10.

[255] Cf. Harnack, 'Das "Wir" in den Johanneischen Schriften', *Sitzungsberichte der preussischen Akademie der Wissenschaften, philosophisch-historische Klasse* 1923, 96–113.

[256] P. H. Menoud, *L'Évangile de Jean d'après les recherches récentes*, 77.

mists of prehistoric time. As the Scandinavian Birger Gerhardsson has stressed,

> For the pioneer form critics, Dibelius and Bultmann, it was a fundamental idea . . . that the Synoptic tradition had anonymous origins in the early Christian congregations, that it arose among people whose names are unknown.

Yet, he insists that

> . . . the early Christian congregations are nowhere described in our sources as grey masses of unnamed equals. Everywhere we see that certain persons have greater authority than others. And clearly one of the factors which gave a man authority in the early church was what he knew about Jesus.[257]

And not only that he knew about Jesus, but that he stood in a relationship of 'discipleship' to him who was called 'rabbi' and 'master', that he was one of those called to 'follow' him and chosen to be 'with him'. This relationship was a well-understood one in contemporary Judaism, and no one who did not share it could speak with authority of what the teacher said or claim to represent him faithfully.[258] Moreover, within that relationship not all were equal. In Jesus' case, twelve were set apart from the rest, and within these some were closer than others and were given or subsequently acquired pre-eminence. Hence their authority within the teaching-fellowship was established: their names were known and respected, they were recognized as 'pillars' (Gal. 2.9).

If this is true of the Synoptic Gospels, which are primarily what Gerhardsson is writing about,[259] it is still more true of John. The

[257] *The Origins of the Gospel Traditions*, 59.

[258] Cf. ibid., 60–65.

[259] Neither here nor in his *Memory and Manuscript* does he seriously consider the Johannine material. There are refreshing signs of the self-questioning of many of the presuppositions of 'classical' form criticism (I take the phrase from Riesner below) including a re-opening of the question of the *Sitz im Leben* of the sayings of Jesus and even of written tradition within the ministry itself, but they too seem so far to have been confined to a reconsideration of the Synoptic tradition. Cf. E. E. Ellis, 'New Directions in Form Criticism' in G. Strecker, ed., *Jesus Christus in Historie und Theologie: Neutestamentliche Festschrift für Hans Conzelmann zum 60. Geburtstag*, Tübingen 1975, 299–315; R. Riesner, 'Der Ursprung der Jesus-Überlieferung', *TZ* 38, 1982, 493–513; *Jesus als Lehrer: eine Untersuchung der Evangelien-Überlieferung*, WUNT 2.7, Tübingen 1981; and earlier H. Schürmann, 'Die vorösterlichen Angfänge der Logientradition: Versuch eines formgeschichtlichen Zugangs zum Leben Jesu' in H. Ristow and K. Matthiae, edd., *Der historische Jesus und der kergymatische Christus*,

relationship of 'discipleship' – and 'the disciples' are always so styled in John rather than 'apostles' – of 'following' or 'coming after', is constantly stressed. Above all the relationship of one 'disciple whom Jesus loved' and who lay in his bosom is central to its tradition. If his name is not given, this is certainly not because it was unknown to the community but because it was too well known to be mentioned (John 21.24; III John 12). It is intimacy rather than anonymity that rules.

Moreover Brownlee has made the important observation that more than personal closeness is here involved:

> The description of the beloved disciple as reclining in the bosom of Jesus means far more than a relationship of affection and intimacy, as is shown by Jubilees 22.26 where 'Jacob slept in the bosom of Abraham'. This occurred when the older patriarch was about to die, but he first conferred his final blessing (along with much moral exhortation) on his grandson. Lying in the testator's bosom seems to designate one as the true son and heir. In Luke 16.19–23 it is Lazarus the poor beggar who lies in the patriarch's bosom. It was just like Jesus to show in this way that the social outcast rather than the rich man is the true son of Abraham. Jubilees 22.26 is in the context of Abraham's final blessing and testamentary exhortation. It is on a like occasion that the beloved disciple lies on Jesus' breast. This means that he and all true disciples (whom he symbolizes) inherit the task, the Spirit, and the peace which Jesus has bequeathed.[260] Similarly, the divine Logos as God's only begotten is one 'in the bosom of the Father' (1.18), for he is the heir of all things, to whom all that the Father has belongs (16.15).[261]

This would link up with Brown's observation[262] that the beloved disciple is only designated as such at the last supper, where the name

---

Berlin 1960, 342–70; *Traditionsgeschichtliche Untersuchungen zu den synoptischen Evangelien*, Dusseldorf 1968, especially 39–68.

[260] And, he adds in a note, the 'new commandment' (13.34; 15.12), which has the same background. As the Testaments of the Twelve Patriarchs indicate, the Greek διαθήκη (testament) and the Hebrew *ṣawwah* (command) are equivalent.

[261] 'Whence the Gospel of John?' in Charlesworth, ed., *John and Qumran*, 193f. He has written to me subsequently: 'Since you were here, I gave a lecture on "The Testament of Jesus", pointing out that lying in the bosom of another was used in connection with ancient adoption ceremonies. The beloved disciple represents all disciples who are Christ's adopted children, who are immediately thereafter addressed as τεκνία (13.33) and are not to be left as ὀρφανοί (14.18).' There is thus a link here with the Pauline idea of υἱοθεσία as the basis of the Christian life.

[262] *Community*, 33.

first appears (13.23). Before that (in 1.35, 40) he is the same man but has not acquired the identity. In the same way Peter is designated 'the rock' in Matt. 16.18, a passage which Cullmann[263] has plausibly argued also belonged originally to the context of the last supper. (John 1.42 has this designation at the beginning, but in the future tense, 'You will be called', as opposed to Matthew's 'You are': so there may be no real difference.)

Who this beloved disciple was and whether he wrote the Gospel or lived to see it finished are all debatable. What is not in doubt, in this tradition above all, is that the link is highly personal, and is that not simply of the collective 'we' but of the individual 'I' (21.25; and II and III John *passim*).

Let us then turn to the evidence, starting, as before, with the external.

This has been worked over so many times that it is unnecessary to do more here than to summarize. But it is worth stressing that, as with the tradition about place (Ephesus), the tradition about person (John) is virtually unchallenged. There were those in early times who repudiated it, but for the entirely tendentious reasons that they did not like its teaching on the Holy Spirit[264] or the Logos.[265] For the rest the tradition is entirely solid.

Even the evidence which used to be used against apostolic authorship (it is now pretty well abandoned as so palpably inferior) in the supposed early martyrdom of the apostle John in fact points the other way. The epitomist of the historian Philip of Side (*c.* 430), whom Lightfoot characterized as 'a notoriously pretentious and careless writer',[266] and Georgius Monachus (alias 'George the Sinner', of the ninth century) quote Papias as saying that John, like his brother James, was 'killed by Jews', thus fulfilling, according to George, the prophecy of Mark 10.39. Yet neither asserts that he was killed *at the same time*.[267] In fact Philip says that while some think that John the elder wrote II and III John and the Apocalypse, authorship of the Gospel and First Epistle is not in doubt, and George specifically records that John

[263] *Peter: Disciple, Apostle and Martyr*, ET London and Philadelphia [2]1962, 188f.

[264] Irenaeus, *Adv. haer.* 3.11.9.

[265] The 'Alogoi' – although, as Dodd says (*Historical Tradition*, 13 n. 1) there never was a sect of this name; it is merely Epiphanius' nickname for them (*Haer.* 51.3). For a fuller discussion see, still, Lightfoot, *Biblical Essays*, 117–19.

[266] *Biblical Essays*, 95.

[267] This stronger assertion is implicit in two martyrologies, of which the earlier is from Edessa and dated AD 411. But these two sources 'can hardly stand as independent witnesses' (Barrett, *John*, 104).

was 'the sole survivor of the twelve Apostles, and *after* writing his Gospel received the honour of martyrdom'.[268] Polycrates also describes John as 'martyr and teacher', though he knows that he died at Ephesus.[269] So the evidence is not for an early martyrdom (which in any case is contradicted by the first-hand testimony of Paul in Gal. 2.9, that John was alive in Jerusalem in 48, at least four, and more probably six, years after his brother's death under Herod, who died in 44) nor for his not having written the Gospel.[270]

Apart from its specific ascription to John by Theophilus of Antioch about AD 170,[271] the Gospel is attributed by Irenaeus (*c.*180) to 'John, the disciple of the Lord, the same who leant back on his breast'[272] and he clearly identifies him as 'the apostle'.[273] Polycrates (bishop of Ephesus, 189–98) uses very similar language,[274] though he does not mention the actual writing of the Gospel. But the strength of Irenaeus' testimony rests on his vivid memory as a boy in Lower Asia of the ancient Polycarp, bishop of Smyrna, who was born *c.* 70 and spoke of 'his intercourse with John and with the others who had seen the Lord' and 'how he would relate from memory their words'.[275] It is true, as

[268]The full texts are in Lightfoot's *Apostolic Fathers*, abridged ed., J. R. Harmer, ed., London and New York 1891, 518f., translated 530f.

[269]Eusebius, *HE* 5.24.3.

[270]Cf. also Armitage Robinson, *Historical Character of the Fourth Gospel*, 70–86, 'On the Alleged Martyrdom of St John the Apostle', who makes the point that 'It is almost inconceivable that, if Papias really said this, Irenaeus, Eusebius and others who had read Papias should not have referred to it' (85); and C. F. Nolloth, *Fourth Evangelist*, 72–82, who exposes how utterly confused and unreliable the evidence is. Perhaps the comment of a secular historian may be permitted: 'There could be no better example of a vice which microscopic research seems often to induce, that of abnormal suspiciousness towards the evidence which suffices ordinary people, coupled with abnormal credulity towards evidence which is trifling or small' (Lord Charnwood, *According to John*, London and Boston, Mass. n.d. [1925], 35). Howard preserves this in his *Fourth Gospel in Recent Criticism*, 45. But unfortunately the book contains little else that is memorable.

[271]*Ad Autol.* 22.2.

[272]*Adv. haer.* 2.22.5; 3.3.1–4; quotes, Eusebius, *HE* 3.23.3f.; 5.8.4. As Bernard points out, *John* I, xlvii, he applies 'the disciple of the Lord' to no one else.

[273]Thus he quotes John 1.14 with the words 'the apostle says' (*Adv. haer* 1.9.2; cf. also 2.22.5; 3.3.4; quoted Eusebius, *HE* 5.24.16; and 5.20.6, where he is among those who had 'seen the Lord').

[274]Eusebius, *HE* 3.31.3; 5.24.3.

[275]*Ad Florinum*, quoted, Eusebius, *HE* 5.20.4.–8; cf. 4.14.3–8. It is scarcely a serious objection that the short *Epistle of Polycarp* does not quote the Gospel of John. For it quotes I John (4.3f. in *Ep. Polyc.* 7), which clearly presupposes the Gospel. Similarly Eusebius says that Papias quoted I John (*HE* 3.39.17) but not that he quoted the Gospel, which he certainly knew.

Barrett points out,[276] seeking to minimize the evidence, that it never actually tells us that Polycarp knew John *in Asia* or said that he wrote the Gospel. But both of these are inferences which one may be reasonably sure that Irenaeus intended. As Dodd said, though he did not accept it as settling the matter,

> His evidence is formidable, even if it is not conclusive. Anyone who should take the view that in the absence of any cogent evidence to the contrary it is reasonable to accept Irenaeus' testimony is on strong ground.[277]

It is possible to weaken the credibility of Irenaeus' witness by showing that he was unreliable on other things, e.g., the common authorship or date of the Apocalypse or his statement that Papias was 'a hearer of John and a companion of Polycarp',[278] which Eusebius claims, on Papias' own authority, refers to another John. For he quotes him as saying,

> If anyone chanced to come who had actually been a follower of the elders, I would enquire as to the discourses of the elders, what Andrew or what Peter said, or what Philip, or what Thomas or James, or what John or Matthew or any other of the Lord's disciples; and things which Aristion and John the elder, disciples of the Lord, say,

and he goes on to comment,

> Here it is worth noting that twice in his enumeration he mentions the name of John: the former of these Johns he puts in the same list with Peter and James and Matthew and the other apostles, clearly indicating the evangelist; but the latter he places with the others, in a separate clause, outside the number of the apostles, placing Aristion before him; and he clearly calls him 'elder'.[279]

But it is to be observed that it is Eusebius, not Papias, who introduces the distinction between 'apostles' and 'elders'. Papias calls them all 'elders', while Eusebius goes on to refer to what Papias called 'the

[276] *John*, 132. In similar, as I believe, hypercritical vein, Kümmel, *Introduction to the NT*, 240f.

[277] *Historical Tradition*, 12.

[278] *Adv. haer.* 5.33.4; quoted, Eusebius, *HE* 3.39.1.

[279] *HE* 3.39.4f.; tr. H. J. Lawlor and J. E. L. Oulton, *Eusebius, The Ecclesiastical History and the Martyrs of Palestine*, London and New York 1927.

discourses of the elders' as 'the discourses of the apostles'.[280] There is not for Papias, nor I believe for Eusebius, any generation gap between apostles and elders such as is regularly read into this passage.[281] For the last two elders were equally 'disciples of the Lord'. Nor does Eusebius imply that the elders are what he earlier calls 'pupils'[282] of the apostles (these are the 'followers' of the first group of elders, whom he identifies with the apostles).[283] What Eusebius is anxious to establish is not two *generations* but two individuals, because, following Dionysius of Alexandria's notable anticipation of modern literary criticism,[284] he quite reasonably wants to find a second John as author of the

[280]Cf. *HE* 3.39.4. 'If anyone chanced to come who had actually been a follower of the elders, I would enquire as to the discourses of the elders', with 39.7, 'Papias, of whom we are now speaking, acknowledges that he received the discourses of the apostles from those who had been their followers.' It is remarkable that neither Streeter, who argued strongly for John the Elder as the evangelist, nor Dom John Chapman in his exhaustive study *John the Presbyter and the Fourth Gospel*, Oxford and New York 1911, once cites this latter passage, which follows so closely upon the other. Chapman argues, contortedly, that the earlier mentioned elders were *not* apostles (but their successors) but that John the Elder, as a disciple of the Lord, was. To do this he has in the second case to give the word πρεσβύτερος a different sense, the 'Ancient' or 'Grand Old Man' (which indeed may well have attached to John as the elder *par excellence*). But I believe he is simply wrong in the first case to say that the elders, described as 'disciples of the Lord', were not themselves also apostles. Cf. D. Smith, *The Expositor's Greek Testament*, London 1897–1910, V, 161: 'ὁ πρεσβύτερος Ἰωάννης must mean "the Apostle John" since the Apostles have just been called "the Elders" (τοῖς πρεσβυτέροις), and it is impossible that the term should bear different meanings within the compass of a single sentence.' He adds for what it is worth: 'In his phrase "from the Truth itself (ἀπ' αὐτῆς τῆς ἀληθείας)" Papias echoes III John 12, and this renders it more than likely that he called St John ὁ πρεσβύτερος because the latter had so styled himself in each of the [second and third] Epistles.' For the equivalence of 'apostle' and 'elder' cf. I Peter 1.1 and 5.1. There is no argument for saying II and III John cannot be apostolic because they are ascribed to 'the Elder'.

[281]E.g., the stemma in Barrett, *John*, 107. Similarly G. Bornkamm, *TDNT* VI, 627. Lawlor and Oulton in their notes, *Eusebius* II, 112–14, oppose this interpretation on the ground that Eusebius himself clearly equates the elders and apostles.

[282]*HE* 3.39.2.

[283]See further T. Zahn, *Introduction to the New Testament*, ET Edinburgh and New York 1909, II, 452 (though cf. the crucial slip I noted in *Redating*, 309, n. 228); Nolloth, *Fourth Evangelist*, 50–71; Headlam, *Fourth Gospel as History*, 55–9; G. M. Lee, 'The Presbyter John: A Reconsideration' in E. A. Livingstone, ed., *StEv* VI, TU 112, Berlin 1973, 311–20. It is remarkable that Lightfoot, *Biblical Essays*, 63, merely says of Papias, 'Whether he was a personal disciple of the Apostle St John, as asserted by Irenaeus, or only of a namesake of the Apostle, the Presbyter John, as Eusebius supposes, I will not stop to enquire.' But cf. his *Essays on the Work entitled Supernatural Religion*, London and New York 1889, 142f. Westcott also ignores the question.

[284]*De prom.*; quoted, Eusebius, *HE* 7.25.6–27.

Apocalypse, and he fastens on John 'the Elder'. *If* indeed this man composed anything, it is more logical, with others,[285] to ascribe to him II and III John, which are written under this designation. But as author of the Gospel he is a mere construct of modern scholarship.[286] In fact it is at least doubtful whether he ever even existed as a second character (he is not alluded to anywhere else in ancient literature), let alone lived in Ephesus,[287] though one does not have to share Eusebius' jaundiced view of Papias[288] to wish that he could have expressed himself more clearly. C. S. Petrie[289] has urged that *ὁ πρεσβύτερος Ἰωάννης* (not *Ἰωάννης ὁ πρεσβύτερος*) means, when the name is repeated with the article, 'the aforementioned elder John'.[290] All that we can be sure of is that Papias distinguishes between those elders/apostles who are dead ('what they said') and those who are still alive ('what they say'). And in the second, much smaller class he also places John, which bears out rather than impugns Irenaeus' statement that Papias, like Polycarp, was 'a hearer of John'. Indeed for Papias this John is almost certainly the one he describes as 'the Elder' without need of further designation, as in the address of II and III John. For Eusebius has just referred to Papias' 'traditions of the elder John' and then proceeds to cite one, from 'the Elder', on the origin of the Gospel of Mark.[291] This would imply that the account of the Petrine origin of Mark goes back to John, who, if he *is* the Apostle, is a very good authority indeed.[292] It would also explain why Eusebius has something to quote from the Elder about the Gospels of Mark and Matthew but not John: at that point Papias was in touch with source, the 'living voice', as he claims.[293]

[285]It is the opinion of 'many' according to Jerome, *Vir. ill.* 18.

[286]Lee, 'The Presbyter John', 312, 320, says that Streeter built up John the Presbyter into 'a sort of snowman, heaping borrowed properties on him and thrusting the Gospel and Epistles into his chill hands. . . . Perhaps we shall yet see the snowman's liquidation. The era of the Presbyter may be nearing its close.' Using another image Armitage Robinson said long ago: 'That mole never made such a mountain' (*Historical Character of St John's Gospel*, 102).

[287]It is only Eusebius who combines Papias' supposed reference to him with Dionysius of Alexandria's inference that there must have been two Johns in Asia because there were two 'memorials' to John in Ephesus. His statement that *Papias* 'proves this to be true' is clearly unfounded.

[288]*HE* 3.39.13.

[289]'The Authorship of "The Gospel According to Matthew": A Reconsideration of the External Evidence', *NTS* 14, 1967–8, 15–32; specif. 21.

[290]It is to be noted that only he and not Aristion is designated 'the elder', both here and in *HE* 3.39.14.

[291]*HE* 3.39.14f.

[292]So Sanday, *Criticism of the Fourth Gospel*, 254.

[293]*HE* 3.39.4.

So one must, I think, agree with Brown[294] that 'Irenaeus' statement is far from having been disproved'. Yet ultimately the external tradition must abide the test of the internal, and on that test I would myself judge that Irenaeus' views on the authorship and date of the Apocalypse are not to be trusted.[295] So his tradition on the Gospel cannot be decisive.

There is one piece of evidence which is on the borderland between the external and the internal, and that is the conclusion to the Epilogue (John 21.18–25), which we have already looked at from the point of view of the link in time. If the Epilogue is an integral part of the Gospel and by the same hand, it is internal evidence; if it is added, then it is very early external testimony indeed, for no copy of the Gospel is known to have circulated without ch. 21, not even the recently discovered **P**^{66}, though this has unfortunately been broken off at 21.9. In any case the penultimate verse, 21.24, 'It is this same disciple who attests what has here been written. It is in fact he who wrote it, and we know that his testimony is true', must be an appended certificate by the Johannine community, with the final verse reverting to the first person singular.[296]

Two uncertainties beset it, whether 'what has here been written' (*ταῦτα*) refers simply to the Epilogue or to the Gospel as a whole, and precisely what the word 'wrote' implies.

On the first point, Dodd[297] argued that *ταῦτα* simply meant the Epilogue. But this is not how it has naturally been understood in ancient or modern times; and the close parallel with the *ταῦτα γέγραπται* in 20.31, that these are written out of the many that could have been included, suggests that it echoes and takes it up.[298] In any case to make the beloved disciple the author of the last stage of the Gospel only, especially if, as seems to be implied by the present tense[299]

[294] *John* I, xcii.

[295] Again I must refer to ch. VIII, on the Book of Revelation, in my *Redating*, 221–53. Apart from the linguistic improbabilities of the Apocalypse being the work of the same hand as the Gospel and Epistles, it claims a very different authority, not that of the apostle or elder but of the prophet. I believe it is by another John from the Ephesus area, who unlike the author of the Gospel and Epistles names himself (Rev. 1.1). The two became so inextricably mixed in the tradition, at least from Justin onwards, that it is by now impossible to sort out which stories belong to which. I also argue that Revelation was written shortly after the death of Nero (*c.* 69) and not at the end of the reign of Domitian (*c.* 95) as Irenaeus asserts (*Adv. haer.* 5.30.3, though his meaning is not absolutely certain).

[296] Brown, *John* I, xciii, says that 'the statement in 21.24 clearly distinguishes the disciple from the writer of ch. 21 (the "we").' On the contrary, the writer of the chapter is the 'I' of v. 25 and the 'we' attests his identity and credentials.

[297] 'Note on John 21.24', *JTS*, n.s. 4, 1953, 212f.

[298] So, rightly, Bultmann, *John*, 717 n. 4.

[299] Westcott, *John* I, lvi, argued similarly from the perfects (ὁ ἑωρακὼς μεμαρτύρηκεν) rather than aorists in 19.35. They are followed by the two presents 'his evidence is to be trusted. He knows that he speaks the truth.'

of μαρτυρῶν, 'attests', in contrast with γράψας, 'wrote', he is present with the community (as well as having been at the last supper), raises more difficulties than it solves – particularly for those who would say that he may originally have *underlain* the tradition but is now dead.

On the second point, it has been maintained that 'he wrote it' need mean no more than 'he caused it to be written', as presumably it does with Pilate in 19.22. But the use of γράφειν of a private individual to imply more than the employment of an amanuensis cannot be paralleled, and this would still mean that the beloved disciple wrote the Gospel of John as much as Paul wrote the Epistle to the Romans (15.15, ἔγραψα), even if Tertius (described in 16.22 as ὁ γράψας) actually penned it.

Rather than try to make John 21.24 say something other than that the beloved disciple wrote the Gospel it would seem to me more honest to accept the plain meaning of the text and conclude, with the majority of modern commentators, that the attribution is simply wrong.

But who was this 'disciple whom Jesus loved'? The external tradition again is solid, that it was John, the apostle, disciple of the Lord and son of Zebedee (which designation he is given cannot affect which John is intended: it is hypercriticism to try to drive a wedge at this point). Again of course this may simply be wrong, though two points have always been made by the conservatives in support of it from the internal evidence. The first is that John, with his brother James, who are so close to the centre in the Synoptic tradition and Acts, would be otherwise unaccountable absentees in the Fourth Gospel. This would be the more remarkable since all the other disciples who feature early in the Synoptic lists, Peter, Andrew, Philip and Thomas, have a major place in the Johannine story. Moreover 'the sons of Zebedee' do appear once in John, in 21.2 in the company of seven disciples on the Sea of Tiberias, and the beloved disciple must be either one of them or one of the two unnamed disciples. But this could point either way, since the veil of anonymity could be being preserved (as usual) or dropped (at last).[300]

The other, more subtle, point is that John the Baptist uniquely in this Gospel is always and simply called 'John' without further qualification, even when he is first introduced out of the blue in 1.6 (contrast Mark 1.4 and pars.). Such a style, as Westcott points out,[301] is

[300]Cullmann, *Johannine Circle*, 76, surely goes too far in saying: 'Chapter 21 seems to me virtually to exclude the possibility that the redactor who wrote it was thinking of John the son of Zebedee.'

[301]*John* I, xlvii.

moreover in contrast with his usual fuller designations – Simon Peter, Thomas Didymus, Judas son of Simon Iscariot, and Judas *not* Iscariot (14.22). Only, it is said, from the point of view of John the son of Zebedee would it appear superfluous to have to distinguish this John from the Apostle. This consideration cannot be conclusive, but it carries some weight.

But what of the positive indication of his identity from within the Gospel itself? It has been said[302] that while the external evidence points to John the son of Zebedee the internal points to Lazarus, as the one person in this Gospel of whom it is specifically said that Jesus loved him.[303] This identification of course has often been canvassed[304] – though it is interesting that in the comparable story from the so-called 'Secret Gospel of Mark' the (unnamed) central character would seem to be nearer to the rich young man of whom it is also said that Jesus loved him (ἠγάπησεν, Mark 10.21). But the real difficulty is that John gives no hint whatever to the reader that Lazarus and 'the disciple whom Jesus loved' are intended to be identified. Lazarus is never called a 'disciple', and after his raising Jesus goes away to Ephraim 'with his disciples' (11.54), to return later to Bethany where Lazarus is (12.1f.).

The beloved disciple on the other hand is always to be found in the company of the other disciples, and in particular of Peter (13.23f.; 20.2–9; 21.7, 20–22), the only exception being at the cross (19.26f.) where Peter has deserted. The close association of Peter and John both during and after the ministry of Jesus in the Synoptists and Acts would certainly support the traditional identification. This is powerfully argued by Brown in his commentary, who maintains that 'his closeness to Jesus seems to have given him a position along with Peter as one of the most important figures in the ministry'; he 'would have had to be a

[302]Brownlee in Charlesworth, ed., *John and Qumran*, 191–4.

[303]But only in 11.5 is the word ἀγαπάω used, and that of his sisters as well as of him. In 11.3 and 36 it is φιλέω, and in 11.11 he is described as '*our* friend'. Of the disciple whom Jesus loved ἀγαπάω is always used except in 20.2. But it would be wrong to press this distinction too far, as clearly in 20.2 (if not in 21.15–17) the two verbs are used synonymously.

[304]E.g., F. V. Filson, 'Who Was the Beloved Disciple?', *JBL* 68, 1949, 83–8; J. N. Sanders, *Fourth Gospel in the Early Church*, 45 (*very* tentatively); '"Those whom Jesus Loved" (John 11.5)', *NTS* 1, 1954–5, 29–41; 'Who was the Disciple Whom Jesus Loved?' in Cross, ed., *Studies in the Fourth Gospel*, 72–82. He espouses the improbable view that the disciple ὃν ἐφίλει ὁ Ἰησοῦς (20.2) was not the same person as the disciple ὃν ἠγάπα ὁ Ἰησοῦς (13.23; 19.26; 21.20). This 'other disciple' (cf. 18.15) is identified with John the Elder, who is, even more improbably, equated with John Mark (whom Papias clearly distinguished) and who was not (as Papias said) the author of the second Gospel. To be reduced to such a string of improbabilities hardly inspires confidence.

man of real authority in the Church, a man of status not unlike Peter's'.[305] His presence and position on one side of Jesus at the last supper (13.23–6),[306] which according to the Synoptists (Mark 14.17 and pars.) was confined to the Twelve,[307] would rule out, Brown maintains, not only Lazarus but John Mark, whose claim has been advanced by others,[308] and any other 'unknown'. But in his later book, *The Community of the Beloved Disciple*, he shifts his position. Though it is introduced rather casually with the words 'parenthetically, I am inclined to change my mind', the book is written on the firm assumption that the beloved disciple is *not* John the Son of Zebedee or one of the Twelve. He says:

> I now recognize that the external and internal evidence are probably not to be harmonized.[309] By setting the Beloved Disciple over against Peter, the Fourth Gospel gives the impression that he was an outsider

[305]*John* I, xcif. Cf. his strong remarks in 'The Problem of Historicity in John', *NT Essays*, 150; Streeter, *Four Gospels*, 432, to the same effect; Bernard, *John* I, xxxiv–xxxvii; and Strachan, *Fourth Gospel*, London 1941, New York 1942, 31, 82–9. Barrett, *John*, 117, 119, also believes that the evangelist intended the beloved disciple to be identified with John the Son of Zebedee, though equally denying him to be the evangelist.

[306]Cf. John Lightfoot, *Horae Hebraicae et Talmudicae* III, 391–3, on John 13.23, who quotes evidence that 'when there were three, the worthiest person lay in the middle; and the second lay above him; and the third below him'. Reclining on the left side meant that the one below him, lying at his feet, was the one who could speak with him without turning round. Westcott, quoting this, uses it as an indication that Peter, who is evidently the other side (Brown, *John* II, 574, suggests improbably that it is Judas) still has precedence in John (*John* I, xlviiif.; 154f.).

[307]The presence of any but the Twelve clearly cannot be ruled out by the Synoptists' statements (though contrast Luke 22.14 with 24.33 where he specially says others were there), but their silence on anyone else especially in such a position of prominence *combined with* the silence throughout the Fourth Gospel on John the son of Zebedee would normally lead the suspicious mind to put two and two together. But to do so in this case seems to be regarded as the mark of the credulous!

[308]E.g., P. Parker, 'John and John Mark', *JBL* 79, 1960, 97–110, who believes him also to have been the evangelist, and is followed by Marsh, *John*, 24. J. N. Sanders, 'Those Whom Jesus Loved', 33f. 1; 'St John on Patmos', *NTS* 9, 1962–3, 75–85; *John* (ed. Mastin), 29–52, argues for him as the evangelist but not the beloved disciple, while G. J. Paul, *St John's Gospel: A Commentary*, Madras 1965, 25–8, contends for him as the beloved disciple but not the evangelist. Since the *second* Gospel is regularly in the tradition ascribed to Mark, the last would seem the most defensible of the options. But I am not convinced of the necessity for any of them. How and why John Mark and John the son of Zebedee should have become confused, against all the biblical and patristic evidence, quite escapes me.

[309]But this is not the point, and the weaknesses he adduces in the 'second-century information about the origins of the Gospels' all relate to authorship. Whether the beloved disciple was the *evangelist* is a different question, on which Brown has not changed his mind: he was not.

> to the group of best-known disciples, a group that would have included John son of Zebedee,

though he admits that 'the relative silence of the Fourth Gospel' about the sons of Zebedee 'remains a mystery'.[310] But he has not answered his previous arguments about the status and authority of the beloved disciple; he has merely abandoned them. The 'impression' that he was 'an outsider' has certainly not been shared by most readers of the Gospel. Rather, he appears to belong to the innermost circle of those whom in his Gospel Jesus calls 'his own' (13.1), his 'friends' (15.14f.), and his place at the supper table strongly reinforces this. I prefer the former to the latter Brown.

But if the beloved disciple is not John the son of Zebedee, who is he? Brown has not moved from his conviction that he cannot be a purely symbolic or ideal figure:[311] 'He is a real human being whose actions are important on the Gospel scene',[312] or, as he subsequently prefers to put it, 'a figure who can scarcely be left in suspension if one wants to be faithful to the Gospel's own sense of history'.[313] He would now concur with Cullmann that he is an unknown Judaean adherent of Jesus and a partial eyewitness[314] who was

> a former disciple of John the Baptist. He began to follow Jesus in Judaea when *Jesus himself was in close proximity to the Baptist.* He shared the life of his master during Jesus' last stay in Jerusalem. He was known to the high priest. His connection with Jesus was different from that of Peter, the representative of the Twelve.[315]

What neither of them, or Schillebeeckx, explains is why this Judaean or Jerusalem disciple should be found fishing in Galilee in ch. 21 in the same boat as Peter. It would be far simpler to explain if he were one who with his brother (also present) was in partnership with Peter (Luke

[310] *Community*, 33f.

[311] *Contra* Bultmann, *John*, 484. (He has to admit that he must represent a real person in ch. 21 – but that of course is the work of the redactor.) For others who have held this view cf. Kümmel, *Introduction to the NT*, 238, who rightly regards it as 'extremely improbable'.

[312] *John* I, xcv.

[313] *Community*, 174; cf. 31.

[314] This as we saw (p. 59 n. 115 above) is a revival of the theory put forward by H. Delff. For his writings and a critique of them, cf. Sanday, *Criticism of the Fourth Gospel*, 17, 99–108. Similar views are expressed by R. Schnackenburg, 'Der Jünger, den Jesus liebte', *EKK* 2, Zürich 1970, 97–117; and 'On the Origin of the Fourth Gospel' in D. G. Miller, ed., *Jesus and Man's Hope*, Pittsburgh 1970, I, 223–46, especially 233–43 (who also abandons his previous identification of the beloved disciple with John); and Schillebeeckx, *Christ*, 344–6.

[315] *Johannine Circle*, 78, italics his; quoted, Brown, *Community*, 34.

5.7) and, as far as one can see from this story, stood in exactly the same relationship to Jesus.

It is clear from the above quotation that both Cullmann and Brown identify the beloved disciple with two other unnamed disciples in this Gospel, the one in 1.35–40, who was a disciple of John the Baptist, and the one in 18.15f., who was known to the high priest. The fact that each again appears in close association with Peter and that the phrase 'the other disciple' in 18.16 is also used of the beloved disciple in 20.3f. makes this identification indeed very probable. Where Cullmann and Brown still differ is that Cullmann agrees with John 21.24 that the beloved disciple is the evangelist, whereas Brown will only put him behind the tradition. Yet each of them would concur in what Cullmann calls 'the possibility of tracing "the Johannine circle" back into the time of Jesus'.[316] And that, rather than the precise author of the finished Gospel, is for our present purposes the important thing.

But now let us move from the identity of the beloved disciple to that of the evangelist. What does the internal evidence tell us about him?

First it tells us that he was a Jew who wrote in Greek. Indeed Dionysius of Alexandria, whose own language it was and who reveals himself to have had a keen sense of style, says of the Gospel and the Epistles in contrast with the Apocalypse, about whose barbarous idioms and inaccurate Greek he is scathing, that they are written in 'faultless Greek', with 'the greatest literary skill' (though this is clearly an exaggeration, except in comparison with the Apocalypse) and 'a complete absence of any barbarous word, or solecism, or any vulgarism whatever'.[317] Yet there is also no doubt that it is a flat, simple Greek, of limited syntax and vocabulary,[318] with an Aramaic ring and numerous Semitisms[319] though no solecisms or classicisms. In fact, as Kilpatrick has indicated, 'the language of the Fourth Gospel is, with little exception, the language of the Septuagint'.[320] The relation

[316] *Johannine Circle*, 84f.

[317] *De prom.*, quoted, Eusebius, *HE* 7.25.25f.

[318] Cf. Barrett, *John*, 7f., and for a sample analysis Bultmann, *John*, 635f. on the style of the passion narrative. He says that 'the sentence construction is very simple' and 'the connections of sentences are very primitive'. Yet this like most judgments can be exaggerated. Meeks, 'Man from Heaven', 61 draws attention to 'the remarkable sentence in 13.1–5, the elegant periodic structure of which contrasts with the usual Johannine style'.

[319] For a cautious summary, cf. Barrett, *John*, 9f.

[320] 'The Religious Background of the Fourth Gospel', in Cross, ed., *Studies in the Fourth Gospel*, 43.

between these phenomena has given rise to many hypotheses. Without being an Aramaist, I am ready to be convinced by the careful survey of Barrett, building on what he calls the 'fine article by Schuyler Brown',[321] that it does not look as if any theory of translation from the Aramaic is necessary or compelling. For what it is worth, there is also no external evidence that – unlike the Gospel of Matthew or Josephus' *Jewish War*[322] – the Gospel of John ever existed in any other language. 'The Fourth Gospel', says Barrett, 'is a Greek book.' But, he goes on, 'we must see in the Semitisms an essential hallmark of the evangelist himself'[323] – and not just of his supposed sources. In other words, he wrote good, if unambitious, Greek with an Aramaic accent.[324]

Why he should have done this if he had been, as Dodd suggested, an Ephesian elder at the end of the first century, Dodd never explains. His roots were clearly in Palestine, but if he had simply been a refugee in mid-life it is doubtful if Dionysius would have vouched that he wrote without a single slip (ἀπταίστως). It is more the Greek of a man who has had it as his second language from youth but who still writes it with an

[321]'From Burney to Black: the Fourth Gospel and the Aramaic Question', *CBQ* 26, 1964, 323–39. The allusion is to C. F. Burney, *The Aramaic Origin of the Fourth Gospel*, and M. Black, *An Aramaic Approach to the Gospels and Acts*, ²1954, ³1967.

[322]*BJ* 1.3. R. O. P. Taylor, whose seminal book, *The Groundwork of the Gospels*, Oxford and New York 1947, has not received the recognition it deserves, points out (99) that this Aramaic version was not intended for local use in Galilee, where Greek would have been perfectly well understood, but as dissuasive propaganda on behalf of the Emperor Vespasian to the non-Greek-speaking population of Upper Syria (the ἄνω βάρβαροι), further specified in 1.6 as the 'Parthians, Babylonians, the most remote tribes of Arabia, our countrymen beyond the Euphrates and the inhabitants of Adiabene'. See further chs. 11 and 12 of Taylor's book.

[323]*The Fourth Gospel and Judaism*, 59f.

[324]The situation is quite different from that of Josephus, who tells us that he worked very hard to cultivate a polished Greek written style without trace of an Aramaic accent (though he admits still speaking it with one) and relied on some assistance with his Greek (*Ant.* 20.263; *Contra Ap.* 1.50). Cf. the judgment of his translator H. St J. Thackeray: 'He clearly took immense pains to acquire a good style and, though his work is very unequal, portions of it attain a very high level. No trace of his native Aramaic is allowed to sully the pages of the Greek version of his *Jewish War*, and the one trace of Semitism thought to have been discovered elsewhere proves illusory. He must further endeavour fastidiously to abjure the "vulgarisms" of the later Alexandrian speech, which were not disdained even by such a writer as Polybius. The style is an excellent specimen of the Atticistic Greek of the first century, modelled on, if not quite on a level with, that of the great masters of the age of Pericles' (*Josephus, the Man and the Historian*, 102, 104). There is no reason to think that the author of the Fourth Gospel and Josephus did not *start* in much the same position, with a working Greek as their second language. But for the purposes of commending the history of his people to the Graeco–Roman world Josephus could not afford to remain there (cf. *Ant.* 14.2).

accent.[325] In other words, he would have come from a bilingual part of Palestine and been perfectly competent in Greek even though it was not his native tongue. This cannot be more than a possible profile of the author, but it would certainly not rule out on purely linguistic grounds a personal link with the origins of the Christian movement, whether in Galilee or in Jerusalem.

The question of whether we are dealing with a single hand throughout the Johannine material is not, as I said, one by which this link stands or falls. The homogeneity of style through the body of the Gospel has already been observed and counts against, though it cannot rule out, the detection of sources or redactors. The Epilogue shows marginal differences from the body of the Gospel,[326] but it is clear from the balance of scholars on both sides that the linguistic evidence cannot in itself be decisive.[327] In fact those who argue for a second hand do it for the most part for other reasons,[328] not least because they believe the beloved disciple or the evangelist, or both, to have been dead[329] and the

[325]Lightfoot, *Biblical Essays,* 16. Cf. his detailed analysis, 128–35. He goes on to argue for his knowledge of the Hebrew as of the Greek Bible (135–40). For the subsequent debate on this, cf. E. D. Freed, *Old Testament Quotations in the Gospel of John, NovT* Suppl 11, Leiden 1965; F.–M. Braun, *Jean le Théologien,* II, *Les grandes traditions d'Israël et l'accord des Écritures selon la Quatrième Évangile,* 1964; J. O'Rourke, 'John's Fulfilment Texts', *Sciences Ecclésiastiques* 19, 1967, 433–43; G. Reim, *Studien zum alttestamentlichen Hintergrund des Johannesevangeliums,* SNTSMS 22, Cambridge 1974; and the summing up in Kysar, *Fourth Evangelist and His Gospel,* 104–7. At any rate it is agreed that John's tradition is deeply rooted in a Jewish, Old Testament milieu.

[326]Cf. Lightfoot, *Biblical Essays,* 59f., who draws out the marked similarities as well as isolating the differences; Boismard, 'Le chapitre xxi de saint Jean: essai de critique littéraire', *RB* 54, 1947, 473–501; Barrett, *John,* 576f., Brown, *John* II, 1079f.; G. R. Osborne, 'John 21: Test Case for History and Redaction in the Resurrection Narratives', in France and Wenham, edd., *Gospel Perspectives* II, 294–6.

[327]Cf. Barrett, *John,* 577: the 'linguistic and stylistic considerations, when weighed against the undoubted resemblances between chs. 1–20 and ch. 21, are not in themselves sufficient to establish the belief that ch. 21 was written by a different author'; similarly Lindars, *John,* 622. B. de Solages, *Jean et les Synoptistes,* Leiden 1979, 191–235, argues that ch. 21 is closer to chs. 1–19 than is ch. 20 and concludes that 'it is scarcely possible to attribute this chapter to another pen than the rest of the Gospel of John' (234).

[328]Barrett's argument, *John,* 577, that only a redactor would have added the supplementary material 'in so clumsy a manner', instead of before 20.30, is surely very subjective, especially in view of the many other signs of rough or unfinished connections. Authors have been known to write postscripts as well as prefaces to their second editions. Luke appears to have added the first two chapters to his Gospel without disturbing the original elaborate opening and dating of 3.1.

[329]So Brown, *John* I, xciv, 'Reading between the lines, we may assume that the disciple has died' (cf. II, 1118f.) and he thinks the evangelist as well. Cullmann, *Johannine*

time-span such as to require the literary activity of more than one man. If one questions both of these, as I would, then the grounds are far less compelling, and the similarity of style is so great that one is bound to posit deliberate imitation of the master's voice. As H. J. Cadbury asked of Ephesians,

> Which is more likely–that an imitator of Paul in the first century composed a writing ninety or ninety-five per cent in accordance with Paul's style or that Paul himself wrote a letter diverging five or ten per cent from his usual style?[330]

In the case of the Johannine Epilogue the degree of similarity is certainly greater than that between Ephesians and Colossians, and I should prefer to put down any divergences to a change of circumstances and a not inconsiderable lapse of time.

With regard to the Gospel and the Epistles of John the case is more open[331] and leading scholars have come down on both sides[332] though undoubtedly the trend at the moment is towards diversity of author-

---

Circle, 71, is much more dogmatic and says: 'It is quite clear that the redactor feels obliged to make this correction because the disciple *had* in fact meanwhile died, probably a short time beforehand.' I see no evidence for this, and the present tense in 21.24 is against it. Hoskyns rightly protests (*Fourth Gospel*, II 670) against Moffatt's translation: 'This *was* the disciple who bears testimony to these facts.' The actual death of the disciple is only one possible reason why the prediction that he would not die was mistaken, and it is not an inference drawn by anyone in antiquity, as Brown recognizes. Such a statement as Culpepper's 'the death of the Beloved Disciple, which is referred to in 21.23' (*Johannine School*, 269) goes far beyond the evidence.

330 'The Dilemma of Ephesians', *NTS* 5, 1958–9, 101.

331 A convenient summary of the similarities and differences is given by Barrett, *John*, 59f.

332 For separate authorship: H. J. Holtzmann, 'Das Problem des ersten Johannesbriefes in seinem Verhältnis zum Evangelium', *Jahrbuch für protestantische Theologie* 7, 1881, 890–712; 8, 1882, 128–52 (especially), 316–42, 460–83; Dodd, 'The First Epistle of John and the Fourth Gospel', *BJRL* 21, 1937, 129–56; *The Johannine Epistles*, xlvii–lvi; Schnackenburg, *Die Johannesbriefe*, ²1963, 41; Bultmann, *Johannine Epistles*; 1; Brown, *Community*, 94–6; *The Johannine Epistles* (Anchor Bible 30), 1982, 19–30, 96f., 100f.

For common authorship, R. Law, *The Tests of Life*, Edinburgh 1909, 339–63; A. E. Brooke, *The Johannine Epistles* (ICC), Edinburgh and New York 1912, i–xix; W. F. Howard, 'The Common Authorship of the Johannine Gospel and Epistles', *JTS* 48, 1947, 12–25; reproduced with a summary of the linguistic evidence in *Fourth Gospel in Recent Criticism*, 276–96; W. G. Wilson, 'An Examination of the Linguistic Evidence Adduced against the Unity of Authorship of the First Epistle of John and the Fourth Gospel', *JTS* 49, 1948, 147–56; and T. W. Manson, *Studies in the Gospels and Epistles*, 119.

ship.[333] There are certainly differences. One of the major ones, curiously not noticed by Dodd or Holtzmann before him in his fifty 'peculiarities' of the First Epistle, is the predominant use of ὁ Χριστός as a title in the Gospel[334] and of Χριστός as a proper name in the Epistles.[335] But this is certainly explicable as the difference between a document concerned to bring Jews to the belief in Jesus as their Messiah and Son of God (John 20.31) and a document concerned to stablish Christians who already believe this and know him as Jesus Christ (I John 5.13). For the rest I am not personally convinced that the discrepancies of style and vocabulary are not again better explained by one man responding to a new situation after the lapse of perhaps a decade.[336] It could also account for the fact that the Aramaic 'accent' is by now less pronounced.[337] But in the last analysis if the Epistles and Epilogue, and I believe one would have to say the Prologue, were by a different member of the same tight circle (the linguistic situation is entirely different from that of the Apocalypse),[338] it would still make no fundamental difference to the issue that here concerns us. It is simply that I personally do not see the evidence to require the positing of more hands.[339] Moreover the question has to be faced as to why the beloved disciple, if he is the authority behind the message and the

[333]Whereas earlier the *presumption* was of common authorship, D. Moody Smith writes, 'If the evidence so far adduced in the scholarly discussion does not preclude the traditional view of common authorship, it has certainly deprived it of the status of a foregone conclusion' ('Johannine Christianity', *NTS* 21, 1974–5, 234).

[334]With only two exceptions, one in the Prologue (1.17) and one in 17.3, which, I shall argue, was also added after the Epistles. See below, ch. VII, p. 328 n. 93.

[335]Again with only two exceptions (I John 2.22; 5.1). II John 9 is ambiguous.

[336]It is absurd to say with Bultmann (following Haenchen) that the fact that John and I John are directed against different fronts is a 'decisive argument' against common authorship (*Johannine Epistles*, 1). Cf. Streeter, *Four Gospels*, 458: 'The minute differences in thought and temper which some scholars think they have detected between the Gospel and First Epistle are far less than those which divide the earlier, middle and captivity epistles of Paul, or the *Dialogues* written by Plato at different periods of his life. It is only a dead mind that shows no change.' But it must be admitted that Streeter had a vested interest in common authorship – to make 'the Elder' of the Epistles the writer of the Gospel.

[337]Cf. Manson, 'The Fourth Gospel' in *Studies in the Gospels and Epistles*, 115–17; and *On Paul and John*, ed. M. Black, 1963, 86, commenting on Burney's evidence. It has been urged too that there are no 'Aramaisms' in ch. 21, but the sample is too small for judgment.

[338]This does not seem to me to be sufficiently recognized in Barrett's reconstruction (*John*, 133f.).

[339]It is interesting that while historically, as Culpepper recognizes in ch. 1 of his well-argued thesis, *The Johannine School*, one of the main motives in Johannine

founder of the 'school', is not referred to in the Epistles (especially if he is now dead), in the way that the Teacher of Righteousness is in the Qumran literature. As Culpepper says, 'It is puzzling that there was no direct appeal to his authority.'[340] It is much easier to believe that he *is* the authority recalling his own children (τεκνία μου: I John 2.1; cf. III John 4) to his own teaching.

But this still leaves open the question of who the 'I' or the 'we' (and the line between them is obviously very fine)[341] may be. What sort of person are we looking for? The geographical connections of the Gospel are with Galilee, Samaria and above all with Jerusalem and its environs. Now apart from Peter, with whom in each case the beloved disciple is closely connected, there is no other New Testament character known to us who has such associations except John. He comes from the Sea of Galilee, and is identified in Acts with 'bringing the good news to many Samaritan villages' (8.25) and more continuously with the early Christian mission to Jews in Jerusalem (1.13–8.25; cf. Gal. 2.9). Indeed of the five locatable references to him during the ministry, apart from his membership of the inner circle of disciples (Mark 5.37; 9.2; 13.3; 14.33; and pars.), three are linked to Galilee (Mark 1.19f. = Matt. 4.21f.; Luke 5.10; 9.49), another to Samaria (Luke 9.52–56), and the last, to the finding of the Passover room in

scholarship for embracing this hypothesis has been to accommodate the scenario of multiple editorial activity in close association, the parallels which he draws with other 'schools' in the ancient world, Greek and Jewish, do not exhibit the phenomenon of a number of disciples creating the primary literature of the sect (e.g., the works of Plato, Aristotle or Philo); nor in his closing summary is this one of the defining marks of a 'school'. In other words, though this hypothesis can be used to account for the literary phenomena (supposed or real), they are not cogent arguments for it nor does it point to them. The phrase 'a school of St John' goes back at least as far as Westcott, *John* I, lxv, but he certainly did not use it to imply multiple authorship (cf. Streeter, *Four Gospels*, 459f.). The case for a 'school' must be established on its own merits, which are considerable as long as the scholastic overtones of the word (ironically itself never actually used of any of the examples) are not pressed. But in contrast with the scribal 'school of Matthew' I should be happier with Cullmann's more neutral 'Johannine circle'.

[340] *Johannine School*, 282. It is a merit of Culpepper's that he faces this problem squarely (282–4), but his answer, the supposition that the false teachers were themselves claiming his authority (and that he *was* something of the 'naive docetist' Käsemann makes him in his *Testament of Jesus*, ET 1968, 26, 45, 70) is equally without evidence and raises more difficulties than it solves. He admits that 'the absence of any specific reference to the beloved disciple in the Epistles is still a problem' – unless, of course, it is he who is writing.

[341] E.g., John 21.24f. and the alternation of 'I' and 'we' in the Epistles. Despite the dominant 'we' of I John, only once does the author say 'we write to you' (1.4). The remaining twelve instances are in the singular, as regularly in II and III John.

Jerusalem, with the knowledge of the city which that implies (Luke 22.8–13).

But one can perhaps narrow the associations down still further. For the place in Galilee which receives more mention in this Gospel than any other (so far from being 'played down') is, as we have seen, Capernaum. And this we may deduce is where the Zebedees had their business. In Mark Jesus first enters the house of Andrew and Simon, which was in Capernaum (1.21–29) (though John 1.44 tells us that they originally came from Bethsaida), with James and John, whom we are told he had just found 'a little further on' from where the other two were at work (1.19). If, as Luke independently confirms (5.1–11), these pairs of brothers were in partnership, then Zebedee and his family lived in Capernaum as well. So the synagogue at Capernaum (Mark 1.21, etc.), the only one mentioned in John (6.59), where Jesus is spoken of as teaching 'in synagogue' as we should say 'in church', would have been extremely familiar ground.

Yet if the clues point suspiciously to John the son of Zebedee, as the external tradition attests, *could* he have been the evangelist? What of the 'moral certainty' that he was not?[342] In the second edition of his commentary, responding to the re-presentation of the conservative case by Leon Morris,[343] Barrett qualifies this phrase by saying:

> It must be allowed to be not impossible that John the apostle wrote the gospel; this is why I use the term 'moral certainty'. The apostle may have lived to a very great age; he may have seen fit to draw on other sources in addition to his own memory; he may have learnt to write Greek correctly; he may have learnt not only the language but the thought-forms of his new environment (in Ephesus, Antioch, or Alexandria); he may have pondered the words of Jesus so long that they took shape in a new idiom; he may have become such an obscure figure that for some time orthodox Christians took little or no notice of his work. These are all possible, but the balance of probability is against their having all actually happened.[344]

But none of the arguments that I should wish to use depend on *any* of them happening!

[342] Kümmel, *Introduction to the NT*, 245, simply says that it is 'out of the question'. The least I would wish to insist is that it is in question.

[343] 'Was the Author of the Fourth Gospel an "Eyewitness"?' and 'The Authorship of the Fourth Gospel', *Studies in the Fourth Gospel*, 139–292.

[344] *John*, 132 n. 2.

Yet the understandable doubts focus on whether he could have had:

(*a*) the Greek, however simple. But that, as we have seen, becomes increasingly doubtful as a serious objection in first-century Palestine, especially in Galilee, which would have enjoyed the phenomenon of Aramaic for everyday speech, Hebrew for formal occasions like the cult, with Greek as the *lingua franca*.[345] With all the coins in Greek, no one could have got far without Greek as a second language. And, as we have seen, the Greek of the Gospel remains within the compass of anyone who knew his Bible well, as this evangelist evidently did, quoting both the Septuagint and the Hebrew apparently freely 'from memory'.[346]

(*b*) the education. Yet the observation in Acts 4.13 that Peter and John were *ἀγράμματοι* does not mean that they were illiterate but 'untrained laymen' (NEB), like Jesus himself according to John 7.15: 'How does this man know *γράμματα, μὴ μεμαθηκώς*?', without, that is, having completed a rabbinic education giving him the rights of an ordained teacher.[347] The astonishment in each case is how competent they were, not how ignorant. Moreover the Zebedees were evidently not poor. Salome, if she was his wife,[348] was among the women of Galilee who contributed to the support of Jesus (Mark 15.40f.) out of their resources (Luke 8.2f.). They owned their own boats (Luke 5.3) and employed servants (Mark 1.20), like the father of the prodigal, who was a man of modest substance. In more than one of John's parables the point rests in the contrast between the position in the household of servants and sons (8.35; 15.15). The social level of Galilean fishermen would not have been particularly depressed.[349]

(*c*) the contacts, especially in Jerusalem and high-priestly circles (assuming, that is, that the beloved disciple and the disciple of 18.15f. are the same). But fishing on the Sea of Galilee was good business. The Lake had a rich variety[350] and the industry had been much expanded in Hellenistic times,[351] giving its name to the town of Tarichaeae or

345 Cf. C. Rabin, 'Hebrew and Aramaic in the First Century', *Compendia* I. 2, 1007–39, especially 1008f., 1036; Freyne, *Galilee*, 144f.

346 Cf. C. Goodwin, 'How Did John Treat his Sources?', *JBL* 73, 1954, 61–75.

347 Cf. K. Rengstorf, *μανθάνω*, *TDNT* IV, 408; Jeremias, *Jerusalem in the Time of Jesus*, 236.

348 Cf. below, p. 119.

349 Cf. W. H. Wuellner, *The Meaning of 'Fishers of Men'*, Philadelphia 1967, 26–63.

350 Josephus, *BJ* 3.508, 520.

351 Cf. M. Avi-Yonah, *The Holy Land from the Persian to the Arab Conquests: An Historical Geography*, 105; Abel, *Géographie de la Palestine* II, 476f., 373; Hengel, *Judaism and Hellenism* I, 46; II, 37.

Saltings, which features prominently in Josephus.[352] Galilee supplied the whole of Palestine except the coast, as it does today. That there should be fishermen at En Gedi on the Dead Sea was an eschatological vision (Ezek. 47.7–10) that not even the Israeli government has so far been able to realize! Fish came into Jerusalem from the north (cf. Neh. 13.16) and the Fish Gate (Neh. 3.3; 12.39; Zeph. 1.10; II Chron. 33.14) lay at the intersection of the second (northern) wall and the Tyropoeon Valley.[353] So the tradition is not altogether fanciful, which is said to go back to the *Gospel of the Nazaraeans*,[354] that John's acquaintance with the girl on the gate and the high-priestly household derived from these commercial contacts and that he was more familiar with the trademen's entrance. If he had a place in the city (19.27), he could even have been his father's 'agent', another parable or metaphor (13.16) which plays a large part in this Gospel.[355] Indeed it is perhaps worth observing that the distinctive name for cooked fish (ὀψάριον),[356] in which the trade would have been conducted,[357] occurs five times in this Gospel but nowhere else in the New Testament.[358]

None of this of course proves anything, though it does something perhaps to answer the more dismissive objections. But we should go far to find anyone else known to us with the same qualifications. I believe it is unscientific to invent unknown characters such as the author of this major contribution to New Testament literature and theology who have left no other trace behind them. If I may repeat what I said in my *Redating*, the creation as the real evangelist of what Brown calls a 'master preacher and theologian', a 'principal disciple marked with dramatic genius and profound theological insight' who was yet 'not famous',[359] raises far more problems then it solves. And to say,

[352]Strabo, *Geogr.* 16.764. It was evidently a large town (Josephus, *BJ* 2.608) and ran to a hippodrome (*BJ* 2.599; *Vit.* 132).

[353]Jeremias, *Jerusalem*, 20. Unfortunately he says nothing about the fish trade among the industries of Jerusalem.

[354]Fragment 33; *NTApoc* I, 152.

[355]Cf. below, ch. VIII, p. 373.

[356]As opposed to the ordinary name for fish (ἰχθύς), which John uses of fish fresh from the sea (21.6, 8, 11) in contrast to the ὀψάριον that Jesus is cooking on the shore (21.9) (he tells them indeed to bring 'from the ὀψάρια which they have caught' (21.10), but in 21.13 the ὀψάριον which he takes is still singular). In the desert feeding John is obviously correct in alone calling what they had with them ὀψάρια (6.9, 11).

[357]For the variety cf. M. *Ned.* 6.4.

[358]Did a fisherman notice afterwards on land that, contrary to what might have been expected (Luke 5.6), the net was not torn (John 21.11)? Cf. the picture of James and John overhauling the nets in Mark 1.19; Matt. 4.21.

[359]*John* I, xxxv, ci.

casually, with Barrett, that 'the evangelist, perhaps, after Paul, the greatest theologian in all the history of the church, was now forgotten. His name was unknown'[360] is to show an indifference to the evidence (or rather the lack of it) which makes one wonder how, like many others (e.g., Sanders), he can appeal to the silence on the use of John in the second century, which I believe in any case to be much exaggerated,[361] as a powerful argument against apostolic authorship. Geniuses, like entities, are not to be multiplied beyond necessity.

This does not in the least mean that apostolic authorship is a hypothesis without any difficulties, nor is it one, as I said at the beginning of this section, on which everything turns. Yet I have gradually been driven back to regard it as the one least open to objection and therefore the most scientific.[362] So I would conclude, with Cullmann[363] (though he does not believe the person concerned to be John), that the ascription of the Gospel to the beloved disciple must be allowed to mean what it says; and that the role of the Johannine community is basically confined to that of which we have positive evidence, namely, their certificate, given in his presence, that it is true (21.24).

But if it *is* true, then we are very close to source indeed, not only to an apostle, and one of the inner circle of the apostles, but to the one who

[360] *John*, 134.

[361] For the evidence, cf. Lightfoot, *Biblical Essays*, 45–122; Stanton, *The Gospels as Historical Documents I;* Sanders, *The Fourth Gospel in the Early Church*; F.-M. Braun, *Jean le Théologien et son Évangile*. Cf. Brown's conclusion, *John*, *I*.lxxxi: 'An objective evaluation would seem to indicate that the argument for the late dating [or, I would add, against the apostolic authorship] of John because the Gospel was not used in the second century has lost whatever probative force it may have had.' Cf. earlier Sanday, *Criticism of the Fourth Gospel*, 258: 'When use is made of the argument from silence, the first question to be asked is, 'What is silent?' It may well be that the literature supposed to be silent is so small that no inference of any value can be drawn from it'; and Lightfoot, *Biblical Essays*, 67: 'Early references to a Gospel which was universally acknowledged had no interest for anyone, unless they contained some curious or important fact.'

[362] Cf. Teeple, *Literary Origin of the Gospel of John*, 122: 'In our surveys of the literary origin of John, we found bias to prove apostolic authorship, bias to preserve the unity of the book, bias to preserve the earliness (and hence the authority) of at least a portion of the gospel, and bias for certain other types of theory. Theological prejudices have been excused on the grounds that even a scientist has presuppositions. That excuse overlooks the fact that a genuine scientist is willing to change his presuppositions in accordance with new knowledge, whereas a biased person will not change them *regardless* of the evidence.' That a person might actually change them to *become* convinced of early dating, apostolic authorship and the rest apparently never occurs to him.

[363] *Johannine Circle*, 84.

was what we should call Jesus' 'bosom friend'. Yet that is not all. For he may have been not only a close friend but a close relative.

According to John 19.25, the mother of Jesus had a sister. She is unnamed, like the mother of Jesus herself in this Gospel, a fact which, as with the beloved disciple, must be taken as a sign of intimacy rather than ignorance. For at least there is the possibility, if not the probability, that she was the mother of John himself. If we try to correlate the figures of the women at the cross in the various Gospels (Matt. 27.55f.; Mark 15.40f.; John 19.25; Luke mentions no names at this point, though cf. 24.10), we find that Mary Magdalene appears in all of them, Mary the mother of Jesus in John alone. In the Synoptists two others are named. The first is Mary the mother of James and Joses (or Joseph), whom Matthew subsequently calls simply 'the other Mary' (27.61; 28.1). The second is, according to Mark, Salome, in whose place Matthew has 'the mother of the sons of Zebedee' (as in 20.20), evidently intending the same person. In John, as we have seen, there is Jesus' mother's sister (and?) Mary (the wife?) of Clopas. The first question is whether these two figures stand in apposition (there is no conjunction in the Greek) or whether they are separate persons. The probability must be that they are separate persons. Otherwise we should have two sisters in the same family called Mary. If they are separate, then it is reasonable to equate 'Clopas' Mary' with the other Mary, the mother of James and Joses.[364] This leaves us with Jesus' mother's sister and Salome the mother of the sons of Zebedee. Are they too to be equated? There is nothing to compel it, for it is made clear that there were other women besides those named (Mark 15.40f.; Luke 23.49; cf. 8.3; 24.10). Yet since all the others singled out appear to correspond, it is legitimate to presume that not only Matthew and Mark but John are referring to the same person in different ways.[365] If so, then she and Mary the mother of Jesus were sisters and John the son of Zebedee was Jesus' first cousin. This cannot be more than a hypothesis, and the fact that the relationship is not taken up elsewhere

[364]Eusebius, *HE* 3.11, records Hegesippus (a good source) as relating that Clopas 'of whom the book of the Gospels makes mention' was Joseph's brother. This Mary would therefore have been sister-in-law to the mother of Jesus and so part of the family, and thus her presence at the cross and at the tomb would be explained.

[365]So Westcott, *John*, ad loc. and (tentatively) Brown, *John* II, 906. The equation was strongly urged by Zahn, 'Brüder und Vettern Jesu', *Forschungen zur Geschichte des neutestamentlichen Kanons* 6, Leipzig 1900, 338–52, specif. 341; *Evangelium des Johannes* (KNT 4), Leipzig [1–2]1908, 644–7. So too Askwith, *Historical Character of the Fourth Gospel*, 122.

speaks neither for nor against it. For it was certainly not exploited by the church[366] and may therefore be presumed not to have been created by it. One can only test the hypothesis by what it might help to explain.

The first thing it could well explain is the commission in John 19.26f. to the beloved disciple, assuming he is John, to take into his care[367] her who on this supposition would be his aunt. It might have been expected that this duty would have fallen on one of Jesus' brothers, whether or not they were Mary's own sons, since they are elsewhere always associated with her. But Jesus' response to family claims, 'Who is my mother? Who are my brothers?' (Mark 3.31–35 and pars.; cf. 10.29f. and pars.; Matt. 10.37 = Luke 14.26) indicates that spiritual affinity overrode for him natural ties with unbelievers, as his brothers then were (John 7.5). The handing over of his mother to her closest nephew would thus be entirely explicable. Less explicable is the designation of Mary as his 'mother' in the presence of his own natural mother. But this like 'son' obviously here implies a spiritual relationship (as in Rom. 16.13, 'whom I call mother too'; cf. I Peter 5.13), which again takes priority over the natural. The 'favourite son' relationship could also help to account for the designation 'the disciple whom Jesus loved', which sounds to us somewhat arrogant, and for the presumption of the sons of Zebedee (Mark 10.35–45) or their mother on their behalf (Matt. 20.20–28) to privileged seats in the kingdom, and it would explain why the two nephews, with Peter the designated leader, should have formed the inner nucleus of the Twelve. It might also explain the easily overlooked detail of the absence of Salome, or the mother of the sons of Zebedee, from the entombment of Jesus in Mark 15.47; Matt. 27.61. For John could well have taken his mother, with her sister, back at that point to his own home (John 19.27). She re-emerges, with the other two Maries, on the Sunday morning (Mark 16.1; though not in Matthew).

Earlier in the Gospel story the relationship may also throw light on why Jesus went to live with his mother and brothers in Capernaum (his sisters had apparently married local boys in Nazareth and are

[366] J. Blinzler, *Die Brüder und Schwestern Jesu*, Stuttgarter Bibelstudien 21, Stuttgart 1967, 113f., who argues against, makes the point that the sons of Zebedee never appear as cousins of Jesus.

[367] This probably has legal and not merely pastoral force. As head of the family Jesus would have had the responsibility of providing for his widowed mother. 'The instruction of a man on his death bed has the same force as a written document' (b. *Gitt.* 13a). By taking her into his own home the beloved disciple accepts legal responsibility for her.

described by the townsfolk in Mark 6.3 as 'here with us'). For Capernaum was Jesus' own town during the ministry (Matt. 4.13; 9.1; Mark 2.1; 3.20; Luke 4.13; etc.), where his family are (Mark 3.21, 31), and to which he is recorded as going down after the wedding in Cana with his mother, his brothers and his new-found disciples for what looks like a brief visit home (John 2.12).[368] Since, as we have seen, Capernaum was also the home of the Zebedees, what more natural, if Mary and Salome were sisters, than that, on the death of Joseph, Jesus as head of the family (note the singular in Matt. 4.13: 'leaving Nazareth he went and settled at Capernaum on the sea of Galilee') should have taken her and the family to live in the same town and perhaps the same extended family?[369] It is perhaps no accident too that Matthew should combine this information about the move with his distinctive interest in 'the mother of the sons of Zebedee' (20.20; 27.56).

But the interrelationships do not end here. For, according to Luke, Mary the mother of Jesus was a cousin or other close relative of Elizabeth the mother of John the Baptist (1.36). So her sister Salome and her sons James and John would also have been cousins of the Baptist, which could explain why, according to John, they joined his movement so far from home in the first place and why, according to all the Gospels, Jesus did later, apparently independently. Furthermore on his mother's side as well as his father's John the Baptist is said to have been of priestly descent (Luke 1.5), which is entirely probable since priests usually tried to marry into priestly families.[370] Indeed according to the Talmud it is said of Mary that 'she was the descendent of priest-princes (*seganim*)'. But 'she played the harlot with carpenters' (b. *Sanh.* 106a)[371] – instead, presumably, of marrying respectably into a priest's family like her cousin Elizabeth! Now *sagan* is the title for the 'prefect', the second in rank to the high priest and the chief officer of the temple, known in Greek as the στρατηγός, the captain or controller of the temple

[368] A great deal of heavy weather is made out of this verse by Brown, 'The Problem of Historicity in John', *NT Essays*, 156–8; *John* I, 112f. This fairly obvious interpretation is not even considered. I think that Sanday's comment is still worth recording: 'The apparent aimlessness of this statement seems to show that it came directly from a fresh and vivid recollection, and not from any floating tradition. It is not the kind of fact that a tradition handed from mouth to mouth would preserve' (*Authorship and Historical Character of the Fourth Gospel*, 53).

[369] Cf. S. Safrai, 'Home and Family', *Compendia* I. 2, 729.

[370] Jeremias, *Jerusalem*, 218. Great care was taken in preserving the purity of priestly lineage (Josephus, *Contra Ap.* 30–6).

[371] Quoted, E. Stauffer, *Jesus and His Story*, London 1960, 45f. The Munich ms. has 'a carpenter'. It is not indeed certain that this refers to Mary, but cf. R. T. Herford, *Christianity in Talmud and Midrash*, London 1903, 48.

(Acts 4.1; 5.24). He would certainly have been chosen from the families of the priestly aristocracy (we know of two who were sons of the high priest Ananias).[372] Indeed his office was regarded as a necessary step to the high priesthood.[373] So if Mary and her sister came from such stock (and it is difficult to see what motive there would have been for inventing this connection in such a defamatory context) it could help to explain the family's high-priestly contacts (John 18.15f.) and even the curious statement of Polycrates that 'John was a priest wearing the sacerdotal plate' (πέταλον; cf. Exod. 28.36),[374] which is also ascribed to his cousin James the Lord's brother by Hegesippus.[375] John 1.19 contains the only reference to the stock division within Judaism between the priests and levites (apart from the mention of these characters in the parable of the Good Samaritan; Luke 10.31f.). This is scarcely significant, though it is surprising (in strong contrast e.g. with the Qumran literature), and it leads Dodd to the comment: 'The interest shown by our evangelist in the levitical ministry could be accounted for if the tradition he followed had somewhere in its background an association with priestly circles'[376] – or we might add 'he himself'. If so John might naturally have found himself drawn to a mission among the hierarchy ('the Jews' *par excellence* of the Gospel); and the fact, which he alone notes, that 'many from the members of the Sanhedrin became believers' (here contrasted with the Pharisees; 12.42), could have led to and be reflected in the otherwise surprising statement of Acts that 'a large crowd of the priests' subsequently did the same (6.7).

Of course all these connections are highly tentative and *nothing* hangs on them. But at least a good deal begins to come together and make sense if the hypothesis is accepted, on its own merits, that the man behind John's Gospel, the beloved disciple, is indeed the son of Zebedee, as tradition has unanimously asserted.

The links therefore with 'the beginning' in place, time and person are, I suggest, sufficiently plausible at least to make it worth while to follow up and test out the presumption that the Fourth Gospel could take us as far back to source as any other – and on the assumption that it really does come from the apostle John a good deal further.

[372]Ananus in AD 52 (Josephus, *BJ* 2.243; *Ant.* 20.131) and Eleazar in 66 (*BJ* 2.409; *Ant.* 20.208).

[373]J. *Yom.* 3.8, 41a.5, quoted by Jeremias, *Jerusalem*, 162; Safrai, 'The Temple', *Compendia* I.2, 875.

[374]*Ep. ad Victorem*, quoted, Eusebius, *HE* 5.24.3.

[375]Quoted, Epiphanius, *Haer.* 29.4; 78.14. Cf. Lawlor and Oulton, *Eusebius* II, 74.

[376]*Historical Tradition*, 263 n.1.

III

The Chronology of the Ministry

The chronology of the ministry of Jesus is one of those areas where it might seem that by now only fools would step in. It has been worked over so much to so few agreed or positive results. The general impression purveyed to the student by the textbooks is that the Synoptics and John give two hopelessly divergent pictures, of a one-year and of a three-year ministry respectively; that if priority is to be given it must be to the Markan outline, although it is very sketchy until we get to the passion narrative and cannot with any confidence be traced behind the evangelist; and that in any case the order of the material in all the Gospels is determined more by topical and theological interest than by topographical or chronological information.[1] The upshot is that we must be content to remain agnostic,[2] with the further corollaries often drawn that it does not matter much anyhow and that the early church itself neither knew nor cared about such points.

I believe that this scepticism is unwarranted by the evidence and requires to be challenged.

[1]Cf. typically on John, Barrett, *John*, 15: 'Since the material is disposed in accordance with a theological literary scheme, it is idle to seek in John a chronology of the ministry of Jesus.' Of course John has his theological and literary scheme, as do the other evangelists, but this does not mean *ipso facto* that the theology or the literary structure determines the chronology rather than *vice versa*. That has to be judged *a posteriori* on its own merits.

[2]Perhaps a surprising witness to this position is the early Westcott, who wrote in 1855 to the Revd J. F. Wickenden, one of his first pupils (and incidentally the only one of his friends to address him by his Christian name!): 'Will you not excuse me if I decline to attempt to settle any chronological point in the Gospels? The data are far too uncertain to give more than a probable conclusion; and in many cases the order of time

In the first place, it is simply not true that the Synoptic and Johannine pictures are so divergent or incompatible. On the contrary, I shall argue that both presuppose a two-year ministry, and that while the Johannine chronology cannot be fitted into the Markan because the latter is too fragmentary the Markan can be fitted into the Johannine.

Secondly, I believe that the presumption of the priority of the Synoptists over John must be questioned. At any given point priority must be established on its own merits, and I hope to show that when there *are* genuine incompatibilities it is John who, on the strength of the evidence, is to be preferred.

Thirdly, I do not believe there is reason to suppose that the early Christians neither knew nor cared about such things. On the contrary, I think they took for granted a great deal more knowledge among themselves and in their audience than we have. 'I need not tell you', Peter is represented as saying at Caesarea, 'what happened lately over all the land of the Jews, starting from Galilee after the baptism proclaimed by John. You know about Jesus of Nazareth' (Acts 10.37f.). Or, as Paul says of King Agrippa, 'I do not believe that he can be unaware of any of these facts, for this has been no hole-and-corner business' (Acts 26.26; cf. also Acts 2.22 and John 18.20).

And, finally, I do not accept that excessive scepticism is a matter of indifference. It is corrosive, at this and many other points, of our confidence in possessing any firm knowledge about the Jesus of history, who, I am convinced, in the twentieth century as in the first, remains an integral part of the Christ of faith.

The chronology of the ministry is in fact a good example of what happens if one allows a genuine openness to the priority of John's evidence, rather than presuming the priority of the Synoptists' and taking the Johannine material seriously only if it confirms, supplements or at least does not contradict the former.

If one starts from the priority of the Synoptic evidence it is true that one cannot construct any sustained or coherent chronology of the ministry of Jesus. Indeed, apart from the Markan outline, or what I would prefer to call that of the triple tradition (for I do not believe that the Second Gospel always or necessarily represents the most primitive form of it),[3] there is virtually nothing to

is wholly – hopelessly uncertain' (A. Westcott, *Life and Letters of Brooke Foss Westcott*, London and New York 1903, I, 233).

[3]Cf. 'The Parable of the Wicked Husbandmen: A Test of Synoptic Relationships', *Twelve More NTS*, 12–34.

go on.[4] The double (or Q) tradition has no temporal framework. The special Matthaean material adds nothing of chronological significance. And even the special Lukan tradition, except before and after the period of the ministry, provides no additional or alternative information. Indeed in the extended central section from Luke 9.51 to 18.14, where Luke is on his own, there is not a single firm indication of either time or place, and the thread of the journey up to Jerusalem on which the beads are strung is clearly his own editorial expansion of the common tradition. Nor does starting from the Synoptic material make it at all easy to incorporate the Johannine, with its many indications both of topography and of chronology. On the other hand, if one starts from the Johannine framework, the Synoptic material can not only be fitted in but be made intelligible to itself.

For it is often said that the Synoptists present a perfectly consistent self-authenticating picture of a one-year public ministry which is capable of standing on its own as a credible and better attested account than the Johannine[5] – though of course there are plenty who believe that *none* of the Gospels supplies us with an outline of anything but topical and doctrinal interests. But in fact this is not true. As Scott Holland insisted, the Synoptic chronology is a mystery to itself, full of hints which are not self-explanatory. Above all the Synoptists are saying to us in all sorts of subtle ways of Jesus in Jerusalem, 'He has been here before.'

> How is it that, at Bethany, there is a house where he can always make his home, with those who passionately love him, and will stand by him in the day of peril? How is it that there is a man with a colt in a village near, who will yield it at once to his service at the word, 'Our Master needs it' (Mark 11.3)? How is it that a man, whose very name they fail to give, is so loyal in his faith, that in the very darkest hour

[4]Cf. Streeter, *Four Gospels*, 424: 'To speak . . . of a Synoptic chronology, as though there were a three-to-one agreement against John, is quite misleading. The chronology of the Life of Christ is simply a question of Mark against John', and of Mark he says, 'the term chronology is really a misnomer in connection with a work of this character.' 'John is the first and the only one of the Evangelists who attempts a chronology.' This is interesting from one who sees John as dependent on Mark, writing some 25 years after him (470), and yet producing, with few exceptions, a more credible chronology both of the ministry and of the crucifixion (419–24).

[5]The shift in scholarly presuppositions is nicely illustrated by J. B. Lightfoot's remark, *Biblical Essays*, 57 n.1: 'St John is our authority for the chronology of the ministry. In the Synoptic Gospels it is highly probable that the sequence of events is not strictly chronological, but that in places incidents are grouped according to subject and treatment.'

> he will keep an upper room ready for him at a moment's notice? Who is this with whom he can trust himself to communicate, just when all the world is against him, by a pre-arranged code of signals? 'Go into the city, and a man will meet you carrying a jar of water. Follow him, and when he enters a house give this message to the householder: "The Master says, 'Where is the room reserved for me to eat the Passover with my disciples?'" He will show you a large upper room, set out in readiness. Make the preparations for us there' (Mark 14.13–15). How did Joseph of Arimathaea arrive at his belief?[6]

Most obviously is this true of the apostrophe of Jerusalem, firmly anchored in the double tradition: '*How often* have I longed to gather your children, as a hen gathers her brood under her wing; but you would not let me' (Matt. 23.37 = Luke 13.34). As Scott Holland says,

> The words cannot, surely, refer to a desire which he never put into act. The judgment pronounced, 'Behold! thy house is left unto thee desolate', is inconceivable, unless the 'visitation' had been an actual fact.
>
> It would be strange if he who wept over the city had never sought to win it.[7]

Moreover there are other intimations of a ministry stretching over a longer period which afford no chronological framework in themselves but which fall into place and make sense when another is presupposed. Above all the myth of a 'Galilean springtime', of a ministry extending simply from one Passover to another, is palpably contradicted by the Synoptic story itself. The only allusion to spring is to the 'green grass' at the feeding of the five thousand in Mark (6.39), which certainly betokens a season before the summer heat scorches everything brown; and John, who also notes the abundance of the grass (6.10), dates it specifically in the pre-Passover period, in late March or early April. But this event occurs at the climax and close of Jesus's public ministry in Galilee. By then so much has already happened, most of it out of doors, that it is inconceivable that it could all have taken place in the spring of

[6] *The Fourth Gospel*, 131. I have substituted the NEB in the biblical quotations. Cf. Dodd, *Interpretation*, 88 n. 1: 'I see no reason to reject the *prima facie* implication of the Synoptic Gospels that Jesus had at least three friends or adherents in Judaea, namely: the owner of the donkey borrowed for the entry into Jerusalem, the landlord of the house in which the Last Supper was eaten, and "Simon the leper" of Bethany.'

[7] *Fourth Gospel*, 131, 133. Cf. also Sanday, *Authorship and Historical Character of the Fourth Gospel*, 55–8; Askwith, *Historical Value of the Fourth Gospel*, 246–58.

that year. Indeed there is one incident located by Mark and the other Synoptists well before it (Mark 2.23–28; Matt. 12.1–8; Luke 6.1–5), the plucking of the ears of grain one sabbath, which must come from the time of corn-harvest, in May or June. So on his own showing Mark takes the ministry back nearly a year, at least, before the springtime of ch. 6, and thus nearly two years before the final Passover. Of course this does not mean that Mark, and the others, may not have put the incidents in the wrong order – only that the Synoptic evangelists themselves clearly imagine a ministry of more than one year.

But let us now turn to the Johannine account, taking it not necessarily as the primary datum but as a primary datum. For whatever John's overall literary relationship to the Synoptists, his chronological notices certainly cannot be derived from them, with the possible exception of the dating of the desert feeding just mentioned. All his other indications of time, even in the passion narrative, are quite evidently independent of, and at times divergent from, the Synoptic.

The most obvious difference is that John specifically mentions three Passovers, one at the beginning of Jesus's public ministry (2.13, 23), one in the middle (6.4), and one at the end (12.1; 13.1 etc.). This in itself does not add up to a three-year but to a two-year ministry. So, however much fuller is the information John provides, his overall span need not be significantly different; and, as we shall argue, the Synoptic indications of time and place can well be accommodated to it.

Let us then look at his picture in detail and evaluate it on its own merits.

Apart from an early record of day-to-day and even hourly movements which are remarkably precise if they are not intended to be taken literally – 'the next day' (1.29), 'the next day again' (1.35), 'the rest of the day. It was then about four in the afternoon' (1.39), 'the next day' (1.43), 'on the third day' (2.1)[8] – the first public time-reference supplied by John is in 2.13. We are told that Passover was 'near' when Jesus went up to Jerusalem and cleansed the temple (2.14–22).

This at once presents us with the first clash with the Synoptic chronology, and it is presumed by most scholars (including Dodd[9] who defends the historicity of John at many other points) that the Synoptists are right in recording this incident at the end of the ministry, in close

[8]On the meaning of this, not as an interval, see below, ch. IV, pp. 165–7.

[9]*Interpretation*, 300–3, 384f., 448; *Historical Tradition*, 162, 211. One scholar who defends the Johannine placing is, ironically, Vincent Taylor in his commentary on Mark, *The Gospel According to St Mark*, London and New York 1955, 461.

conjunction with the passion narrative.[10] I can only say here very summarily[11] that I have long been persuaded, without commitment to any particular chronological schema, that John's placing is far more convincing. The Synoptists, if they are to record the incident at all, have no option but to put it where they do, since it is one of the few incidents in Jesus' ministry that must have occurred in Jerusalem and they record only one visit there. Since John records many, he is able to associate it correctly with the pre-Passover period when, according to the Mishnah (*Shek*. 1.3), the tables of the money-changers for converting the annual half-shekel tax were set up in the temple court from the twenty-fifth day of Adar, that is, three weeks prior to the feast. And of the three Passovers John mentions, for only two of which Jesus was in Jerusalem, he is clear that it was the first. I believe there are considerations in all the Gospels which suggest that he is right.

First, Mark's connection between Jesus' action in cleansing the temple and the final determination of the authorities to do away with him looks like his own editorial construction (11.18). The other Synoptists do not follow him at this point[12] and the incident is not brought up at the trial, as one would expect if it were the *casus belli* – only some alleged *words* about *destroying* the temple (Mark 14.57f. = Matt. 26.60f.; cf. Mark 15.29 = Matt. 27.39f.; and Acts 6.14). Brown, while arguing with most commentators for the later dating for the cleansing, agrees that the saying about the temple's destruction could scarcely have left such a dim and divisive memory at the trial (cf. Mark 14.59) if it had only been uttered a few days beforehand. He therefore allows that this points to an earlier context for the saying.[13] Moreover,

[10]The shift in presuppositions is again illustrated by the comment in the manuscript of Lightfoot's unpublished lectures on St John's Gospel in the Durham Cathedral Library. Of the two accounts of the cleansing he said, 'If it were necessary to identify the one with the other St John has the higher claim to our absolute deference and the historic truth of the Synoptic narratives must yield. As a rule ['in all things' crossed out] the Synoptists are to be interpreted by St John and not conversely. For St John is precise and definite. But the incident may well have occurred twice.' It is noticeable that in the material in the *Biblical Essays* he avoids any discussion of the conflict of the Johannine and Synoptic chronologies either here or in the dating of the last supper and crucifixion. But in the latter case too he clearly gave preference to John's evidence.

[11]See more fully below, ch. IV, pp. 185f.

[12]Matthew omits the connection altogether and Luke says that it was Jesus' *teaching* in the temple that decided them to act. In fact in all four Gospels his teaching is given as the real ground (whatever the occasion) of their opposition (Mark 11.18; 12.12 and pars.; 14.64 and pars.; Luke 19.47; 20.1; John 18.19–21; 19.7).

[13]*John* I, 118. So earlier Askwith, *Historical Value of the Fourth Gospel*, 246–50, who observes that '*We* heard him say, I will destroy *this* temple' (Mark 14.58) presupposes in this case a previous visit to Jerusalem.

if such a disturbance had occurred in the highly-charged atmosphere following his excited public welcome into the city (John 12.12–18; Mark 11.8–10) it is surely remarkable that Jesus was not arrested on the spot,[14] as S. G. F. Brandon says, unless as he also says, without a shred of evidence, he was accompanied by a *force majeure* which rendered this impossible.[15] But it is Jesus' response to the challenge to his authority in so acting that I believe provides the positive clue to its true setting. His counter-question, 'The baptism of John: was it from God, or from men?' (Mark 11.28–30 and pars.), appears in its Synoptic setting to be merely a clever riposte to put his opponents on the spot. For what has the Baptist to do with the case, and why should the authorities still fear the people's response to him when he has been out of the picture for so long?[16] But in John's setting the question is immediately relevant. For what Jesus is doing at that stage of his ministry is, as we shall be arguing, directly under the Baptist's influence and inspiration. And what was the coming mighty one of Malachi's prophecy to do but come suddenly to the temple and purify the sons of Levi and cleanse them like gold and silver, so that they should be fit to bring offerings to the Lord (Mal. 3.1–3, 8f.)? Jesus' right to act as he did can be accepted only if the source and sanction of the Baptist's ministry is acknowledged: for the authority behind the one is the authority behind the other. If the question about the Baptist's activity had occurred in John and the Johannine chronology in the Synoptists instead of the other way round, no one I think would have doubted that the cleansing of the temple belonged most naturally to the period when

[14]Cf. Josephus, *Ant.* 17.149–63, where two men with good Maccabean names, Judas and Matthias, suffer this fate for tearing down the golden eagle set over the great gate of the temple by Herod. The situations are not fully parallel, since clearly this act was a highly political as well as a religious protest. I have argued in my chapter 'His Witness is True: A Test of the Johannine Claim' in *Twelve More NTS*, 112–37, specif. 114–21, on which I have drawn here and elsewhere, that Jesus' act was, according to all the Gospels, motivated by purely religious zeal (as John makes most explicit; 2.17); yet the *context* in which the Synoptists set it makes it difficult to believe that it would not have provoked response from the watchful guard on the roof of the Antonia, as in Acts 21.30–6.

[15]*The Fall of Jerusalem and the Christian Church*, London [2]1957, 103f.; *Jesus and the Zealots*, Manchester and New York 1967, 332–4; *The Trial of Jesus of Nazareth*, London and New York 1968, 83f. Cf. also E. Trocmé, 'L'expulsion des marchands du Temple', *NTS* 15, 1968–9, 1–22; *Jesus and His Contemporaries*, ET London (= *Jesus as Seen by His Contemporaries*, ET Philadelphia) 1973, 112–15.

[16]Cf. H. E. Edwards, *The Disciple Who Wrote These Things*, 191: 'Is it likely that if John the Baptist had disappeared from public view *two years before* this incident it would still have been dangerous for any member of the Jerusalem aristocracy to disavow belief in him?'.

the people were still 'all wondering about John, whether perhaps he was the Messiah' (Luke 3.15). Moreover, the cursing of the barren fig- tree, equally symbolic of the fate of Israel (cf. Hos. 9.10, 16f.; Luke 13.6–9), which is closely intertwined with the Synoptic account of the cleansing (Mark 11.12–14, 20–23; Matt. 21.18–21) and must also belong to the season of early spring (Mark 11.12f.)[17] appears equally to reflect the Baptist's influence. Indeed it might have been designed as an act of prophetic symbolism to spell out his warning: 'Prove your repentance by the fruit it bears. . . . Every tree that fails to produce good fruit is cut down and thrown on the fire' (Matt. 3.8–10 = Luke 3.8f.).

Furthermore the fourth evangelist supplies an incidental but very specific time-reference which confirms the date of the Passover concerned. For the Jews say that at the time of Jesus' action the temple had been under construction for forty-six years (2.20). We shall return to the significance of this figure when we ask at the end whether it is possible to set any absolute dating on the span of the ministry. For now it is enough to say that if, as Josephus tells us, Herod the Great started his rebuilding programme 'in the eighteenth year of his reign'[18] (20–19 BC),[19] then forty-six years on would bring us, counting inclusively, to

[17]It reflects the situation in March–April when the bursting of the fig-leaves (cf. Mark 13.28 and pars.) is preceded and accompanied by small green figs, which can be eaten if one is really hungry (cf. Mark 11.12), but which never ripen and subsequently drop off. 'The season of figs' proper is not till late summer, but the absence of these early figs (from my observation not an uncommon phenomenon) is an indication that the tree will later be barren. So it represents a perfectly reasonable parable or 'sign', not an act of irrational petulance. Cf. C. E. Padwick, *With Him in His Temptations*, London 1949, 33. T. W. Manson's resort in 'The Cleansing of the Temple', *BJRL* 33, 1950–51, 271–82 (277f.), to excising Mark 11.13b ('for it was not the season of figs') is gratuitous and unnecessary.

[18]*Ant.* 15.380: *Ὀκτωκαιδεκάτου γεγονότος ἐνιαυτοῦ*. It appears arbitrary to take this, with J. Finegan, *Handbook of Biblical Chronology*, Princeton, N.J., 1964, 277, to mean that the eighteenth year had passed and that it was now his nineteenth year. Josephus uses a different expression in *Ant.* 15.354 when he wants to say that Herod 'had completed the seventeenth year of his reign' (ἑπτακαιδεκάτου παρελθόντος ἔτους).

[19]Schürer, *History* I, 292 and the bibliography there cited; Finegan, *Chronology*, 276–80. In principle the date depends on whether Herod's reign is reckoned from his *de jure* appointment by the Romans in 40 BC or its *de facto* start with his capture of Jerusalem in 37 BC. (Josephus is aware of the different reckonings himself: *BJ* 1.665; *Ant.* 17.191.) But it is clear that Josephus is counting from the latter here. His previous time-reference, in *Ant.* 15.354, to the completion of his seventeenth year, is to date Augustus' arrival in Syria, and this we know was in 20 BC (Dio Cassius, *Hist.* 54.7.6, when Apuleius and Nerva were consuls). In *BJ* 1.401 he puts the restoration of the temple in the fifteenth year of Herod's reign, and it is tempting to try to harmonize the two statements by deriving the eighteenth year from 40 BC and the fifteenth from 37 BC. But this would yield the year 23–2, not, as Jeremias wishfully asserts (*Jerusalem in the Time of Jesus*, 21f.), 20–19.

AD 27–8. This would be a date entirely consistent with the Johannine placing, but too early for the Synoptic.[20] Since it is hard to find any plausible symbolic reason for the figure,[21] it would suggest that the evangelist or his tradition is neither uninterested nor uninformed when it comes to matters of chronology.

We may then, I believe, accept this initial time-reference in the story of Jesus's public ministry as a point from which we can with reasonable confidence move both backwards and forwards.

Behind it we have both the baptism of Jesus (which the Gospel of John does not describe but evidently presupposes) and the preaching of the Baptist. All the evangelists agree that the Baptist had been preaching and baptizing for some time before Jesus' arrival at the Jordan (Matt. 3.13–17; Mark 1.9; Luke 3.21), and John tells us that he had already built up a following of disciples and attracted an official deputation from the Jerusalem authorities (1.19–35). So if Jesus was in Jerusalem shortly before Passover, in March/April, and prior to that had as John tells us spent a limited time in Cana and Capernaum (2.1–12), it must have been in the early part of that year, at the latest, when he was baptized, and the autumn before, if not earlier, when John the Baptist had started his preaching in the Jordan valley. In fact it is inherently unlikely that John would have drawn large crowds in or to that area in the heat of the summer when, as Josephus says, 'the plain is burnt up, and the excessive drought renders the surrounding atmosphere pestilential' (*BJ* 4.457). Indeed it has been persuasively argued by Sydney Temple,[22] that John began his mission there when he did because he would have had someone to preach to. Because it was so much lower and warmer than Jerusalem, Jericho had been extended by Herod the Great to form a winter-capital for the court. 'The climate is so mild', says Josephus, 'that the inhabitants wear linen when snow is falling throughout the rest of Judaea' (*BJ* 4.473). The new area included a hippodrome, an amphitheatre, swimming pools and commodious accommodation for guests, as well as the palace, later sumptuously restored by his son Archelaus;[23] and after the end of the

[20]If it were started in the fifteenth year it would make the Synoptic timing even more difficult.

[21]Augustine, *In Joh*. 10.12, noting that the Greek letters of 'Adam' had the numerical value of 46, applied it to Jesus' own age (cf. John 8.57, 'not yet fifty years old'). But this bears no relation to the plain sense of the text.

[22]*Core of the Fourth Gospel*, 17f.

[23]*BJ* 1.407, 659, 666; 2.57; *Ant*. 15.53f.; 17.161, 175, 194, 274, 340. For a summary of the archaeological confirmation, cf. M. Avi-Yonah, *Encyclopaedia of Archaeological Excavations in the Holy Land* II, 1976, 564–70; and in more detail the works of D.

monarchy it doubtless continued to serve as a riviera for the wealthier citizens of Jerusalem. We may even catch behind the tones of 'Who warned you to escape from the coming retribution?' addressed to 'many of the Pharisees and Sadducees coming for baptism' (Matt. 3.7), a dig at the hotel population of New Jericho! At any rate we shall probably not be far wrong if we place the initial baptizing mission of John in the autumn and winter preceding that first Passover.

Going forward now from that Passover, for which Jesus stayed on in Jerusalem (John 2.23) and which saw his first contact with Nicodemus (3.1–21), we are told that 'After this, Jesus went into the countryside[24] of Judaea with his disciples, stayed there with them and baptized' (3.22). It is impossible to be sure how long this period lasted. The only other time when John uses the same word, διέτριβεν, namely in 11.54 (if it is there the correct reading),[25] it refers to what was evidently a short stay, spending time (as the root of the word would suggest) rather than settling down. It looks as if Jesus merely 'took his time' returning from Passover (cf. Luke 2.41–52!). For when eventually he reaches Galilee, after going through Samaria, 'the feast' on which the Galileans look back, and at which they too had been present, is still the same Passover (4.45). So there is no *a priori* reason to predicate an extended period of residence in Judaea, as some have, postulating yet a further, unrecorded, Passover and adding an extra year to the ministry.

The only reason why Finegan and others are forced to do this is because they take the next time-reference, to there being four months till harvest (4.35), as an indication that Jesus was in Samaria in the early part (January or February) of the following year.[26] This is a possible and perfectly proper inference from the verse,[27] but it is nevertheless one which I would seriously question. For this is the only

C. Baramki, J. B. Pritchard and E. Netzer in the bibliography in *Compendia* I.2, 1002–6.

[24]The distinction is usually expressed by χώρα (John 11.55; Mark 1.5; Luke 21.21; Acts 26.20), but for γῇ in this sense cf. Bultmann, *John*, ad loc.

[25]The manuscripts and the editors are fairly evenly divided, but διέτριβεν seems more likely to have been altered to the typically Johannine ἔμεινεν rather than *vice versa*.

[26]*Biblical Chronology*, 283–5. So too H. W. Hoehner, *Chronological Aspects of the Life of Christ*, Grand Rapids, Mich., 1977, ch. 3. Finegan together with E. F. Sutcliffe, *A Two Year Public Ministry Defended*, London 1938, and C. J. Cadoux, *The Life of Jesus*, West Drayton 1949, argue that a two-year ministry involves reversing John 5 and 6 (which Hoehner, I think rightly, declines to do). But it involves nothing of the sort *unless* John 4.35 is taken to refer to January–February of the following year.

[27]Dodd's comment, 'That it is to be understood as a banal remark upon the time of year (as many commentators have assumed, in their anxiety to discover data for a calendar of the Ministry of Jesus) I find entirely incredible; *such remarks did not find a place in the gospel tradition*', is quite arbitrary (*Historical Tradition*, 394; italics mine).

hint of a time-span which would require the passing over in silence of a whole year's cycle of feasts; and there are a number of indications that point the other way – not least, as we have seen, the clear reference in 4.45 back to the same Passover mentioned in ch. 2.

It looks as though those are right who see here a proverbial saying introduced by the words 'Do you not say?',[28] just as two verses later in 4.37 Jesus refers to the 'saying' (λόγος), 'One does the sowing, another the reaping.' The objection to this interpretation, which I myself felt earlier,[29] has been the opening ἔτι ('There are *yet* four months to harvest'), but with its omission now by **P**[75] as well as by a cross-section of other authorities[30] it looks as if it may have got into the text either by dittography (ὅτι ἔτι) or in an attempt to improve the sense. Without it the saying would refer to the sort of popular schema of the agricultural year to be found in the ancient Gezer calendar (which dates back at least to the tenth century BC). This specifies the month or months the farmer works at a particular operation, starting with autumn:

His two months are (olive) harvest (Sept/Oct; Oct/Nov);
His two months are planting (grain) (Nov/Dec; Dec/Jan);
His two months are late planting (Jan/Feb; Feb/Mar);
His month is hoeing up of flax (Mar/Apr);
His month is harvest of barley (Apr/May);
His month is (wheat) harvest and festivity (May/June);
His two months are vine-tending (June/July; July/Aug);
His month is summer fruit (Aug/Sept).[31]

Such schematizations are obviously rough and ready and take no account of the wide climatic variations in Palestine. The Jordan valley is a good month ahead of the Judaean highlands, and there the barley-cycle, unlike that of the longer-ripening wheat, does in fact occupy the four months between December and April.[32] The saying could then be

[28]In Matt. 16.2 (whether it is part of the text or a scribal addition) a similar saw from nature is introduced with the word λέγετε.

[29]Cf. 'The "Others" of John 4.38', *Twelve NTS*, 65.

[30]D L 0133 Φ pm l sy^{c} Or^{pt} Cyr.

[31]Tr. W. F. Albright, 'The Gezer Calendar', *BASOR* 92, 1943, 2f. It is reproduced in J. B. Pritchard, *Ancient Near Eastern Texts*, Princeton [3]1969, 320, and quoted in Finegan, *Biblical Chronology*, 33f. See R. A. S. Macalister, *The Excavation of Gezer* II, London 1912, 24–8, for fuller discussion.

[32]I have myself seen barley ripe in the Jordan valley in early April. Cf. Macalister, *Gezer* II, 23; J. Lightfoot, *Horae Hebraicae et Talmudicae* III, 288; Strack-Billerbeck, *Kommentar zum NT* II, 439. The barley for the *Omer* was got from near to Jerusalem if

part of a popular jingle, on the level of 'Thirty days hath September, April, June and November', since, as has often been observed,[33] it forms a crude iambic trimeter:

τετράμη|νός ἐσ|τι χὼ | θερισ|μὸς ἔρ|χεται.

The paratactic syntax ('It is four months and harvest comes') bespeaks a Semitic origin[34] and it is no objection that it should have been current in a Greek version in first-century Palestine.[35]

The passage would then mean: Doesn't the nature-rhyme run: 'From sowing to harvest four months'? But look at the fields. You can see they are white to harvest, and the reaping-men are even now at work and receiving their wages.[36] And this is a parable of our work. It is still true, as again the saying goes, 'One sows, another reaps.'[37] I have sent you to reap what you haven't worked on. Others have laboured and you have come in for the fruits of their labour. Yet so instantaneous has been the harvest that sower and reaper can join together in the festivity.

If this is the correct interpretation, then the chronological reference will be to the present state of the grain-fields in the plains around Sychar[38] where the barley-harvest (implied in the four-month interval)

---

possible (in the Kedron valley), but if not from further afield (M. *Men.* 10.2).

[33]See the commentaries, e.g., of Westcott, Bernard and Brown, ad loc., and Dodd, *Historical Tradition*, 394. The reconstructions differ according to whether the initial ἔτι is regarded as part of it.

[34]Cf. Dodd, *Historical Tradition*, 395, and the references there given. John himself uses the same construction elsewhere, both with ἔτι (14.19) and without (16.16f.).

[35]Apart from the literature already cited, cf. S. Lieberman, *Greek in Jewish Palestine*, New York 1942, 144–60 ('Greek and Latin Proverbs in Rabbinic Literature'); and A. W. Argyle, 'A Note on John 4.35', *ExpT* 82, 1970–1, 247f.

[36]For this as a metaphor for the harvest of the Spirit, cf. II John 8, where Bultmann (*Johannine Epistles*, 113, following Schnackenburg, *Johannesbriefe*, 314) quotes it as a surprising Jewish expression in what he regards as a gnosticizing Hellenistic author.

[37]For harvest, unlike sowing, involves getting in hired labour (4.36; cf. James 5.4; b. *B.M.* 76b), though doubtless as a proverb it is a reflection, as Barrett says ad loc., on 'the sad inequality of life' (cf. Job 31.8; Micah. 6.15; and especially the Greek proverb ἄλλοι σπείρουσιν, ἄλλοιδ' ἀμήσονται and other parallels cited by Bultmann, *John*, 198, n. 2).

[38]'Sychar' in John 4.5 is either a corruption of Shechem (Balatah), a mile and a half east of Nablus (Neapolis), or else the village of 'Askar, three quarters of a mile to the north of Balatah. Brown, *John* I, 169, and Schein, *Following the Way*, 70–75, 205, argue for Shechem. Kopp, *The Holy Places of the Gospels*, ET New York and London 1963, 155–66, argues strongly for 'Askar, which has been defended by, among others, George Adam Smith, Dalman, Barrett, Schnackenburg and Lindars and is supported by Boismard. I am inclined towards the latter. There are springs in both places. So the question arises, Why did the Samaritan woman have to 'come all this way' (διέρχεσθαι; John 4.15) further down the valley to Jacob's well? (This site is beyond doubt and still clearly visible. For a photograph of it before it was enclosed by the unfinished Russian

is ready in May.[39] And this would fit well with a stay of some weeks in Judaea after Passover, the precise duration depending on the date of the festival that year, to which we shall return.

It would synchronize too with the parallel activity of John the Baptist, who, we are told, had moved his scene of operations from the Jordan valley to Aenon near Salim (3.23). Now this in all probability is to be located in the same region of Samaria,[40] Salim being clearly

---

Orthodox church, see Sanday, *Sacred Sites*, plate XXIX.) My Palestinian guide, Najib Khouri from St George's College, Jerusalem, who acted as interpreter to the American scholars interviewing the goat-herd who first discovered the Dead Sea Scrolls and is mentioned by Brownlee, in Stendahl, ed., *The Scrolls and the NT*, 33, and to whom I am greatly indebted, gave an explanation which I found wholly convincing. Because the woman was of dubious repute (John 4.16–18) she would have been boycotted by the other women at the village spring, and was forced to go to the well on the main trade-route used by the caravans. This would also explain why she came to be there at midday (4.6) rather than 'towards evening, the time when the women came out to draw water' (Gen. 24.11). The slightly greater distance of the well from 'Askar than Shechem would therefore be no objection: she was not going there for convenience.

[39] So Brown, *John* I, 174. E. L. Martin, 'The Year of Christ's Crucifixion', *Exposition* (Foundation for Biblical Research, Pasadena, Ca.), 1983, adopts the same position and the same overall dating but, retaining the ἔτι in 4.35, argues that though the corn was ripe it still had to stand for four months, since Sept. 27–Sept. 28 was a sabbatical year. The theory is ingenious but without any basis in the narrative. Someone had laboured to sow it in 4.38 and in fact in v. 36 'the reaper *is* drawing his pay' – presumably not as unemployment benefit.

[40] It was put in ancient times some 8 miles south of Scythopolis, not far from the Jordan, and the location is still supported today (e.g., by Finegan, *The Archaeology of the New Testament*, 12f.). Yet it has been strongly argued by Albright, 'Some Observations Favoring the Palestinian Origin of the Gospel of John', *HTR* 17, 1924, 193f.; 'Recent Discoveries in Palestine and the Gospel of St John' in Davies and Daube, edd., *The Background of the New Testament and its Eschatology*, 159f.; and M.-É. Boismard, 'Aenon, près de Salim (Jean 3.23)', *RB* 80, 1973, 218–29, that Salim is the village of that name, still inhabited, some 3 miles east of Shechem in Samaria. It was favoured by Edward Robinson, *Biblical Researches in Palestine, Mount Sinai and Arabia Petraea*, London 1841, III, 118. Westcott, *John* I, 126, quoted the *Palestine Exploration Report*, 1874, 141f. (cf. 1876, 99) for an Aynun 'not far from a valley abounding in springs to the north of Salim which lies not far to the east of Nablus'. With this I would completely agree. As Albright says, the comment that 'there was much water there' is evidently 'intended to explain why he chose a place so far removed from the Jordan as Aenon'. But I would question their more precise identification of it with Khirbet 'Ainun (Ruin of Springs), north of the Wadi Far'ah near the old town of Tirzah, once the capital of the northern kingdom. There is no spring there (as Albright admits), nor is there ever likely to have been on the barren hillside, and it seems improbable that it would have been described as 'near Salim' (rather than Tirzah), which is some seven or eight miles away even as the crow flies, the other side of a chain of hills. (All this was said by Sanday, *Sacred Sites*, 33f., who however opted for the site near Scythopolis.) Far more convincing is Wadi Beidan, three miles from Salim (four by road), and less than two from the edge of the Salim plain. It has a dozen springs, feeding, as I have seen, four streams of plentiful water which do not dry up. This case is argued by Schein, *Following*

visible across the valley from Jacob's well. This proximity would then explain the reference to the 'others' in 4.38, which, I have long believed, relates to the work of the Baptist's movement,[41] and would account for the fact that Jesus found himself able immediately to reap the fruits of their labours. If we ask why John had chosen this spot the reason given is that water was plentiful there. The very name Aenon ('springs') shows that this was not river-water and suggests that John had moved with the coming of the summer season, which would not only dry up the wadis, which were simply winter-torrents (χείμαρροι), but cause his audience to disperse. In Schein's words,

> As Judaeans go to the area of the Jordan valley to escape the chilling cold of winter, so Samaritans go to Aenon for relief from the stifling heat of summer. By mid-May the Jordan Valley can be unbearably hot, people no longer vacation in Jericho of Bethany of Peraea. John has moved from there to a Samaritan holiday center.[42]

But there is no indication that this phase of the Baptist's activity lasted long. Indeed, according to the summary of Acts 13.25, which Dodd[43] has argued preserves several interesting features independent of the Synoptic tradition (and incidentally closer to John's), the Baptist was already 'nearing the end of his course' before he even spoke of the one coming after him. John 5.35 suggests in fact that his entire ministry was a short-lived phenomenon, a blazing torch in whose light men were happy to exult 'for a while' (πρὸς ὥραν), a phrase which elsewhere in the New Testament always describes a passing moment or a brief period (II Cor. 7.8; Gal. 2.5; Philem. 15; cf. I Thess. 2.17). His activity was in any case brought to a premature end by his arrest, which the fourth evangelist again does not describe[44] but alludes to in the very next verse after the mention of his activity at Aenon: 'This was before John's imprisonment' (3.24).

In the Markan account the incarceration of John is the turning-point that marks Jesus' move from Judaea to Galilee (1.14). It is not actually

---

the Way, 68f., 203, and I found Boismard in conversation happy to agree. There is no known village called Aenon in these parts but, as Boismard says, it could mean simply that John baptized 'at the Springs near Salim'.

[41] 'The "Others" of John 4.38', *Twelve NTS*, 61–6. C. H. H. Scobie, *John the Baptist*, London and Philadelphia 1964, 175f. concurs.

[42] *Following the Way*, 68.

[43] *Historical Tradition*, 255–8.

[44] Wherever Aenon is located it was not within Herod's jurisdiction, so he must have moved from there.

said that it is the cause of it, though Matthew suggests as much by saying that Jesus 'withdrew' upon hearing of it (4.12). But the Fourth Gospel gives a specific reason for it: 'A report now reached the Pharisees: "Jesus is winning and baptizing more disciples than John"; although, in fact, it was only the disciples who were baptizing and not Jesus himself. When Jesus learned this, he left Judaea and set out once more for Galilee' (4.1–3). One can only surmise from this curiously circumstantial statement that Jesus sensed that with the growing success of his movement (3.26–30) the unwelcome attention that had been focused on John would now be turned upon himself. Yet the fourth evangelist makes the important point that it was not Herod whom Jesus was fearing (as we might deduce from the Synoptists) but the Pharisees, who, all the Gospels agree, constituted for him the real source of opposition.

So Jesus makes the decisive transition to Galilee in what we have already had reason to think is about May. And John's note about the route he takes supplies perhaps a further pointer to the time of year, for he tells us (4.4) that it meant 'having' to 'go *through*' Samaria (there is a double διά in the Greek). That he should take the trouble to note this is intelligible only if the implied contrast is with skirting Samaria by the Jordan valley route. No mention is made of this necessity on Jesus' previous journey to Galilee in 1.43–2.1, which, especially from where he was on the east bank, would naturally have been by the valley road. But that had been in the new year. By May this would have gone through a region where in summer, as Josephus tells us, 'no one goes out if he can help it' (*BJ* 4.471). The obvious route north from Jerusalem would then be by way of the high ground.[45] Yet John goes out of his way to say that Jesus did not spend more than two days in Samaria (4.40, 43). So his time of arrival in Galilee is still probably to be set in late May.

This inaugurates an extended period of public preaching and healing, which in John is presupposed (cf. 6.2; 18.20) rather than described. The Synoptists here provide far the fuller record. From the point of view of plotting the course of the ministry, however, the difficulty is that it is impossible with confidence to place their material in chronological sequence, since the connections are for the most part topical rather than temporal.

There is one story however that contains, as we have seen, a built-in

[45]The point about the climate is well made by Temple, *Core of the Fourth Gospel*, 18f. For this as the customary route of Galileans to festivals in Jerusalem, cf. Josephus, *Ant*. 20.118. It was the quickest, and the journey could be done in three days (*Vit*. 269).

time-reference, that of the plucking of grain on the sabbath (Mark 2.23–28; Matt. 12.1–8; Luke 6.1–5). The triple tradition sets this among the early conflict stories, though there is no guarantee of course that these could not have been assembled from later incidents. But the story, which appears to come from the Galilean wheat-harvest in June,[46] is immediately preceded in this same tradition (according to Mark and Luke; Matthew sets it earlier still) by one which contrasts the fasting-disciplines of the followers of John and of Jesus (Mark 2.18–22; Luke 5.33–39; Matt. 9.14–17). This suggests a period when the two movements were still actively operating in parallel. Indeed the saying which forms the heart of this encounter, designating Jesus as the bridegroom, who it is stressed (unlike the Baptist?) is still with them, receives its Johannine parallel (cf. John 3.29f. with Mark 2.19f.) in a dispute of John's disciples (with Jesus?)[47] before their master's imprisonment (3.23f.). Moreover, if the incident in the cornfields were to be placed a year later it would fall in the period when, as we shall see, Jesus has already withdrawn from public contact and dispute. So in all probability it properly belongs where the Synoptists set it, in the summer of that first year, and would independently confirm what we should gather from the Gospel of John about when the Galilean ministry began.

However, according to John, after a relatively short period Jesus is back again in Jerusalem for 'a feast of the Jews', or Judaeans (5.1).[48] Pentecost in May/June is obviously too soon and the Encaenia or Dedication festival in mid-winter would have been too cold in Jerusalem for the sick to be lying around waiting for the waters to move (5.3–9).[49] So the probability must be in favour of Tabernacles, in

[46]Wheat from Capernaum and Chorazin was regarded as being of the top quality (b. *Men.* 85a; quoted, Jeremias, *Jerusalem in the Time of Jesus*, 41).

[47]Following the emendation τοῦ Ἰησοῦ in 3.25 for the very difficult, but best attested, Ἰουδαίου. See below, ch. IV, p. 17 n. 37.

[48]The weight of the manuscript evidence (P^{66} and P^{75} as well as Vaticanus etc.) is now fairly heavily against reading with Sinaiticus, '*the* feast', which *could* be interpreted as another Passover, though it would more naturally refer to Tabernacles, which Josephus tells us was the greatest and most observed festival (*Ant.* 8.100, 15.50). In *Ant.* 13.372 we actually find 'the feast' designating Tabernacles (cf. the note in the Loeb edition, 413; the parallel passage in *BJ* interestingly has 'a feast'). For the expression in the Tannaitic literature see S. Safrai, 'The Temple', *Compendia* I.2, 894; 'The Temple and the Divine Service' in M. Avi-Jonah and Z. Baras, edd., *The World History of the Jewish People* VII, Jerusalem 1975, 311.

[49]Bowman, *The Fourth Gospel and the Jews*, 36, admits this as an objection to Purim (February–March), but says 'This takes no account of the claim that he had been lying there for thirty-eight years' (John does not actually say this; but presumably it is implied that the paralytic had become inured to the cold!). In fact Bowman opts for Purim

October, which would in fact fit very well. The setting of the incident at Bethesda we have already discussed sufficiently.[50]

On this view Jesus evidently returns to Galilee, where (unless we transpose John 5 and 6) he still is at the beginning of ch. 6 some six months later. In any case there is much more of the Galilean ministry to be fitted in, including other Synoptic passages which, if they are taken from life, would fit a later period of the agricultural year. In Mark 4.2–41 there are three parables about seeds, followed by a violent squall on the lake, and Stauffer has suggested that these would belong naturally to December, 'the time of sowing and of storms'.[51] Obviously nothing can be based on that, but it would fit well.

In the course of the Tabernacles visit reference is made to John the Baptist in the past tense (5.33–35). But it is not said that he was dead, simply that the lamp of his witness was now a thing of the past. It need imply no more than when, according to the Q tradition, Jesus asks: 'What was the spectacle that drew you to the wilderness?' (Matt. 11.7 = Luke 7.24), when John is still alive in prison (Matt. 11.2 = Luke 7.18). John's death, which again is not narrated in the Fourth Gospel, cannot be dated precisely. According to Matthew (14.12f.), it was the news of it which led to Jesus withdrawing to the wilderness prior to the desert feeding early in the following spring. This cannot with confidence be attributed to more than his editorial treatment of the Markan material, which makes no such direct connection. But that does not mean that Matthew may not have been right in placing it towards the close of the Galilean ministry. For reflection on the fate of John seems also to have been preoccupying Jesus in the conversation following the Transfiguration (Mark 9.11–13; Matt. 17.10–13). Furthermore, if the banquet to which, according to Mark (6.21), Herod Antipas had invited 'his chief officials and commanders and the leading men of Galilee' was really held, as the story seems to imply, at Machaerus, where Josephus tells us he had imprisoned John (*Ant.* 18.119) and where his father, Herod the Great, had 'built a palace with magnificently spacious and beautiful apartments' (*BJ* 7.175), then it may well be that it was during the winter season, the only time of year

simply because he takes the 'four months to harvest' to require a feast between January (ch. 4) and Passover (ch. 6). But on it he erects his fantastic superstructure of parallels with the book of Esther which according to Mishnah *Megillah* was in the second century read exclusively at this feast. Cf. his earlier 'The Identity and Date of the Unnamed Feast of John 5.1' in H. Goedicke, ed., *Near Eastern Studies in Honor of William Foxwell Albright*, Baltimore and London 1971, 43–56.

[50]Above, ch. II, pp. 54–9.

[51]*Jesus and His Story*, 71.

at which such a place, even though well above the level of the Dead Sea, would have been agreeable for entertaining VIPs from Galilee. So in agreement with Matthew we may not be far wrong in setting John's death early in the following year.

Our next time-reference, in John 6.4, is once again to the approach of Passover. This, as we have seen, makes specific what could be deduced from the mention of the 'green grass' in Mark's description of the same incident, the feeding of the five thousand. That Jesus spent a Passover at the height of his public ministry in Galilee when he did *not* go up to Jerusalem could also be inferred from Luke 13.1: 'At that very time there were some people present who told him about the Galileans whose blood Pilate had mixed with their sacrifices.' It is impossible to identify or date this incident from Josephus, though it is thoroughly in line with other things he tells us of Pilate's character (*BJ* 2.169–77; *Ant.* 18.55–62). But it is probably to be placed at Passover-time, which was the only feast at which the people had to be involved in the killing of their own animals.[52] Another incident which could bear out a Passover spent in Galilee is that of the temple-tax in Matt. 17.24. The collectors of the two-drachma tax are in Capernaum, and according to the Mishnah this annual levy was made in the month before Passover.[53] Again it is characteristic that John supplies the firm date, while three separate Synoptic traditions (Mark, L and M) each drop hints on which little could be based but which independently confirm it.

After the desert feeding comes a section of the gospel story which is both remarkably well documented and unusually confused. There is a strong sequence of events, a feeding in the wilderness, a crossing of the lake by the disciples, Jesus's walking on the water, a discourse about bread, and a questioning of the faith of the twelve, which is repeated in whole or in part in Mark 6, Mark 8 and John 6. I shall be looking at this more closely later,[54] but here would simply say that I believe the most satisfactory explanation to be that these represent three traditions of a

[52]Cf. Philo, *Spec. leg.* 2.145; *Quaest. in Ex.* 1.10; and M. *Pes.* 5.6: 'An Israelite slaughtered his [own] offering and the priest caught the blood.' Cf. P. Winter, *On the Trial of Jesus*, Berlin 1961, 176f., and the bibliography given, especially Blinzler, 'Die Niedermetzelung von Galiläern durch Pilatus', *NovT* 2, 1957–8, 24–49, who actually dates the incident (32) to Monday, 18 April, AD 29 (Nisan 14), which would fit the chronology proposed at the close of this chapter.

[53]'On the first day of Adar they give warning of the Shekel dues. . . . On the 15th the tables of the money-changers were set up in the provinces; and on the 25th they were set up in the temple' (M. *Shek.* 1.1, 3). In Matthew the incident is placed after the disciples' return from the north, and therefore apparently *after* Passover, but it is evidently a floating story which he has inserted into the Markan narrative after Mark 9.33a.

[54]See below, ch. V, pp. 190–211.

critical transition in the ministry of Jesus, which was vividly but variously remembered and to which John alone gives us the interpretative clue in the attempt to make Jesus king (6.15). The two accounts of the feeding, of the five thousand and of the four thousand, are probably best regarded as doublets; so Luke appears to have recognized by omitting the whole of the second sequence, though leaving traces of the tradition that he chooses not to use, like the reference to Bethsaida in 9.10 (cf. Mark 6.45; 8.22). John's account has features that are paralleled both in Mark 6 and in Mark 8. But it is the chain of events following the feeding, including the Transfiguration, which is specified (quite unusually for the Synoptists) as occurring a week later than the testing of the disciples' faith (Mark 9.2 = Matt. 17.1: 'after six days'; Luke 9.28: 'after about eight days'), that introduces one of the most bewildering sections of the public ministry. For at this point John fails us, and for the most part Luke too. We have to try to piece together as best we may the two sequences from the tradition represented in Mark and Matthew – and the fact that they do not recognize them as doublets (if that is what they are) must diminish our confidence in their chronology.

According to the first sequence, Jesus and his disciples make excursions outside Israelite territory to the region of Tyre and Sidon in Phoenicia, and thence in a wide circle through the territory of the Decapolis back to the Sea of Galilee (Mark 7.24, 31; Matt. 15.21, 29 abbreviates and conflates). According to the second sequence, they visit 'the villages of Caesarea Philippi' (Mark 8.27; Matt. 16.13), a thoroughly Hellenized area which was also at that period regarded as belonging to Phoenicia,[55] and go from there through Galilee (Mark 9.33; Matt. 17.24). During this period Jesus seems to have been taking deliberately evasive action, and it is reiterated in Mark that he did not wish his presence to be known (7.24; 9.30) or his actions reported (7.36; 8.26). No reason for this secrecy is given, and indeed all trace of it has disappeared from Matthew and Luke. John alone provides a clue, by saying in 6.15 that he 'withdrew', or more probably 'fled' (for the well-attested variant φεύγει[56] would scarcely have been invented), from the dangerous political implications of the crowd's intentions. Since John has no interest in the Gentile mission he omits any reference to Jesus leaving Jewish territory, but he too says that at this time, after the defection of many of his followers (6.66), Jesus 'went about' in Galilee (7.1) preserving his seclusion (7.4, 10) and biding his time before appearing again in public.

[55] M. Avi-Yonah, 'Historical Geography of Palestine', *Compendia* I.1, 103.
[56] ℵ lat sy[c]. It is adopted by Brown, *John*, ad loc.

During this period there are persistent intimations in all the Gospels that he is beginning to set his face and prepare his disciples for Jerusalem and for his death (Mark 8.31–9.32 and pars.). It is Judaea that calls and looms (John 7.1–9). And it is to this time that there apparently belongs a saying from the L tradition which Luke, who telescopes the whole period drastically, sets on the journey to Jerusalem but which must come from when Jesus was still within Herod's jurisdiction:

> At that time a number of Pharisees came to him and said, 'You should leave this place and go on your way; Herod is out to kill you.' He replied, 'Go and tell that fox, "Listen: today and tomorrow I shall be casting out devils and working cures; on the third day I reach my goal." However, I must be on my way today and tomorrow and the next day, because it is unthinkable for a prophet to meet his death anywhere but in Jerusalem' (13.31–33).

The motivation of the Pharisees is left ambiguous. Their solicitation, though seemingly well intentioned, may be an attempt to lure Jesus from Galilee to Judaea, and in that case the passage is parallel to the exchange in John 7.3–9 in which his brothers urge him, from whatever different motives, to make the same journey. But in each case Jesus shows himself determined to take his time. His 'hour' and his 'goal' cannot be rushed, though their place is determined.

When finally he does move from Galilee to Judaea, which is recognized as the turning-point of the ministry in all the traditions (Mark 10.1; Matt. 19.1; Luke 9.51) and is reflected in the Acts summaries (10.37; 13.31), it is John again who alone provides us with a date – the feast of Tabernacles in October (7.2, 10). In the Synoptists there is absolutely no indication of the passage of time between the Passover spent in Galilee and the same festival twelve months later. This is a long span, common to all the traditions. It is John who breaks it up for us with references to the feasts for which Jesus was present in Jerusalem, Tabernacles in ch. 7 and the Dedication or Encaenia in ch. 10. While the former was celebrated in booths out of doors, the latter, which fell in December, is specifically noted by the evangelist to be in winter, and Jesus takes advantage of the shelter of Solomon's cloister (10.22f.; cf. Jer. 36.22 of the same month in Jerusalem!). Where he spent the ten weeks or so that separated the two festivals we are not told, but there is no indication in any of the Gospels that he returned to Galilee once he had left. Indeed the challenge, both in the triple and the double traditions, to renounce family and leave home as an integral part of denying oneself and taking up the cross, which Jesus laid upon every would-be disciple (Mark 10.29f. = Matt. 19.29 = Luke 18.29f; Matt. 10.37f. = Luke 14.26f.) and which Peter and the rest claimed to have followed literally (Mark 10.28 = Matt. 19.27 = Luke 18.28), cannot be understood unless he himself had made the same break. In fact the last references in Mark to 'the house' in Capernaum that for him was home (2.1; etc.) occur shortly before this saying (9.28, 33; 10.10). Henceforth he is no longer to be found ἐν τῇ οἰκίᾳ or ἐν οἴκῳ, 'at home' but ἐν τῇ ὁδῷ, 'on the road' (10.32), the same sequence being preserved also in Matthew (13.1, 36; 17.25, followed by 19.27 and 20.17). There is a similar transition in Luke's independent tradition (9.57), and it is in his very next verse that he records the Q saying (set by Matthew, less probably, in Galilee [8.18–20]) that while the foxes have their holes and birds their roosts 'the Son of man has nowhere to lay his head' (9.58), a saying which Matthew follows by two others about burying one's father and saying good-bye to the people at home (9.59–62).

If we ask where this time 'on the road' took them, which Luke recognizes must have lasted for a considerable period, occupying, as it does, over a third of his gospel (9.51–18.14), we are given most imprecise indications by the Synoptists. Mark says, according to the best texts, that 'he came into the regions of Judaea and Transjordan' (10.1); Matthew (19.1) says that 'he came into the region of Judaea across Jordan' (which is strictly non-existent); and Luke, after noting his rejection by a Samaritan village (9.52–6), tells us only (and that much later) that on the way to Jerusalem he travelled 'through the midst of Samaria and Galilee' (17.11) – in that order! In so far as this is intelligible, it could mean along the borderland between the two[57] or simply, as in John 4.4, that he took the route down the spine of the country rather than through the Decapolis and Jordan valley. All we know is that finally all the Synoptists have Jesus coming up to Jerusalem from the Jordan valley via Jericho (Mark 10.46 and pars.), Bethphage, Bethany and the Mount of Olives (Mark 11.1 and pars.).

John as usual is much more specific, separating out what in the Synoptists looks like a conflation of various journeys. He also records Jesus as being in Judaea (for Tabernacles and the Encaenia) and in Transjordan. After the second visit to Jerusalem in midwinter he says specifically that 'Jesus withdrew again across the Jordan, to the place where John had been baptizing earlier. There he stayed (ἔμενεν), while

[57]So, probably correctly, RSV, NEB, TEV. Cf. below, ch. VI, p. 214.

crowds came to him. . . . Many came to believe in him there' (10.40–42). This seems to correspond to the note in Mark 10.1: 'He came into the regions of Judaea and Transjordan; and when a crowd gathered round him once again he followed his usual practice and taught them.' John, characteristically, records the actual place, Bethany beyond Jordan (cf. 1.28), and tells us that Jesus 'went away *again* beyond Jordan'. Unfortunately the expression is ambiguous. It could mean that he revisited the spot where he had been with John the Baptist at the beginning or that he had already been staying there between Tabernacles and Dedication. Since the former occasion was so remote, the second interpretation is just possibly the more likely.[58] In any case it seems probable that if Jesus and his disciples were to spend the winter months with no fixed abode they would have headed for the warmer climate of the Jordan valley. For winter was no time to be out in the hill-country of Judaea (Mark 13.18 = Matt. 24.20). And the welcome they were to find where John had worked made it an obvious place of retreat.

From the Synoptists we should learn nothing of any movement by Jesus from the Jordan valley until his last journey to Jerusalem shortly before Passover. But John again is much more specific. Some time prior to that Jesus makes a reluctant visit from Bethany in Peraea to Bethany in Judaea (11.1–44), whose location the evangelist could not have given more precisely (11.18), and he tells us exactly where he stayed. Then, following the furore provoked by the raising of Lazarus, a formal meeting of the Sanhedrin is convened (11.47), as a result of which Jesus is publicly declared a wanted man and a warrant, and doubtless a reward, is put out for his arrest. Such a proceeding would be in line with the early rabbinic tradition (b. *Sanh.* 43a) of a gap of forty days between Jesus' incrimination and condemnation[59] for which

[58]So Westcott, *John* II, 73. Interestingly the word *πάλιν* appears twice, both times obscurely, in the corresponding verse in Mark 10.1 (smoothed over in the NEB translation); both instances have disappeared from Matthew and Luke. We read that on Jesus' arrival in Judaea and Transjordan 'crowds came together to him again and as he was used to he taught them again.' This must presumably be interpreted as it stands in Mark's Gospel to mean 'as he had in Galilee'. But H. E. Edwards' question is at least in order: 'Who are these "multitudes"? Up to the present the whole public ministry of our Lord has taken place in Galilee, and we have no record of any preaching in Judaea or, indeed, of any visit to Judaea. Yet there are "multitudes" all ready to come out to meet him, and the significant adverb "again" is twice repeated. This is one of those hints, dropped by the Evangelist, as it were, in passing, which show that there had been a Judaean ministry as well as a Galilean ministry' (*The Disciple Who Wrote These Things*, 170).

[59]See below, ch. VI, pp. 225f.

the Synoptists leave no room but John does. If we may use this datum then the visit to Bethany would probably have taken place in February.

As a result of the court summons John tells us that 'Jesus no longer went about publicly in Judaea, but left that region for the country bordering on the desert, and came to a town called Ephraim, where he stayed (διέτριβεν, if that is the right reading) with his disciples' (11.54). Again it was a place where presumably he knew he would be safe. It is to be located, in all probability, some miles north-east of Bethel,[60] bordering on the barren hills leading down to the Jordan. Identifying the site with 'Ein Samiya, Albright wrote more than fifty years ago:

> In this beautiful valley, warm and lovely in February and March, with an abundance of water, and countless grottoes, Jesus could pass a quiet month or so before going up to Jerusalem for the Passover. Moreover, the valley is one of the hardest places in Palestine to reach, since it is far removed from the roads and accessible only by an arduous descent over the worst path in Palestine. Jesus could find here the seclusion he wished, as well as the surroundings necessary for the band of disciples.[61]

The place is now approachable by road but remains isolated and strangely peaceful.

Yet it was not to be a long stay, for already Passover was at hand and the pilgrims were beginning to come up for the preliminary purifications (11.55f.). Then with another precise time-reference, where the Synoptists give us none, John tells us that Jesus went back to Bethany, to the home of Lazarus, Martha and Mary, six days before Passover (12.1f.). Counting back inclusively from John's date for Passover, the Friday, yields not Saturday, but Sunday, and this is

[60]Cf. II Sam. 13.23; II Chron. 13.19; Josephus, *BJ* 4.551.

[61]'Ophrah and Ephraim', *AASOR* 4, 1922–3, 124–33 (127). Albright is followed by Avi-Yonah, *Map of Roman Palestine*, Oxford 1940, and by Schein, *Following the Way*, 143, 213f. See also B. Schwank, 'Ephraim in Joh. 11.54' in *Évangile*, 377–83, who insists that John, unlike Luke, knows Palestine and must be taken very seriously on geographical detail; but strangely he does not attempt to locate Ephraim! Previously it was identified with et-Taiybe, a few miles further south (so Dalman, *Sacred Sites*, 217–20; F.-M. Abel, *Géographie de la Palestine*, Paris 1933–8, II, 318, 403; Kopp, *Holy Places*, 254–6). But this is a village set on a hill at 2,800 ft. and would not make an obvious place of concealment, especially in winter; nor is it 'on the edge of the wilderness'. 'Ein Samiya at half the height is in a secluded and fertile valley fed by a copious spring (now supplying Ramallah with its water), which leads down through the wilderness to the Jordan. There are numerous caves for shelter and the ruins of a Roman aqueduct. It is an altogether more convincing site.

almost certainly correct. Otherwise Jesus and his disciples would have made the journey of over twenty miles on the sabbath, and there is no ground for supposing that he would have breached the sabbath law for this reason.[62] This means that the entry into Jerusalem the following day (12.12) would be on the Monday and not, as in later ecclesiastical tradition, Palm Sunday. At the close of that day Mark and Matthew, confirming John's tradition, say that he returned to lodge at Bethany (Mark 11.11; Matt. 21.17; Luke has him go each evening to the Mount of Olives, 21.37). The Synoptists of course introduce at this point the cleansing of the temple, the cursing of the fig-tree and the question about authority (Mark 11.12–33 and pars.), all of which fit better, as we have argued, into the period when Jesus was still acting very much under the Baptist's influence.

The lament over Jerusalem, which Matthew (23.37–39) inserts into the teaching in the temple that follows, but which Luke (13.34f.) has added, apparently by catchword, to an earlier saying about a prophet not perishing except in Jerusalem (13.33), is strong testimony in the Synoptic tradition to the fact that Jesus had tried on previous occasions to win a following in the capital:

> O Jerusalem, Jerusalem, the city that murders the prophets and stones the messengers sent to her! How often have I longed to gather your children, as a hen gathers her brood under her wings; but you would not let me.

Moreover, earlier in the chapter in which Luke places it he has the parable of a fig-tree in a vineyard (13.6–9), whose central figure, as in that of the vine-dressers (Mark 12.1–12 and pars.), is scarcely intelligible unless it is intended to refer to Jesus himself:

> A man had a fig-tree growing in his vineyard; and he came looking for fruit on it, but found none. So he said to the vine-dresser, 'Look here! For the last three years I have come looking for fruit on this fig-tree without finding any. Cut it down. Why should it go on using up the soil?' But he replied, 'Leave it, sir, this one year while I dig round it and manure it. And if it bears next season, well and good; if not, you shall have it down.'

The Semitic idiom 'it is now three years since I have come' implies, on the Jewish reckoning, that two years have now elapsed since Jesus first

[62]So Lindars, *John*, 415. But to say that the date probably attached originally to the triumphal entry rather than the arrival at Bethany is entirely arbitrary.

made his appeal to the nation. Indeed he may specifically be referring back to the prophetic action of cursing the barren fig-tree of Israel, which, we have argued above, properly belongs with the cleansing of the temple just that time ago. A further year of grace is requested as a last chance for repentance. But it was not to be taken. That spring, as the Markan parable of the fig-tree (13.28f. and pars.) vividly portrays, things were bursting to a head: the decisive moment was at hand. All these parables appear to belong to the final period of teaching in Jerusalem, and the Lukan story provides further confirmation that the Synoptic tradition implicitly presupposes the two-year chronology of the ministry that John makes explicit.

Finally, we come to the chronology of the passion itself. There are two specific time-references in the Synoptic tradition. The first is to 'two days before Passover' (Mark 14.1 = Matt. 26.2; though Luke here is typically vague in 22.1), when, according to Mark (14.3–9) and Matthew (26.6–13), Jesus is once again in Bethany for the anointing (which John had set four days earlier) and when the chief priests and scribes, casting around for a plan to seize him by stealth (Mark 14.1f. and pars.), receive the unexpected windfall of Judas's offer (14.10f. and pars.). The next reference is to 'the first day of Unleavened Bread, when they sacrificed the Passover' (Mark 14.12 and pars.),[63] and the last supper (a Passover meal) is prepared for that evening. John has a clearly different tradition, that the last supper was eaten the night before Passover (13.1),[64] and he consistently affirms that the Paschal meal had yet to be eaten when Jesus was being tried (18.28; cf. 13.29) and that he was executed on the eve of Passover (19.14). Where Mark (15.42) and John (19.31) agree is that Jesus died on the Friday

[63]Actually, of course, the Passover was killed, as opposed to being eaten, *before* the first day of Unleavened Bread. Matthew (26.17), apparently knowing better, omits 'when they sacrificed the Passover' but still presupposes that the disciples were *preparing* for Passover on the first day of the feast! Luke (22.7) if anything compounds the confusion by speaking of '*the* day of Unleavened Bread, on which the Passover had to be sacrificed', as if there was only one. This is not the sort of carelessness which is to be found in John. Cf. Askwith, *Historical Value of the Fourth Gospel*, 227: 'If . . . the Gospel of Mark is inaccurate here, it may be also inaccurate in making the Last Supper a paschal celebration, this inaccuracy being taken over in Matthew and by St Luke.'

[64]From the number of parallels with the Synoptic accounts (cf. Brown, *John* II, 557), despite the absence in John of the institution of the Eucharist, there can be no doubt that they are both referring to the same meal. John Lightfoot, *Horae Hebraicae* II, 334–40, maintained that the supper of John 13.1 was to be identified with the meal at Bethany at the house of Simon the leper two days before Passover (Matt. 26.2; Mark 14.3), thus introducing two anointings at Bethany at four days' interval, one of Jesus' feet and the other of his head! The version in Luke 7.36–50 would be yet a third, though he makes no effort to correlate them.

afternoon, the eve of sabbath. Where they disagree is whether Nisan 14, the day on which the Paschal lambs were killed, fell that year on a Thursday, with the festival beginning on the Thursday night, as the Synoptists say, or on a Friday, with the festival beginning on the Friday night and thus coinciding, as John says, with the sabbath (19.31).

This is an enormously wide-ranging question, full discussion of which would take us far afield. One may perhaps begin with the observation that if the tradition had stood in the Synoptics that the entire proceedings against Jesus were got out of the way before the festival began – as does the *intention* that they should be (Mark 14.2 and pars.)[65] – and the tradition that it all went on during the festival had stood in John, no one would seriously have questioned that the Synoptists were right. As it is, it is only because of the presumption that the Synoptists must be given preference that the reverse is so vehemently argued. A case can be and has been made for it – notably by Jeremias,[66] who is supported by Barrett[67] – though I believe it to be a *tour de force*. With sufficient ingenuity it can be shown at each individual point that what is recorded as going on would not have been illegal during the feast – or at any rate would have been just as illegal on the eve of the feast – and even that it *must* have been done on the feast-day.

For this last point the procedure is invoked for the execution of a 'rebellious elder', assuming for the time being that the later evidence of the Mishnah can be used for this period.[68] According to *Sanh.* 11.4, 'he was kept in guard until one of the [three] Feasts and he was put to death on one of the [three] Feasts, for it is written "And all the people shall hear and fear, and do no more presumptuously" (Deut. 17.13).' But this refers to a specific case during the period when the court sat at Jamnia (AD 70–118), and Rabbi Judah gave a contrary opinion: 'They should not delay his judgment but put him to death at once.'[69] There is

[65]It has often been suggested that ἐν τῇ ἑορτῇ in this verse means not 'during the festival' but 'in the presence of the festival crowd'. But this is an unnatural way of taking the phrase and cannot be based on its meaning this in John 2.23 and 7.11, as Jeremias argues (*The Eucharistic Words of Jesus*, ET London and New York ²1966, 72). Moreover it scarcely helps the chronology. The festival crowd is very much present during the trial in the Synoptists (Matt. 27.17–25; Mark 15.8–15; Luke 23.4, 13, 18–25, 27). In Matt. 27.24 there is the very θόρυβος or riot that the Synoptic timing was intended to avert. In John, by contrast, the crowd is not mentioned, only the leadership.

[66]*Eucharistic Words*, 49–84.

[67]*John*, 48–51.

[68]On this see below ch. VI, pp. 251f.

[69]Jeremias, *Eucharistic Words*, 79, cites at this point not the Mishnah but the Tosefta (*Sanh.* 11.7), where the provision is extended: 'A stubborn and rebellious son, a

no indication whatever that this ruling was earlier invoked in the case of Jesus, who was not 'an elder who rebels against the decision of the court' (*Sanh*. 11.2–4, which clearly applies, as it was later interpreted, to a professional rabbi)[70] but an untrained layman (John 7.14f.; cf. Mark 6.2 and par.). Furthermore, according to the Mishnah (loc. cit.), the punishment for a rebellious elder is strangulation, and this is never associated with Jesus even in Jewish tradition. This crime is I believe quite irrelevant to the case of Jesus, and therefore to the day of his execution. Indeed the burden of proof must lie overwhelmingly on those who wish to argue that the whole process of the arrest, trial and execution took place during the feast as officially celebrated by the temple authorities (whatever calendar may or may not have been observed by sectarian groups). This applies particularly to its first day (Nisan 15), on which *all* work was explicitly forbidden (Lev. 23.6f.). Moreover, it was specifically laid down that an execution could not take precedence over a sabbath (b. *Sanh*. 35a–b) or a feast-day (36a). For 'any act that is culpable on the sabbath . . . is culpable also on a festival-day [including, specifically, 'sitting in judgment'][71]. . . . A festival-day differs from the sabbath in naught save in the preparing of needful food' (M. *Betz*. 5.2).

It is indeed possible, though one cannot say more, that Jesus and his disciples had themselves eaten the Passover the night before in accordance with some other calendar. Attempts have been made to differentiate between Galilean and Jerusalemite or Sadducaic and Pharisaic reckonings, and, more recently, to argue that Jesus and his disciples were following the solar calendar observed at Qumran, by which Passover was always kept on a Tuesday night.[72] The argument is

defiant elder, a beguiler to idolatry, one who leads a town astray, a false prophet, and perjurers, are not killed at once, but brought up to the great court at Jerusalem and kept in prison till a feast and killed at a feast, for it is written: "And all the people shall hear and fear, and do no more presumptuously"' (tr. H. Danby, *Tractate Sanhedrin: Mishnah and Tosefta*, London and New York 1919, 111). This judgment is attributed to R. Meir (slightly later in the second century AD than R. Aqiba), though again opposed by R. Judah. That the ruling of the Mishnah, not to mention the Tosefta, applied in the time of Jesus remains to be demonstrated. And even referring the *baraita* b. *Sanh*. 43a (see below, pp. 225f.) to a different Yeshu, Jeremias cannot possibly use it to show that anyone was executed '*at* the feast'; it clearly specifies 'the *eve* of Passover'.

[70]This is fully admitted by J. Bowker, *Jesus and the Pharisees*, Cambridge and New York 1973, 46–51, who nevertheless seeks to argue this case.

[71]So earlier Philo, *Migr. Abr*. 91.

[72]A. Jaubert, *The Date of the Last Supper*, ET New York 1965; supported by E. Ruckstuhl, *Chronology of the Last Days of Jesus*, ET 1965. For criticism cf. P. Benoit's review in *RB* 65, 1958, 590–4, reprinted as 'The Date of the Last Supper' in his *Jesus and the Gospel* I, ET 1973, 87–93; Blinzler, 'Qumran-Kalendar and Passions

undoubtedly clever, but there is no evidence that Jesus belonged to such a sectarian group.[73] Indeed, on all the other occasions he shared in the publicly celebrated feasts in the temple (cf. especially John 7.14, 37). Nor is there a hint in the Gospels that the arrest of Jesus after the supper was not followed overnight by his trial and death. We should have to find a reason why *all* the evangelists shortened the period so drastically and created the legal difficulties of which ever since scholars have accused them or sought to clear them.

Of course, whichever night the last supper was held, it would have had Paschal associations which could have led the Synoptists actually to identify it with the Passover meal. The most obvious objection to the supper *being* the Passover is the complete absence in all the traditions of any reference to the lamb (with which Jesus might more obviously have identified his flesh/body than the bread). Jeremias' attempts to show how, despite his chronology, John's description of the supper implies that it was a Passover are very weak.[74] The word used for 'recline' (ἀνάκεισθαι) in John 13.23, 28, to which he attaches very specific significance, is used frequently in the Gospels of meals in general (including the supper at Bethany in John 12.2). The ψωμίον, sop, in 13.26–30 is in all probability a piece of bread (so NEB), whereas the Passover *haggadah* mentions only the dipping of the bitter herbs in the sauce. And the fact that the meal was in Jerusalem (18.1) at night (13.30; cf. I Cor. 11.23) cannot be used to *imply* that it was the Passover, even though the Passover had to be eaten within the city bounds and after dark. Rather I would agree with Brown's cautious conclusion that

For unknown reasons, on Thursday evening, the 14th of Nisan by

---

chronologie', *ZNW* 49, 1958, 238–51; *Der Prozess Jesu*, [4]1969, 109–26; M. Black, 'The Arrest and Trial of Jesus and the Date of the Last Supper' in A. J. B. Higgins, ed., *New Testament Essays; Studies in Memory of T. W. Manson*, 1959, 19–33; R. E. Brown, 'The Date of the Last Supper', *The Bible Today* 11, 1964, 727–33; reprinted in his *NT Essays*, 160–7.

[73]All that can be advanced, e.g., by Ruckstuhl, *Chronology*, 117–24, are *contacts* of Jesus and his disciples with the Essene tradition, e.g. via John the Baptist, and the absence of any polemic against, or indeed mention of, the Essenes in the Gospels, in notable contrast with the Pharisees and Sadducees. Yet, as he admits, 'By His attitudes and by His teaching, Jesus challenged their existence and goals as well. His freedom from the Mosaic law, his lack of respect for the laws of ritual purity, His teaching of love for one's enemies, His contacts with sinners, the rejects and the infirm, separated Him not only from the Pharisees but also from the Essenes' (119f.).

[74]But not as weak as the very strained efforts to demonstrate the same (on the Tuesday night) in Jaubert, 'The Calendar of Qumran and the Passion Narrative in John' in Charlesworth, ed., *John and Qumran*, 62–75.

the official calendar, the day before Passover, Jesus ate with his disciples a meal that had Passover characteristics. The Synoptists or their tradition, influenced by these Passover characteristics, too quickly made the assumption that the day was actually Passover; John, on the other hand, preserved the correct information.[75]

It is difficult to believe, with Lindars,[76] that 'the death of Jesus on the eve of the Passover is a purely Johannine invention'.[77] It is clearly stated in an early Jewish *baraita* (b. *Sanh*. 43a) that he was 'hung on the eve of Passover', the Florentine manuscript adding 'and on the eve of Sabbath'. The custom reported in all the Gospels of releasing a prisoner at the feast (John alone specifying Passover) *could* be reflected in the reference in the Mishnah to killing the lamb 'for one whom they have promised to bring out of prison' (*Pes*. 8.6),[78] and this would only make sense, if he were to eat it, on the Johannine chronology. In the extra-canonical Christian tradition too Jesus is delivered to the people, according to the Gospel of Peter (2.5), 'on the day before the unleavened bread, their feast', though this historically worthless document is a mishmash of Gospel traditions, including that of the fourth (e.g. 5.14; 6.21, 24; 14.59f.).

That John was at this point deliberately setting out to correct the dating of the Synoptists is without any trace in the material, and the only reason which has been advanced is that he is switching the date and time of the crucifixion in order to make it coincide for theological reasons with the slaughter of the Passover lambs. But this is questionable on both chronological and theological grounds.

According to Exod. 12.6 the Paschal lamb had to be slaughtered 'between the two evenings' (NEB 'between dusk and dark').[79] But by New Testament times it was no longer done at home but by the priests

[75]*John* II, 556.

[76]*John*, 446.

[77]Furthermore Dodd argues (*Historical Tradition*, 110f.) that the church calendar in the province of Asia, by which in the second century the passion and resurrection of Christ was celebrated not according to the day of the week, as became the universal custom, but on Nisan 14 as the date of his death, was grounded not on appeal to the authority of the Fourth Gospel but to uninterrupted tradition derived from the fathers of their church, including John but also many others (Eusebius, *HE* 5.24.1–8; Theodoret, *Haer. fab*. 3). However, the interpretation of this controversy is itself highly controversial and nothing can securely be rested on it.

[78]See further below, ch. VI, pp. 261.

[79]For the rabbinic interpretation of this, cf. b. *Pes*. 58a and Finegan, *Biblical Chronology*, 13f.

in the temple[80] and the great numbers of pilgrims meant that it had to be started earlier. Josephus (*BJ* 6.423) says it was done 'from the ninth to the eleventh hour', between 3 p.m. and 5 p.m., that is, after Jesus would have been dead. But the Mishnah (*Pes.* 5.1) records arrangements for it to be started earlier on the eve of a sabbath. Usually the evening offering was slaughtered each day at 2.30 p.m. and offered at 3.30 p.m. (Josephus, *Ant.* 14.65, 'about the ninth hour'). On the eve of Passover it was slaughtered at 1.30 p.m. and offered at 2.30 p.m., 'whether it was a week day or the sabbath'. But 'if the eve of Passover fell on the eve of sabbath, it was slaughtered at 12.30 p.m. and offered at 1.30 p.m. and, after this, the Passover-offering [was slaughtered].' If Josephus is presupposing the *normal* Passover timing, then half an hour elapsed between the offering of the daily sacrifice and the beginning of the slaughter of the lambs. When therefore the eve of Passover coincided with the eve of sabbath, as John says it did that year, the slaughtering would have been done between 2 p.m. and 4 p.m. If these regulations were then in force,[81] the correspondence with Jesus' actual death would thus be approximately right. But it is hard to believe that readers of the Gospel in Asia Minor could be expected to know these details or to guess that the synchronicity was the significant point, when no attempt is made by the evangelist to explain it or to draw attention to it – especially when he is so insistent in drawing attention to the customs of Palestinian Judaism elsewhere. Above all, as Ruckstuhl pertinently asks, 'Why did he not mention the hour of Jesus' death that was linked with the slaughter of the paschal lambs, while he indicated the time of his condemnation (19.14)?'[82]

Theologically too there is little ground for supposing that this is the point that John is intending to make or asking the reader to see.[83] It is Mark (14.12) and Luke (22.7), not John, who draw attention to the day on which the Passover lamb had to be killed. If it were really with this in mind that he is altering the entire chronology of the passion one might think that he would at least have alluded to it. Moreover there is no compelling evidence that he sees the death of Christ in terms of the

[80]Cf. Jeremias, *Jerusalem in the Time of Jesus*, 78f.

[81]According to the (much earlier) Qumran Temple Scroll the Passover was sacrificed *before* the daily offering (J. Milgrom, *BA* 41, 1978, 115f.). In Jubilees 49.10 the Passover offering can start 'from the third part of the day', i.e. 2 p.m. onwards, but in 49.19 this is further specified as meaning 'in the evening, at sunset'. Philo, *Spec. leg.* 2.145, says simply that the sacrifice took place 'from noon till eventide'.

[82]*Chronology of the Last Days of Jesus*, 16.

[83]Cf. again Scott Holland, *The Fourth Gospel*, 194f.

sacrifice of the Paschal lamb. The sole reference to Jesus as the Lamb of God (with no mention of his death) occurs back in ch. 1 and there is no ground there for supposing that the Paschal lamb is particularly in mind. Only in John 19.36, 'no bone of his shall be broken', could there be any obvious allusion to the Paschal ritual (Exod. 12.46; Num. 9.12),[84] but here the reference to scripture is more probably to Ps. 34.20 describing the sufferings of the righteous one: 'The Lord delivers him out of them all. He guards every bone of his body, and not one of them is broken' (*οὐ συντριβήσεται* – exactly as in John).[85] The symbolism of Christ as the Paschal sacrifice, drawn out by Paul in I Cor. 5.7, is more likely to have been derived from reflection on the chronology to which John bears witness than so early to have created it.

But finally there is also the astronomical evidence, which may lead us to ask in closing whether it is possible to set any absolute dating on the years of Jesus's ministry. This is far too complex a subject to go into in detail, even if I were competent, and all I can do is to summarize drastically the work of others.[86] What we are looking for is a year when the afternoon on which the Passover was sacrificed (Nisan 14) fell on a Thursday (as the Synoptists say) or a Friday (as John says). Within the outside limits available (AD 27–34), only three years in fact present themselves: 27 when it was on a Thursday, 30 when it was on a Friday, and 33 when it would have been on a Friday unless, as is probable that year, an extra month had been intercalated, when it would have fallen

[84]Echoes have also been seen in the reference to 'hyssop' in 19.29, which played a part in the Passover observance (Exod. 12.22), though for an entirely different purpose; but I agree with the NEB that *ὑσσώπῳ* is probably not what John intended to write anyhow (see below, ch. VI, p. 279). Attention has also been drawn to the 'mingled blood' of 19.34 by J. M. Ford, '"Mingled Blood" from the Side of Christ (John 19.34)', *NTS* 15, 1968–9, 337f.; but if Paschal allusions were present in John's mind he does nothing to alert the reader to them in his studied comment on the incident.

[85]See Dodd, *According to the Scriptures*, 1952, 98f.; *Historical Tradition*, 42–4, who points out that all the other Johannine passion testimonia are from the Psalms or the prophets, not from the Pentateuch. The same point was made by Hort, who said in a letter to W. Milligan, 'I wish I could see as clearly as you do that St. John treats our Lord as the Paschal Lamb at all. Why are the quotations so little distinctive? . . . the want of clear evidence is to me most perplexing' (A. Hort, *Life and Letters of F. J. A. Hort* II, 221).

[86]Cf. especially J. K. Fotheringham, 'The Evidence of Astronomy and Technical Chronology for the Date of the Crucifixion', *JTS* 35, 1934, 146–62; R. A. Parker and W. H. Dubberstein, *Babylonian Chronology 626 BC – AD 75*, Brown University Studies 19, Providence, R.I. 1956, 46 (for the calendrical tables); G. B. Caird, 'Chronology of the NT', *Interpreter's Dictionary of the Bible*, New York and Nashville 1962, I, 602f.; Finegan, *Biblical Chronology*, 291–6.

on a Saturday.[87] 27, it is generally agreed, is simply too early to fit plausibly with the other evidence and would in any case require a one-year ministry which, as we have seen, the Synoptists implicitly deny. Of the other two 30 is widely accepted as the more likely, 33 (even if the day was right) making the chronology of the apostolic age almost impossibly tight. In either case John's day of the week is vindicated and that of the Synoptists effectively excluded. As Finegan puts it, 'in terms of the standard Jewish calendar, the representation of the day in the Fourth Gospel appears to be confirmed.'[88]

If then we may provisionally accept 30 as the date of the last Passover, when Nisan 14 fell on Friday April 7, then the first Passover will be that of 28.[89] There is an element of doubt whether in that year it was observed on Tuesday March 30 or, more probably, Wednesday April 28. This turns again on whether an extra month was inserted, as had to happen every few years (seven in every nineteen to be precise)[90] when the lunar cycle got too far out of step with the solar and Nisan

[87]Cf. Parker and Dubberstein, *Babylonian Chronology*, 46. It is remarkable that Stauffer, who offers an extremely detailed chronology of the life of Jesus (*Jesus and his Story*, 17f.) takes no account of the calendrical evidence for the date of his death, while relying on the far more dubious astronomical data for determining his birth. He opts for 32 as the date of the crucifixion (when Nisan 14 fell on Monday!) solely because he believes Pilate's insecurity attested in John 19.12f. reflects the fall of Sejanus on 28 October 31 (108). But this is entirely hypothetical, and the ministry of Jesus is then extended to fill the time available between 28 (his dating for the 15th year of Tiberius in Luke 3.1) and 32, including no less than five Passovers (and what he calls 'ten quiet months' slipped in between John 4 and 5!). The schema reflects the combination of erudition and arbitrariness of judgment which, alas, makes his book so much less valuable than it might have been.

[88]*Biblical Chronology*, 296. Too much weight cannot however be placed upon such calculations. The dates reflect the 'true' days of the appearance of the new moon which marked Nisan 1 (and therefore of Nisan 14). But this was determined by observation and not calculation (for a summary of the procedure, cf. M. D. Herr, 'The Calendar', *Compendia* I.2, 845–50), and if it was missed (e.g., by being clouded over) the first of the month, and subsequently the Passover, could have been celebrated one day late (though never more than one). This means that Nisan 14 might have been observed on a Thursday when it should have been on a Wednesday, as was the case in 28 and 31 if a month was intercalated (otherwise not till 34). The calendrical data can only be used to reinforce other probabilities, though they can eliminate some. On balance the Johannine chronology still remains the most likely, as even Jeremias (*Eucharistic Words*, 41) admits, though he stresses the uncertainty of the results.

[89]It is interesting that these outside limits correspond exactly with those already arrived at on the basis of nineteenth-century calculations by C. E. Caspari, *A Chronological and Geographical Introduction to the Life of Christ*, ET Edinburgh 1876.

[90]Cf. Herr in *Compendia* I.2, 838.

started too early. One of the reasons[91] was that the first-fruits of barley offered on Nisan 16, which was the signal for the harvest to begin,[92] would not have been ripe. So the previous month, Adar, was observed again. But in that first year of the ministry nothing depends on the precise date, except the length of time Jesus would have stayed in Judaea before reaching Galilee at the end of May. Probably it was only two or three weeks. More importantly, the Passover of 28 would in fact fit exactly with the figure of forty-six years given in John 2.20. The correlation cannot be pressed too hard, since there is always the possibility of a year's difference in computing. But the fit is remarkable, and, as we saw, does not work if the cleansing of the temple is set, with the Synoptists, at the close of the ministry.

The chronology we have followed would put the appearance of John the Baptist towards the end of 27. As a final test, how does this accord with Luke's dating of this 'in the fifteenth year of the Emperor Tiberius' (3.1)? Unfortunately, precise as it sounds, this is one of the most indeterminable dates in the New Testament. Finegan offers no less than sixteen different tables by which it may be calculated![93] There is disagreement as to whether the reign of Tiberius is to be reckoned as beginning from his co-regency with Augustus in AD 12 or (more likely) from the death of Augustus on 19 August AD 14. It also depends on whether the portion of the new reign prior to next new year's day was counted as a full year and on what date the new year was reckoned to start. On the probable assumption that in Syria the Macedonian calendar was followed with new year's day on October 1 and that this marked the beginning of the second year of his reign, then the fifteenth year would be October 27–October 28.[94] If so, then Luke's dating would fit precisely with the chronology to be derived from John. But it must be stressed that nothing can be based on this. In fact it is the Johannine timings of the cleansing of the temple and the crucifixion which provide the framework of absolute dating into which the Synoptic evidence can be fitted. These indeed are the only two major points at which John's chronology diverges from that of the Synoptists, and on both occasions

[91] Cf. b. *Sanh.* 11b and Finegan, *Chronology*, 42–4; Herr, *Compendia* I.2, 853–5.

[92] Josephus, *Ant.* 3.251. The wheat-harvest was inaugurated seven weeks later at Pentecost (3.252).

[93] *Biblical Chronology*, 259–73.

[94] So I. H. Marshall in his commentary *The Gospel of Luke*, London 1978, 133; Caird, *IDB* I, 601; Blinzler, *The Trial of Jesus*, ET 1959, 73–8; *Der Prozess Jesu*, revised and enlarged, [4]1969, 101–8; Brown, *John* I, 116; and Ruckstuhl, *Chronology*, 1–9.

I believe that he is right. For the rest, as we have seen, their material can be fitted into his outline but not *vice versa*.

Let me end with a chronological table of the ministry of Jesus. Though many of the datings are of course approximate I believe we may have a good deal more confidence in it than most modern scholarship, starting from the Synoptists and dismissing John, would suggest was possible. The days of the month are taken from the dates of the festivals in the years concerned[95] correlated with the notices of Jesus' movements in the Fourth Gospel. It coincides almost exactly, and quite independently, with the chronology worked out by Schein.[96]

[95]Following Parker and Dubberstein, *Babylonian Chronology*, 46, and allowing for the intercalation of a month in 28, the only year affected.

[96]In an independently produced chronological map for private circulation reflecting the position taken up in his *Following the Way*. The only major divergence is that he makes Jesus stay on in Jerusalem from Tabernacles in October 28 till just before Passover in April 29, for which I see no evidence or reason (cf. below, ch. V, p. 202 n. 27).

Perhaps I may also be allowed to quote from a personal letter of 27 October 1982 from Professor Jack Finegan, who says that he has now turned to other studies: 'Nevertheless I am very impressed and very pleased by your work. I have long felt that John is early and trustworthy and is to be taken seriously in his historical as well as theological sense and not to be relegated to a secondary position after the Synoptics. Now you are working this out systematically and penetratingly and, as far as I can see, convincingly.'

Summary of the Ministry of Jesus

27	autumn (?)	Appearance of John the Baptist
28	March (?)	Baptism of Jesus
	April	In Cana and Capernaum
		In Jerusalem before, and during, Passover and the feast of Unleavened Bread (April 28–May 5)
	May	In Judaea baptizing
		Arrest of John the Baptist
		Departure for Galilee
	June–October	In Galilee
	October 23–31	In Jerusalem for Tabernacles
	November–April	In Galilee
29	early (?)	Death of John the Baptist
	April	Desert feeding, before Passover (April 18)
	May–September	In Phoenicia, Ituraea and Galilee
	October 15	In Jerusalem for Tabernacles (October 12–19)
	November–December	In Judaea and Peraea
	December 20–27	In Jerusalem for Dedication
	January–February	In Bethany beyond Jordan
30	February (?)	In Bethany in Judaea
	March	In Ephraim
	April 2–6	In Bethany and Jerusalem
	April 7	Crucifixion

IV

The Story: The Beginning

The opening chapters of the Fourth Gospel, up to the moment when Jesus leaves Judaea for Galilee in 4.43, describe a period in the ministry for which the other Gospels offer no parallel. John is here on his own, and for that reason alone his evidence has been discounted as a serious contribution to the history. It has also been deemed to betray a tendentious theological motive of a polemical character. That there is a theological and not a mere historical purpose in all that John writes goes of course without saying. The only issue here, or elsewhere, is whether the theology creates the history or the history the theology. This cannot be settled *a priori* but only by a careful examination of the material, and later we shall examine the charge that the theological axe John has to grind has so distorted the record as to render his contribution historically worthless.

But the first question is where, or rather how, in this Gospel the history begins. For the first seemingly historical statement, 'There appeared a man named John, sent from God' (1.6), is so involved with the highly theological prologue as to make their relation problematic from the start. It has always been recognized that the prologue combines different levels of writing – hymnic ode, theological commentary and historical statements. These last appear to interrupt the movement of the whole and have more often than not been regarded as insertions. I have sought to establish the opposite thesis,[1] namely, that the historical statements came first and the prologue was subsequently written round them to set the history in a larger, cosmic context, performing much the same function though at a deeper level as the prologues of Matthew (1–2) and Luke (1–2) and indeed of Mark (1.1).

[1]'The Relation of the Prologue to the Gospel of St John', *Twelve More NTS*, 65–76.

The first edition of the Gospel, I believe, opened with the historical statements, 'There appeared a man named John, sent from God; he came as a witness to the light, that all men might become believers through him' (1.6f.), leading in due course into 'Here is John's testimony to him: he cried aloud, "This is the man I meant when I said, 'He comes after me, but takes rank before me'; for before I was born, he already was"' (1.15) and 'This is the testimony which John gave when the Jews of Jerusalem sent a deputation of priests and Levites to ask him who he was. . . . ' (1.19ff.). Round and into this opening narrative has been built the present prologue. But it has not left the original masonry undisturbed. So we cannot now tell precisely where one ends and the other begins. (This is particularly true of the references to 'the light' in 1.7–9, which clearly take up what has been said in 1.4f.). Moreover we cannot reconstruct the original opening without loss. The narrative verses do not run into each other, and the first words of the Baptist 'This is the man I meant when I said' suggest that some previous material may have disappeared. There could well have been more narrative to set the scene which has since been sacrificed.

Nothing that follows will depend on this reconstruction. I mention it because, if true, it reinforces the conviction that the history belongs to the bedrock of the Johannine tradition: it cannot be dismissed as merely illustrative of the theological themes played over in the prologue, for the history came first. I am convinced that we take John most seriously as we take it most seriously. And just because he is here on his own there is no reason for treating this section of the Gospel any less seriously.

Indeed, according to Eusebius (*HE* 3.24.7–13), who claims to be citing oral tradition ('it is said'), John's motive in writing his Gospel at all (and that 'under compulsion', 3.24.5) was to supply information lacking in the others about the early period of Jesus' ministry. It is scarcely credible that this was his main motive, since the material occupies less than a fifth of the Gospel. Nor, as we have seen, is there evidence that he was conscious of supplementing or correcting the accounts of others. Certainly he shows no sign of it at this point. He appears to be telling the story as he believed it to have been – and indeed as he personally experienced it. For there are more signs than usual in this section of eyewitness testimony.[2] However, this is a

[2]Cf. L. Morris, 'Was the Author of the Fourth Gospel an "Eyewitness"?' in his *Studies in the Fourth Gospel*, 139–214 (especially here, 139–42), who builds up a formidable case. Judgments on either side of the question are however heavily affected

notoriously difficult category to establish to general satisfaction, and I should wish to rest little on these signs, since they will always be open to other interpretation.

But before considering the details in this section it may be worth drawing attention to what long ago J. B. Lightfoot noted as 'the conversational character of the Gospel' as it was shared with 'an immediate circle of hearers'.[3] Similarly Adolf Deissmann made the observation that 'St Luke's is written Greek; but St John's is *spoken* Greek'. And H. E. Edwards, who quotes this,[4] suggests that the characteristic Johannine links like οὖν, 'so then',[5] or μετὰ ταῦτα, 'another time', or unnecessary repetitions, which would be merely slovenly in literary composition, reflect resumptions in spoken and frequently episodic teaching material (which except in ch. 6 and perhaps ch. 3 is probably a better designation than preaching material) given to groups of disciples. An interesting phenomenon in this connection is the curious and apparently uncontrived use of οὕτως, which *could* represent little more than a gesture of the hands in the telling.[6] It occurs twice in John. The first time is in 4.6, where Jesus sat at the well οὕτως, 'thus' or 'like this'. It is virtually untranslatable in print and is omitted in many modern translations, as in the old Latin, Syriac and Coptic versions both here and in the second passage; or it is taken, illegitimately I believe, with the previous clause (e.g. in the RSV's 'tired as he was'). The usage recurs in 13.25, 'he therefore dropped back *thus* upon the breast of Jesus.' Bernard seeks to make sense of both of them by rendering 'just as he was'. But in the latter instance this interpretation, i.e. taking it to mean leaning back, keeping the same attitude that has been described in v.23,[7] ignores a significant distinction to which Lightfoot drew attention in his book *On a Fresh Revision of the New Testament*.[8] The AV, he pointed out (and the RSV goes back on the differentiation he succeeded in getting into the RV),

---

by the presuppositions brought to them. It is a pity that he so constantly sets his up against 'inventions' of some 'writer of fiction in the second century'. There are other alternatives.

[3] *Biblical Essays*, 197f.

[4] *The Disciple Who Wrote These Things*, 28 (cf. 27–34). I have not been able to trace the original quotation.

[5] Depending on the textual variants, οὖν occurs in John almost twice as often as in all the other Gospels put together. With his epexegetic use of ἵνα, '(in order) to', it must be reckoned as his most distinctive stylistic trait.

[6] I find, re-reading Edwards after nearly thirty years, that he makes this point and I may have got it from him, but what follows was written independently.

[7] *John* II, 472f.

[8] London and New York [3]1891, 80f.

> makes no distinction between the reclining position of the beloved disciple throughout the meal, described by ἀνακείμενος, and the sudden change of posture at this moment, introduced by ἀναπεσών. This distinction is further enforced in the original by a change in both the prepositions and the nouns, from ἐν to ἐπί, and from κόλπος to στῆθος. S. John was reclining on the bosom of his Master, and he suddenly threw back his head upon His breast to ask a question.

The οὕτως refers to the movement (which is recalled in 21.20) not to the position.[9] I find it difficult to account for this vivid touch (which has dropped out of some manuscripts as apparently meaningless) except on the basis of some personal reminiscence recalled in the telling – though of course traces of oral communication are not the same as signs of first-hand witness.

Similarly in the section before us there are indications that the material originated with some group or individual (and many have pointed to the unknown disciple of 1.35–40), who had shared directly in the movement of the Baptist and had 'followed Jesus after hearing what John said' (1.37, 40). The twice repeated 'This is the man of whom I spoke when I said' (1.15, 30) suggests that it comes from a circle privy to a previous announcement or conversation which has not, now at any rate, been included in the evangelist's narrative. And in 3.28 there is a similar reference to what John 'said', the first part of which, 'I am not the Messiah', has been previously recorded by the evangelist (1.20) but not the second, 'I have been sent as his forerunner.'

Then there is the unique collocation of specific notes of time to be found in this section: 'the next day' (1.29), 'the next day again' (1.35), 'it was then about four in the afternoon' (1.39), 'the next day' (1.43), 'on the third day' (2.1). The usual explanation of these is that they are purely symbolic – sketching out a first week of the new creation,[10] modelled (perhaps) on Genesis 1 (cf. John 1.1) and coming (perhaps) to a climax on 'the third day' with its anticipation of the wedding banquet of the resurrection age. No one can deny that there are theological and symbolic overtones to be heard throughout John's narrative. Indeed one might be tempted to say that what he writes is symbolic until proved otherwise – though that still would not mean that the theology

[9]Cf. the contrast between the same verbs in Mark 6.39f.

[10]Cf. for example T. Barosse, 'The Seven Days of the New Creation in St John's Gospel,' *CBQ* 21, 1959, 507–16.

creates the history. Yet this criterion would be far too imprecise to be useful. For one can never *prove* that what he writes is *not* symbolic of something. To establish intention there must be some indication that the evangelist means his readers to see the symbolism involved – otherwise we are dealing with eisegesis rather than exegesis. Sometimes this is explicit – notably in 9.7 where the drawing-out of the meaning of Siloam as 'sent' is quite evidently intended to point to the deeper source of the healing, though this does not imply that the evangelist invented the place-name (which he clearly did not) or the incident: he simply sensed its overtones.[11] More often, of course, the reader is left to catch these overtones for himself in the rich vocabulary and *doubles entendres* of the Gospel.[12] I have no wish whatever to impose a minimizing interpretation or to suggest that any incidents have a purely factual (any more than a purely symbolic) significance. Indeed the evangelist is clear that the barely historical *per se*, judging merely as the eyes see, avails nothing (6.63; 7.24; 8.15). Nevertheless there are limits to responsible exegesis which may be overstepped by appeals to symbolism which is either too far- fetched or not suggested by anything in the context. An example which fails on both counts is seeing in the forty-six years of 2.20 the numerical value of Adam's name and (thus) Jesus' age: the number is clearly presented as a straight statement of time, whether it is correct or incorrect.[13]

With this in mind it is worth analysing more closely the supposed symbolism of the first 'week' of Jesus' ministry, since the judgments involved have wider application.

First, there is no clear statement that a week is meant – in contrast, for instance, with 20.26, where the 'after eight days' is properly

[11]Recall, on the supposed symbolism of John's geography, the discussion above, ch. II, pp. 49f.

[12]Barrett, *John*, 208 gives a useful, and reserved, list of them: 'Among words of double or doubtful meaning (other than simple metaphors) are: ἄνθρωπος (19.5), ἄνωθεν (3.3, 7), ἀποθνήσκειν ὑπέρ (11.50f.; cf. 18.14), βασιλεύς (19.14f., 19, 21), εὐχαριστεῖν (6.11, 23), καθίζειν (19.13), καταλαμβάνειν (1.5), ὕδωρ (4.10), ὑπάγειν (8.21; 13.33), ὕπνος (11.13), ὑψοῦν (3.14; 8.28; 12.32, 34).' The list could be extended indefinitely, but πνεῦμα (3.8) is a surprising omission. I would also include δόξα (1.14), which here also I think carries the meaning of reflection or image (as in I Cor. 11.7) or a father in his only son.

[13]See pp. 130f. above. Similarly I would agree with Lindars, *Behind the Fourth Gospel*, 65 that the reference to the Samaritan woman's 'five husbands' in 4.18 'has nothing whatever to do with the five pagan nations with which Samaria was populated according to II Kings 17.24', though this view is constantly reiterated. As Brown, *John* I, 171, rightly says, 'Such an allegorical intent *is* possible; but John gives no evidence that it was intended.'

interpreted by the NEB as meaning 'a week later' than 'the first day of the week' in 20.1. The so-called week has to be extracted from the material with considerable ingenuity. Day One is not mentioned as such, but must be presumed to occupy 1.19–28. Day Two lasts from 1.29 to 1.34. Day Three starts at 1.35 and ends with the statement of 1.39: 'they . . . spent the rest of the day with him. It was then about four in the afternoon.' Day Four begins at 1.43, when Jesus (apparently, though the subject is vague) 'decided to leave for Galilee' and, it seems, met Philip, who in turn introduced Nathaniel (1. 43–51). The next and last indication of time is in 2.1: 'On the third day there was a wedding at Cana-in-Galilee.' If this means on the third day after the one previously mentioned it must, all agree, indicate on Jewish inclusive reckoning 'two days later'. But that only adds up to six days. So another day must be found somewhere, which is usually done by adding another to day three, either by reading in 1.41 πρωΐ (in the morning) instead of πρῶτον or πρῶτος, or by assuming that the two disciples stayed on with Jesus for the next day as well, perhaps because it was the sabbath. But the variant reading is far too weakly attested (it does not occur in a single Greek manuscript), and the assumption of an extra day's stay, though no doubt quite reasonable, hardly provides grounds for asserting that the evangelist is intending the reader to count up the figures. And when he wants to say that anyone spends two days in a place he says so quite clearly (4.40; 11.6).

But at least the computation yields a 'seven', and here, it is said, is just another example of the pattern into which everything in this Gospel falls – seven signs, seven discourses, seven instances of 'I am', seven titles in ch. 1, seven periods of Jesus' life, etc. etc.[14] But I agree with Brown[15] that this process is highly subjective and selective. It involves, for instance, having to treat the walking on the water as a sign, though it is never so designated,[16] or else the crucifixion[17] or the resurrection appearance on the Sea of Galilee.[18] And those who see

[14]Cf., most uninhibitedly, M.-É. Boismard, 'L'Évangile à quatre dimensions', *Lumen Vitae* 1, 1951, 94–114.

[15]*John* I, cxlii and 106, who cites and argues against Boismard.

[16]It is possible, though not I think probable, that it may not even be intended by John to be seen as walking on the water, ἐπὶ τῆς θαλάσσης in 6.19 having the same meaning as in 21.1, 'by the sea'. It is remarkable that this is not even referred to in the recent study by C. H. Giblin, 'The Miraculous Crossing of the Sea (John 6.16–21)', *NTS* 29, 1983, 96–103.

[17]Marsh, *John*, 65.

[18]Fortna, *Gospel of Signs*, 108. This episode is again never called a sign, and his treatment means that the epilogue has from the beginning to be regarded as an integral

seven as the mystical number of the Gospel have to explain why it is the only cardinal number between one and eight which never occurs in it (in striking contrast with the Book of Revelation). To find subtle theological significance in 'the seventh hour' at which the fever abated in 4.52 (properly rendered again by the NEB 'at one in the afternoon') is as misplaced as searching for it in the tenth hour of 1.39, the twenty-five to thirty stades of 6.19, the thirty-eight years of 5.5 or, again, the forty-six years of 2.20. This is not to say that number symbolism is never to be found in the Fourth Gospel. Clearly the twelve baskets of fragments collected after the feeding of the five thousand (which of course is not of John's creation, being found in all the traditions) must be symbolic – though not, I believe, as most commentators seem to assume, to match the number of the apostles (so that each conveniently had one) but to represent the fullness of Israel yet to be gathered in. Of course, too, the one hundred and fifty-three fishes of 21.11 cry out for esoteric interpretation – and when anyone produces a really convincing allegorization I will gladly accept it. Till then, having studied the attempts, whose mathematical ingenuity one cannot but admire,[19] I confess to being innocent enough to believe that fishermen do actually count their catch, particularly a bumper one ('one hundred and fifty-three big fish'),[20] and especially when a partnership is involved.[21] The figure may be no more symbolic[22] than the 'about two hundred cubits' (or a hundred yards) which (v. 8) the boat was from the shore.[23]

---

part of the structure of the Gospel. The order of what Fortna regards as the original arrangement of the signs (those of chs. 2, 4, 21, 6, 11, 9, 5) simply plays ducks and drakes with any chronological framework based on the feasts, and appears wildly arbitrary. He also suggests (p. 101) that the evangelist has reproduced all the seven miracle stories which his source contained (despite 20.30!).

[19]Apart from what is offered in the standard commentaries, cf. R. M. Grant, *HTR* 42, 1949, 273–5; J. A. Emerton, *JTS* 9, 1958, 86–9; 11, 1960, 335f.; P, R. Ackroyd, *JTS* 10, 1959, 94; N. Z. McEleney, *Bibl* 58, 1977, 411–17; J. A. Romeo, *JBL* 97, 1978, 263f.

[20]Cf. Green-Armytage, *John Who Saw*, 13: 'In my world, if a fisherman makes an unusually good catch, he counts and weighs and measures each fish and can accurately (even maddeningly) recall these statistics to memory until the end of his life.'

[21]A point made by R. A. Edwards, *The Gospel according to St John*, 180.

[22]Bultmann, *John*, 709, says 'it must have an allegorical meaning, since it is not a round number'! But his footnote finds all the explanations he lists unconvincing.

[23]Brown, *John* II, 1074–6, after summarizing the proposed solutions, concludes: 'One cannot deny that some of these interpretations (they are not mutually exclusive) are possible, but they all encounter the same objection: we have no evidence that any such complicated understanding of 153 would have been intelligible to John's readers. We know of no speculation or established symbolism related to the number 153 in early thought. On the principle that where there is smoke there is fire, we would concede to the above-mentioned interpretations the likelihood that the number may be meant to

But this still leaves 'the third day' of 2.1. As Walter Wink, who supports a seven-day schema, confesses, '"on the third day" is admittedly an awkward way of designating the seventh day'.[24] Moreover if it is really intended to be anticipatory of Easter day (and John in fact never uses 'the third day' of the resurrection), then some further work has got to be done on 'the week'. So by various means an eighth day is discovered. But the basic assumption of all these reconstructions is that 'on the third day' marks yet another *interval*, following the decision to travel to Galilee, which is occupied by the journey. Since the journey is never mentioned – only the intention to make it – nothing can usefully be said about when it occurred[25] or how long it took. What can be asserted is that it would be quite impossible to do it on foot in two days. Josephus tells us (*Vit.* 269f.) that 'for rapid travel, it was essential[26] to take that route' (viz. through Samaria), 'by which Jerusalem may be reached in three days from Galilee', and it is clear from the context that he means 'from the frontier of Galilee' (where the dangerous section began). Now the journey which Jesus and his disciples were taking was not from Jerusalem but from the other side of the Jordan valley, in all probability at the southern end of it,[27] and they were making not for the frontier of Galilee but for a hill-

---

symbolize the breadth or even the universality of the Christian mission. But we are inclined to think that because this symbolism is not immediately evident, it did not prompt the invention of the number; for certainly the writer, were he choosing freely, would have come up with a more obviously symbolic number, for example, 144. The origin of the number probably lies in the direction of an emphasis on the authentic eyewitness character of what has been recorded (21.24). The Beloved Disciple is present. In 19.35 he was seemingly the one who transmitted the fact that blood and water flowed from the side of Jesus; in 20.7 he was the source for the exact description of the position of the burial wrappings; so here perhaps we are to think of his reporting the exact number of fish that the disciples caught. The number would have been retained in the story because it was so large.' It could then have formed the basis for later symbolic interpretation. He adds characteristically: 'By way of caution we should note in conclusion that the explanation we have offered of the number's origin is not a solution to the problem of historicity.' Not a solution, but surely, if true, relevant evidence.

[24] *John the Baptist in the Gospel Tradition*, SNTSMS 7, Cambridge and New York 1968, 93.

[25] So Hoskyns and Davey, *The Fourth Gospel* I, 187. Some, e.g. Lindars, *John*, 116, set it *before* the finding of Philip in 1.43.

[26] *Ἔδει*, the same word as used in John 4.4.

[27] John, characteristically, alone gives a precise location for it, Bethany beyond Jordan (1.28), yet unfortunately the site and even the name are uncertain. 'Bethabara' of the AV is derived from inferior manuscripts favoured by Origen because he could find no evidence of a Bethany in this area. But the pilgrim traditions concur in locating it near the crossing of the Jordan below Jericho. It must have been close enough to Jerusalem to invite the attention it did from the capital (Mark 1.5; Matt. 3.1, 5, 7; John

village lying beyond Nazareth and Sepphoris.[28] Nor is there any reason to think that on this occasion (unlike 4.3f.) they took the route through Samaria. Indeed from Bethany-beyond-Jordan the obvious way would have been up the east side of the Jordan valley. The idea that the entire journey could be done in two days reveals the commentator's comfortable ignorance. Of course the conclusion often drawn is that it shows that *John* had no idea of what he was talking about – despite the many signs that he is remarkably well-informed on distances both of space and time.[29]

But whatever the symbolic overtones (if any) that 'the third day' carried for the evangelist, there is no hint in the narrative that he saw it as the third day *after* anything. When Josephus, in the same passage in which he mentions the travelling-time from Galilee to Jerusalem (*Vit.* 268), wishes to express this he says, quite naturally, ἡμέρᾳ τρίτῃ μετά. But here there is no indication of interval. Though I have not seen it in any commentary, I was immediately persuaded by the interpretation when I was given it in Jerusalem that it simply means what it says, 'on the third day', namely, 'on the Tuesday'. For there was and still is today in Greek or Hebrew no other way of designating that day of the week.

1.19). Schein, *Following the Way*, 189, locates it near Wadi Abu Aruba which carries much water in winter and is about half a mile from a sector of the Wadi el-Kharrar with a good spring. This is about a mile from the traditional area of John's ministry at the Jordan. All agree there is no place with such a name now. Yet it is hardly likely to have been invented by the evangelist, who has Jesus going directly from one Bethany to the other in 10.40–11.1. Brownlee, 'Whence the Gospel of John?' in Charlesworth, ed., *John and Qumran*, 167–74, revives a theory that Bethany beyond Jordan refers to Batanaea, the highlands of upper Transjordania. This is entirely based on the calculation that it took two days to get from there to Cana and four to the other Bethany. But I shall argue below that 'on the third day' of 2.1 is not an interval, and no deduction can be made from the fact that by the time Jesus arrived in Bethany Lazarus had been dead for four days (11.17), since it is nowhere stated when he actually died (11.3, 6, 11–14, 21).

[28]According to Josephus, who had his quarters there for a time (*Vit.* 86), Cana-of-Galilee, correctly so designated by John (2.1, 11; 4.46; 21.2) to distinguish it for instance from Cana near Tyre (cf. Josh. 19.28), lay a full night's march from Tiberias (*Vit.* 90). There is now general agreement that it is to be identified with Khirbet Kana (now a ruin) about nine miles north of Nazareth. Its subsequent identification with Kafer Kenna (the Village of the Daughter-in-Law) came with the re-routing by the Crusaders of the main road from Nazareth to the Sea of Galilee. It was designated the Cana of the Gospel story by the Franciscans, for the convenience of pilgrims. Cf. Dalman, *Sacred Sites and Ways*, 100–6; F.-M. Abel, *Géographie de la Palestine* II, 412f.; C. Kopp, *The Holy Places of the Gospels*; 143–54. For the Franciscan case, cf. P. B. Bagatti, 'Le Anticheta de Kh. Qana di Kefer Kenna in Galilee', *Liber Annuus*, 1964–5, 251–92.

[29]'John's topographical care deserts him at this point', according to Lindars, *John*, 116. But he then makes the journey take *one* day (128)!

Moreover the third day I discovered is regularly regarded as particularly propitious for weddings – for that day of creation is the only one of which it is *twice* said that God saw that what he had done was very good (Gen. 1.10, 12). So well understood is this that wedding invitations, I am told, are sent out for 'the day that good is mentioned twice', without bothering to specify Tuesday. John 2.1 would be far the earliest evidence for such a wedding custom and of course there is nothing in the Cana story to suggest that the third day was the natural one for weddings, as Saturday is for us. The Mishnah (*Ket.* 1.1) and Talmud (b. *Ket.* 2a) recommend the fourth day, Wednesday, for virgins (and the fifth, Thursday, for widows), but this is determined by the fact that 'in towns the court sits twice a week, on Mondays and Thursdays, so that if the husband would lodge a virginity suit he may forthwith go in the morning to the court'! But town practice in Judaism after Jamnia is no sure guide to village custom before 70. At any rate it cannot affect the likelihood of 'on the third day' meaning 'on the Tuesday' (presumably the one following Jesus' arrival in Galilee) – though no one can say that for Christians it would not *also* carry overtones of the resurrection, despite the fact that this was firmly attached to 'the first day of the week'.

In any case the supposed symbolic week is in tatters. For no allowance is made for the time-consuming journey north, and since John does not even mention it it seems that he attached no great significance to it. For the rest he is giving some very precise details of when certain things occurred, even to the hour and day of the week. If these have no esoteric meaning, then the simplest explanation is surely that they were remembered to have happened like that and may reflect the experienced fact that the early days and hours of a conversion (as of an engagement) tend to be especially significant and memorable.[30] But

[30]So Sanday, *Authorship and Historical Character of the Fourth Gospel*, 46: 'If the author of the Gospel was really the Apostle, and if he had really been a disciple of John in his youth, then we can well understand how the events of those few days would cling tenaciously to his memory, because to him they were the turning-point of his life.' Similarly Scott-Holland: 'It is impossible to read these words without recognising that their significance belongs to them solely because they represent the personal record of the first experience of a disciple. . . . the precise minuteness of the tiny details, so unimportant in themselves, convey the intensity of a vivid personal memory. They are there for no other purpose' (*Fourth Gospel*, 171f.). Naive as this may now sound in scholarly circles, it is an impression easier to smile at than to refute and one that is not, I believe, incompatible with a more sophisticated theological purpose to the chapter. Even Bultmann thinks it probable that 'the evangelist himself was among these disciples' (*John*, 108), but then, as we have seen, he arbitrarily denies the element of first-hand witness.

again I would wish to rest no great weight on the eyewitness character of the narrative, simply to counter what would seem to be illegitimate inferences in the opposite direction, that symbolism, not history, is the dominant factor.

But let us now pass from the form of the story to its content.

It might appear that the material of these early chapters is so divergent from the Synoptic accounts that it can carry little credibility. Yet in fact the Synoptic tradition is not entirely self-consistent, nor, as we shall see, self-explanatory.

That, as John tells us, Jesus already had some disciples, including Peter, *before* the Galilean ministry started seems to be implicitly confirmed in Peter's speech prior to the day of Pentecost in Acts 1.21f., (which indeed echoes the word of Jesus himself in John 15.27, 'You are . . . my witnesses because you have been with me from the beginning'): 'Therefore one of those who bore us company all the while we had the Lord Jesus with us, coming and going, *from John's baptism* until the day when he was taken up from us – one of those must now join us as a witness to his resurrection.' As Brown comments, 'Since this observation does not match Luke's own account in the Gospel, there is every reason to take it seriously.'[31] For the rest of the Synoptic tradition has 'the beginning' as 'starting *from Galilee*' '*after* the baptism proclaimed by John' (Acts 10.37) and indeed after John's imprisonment (Mark 1.14 and pars.). Peter and the rest of the apostles come upon the scene only after John has disappeared from it, and there would be no reason to suppose they had any contact with him, let alone belonged to his following. In fact the relation of the two movements is presented as one of temporal succession and sharply contrasting character. John came as a life-long ascetic (Luke 1.15), neither eating nor drinking; Jesus came doing both, earning the reputation of a glutton and a drinker (Matt. 11.18f. = Luke 7.33f.). In John's message the mission of the coming one would be to separate the wheat from the chaff (Matt. 3.12 = Luke 3.17); Jesus by contrast thought of the kingdom as a *corpus permixtum* (Matt. 13.24–30) and went out of his way to consort with tax-gatherers and sinners (Matt. 11.19 = Luke 7.34). Whereas John's disciples like those of the Pharisees fasted, Jesus' did not (Mark 2.18 and pars.). The prayer which John taught his disciples (Luke 11.1) was evidently similar to those of the Pharisees (Luke 5.33; cf. for an example 18.11f.), while the manner of praying that Jesus taught stood in strong contrast with that of 'the hypocrites'

[31] *John* I, 77; cf. earlier Askwith, *Historical Value of the Fourth Gospel*, 268f.

(Matt. 6.5f.). There does not appear to be much overlap or common ground.

This antithetical picture is not of course the full one. There was also a positive relation between John and Jesus to which the Synoptists testify. Thus:

Of *John's relation to Jesus* they tell us that he was herald and forerunner (Mark 1.2f.; Matt. 11.10 = Luke 7.27; Mark 9.13; Matt. 17.12f.), though the contrast between John and the mightier one announced is again stressed. John would not be fit to unfasten his shoes, and whereas he baptized in water the coming one would baptize in holy Spirit (and fire) (Mark 1.7f. and pars.). Again while John was a prophet, and more than a prophet (Matt. 11.9 = Luke 7.26), greater indeed than any other mother's son (Matt. 11.11 = Luke 7.28), and his baptism and 'way of righteousness' (Matt. 21.32) was evidently 'from God' and not just 'from men' (Mark 11.30 and pars.), yet 'the least in the kingdom of Heaven is greater than he' (Matt. 11.11 = Luke 7.28).

Of *Jesus' relation to John* the Synoptists tell us little. The most obvious fact is that he came to John for baptism (Mark 1.9 and pars.). Yet there is no sign that John recognized in Jesus the coming one of his preaching – except in the clearly apologetic addition in the Gospel of Matthew where we read that John sought to dissuade him. '"Do you come to me?" he said; "I need rather to be baptized by you"' (3.14). Nevertheless when later the question is raised by John from prison, 'Are you the one who is to come, or are we to expect some other?' (Matt. 11.3 = Luke 7.20), the presumption behind the Synoptic narrative is that the question is asked not out of ignorance but disillusionment. For 'happy is the man', says Jesus, 'who does not find me a stumbling-block' (Matt. 11.6 = Luke 7.23). The question, I believe, assumes rather than rules out that John had once seen in Jesus the fulfiller of his hopes.[32]

Yet from the Synoptics we get no clear impression of Jesus' deeper relation to John. He accepted his baptizing mission, but we are not told why. The answer given in the Matthaean community, 'Let it be so for the present; we do well to conform in this way with all that God requires' (Matt. 3.15), does not take us very far. It is difficult from the Synoptists to discover just what the two had in common. True, according to Matthew (3.2; 4.17), they proclaimed an identical

[32]'It may be inferred', commented Stanton, from the implication that John was 'offended', 'that the Baptist having at one time believed was now experiencing doubt and perplexity, because of the line of conduct followed by Jesus' (*Gospels as Historical Documents* III, 223).

message, 'Repent; for the kingdom of Heaven is upon you.' But John's message is evidently here being assimilated to that of Jesus (Mark 1.15 and pars.) rather than the other way round; it gives us no ground for supposing that Jesus took over what the Baptist said or identified with it. And yet we have the mysterious testimony that there were some who said that he *was* John the Baptist (Mark 6.14 and pars.; 8.28 and pars.).[33] Those who shared this view evidently saw the same spirit and power at work in Jesus: now that John was gone, he represented what John stood for. Yet for this view, that Jesus was somehow in the line of John, the Synoptists provide no basis or explanation.

That the two movements were, or had been, closer than the Synoptists suggest, that there was a deeper affinity which led Jesus to identify with John and John to set his hopes on Jesus, but that this relationship underwent change, is, I submit, presupposed in the first three Gospels. But it is nowhere accounted for. The Fourth Gospel, however, provides us with a picture, which if allowed to stand in its own right, can help explain the others to themselves. For not only does it give us the account of an earlier Jesus – supplying evidence of contemporaneous and indeed complementary work with John the Baptist in Peraea, Judaea and Samaria, rather than a bare succession – but it enables us to glimpse a new Jesus, a Jesus who was for some time the disciple and protégé of the Baptist. Only this, I believe, makes intelligible subsequent developments in the gospel story, alike in the Synoptists and in John.

Yet before we examine what the Fourth Gospel tells us new about Jesus, we must look at what it tells us new about the Baptist – and before that ask whether it affords any historical information of worth at this point at all. For ever since Wilhelm Baldensperger[34] Johannine criticism has been dogged by the notion that the entire treatment of John the Baptist in this Gospel is motivated – and thoroughly distorted – by polemic against the Baptist groups opposed to the early church. There are a string of denials and disclaimers which, it is said, can make sense only as rebuttals of counter-claims that John the Baptist *was* all these things – the true light (1.8; cf. 5.35), the superior in rank (1.15, 30; 3.30), the Messiah, Elijah, the prophet like Moses (1.19–21; 3.28). That there is theological motivation at work here – as throughout the

[33]In 6.14 there is a division of textual witnesses, some implying that this view was a peculiarity of Herod Antipas' – which Matthew's version supports but not Luke's. In 8.28 and pars. the plural is not in doubt.

[34]*Der Prolog des vierten Evangeliums: sein polemisch-apologetischer Zweck*, Tübingen 1898.

Gospel – cannot be doubted. The sole question is whether it distorts the history and provides evidence merely for the life-setting of the Johannine community rather than affording any reliable information about the Baptist and his mission.

First it must be observed that the denials are not just created by the fourth evangelist but are reflected in the Synoptic tradition. The words 'After me comes one who is mightier than I. I am not fit to unfasten his shoes' (Mark 1.7 and pars.; John 1.27) occur in all the Gospels in closely similar form, and in the Acts summary they are combined with the disclaimer on John's lips 'I am not what you think I am' (13.25),[35] referring evidently to the speculation 'whether perhaps he was the Messiah' (Luke 3.15). The subordination of John to Jesus is, as we have seen, a dominant trait of the whole Synoptic witness. Oscar Cullmann, who argues strongly for the polemical strain in the Johannine record, admits that the denials could well fit the historical situation.[36] In fact, there is no element of dispute between John and Jesus (as opposed to one between the disciples of John and 'a Jew'),[37] and their relations are represented as uniformly friendly throughout the Gospel. There is absolutely no evidence for such a statement as that of M. Goguel[38] that John regarded Jesus as a renegade. Indeed if my interpretation is right[39] Jesus saw the mission of the Baptist as sowing the seeds of his harvest (4.38). It is significant too that when later Jesus is forced to flee from Judaea he deliberately seeks refuge in Bethany-beyond-Jordan where John and he were first associated (1.28; 3.26) and there finds a ready following among those who recall John's teaching (10.39–42). This hardly suggests that the groups were at daggers drawn, either then or

[35]Dodd, *Historical Tradition* 255–8, has cogently argued that the historical summary in Acts 13.24f. is independent of the Synoptic Gospels and represents good early tradition. He also points out that in three details it sides with John's Gospel over against Luke 3.16.

[36]*Christology of the NT*, 29.

[37]So the best-attested (including $\mathbf{P}^{75}$), and hardest, reading in 3.25. 'The Jews' is too obviously a correction (despite $\mathbf{P}^{66}$). I am much drawn to the conjecture, going back to Bentley, of 'Jesus' or 'those of Jesus'. But this would still only mean that the rival movements differed over ritual requirements (which we already know: cf. Mark 2.18 and also 7.3, where John's disciples would almost certainy have been in solidarity with 'the Jews in general'), not that the principals quarrelled. Dodd, *Historical Tradition*, 280f., suggests that John 3.25 reflects a purely intra-Jewish dispute, possibly with the men of Qumran where lustrations were given such emphasis. But if so, as he says, it leads on to nothing. What follows is all about relations with Jesus, which gives force to the emendation.

[38]M. Goguel, *Au seuil de l'évangile: Jean-Baptiste*, Paris, 1928, 274.

[39]See above, ch. III, pp. 135f., and again my article, 'The "Others" of John 4.38', *Twelve NTS*, 61–6.

later. It is much easier to think that the fourth evangelist had an eye to *persuading* those who (like him?) were brought up on the Baptist's teaching to believe in Jesus as the one to whom John pointed.[40]

But the real difficulty is to find any evidence for the existence of Baptist groups claiming John as Messiah, with whom the Johannine community, and the church generally, are supposed to have been in running conflict. Often the existence of this rival sect is simply deduced, by circular argument, from the signs of polemic within the Gospels themselves.[41] But after the disciples of John bury their master, and significantly come to tell Jesus (Matt. 14.12), we hear nothing more of them in the New Testament. Even if those in Acts 18.24–19.7 who knew only the baptism of John were not already in some sense Christians, as the use of the word 'disciples' is generally admitted to imply,[42] they certainly do not fulfil the necessary conditions of a rival group proclaiming John as Messiah: if Apollos had belonged to such a group, whatever the limitations of his theology, Priscilla and Aquila could hardly have vouched that he 'taught accurately the things about Jesus'! The sole direct evidence that there was such a group at any time is in fact confined to two passages in the *Clementine Recognitions* (1.54 and 60), which are notoriously unreliable as history and cannot at best take us back beyond the second and third centuries AD.[43] For detailed assessment of the evidence I must refer to an earlier article on which I have here drawn, but I quote its conclusion: 'That there were elements of John's following which did not find their way into the Church is indeed very probable; that these elements constituted a rival group to Christianity in the first century, with a competing Christology, is, I believe, without any foundation whatever.'[44]

Yet the question whether the Johannine account of the Baptist is purely or largely tendentious cannot be settled *a priori*. Obviously apologetic motives are at work, but whether they distort the history can be judged only by the probabilities or improbabilities of the emerging picture. Does John afford us a basically credible or incredible

[40]So Dodd, *Historical Tradition*, 300. Wink, who quotes Dodd with approval, agrees, while being open to the apologetic motivation (*John the Baptist*, 98–105).

[41]E.g., Goguel, *Jean-Baptiste*, 104: 'The existence of this literature [viz. the Lukan birth narratives and John 3 and 4] establishes that of a Baptist group.'

[42]Cf. B. T. D. Smith, 'Apollos and the Twelve Disciples at Ephesus', *JTS* 16, 1915, 241–6.

[43]Cf. again Dodd's judgment: 'To base a theory upon the evidence of the late and heretical Clementine romance is to build a house upon sand' (*Historical Tradition*, 298).

[44]'Elijah, John and Jesus', *Twelve NTS*, 28–52. I quote here from p. 50.

account of the Baptist against his historical background?

The first thing to be said is that it is not wildly out of line with the Synoptic presentation. The contrast between John in his menial role of baptizing with water and the one coming after him who will baptize with holy Spirit (John 1.26f., 33) is, as we have seen, closely parallel with that in the Synoptic traditions (Mark 1.7f. and pars.). The reference to him as 'a voice crying aloud in the wilderness, "Make the Lord's highway straight"' (Isa. 40.3) is also common to all the reports (Mark 1.3 and pars.; John 1.23), the only difference being that John sets it on the Baptist's own lips.[45] Again, though the Fourth Gospel does not actually narrate the baptism of Jesus it clearly presupposes it, and it has a parallel disclosure of him as God's servant-son accompanied by the descent of the Spirit like a dove (Mark 1.9–11 and pars.; John 1.32–34). And again, the report of this event and disclosure is attributed to John the Baptist himself.[46] Moreover it is made clear that the Baptist recognized Jesus as the coming one only at this moment (1.31, 33), a recognition which is explicit in Matthew 3.14f. and, we argued above, implicit in John's subsequent question from prison (Matt. 11.2–6 = Luke 7.18–23).

But it is the further material which the Fourth Gospel alone gives us that helps to illumine the purpose of the Baptist's mission against its historical background and supplies possible motives for Jesus' association with it. In recent years our understanding of this background has been greatly enriched by the evidence from Qumran and it is the Johannine picture that is most interestingly vindicated by it.[47] I have argued that just as disciples of John transferred their allegiance to the Christian church (as John 1 asserts and Acts 18–19 presupposes), so John himself is best explained on the hypothesis (however guardedly stated) that he had perhaps earlier been brought up in the Qumran

[45] Askwith, *Historical Value of the Fourth Gospel*, 33f., argues the greater likelihood of this last. 'If the Baptist in his humility had made his own this appellation – a voice crying in the wilderness – we can well understand the application of it to him in the Synoptists, whereas it is not easy to understand that those who believed in his divine mission and took him for a prophet sent by God would have applied to him a description which might seem derogatory.'

[46] Cf. Askwith, ibid., 51: 'It must have been from him that the story of the baptism of Jesus came.' He argues that this accounts for the otherwise unexplained source of the tradition in the other Gospels (66).

[47] Cf. B. Reicke, 'Nytt ljus över Johannes döparens förkunnelse', *Religion och Bibel* 11, 1952, 5–18; W. H. Brownlee, 'John the Baptist in the New Light of Ancient Scrolls', *Interpretation* 9, 1955, 71–90; reproduced in revised form in Stendahl, ed., *The Scrolls and the New Testament*, 33–53 (esp. 45–52); and my own article, 'The Baptism of John and the Qumran Community', *Twelve NTS*, 11–27.

community, or at any rate that his baptism of repentance is more fully understandable against that background than that of the other contemporary baptist sects[48] or Jewish proselyte baptism. I shall not repeat the arguments for this, which for me have lost none of their cogency, but simply restate and draw out the corollaries for the Johannine picture.

First, there are two points of contact with Qumran which John shares with the Synoptists. For the citation of Isa. 40.3 was also used in their Manual of Discipline to describe and justify what the Qumran covenanters aimed to do:

> Now when these things come to pass in Israel to the community, according to these rules, they will separate themselves from the midst of the session (or habitation) of perverse men, to go into the wilderness to clear there the way of (the Lord), as it is written:
> In the wilderness clear the way (of the Lord);
> Level in the desert a highway for our God.[49]

At first sight it might look as if this is a description of the present life of the community and without doubt it represents an ideal which it is already seeking to practise and perfect. But when the opening phrase 'now when these things come to pass in Israel' is used twice again in neighbouring passages (8.4 and 9.3), it evidently indicates a future, eschatological stage which has not yet been reached. The conception appears to be that by its present life and discipline, and through an inner group dedicated to perfection, the community as a whole will stand forth, purified of every contamination, to be the instruments of Yahweh's atoning work and judgment. *Then*, it seems, it will complete its separation from the world and every contact with evil (cf. 9.6) by marching out into the desert, ready for whatever he may require of it (presumably, to judge from the War Scroll, the final conflict with the sons of darkness) and prepared for the coming of the Prophet and the Messiahs of Aaron and Israel (9.11). This interpretation is supported by the only other reference to the moment of clearing a way in the desert – an obscure allusion in 9.20. In the context (9.12–24) it is made clear that in this present time the life of purification and perfection has still to be lived to a great extent 'in the midst of men of perversity'. But the ultimate purpose of all the teaching, instruction and discipline of

[48]For these cf. J. Thomas, *Le Mouvement Baptiste en Palestine et Syrie*, Gembloux 1935.

[49]1QS 8.12–14. Tr. W. H. Brownlee, *BASOR Supplementary Studies* 10–12, 1951.

the sect is to perfect a group which 'may walk perfectly each with his fellow in all that was revealed for them'. And '*that is the time* of clearing the way in the wilderness', i.e., when the community is finally ready 'to separate from everyone' to meet the messianic age.

If this interpretation is correct we *could* have the clue to why John left the community – for it is certain that by the time we meet him baptizing in the Jordan valley he is on his own. On this showing, he severs himself from the relative civilization even of Qumran because, under the constraint of the word of God (Luke 3.2), he becomes convinced that the eschatological moment is nearer even than they believe. He deliberately goes out into the wilderness to announce the imminent coming of the Prophet and Messiah and to prepare the faithful of Israel for a final dedication to their God. So the Fourth Gospel, the only one also to mention 'the prophet' in this or any other context, could well be right in placing upon John's own lips the justification of his mission in terms of Isa. 40.3.

The second point of contact between this Gospel and Qumran shared with the Synoptists is the reference to a baptism still to come. Of this there is no suggestion in the rite of proselyte baptism or in any other of the baptist sects. 'The very reason why I came, baptizing in water, was that he might be revealed to Israel', 'he', that is, 'who is to baptize in holy Spirit' (John 1.31, 33; so Mark 1.8; Acts 1.5; 11.16; in Matt. 3.11 = Luke 3.16 it is 'in holy Spirit and fire'). Despite the fact that it is the term common to all the versions, many critics have hitherto been reluctant to believe that John spoke of holy Spirit (though always, to be noted, without the article) and have seen in it a reading back of Christian theology. But now from Qumran we have clear evidence that the covenanters too regarded the dispensation of water, and with it all the present rules and discipline under which the community lived as being merely provisional until the coming of the messianic age (1QS 9.10f.; cf. CD 15.4), when it would be superseded by a new dispensation of holy Spirit:

> And then [namely, at 'the season of visitation' when 'the truth of the world will appear for ever'] God will purge by his truth all the deeds of men, refining for himself some of mankind in order to abolish every evil spirit from the midst of his flesh, and to cleanse him through a holy Spirit from all wicked practices, sprinkling upon him a Spirit of truth as purifying water (1QS 4.20f.).

Here are the characteristic themes of the Baptist's preaching – refining, cleansing, water and holy Spirit – all set in the context of the fire of judgment (4.13),[50] the abolition of evil (4.19f.) and 'the making of the new' (4.25).[51] Here too we may see a background for some of the distinctively Johannine language associated with the Baptist which is not shared with the Synoptists. There is still no satisfactory parallel for 'the Lamb of God' and until further evidence emerges I would agree with Dodd[52] and Brown[53] that its most likely associations *on the Baptist's lips* are with the apocalyptic tradition, for it is immediately equated by Andrew with 'the Messiah' (1.41). But certainly his function of 'doing away' sin (1.29; cf. I John 3.5, paralleled in I John 3.8 by 'undoing the devil's work') is closely reflected in the Qumran hope, as is the phrase 'the elect of God' with which in all probability the Baptist hails Jesus in John 1.34[54] – the same expression being used in the plural of the community itself in 1QpHab. 10.13 (cf. 1QS 8.6), of the Righteous Teacher in 1QpHab. 9.12 and perhaps of the Messiah in 4QMess. ar.[55]

But it is when we come to ask what Jesus saw in John, rather than what John saw in Jesus, and why he came to identify with his movement, that the Qumran background becomes most interesting. Something more seems necessary to explain Jesus' submission to John's baptism of repentance than that he believed it to be 'from God' and not merely 'from men'. It has indeed been customary[56] to see in this act Jesus' first recognition of his redemptive mission and his willingness from then on to be 'numbered among the transgressors'. The difficulty is that there is nothing in the Synoptists to suggest that the Baptist's movement was in any way a *redemptive* group to which a man might attach himself from this kind of motive – in order, that is, to share in

[50]Cf. the vivid description of the final judgment of the world by fire in 1QH 3.29–36.

[51]This is probably a reference to Isa. 43.19, where significantly the 'new thing' which God promises is to make a way in the wilderness. This would confirm that the time of the way in the wilderness is 'the period of the decree', i.e. the end.

[52]*Interpretation*, 230–8; cf. his *Historical Tradition*, 269–71, where he argues that there is no good reason why it should not have been used by John the Baptist. He is followed by Fortna, *Gospel of Signs*, 233.

[53]*John* I, 58–60; cf. earlier his 'John the Baptist in the Gospel of John', *NT Essays*, 136–8. That, as he says, it may carry further overtones for the evangelist is very probable.

[54]Following the well-attested variant ὁ ἐκλεκτὸς τοῦ θεοῦ, which is a good deal more likely to have been assimilated to 'the Son of God' than the other way round. It is preferred by Harnack, Jeremias, Cullmann, Barrett, Brown, the NEB text, etc.

[55]Cf. J. A. Fitzmyer, 'The Aramaic "Elect of God" Text from Qumran Cave 4' in his *Essays on the Semitic Background of the New Testament*, London 1971, Missoula, Mont., 1974, 127–60, who however questions whether the Messiah is in mind in this fragmentary and obscure text.

[56]So Cullmann, *Christology*, 66–9.

making atonement and removing sin. But if there does lie behind John's mission the kind of thinking represented at Qumran, this link is supplied. For this community saw its function precisely in these terms: 'to lay a foundation of truth for Israel . . ., to atone for all those who dedicate themselves for holiness in Aaron and for a house of truth in Israel' (1QS 5.5f.), 'to make atonement for the guilt of transgression and sinful infidelity' (9.4). If this was the kind of outlook in which John was nurtured and in some way also the *raison d'être* of his own movement – repentance, that is, not merely to escape the coming judgment, but to create a pure and purifying remnant – then we may have a clue to why Jesus felt compelled to identify himself with it.

New light may also be shed on the connection between Jesus' baptism by John and the subsequent descent upon him of the Holy Spirit. This latter is accompanied by the declaration in the Synoptists, 'Thou art my Son, my Beloved; on thee my favour rests' (Mark 1.11 and pars.) and in John by the very similar testimony of the Baptist, 'I saw it myself, and I have borne witness. This is God's Chosen One (or, Son)' (John 1.34). It is generally recognized that behind these words stand those of Isa. 42.1: 'Here is my servant, whom I uphold, my chosen one in whom I delight; I have bestowed my spirit upon him.' But what is the link between Jesus' baptism with water and his anointing with the Spirit as the servant-son of God? The Synoptists (for John does not actually mention the baptism) are content merely to stress the immediacy of the connection (Mark 1.10 and pars.). Part of the reason has already been suggested, namely that water-baptism meant setting one's foot on the path of the servant. But what is the relation between this baptism and that unique event which followed for Jesus but for none of the others who partook of John's rite?

Again the outlook of the Qumran sect is instructive. As we saw, they expected their present washings to give place to a 'baptism' with holy Spirit that God himself would administer. And to hasten the day there was to be built up within the community as a whole a dedicated nucleus of 'Israelites who walk in perfection' in contrast with 'the men of deceit' (1QS 9.6 and 8).[57] Then, 'when these things come to pass in Israel [i.e. when such purification and dedication is fully perfected], the council of the community [viz., the whole body] will have been established in truth:

> As an eternal planting, a holy house of Israel,

[57]The words in John 1.47, 'Here is an Israelite worthy of the name: there is nothing false in him', could reflect the Baptist's ideal taken over by Jesus.

A most holy institution of Aaron,
True witnesses with regard to religion
And the chosen of divine acceptance to atone for the earth.[58]

In other words, the final object of all the sect's discipline, repentance and purification is that the community itself may become the elect of God for his atoning work. And in Jesus this ideal is already declared by the divine voice, *and in John testified by the Baptist*, to have found its fulfilment. Here and now, in this man is God's purified instrument 'to serve the purpose of grace to make atonement for the earth' and 'to establish the new and eternal covenant' (8.9–10). Baptized by John, and without further need to be made perfect, Jesus is designated what the covenanters, and according to the Fourth Gospel John too, envisaged as the agent by whom the messianic period would be ushered in.

But it may even be that the sect actually expected this servant ideal to be embodied in the community only through an *individual*, whom God must purify and anoint with the Spirit, to be the means of communicating his knowledge of God to the rest. Brownlee has given an interpretation to a passage from the Manual of Discipline quoted earlier (1QS 4.20–22) which would suggest that the sect looked for such an eschatological figure delineated in terms of the suffering servant:[59]

> And at that time God will purify by his truth all the deeds of *a man*; and he will refine him more than the sons of men, in order to consume every evil spirit from the midst of his flesh, to cleanse him through the holy Spirit from all wicked practices; and he will sprinkle upon him the Spirit of truth as purifying water so as to cleanse him from all untrue abominations and from being contaminated with the Spirit of impurity, so that he may give the upright insight into the knowledge of the Most High and into the wisdom of the sons of heaven.

[58] 1QS 8.4–6. Tr. as revised by Brownlee, *BASOR* 135, Oct. 1954, 34.

[59] 'The Servant of the Lord in the Qumran Scrolls, II', *BASOR* 135, 1954, 33–8. He has followed it up in 'Jesus and Qumran' in F. T. Trotter, ed., *Jesus and the Historian*, Philadelphia 1968, 59–64, where he suggests that 'the Man' of Hebrew messianic expectation is seen as fulfilled in the ἄνθρωπος of John 19.5; and in 'Whence the Gospel of John?' in Charlesworth, ed., *John and Qumran*, 174–9, where he further adduces the peculiar reading of Num. 24.15f. in 4Q Testimonia about 'the Man whose iniquity is purged' and who 'knows the knowledge of the Most High'. B. Reicke, *Religion och Bibel* 11 (see n. 47 above), and J.-P. Audet, 'Affinités littéraires et doctrinales du Manuel de Discipline', *RB* 60, 1953, 74, come independently to a similar interpretation.

With that we may compare a passage from the Testaments of the Twelve Patriarchs: 'The heavens will be opened . . . and the glory of the Most High shall burst forth upon him. And the spirit of understanding and sanctification shall rest upon him [in the water]. For he shall give the majesty of the Lord to those who are his sons in truth for ever.'[60] In the light of the parallel from the Manual of Discipline it may not be so certain that the bracketed words are simply a Christian interpolation.[61]

If this is the true interpretation, it provides the connection we are looking for between the baptism of Jesus and his anointing with the Spirit as the servant of the Lord for his consummating work of revelation and redemption. Moreover, if the Baptist was brought up to look for such a figure, it could explain how he could have seen as the rationale of his baptizing work, as the Fourth Gospel asserts, 'that he might be revealed to Israel' (1.31; a very Qumranic limitation). For 'He who sent me to baptize with water had told me, "When you see the Spirit coming down upon him and resting on him you will know that this is to be he who is to baptize in holy Spirit"' (1.33). The Dead Sea Scrolls, to be sure, have provided no exact parallel for the idea that it is *through* the 'coming one' that God would baptize his people with holy Spirit.[62] But given the fact that this was John's message – and such is the unanimous testimony of the Gospels – we may now be able to see why he should have expected to recognize this figure in one who was himself to be baptized with the Spirit before he could communicate his wisdom and knowledge to others.

The purpose of John's coming into the wilderness was, we may say, precisely to force the eschatological issue. The identity of the coming one remained indeed at that stage hidden from him as from the rest (1.26, 31, 33). What distinguished John was his certainty that this figure stood among them, waiting to be revealed (1.26). So he emerges, at the prompting of God, to set the last things in motion by his baptism of water. For that was the divinely ordained preliminary to that other baptism by the Spirit which was to consecrate the coming one for his mission, the final work of God in taking away sin from the earth (1.29) and pouring out upon men the holy Spirit of the new age.

[60]Test. Levi 18.6–8; ET in J. H. Charlesworth, ed., *The Old Testament Pseudepigrapha*, I, New York and London 1983, 795.

[61]So too Brownlee in Stendahl, ed., *Scrolls and the New Testament*, 253 n. 14, citing A. Dupont-Sommer.

[62]The nearest parallel is CD 2.12: 'And through his Messiah he shall make known to them his holy Spirit' (Charles' translation). But this refers, like the rest of the passage, to the past history of Israel.

Such is the picture offered by the fourth evangelist. Its historicity has not been highly regarded. Yet the material from Qumran must make us consider whether it does not make surprising sense as an interpretation of John's work.[63] If it is thus rooted in the contemporary expectation of Palestinian Judaism it cannot so easily be dismissed as evidence of little more than the internal debates of the Christian church in the latter part of the first century AD.

Yet the Fourth Gospel's distinctive contribution is far from exhausted. It is what it tells us of the period *after* Jesus' designation by John as the coming one that is most significant.

According to the Synoptists Jesus separates himself immediately from John, first by retreat to the wilderness and then, after John's arrest, by withdrawal to Galilee. From the moment of his baptism onwards we should not guess that he had any further contact – or affinity – with John.

The picture in the Fourth Gospel is strikingly different. Just as immediately, in fact the very next day, Jesus, still in the company of John, begins to attract to himself his first disciples. We have already seen that Acts 1.21f. presupposes that Jesus had disciples, including Peter, who had accompanied him 'from the baptism of John' – and this indeed would suggest through whom the account of the Spirit's descent and the words at the baptism reached the Gospels. It also helps to explain the otherwise totally abrupt acceptance in Mark 1.16–20 and pars. of Jesus' call to his first disciples to drop all and follow him.[64] For it is not implied in the Johannine story that he had earlier called them (they had come to him) to permanent or continuous attachment.[65] Of these early disciples we are given the names in John only of Andrew and Simon. That Andrew is at first given precedence over his brother (1.40, 44) is a feature hardly likely to have been invented.[66] But the close association of the call of Simon and Andrew with that of James and John both in Mark (1.16–20) and in the independent Lucan account (5.1–11) has strongly suggested that John, who with his brother James is otherwise unaccountably missing from this Gospel (apart from

[63]So also Dodd, *Historical Tradition*, 288–90; Brown, 'John the Baptist in the Gospel of John', *NT Essays*, 132–40.

[64]The abruptness is less apparent in Luke, who displaces the call of the first disciples to 5.1–11. This move however leaves the mention of Simon in 4.38 without introduction or explanation.

[65]Cf. Stanton, *Gospels as Historical Documents* III, 224f.

[66]Contrast Mark 1.16: 'Simon and his brother Andrew'. Andrew is not explicitly mentioned in Luke 5.1–11, but cf. the plurals in vv. 5–7 and also 6.14 where he is called Simon's brother.

21.2), is intended by the unnamed disciple of 1.35 and 40. That Andrew first (πρῶτος), or more probably first of all (πρῶτον), 'found his *own* brother' (1.41) cannot, admittedly, be pressed to sustain the inference that the anonymous disciple was also one of a pair, since in New Testament Greek ἴδιος can have an 'exhausted' sense, meaning no more than 'his'.[67] But John's usage of the word does support the emphatic meaning here.[68] When he merely wants to say 'his' he regularly uses αὐτοῦ, and in the fourteen other occurrences of ἴδιος the translation 'own' is necessary to the sense, not least in 5.18, where it is only by Jesus' 'calling God his own Father' that a supposed claim to 'equality with God' is implied.[69] So the inference that in 1.41 John is meant certainly cannot be ruled out,[70] and in view of the association in this as in every other instance of an unnamed disciple in this Gospel with Simon Peter (18.15 and all the occurrences of 'the disciple whom Jesus loved'),[71] I should regard it as probable. It is also borne out by the fact that in all the Synoptic lists of the Twelve (Matt. 10.2f.; Mark 3.16–18; Luke 6.14; Acts 1.13) Peter, Andrew, James, John and Philip are the first five. Moreover, in Mark and Acts Andrew is bracketed not with his brother Simon (as one would expect, and as one finds in Matthew and Luke) but with Philip, an association only explained by the information John gives us that they came from the same town, Bethsaida (1.44; 12.21). Furthermore when the explanation is given of how Simon came to be nicknamed Peter – which in Mark (3.16) and Luke (6.14) is simply stated as a fact – John's account (1.42), which is quite evidently independent of Matthew's (16.17f.), nevertheless concurs with Matthew in giving Simon's father's name as John or Jona[72] (cf. 21.15–17); and he alone supplies the Aramaic *Kēphas* on which the pun is based, a designation otherwise only (but amply)

[67]Cf. F. Blass and A. Debrunner, *A Greek Grammar of the New Testament and other Early Christian Literature*, ET, ed. R. W. Funk, Cambridge and Chicago 1961, § 286, followed by Brown and Barrett, ad loc. But cf. J. H. Moulton, *A Grammar of New Testament Greek* I, 1908, 90, who regards the emphasis of ἴδιος here as 'undeniable'.

[68]So Howard, *Fourth Gospel in Recent Criticism*, 292.

[69]In fact Barrett here italicizes it in his commentary, p. 256!

[70]Zahn, *Das Evangelium des Johannes*, 129–32; N. Turner, *Grammatical Insights into the New Testament*, 135–7; Schlatter, *Der Evangelist Johannes*, 55, who cites Josephus, *Ant.* 11.300: 'Joannes, the high priest . . . had murdered his own brother (τὸν ἴδιον ἀδελφόν) in the temple.'

[71]See above, pp. 106, 109.

[72]Whether or not the two are alternative transliterations, Dodd argues strongly for the independence of the Johannine version, for which he finds support in the Gospel according to the Hebrews (*Historical Tradition*, 306f.).

confirmed as very primitive by Paul (I Cor. 1.12; 3.22; 9.5; 15.5; Gal. 1.18; 2.9, 11, 14).

So the witness of the Fourth Gospel to the early disciples of Jesus cannot be lightly dismissed: it bears out or explains much that would otherwise be unaccountable.

Now John tells us what we should elsewhere have had no grounds for suspecting, that Jesus' original inner circle had been disciples of the Baptist. But, more importantly, he tells us that Jesus also so began. We might of course infer this from the fact that he accepted John's baptism, and the words 'Do you come to me?' in Matt. 3.14 may reflect a technical phrase for coming to a teacher to be his disciple.[73] Jesus' extraordinary words of praise for John in Matt. 11.11 (par. Luke 7.28) point in the same direction. Moreover it has been argued that in the second half of this same verse, the expression 'in the kingdom of Heaven' should be taken adverbially, so that the meaning is 'he who is least, is greater than John in the kingdom of Heaven'. 'He who is least' (or 'a lesser one', *μικρότερος*) then sounds like a self-designation by Jesus speaking as an ex-disciple of John. If this interpretation is correct[74] the whole saying concerns the reversal in status between the two, and coheres remarkably with the Johannine picture, as we shall see. Beyond these hints, however, the Synoptists afford no evidence that Jesus had any continuing association with John, whether before or after his baptism.

Such evidence is what we find in John 1.15, 30, where Dodd has, I believe convincingly, argued[75] that, whatever further meaning of temporal posterity (as in 1.27) and timeless pre-existence the words may carry for the evangelist, the statement including the phrase *ὁ ὀπίσω μου ἐρχόμενος* would on the lips of the Baptist naturally mean 'There is a man *in my following*[76] who has taken precedence of me, because he is and always has been essentially my superior.'[77] And he concludes that at this point

[73]E. Fascher, 'Jesus der Lehrer: Ein Beitrag zur Frage nach dem "Quellort der Kirchenidee"', *TLZ* 79, 1954, 325–42, specif. 328.

[74]So F. Dibelius, *ZNW* 11, 1910, 190–2 recalling also the exegesis of Tertullian, Chrysostom and Hilary. This interpretation is favoured over other possibilities (without any reference to the Fourth Gospel) by P. Hoffmann, *Studien zur Theologie der Logienquelle*, Neutestamentliche Abhandlungen, N. F. 8, Münster 1972, 220–4.

[75]*Historical Tradition*, 273–5; quotation from 275.

[76]So Fascher, 'Jesus der Lehrer', 327–31; cited with approval by Culpepper, *Johannine School*, 222.

[77]Brown, *NT Essays*, 138–40; *John* I, 64, suggests that as spoken by the Baptist *ἔμπροσθέν μου γέγονεν* is a specific but veiled reference to Jesus as Elijah, since he lived some 900 years before him. This is certainly *possible* and would fit the other indications that the Baptist saw the coming one in this role.

> We are reaching back to a stage of tradition scarcely represented elsewhere in the gospels, . . . namely that Jesus was at one time regarded as a follower or adherent of John the Baptist. If, as the Synoptic Gospels report, he accepted baptism at his hands, how else should he be regarded? That the fact should be obscured in the development of the tradition of the Church was to be expected.

As Goguel put it earlier, 'When Jesus preached and baptized in Peraea, it was as a disciple of John the Baptist that he did it',[78] or Stauffer, still more strongly, 'This early period of Jesus' ministry is only a chapter in the story of the Baptist's movement.'[79]

Yet clearly he was no ordinary disciple. The norm is that 'the disciple is not above his master. . . . It is enough for the disciple to become as his master' (Matt. 10.24f.; cf. Luke 6.40; John 13.16). But John himself reiterates that in this case the rule is broken (John 1.15, 30) – though not, be it noted, because Jesus takes his own disciples: that was the regular way by which rabbinic schools grew, and it is in no way suggested that this represented an affront to the Baptist. Rather it was because, on John's recognition, Jesus was the mightier one for whom his own role had been merely preparatory: he was the one whose shoes he was not good enough to unfasten (1.27) and who would baptize in holy Spirit (1.33), the Lamb of God who was to remove sin from the world (1.29, 36), the Christ before whom he had been sent (3.28), the bridegroom at whose side the best man is content to stand (3.29). Indeed if we look for the role-definition of this 'disciple' it is implicitly given in the titles which the Baptist denies to himself in 1.20f. – the Messiah, Elijah, the Prophet. It is in fact likely[80] that the ἐγώ here, and in 3.28, is emphatic, '*I* am not the Messiah', as it evidently is in 1.26, '*I* baptize with water, but among you . . . stands one'. Jesus is the one that John is not. And it is significant that the Gospels preserve the tradition that each of these titles was attributed to Jesus (Mark 6.15; 8.28f.; John 1.41; 4.25; 6.15; 7.40f.) even though he was to distance or dissociate himself from them. It is indeed particularly remarkable that the Johannine tradition should retain the memory that John denied he was Elijah when Jesus was to say that was just what he was (Matt. 11.14; 17.12.; Mark 9.13) and also that John denied being Elijah while still claiming to be the forerunner of the Messiah (3.28) when the

[78] M. Goguel, *Jean-Baptiste*, pp. 250f.; cf. 235–57 as a whole.
[79] *Jesus and his Story*, 60.
[80] So Barrett, *John*, ad loc.

Christian church subsequently equated the two roles by identifying 'the Lord', for whom Elijah prepared, with Christ. In both I believe the memory is historically correct.[81]

If therefore Jesus is to be seen as a disciple of the Baptist it is not because he does what *he* does but because he does what he said the coming one would do; because, in other words, Jesus accepts the role John marks out for him and thus 'fulfils' his hopes (3.29f.). And this is precisely what the fourth evangelist represents and proceeds to spell out: the early Jesus is to be understood as *John's* coming one. I owe this insight to my uncle J. Armitage Robinson's little book *The Historical Character of St John's Gospel.*[82] He argued that during the period which the evangelist goes out of his way to specify as 'before John's imprisonment' (3.24) Jesus' activities are to be correctly interpreted only in the light of the Baptist's message. Jesus starts, at any rate, by adopting John's rite of baptism, and soon outdoes him (3.22, 26; 4.1). Even though the evangelist later says that Jesus himself did not baptize,[83] he evidently did not deter his disciples from doing so (4.2). In fact without this precedent (with or without some Dominical command such as is recorded, or read back, in Matt. 28.19) it is difficult to explain the instant and uncontested adoption of baptism as the means of entry into the Christian church (Acts 2.38 and the Epistles *passim*),[84] especially since the logic of the quoted word of Jesus that 'John baptized with water, but you will be baptized with the Holy Spirit' (Acts 1.5; 11.16) would have suggested the leaving behind of water-baptism.

Armitage Robinson draws attention in this connection to the significance of the exchange with Nicodemus in John 3.3–5. Noting that 'seeing' or 'entering the kingdom of God' is very untypical Johannine vocabulary[85] and therefore not likely to be of his own

[81]For the complex situation here I must refer again to my 'Elijah, John and Jesus', *Twelve NTS*, 28–52.

[82]Cf. above, ch. I, p. 8 n. 16.

[83]I should be less confident than Dodd (*Historical Tradition*, 285f.) and most commentators that this is patently the work of a redactor rather than a self-correction by the evangelist (cf. Brown, ad loc.: 'almost indisputable evidence of the presence of several hands in the composition of John'). In any case the thrice-repeated statement that Jesus *did* baptize must be given priority and, as Dodd says, its subsequent embarrassment to the church increases its historical credibility.

[84]Cf. W. F. Flemington, *The New Testament Doctrine of Baptism*, London 1948, New York 1949, 31 (quoted by Barrett, *John*, 230): 'If . . . baptism were practised with the approval of Jesus, it becomes easier to explain why, immediately after Pentecost, baptism took its place as the normal rite of entry into the Christian community.'

[85]Both phrases are to be found in Mark (9.1; 10.15) and in the latter case the parallel with John is very close. It is still closer in the apparently independent tradition of Matt.

creation, he comments: 'When Nicodemus was told, "Except a man be born of water and spirit he cannot enter the kingdom of God", he would necessarily be reminded of the Baptist's works and words: the whole of John's mission lies behind the saying.'[86] For what Jesus is insisting on is 'the sequel of the message of the Baptist – the axe is laid at the root of the tree. It is John's baptism raised to a higher power – water and spirit, as he had foretold. Reform is not enough: reconstitution only will avail.'[87] Yet the fact that what is required is water *and* spirit, and not spirit in place of water, emphasizes the continuity as well as the discontinuity between the two movements. The one grew out of the other, in both senses.

However, the most notable example of Jesus acting out the programme laid down for him by John is, as I argued earlier in the context of the chronology of the ministry, to be found in the cleansing of the temple, set where the fourth evangelist sets it, as Jesus' first public demonstration to the nation. For what was the mighty one, whose role of axing, winnowing and burning had been so vividly defined by the Baptist (Matt. 3.10–12 = Luke 3.9, 16f.), expected to do?

> Suddenly the Lord whom you seek will come to his temple; the messenger of the covenant in whom you delight is here, here already, says the Lord of Hosts. Who can endure the day of his coming? Who can stand firm when he appears? He is like a refiner's fire . . .; he will purify the Levites and cleanse them like gold and silver, and so they shall be fit to bring right offerings to the Lord. . . . The day comes, glowing like a furnace; all the arrogant and evildoers shall be chaff and that day when it comes shall set them ablaze, says the Lord of Hosts, it shall leave them neither root nor branch. . . . Look, I will send you the prophet Elijah before the great and terrible day of the Lord comes (Mal. 3.1–3; 4.1, 5).

It is true that the Malachi passage is not cited in any of the Gospel accounts of the temple cleansing, but it evidently lies behind the understanding of the Baptist's work, not only in Mark (1.2), Matthew (11.10) and Luke (7.27), but also, by allusion rather than quotation,[88]

18.3: 'I tell you this: unless you turn round and become like children, you will never enter the kingdom of Heaven.'

[86] *Historical Character of St John's Gospel*, 31.

[87] Ibid., 27f.

[88] The ἔμπροσθεν ('ahead of'), common to Q and John, suggests a Christian testimonium from a non-septuagintal version of Mal. 4.5.

in John (3.28); and John alone sets it on the Baptist's own lips, like the prophecy from Isa. 40.3. Moreover both the cleansing of the temple and, I suggested, the cursing of the barren fig-tree of Israel with which it is intertwined in the Synoptic account are best understood as inspired and sanctioned by the work of John, as indeed the Synoptists indicate: the authority behind the one is the authority behind the other (Mark 11.11–33 and pars.). Yet it is the Fourth Gospel alone which brings them into what I believe is their proper conjunction and allows us to understand them in a temporal context in which the authorities who have spurned John still have reason to fear his popularity (cf. Mark 11.32; Luke 3.15; 7.29f. = Matt. 21.31f.).[89]

Yet it is also clear that this role cast for Jesus by John is subsequently repudiated by him, however much two disciples who, if we are right, had been with him from the earliest days still expect him to sanction it. The incident is placed by Luke considerably later (9.52–56); for being tied to Samaria, it must be set in the only passage through Samaria which he knows, namely, Jesus' last journey to Jerusalem. We cannot say that it does not belong there, though most of the material in his 'travel' section seems, as we shall see,[90] to have its original context elsewhere. But it would gain considerable force if in fact it originally had had its setting in an earlier occasion when 'he had to pass through Samaria', namely, on the journey from Judaea which marked his final break with the Baptist (John 4.1–4). Of the unresponsive Samaritans James and John ask, 'Lord, may we call down fire from heaven to burn them up?', and the scribal gloss 'as Elijah did' merely draws out what they meant. But, we read, 'he turned and rebuked them'. The words which follow in the received text, though again no doubt the commentary of the church, describe sufficiently the difference of conception: '"You do not know", he said, "to what spirit you belong; for the Son of man did not come to destroy men's lives but to save them."'

The 'spirit' has indeed changed: the conception of his role and function has altered. Jesus has come as the proclaimer of deliverance rather than judgment, of the acceptable year, rather than the terrible day, of the Lord. Thus it is that Luke, programmatically, represents the new, Galilean gospel from the beginning (4.16–21). So for the fourth evangelist too it is at this point that the healing ministry of Jesus begins (John 4.46–5.15), a mission, it is stressed, which is primarily to give life, to save rather than to judge (5.19–47; cf. 3.17; 12.47). These

[89] Recall the argument in ch. III above, pp. 127–30.

[90] See below, ch. VI, p. 215f.

'signs' are precisely what distinguish the ministry of Jesus from that of John (10.41). Since they are the Father's works they rest on 'a testimony higher than John's' (5.36), meaning not the testimony which John had – for his authority too was 'from God' (1.6; cf. Mark 11.30 and pars.) – but the testimony that John gave (5.33; cf. 1.19),[91] which was but human testimony (5.34; cf. 3.31–34). Up till now Jesus had indeed based his work on what John said – and as far as it went it was true and salvific (5.33–35; 10.41). But now there was the witness of 'another' to whom he must defer (5.32).

If the change of conception receives its first outward expression in the decisive move from Judaea to Galilee, then the memory preserved in both the Markan (1.12f.) and Q traditions (Matt. 4.1–11; Luke 4.1–13) of a wrestling in the wilderness may give dramatic form to the struggle that preceded it. The Synoptists agree in placing this between Jesus' baptism with the Spirit and the arrest of John (for which they give no indication of date). If a Judaean ministry occupied that interval, then the crisis could as well have come after it as before. Mark indeed, as we have seen, places the temptation 'immediately' after the baptism, but his constant use of this word inspires no confidence in it as a serious time-reference. John provides a different and much more circumstantial account of the immediate sequel to the Baptist's recognition of Jesus. We must choose between them. But there is one indication that the crisis is more probably to be located at the end rather than the beginning of the period. The reason given in the Gospel of John for Jesus' withdrawal to Galilee is a curious one if it has not behind it some historical tradition: 'A report now reached the Pharisees: "Jesus is winning and baptizing more disciples than John"' (4.1). The decision to shun the temptations of success could well reflect the same struggle represented in the more mythological categories of the Q story and presuppose that the dangers of success were already a reality to be reckoned with. If the temptation story does reflect in part at least this crisis, it may be seen as marking Jesus' resolution to model himself henceforth not on the mighty one of John's preaching but on the servant-son of the baptismal voice. For the call to be God's son found its archetypal expression in the call to Israel to go out into the wilderness (Hos. 11.1), and thus it is that Jesus responds to the repeated 'If you are the Son of God' with the classic words of Deuteronomy (8.3; 6.13f.; 6.16)[92] – just as later he was to use those of Isaiah (29.18; 35.5f.; 61.1) to say in effect to the disillusioned John,

[91] So Brown, *John* ad loc.
[92] Cf. my article, 'The Temptations', *Twelve NTS*, 53–60.

'Yes, I am the coming one, but the role is indeed very different from that based on Malachi which you proclaimed' (Matt. 11.2–6 = Luke 7.18–23).

If there was this shift of function, then the utterances of Luke 12.49–53 could well embody Jesus' subsequent reflection upon it. 'I came', he says, 'to set fire to the earth.' That was the role of Elijah (cf. Ecclus. 48.1, 'Elijah appeared, a prophet like fire, whose word flamed like a torch').[93] The words that follow, καὶ τί θέλω εἰ ἤδη ἀνήφθη, are usually taken to mean 'and how I wish it were already kindled!' But they could, more naturally, be translated, 'But what do I care if it is now kindled?' – for that baptism with fire belongs to another conception of my work. In any case, Jesus goes on, 'I have a baptism to undergo (rather than to dispense), and how am I constricted until it is accomplished!' What follows could also contain a reference to that mission of Elijah which some still think he is aiming to fulfil: 'Do you suppose I came to establish peace on earth?' Now this was, *par excellence*, to be the function of Elijah, to 'reconcile fathers to sons and sons to fathers' (Mal. 4.6; Ecclus. 48.10; Luke 1.17; cf. II Esdr. 6.26), which was interpreted by the rabbis to mean to settle all disputes, 'to make peace in the world'.[94] 'That', says Jesus, 'is the work of the restorer prior to the end, to set everything right (Mark 9.12); but it cannot describe what I have come to do. The effect of my mission is to bring not peace but division, to set father against son and son against father. For this is the period of the end itself, the time when prophecy has declared that family strife is bound to come' (I Enoch 100.1f.; II Baruch 70.3–7; II Esdr. 5.9; 6.24; cf. Micah 7.6; Isa. 19.2; Ezek. 38.21).

The most fundamental change is the recognition that Jesus has a baptism not simply, as John said, to dispense but himself to suffer. This is the baptism to which he refers those same two disciples, James and John, who still view the kingdom in triumphalist terms: 'You do not understand what you are asking. Can you drink the cup that I drink, or be baptized with the baptism I am baptized with?' (Mark 10.35–40).

[93] It is possible that the phrase 'John was a [Greek 'the'] lamp burning brightly' in John 5.35 may contain an echo of this verse, though the LXX has λαμπάς and John λύχνος. If so we *could* have the Johannine version of *Jesus*' identification of John with Elijah, despite John's own disclaimer. But in the context the primary contrast must be between the eternal Light which the Baptist was not (1.8) and the torch which burns itself out.

[94] M. *Eduy.* 8.7; Schürer, *History* II, 515f.; Strack-Billerbeck, *Kommentar zum NT* IV, 796f.; J. Klausner, *The Messianic Idea in Israel*, ET New York 1955, London 1956, 454.

And that painful scene is followed by the classic redefinition of 'the mighty one' in terms not of the potentate but the slave. 'For even the Son of man did not come to be served but to serve, and to surrender his life as a ransom for many' (10.41–45).

The full recognition of this change, that as the Son of man Jesus could fulfil God's purpose only through suffering and death, is again bound up with reflection upon the Baptist. For the 'constriction' began with him. 'Ever since the coming of John the Baptist the kingdom of heaven has been subjected to violence and violent men are seizing it' (Matt. 11.12). This violence has already engulfed John: they 'worked their will upon him; and in the same way the Son of man is to suffer at their hands' (Matt. 17.12f.; Mark 9.12f.).

But this is to run further ahead than we have yet reached in the story, and we shall return to this second and still more agonizing crisis of reappraisal in the next chapter. For the image of the charismatic messianic liberator depicted in Luke 4.16–21 which dominates the Galilean period will itself need correcting. And we shall see that the evidence of the Fourth Gospel is again decisive for understanding the change, even though we are almost entirely dependent on the Synoptic tradition for the Galilean period itself. Yet the same second transition is detectable in John – from the Son who quickens whom he wills (5.21) to the one who gives life only by giving his life (6.51–58; 10.10f.); from the wine flowing freely and joyously (2.1–11) to the blood which must be drunk as the condition of receiving eternal life (6.53–56); from the Spirit given in the present tense without measure (3.34),[95] to its constriction to believers hereafter; 'for the Spirit had not yet been given, because Jesus had not yet been glorified' (7.39).

To all this we must come back. But what John does at the beginning is to fill in an initial self-understanding of Jesus of which the Synoptists at best give hints, an estimate which was to linger on in others' hopes and with which the Baptist was much associated. The long shadow cast over the Gospel story by John the Baptist is not really intelligible from the Synoptic record. But the Johannine tradition if taken seriously as an independent and, I believe, first-hand witness can here as elsewhere explain much.

[95] I am inclined to agree with Brown, *John*, ad loc., that 'he whom God sent speaks the things of God, for he gives the Spirit without measure' probably refers throughout to the Son, though whether instead the Spirit is given by God (so NEB and as interpreted in some manuscripts) through the Son makes little difference. In the context it is probably the evangelist's comment reflecting on the difference between the Baptist and Jesus, who dispenses the Spirit freely.

V

The Story: The Middle

If the ministry of Jesus was seen by the early church to have a clear beginning and end – 'from John's ministry of baptism until the day when he was taken up from us' (Acts 1.22) – so it had a scarcely less recognizable middle, which marked the transition, also reflected in the Acts summaries, 'from Galilee to Jerusalem' (10.37; 13.31). But this mid-point was not a single or a sudden moment. Though the hour when Jesus 'set his face resolutely towards Jerusalem' (Luke 9.51) and left Galilee for the last time for Judaea and Transjordan is clearly recorded in all the Gospels (Matt. 19.1; Mark 10.1; Luke 9.52; John 7.2–10), yet the decision was preceded by a sequence of events and a period of reappraisal which evidently occupied a considerable time. John indeed enables us to determine it precisely, as the six months between Passover in mid-April (6.4) and Tabernacles in mid-October (7.2) of the year 29. What was the significance of this broad watershed and how are we to interpret what happened in it?

There is no lack of material. In fact it is because there is so much in the various and varying traditions, not because there is so little, that reconstruction is difficult – though of course we should like more, particularly towards the end of the time when the trail seems almost deliberately to go cold. For we have for this period an overlap and apparent duplication of sources which is to be paralleled only in the Passion narrative. In fact this section of the Gospel story, covered by Mark 6–8 and its parallels in the triple tradition and John 6, contains the only major incident in Jesus' life outside the story of the passion that is recorded by all four evangelists in the same position, namely, the feeding of the five thousand. (The cleansing of the temple comes in all of them, but is set by John and the Synoptists at opposite ends of the ministry.) Yet this is but one item in a cluster of events which is reproduced by John and two or more of the Synoptists in the same sequence:

1. Jesus and his disciples cross the Sea of Galilee to a deserted spot
2. He miraculously feeds the crowds
3. The disciples re-cross the lake
4. Jesus joins them, walking on the water
5. The Jews ask for a sign
6. Jesus speaks about bread
7. He tests the disciples' faith
8. He forewarns of betrayal and death.

This should not cloak the fact that there are also great differences in the common material as well as much that is not shared by John and the Synoptists. Indeed the lack of agreement, especially verbal, is just as significant and puts a big question-mark against the obvious inference that John is here dependent for his material and its order upon the Synoptists. This has been the traditional critical conclusion and is still upheld by C. K. Barrett even in the revised edition of his commentary. Indeed so little does he think John's account of separate historical significance that he says: 'A discussion of what may be supposed actually to have taken place in this incident belongs rather to a commentary on Mark than to one on John.'[1] But Barrett is now in a minority of scholars and the independence of the Johannine tradition, even at this point, has in my judgment been decisively argued by Dodd[2] and Brown.[3] Except in the accounts of the feeding of the five thousand and the walking on the sea (items 2 and 4 above), there is no agreement in wording; and in the former it is virtually limited to the figures (two hundred denarii, five loaves, two fishes, five thousand men and twelve baskets), while in the latter, apart from the reply, 'It is I, do not be afraid' (John 6.20, where the last half, missing from the Curetonian Syriac, may even be an assimilation to the text of the Synoptics),[4] there is the minimum of common vocabulary required to tell the story at all (embarking, boat, across, sea, wind, rowing, walking on the sea).[5] The

[1] *John*, 271.

[2] *Historical Tradition*, 196–211.

[3] *John* I, 236–44; so too Lindars, *John*, 234–8. Cf. the observation quoted from Fortna above (ch. I, p. 24) that no one would think of explaining the comparable similarities in Mark 6 and Mark 8 by literary dependence.

[4] So Brown, ad loc.

[5] Also 'stades' in Matthew, with whose account there is no reason to see independent affiliation, and John alone gives the precise figures '25 or 30'.

conclusion is that they are a good deal more likely to represent independent traditions of the same remembered events.[6]

Furthermore within the Synoptic tradition itself there are two phenomena which make this section of the Gospel story unusual if not unique. First, in Matthew and Mark there are two cycles of material with similar features: a second feeding (of four thousand), another boat-crossing (though this time of Jesus with the disciples and no storm), journeys outside Galilee (the first time to Tyre and Sidon, the second to Caesarea Philippi) and, in Mark, two strikingly similar healings (of the deaf-mute and the blind man). It looks again as if these may be parallel versions of the same events, so that we should have three independent cycles of tradition, one in Mark 6–7, one in Mark 8 and another in John 6. Of the incidents in John 6 listed above, items 1–4 are paralleled in Mark 6, while items 5–8 have (more remote) equivalents in Mark 8.

Secondly, this stretch of material is marked not only by duplication but by equally significant omissions. This is the scene of Luke's so-called 'great omission', where not only is the entire second cycle in Matthew and Mark missing but everything between the feeding of the five thousand and the testing of the disciples' faith, including the walking on the water and the first trip to Gentile territory (which might have been thought well-suited to Luke's missionary purpose). In fact of the eight incidents Luke has only items 2 (the feeding), 7 and 8 (the testing of the disciples' faith and the passion prediction). He even manages to avoid any reference to the sea or to boats, whether before or after the feeding. That this is deliberate omission and that he is aware of material he chooses not to use is suggested by the reference to

[6]Cf. Brown's comments on the walking on the water: 'Since it would have been simpler for the fourth evangelist, if he were simply a creative artist, to have placed the discourse on bread immediately after the multiplication, his inclusion of the walking on the sea indicates that he was controlled by an earlier tradition in which the multiplication and the walking on the sea were already joined' (*John* I, 252). (I should prefer to say the remembered history.) Then on the details: 'John's account patently has a claim to be considered as the more primitive form of the story. John's brevity and lack of emphasis on the miraculous are almost impossible to explain in terms of a deliberate alteration of the Marcan narrative. . . . Thus, John's account of the walking on the water seems to represent a relatively undeveloped form of the story' (254). He observes too that what might be thought to be the theological *leitmotiv* of the Johannine story – the ἐγώ εἰμι of its climax – occurs also in the Synoptists and 'may be considered as belonging to the primitive form of the tradition' (256). Moreover, if as some have argued, the walking on the water is intended to evoke the Passover theme of crossing the Red Sea, prior to the giving of the manna, John makes no attempt whatever to bring out this theme, and Lindars, I believe, rightly dismisses it (*John*, 246).

Bethsaida in 9.10 (as the site of the feeding of the five thousand), which could have come from Mark 6.45 (where the disciples make for Bethsaida after the feeding) or 8.22 (where Jesus and his disciples came to Bethsaida before leaving for Caesarea Philippi), and by the mention of Jesus 'praying alone' in 9.18 (as an introduction to the testing of the disciples' faith) which could have come from Mark 6.46f. (where Jesus is alone in prayer after the feeding of the five thousand). But Luke does not even mention the name Caesarea Philippi or suggest any journey or location.

Yet his are not the only omissions. For while for the most part Matthew and Mark run closely parallel not only in order but in wording (far more so than Luke where he does have an equivalent in the feeding of the five thousand), this stretch of material is also notable for Matthaean omissions.[7] Not only are both the healing stories of Mark 7.32–37 and 8.22–26 uniquely missing from Matthew (in place of the former he has a generalized account of healings) but also a surprising number of other Markan verses (6.31, 37b–38a, 40, 52, 56; 7.2–4, 9.24b; 8.14b, 17b–18). Some of these, like his overall reduction of words in other verses, reflect no more than Matthew's usual trimming of Mark. But unusually they amount to more than Matthew's own additions, namely, the two pericopae about Peter walking on the water (14.28–31) and being acclaimed as the foundation of the church (16.17–19) and the two parabolic sayings found also in the double, or Q, tradition about the blind leading the blind (15.14) and about discerning the signs of the sky (16.2f.). The effect of these omissions is not only to play down Mark's stress on the disciples' obtuseness, which may represent his own editorial emphasis, but to cut out the references to Jesus' insistence on seclusion and secrecy during this period (Mark 7.24, 36; 8.26; 9.30), to which John also testifies (7.4, 10).

The question arises why the tradition at this point is both so thick in the first instance and why (unlike that of the passion narrative) it has apparently been so thinned. Is it perhaps because the period was particularly significant for the development of the story of Jesus and because subsequently its significance came to be lost for the church?

In Mark the period is treated as one of slow and painful progress in

[7] I have assumed here the hypothesis of Markan priority, though I should be quite open to the supposition that Mark may at points have added material for his own editorial purposes to the triple tradition. In the feeding of the five thousand there are also some (minor) agreements between Matthew and Luke which could be put down to Mark having changed the underlying common source.

overcoming the disciples' blindness and dullness of understanding of who Jesus was. Three times he has to upbraid them, despite the evidence of the two feedings (6.52; 7.18; 8.17–21); and the healings of the deaf-mute and the blind man, both needing considerable physical effort, are evidently intended to be symbolic of what is required to open the disciples' minds. And yet when Peter does come out with the answer that Jesus is the Messiah he is silenced and subsequently snubbed (8.27–33). Three times in four verses the word ἐπιτιμάω, rebuke, is used; and instead of his faith being hailed as a revelation from heaven, as in Matthew's addition (16.17–19),[8] Peter receives the appelation Satan, which in John's parallel scene is reserved for Judas (6.70f.). It looks as if Mark may have imposed on the sequence of events an interpretation which it will not bear, and it is perhaps not surprising that the other Synoptists do not follow him. Luke makes drastic cuts and offers no interpretation of why the testing of the disciples' faith should follow directly on the feeding of the multitude. Matthew, as we have seen, plays down the theme of opening the disciples' minds and makes Peter's confession the climax which we might have expected it to be in Mark. In all the Synoptists the incident at Caesarea Philippi prepares for the future and the need for suffering and death. But it seems to come out of the blue. None of them offers any hint as to how it arises from the six preceding items in the cluster of events with which in Mark and Matthew it is closely associated. It looks as if this is a further example of where the Synoptic Gospels are not self-explanatory and indeed where in the developing tradition the significance of the connection gets lost rather than deepened. Can John help us to a better understanding? What here is the effect of giving priority to his independent tradition?

The first thing to say is that whatever help John may give us in interpreting the events following the feeding he is of no use in elucidating what led up to it. In fact we have here one of the most blatant Johannine *aporiae* or failures of connection. At the end of ch. 5 Jesus is in Jerusalem. Then in 6.1 we read he 'withdrew to the farther

[8]Cullmann has convincingly argued, following J. Bieneck, *Sohn Gottes als Christusbezeichnung der Synoptiker*, ATANT 21, Zürich 1951, 50 n. 15, that Matthew's addition 'the Son of the living God' which 'flesh and blood has not revealed, but my Father in heaven' refers not to Messiahship but to the Father–Son relationship that constitutes the secret heart of Jesus' life (cf. ch. VIII, pp. 359–63 below), and he suggests the words belong to the context of Luke 22.28–34. See his *Peter: Disciple, Apostle, Martyr*, 176–91; 'L'apôtre Pierre instrument du diable et instrument de Dieu: la place de Matt. 16.16–19 dans la tradition primitive' in A. J. B. Higgins, ed., *New Testament Essays*, 94–105; *Christology of the NT*, 280f.

shore of the Sea of Galilee'. Many have favoured a simple transposition of chs. 5 and 6. For at the end of ch. 4 Jesus is in Galilee (though in Cana in the hill-country rather than on the lake-side). Chapter 6 would then follow, succeeded by 5.1, 'Later on Jesus went up to Jerusalem for one of the Jewish festivals', and 7.1, 'Afterwards Jesus went about in Galilee. He wished to avoid Judaea because the Jews were looking for a chance to kill him.' It is also urged that the statements in 7.1 and 19–21 about the Jews trying to kill him in connection with a sabbath healing are more natural following closely upon 5.18 – though 7.3 would equally seem to imply that Jesus had *not* been seen recently in Jerusalem performing his mighty works. The transposition is tempting, and it has been adopted by many commentators including Bernard and Bultmann. But the vogue for it seems to be passing and Hoskyns, Dodd, Barrett, Brown and Lindars are united in rejecting it. There is absolutely no manuscript evidence for it, and while it may ease the topography it makes the chronology more difficult. If, as we have argued, both from the Synoptic evidence and from John 4, Jesus arrived in Galilee at the end of May following the Passover of 28, then if ch. 6 follows immediately on ch. 4 almost an entire year elapses with nothing to show for it until another Passover is at hand (6.4). The unnamed feast for which Jesus visits Jerusalem in 5.1 would then have to be Pentecost, for he goes up again at Tabernacles in 7.2, though all the Synoptic evidence suggests that Jesus went north rather than south in the period following the feeding(s). Moreover, as Stanton rightly remarked,

> The account of the crisis in the work of Jesus in Galilee given in the latter part of ch. 6, if retained as part of the narrative and transposed with the rest, would come too early. Where it stands at present it is brought near to his final departure from Galilee. This is in itself more likely, and is certainly more in accord with the Synoptic outline, than that He should have thought it worth while to return there after that crisis had occurred and after a visit to Jerusalem.[9]

It seems better to conclude that in 6.1 John is introducing a new and disconnected incident with his vague and resumptive phrase μετὰ ταῦτα, which the NEB here correctly renders 'some time later'. When he wants to be he can be quite precise about notices of time (1.29, 35, 43; 2.1, 12; 4.40, 43; 6.22; 11.6, 17; 12.1, 12; 20.26); but, in contrast with μετὰ τοῦτο (after this), which always seems to refer back to the

[9] *Gospels as Historical Documents*, III, 68.

immediately preceding incident (2.12; 11.7, 11; 19.28), *μετὰ ταῦτα* is his regular way of indicating an indefinite interval of any duration (3.22; 5.1, 14; 6.1; 7.1; 13.7; 19.38; 21.1). So we should infer that he is making no attempt to link the events of ch. 6 geographically or temporally to what has gone before. In his highly selective presentation of scenes from the ministry of Jesus (cf. 21.25) he is simply starting again.

In so doing John provides us with less light at this point than the Synoptic tradition. For in the latter the withdrawal to a deserted spot prior to the feeding is connected with two preceding incidents. In Mark (6.30–32) and, more summarily, in Luke (9.10) it is linked to the return of the Twelve from their preaching mission: Jesus calls them apart for a period of rest and reflection. In Matthew the mission of the Twelve is set earlier (10.1–16) and is made the occasion of a typical Matthaean discourse occupying the rest of the chapter – and surprisingly we are never told of their return. Instead Matthew has linked Jesus' withdrawal to the story of the Baptist's death. This story indeed comes in the same place in Mark (6.17–29), but whereas in Mark it is told as an incident from the past, to explain Herod's reference to 'John whom I beheaded' (6.16), in Matthew (14.3–12) it is the report of John's death which directly prompts Jesus' retreat (14.13). The link is fairly clearly the editorial work of Matthew. For he has used exactly the same phrase (*ἀκούσας . . . ἀνεχώρησεν*) of the news of John's death as he had used earlier (4.12) of his arrest. But the question remains whether he may not be correct in connecting violence done to John with reappraisal by Jesus of his own mission. Certainly reflection upon the fate of John was still preoccupying Jesus not long afterwards, according to the Markan as well as the Matthaean tradition (Mark 9.11–13; Matt. 17.10–13; Luke again omits). For the moment we may leave the connection open and return to it in the light of the Johannine interpretation of the feeding. In any case the need for withdrawal and reassessment seems to have been forced upon Jesus by either or both of the factors (the return of the Twelve or the news of John's death) with which the Synoptists associate it.

Let us now examine the narratives of the feeding itself and begin by asking how we may locate it both in time and space. In time John is quite precise: 'Passover was at hand' (6.4), confirming what could be inferred from the greenness of the grass in Mark 6.39, that it had not yet been scorched by the searing wind and sun of summer. Matthew and Luke eliminate any indication of time, and there is nothing to be deduced from the duplicate tradition of the feeding of the four thousand. It has however been pointed out that the discussion which follows this in Mark 8.15 and Matt. 16.6 about the 'leaven' of the Pharisees would have been particularly topical at Passover time when the leaven had to be purged out (cf. I Cor. 5.6–8). But this is purely inferential and any such connection has been lost in the parallel in Luke 12.1f.[10]

About the place, in contrast, there is a confusing welter of information.

We may start by looking at three supposedly precise locations in the tradition, which could settle the issue.

The first is in Luke 9.10, where it is said that Jesus withdrew privately with the apostles 'to a town called Bethsaida' (at the north-east end of the Lake). Apparently the feeding takes place there, since there is no indication of further movement. But later the Twelve approach Jesus and say: 'Send these people away; then they can go into the villages and farms round about to find food and lodging; for we are in a lonely place here' (9.12). Clearly there is a contradiction at this point and Luke's geography must here as elsewhere in the Galilee area be regarded as unreliable, except perhaps as an indication of the *direction* in which Jesus and the disciples set out. As we said earlier, it looks as if he may have taken over the place-name from Mark 6.45 or 8.22, but in neither instance is it there given as the location of a feeding.

Secondly, there is a variant reading in John 6.1, which if original would indicate at any rate the area of the feeding. In place of the awkward phrase 'across the Sea of Galilee of Tiberias', which seems to duplicate alternative names for the Lake (cf. 21.1),[11] some (not very impressive) manuscripts[12] read 'across the Sea of Galilee to the parts

[10]If there is any parallelism to be seen between the *barley* loaves peculiar to John (6.9), and the incident in II Kings 4.42–24, then it may be significant that this was also at Passover-time:

> A man came from Baal-shalisha, bringing the man of God some of the new season's bread, twenty barley loaves, and fresh ripe ears of corn. Elisha said, 'Give this to the people to eat.' But his disciple protested, 'I cannot set this before a hundred men.' Still he repeated, 'Give it to the people to eat; for this is the word of the Lord: "They will eat and there will be some left over."' So he set it before them, and they ate and left some over, as the Lord had said.

John's word παιδάριον is also used in the LXX of Elisha's servant, Gehazi, earlier in the same chapter (II Kings 4.12, 14, 25), but here the word is λειτουργός. It is very difficult to be sure that the evangelist intended the parallel.

[11]Josephus, *BJ* 3.57, confirms the name 'Lake of (lit. 'by') Tiberias' as well as Lake of Gennesar (3.506 etc.).

[12]D, Θ, *892* and other minuscules, some Old Latin manuscripts, the Georgian version and Chrysostom.

(or region) of Tiberias'. But, despite its advocacy by Boismard,[13] this looks suspiciously like a correction of the harder reading. As B. Metzger says, 'If this reading were original, it would be difficult to account for the rise of the others.'[14] We may therefore agree with Barrett[15] that 'the clumsy text is no doubt the original'. On it turns also the translation of 6.23: 'But (or, Other) boats came from Tiberias near the place where they ate the bread.' If the variant reading in 6.1 were adopted, then 'near the place where they ate the bread' would have to refer to the point of departure rather than arrival of the boats, but this is a much less natural way of taking it.[16] So it does not look as though John intends to locate the feeding in the vicinity of Tiberias.

Thirdly, there is the site adopted by later tradition, namely, Tabgha or Heptapegon (the Seven Springs), on the north-west corner of the Lake. This is mentioned by the pilgrim Egeria at the beginning of the fifth century AD[17] and a church dedicated to the Multiplying of the Loaves and Fishes stands there to this day. But she tells us that Tabgha was also commemorated as the site of the resurrection appearance in John 21.1–14 and of the Sermon on the Mount. It would in fact fit the scene of John 21 very well (which also involves loaves and fishes) since shoals of fish still congregate round the warm springs that issue into the Lake at this point.[18] But there is little to be said for it as the site of the feeding. For it cannot be held to be on the 'other side' of the Sea from Bethsaida (Mark 6.45) or Capernaum (John 6.17), let alone Gennesaret (Mark 6.53; Matt. 14.34) or Magdala (Matt. 15.39).[19] It looks as if the various tourist sites came to be brought together in one accessible spot for the convenience of pilgrims.[20]

[13]*RB* 60, 1953, 362–6; 64, 1957, 369.

[14]*A Textual Commentary on the Greek New Testament*, London and New York, 1971, 211.

[15]*St John*, ad loc.

[16]There is in 6.23 a variant in ℵ* (which, as Brown says, has here 'a remarkably aberrant form of the text'), b and r: 'Tiberias which *was near* the place'. But it can hardly be taken as anything but one more of many attempts to improve a confused piece of writing.

[17]Wilkinson, *Egeria's Travels*, 196.

[18]Cf. Kopp, *The Holy Places of the Gospels*, 216: 'Where the water from Seven Wells pours into the lake is the richest fishing-ground on the whole west bank of the Lake.' G. Dalman, *Sacred Sites and Ways*, 135f., gives a vivid description of fishing in this neighbourhood.

[19]S. Loffreda, *The Sanctuaries of Tabgha*, Jerusalem 1975, who defends the traditional site, makes no attempt to explain this.

[20]So Kopp, *Holy Places*, 215.

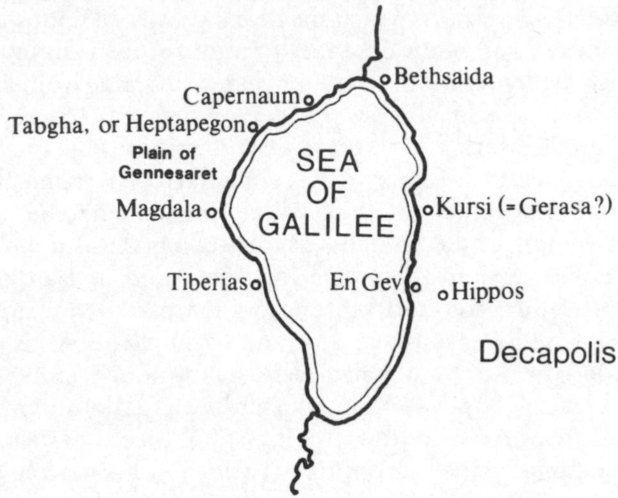

So if none of the specific localities mentioned in Scripture or later tradition is convincing, what are the probabilities?

We may begin by taking up the implications of the phrase 'the other side' which occurs in some form or other in all the accounts.

There are two expressions in the Gospels, *πέραν τοῦ Ἰορδάνου* and *τὸ πέραν*. The former, 'beyond Jordan', always indicates a specific geographical area, the other half of Antipas's territory, known as Peraea – a name which, though frequent in Josephus, is never found in the New Testament, except as a variant addition to Luke 6.17. It would simplify matters if *τὸ πέραν* were similarly a quasi-technical term for 'the east bank'. But unhappily it is not so simple.

Τὸ πέραν first occurs in the Gospels in Mark 4.35 and parallels: 'Let us go to the other side.' According to Matthew (8.5–18) Jesus says this in Capernaum; according to Mark (4.1–35) in a boat evidently near by. Luke (8.4–22) is characteristically unspecific. After a storm in which the boat nearly sinks they arrive at what the best texts of Mark (5.1) and Luke (8.26) call 'the country of the Gerasenes'. (That of Matthew (8.28) has 'the country of the Gadarenes', but despite the familiarity of 'the Gadarene swine', this was certainly not Gadara, which is situated many miles to the east and far from the sea into which the pigs rushed down.) Gerasa is probably the modern Kursi, about mid-way down the east coast of the Sea of Galilee.[21] Anyhow it was clearly, from the keeping of

[21] Finegan, *Archaelogy of the NT*, 62.

pigs, in a Gentile area and according to Mark (5.20) in the neighbourhood of the Decapolis, to which the near-by city of Hippos belonged. But in his next verse Mark describes Jesus crossing again to 'the other side', which evidently means back to where they came from and which Matthew (9.1) specifically says is his 'own town' (ἰδία πόλις), i.e. Capernaum (cf. Mark 2.1). So far everything is fairly plain, though it already shows that 'the other side' is not a fixed geographical location but designates the opposite side to where you happen to be.

When we come to the accounts of the feeding(s) it is to be observed that in Luke's version of the five thousand, and in Matthew's and Mark's of the four thousand, there is no prior sea-crossing. In fact only John (6.1) actually says that Jesus (and by implication his disciples) went 'across' the Sea, though he never uses the noun τὸ πέραν but only the adverb πέραν. Mark (6.32) and Matthew (14.13) simply say that they went away or withdrew by boat to a lonely or desert place, Matthew adding vaguely 'from there', which in his writing generally seems to imply Capernaum (on the middle of the north coast). The only clue, apart from Luke's statement that the journey at least took them through Bethsaida (9.10), is that in Matthew (14.13) and Mark (6.33) the crowds 'from (all) the towns' follow 'on foot' and in Mark get there before the boat. So it would appear that it could not have been too far round the north-east corner of the Lake. Then after the feeding of the five thousand Matthew, Mark and John agree that the disciples went back by boat by themselves to 'the other side' or 'across the sea'. John says they set off for Capernaum and in due course arrived there (6.17, 21), Mark (6.45) that Jesus made them embark for Bethsaida (on the north- east coast) 'ahead of him, while he himself sent the people away' (meaning to catch them up at Bethsaida?). Cf. John 6.17, 'Jesus had not yet joined them', but, as Matthew agrees (14.34), they landed up at Gennesaret (Mark 6.53) at the north-west corner. For during the trip they had been blown off course 'many stades' (Matt. 14.24) 'into the middle of the sea' (Mark 6.47), or as John puts it with characteristic precision 'twenty-five to thirty stades' (6.18), that is, three to four miles out.[22]

In the parallel accounts of the feeding of the four thousand Jesus had previously come down by land from the district of Tyre and Sidon and had reached the shore of the Sea of Galilee, according to Mark (7.31), 'through the territory of the Decapolis', which again would imply the east coast. Thereafter he goes by boat (with his disciples in Mark) to the

[22]Josephus (*BJ* 3.506) says that the lake measured 40 stades across; in fact it is 7 miles, but only at its broadest point.

district of Magadan or Magdala (Matt. 15.39) or in Mark (8.10, where the text is probably corrupt) Dalmanutha. Shortly afterwards he leaves there once more, according to Mark (8.13) by boat, though not specifically so in Matthew (16.4f.), for 'the other side' (which again shows the contextual character of the phrase), arriving in Bethsaida (Mark 8.22), whence he travelled up to 'the villages (or, district) of Caesarea Philippi' (Mark 8.27; Matt. 16.13).

From this confusion of statements, which it is clearly impossible fully to harmonize, it looks as though the Synoptic evidence points to the feeding(s) having taken place on the north-east side of the Lake and having been followed by a boat-crossing to the north-west corner. But there are many duplications and loose ends.

To this evidence John adds a fascinating coda (6.22–25), which appears to have no obvious theological motive. Though it is not without ambiguity and could certainly have been expressed more clearly, it reads with something of the circumstantiality of a detective story. In the NEB it runs:

> Next morning the crowd was standing on the opposite shore. They had seen [taking the aorist, necessarily, as a pluperfect] only one boat there,[23] and Jesus, they knew, had not embarked with his disciples, who had gone away without him. Boats from Tiberias, however, [or, other boats from Tiberias] came ashore near where the people had eaten the bread over which the Lord gave thanks.[24] When the people saw that neither Jesus nor his disciples were any longer there, they themselves went aboard these boats and made for Capernaum in search of Jesus. They found him on the other side. 'Rabbi', they said, 'when did you come here?'

Although we might have also expected their question to be 'how?', they evidently presumed, correctly, that Capernaum was where Jesus and his disciples would be making for. From this gratuitous piece of itinerary we can deduce that the place of the feeding lay across the sea not only from Capernaum but also from Tiberias (on the south-west side). An obvious port of call for boats from Tiberias

[23]Cf. Sanday, *Authorship and Historical Character of the Fourth Gospel*, 126f.: 'This, we may remark in passing, confirms the statement of the Synoptics that the people themselves had come round by land, just as the fact that they are now ready to cross the sea tends to show that they were not, at least that part of them, on the way to the passover at Jerusalem.'

[24]The last six words are omitted by D and a number of versions, and may well not be part of the true text. But this does not affect the geography.

would be En Gev, the harbour of Hippos, to the south of Kursi (as it still is for lake-crossings today both from Capernaum and Tiberias). Since the place of feeding was near rather than at this point and since it was in all the accounts a deserted spot (this is not specified in John but is implied by the parallel with Moses giving manna 'in the wilderness' in 6.31, 49), it would fit well with the Synoptic evidence if it lay further up the east coast between Kursi and the plain of Bethsaida.[25] It would probably be a mistake to attempt to identify 'the mountain' (τὸ ὄρος) with which Mark (6.46), Matthew (14.23) and John (6.3, 15) associate the feeding of the five thousand and Matthew (15.29) also that of the four thousand, since there are not, properly speaking, 'mountains' within striking distance of the Lake. The NEB is surely correct in simply referring to it as 'the hill-side' – and there are several possibilities between the wadis on that part of the coast, all with 'plenty of grass' (John 6.10) at that time of the year.[26] It is perhaps further confirmation of the place being not too far from Bethsaida that the question in John 6.6, 'Where are we to buy bread to feed these people?', should be addressed to Philip who, John tells us, was a native of that town (1.45) and could be presumed to have local knowledge.[27]

We may conclude then that in regard to both time and place John's account of the feeding confirms and articulates the more vague and confused information to be pieced together from the Synoptic traditions.

[25]Dalman, *Sacred Sites*, 172–6, places it between En Gev and Kursi, but the Synoptic evidence would favour a spot further north.

[26]Dalman, *Sacred Sites*, 174f., refers to 'the exuberant wild growth of herbs which, in the spring and through the greatest portion of the rainy season, cover the whole uncultivated ground in the lake district, and even the mountains (Lev. R. 27.72a).'

[27]Mention should perhaps be made of another reconstruction favoured by Schein in *Following the Way*, 100–6, 210f., since in almost every other respect he argues for the same chronology as I have adopted. But in order to avoid the break in itinerary at 6.1, instead of reversing chs. 5 and 6, he has Jesus staying on in Jerusalem from the visit of ch. 5 (which he agrees was at Tabernacles) throughout the winter almost till Passover (why he should have left just *before* the Feast he does not explain). Then he makes him cross the Sea of Galilee from the south to Magdala on the north-west coast, which he claims is supported as the site of the feeding by the pilgrim Arculfus. But this is neither in the vicinity of Tiberias (for he accepts the D reading in 6.1) nor can it be squared with any of the Synoptic geography (which he simply has to dismiss). Nor is it compatible with John 6.22f., which he interprets of people from Tiberias hearing of the miracle going to the scene by boat to Magdala, finding the wonder-worker gone, and then being joined by others from the village to cross to Capernaum. But this is not what the text says. The crowd is part of that which had been standing on the other side since the feeding and which then takes the boats coming from Tiberias. Also from Magdala Jesus could easily have walked round to Capernaum during the night, thus making the question of 6.25, 'When did you get here?', redundant.

But its most important contribution has yet to be considered. Though it gives us no insight as to what led up to it, it provides a vital clue to interpreting its significance and thus to understanding what led from it.

This clue is supplied in the crowd's reaction to the miracle, of which no hint surprisingly is offered in the Synoptic accounts of either the five thousand or the four thousand:

> When the people saw the sign Jesus had performed, the word went round, 'Surely this must be the prophet that was to come into the world.' Jesus, aware that they meant to come and seize him to proclaim him king, withdrew again to the hills (τὸ ὄρος as in 6.3) by himself (6.14f.).

There is some manuscript support for reading, in place of 'withdrew', φεύγει ('fled'),[28] which is hardly likely to have been invented, and is adopted by both Brown and Boismard.[29] In any case Jesus' hand is forced and he finds himself compelled to rapid evasive action. Suddenly we become aware of the political and paramilitary dimensions of this messianic meal, which have been explored by T. W. Manson,[30] H. W. Montefiore,[31] C. H. Dodd[32] and earlier, as one discovers so often, J. B. Lightfoot.[33]

We could never have deduced its existence from the Synoptic accounts, but with the clue in our hands a number of things become perspicuous. In Mark (6.32–44) one can sense the manic excitement of the mob, rushing together[34] ahead of the boat, in their lost and dangerous condition of lacking and looking for a leader. For the reference to their being like 'sheep without a shepherd' has a political background in the Old Testament (Num. 27.17; I Kings 22.17; Ezek. 34.5). The companies of hundreds and fifties in which they were formed[35] may

[28]It is read by the original hand of Codex Sinaiticus, many manuscripts of the Old Latin, the Vulgate, the Curetonian Syriac, the Diatessaron, Tertullian and Augustine.

[29]*Synopse des Quatre Évangiles*, III, *L'Évangile de Jean*, 178.

[30]*The Servant Messiah*, Cambridge and New York 1953, 69–71.

[31]'Revolt in the Desert', *NTS* 8, 1961–2, 135–41.

[32]*Historical Tradition*, 212–17; *The Founder of Christianity*, 1970, 131–9.

[33]*Biblical Essays*, 24–6, 151–3. It is noteworthy that it escaped B. F. Westcott. In what follows I have paraphrased some material from my chapter 'His Witness is True: a Test of the Johannine Claim' in *Twelve More NTS*, 112–37.

[34]Cf. the scenes in Acts 3.11 and 21.30 where the same language is used.

[35]I am persuaded (*pace* C. F. D. Moule, *An Idiom Book of New Testament Greek*, Cambridge ²1963, 59f.) that the κατὰ ἑκατὸν καὶ κατὰ πεντήκοντα in Mark 6.40 must be distributive, as regularly with numerals (Blass-Debrunner, *Greek Grammar of the NT*, § 248 (1)), 'in hundreds and fifties', and cannot mean, as in the NEB, 50 × 100 (= 5000). But with Moule I am prepared to be sceptical about the military overtones of the formation.

perhaps, as Montefiore suggests,[36] have quasi-military overtones and recall the divisions of the Israelites during their wilderness wanderings (cf. Exod. 18.21; Deut. 1.15) and find their parallel in the War Scroll of the Qumran community (1QM 4.2–5; 6.10; cf. 1QS 2.21; CD 13.1). Then there is the significance, if we were looking for it, of the fact that they were all males (ἄνδρες: Mark 6.44; Luke 9.14; John 6.10). Matthew appears to miss the point, perhaps to heighten the miraculous, by adding in each of his accounts[37] 'besides women and children' (14.21; 15.38).[38] For the context of this gathering in the desert is evidently the same as that described in Acts 21.38: 'Then you are not the Egyptian who started a revolt some time ago and led a force of four thousand terrorists (ἄνδρας τῶν σικαρίων) out into the wilds?' The wilderness, not least at Passover-time, that annual reminder of Jewish 'liberation theology', when another Moses should appear to perform mighty works in the wilderness (cf. John 6.30f.),[39] was the natural place from which nationalist leaders might be expected: 'Impostors will come claiming to be messiahs or prophets, and they will produce great signs and wonders. . . . If they tell you, "He is there in the wilderness", do not go out' (Matt. 24.24–26). Josephus testifies later[40] to several abortive risings by men calling a mob to follow them into the desert, promising signs (σημεῖα ἐλευθερίας) and giving themselves out to be prophets.[41] Of that same Egyptian that Acts mentions Josephus writes:

> A charlatan, who had gained for himself the reputation of a prophet, this man appeared in the country, collected a following of about thirty thousand dupes, and led them by a circuitous route from the desert to the mount called the mount of Olives. From there he proposed to force an entrance into Jerusalem and, after overpowering the Roman garrison, to set himself up as tyrant of the people, employing those who poured in with him as his bodyguard.[42]

[36]'Revolt in the Desert', 137.

[37]In the second feeding Mark (8.9) has simply 'four thousand' without a noun.

[38]Unless, as Dodd suggested to Montefiore ('Revolt in the Desert', 137) χωρίς could here mean 'without any admixture of women and children', or 'unencumbered by women and children'. But he did not repeat this in his own discussion of the passage.

[39]Cf. b. *R. Sh.* 11a: 'During the month of Nisan they were redeemed and in the month of Nisan they will be redeemed again'; and R. Le Déaut, *La nuit pascale*, Analecta Biblica 22, Rome 1963, specif. 279–91.

[40]*BJ* 2.258–60; *Ant.* 20.97–9, 167–72, 188.

[41]Cf. P. W. Barnett, 'The Jewish Sign-Prophets – AD 40–70. Their Intentions and Origin', *NTS* 27, 1980–1, 679–97.

[42]*BJ* 2.261f.; tr. H. St. J. Thackeray, LCL.

Such, no doubt, was the kind of programme that many in that crowd were expecting from Jesus in the wilderness. And John's evidence in 6.14f. is our earliest for such a complex of expectation: when they saw the *sign* he did, they concluded he was a *prophet* and immediately tried to make him *king*. By this they need have meant no more than when Josephus uses the same word to describe how, 'as the several companies of the seditious lighted upon anyone to head them, he was immediately created a king (βασιλεύς)'.[43] Yet a bid for the throne of Israel was a serious possibility, for, as Josephus says again, with 'the country . . . a prey to disorder . . . the opportunity induced numbers of persons to aspire to sovereignty (βασιλεία),[44] and he catalogues a number of them individually.[45] Indeed of John 6.15 Sanday wrote many years ago: 'There is no stronger proof both of the genuineness and of the authenticity of the Fourth Gospel than the way in which it reflects the current Messianic idea.'[46]

This clue also explains the sudden and otherwise unaccountable ending to the story of the feeding of the five thousand in Mark: 'As soon as it was over he forced (ἠνάγκασεν) his disciples to embark and cross to Bethsaida ahead of him, while he himself sent the people away' (6.45). Evidently Jesus could not trust his closest associates not to share in the popular surge and constitute themselves his bodyguard. Then, we read, after dismissing the crowds 'he went away εἰς τὸ ὄρος to pray' (6.46) or in John 'he withdrew (or, fled) again εἰς τὸ ὄρος by himself alone' (6.15). Here perhaps we may have the setting in life for the temptation to a populist programme of material sovereignty which the Synoptists represent him as rejecting in principle from the beginning in the symbolic stories of his temptation in the wilderness (Matt. 4.1–4, 8–10; Luke 4.1–8) but which could well have taken their particular form from the loaves and mountain (cf. Matt. 4.8: εἰς ὄρος) of this desert crisis.[47]

[43]*Ant.* 17.285. I have preferred here the translation of A. N. Sherwin-White in his *Roman Society and Roman Law in the New Testament*, 1963, 25. The Loeb edition (R. Marcus) takes προϊστάμενος to mean 'made himself king', which is perhaps less likely in the context. But cf. John 19.12, 'Anyone who makes himself a king'.

[44]*BJ* 2.55.

[45]*Ant.* 17.271–84; cf. Acts 5.36f.

[46]*Authorship and Historical Character of the Fourth Gospel*, 124. Similarly Dodd, *Historical Tradition*, 120, 216f., 222.

[47]Cf. R. E. Brown, 'Incidents that are Units in the Synoptic Gospels but Dispersed in St John', *CBQ* 23, 1961, 153f. His article concludes: 'In the cases we have studied, an interesting case can be made out for the basic historicity of the Johannine picture and for theological reorganization on the part of the Synoptic Gospels. We are coming to realize more and more that the critics have played us false in their minimal estimate of the historicity of the Fourth Gospel' (160).

If so they will apply, not so much to the first reappraisal in Jesus' self-understanding we looked at in the last chapter, from the role of the mighty one of Malachi 3 and 4 which John the Baptist had marked out for him to that of the anointed liberator of Isaiah 61 and 35 which characterized him during the Galilean period (cf. Luke 4.16–30; 7.18–23; Matt. 11.2–6), but to the second turning-point in his ministry, occasioned by the dangerous misunderstanding to which the title 'messiah' or 'anointed one' came to be exposed. I am much attracted to the view put forward by A. E. Harvey in his Bampton Lectures[48] that 'the Christ' in the weak sense of 'the anointed or appointed one' derived from his use of Isaiah 61.1, could already have stuck to Jesus during his lifetime as a popular designation or nickname to distinguish him from many others.[49] He was 'Jesus called the Christ' (Matt. 1.16; 27.16f. [contrasted with 'Jesus Barabbas'?]; 27.22; Josephus, *Ant.* 20.200). Just as Josephus speaks of 'John surnamed the Baptist' (*Ant.* 18.116), which becomes in the Gospels simply 'John the Baptist', so it is quite likely that 'the Christ' may at first have attached itself to Jesus as a popular designation without any great or pre-established theological significance.[50] If so it became an embarrassing title, for it was open to be interpreted not only in religious but in political terms, as the equivalence of 'Christ' and 'king' in popular usage makes clear (Mark 15.32; Luke 23.2, 35–7). The accusation was later to be made of Christians that they 'assert that there is a rival king, Jesus' (Acts 17.7) (and this indeed could well explain the silence on the political dimension of the desert feeding in Mark, if he was writing for the Roman church). When therefore this same conclusion is drawn by the crowds at the climax of the messianic meal, Jesus is compelled to urgent corrective and evasive action beginning with the Twelve.

First he must isolate them from the dangerous enthusiasm of the mob (Mark 6.45). Then he must take them away to test and re-educate them in the terms of their loyalty to him. Peter's reply that he is the Messiah is silenced rather than acclaimed (Mark 8.27–30). They must

[48] *Jesus and the Constraints of History*, 80–82; 139–43; 149–53.

[49] Harvey points out that Josephus mentions 21 Jesuses, compared with 18 Josephs and 11 Johns.

[50] It could even perhaps explain Josephus, *Ant.* 18.63 as genuine Josephus: 'He was "the Christ".' F. Scheidweiler, 'Das Testimonium Flavianum', *ZNW* 45, 1954, 230–43, suggests that this passage, like 20.200 also, originally read ὁ λεγόμενος Χριστός. Jerome, *Vir. ill.* 13, in his quotation of 18.63 reads 'credebatur esse Christus'. Cf. Feldman, 'The *Testimonium Flavianium*' in Berkey and Edwards, edd., *Christological Perspectives*, 192.

be detached from this triumphalist category to follow a Son of Man whose victory could come only the other side of suffering and death (Mark 8.31) and whose scriptural model was this time to be Daniel 7 and Isaiah 53. A similar challenge in face of disappointment and defection is issued in John 6.66–69. Peter responds in terms of 'the Holy One of God', another designation of the consecrated or anointed one (in Ps. 106.16 it is used of Aaron).[51] There is no explicit praise or disapprobation, but similar words are used of Judas in John (6.70f.) as are addressed to Peter in Mark for failing to see that the way of violence must be disavowed. Perhaps, it is implied, Jesus could see even at that stage that Peter was only half convinced and Judas not at all.

In the Synoptic account the questioning of the disciples' faith, which has often been seen as the climax and watershed of the Markan narrative,[52] is presented without motive or explanation. This exercise in theology by Gallup poll, which ends apparently in rebuke and recrimination, has no obvious occasion or interpretation. As Goguel said, 'As we read the Synoptic narrative we feel that something must have happened at this point which Mark has not mentioned, and that this unknown element must have exercised a direct influence on the following course of events.'[53] In John, however, we can see it as the consequence (rather than the climax) of an earlier turning-point or dangerous corner in the ministry. The Johannine setting, again, explains not only the need for forced withdrawal and the sharp rebuke of the disciples, but the reiterated suppression by Jesus in the Markan narrative of all publicity (7.24, 36; 8.26, 30; 9.9, 30). Except for the charges to silence after Peter's confession (8.30) and the Transfiguration (9.9), this gets lost, as we have seen, in Matthew and Luke, though it is preserved in John (7.1–10). John also alone tells us of the background of disaffection among 'disciples' at the time (6.66f.).[54] This not only gives a reason for testing the loyalty of the Twelve but would explain the reference in Mark 8.38 and parallels (cf. Matt. 10.33 = Luke 12.9) to those who are 'ashamed' of Jesus, and the

[51] I cannot follow Cullmann, *Christology of the NT*, 285, in thinking this is the equivalent of 'Son of God'.

[52] Notably by T. W. Manson in *The Teaching of Jesus*, Cambridge 1935, specifically 210.

[53] *Life of Jesus*, ET London and New York 1933, 369; quoted, Montefiore, 'Revolt in the Desert', 141.

[54] Dodd suggests that the ἐκ τούτου here may originally have referred not to the immediately preceding Johannine discourse but to 'the whole episode described earlier in the chapter, especially in v. 15, *possibly* with the demand for a sign which may have followed' (*Historical Tradition*, 220).

repeated language of the Gospels about those who are offended or do not stay the course (e.g. Mark 4.17 and pars.; Matt. 11.6 = Luke 7.23; Luke 9.62; 22.28; Mark 14.27–29 and pars.; John 16.1).[55]

John 6.15 affords a vital glimpse into how easily Jesus could have been swept to Jerusalem twelve months earlier as a sort of king whose followers *would* fight (John 18.36): that to the end remained a real possibility (cf. Matt. 26.52; John 18.11), and even when Jesus was arrested it was as if he were an armed revolutionary (Mark 14.48 and pars.). The onset of this previous Passover could so swiftly have led to a passion narrative before its time. Indeed the refrain 'the Passover was near' (ἐγγὺς τὸ πάσχα) tolls as a bell through John's Gospel (2.13; 6.4; 11.55) rather like the passion predictions in the second half of Mark's (8.31; 9.31; 10.33). Perhaps this is why the sequence of these events, together with intervals of time (Matt. 17.1; Mark 9.2; Luke 9.28), unique to the Synoptic story of the ministry, imprinted itself upon the tradition of the apostolic church almost as deeply and diversely as the passion itself.

Blinzler[56] makes the interesting suggestion that Jesus' refusal to go to Jerusalem for Passover that year was directly influenced by this event, and that the politically-aroused mob from Galilee who *did* go up provoked Pilate to the blood-bath recounted in Luke 13.1–3, with its warning to change direction or expect the same end. He also suggests that the alienation between Herod and Pilate (Luke 23.12) and Herod's presence in Jerusalem the next Passover (23.7) were related to this incident involving his own citizens. Pilate by acknowledging Herod's jurisdiction over Jesus as a Galilean heals the diplomatic breach. None of this can be more than speculative, but it would certainly enable us to integrate otherwise disconnected features of the Gospel story into a coherent political picture, to which John's account of the desert feeding alone provides the clue.

Thenceforward, care to avoid premature dénouement, which this crisis so nearly provoked, became decisive. The watershed had been crossed. Now everything began to flow for Jesus inexorably in a new direction, towards Jerusalem and death. But the timing and the tactics must be his own (John 7.2–14, 30; 8.20; 12.23, 27; 13.1; cf. Luke 13.31–35). That was the lesson of this climactic moment.

Reading back, the church was able to recognize in the messianic

[55]So Dodd, ibid., 221, who points out that John alone gives explicit evidence for such a larger body of 'disciples' which all the Gospels presuppose.

[56]'Die Niedermetzelung von Galiläern durch Pilatus', *NovT* 2, 1957, 24–49, specif. 43–7.

meal in the desert and in Jesus' actions in taking, blessing, breaking and distributing the bread an anticipation of that final act of prophetic symbolism which was to place his own interpretation on his life-giving death. And so it comes about that the Synoptic telling of it, and not only the Johannine, is instinct with eucharistic overtones. As Brown rightly insists, 'the eucharistic elements in the various multiplication accounts are about the same in number, even though different in detail.'[57] What John does here as elsewhere is to evoke rather than invent, and by placing the emphasis of his sacramental teaching on the discourse at Capernaum (6.26–59) rather than on the last supper he brings out more than the others the shadow of the end under which these events fell. But he does it, as usual, not by developing the theology at the expense of the history but by being faithful to the history in all its temporal, geographical and political detail.

Finally, we may return to the part of the history of which John says nothing, namely, to what led up to and provoked the withdrawal to the wilderness in the first instance. For although John is here silent, his clue to what follows it can again, I suggest, help to interpret and assess what the Synoptists give us.

It will be remembered that the withdrawal is precipitated in Mark (6.30) and Luke (9.10) by the return of the Twelve from their mission, and in Matthew (14.12) by the news of the Baptist's death. Now it is interesting that the first 'withdrawal' of Jesus from Judaea and the reassessment of his role,[58] was equally occasioned, according to John (4.1–3), by the very success of Jesus' mission and, according to Matthew (4.12), by the arrest of the Baptist. We may perhaps see the same factors at work in this second and more agonizing reappraisal. The Twelve had been sent out, as Luke summarizes it, 'to announce the kingdom of God and to heal' (9.2), and in his parallel charge to the seventy, to 'say to them, The kingdom of God has come upon you' (10.9). The success of the mission of the Twelve is not recorded (Mark

[57]*John* I, 248. Cf. the chart (243) and the whole discussion, 246–9. Even John's use of *εὐχαρίστειν* rather than *εὐλόγειν* cannot be held to be especially significant or technical. It occurs also in both Synoptic accounts of the feeding of the four thousand. Both words are to be seen rendering the Hebrew root *brk* and are used indifferently in the institution narratives of 1 Corinthians and the Gospels. Cf. J. -P. Audet, 'Esquisse historique du genre littéraire de la "bénédiction" juive et de l'"eucharistie" chrétienne', *RB* 65, 1958, 371–99. One of the most striking *absences* in John 6 (and perhaps even more significantly in 21.13; contrast Luke 24.30, 35) is any mention of the *breaking* of the bread, common to both the Synoptic feeding and all accounts of the last supper, though of course John refers to the *κλάσματα*, fragments, like the rest.

[58]See above, ch. IV, p. 187.

6.30; Luke 9.10), but that of the sending of the seventy (which belongs to Luke's non-Markan material and may well be a doublet) is reported with ebullience, though the outward signs of it are played down by Jesus (Luke 10.17–20). In Luke (10.21–24) this marks the moment of the *Jubelruf*, when Jesus sees the fulfilment of the Father's deepest purpose for his life. In Matthew (11.25–30) this saying is followed by the call to all who 'labour' (the word used of missionary work in John 4.38) to be 'rested' (the same word as in Mark 6.31). It could well be that the 'all you' is not originally a general invitation to the public (who are far away at this point) but a call to the returning missionaries to come apart. If the misunderstanding of the kingdom in political terms was indeed becoming a source of anxiety to Jesus, then the report of their triumph[59] *coupled with that of the Baptist's execution* could well have been what triggered his reaction.

For in the latter was to be seen most vividly where the way of those who would take the kingdom by violence could lead. The men who wished to 'seize' (ἁρπάζειν) Jesus to make him king are precisely the βιασταί, the men of violence, who would also 'seize' the kingdom by force (Matt. 11.12). And, says Jesus significantly, these have been at work 'from the days of John the Baptist until now'. Though there is no hint that the Baptist himself had encouraged such violence, it is significant that Josephus attributes Herod's action in arresting him to the fear that his movement could give rise to just this response. He writes:

> When others too (i.e., those who were not motivated purely by moral reformation) joined the crowds about him, because they were aroused (or, delighted) to the highest degree by his sermons, Herod became alarmed. Eloquence that had so great an effect on mankind might lead to some form of sedition (or, revolt), for it looked as if they would be guided by John in everything that they did. Herod decided therefore that it would be much better to strike first and be rid of him before his work led to an uprising, than to wait for an upheaval, get involved in a difficult situation and see his mistake.[60]

If there were those who would use the Baptist's movement for their own political ends, then with his violent removal from the scene they were in that dangerously lost condition of being 'like sheep without a

[59]Cf. the reiterated theme of 'subjection' in Luke 10.17–20.

[60]*Ant.* 18.118; tr. L. H. Feldman, LCL. For the textual variants see his notes.

shepherd' (Mark 6.34);[61] and it is not at all unlikely that they should have turned to Jesus as his replacement. Are these the 'some' who at this stage in the narrative say mysteriously that he *is* John the Baptist (Mark 8.28 and pars.)? Herod seems to have agreed with them (Mark 6.14–16 and pars.) – with the consequence that he turned his sights now from John onto Jesus (Luke 9.7–9; 13.31). If such a switch of loyalty was already in the air, so that Jesus could sense their mood (Mark 6.33f.; John 6.15) – and it did not require supernatural insight – then it is thoroughly explicable that under the pressure of swelling crowds he should have felt it necessary, in Mark's vivid description, to say to the Twelve, 'Come with me, by yourselves, to some lonely place where you can rest quietly [if we are right in the location, out of Herod's territory]. For they had no leisure even to eat, so many were coming and going' (6.31). It could explain too the cryptic warning after the second account of the feeding in Mark, 'Beware, be on your guard against the leaven of the Pharisees *and the leaven of Herod*' (8.15). This dimension is lost in Matthew, where we have 'the leaven, or teaching, of the Pharisees and Sadducees' (16.6, 12). Luke of course omits the second feeding altogether, but in 12.1 has a parallel warning against the leaven of the Pharisees (only) in the midst of Q material, which is interrupted and introduced by the words, 'Meanwhile, while a crowd of many thousands [literally, tens of thousands] had gathered, packed so close that they were treading on one another, he began to speak first to his disciples.' This could well have come originally from the same context of manic excitement that marked the watershed of the Galilean ministry.

Thus the political dimension which John opens up may allow us again to appreciate connections on which he is silent. If we are prepared to treat him as being also among the Synoptists and to permit his witness to have interpretative priority, much can be illumined.

[61]E. M. Sidebottom, *Good News of God*, London 1982, 54, suggestively refers this saying to the aftermath of the Baptist's murder.

VI

The Story: The End

The end-period of the ministry falls naturally into two halves – Jesus' approach to Jerusalem for the last time and the final stay in Jerusalem culminating in his trial, death and resurrection. The former is much longer in duration, and although naturally covered in far less detail in all the Gospels, with much greater variation in detail among them.

1. *The Approach to Jerusalem*

The period concerned, though only John gives us the material for dating it either relatively or absolutely, occupies almost a quarter of the total span of the ministry as we have computed it, namely, the six months between the feast of Tabernacles in the autumn of 29 and the approach to Passover in the spring of 30. The Synoptists also presuppose, though they do not specify, an extended period, since a considerable time has to elapse between the last datable *allusions* to a Passover period for which Jesus was in Galilee (Mark 6.39; Matt. 17.24; Luke 13.1) and the next Passover in Jerusalem, a period which must be divided between excursions in the north and the final journey south. John alone tells us that these occupied more or less equal time.

The pivotal point in all the Gospels is clearly marked (Matt. 19.1; Mark 10.1; Luke 9.51; John 7.2), and, as we have seen, there is no suggestion in any of them that Jesus ever thereafter returned to Galilee. But the coverage of the period which follows is remarkably uneven. Mark devotes one chapter to it (10), Matthew two (19–20, though in fact he produces only one extra block of material, the parable of the labourers in the vineyard in 20.1–16), while Luke gives it nearly ten of his twenty-four chapters (9.51–19.27) and John the best part of five (7.2–11.54).

The Synoptists and John have basically the same geographical framework: from Galilee via Judaea and Peraea to Jerusalem. But there the similarities end. After a first sketchy indication of the itinerary in Mark (10.1) and a still vaguer one in Matthew (19.1) neither gives any further indication of place (or for that matter of time), except to mention, somewhat confusedly, the passage through Jericho, where Luke joins up again with the other two. Matthew (20.29) never actually says that they came to Jericho, only that they left it. Mark says that they did both (10.46), as does Luke, except that while the other two put the healing of Bartimaeus on the way out of the city Luke places it as Jesus approaches Jericho (18.35), so that he can fit in the call of Zacchaeus while Jesus is there (19.1) – though he could have reversed the incidents and preserved the topography of the triple tradition. But this simply shows that such details were unimportant to him, as emerges from the long previous section, 9.51 to 18.14, when he is on his own.

The editorial history of this so-called 'central section' has provoked many theories. I am still inclined to favour some version of the proto-Lukan hypothesis,[1] that a collection of traditions (of the so-called 'Q' and 'L' material) was strung together by the evangelist on the thread of a last journey to Jerusalem before he incorporated it into the framework of triple (or Markan) tradition. Others believe that it presupposes the Markan framework;[2] others again that Luke created it from Matthew and his own special material, whether or not Mark was already in existence.[3] In any case it is here if anywhere that Luke is to be looked to for his independent contribution to the story; and, as we have seen, there is no lack of material.

But it gives a singularly disappointing yield from the point of view of reconstructing the history or the geography. Indeed it is chaotic.[4] There is not even, as in Mark or Matthew, an overall sketch of the itinerary and there is no mention of Peraea (or for that matter of Judaea), simply the insistent thrust towards Jerusalem (9.51, 53; 13.22, 33; 17.11; 19.11). Moreover, till we rejoin the triple tradition at Jericho there is no single indication of place or time, apart from two unspecific

[1]Cf. Streeter, *Four Gospels*, ch. 8.

[2]E.g., C. F. Evans, 'The Central Section of Luke's Gospel' in D. E. Nineham, ed., *Studies in the Gospels in memory of R. H. Lightfoot*, Oxford 1955, 37–53.

[3]A. M. Farrer, 'On Dispensing with Q' in Nineham, ed., *Studies in the Gospels*, 55–86; B. Orchard, *Matthew, Luke and Mark*, Manchester 1976, especially 60–64.

[4]Cf. C. C. McCown, 'The Geography of Luke's Central Section', *JBL* 57, 1938, 51–66.

references to Samaria. The first is at the very beginning:

> As the time approached when hc was to be taken up to heaven, he set his face resolutely towards Jerusalem, and sent messengers ahead. They set out and went into a Samaritan village to make arrangements for him; but the villagers would not have him because he was making for Jerusalem. When the disciples James and John saw this they said, 'Lord, may we call down fire from heaven to burn them up?' But he turned and rebuked them, and they went on to another village (9.51–56).

Though one may presume that the other village was also Samaritan, there is no actual indication that Jesus himself went into rather than round Samaria. In any case, as we have suggested above,[5] we can have no confidence that this, the only brush with Samaria which Luke records, may not belong with equal if not greater probability to that other earlier journey Jesus made through Samaria on his way from association with the Baptist in the south towards Galilee. It gives us nothing firm on which to build.

Even more tantalizing is the second reference to Samaria towards the end of the journey in 17.11, occasioned by the fact that one, out of ten, of the inhabitants of an unnamed village was a Samaritan (17.12–19). It runs: 'In the course of his journey to Jerusalem he was travelling through the borderlands (διὰ μέσον) of Samaria and Galilee' (NEB), or 'along between Samaria and Galilee' (RSV), or 'through the midst of Samaria and Galilee' (AV and RV). The last way of taking it could indicate that he took the spine-road direct to Jerusalem, though the order 'Samaria and Galilee', rather than 'Galilee and Samaria', is very difficult, and the Greek for this would ordinarily be διὰ μέσου (as in Luke 4.30 and as in inferior manuscripts here). Probably, it is to be seen as corresponding to the phrase 'on the border (ἐν μεθορίῳ) between Samaria and the Great Plain (of Esdraelon)' in Josephus, *Ant.* 20.118, where in a similar context, of Galileans going up to a festival in Jerusalem, he alludes to the village of Ginaë (Jenin). But Josephus is far more specific in every way. In any case if Jesus was in this border-country it would have been very much earlier on the journey than Luke sets it.

Any coherent itinerary is obviously impossible to reconstruct from the Lukan narrative. For the rest incidents are strung together with but the vaguest of introductions: 'as they were going along the road'

[5] Ch. IV, p. 186.

(9.57), 'on one occasion' (10.25), 'while they were on their way Jesus came to a village' (10.38), 'once in a certain place' (11.1), 'one sabbath he was teaching in a synagogue' (13.10), 'he continued his journey through towns and villages' (13.22), 'one sabbath he went to have a meal' (14.1), 'another time, the tax-gatherers and other bad characters were all crowding to listen to him' (15.1), 'as he was entering a village' (17.12), and so on.

If we try to place the sayings or incidents in their most natural setting in life it becomes clear that this central section is a rag-bag of material from all periods. There is little that one can say *must* belong to this six months. Thus, the apostrophe of the Galilean towns, 'you, Chorazin . . . you, Bethsaida . . . you, Capernaum' (10.13–15), is surely more likely to have been spoken in Galilee. The lawyer's question in 10.25–8, which has a (probably independent) parallel in Mark 12.28–31, seems more appropriate to the confrontation in Jerusalem where Mark and Matthew place it and from which Luke subsequently omits it; and this inference is reinforced by the locale of the attached parable of the Good Samaritan (10.29–37) on the road from Jerusalem to Jericho. The Beelzebub controversy in 11.14–23 is provided with no setting whatsoever. Mark, followed by Matthew, is much more specific in setting it in Galilee, where it is provoked by scribes who had come down from Jerusalem (3.22) – in Matthew (12.24) it is the Pharisees, in Luke (11.15) simply 'some of the people'. Luke 13.1–4, on the Galileans whose blood Pilate had mixed with their sacrifices, looks, as we have seen, as if it comes from a Passover-time when Jesus was in Galilee; while 13.6–9, with its phrase 'For the last three years I have come looking for fruit on this fig-tree', like the parable of the tenants in the vineyard of Mark 12.1–12 and pars., appears to have been provoked by the final challenge to the nation and its leaders in Jerusalem. 13.31–3 ('Go and tell that fox') clearly presupposes that Jesus is still in Herod's jurisdiction, almost certainly in Galilee,[6] whereas the following verses (13.34f.) with their apostrophe of Jerusalem are most naturally at home where Matthew sets them (23.37–9), in the capital. Again, the charge in 15.1f. against Jesus of consorting with tax-gatherers and other bad characters seems to belong to Galilee where the triple tradition places it (Mark 2.16 and pars., including this time the doublet Luke 5.30), while if the parable of the Pharisee and the publican in 18.9–14 has a local setting it is more

[6]Dodd draws attention (*Historical Tradition*, 322f.) to the striking parallel both in form and content between these verses and John 7.3–8 which presuppose the same Galilean milieu.

likely, like the observation on the widow's mite (Mark 12.41–44; Luke 21.1–4), to be that of the temple worship.

So one could go on. Luke, for all his extra material, cannot be said to add anything to our knowledge of the period leading up to Jesus' final arrival in Jerusalem. It is a period for which the Synoptists are as thin as John is for the Galilean ministry. But John here by contrast supplies a great deal more. To begin with, he dates the period with a precision that allows us almost to define it to the day at each end. When Jesus arrives in Jerusalem from Galilee it is half-way through the feast of Tabernacles. This lasted seven days (with an extra day of 'rejoicing' as an eighth), starting on the fifteenth day of the seventh month (Tishri).[7] In the year 29 this would have fallen on 12 October, and if Jesus arrived when the festival was half over (John 7.14) we can thus date his appearance on or about 15 October. Equally, at the other end, Jesus arrived in Bethany six days before Passover (12.1) and in Jerusalem the day after (12.11). Since in the year 30 Passover (Nisan 14) fell on 7 April, he would have reached Bethany (on the regular inclusive reckoning) on 2 April and entered Jerusalem on 3 April. So the period defines itself as one of six months – less just under a fortnight. Such precision is inconceivable in the Synoptists.

In locale too there is no lack of precision in John as to where Jesus is. He is teaching in the temple (7.14) and specifically later on in the treasury (8.20); and it is often observed in the commentaries that the detail of the Tabernacles ritual is clearly reflected in the claims that Jesus makes about himself as the water (7.37f.) and the light (8.12). In 7.37 we have the specific date: 'the last and great day of the feast', i.e. 18 or 19 October. Which it was depends on whether the eighth day, of Rejoicing, which was strictly not part of the feast (Deut. 16.13–15; Ezek. 45.25) was or was not counted in (for its inclusion cf. Num. 29.35; Neh. 8.18; II Macc. 10.6; Philo, *Spec. leg.* 1.189; Josephus, *Ant.* 3.245–7). Brown favours the seventh, Barrett the eighth. I would side with the latter,[8] since the Mishnah (*Sukk.* 4.8) specifically calls the eighth day 'the last festival-day of the feast' and speaks of 'the honour due to it'. True, the water-libation ceased on the seventh day (4.1), but the symbolism would fit in as well, if not better, if Jesus proclaimed himself as the true and living water on the eighth day *after* the seven days of Jewish ritual to bring rain. If so this is one piece[9] of Jesus'

[7]Lev. 23.33–36, 39–43; Josephus, *Ant.* 3.244–7; M. *Sukk.* 4.

[8]Also Lightfoot, *Biblical Essays*, 166f.

[9]L. Morris, *The New Testament and the Jewish Lectionaries*, London 1964, 64f., makes a case for this not being a continuous dialogue (though of course the intrusive

teaching we can actually place to the day, 19 October AD 29, as well as perhaps to the precise spot, the treasury (8.20; cf. Mark 12.41), which was in the Court of the Women where the light of the great golden candlesticks was lit at the close of the first day (*Sukk.* 5.2f.). Subsequently he leaves the temple (8.59), but is still within range of the Pool of Siloam lying near by to the south (9.7). It is not clear just how long Jesus remains in the capital, but the whole narrative down to 10.21, with its reference back to the healing of the blind man in ch. 9, appears to belong to the same Tabernacles visit.

The next reference, in 10.22, is to the festival of the Dedication, which started on the twenty-fifth day of the ninth month (Chislev) and lasted for eight days (I Macc. 4.59; Josephus; *Ant.* 12.316–25). That year it would have been 20–27 December. Where Jesus spent the interval between the feasts is unfortunately a matter of ambiguity, since it is uncertain whether the 'again' in 10.40 ('Jesus withdrew again across the Jordan, to the place where John had been baptizing earlier') refers to the period immediately before the festival of the Dedication or to his original time there with John the Baptist. But once again the details are vivid. It was winter (10.22), and, this time no doubt to keep warm, 'Jesus was walking in the temple precincts' (a habit also referred to in Mark 11.27 though not in Matthew or Luke) 'in Solomon's Cloister' (10.23). This location is attested not only by Acts 3.11 and 5.12 but by Josephus, who tells us that it was the oldest portico, running along the eastern wall of the temple mount (*BJ* 5.18f.; *Ant.* 15.396–401; 20.220f.).

After Dedication Jesus certainly this time returns to the relative warmth of Bethany beyond Jordan, and there 'stays' long enough for crowds to be attracted and a following built up (10.40–42). We must presume that we are now well into what we should call the opening months of the year 30.

Then, knowing that 'not long since' the Judaeans were wanting to stone him (11.8; cf. 8.59; 10.31), Jesus reluctantly returns to Judaea on hearing of the illness and death of Lazarus. He leaves Bethany beyond Jordan for Bethany near Jerusalem, the home of Martha and Mary (11.1–16) – hardly what anyone inventing an itinerary would have thought of. The contrast again with the special Lukan material is particularly striking. In Luke 10.38–42 a visit is also made during this

---

7.53–8.11 which breaks it up is non-Johannine anyhow). The reference to the last day of the feast in 7.37 looks as if this may be intended to mark the end of this particular occasion. The πάλιν in 8.12 and 21 could introduce separate blocks of teaching, though the same formula in 10.7 immediately takes up and interprets 10.1–6.

overall period to the same house, and the characterization of the two sisters is strikingly similar.[10] But the vague way in which it is introduced is typical: 'While they were on their way, Jesus came to a village where a woman named Martha made him welcome in her house.' Luke evidently had no idea of the occasion or the location, except that as it is set nearer the beginning than the end of the journey, and well before Jesus is recorded as passing 'through the borderlands of Samaria and Galilee' (17.11), one would be led to imagine that it was in the north rather than in the south – certainly not within two miles of Jerusalem – and Luke, who knew of Jesus' association with Bethany (19.29; 24.50), never thinks of identifying the two. Yet John is quite precise as to why, when and from where Jesus came to Bethany on two separate occasions (11.17; 12.1). He tells us exactly how far it was from the city – fifteen Roman stades or 'just under two miles' (11.18), which it is.[11]

But the whole Lazarus incident – with the history and geography included in it – has been the object of attack by many scholars as being no original part of the Fourth Gospel and therefore as having nothing to contribute to this part of the story.

Thus Brown[12] contends that 'it would be far easier to reconcile the sequence in John with that of the Synoptics if chs. 11–12 were not considered' and 10.40–2 was followed immediately by 13.1. How in fact it would comport with the Synoptic sequence if Jesus was immediately translated from Peraea to the upper room, with all mention of his entry into Jerusalem (12.12–19) omitted, is not altogether obvious; and it is ironical that 'the switch of locale from the

[10]Cf. Lightfoot, *Biblical Essays*, 37–9.

[11]Bethany of New Testament times lay slightly west of the modern village of el-'Azariyeh named after Lazarus, whose tomb would naturally have been outside the village (cf. 11.31). The vaulting of the rock-tomb claimed to be his dates from crusader times and the present entrance was made by the Franciscans in the sixteenth century, the original one having been blocked by a mosque. But there is no good reason to doubt the site, which has been attested by continuous veneration at least since the fourth century. The precise distance of the village from Jerusalem obviously depends on the route taken (the modern motor road is more circuitous). In all probability the ancient track went through the village of eṭ-Ṭur on the Mount of Olives where the old Roman road from Jericho divided, the right fork going on to Jerusalem, the left to Bethany. Martha would have come out to meet Jesus along this track (11.20). The distance by this route from the Temple mount would be about 15 stades, or slightly under 1¾ miles. By way of comparison, Josephus locates the Mount of Olives 6 stades from Jerusalem (*BJ* 5.70). Cf. Dalman, *Sacred Sites and Ways*, 249–51; Kopp, *Holy Places*, 279–81; J. Finegan, *Archaeology of the NT*, 91–5; Wilkinson, *Jerusalem as Jesus Knew It*, 108–13; J. Murphy-O'Connor, *The Holy Land*, 96–8.

[12]*John* I, 414, 427–30.

Transjordan to Jerusalem' is defended as being 'no more violent than that between chs. 5 and 6' when this is usually regarded as one of the most notorious *dis*locations in the Gospel! The existing sequence, including chs. 11 and 12, is altogether smoother and more circumstantial. It is dismissed by Brown as 'complicated' and 'hard to reconcile with the Synoptic picture wherein before Passover Jesus came from the Transjordan through Jericho to Jerusalem, with Bethany as his domicile'. Yet in fact what John says is precisely this, except that he gives us a great deal more. But apart from having to fit the Procustean bed of the very sparse Synoptic account, what objective reason is there for omitting chs. 11 and 12? Brown agrees that they abound in Johannine features. The only stylistic difference suggested is that 'in 11.19, 31, 33, 36, 45; 12.9, 11, the Jews are not the hostile Jewish authorities but the ordinary people of Judaea and Jerusalem who are often sympathetic to Jesus and even believe in him'. There is something in this. Yet John uses the term 'the Jews' in a far too varied and nuanced a manner for this to be a reliable criterion. It can, as we have seen,[13] have a purely neutral, geographical connotation – as indeed it has in this section in 11.54, which Brown does not mention. Furthermore to fit this thesis, 8.31, with its reference to 'the Jews who had believed in him', has to be excised as an editorial addition, and 11.8 with its 'normal' hostile usage is simply ignored. The arbitrariness of the whole proceeding is evident.

In similar fashion Barnabas Lindars says:

> The Lazarus material (11.1–46; 12.9–11) has been added to prepare for the passion of Jesus. This not only breaks the connection between chapters 10 and 12 [n.b., not this time 13], but also has led John to make further rearrangements for the second edition. . . . In his original edition he had an order of events closer to that of the Synoptics, comprising the Triumphal Entry (12.12–19), the Cleansing of the Temple (2.13–22), the Priests' plot (11.47–53), and the Anointing at Bethany (12.1–8). John has removed the Cleansing to chapter 2 in order to make the raising of Lazarus the prime motive for the Priests' plot, and brought the Anointing into closer relation with the Lazarus material. Originally it had a more obvious connection with the Last Supper (chapter 13).[14]

Yet the only reasons given for all this are that the Synoptic order is to be

[13]Chapter II, pp. 84f.
[14]*John*, 50.

accepted as axiomatic and that the rearrangement gives a supposedly better sequence. It has no more basis than any other re-ordering of the Johannine material and is a supreme example of allowing procedural priority to the Synoptic order. Not only is this the better and truer order, but John must originally have had it too!

One more example is the treatment of the Lazarus material in Sydney Temple's *The Core of the Fourth Gospel.*[15] Here only half the story belongs to the original Johannine 'core'. In its original (and historical) state the story, he suggests, ended at 11.37, with the words 'Could not this man, who opened the blind man's eyes, have done something to keep Lazarus from dying?' The answer sadly was, No. Because the incident represented a failure on Jesus' part it found no place in the Synoptic narratives but a 'rewrite redactor' added the miraculous ending (plus some other verses) and thus established its place in John's Gospel.

But again there is absolutely no objective evidence, textual or stylistic, for such an analysis. In fact of this whole passage Dodd writes, 'Nowhere perhaps, in this gospel, have attempts to analyse out a written source or sources proved less convincing',[16] and even Bultmann is reduced to saying, 'The analyses . . . have achieved no illuminating result, and it is questionable whether one can be reached. The linguistic investigation yields no satisfying criteria.'[17] The reconstructions are governed entirely by the presumption that if it had been genuine historical tradition it must have been reflected in the Synoptic Gospels and because it 'disturbs' the Synoptic order of events it must be secondary.

Until recently the belief was at least not unreasonable that the Lazarus story was a purely Johannine construction – perhaps out of a Synoptic raising miracle and the Lukan parable of Dives and Lazarus.[18] But the appearance of a version of it, in the same location but without

[15]183–93.

[16]*Historical Tradition*, 230. One of the more bizarre flights of critical fantasy is, with Fortna, *Gospel of Signs*, 194, to locate the episode of the Samaritan woman between 11.16 and 17; for Jesus stayed two days in her village (4.40) and in 11.6 'John mentions another arbitrary stay of two days'. By such methods one could reshuffle the entire Gospel.

[17]*John*, 395.

[18]So, among many others, Fortna, *The Gospel of Signs*, 85. Yet as Temple points out the parable does *not* issue in Lazarus being brought back from the dead, a fact which leads him to argue that the Johannine story originally ended in the same way. More plausibly, Dodd, *Historical Tradition*, 229, argues that the Lukan parable (where the occurrence of a proper name is unique to the parables of Jesus) would be explained 'if there existed in pre-Johannine tradition a story about the resurrection of a man called Lazarus, with a general implication that this did not win men to faith in Christ.' Cf. R.

personal names or any obvious traces of Johannine colouring, in the so-called 'Secret Gospel of Mark'[19] must throw serious doubt on this:

> And they come into Bethany. And a certain woman whose brother had died was there. And, coming, she prostrated herself before Jesus and says to him, 'Son of David, have mercy on me.' But the disciples rebuked her. And Jesus, being angered, went off with her into the garden where the tomb was, and straightway a great cry was heard from the tomb. And going near Jesus rolled away the stone from the door of the tomb. And straightway, going in where the youth was, he stretched forth his hand and raised him, seizing his hand. But the youth, looking upon him, loved him and began to beseech him that he might be with him. And going out of the tomb they came into the house of the youth, for he was rich. And after six days Jesus told him what to do and in the evening the youth comes to him, wearing a linen cloth over his naked body. And he remained with him that night, for Jesus taught him the mystery of the kingdom of God. And thence, arising, he returned to the other side of the Jordan.

By any standard this is a much inferior tradition, being largely a pastiche of Markan phrases and clearly influenced by Gnostic motifs. There is no reason to think that John was dependent on it nor, despite Brown,[20] that it is dependent on John. Much the most likely hypothesis would seem to be that the apocryphal version represents an independent, though historically pretty worthless, account of the same incident. If so, it would show that John did not simply create it to illustrate his theology of Jesus as the resurrection and the life. The tradition that Jesus raised the dead (Matt. 11.5 = Luke 7.22) and indeed that the disciples were to do the same (Matt. 10.8) is an inalienable part of the proclamation of the powers of the new age, and what would call for explanation would be if John did not, like the Synoptists, present us with the same picture. As Dodd has pointed out,[21] the Lazarus story, however much Johannine theology it is also made to carry, is not in principle different in form or content from the

---

Dunkerley, 'Lazarus', *NTS* 5, 1958–9, 321–7, who also thinks the parable is based on the miracle rather than *vice versa*.

[19]Morton Smith, *Clement of Alexandria and a Secret Gospel of Mark*, whose translation (447) I have reproduced.

[20]'The Relation of the "Secret Gospel of Mark" to the Fourth Gospel', *CBQ* 36, 1974, 466–85. Fortna, *Gospel of Signs*, 87, regards it as 'obviously independent of John 11'.

[21]*Historical Tradition*, 230–2.

Synoptic stories of the widow's son at Nain (Luke 7.11–17), Jairus' daughter (Mark 5.21–43) or the epileptic boy (Mark 9.14–27). The difference is a matter of degree rather than of kind.

Yet the Lazarus story, unlike these others, cannot simply be separated and detached from the surrounding narrative. It crucially affects the unfolding of the story as a whole.[22] Four times it is referred back to in the subsequent developments (11.45f.; 12.1f., 9, 17f.). Indeed this is why it attracts so much adverse attention from those who adhere to Synoptic priority. For it gives a very different account of what led to the final determination of the authorities to do away with Jesus. If the Synoptic sequence of events is the true one, then the Lazarus incident, or at any rate the key role which it occupies in John, *cannot*, it is held, be historical. 'Where are we to put the scene,' asked Burkitt, 'into the historical framework preserved by St Mark? Can any answer be given, except "there is no room"?'[23] Yet the subsequently-discovered answer of the author of the Secret Gospel of Mark is quite specific: in between (in our texts) Mark 10.34 and 35. He at any rate found it possible to accommodate it. H. E. Edwards[24] goes further and suggests that, just as we contended earlier that something like the attempt to make Jesus king in John 6.14f. was necessary to make sense of the sequel to the desert feeding in Mark, so here there are unexplained features in the Markan narrative which only something like the raising of Lazarus and the subsequent need for concealment would account for. His reconstruction contains some improbabilities,[25] but he argues that only the information John supplies, that Jesus was going about in hiding from the time of the Lazarus incident (11.54–57) right up to the moment of his arrest (cf. 12.36), explains the attempted silencing of Bartimaeus' embarrassing acclamation 'Jesus, son of David' (Mark 10.47f.), the elaborate secrecy in planning the entry into Jerusalem (11.1–7) and the last supper (14.12–16), and the necessity for Judas' action to reveal his whereabouts (14.10f.; cf. John 11.57, 'where he was'). He maintains very plausibly that all the *public* teaching placed by Mark in the final week (11.27–12.44), of

[22]For its place as the turning-point of the Gospel, cf. T. E. Pollard, 'The Raising of Lazarus (John xi)' in E. A. Livingstone, ed., *StEv* IV, TU 112, Berlin 1973, 434–43.

[23]*The Gospel History and its Transmission*, Edinburgh [3]1911, 222.

[24]*The Disciple Who Wrote These Things*, ch. 9, 164–99.

[25]Above all, I fear, the attempt to interpret Mark 11.7 to mean 'They bring the colt to Jesus and put their clothes on him [Jesus], and he sat on it.' That is to say, Jesus was hoping to get into Jerusalem in disguise, with no more intention than to visit the holy places (11.11). But the ploy was frustrated by the crowd's reaction. That he did not *plan* a 'triumphal entry' will indeed be argued, from John's account of it, below (pp. 230–2).

which John knows nothing (the request by the Greeks to see him has to be arranged through intermediaries; John 12.20–22), properly belongs to earlier sessions in the temple described by John, and that the cleansing of the temple with its sanctioning by reference to John the Baptist (and I should add, though he does not, the cursing of the fig-tree) (Mark 11.12–25), come, as we argued earlier,[26] from a visit two years previously. But Mark has no option but to place them all in the only visit to Jerusalem he records.

But whether or not the Markan narrative actually demands, rather than excludes, what John gives us, we shall go on to argue that if the Johannine record is allowed priority many inconsistencies and improbabilities in the Synoptic accounts begin to fall into place. But at this point we are led from the approach to the passion story directly into the trial and death of Jesus itself. For the Lazarus incident and its attendant publicity are in John the trigger which sets the legal process in motion.

2. *The Proscription of Jesus*

John describes the transition in a passage that demands to be reproduced in full.

> Now many of the Jews who had come to visit Mary and had seen what Jesus did, put their faith in him. But some of them went off to the Pharisees and reported what he had done. Thereupon the chief priests and the Pharisees convened a meeting of the Council. 'What action are we taking?' they said. 'This man is performing many signs. If we leave him alone like this the whole populace will believe in him. Then the Romans will come and sweep away our temple and our nation.' But one of them, Caiaphas, who was High Priest that year, said, 'You know nothing whatever; you do not use your judgment; it is more to your interest that one man should die for the people, than that the whole nation should be destroyed.' He did not say this of his own accord, but as the High Priest in office that year, he was prophesying that Jesus would die for the nation – would die not for the nation alone but to gather together the scattered children of God. So from that day on they plotted his death (11.45–53).

Here we have a formally convened meeting of the Sanhedrin at which they 'resolved' or 'passed a resolution' (ἐβουλεύσαντο; cf. Acts

[26] Chapter III, pp. 127–31 above.

5.33; II Cor. 1.17),[27] and not just 'plotted' (NEB), that Jesus should be put to death and at which he is publicly declared a wanted man. For, John goes on, 'the chief priests and the Pharisees had given orders that anyone who knew where he was should give information, so that they might arrest him' (11.57).

Bammel points out that this passage is full of quasi-technical terms:

> διδόναι . . . ἐντολάς describes the issue of a writ. ζητεῖν [cf. 11.56] describes the search which takes place in order to find out the whereabouts of a fugitive. μηνύειν denotes the denunciation of a person who is named in the ἐντολαί . . . Taken together, the terms can easily be considered as indicating the different stages of a προγραφή. This action was undertaken against those who had not been present for the ἀπογραφή.[28]

In particular the word μηνύειν which is the technical word for the activity of an informer (as in Acts 23.30; cf. II Macc. 6.11; Josephus, *Ant.* 15.266) recalls the provision of the Mosaic law, as interpreted by Josephus, if the murderer cannot be found: 'Let them make diligent search for the culprit, offering rewards for information' (*Ant.* 4.220). That the warrant was accompanied by a reward 'for information leading to his arrest' is not stated in any of the Gospels but would provide an entirely probable background for Judas' action.

In subjecting this whole section to close analysis Bammel has

[27]So E. Bammel, 'Ex illa itaque die consilium fecerunt', in Bammel, ed., *The Trial of Jesus*, 1970, 30, quoting K. Bornhäuser, *Das Johannesevangelium eine Missionsschrift für Israel*, Gütersloh 1928. As E. Bickermann observed in his classic article on which Bammel depends, 'Utilitas Crucis: Observations sur les récits du procès de Jésus dans les Évangiles canoniques', *RHR* 112, 1935, 169–241, it is astonishing how little attention has been paid to the juridical importance of this meeting (215). It was however correctly assessed by C. E. Caspari, *A Chronological and Geographical Introduction to the Life of Christ*, 181–4, 224, who drew the same corollaries for the chronology and interpretation of the Johannine trial narrative as we shall. He was quoted by Sanday, *Authorship and Historical Character of the Fourth Gospel*, 191. But subsequently the significance of John 11.47–57 has received little notice. It is for instance passed over in one paragraph in Blinzler's *Trial of Jesus*, ET 57f. (and still in the much enlarged fourth edition, 84, which will regularly be quoted below in addition to the ET which was made from the second edition). In G. S. Sloyan, *Jesus on Trial*, Philadelphia 1973, it is totally ignored, with the remark 'In John there is no reference to the Sanhedrin or to a body of any sort'! Bickermann's article receives but a single passing reference in D. R. Catchpole's *The Trial of Jesus: A Study in the Gospels and Jewish Historiography from 1770 to the Present Day*, 1971, 259 n. 4, which is a remarkable omission in view of the subtitle. Nor is it noticed, except cursorily by Bultmann (*John*, 412, 642), in any of the commentaries I have consulted.

[28]'Ex illa itaque die', 33f.

concluded that its parallels with Jewish tradition afford confidence that it represents reliable and primitive historical material. He notes in it four main points which individually, he says, may look strange but 'together they give a picture which is thoroughly consistent, and is paralleled in more than one detail by traditions which do not merely reproduce the Fourth Gospel.'[29]

He summarizes these distinctive features as follows: (*a*) 'a picture of the prosecution of Jesus which makes the legal proceedings begin a considerable time before the crucifixion'.[30] This is in line with the early rabbinic *baraita*[31] cited earlier:

> On the eve of the Passover Yeshu was hanged. For forty days before the execution took place, a herald went forth and cried, 'He is going forth to be stoned because he has practised sorcery and enticed Israel to apostasy. Anyone who can say anything in his favour, let him come forward and plead on his behalf.' But since nothing was brought forward in his favour he was hanged on the eve of the Passover!
>
> Ulla retorted: Do you suppose that he was one for whom a defence could be made? Was he not a *Mesith* [enticer], concerning whom Scripture says, 'Neither shalt thou spare, neither shalt thou conceal him?' With Yeshu however it was different, for he was connected with the government [or royalty, i.e., influential] (b. *Sanh*. 43a).[32]

This presupposes a considerable delay in Jesus' case between incrimination and execution, which was clearly seen as an exception to be explained, rather than the rule. Usually when a sentence has been passed the execution is to take place on the same day so as not to

[29]Ibid., 35.

[30]There is also an important sense in which the whole of John's Gospel is a trial-narrative and its literary form, like that of the book of Job, that of a lawsuit (*ribh*). Jesus is 'on trial' long before matters come to court. Cf. my 'His Witness is True', *Twelve More NTS*, 128f.; A. E. Harvey, *Jesus on Trial, A Study in the Fourth Gospel*, 1976 and earlier T. Preiss, 'Justification in Johannine Thought', ET in *Life in Christ*, SBT 13, London and Nashville 1954, 9–31. Surprisingly Harvey does not mention this important study, which has been ignored by the commentaries, nor does he discuss the trial narrative itself.

[31]Literally 'extraneous' material of the same period as the Mishnah which was not included in it.

[32]Tr. ed. I. Epstein, *The Babylonian Talmud*, London 1935–52, *Nezikin*, V, *Sanhedrin*, 281f. For a recent discussion of this passage and the objections brought against it, cf. W. Horbury, 'The Benediction of the *Minim* and Early Jewish–Christian Controversy', *JTS*, n.s. 33, 1982, 19–61.

prolong the mental agony.[33] Why then the delay in the case of Jesus? Does it mean that he was one whose guilt was in doubt? No. It is attributed to his 'connections' with the Roman government. In fact it was because the Jewish authorities could not lay hands on him. But the difficulty of a forty days' interval between incrimination and execution would scarcely have been invented in order to be explained away. It looks as if it was a firm memory in the Jewish tradition, for which the Synoptists allow no room but which can easily be fitted into the Johannine chronology.

What then was the status of this initial court action against Jesus? It appears to represent the equivalent in Roman jurisprudence of the προγραφή[34] or *proscriptio*, the decision of the authorities in the absence of the offender to pronounce him guilty until proved otherwise and therefore liable to arrest on sight. This use of proscription (προγραφὴ ἐπὶ θανάτῳ or εἰς θάνατον) is well illustrated in the Roman historian Appian, *Bell. Civ.* 1.2 and 4.1, where those on the proscribed list are subject to search, with large rewards for their finding and killing, and are described as already ἀποθανατούμενοι, marked down for death. Yet in Jewish law at any rate the verdict had subsequently to be ratified by the proper legal procedures. But, as E. Bickermann recognized, in the case of proscribed persons 'incrimination precedes interrogation.'[35] This is the situation which John presupposes of Jesus, and which, alone I believe, makes sense of the rest of the trial process. 'The decision has been made already; it is only the carrying out of the judgement which is to come.'[36]

(*b*) 'The fact that the legal proceedings are started and carried out solely by the Jews'.[37] While in this Gospel as in the others the Pharisees

[33]B. *Sanh*. 35a. The herald called for any appeals against the sentence on the way to the place of execution (M. *Sanh*. 6.1, the passage on which b. *Sanh*. 43a is the commentary).

[34]Bickermann, 'Utilitas Crucis', 213–6; the first known occurrence of the term is said to be in an edict of Tiberius Julius Alexander of AD 68. But cf. within the biblical literature Jude 4: προγεγραμμένοι εἰς τοῦτο τὸ κρίμα, 'marked down for this judgment' (not 'written about before', as in Rom. 15.4).

[35]'Utilitas Crucis', 221 (cf. 210–26 for an excellent study of the Johannine trial narrative). I believe however that he goes too far, as Caspari did, in saying that there was no need for any subsequent Jewish trial and verdict. The prisoner may have been pronounced guilty until proved otherwise, but he still had to be proved guilty, and for this under Jewish law the necessary witnesses in the presence of the accused and a verdict properly arrived at were essential. All the evidence for *proscriptio* which Bickermann cites is Roman, where all lay within the *coercitio* of the governor.

[36]Bammel, 'Ex illa itaque die', 35.

[37]On whether John is particularly biased in an anti-Semitic direction, see below, pp. 272–4.

represent the hard core of the religious opposition to Jesus and his teaching (4.1; 7.32, 47f.; 8.13; 9.13–16, 40; 11.46; 12.19, 42), John is careful to observe that when the judicial authority of the Sanhedrin is involved it is 'the chief priests and the Pharisees' who have to act together (7.32, 45; 11.47, 57; 18.3), or the chief priests alone (12.10; 18.35; 19.6, 15, 21), since they controlled the Council.[38] At this stage the proceedings lie entirely in the hands of the Jewish supreme court, which issues, quite legally, the warrant for the arrest, observing the proper procedural delay, though the implication is that the wanted man is already guilty until proved otherwise. The Roman authorities are not at this point involved, even though fear of what they might do should the situation get out of hand is a powerful motive behind the Jewish initiative (11.48). At this stage too there is no precise charge: that has to be formulated when the prisoner can be interrogated and the evidence established under oath. But it is already defined as a capital case (11.53), with the rules of procedure which, as we shall see, that will imply.

(*c*) 'The part played by Caiaphas and the arguments presented by him.' The high priest, surprisingly, is named in the passion narratives only of John (11.49; 18.13f., 24, 28) and Matthew (more briefly: 26.3, 57),[39] though Luke knows of Caiaphas and of his relationship with Annas which John makes explicit (Luke 3.2; Acts 4.6), and the facts of his career are not in dispute. Matthew confirms the leading role personally played by the high priest, though he only mentions the events of the last forty-eight hours. But from the first John makes it clear that the arguments for removing Jesus are primarily those of expediency ('it is more to your interest'; 11.50) for which legal backing must then be found; and in his account the last word, as well as the first, of the religious establishment is one of religious expediency laced with political opportunism (19.12–16). This fits well with what we know of Caiaphas, who was essentially a 'survivor', retaining the office of high priest for nineteen years,[40] considerably longer than anyone else in the first century. His 'working relationship' with Pilate is confirmed by the

[38]Contrast Barrett, *John*, 420, commenting on 'the Pharisees' in 12.19 in contrast with 'the high priests and the Pharisees' in 11.47: 'It is doubtful whether John clearly distinguished between the two groups.' But the distinction in their roles is consistently observed.

[39]Even more surprisingly he seems never to be mentioned in rabbinic sources (Bammel, 'Ex illa itaque die', 38) though his existence and dates are firmly established by Josephus.

[40]AD 18–37. For this rather than AD 36, cf. Jeremias, *Jerusalem in the Time of Jesus*, 195.

fact that his removal from office soon followed that of the Prefect.[41]

(*d*) 'The withdrawal of Jesus'. 'Accordingly', says John, on hearing, that is, of the resolution to put him to death, 'Jesus no longer went about publicly in Judaea [literally, among the Judaeans], but left that region for the country bordering on the desert, and came to a town called Ephraim, where he stayed [or spent time][42] with his disciples' (11.54). Escape from a series of attempted arrests is another feature which the Jewish tradition about Jesus shares with the Fourth Gospel (7.30, 44; 8.20, 59; 10.39; 12.36).[43] In particular, of the disappearance after the session of the Sanhedrin Celsus' Jew says of Jesus that 'when we had convicted him, condemned him and decided that he should be punished, [he] was caught hiding himself and escaping most disgracefully.' This presupposes precisely the situation which John alone records, namely, an interval *after* a condemnation and decision that he should be punished. It is interesting that Origen, sticking to the Synoptic tradition, simply denies the charge.[44]

The details of this withdrawal[45] are given by John, and he is privy to where Jesus and his disciples lay low, information which could only have been known to the inner circle. He does not tell us how long it lasted, but if there is anything in the Talmudic tradition (and it is difficult to see why it should have been invented) it presumably fell within the forty-day period. But he does tell us when it ended. It was in the time of preparation for Passover, when the pilgrim crowd had begun assembling in Jerusalem to purify themselves prior to the feast (11.55; cf. Num 9.6–12; II Chron. 30.13–19; Josephus *BJ* 1.229; *Ant.* 12.145). A statutory ritual requirement for a variety of other purposes seems to have been seven days (cf. Num. 19.11–13; Acts 21.23–27). According to Josephus, the high priest's vestments were handed over from Roman keeping and purified seven days before each festival (*Ant.* 18.94)[46] and he mentions that 'the people were assembling for the feast

[41]Josephus, *Ant.* 18.89, 95.

[42]There is a slight edge in the manuscript evidence for ἔμεινεν over διέτριβεν, though the latter would have been more likely to be assimilated to the regular Johannine usage than *vice versa*.

[43]Bammel, 'Ex illa itaque die', 30, and W. Horbury, 'The Trial of Jesus in Jewish Tradition' in the same volume (n. 27 above), 103–21.

[44]Origen, *Contra Celsum* 2.9–10; tr. H. Chadwick, Cambridge 1953, 73.

[45]For ἀναχώρησις as a legal term cf. Bickermann, 'Utilitas Crucis', 213f.; Bammel, 'Ex illa itaque die', 33f. The word is not in fact used here, though it is by Origen in his commentary on John 11.54 and the verb appears in John 6.15 and elsewhere in the Gospels.

[46]But in *Ant.* 15.408 it is one day. John 18.28 obviously presupposes that the Jewish leaders were already in a state of purification on the eve of Passover, declining to enter

of unleavened bread on the eighth of the month Xanthicus' (Nisan: *BJ* 6.290), i.e., a week beforehand. This fits well with the expectancy in John of the gathering crowds who 'looked out for Jesus, and as they stood in the temple they asked one another, "What do you think? Perhaps he is not coming to the festival"' (11.56), and with his final arrival for supper in Bethany six days before Passover (12.1).[47]

3. *The Arrival in Jerusalem*

> The next day the great body of pilgrims who had come to the festival, hearing that Jesus was on the way to Jerusalem, took palm branches and went out to meet him (12.12f.).

At this point we are back with the story told by the Synoptists. Yet the traditions are subtly different. Those who see John as using and adapting Mark will naturally see his dependence on him here too.[48] Others will be persuaded of his independence.[49] In fact the case for independence is perhaps as strong here as anywhere. Indeed the only verbal agreement in the whole narrative is the common citation of the

---

the Praetorium so as not to be defiled. Certainly at that time of the year Gentile property could not be guaranteed to be free of leaven, and M. *Ohol.* 18.7 lays down that 'the dwelling-places of Gentiles are unclean' (as the context implies, because 'they throw abortions down their drains': Danby, *Mishnah*, 675 n. 10). (This rule is held specifically to exclude 'the open space in a courtyard': *Ohol.* 18.10; cf. the contrast in John 18.28f.). If the defilement was thus claimed to be the equivalent of contact with a corpse or dead bones, then those contracting it would have been impure for seven days (Num. 19, 11–16) and have been forced to keep Passover a month later (Num. 9.6–12). If it was of lesser degree, they could have immersed themselves and been clean by sunset (Lev. 27.7; Num. 19.7) and thus *eaten* the Passover that night (M. *Pes.* 8.8). But they could not as priests or laymen have sacrificed the Passover that same afternoon nor indeed entered the temple beyond the court of the Gentiles (M. *Zeb.* 2.1; *Kel.* 1.8) Cf. also Morris, *Studies in the Fourth Gospel*, 193f. n. 154.

[47]Mark and Matthew appear to set this meal (though Matthew never even mentions that there was a meal and Mark leaves us to infer it) and the anointing which accompanied it two days before Passover. But this is simply the date given for the meeting of the authorities to plot Jesus' death (Mark 14.1; Matt. 26.2) which immediately precedes it in their narrative. The anointing itself seems to have had no date attached to it in the Synoptic tradition. Luke if he is describing the same event, which Brown doubts (*John* I, 450f.), sets it much earlier, in Galilee (7.36–50). Mark (14.3–9) and Matthew (26.6–13) agree with John in placing it during the last visit to Bethany, though with wide variations. For the independence of the Johannine version, cf. Dodd, *Historical Tradition*, 162–73.

[48]So Barrett, *John*, 415f.; E. D. Freed, 'The Entry into Jerusalem in the Gospel of John', *JBL* 80, 1961, 329–38.

[49]So Brown, *John* I, 459–61; D. M. Smith, 'John 12.12ff. and the Question of John's Use of the Synoptics', *JBL* 82, 1963, 58–64; Dodd, *Historical Tradition*, 152–6.

LXX of Ps. 117 (Heb. 118). 25 (though all the Gospels preserve the transliterated ὡσαννά in place of the LXX interpretation σῶσον δή), and John and Matthew (but not Mark and Luke) both allude to Zech. 9.9, though in a different translation and at a different point in the story. As Dodd says,

> Beyond the quotations from the Old Testament, there is very little similarity between John and the Synoptics. They differ, in fact, in every point where it is possible to differ in relating the same incident. . . . Anyone who should wish to maintain that the Johannine account is in any sense derived from the Marcan must do so on *a priori* grounds, without any support whatever from the actual texts.[50]

In all the records of the triumphal entry there is the same tense mixture of the spiritual and the political.[51] The distinctive emphasis of John is to present Jesus' action as a conscious *corrective* of a planned political ovation. In the Synoptists it is Jesus himself who stage-manages his entry on a donkey (Mark 11.1–7 and pars.) and the crowd that spontaneously throw down their clothes and cut brushwood (or rushes, στιβάδας) from the fields (Mark 11.8) or branches from the trees (Matt. 21.8). In John (12.12f.) it is the crowd which takes the initiative, coming out from Jerusalem to greet him, with a reception calculated to evoke the memories and rekindle the spirit of Maccabaean nationalism. W. R. Farmer has filled in this background to the use of palm branches.[52] The only other use of βαΐα (branches of date-palm) in biblical Greek is in I Maccabees 13.51, where Simon Maccabaeus made his entry into Jerusalem 'with a chorus of praise and the waving of palm branches . . . to celebrate Israel's final riddance of a formidable enemy'. And John's other word, φοινίκων, of palm trees, is used in II Maccabees 10.7 of the rededication of the temple under Judas Maccabaeus: 'So they carried garlanded wands and branches with their fruits, as well as palm-fronds, and they chanted hymns to the One

[50] *Historical Tradition*, 155f.

[51] At this and other points in the story of the passion and trial of Jesus I have expanded what I have written in 'His Witness is True: A Test of the Johannine Claim', *Twelve More NTS*, 112–37.

[52] 'The Palm Branches in John xii.13', *JTS*, n.s. 3, 1952, 62–6; cf. R. H. Lightfoot, *St John's Gospel*, 238; Brown, *John* I, 461f. For another view connecting the palm branches with rain and resurrection, cf. R. Loewe, '"Salvation" is not of the Jews', *JTS*, n.s. 32, 1981, 341–68, specif. 350–60. But the evangelist shows no awareness of this rather far-fetched connection.

who had so triumphantly achieved the purification of his own temple.'[53] Indeed there have been suggestions that the triumphal entry and the cleansing of the temple took place not at Passover but at the feast of the Encaenia or Dedication[54] or that of Tabernacles[55] (with which the Encaenia is specifically compared in II Maccabees 10.6; cf. 1.9), because the waving of the *lulab* (literally 'palm branch', but a bundle made up of palm, myrtle and willow in accordance with Lev. 23.40) was a stipulated part of the ritual as the *hosanna* from Ps. 118.25 was reached (M. *Sukk.* 3.9). But the association of both the entry into Jerusalem and the cleansing of the temple with Passover in all the Gospel traditions, however otherwise divergent, must lay a heavy burden of proof on those who would wish to put them at any other season.[56] But this does not affect the 'triumphalist' associations of palm branches (cf. also Rev. 7.9f.).

Brown, whose commentary is particularly illuminating at this point, observes that in the Testaments of the Twelve Patriarchs, Naph. 5.4, where the same combination of words occurs as in John (βαΐα τῶν φοινίκων), 'the fronds are given to Levi as a symbol of power over all Israel'. He goes on:

> On the basis of this background, the action of the crowd in John's scene seems to have political overtones, as if they were welcoming Jesus as a national liberator. This suggestion may receive some

[53]Attempts have been made to discredit the historicity of John by denying that palm trees grew in Jerusalem. Thus Bultmann, 'who to my knowledge never wanted to visit Palestine and never has visited it' (B. Schwank, 'Ephraim in John 11.54' in *Évangile*, 379) says dogmatically, 'In Jerusalem there are no palm trees' (*John*, 418). He is followed by P. Winter, 'At the high altitude of Jerusalem no palms grow' (*On the Trial of Jesus*, 142). In fact they do, though it is too cold for fruit. Yet palm branches were readily available from Jericho and the Jordan valley (Lev. 23.40) and John says that the crowd 'took (ἔλαβον) the branches of the palms' (which they had kept in their houses from Tabernacles), not that they stripped them from trees on the way (they would mostly have been out of reach anyhow!). Their action was premeditated, not spontaneous. So Dodd, *Historical Tradition*, 155f.: 'They were carried by pilgrims who had planned an ovation beforehand.' Cf. E. E. F. Bishop, *Jesus of Palestine*, London and New York 1955, 301.

[54]F. C. Burkitt, 'W and Θ, Studies in the Western Text of Mark', *JTS* 17, 1916, 139–50; C. G. Montefiore, *The Synoptic Gospels*, London 1927, I, 259f.; B. A. Mastin, 'The Date of the Triumphal Entry', *NTS* 16, 1969, 76–82.

[55]T. W. Manson, 'The Cleansing of the Temple', *BJRL* 33, 1951, 276–80.

[56]The provision, quoted earlier, for the setting up of the tables of the money-changers in the temple court three weeks prior to Passover (M. *Shek.* 1.3) also points in the same direction. Manson's attempt to get round this by saying that 'there would probably always be some tables in the Temple precincts' is weak.

confirmation in the statement that the crowd 'came out to *meet* him (εἰς ὑπάντησιν).' This was the normal Greek expression used to describe the joyful reception of Hellenistic sovereigns into a city.[57]

The line that John 12.13 adds to the citation from Psalm 118.26 also smacks of nationalism. The crowd evidently interprets '*he who comes* in the Lord's name' as the *King of Israel*. The juxtaposition of these two titles is also found in the crowd scene of 6.14f. There the people designate Jesus as 'the Prophet *who is to come* into the world', and Jesus recognizes that this means they will attempt to make him king.[58]

The parallel with the desert feeding, where John again stresses the initiative of the crowd in 'coming' to Jesus (6.5, 15) is important for what follows the palm-waving and the acclamation scene in John. 'But Jesus found a donkey and mounted it' (12.14). The δέ is omitted in the standard English versions or translated 'and'. J. N. Sanders is however surely right in interpreting it as 'a prompt repudiation of the crowd's acclamations'.[59] In the Synoptists it is the procurement of the donkey by Jesus which is planned, the people's reaction which is spontaneous. In John it is the ovation which is premeditated, Jesus' response in 'finding a donkey and sitting on it' which is *ad hoc*. The purpose of this piece of prophetic symbolism is clear. It is to say: 'King of Israel – yes (cf. 1.49); but not that sort of king (cf. 18.36f.)'. He chooses to make his royal entry 'humble and mounted on an ass', not as conquering Messiah riding a war-horse (Zech. 9.9f.; contrast Rev. 19.11–16).[60]

There is no suggestion in John that the disciples had any part in procuring or preparing the donkey (contrast Mark 11.1–7 and pars.) – though, if one wanted to harmonize the traditions, Jesus could still in John 12.14 have used the disciples to 'find it' as in Mark 11.4. Nor are the disciples involved in the demonstration – unless we use this term to

57He cites, *inter alia*, Josephus, *BJ* 7.100: 'The people of Antioch, on hearing that Titus was at hand, through joy could not bear to remain within their walls, but hastened to meet him (ἐπὶ τὴν ὑπάντησιν) and advanced to a distance of over thirty furlongs, not only men, but a crowd of women and children also, streaming out from the city.'

58*John* I, 461f. He recalls too that the *hosanna* shouted by the crowds was also used in addressing kings (II Sam. 14.4; II Kings 6.26).

59*John*, 288. Brown takes the same view.

60It is difficult to judge whether the opening phrase of 12.15, 'Fear no more, daughter of Zion' is simply a free quotation of Zech. 9.9, 'Rejoice, rejoice, daughter of Zion', or, as Brown thinks, contains some allusion to Zeph. 3.14–16 which includes the words 'the Lord is among you as king, O Israel'. In any case it is very doubtful if Zeph. 3 can, as he believes, be read non-nationalistically.

include Jesus' adherents in Jerusalem (specifically mentioned by John in 2.23; 4.1f.; and especially 7.2, 'Go into Judaea, that your disciples *there* may see the great things you are doing'), from whose point of view Dodd indeed sees the triumphal entry in John as written.[61] In this case Luke 19.37, unparalleled in Matthew and Mark, would strikingly bear out the Johannine picture: 'As he approached the descent of the Mount of Olives the whole company of the disciples (τὸ πλῆθος τῶν μαθητῶν, cf. Acts 6.2) in their joy began to shout (cf. John 12.13) the praises of God for all the mighty works they had seen.' This would then be the equivalent of John 12.17f.: 'The people who were present when he called Lazarus out of the tomb and raised him from the dead [i.e., *'Ιουδαῖοι* who believed on him; 11.45; cf. 12.9] told what they had seen and heard. That is why the crowd [of pilgrims; 12.12f.] went to meet him; they had heard of this sign that he had performed.'[62] It may well be that Luke, who has followed the triple tradition closely in 19.29–36, is in 37–40 drawing on separate material (containing most unLucan topographical detail) with other interesting contacts with the Johannine tradition – the addition of 'the king' to the crowd's acclamation (John 12.13) and the reaction of the 'Pharisees' to Jesus' popularity (John 12.19). If so Luke 19.37 could be corroborative evidence for the raising of Lazarus and the fervour it produced. For no other 'mighty works' are recorded as performed by Jesus in the city at that time, though John mentions 'the chief priests and the Pharisees' referring to 'many signs' (11.47; cf. 12.37). Matthew also, in what is evidently independent material, says 'the chief priests and doctors of the law saw the wonderful things he did and heard the boys in the temple shouting "Hosanna to the Son of David!"' and instances how 'in the temple blind men and cripples came to him, and he healed them' (21.14f.). It is significant that these are the very two examples which John gives of Jesus' earlier healing activities in the vicinity of the temple (9.1–7; 5.1–9), though of course Matthew has no alternative but to place them during this last brief visit. So once again John's picture is not as eccentric or unsupported as it may seem at first sight.

To return to the Johannine account of the entry into Jerusalem, the Galilean disciples have no part in the scene. They are simply recorded as not understanding at the time. 'But after Jesus had been glorified

[61] *Historical Tradition*, 156, 246f.

[62] Cf. Bernard, *John* I, clxxxiiif.: 'The Synoptic account of the triumphal entry of Jesus into Jerusalem provides no explanation of the extraordinary enthusiasm with which He was received on His last visit. . . . The only evangelist who gives a sufficient

they remembered that this had been written about him, and that this had happened to him' (12.16).[63] Barrett[64] accuses John of having introduced a 'contradiction' at this point: if the disciples did not understand the royal significance, how could the crowds? But the crowds understood well enough what they were about; it was the disciples[65] who could not comprehend at that time what Jesus was trying to communicate through his acted parable. For the meaning of it all could only be grasped in the light of the distinctive and paradoxical manner in which Jesus was in reality to 'enter upon his glory'. Like all the history in this Gospel it is written 'from the end', and its telling has been shaped by that 'calling to mind' which must await the gift of the Spirit (14.26). Yet what is 'remembered' (cf. 2.22) is not only 'that this had been written about him' but 'that this had happened to him': not merely the interpretation but the event. Sanders' commentary is again apposite at this point:

> So far from being 'hardly possible as history' (Barrett),[66] his [John's] account may well reveal a better understanding than the other evangelists' of Jesus' dilemma, as 'Son of David' by right, and conscious of a mission to save Israel, yet refusing to adopt the only policy that the majority of his people would understand or accept.[67]

For John the entry into Jerusalem, with its tragi-comic 'God bless the king of Israel!', presents the reader in advance with the clue by which the trial of Jesus is to be interpreted, whose proceedings turn more insistently in this Gospel than in any other upon the question, 'Are you

---

reason for this is Jn., . . . he makes the story of the triumphal entry coherent for the first time.'

[63]Literally 'they did this to him'. It refers to the action of the people, not the disciples, and bears out how Jesus is viewed as at the receiving end in the Johannine account (as in 6.15), against the prevailing impression that he is always in control. He is, but only by turning the actions of others to his own purpose (cf. 14.30f.).

[64]*John*, 416, 419.

[65]Schlatter, *Der Evangelist Johannes*, 266, makes the point that only here does the *αὐτοῦ* precede *οἱ μαθηταί* and suggests that the contrast may be implied: 'his own disciples' did not understand the significance of Zech. 9.9, still less the Jerusalemites. He sees the same emphasis in 9.27.

[66]*John*, 1955, 347; it is still repeated, ²1978, 416.

[67]*John*, 288f. – at this point the editorial work of B. A. Mastin. Cf. Lindars, *John*, 421f.: After saying that 'John's account gives very little help in the task of reconstructing what actually happened. The fuller Synoptic versions of the story give a far more plausible picture of the course of the events', he paradoxically goes on, 'In spite of the difference of terminology, John's understanding of the event is in striking agreement with what appears to have been its actual significance for Jesus.'

– or in what sense are you – the king of the Jews?' (18.33).[68]

But before the trial there is an uneasy period of manoeuvring on both sides. Jesus is officially listed as a wanted man, yet is flouting the impotence of the authorities to arrest him. It is a period that not surprisingly has left vivid but confused memories in the various traditions. As with the scene which twelve months earlier could so easily have led to a passion narrative before its time, it is impossible neatly to harmonize the Synoptic and the Johannine pictures or even the Synoptists themselves. Both scenes have in common attempts, defused by Jesus, to proclaim him king of Israel in a manner that John alone fully explains. Yet the excitement of the crowds and the frustration of the authorities in the face of his popular support are attested by all the traditions (Matt. 21.15f., 46; 22.46; 26.5; Mark 11.18; 12.12; 14.2; Luke 19.39f., 48; 20.19, 39f.; 22.2; John 11.47f.; 12.10f., 19, 42f.). So too, if it properly belongs here, is the pattern of Jesus teaching by day in the temple and staying by night at Bethany or camping with the Twelve on the Mount of Olives (Matt. 21.17; 26.55; Mark 11.11, 19; 14.49;[69] Luke 19.47; 21.37; 22.53; and the floating tradition in John 8.1f.). Obviously there would not have been room for them all in the house at Bethany, though John alone accounts for the choice of this village as a base or explains his contacts there (cf. Mark 11.1–6 and pars.; 14.3 and par.). There is also in Mark memory of a day-by-day itinerary such as we saw characterized the critical stages of the beginning and middle of the ministry: 'it was now late' (11.11), 'on the following day' (11.12), 'when evening came' (11.19), 'early next morning' (11.20), 'they came once more to Jerusalem' (11.27). But these notes are not sustained and they have disappeared in Matthew and in Luke, who typically generalizes (19.47; 20.1; 21.37). Yet the recollection that Jesus set off for the temple very early in the day is interestingly preserved independently in Matt. 21.18; Luke 21.38; and in the floating tradition of John 8.2 (which the scribe of the manuscript behind the family 13 intelligently introduced after Luke 21.38). From the Synoptists we should have no idea how long this period lasted, though one gets the strong impression that it was measured in days rather than weeks. John alone tells us that it lasted only four days (from

[68]In John's passion narrative βασιλεύς occurs 12 times (and βασιλεία 3) compared with Matthew 4, Mark 6 and Luke 4. This is the more notable in view of the two occurrences only in John of the phrase 'the kingdom of God'.

[69]For the interpretation of Mark 14.49 and pars. to mean 'by day', as in Luke 19.47 and 21.37f., rather than 'daily', i.e., openly, as in John 18.20, in contrast with the nocturnal arrest of a secret band, cf. Winter, *Trial of Jesus*, 49.

the Monday to the Thursday). But of course, as we said, all the teaching included in the Jerusalem period by the Synoptists need not have been crammed into the sole visit that they record (contrast John 18.20: 'I have always taught in synagogue and in the temple' with Mark 14.49 and pars.: 'Daily I . . . taught in the temple').

The one firm time-reference in the Synoptic record of that week, which John does not mention, occurs at Mark 14.1 and Matt. 26.2, where it is said that the Passover was due 'after two days', i.e., the day after tomorrow (Luke 22.1 characteristically again says simply that it was 'near'). There is a meeting of the authorities to plan how they could lay hands on Jesus to put him to death: '"It must not be during the festival", they said, "or we should have rioting among the people"' (Mark 14.1f. and pars.). This marks the climax of other frustrated attempts both in the Synoptists (Mark 3.6 and pars.; 11.18; 12.12 and pars.) and still more in John (5.18; 7.1, 19, 25, 30, 32, 44f.; 8.20, 40, 59; 10.31, 39; 11.8, 53, 57). Unlike the meeting in John 11.47, this is not called a meeting of the Sanhedrin and the fact that, according to Matthew (26.3), it met in the high priest's palace and not in the Council chamber shows that it could not have been. It was a private caucus summoned in desperation to decide how to implement the resolution of the Council already passed in John 11.53, 57. It concerned what Luke 22.2 calls *τὸ πῶς* – 'the how' rather than the that.

What they decided, if anything, we shall never know. For they had the unexpected benefit of Judas Iscariot coming to talk with them precisely on this matter of 'how to betray him to them' 'without collecting a crowd' (Luke 22.3–6). The 'agreement' to pay him could well arise out of an understanding implicit in John 11.57. Luke's account of this follows immediately upon the meeting of the authorities, as if their hopes were instantly answered. In Mark and Matthew Judas' visit is preceded by the story of the anointing (which Luke has much earlier), but again without any indication of a connection. The explanation of the link is perhaps to be found in John, where the indignation of the disciples (Matt. 26.8), or 'some of those present' (Mark 14.4), is specifically attributed to Judas (John 12.4).[70] This underlying connection, although submerged in the Synoptists, could

[70]This is one of the many features of the account of the anointing in John which point to independent and perhaps first-hand tradition. The *smell* of the perfume filling the house (12.3), which is distinctive to John, has also been noted as something that would particularly have lingered in the memory of someone present. Indeed John is the only evangelist to allude to this, the most reminiscent of the senses, both here and in the story of Lazarus (*ὄζει*, 11.39).

well be the reason why the anointing and the priests' plot were brought together in the Markan tradition and the former transferred from its original position[71] prior to the entry into Jerusalem 'six days before Passover' (John 12.1), to the day of the priests' plot, correctly dated two days before the festival (Mark 14.1; Matt. 26.2).

John does not record Judas' deal with the authorities, though it is presupposed (18.3). Nor, any more than the other evangelists, does he speculate on his motives: the theological ground, not the psychological cause, is what concerns them (John 13.2, 27; Luke 22.3). Judas' position as treasurer of the group – a piece of inside information which John alone discloses – with the opportunity this afforded for 'lifting' (ἐβάσταζεν) from the kitty (12.6), is not advanced as an explanation of his action: at most it is a cover (13.27–29). Yet probing beneath the surface of the Johannine narrative may enable us to make connections that illuminate what the evangelist is content to leave dark (13.30).[72]

The theme of Judas' betrayal is first introduced in John as far back as the testing of the terms of the disciples' loyalty after Jesus had disappointed many of his followers in refusing the role of 'king'. Peter affirms the faith of the inner circle. But 'Jesus answered, "Have I not chosen you, all twelve? Yet one of you is a devil." He meant Judas, son of Simon Iscariot.[73] He it was who would betray him, and he was one of the Twelve' (6.70f.). Is John implying that even then Jesus could see that Judas was not convinced that this role was unacceptable? If so then John's report of the so-called triumphal entry as another damping of the same expectations may help us to see how for Judas that could have been the last straw – following hard upon his burst of irritation the previous evening. If Jesus was thus to throw away such a chance, with the mass support that the Passover offered (11.55; 12.12), then his hand must be forced. Judas would provoke the confrontation between Israel and Rome that, with the world going after him (12.19), Jesus must surely win.

[71] Cf., perhaps surprisingly, Fortna, *Gospel of Signs*, 151: 'There is no reason to doubt that John retains the original setting of the story [of the anointing], that is as preceding the triumphal entry.'

[72] I have here expanded some material from a pen-sketch of Judas in my book *The Roots of a Radical*, 139–43.

[73] John alone gives us the name of Judas' father, Simon Iscariot (6.71; 13.2, 26); and since 'Iscariot' attaches to him and not simply to the son it is likely to indicate his geographical origin (*'ish qeriyyoth*, the man from Kerioth, as some important manuscripts at 6.71 interpret it, as well as the Western text in 13.2, 26 and 14.22) rather than his nickname (*sicarius*, assassin). Kerioth was in the deep south of the country and it may help to explain why Judas as the only non-Galilean among the Twelve (cf. Acts 1.11; 2.7) was the odd man out. Cf. Lightfoot, *Biblical Essays*, 143f.

This of course is highly speculative, but it may be borne out by the scene which Matthew records, as Judas returns the money in disgust: 'When Judas the traitor saw that Jesus had been *condemned*, he was seized with remorse' (27.3). Whether this is true to history or not, it is surely significant that the Matthaean community remained convinced, after the event, that Judas' intention was that Jesus should *not* be condemned but emerge triumphant. Moreover, one has to explain why, according to all the traditions, the rest of the Twelve were, up to the last moment, at a complete loss to know to whom Jesus might be referring at supper (Mark 14.19 and pars.; John 13.22) or, when Judas got up and left, why he did so (John 13.28). This does not read like the action of a man they had long had reason to suspect. It looks as if he fully went along with them, willing Jesus to win perhaps even more intensely than the others. All the subsequent blackening of his character (and no end can be imagined too bad for him: Matt. 27.5; Acts 1.18; and an even nastier one preserved in a fragment of Papias)[74] has not quite succeeded in obliterating this. And if this is the interpretation which best fits the facts, it is again John who may give us the clue to it by tracing things back to the aftermath of the desert feeding.[75]

4. *The Arrest of Jesus*

The discussion of Judas has already led us from the events of 'two days before Passover' to those of the last supper. Whether this was held the next night, one day before Passover, as John says, or on Passover evening, as the Synoptists say, has already been fully discussed and reasons given for thinking that John is right. In either case the departure of Judas from the supper table leads directly into the arrest of Jesus, and here again John has a distinctive contribution to make, focusing once more on the political background.

John's account of the arrest (18.1–12) is verbally almost completely independent of the Synoptic versions (Mark 14.32–52 and pars.). Apart from the minimum of common wording required to tell the story

[74]Reproduced in Lightfoot, *Apostolic Fathers* (abridged ed.), 523f., ET. 534f.

[75]Many of these points were already made by Scott Holland, *The Fourth Gospel*, 175–8: 'We are inside the very atmosphere within which the shock of betrayal had taken place, when they first became aware of what had been going on in their very midst unperceived' (177).

at all, John shares with Mark only the striking of the high priest's servant (though he uses a different word for the cutting off of his ear) and with Luke the fact that it was the right ear (though here the word for ear is different), and John alone names Peter and Malchus[76] as involved. He does not name the place Gethsemane, though he says it lay across the Kedron ravine[77] (surprisingly mentioned only by John in the New Testament), which agrees with the Synoptists' departure from the last supper 'for the Mount of Olives' (Mark 14.26 and pars.). But he further defines the *χωρίον* of Mark and Matthew as a garden (*κῆπος*), Luke again simply having a nameless 'place' (*τόπος*, 22.40), 'into' and 'out' of which Jesus goes, implying that it was an enclosed retreat. John specifically states that Jesus and his disciples had often (*πολλάκις*)[78] used it as a rendezvous (*συνήχθη*)[79] and that is how Judas knew where to find him – the very information the authorities were wanting (*ποῦ ἐστι*, 11.57).[80] Mark and Matthew give no explanation for this, or what it was to which Judas was privy. Luke says that Jesus 'made his way as usual (*κατὰ τὸ ἔθος*) to the Mount of Olives' (22.39), but this probably simply refers to his previous statement that he camped there during that period (21.37) and implies no more prolonged or intimate acquaintance.[81]

However the really significant difference that John introduces lies in the personnel of the party making the arrest. All the Gospels agree on the presence of Judas and representatives of the Jewish authorities –

[76]The lengths to which commentators will go to avoid the simple conclusion that that was actually his name are illustrated by Guilding, *Fourth Gospel and Jewish Worship*, 165f., 232, who sees it as a fulfilment of Zech. 11.6, 'I will deliver every one of them into his neighbour's hand, and into the hand of Malko' (Hebrew for 'his king')!

[77]The true reading is almost certainly the one adopted by Nestle-Aland and the United Bible Societies texts, *τοῦ Κεδρών*, despite the better manuscript support for *τοῦ κέδρου* and *τῶν κέδρων* ('of the cedar(s)') which are explicable as easier corrections from it (so Metzger). This case was cogently argued by Lightfoot, *Biblical Essays*, 172–5, in conscious opposition to Westcott who preferred *τῶν κέδρων* (*John* II, 295f., and the Westcott and Hort text). So too Sanday, *Authorship and Historical Character of the Fourth Gospel*, 240f. There is no reason to suppose that John was under the illusion that cedars grew in it or that it was named for this reason.

[78]As Barrett observes, *John*, 518, 'This is possible if the Johannine account of the ministry is presupposed, but it is inconsistent with the one short visit to Jerusalem of the Marcan.'

[79]Cf. Askwith, *Historical Value of the Fourth Gospel*, 74: 'This is a detail that would be known to the select circle, and the mention of it is intelligible if the writer belonged to that circle.'

[80]So, against wilder theories of the 'secret', Blinzler, *Trial*, 58f.; *Prozess* [4]84–6. Bickermann, 'Utilitas Crucis', 216 relevantly compares *Mart. Polyc.* 6.

[81]So Dodd, *Historical Tradition*, 67. Bernard, *John* II, 584, suggests that the apostles quite reasonably thought they had come there to sleep!

though the Synoptists loosely call them 'a crowd' and Luke improbably suggests that 'the chief priests and captains of the temple and the elders' came out in person (22.52). John alone specifies them as ὑπηρέται, usually translated as 'temple police' but more accurately in this role as 'constables of the court' (cf. Matt. 5.25; 'the judge may hand you over to the constable'), that is, of the Sanhedrin acting in its judicial capacity.[82] John, who unlike the other Gospels (Mark 14.54; Matt. 26.58) distinguishes them from the servants (δοῦλοι) of the high priest (18.18), always uses this word in its judicial context[83] – except when in irony to Pilate Jesus refers to the disciples as his ὑπηρέται (18.36) or 'force'.

But as well as 'the constables of the Jews' John uniquely introduces – and so casually that if it had stood in Mark it would be taken for granted that John was presupposing knowledge of the Synoptic narrative – 'the σπεῖρα' under the command of 'the χιλίαρχος' (18.3, 12). These are the regular terms for the *cohors* and *tribunus* of the Roman army and there is no good reason for doubting that John is using them in their usual technical sense like the rest of the New Testament writers (Matt. 27.27; Mark 15.16; Acts 10.1; 21.31; 27.1).[84] This has been questioned because a full cohort comprised 600 men (though outside the New Testament σπεῖρα also translates the smaller *manipulus*), and this would be absurdly large. But it is pedantic to insist that 'the whole cohort' (subsequently referred to in Mark 15.16 and par.) must have been sent out to arrest Jesus, thus endangering security at the Antonia. Nor does the phrase about Judas 'taking the cohort' mean that John imagined that Judas commanded it (he knew he did not: 18.12), but simply that he 'had got the help of "the cohort"'[85] and 'acted as a guide' (Acts 1.16). Lightfoot[86] also drew attention to the definite article before σπεῖρα as showing John's knowledge of the regular garrisoning arrangement at the Turris Antonia during the great festivals, to which Josephus, like Acts 21.31, refers:

[82]Cf. Blinzler, *Trial*, 63 n. 32; *Prozess*[4], 126–8.

[83]In 7.32, 45f.; 18.3, 12 of constables sent out to make an arrest in the name of the Council (as in Acts 5.21–26); in 18.18, 22; 19.6 of constables in court (as in Mark 14.65).

[84]This is denied by Blinzler, *Trial*, 66–9, *Prozess*[4], 94–8; Catchpole, *Trial of Jesus*, 148–51; and Bammel, in Bammel and Moule, edd., *Jesus and the Politics of his Day*, 439. But see Schürer, *History* I, 372 n. 86, for a clear repudiation of this view.

[85]Bernard, *John* II, 584; so Brown, *John* II, 807. For a Jew procuring the aid of (λαβών, as in John) troops from the Romans, cf. Josephus, *BJ* 7.52.

[86]*Biblical Essays*, 161.

The usual crowd had assembled at Jerusalem for the feast of unleavened bread, and the Roman cohort (ἡ σπεῖρα) had taken up its position on the roof of the portico of the temple; for a body of men invariably mounts guard at the feasts, to prevent disorders arising from such a concourse of people.[87]

But the refusal to accept the obvious meaning of John's language derives from an *a priori* conviction that the involvement of the Romans at this point is incredible. Most commentators, accepting that this is what John means to imply, dismiss it as 'historically improbable'[88] or see it as simply symbolic of 'the world' ranged against Jesus.[89] Even Dodd concludes that 'John assumed without warrant that Roman troops participated in the arrest.'[90] But other writers make the point that Roman participation so goes against John's tendency (as they see it) to load responsibility for the death of Jesus on the Jews and exonerate Pilate that it cannot be regarded as his invention.[91]

But is the Roman presence so astonishing? The one thing that all the Synoptic accounts agree on verbally (and Luke's words may well derive, like his version of the Gethsemane story, from his own source) is the words 'Do you take me for a bandit (ληστής), that you come out with swords and cudgels to arrest me?' Now if we ask whom we should expect to arrest such a terrorist or freedom fighter, there can only be one answer. Who would have arrested Barabbas, whom John also describes as a ληστής (18.40), 'with the rebels (στασιασταί) who had committed murder in the rising' (Mark 15.7), or the two λησταί crucified with Jesus (Mark 15.27 and par.)? Obviously it would have

[87] *BJ* 2.224; *Ant.* 20.106, 192; cf. *BJ* 5.243f., describing the Antonia: 'At the point where it impinged upon the porticoes of the temple, there were stairs [cf. Acts 21.40] leading down to both of them, by which the guards descended [cf. Acts 21.32]; for a Roman cohort (τάγμα) was permanently quartered there, and at the festivals took up positions in arms around the porticoes to watch the people and suppress any insurrectionary movement.' After AD 70 a radical change took place in the garrisoning of Palestine; cf. Schürer, *History* I, 366f.

[88] Barrett, *John*, 516. In *The Gospel of John and Judaism*, 71, he calls it 'astonishing', though he is incorrect in saying that in John 'the Romans *rather than* the Jews arrest Jesus' (my italics).

[89] Bultmann, *John*, 639; Lindars, *John*, 539f.

[90] *Historical Tradition*, 118.

[91] Cf. Winter, *Trial of Jesus*, 44–9; H. Cohn, *The Trial and Death of Jesus*, New York 1977, 78; and earlier M. Goguel, *The Life of Jesus*, 468f., and Gardner-Smith, *St John and the Synoptic Gospels*, 57f. So, on balance, Brown, *John* II, 815f., who judges that 'John's information or approach has considerable plausibility as representing older tradition [than the Synoptic Gospels]'.

been the Romans, taking the precaution of doing it in strength. What was distinctive, and shameful, about the arrest of Jesus is that the Jews took the initiative[92] *and collaborated.*[93] But then the exercise was, as John insists, collaborationist from start to finish.[94] The initiative indeed came from the Jews, and Jesus' subsequent words to Pilate, 'My ὑπηρέται would be fighting to save me from arrest *by the Jews*' (18.37), clearly presuppose that it was they, not the Romans, who were out to apprehend him.[95] Yet they were not above using the services of one of Jesus' own following or of the occupying garrison. Then as later they were no doubt able to obtain the assistance of the Romans by representing him as a danger to the peace. For they needed the force which they alone could command should serious resistance be offered. John's account, as well as being the only one to mention the precaution of taking 'lanterns and torches', speaks of 'weapons' (ὅπλα). The Synoptists refer to 'swords and cudgels'. The latter (ξύλοι, or truncheons) were the equipment of the constables, and Winter argues that the presence of swords implicitly confirms the Johannine tradition that Roman soldiers were also involved.[96] It was an army job and not merely constabulary duty.[97]

But since the prisoner was a wanted man on the Jewish list, for whom (unlike Barabbas) a summons was out from a properly convened meeting of the Jewish high court (11.47–57), it was to this court that he was handed over – by the Romans. It is this fact that has

[92]That the initiative was Pilate's, as Goguel argued ('Juifs et Romains dans l'histoire de la passion', *RHR* 62, 1910, 165–82, 295–322), is without any support. There is no reason to suppose that Pilate personally knew about the arrest, in contrast with the tribune at the Antonia.

[93]According to Cohn the Jews begged to be allowed a part so that they could take Jesus into their protection for the night in order to 'persuade him to co-operate' and thus *save* him from execution by the Romans. The high priest rent his clothes in grief because Jesus refused to be co-operative – after all the trouble and inconvenience of a night-session of the greater Sanhedrin! It is sad to see such legal learning and fair-mindedness on the part of this Israeli judge harnessed to so groundless a construction in the interest of showing that the Jews were 'wholly innocent'.

[94]Cf. the comment of Schlatter, *Der Evangelist Johannes*, 327, that the beginning of the process in John corresponds to its end, since the priests make clear that Caesar is their only king (cf. 19.15).

[95]Cf. F. Hahn, 'Der Prozess Jesu nach dem Johannesevangelium: eine redaktionsgeschichtliche Untersuchung', *EKK* 2, Zurich 1970, 23–96, specif. 40.

[96]'The Trial of Jesus', *Commentary* (The American Jewish Community, New York) 38, September 1964, 36. He believes that Mark, writing in Rome after AD 70, wanted to play down the Roman participation.

[97]For the difference between these two, even then, cf. Josephus *BJ* 2.276, where Pilate intersperses his troops among the Jewish crowds 'armed but disguised in civilian dress, with orders not to use their swords (ξίφη), but to beat any rioters with cudgels (ξύλα)'.

seemed to many a contradiction, discrediting the Johannine evidence.[98] Yet so far from the procedure being improbable or irregular, there are close parallels in the story of Acts 21–23. There too the chiliarch commanding 'the cohort', faced with a riotous assembly at the feast of Pentecost, 'took a force of soldiers with their centurions and came down on the rioters at the double' (21.31f.).[99] He too supposes that he is dealing with a revolutionary, saying to Paul, 'Then you are not the Egyptian who started a revolt some time ago and led a force of four thousand terrorists out into the wilds?' (21.38). For he was on a charge before the Jewish court (22.30; 23.28f.), and it remained within the power of the Council to apply to the commandant to bring him before it for 'closer investigation of his case' (23.15). Subsequently Lysias reports: 'I found that the accusation had to do with controversial matters in their law, but there was no charge against him meriting death or imprisonment' (23.29). That would have been the end of it as far as the Romans were concerned, were it not that, thanks to information received (the same term as in John 11.57), a plot against Paul's life had been uncovered (23.30) and he required further protective custody. But judicially the Romans were acting as law-enforcement officers for the Jewish supreme court, whose jurisdiction, except in capital or political cases, was fully recognized by the occupying power. This is precisely the situation which the Fourth Gospel faithfully reflects.

Yet there was a difference between the situations of Paul and Jesus. In Paul's case the chiliarch handed him over to a meeting of the Sanhedrin, which he had ordered to be summoned, 'to be quite sure what charge the Jews were bringing against him' (22.30). In Jesus' case he handed him over to the high priest to allow him and his confederates to frame the charge or charges. For one thing upon which all the Gospel traditions agree is that Jesus was led off not to the Council chamber but to the palace (*αὐλή* or *οἰκία*) of the high priest (Matt. 26.57f.; Mark 14.53f.; Luke 22.54; John 18.15).

At this point also in all the Gospels the denial of Peter is introduced, though with a welter of detailed differences. John agrees with Mark (14.54, 66–72) and Matthew (26.58, 69–75) in telling the story in two sections, but in the latter two Gospels all the questions come in the

[98]E.g., Bultmann, *John*, 637: 'It is unbelievable that the chiliarch led the prisoner to the Sanhedrin [actually it was to Annas] instead of to the Antonia.' Similarly, Barrett, *John*, 518, quoting E. Haenchen.

[99]We are not told how many troops he took – again obviously not the whole cohort. Later he detailed 200 infantry (a maniple), together with 70 cavalry and 200 other armed men, to convoy Paul, who was under threat of ambush, to Caesarea (23.23).

second part. After the first question Peter goes out into the porch or forecourt (προαύλιον) in Mark or the gateway (πυλών) in Matthew, where the same servant girl (Mark) or another (Matthew) accuses him to the bystanders. Then 'shortly afterwards' (μετὰ μικρόν) the bystanders themselves confront Peter. In Luke the story is told continuously (22.54–62). The servant-girl stares at Peter and says 'This man was with him too.' A little later (μετὰ βραχύ) someone else (male) notices him and says 'You also are one of them,' and then 'after the space of about an hour' another (male) individual speaks more strongly still: 'Of course this fellow was with him.' In John (18.15–18, 25–7) the maid on duty at the door questions Peter directly as he enters. There follows the break in the narrative, though without any indication of time-lapse. Then 'they' (from among the servants and constables) say to him, 'Are you another of his disciples?', and finally, again without any indication of interval, one of the servants insists, 'Did I not see you with him in the garden?' In Matthew and Mark the first and third questions are in the second person, the second in the third; in Luke the first and third are in the third person, the second in the second; in John all three are in the second person. It is obvious that the tradition is as confused as under the circumstances one would expect, but equally clear that we are dealing here with three independent sources of it.[100] All may preserve authentic traits. But John is more circumstantial in identifying the maid as the girl on the gate; in explaining how Peter gained access at all and why he came to be at the porch or gateway (as Mark and Matthew assert); in mentioning the presence of another disciple (which seems to be implied by the question 'Were you *also* [καί] with Jesus of Nazareth?' in all the accounts); and finally in identifying the other servant as a relative of Malchus and thus explaining how he recognized Peter. Dodd comments: 'This vivid narrative, every step of which is clear and convincing, is either the product of a remarkable dramatic flair, or it rests on superior information.'[101]

[100] So Brown, *John* II, 837; Dodd, *Historical Tradition*, 83–6. For the independence of Luke and Mark, cf. Catchpole, *Trial of Jesus*, 160–74.

[101] *Historical Tradition*, 86. There is an interesting discussion of this incident from the point of view of literary representation in E. Auerbach, *Mimesis: The Representation of Reality in Western Literature*, ET Princeton, N.J. and Oxford 1953, 45f. He is analysing the Markan account, but the points he makes apply just as much to the Johannine. 'A scene like Peter's denial fits into no antique genre. It is too serious for comedy, too contemporary and everyday for tragedy, politically too insignificant for history – and the form which was given it is one of such immediacy that its like does not exist in the literature of antiquity. This can be judged by a symptom which at first glance

5. *The Jewish Trial*

In the meantime, while all this is going on outside (Matthew) and downstairs (Mark) Jesus is being interrogated. According to Matthew and Mark this is done by the high priest, whom Matthew again names as Caiaphas, and a gathering of his associates. Luke at this stage has only those who made the arrest beating up the prisoner – and no interrogation (22.63–65). John says that Jesus was led first to Annas, the father-in-law of Caiaphas who was high priest that fateful year (18.13),[102] and only subsequently to Caiaphas (18.24). At first sight it looks as if both these are within the same palace, since Peter is apparently in the courtyard both before (18.15–18) and after (18.24–27). Yet the second round of Peter's ordeal is probably to be understood as going on while Jesus is being interrogated by Annas. There is no indication of the passage of time but the NEB is almost certainly right in rendering the δέ as 'meanwhile'. The 'sending' of him 'bound'[103] to Caiaphas would then indicate not simply a transfer within the palace but more naturally the longer journey across the city to the Council chamber, recorded in Luke 22.66, where the official high priest, who alone could chair the Sanhedrin,[104] was arranging the morning meeting of the Council which John does not mention.[105] In this case it was left to Annas to conduct the preliminary interrogation.

may seem insignificant: the use of direct discourse. The maid says: And thou also wast with Jesus of Nazareth! He answers: I know not, neither understand I what thou sayest. Then the maid says to the bystanders: This is one of them. And, Peter repeating his denial, the bystanders speak up: Surely thou art one of them, for thou art a Galilean by thy speech! – I do not believe that there is a single passage in an antique historian where direct discourse is employed in this fashion in a brief, direct dialogue. Dialogues with few participants are rare in their writings; at best they appear in anecdotal biography, and there the function they serve is almost always to lead up to famous pregnant retorts, whose importance lies not in their realistically concrete content but in their rhetorical and ethical impact.'

[102]It is hardly necessary now to rebut the charge that John's thrice-repeated phrase 'high priest that year' (11.49, 51; 18.13) implies, as even Dodd asserts, that 'he must have thought of it as an annual tenure' (*Historical Tradition*, 94; similarly Bultmann, *John*, 410f.). John's evident knowledge of Judaism was far too deep for him to make so crude a mistake. As Stanton puts it, it 'would imply ignorance so gross as to be inconceivable in view of the amount of knowledge of things Jewish shown in the book' (*Gospels as Historical Documents* III, 155). So too Brown, *John* I, 439f.

[103]Bickermann, 'Utilitas Crucis', 221, sees those words as indicating that according to John, the prisoner, as a 'proscript', has already been incriminated. He is thus 'bound' from the moment of his arrest (18.12). In the Synoptists (Mark 15.1; Matt. 27.2) he is bound only after he has been condemned by the formal verdict of the Sanhedrin.

[104]For the evidence, see Schürer, *History* II, 215–18.

[105]Brown, *John* II, 827, 844, argues for this interpretation, pointing out that the 'they' of 18.28 who take Jesus from Caiaphas to Pilate are evidently the chief priests and

There is little doubt that John is historically accurate[106] in depicting Annas thus as very much a power behind the throne and one who still enjoyed the courtesy title of 'high priest' (exactly as in Luke 3.2; Acts 4.6),[107] though he actually held the office only from AD 6 to 15, being succeeded (after three appointments lasting no more than a year each) by Joseph Caiaphas (AD 18–37).[108] Only John informs us that Caiaphas was Annas' son-in-law, though Josephus says that no less than five of his sons were high priests, 'he himself having formerly enjoyed the τιμή (the office, or honour?) for a very long time'. Not for nothing does he call him the 'luckiest' of men (*Ant.* 20.197f.)![109]

Matthew says that with the high priest at that night session (whom he alone, with understandable confusion, names Caiaphas) were assembled 'the scribes and the elders', and Mark 'all the chief priests and the elders and the scribes'. Though the presence of associates and assessors is entirely possible, as in the former meeting at Caiaphas' house in Matt. 26.3 and pars., there is no suggestion to begin with that this is a meeting of the Sanhedrin, which indeed it could not formally have been in this location.[110] But after the account of Peter's denial

---

the constables of the Sanhedrin (18.35; 19.6). So too Bernard, ad loc., and P. Benoit, 'Jesus Before the Sanhedrin', ET in *Jesus and the Gospel* I, 165f. The RSV incorrectly translates in 18.28 'from *the house of* Caiaphas', which is not in the Greek.

[106]Winter, *Trial of Jesus*, 31–43, seems at this point to go quite wild in his judgment, believing that 'no tradition of any sort existed which preserved the name of the Jewish high-priest in Jesus' time' (33). The whole chapter is indeed an essay in text-, form-and redaction-criticism run riot.

[107]That 'the high priest' in John 18.19, 22 already refers to Caiaphas, as Barrett asserts (*John*, 523), and thus that the sending of Jesus to Caiphas in 18.24 reflects the total incoherence of the narrative (which the Sinaitic Syriac version has attempted to mend by rearrangement of the verses) is a quite unnecessary interpretation. See to the contrary Brown, *John* II, 820f.; and Dodd, *Historical Tradition*, 94.

[108]Josephus, *Ant.* 18.26, 33–5. In 18.34 he still refers to 'the high priest Ananus (Annas)' after his deposition from office. Similarly later on in *BJ* 2.243 he speaks of 'the high priests Jonathan and Ananias' (the Ananias of Acts 4.6, the son of Annas who succeeded Caiaphas; *Ant.* 18.95), even though Jonathan had been deposed some fifteen years earlier (*Ant.* 18.123) – the same interval that separated Annas from office in AD 30. Jonathan later declined reappointment (*Ant.* 19.313–16) but continued to be called 'Jonathan the high priest' till his death (*BJ* 2.240, 256; *Ant.* 20.162). For the principle 'once a high priest always a high priest', cf. M. *Hor.* 3.4 (tr. Danby): 'A High Priest in office differs from the priest that is passed [from his high-priesthood] only in the bullock that is offered on the Day of Atonement and the Tenth of the Ephah. Both are equal in the [Temple-] service of the Day of Atonement' and in all other respects.

[109]For the long arm of the house of Annas, cf. Jeremias, *Jerusalem in the Time of Jesus*, 194–8.

[110]Where precisely the Council chamber was at this point is unfortunately in doubt. We are told that 'forty years before the destruction of the temple' the Sanhedrin went

Matthew (26.59) and Mark (14.55) refer to 'the chief priests and the whole Council (συνέδριον)'. It appears to be a continuation of the same meeting, but Luke is quite clear that what occurred at it took place at a separate meeting in the morning when 'the elders (πρεσβυτέριον) of the nation, chief priests and scribes assembled' and 'Jesus was led off[111] to their συνέδριον' (22.66).[112] Matthew (27.1) and Mark (15.1) also speak of this morning meeting as a gathering of 'the chief priests and elders of the people', Mark again using the phrase 'the whole συνέδριον',[113] but they do not specify that it was at a different location. There can be little

---

into exile from its proper meeting-place in the Chamber of Hewn Stone, one of the south-west chambers of the Court of Priests (M. *Midd.* 5.4; *Sanh.* 11.2, cf. b. *Yom.* 25a), and took its seat at the Hanuyot (shops) (b. *Shab.* 15a; *Sanh.* 41a; *A. Zar.* 8b), perhaps (?) to be located inside the Huldah Gates on the south portico of the temple precincts, near where the money-changers had their stalls. The move to a less holy site may have been forced by popular demand because of the corruption in the high-priestly establishment, though b. *A. Zar.* 8b attributes it to the disorders of the Roman occupation: 'When the Sanhedrin saw that murderers were so prevalent that they could not be properly dealt with judicially, they said: Rather let us be exiled from place to place than pronounce them guilty [of capital offences], for it is written "And thou shalt do according to the sentence, which they of that place which the Lord shall choose shall tell thee" (Deut. 17.10), which implies that it is the place that matters.' But this could well be part of the process, evident in the context, of blaming the Romans for everything wrong in Israel and would imply that the Sanhedrin gave up even sentencing, as opposed to executing, capital cases, which was clearly not the case. The date would exactly coincide with the year of the crucifixion (cf. V. Eppstein, 'The Historicity of the Gospel Account of the Cleansing of the Temple', *ZNW* 55, 1964, 42–58), though 'forty years' may simply be a round figure, as so often in the Bible. Yet such a move must certainly have taken place by the time of the incident in Acts 23.1–10, probably in AD 57, since the Roman troops could never have entered the Council chamber if it was within the Court of Israel. But Josephus (*BJ* 2.344; 5.144; 6.354) locates the Council chamber or βουλή just to the west of the temple mount and joined to it by a bridge (which must be what is now known as 'Wilson's arch') beside the Xystus or on the Xystus (probably an open area of 'polished stone' – hence (?) the name 'chamber of hewn stone' which would not be distinctive in the temple). Josephus is almost certainly to be preferred to the later unconfirmed evidence of the Mishnah and Talmud (so Schürer, *History* II, 223–5). In any case the Council chamber is clearly distinct from the high priest's house.

111 Literally, 'they led him away', but it was clearly done by the ὑπηρέται, not by the councillors.

112 For this localized use, cf. Acts 6.12; 23.20, 28; and probably 4.15.

113 This is clear; yet, despite Benoit who says that 'the only legitimate translation of the expression συμβούλιον λαμβάνειν is "to hold a council"' (*Jesus and the Gospel* I, 150), συμβούλιον does not itself indicate that it is a meeting of the Council. As Sherwin-White, *Roman Society*, 44f., rightly says, this and comparable expressions elsewhere in the Gospels (Matt. 12.14; 22.15; 27.7; 28.12; Mark 3.6) evidently mean to 'take counsel' (cf. the Latin *consilium capere*; so Bauer-Arndt-Gingrich, ad loc.) But this is no ground, with Sherwin-White, for *denying* that it was a meeting of the Sanhedrin.

doubt that there is confusion here and that Matthew and Mark are wrong in describing what happened by night at the high priest's palace as a meeting of the Sanhedrin, which would have been illegal by night, quite apart from being in the wrong place. It looks as if the calling of witnesses, the cross-examination of the prisoner by the high priest, and the verdict that he was guilty and deserving of death (Mark 14.55–64 and pars., though Luke passes over the witnesses[114] and the verdict) belong to the properly constituted Council meeting in the morning.

So what then happened at night? What John says: a questioning of Jesus by Annas about his disciples and his teaching (18.19) and a 'roughing up' of the prisoner by the constables in charge of him (18.22 and Luke 22.63–65; rather than after the verdict as in Mark 14.65 and Matt. 26.67f.). In other words, what took place in the high priest's palace was what today might happen in a police station before the prisoner is brought to court. Or, under the French system, Annas could be said to be performing the preliminary function of *juge d'instruction* or examining magistrate. As Brown puts it,[115] 'We are in the atmosphere of a police interrogation of a newly arrested criminal before any formal trial procedures are begun'; and he attaches considerable historical importance to the whole incident.[116] The object of the interrogation was doubtless to probe the teaching and movement of Jesus for its perversive and subversive elements and if possible to get the prisoner to incriminate himself, which under Jewish law then was probably illegal (as it certainly was later).[117]

According to John, Jesus at this point puts up a vigorous defence:

> I have spoken openly to all the world; I have always taught in the synagogue and in the temple, where all Jews congregate; I have said nothing in secret. Why question me? Ask my hearers what I told them; they know what I said (18.20f.).[118]

[114]Yet Luke 22.71, 'Need we call further witnesses?', implies earlier ones.

[115]*John* II, 834.

[116]*John* II, 834–6.

[117]The earliest positive evidence is not to be found till the commentary by Maimonides (1135–1204) on M. *Sanh.* 6.2: 'Our law condemns no one to death on his own confession.' But Israel Abrahams argued that 'though no such formal rule is given in the Mishnah, it is implied throughout' (*Pharisaism and the Gospels* II, 132).

[118]Cf. Mark 14.49 and pars.; and more directly Plato, *Apol.* 33b of Socrates: 'If anyone says that he has ever learnt or heard anything from me in private, which all others could not have heard, know that he does not speak the truth.' This is quoted by Bernard, *John* II, 600, who adds: 'It is noteworthy that the strongest repudiation in the Gospels of cryptic or esoteric teaching in the words of Jesus is found in John' (601). There is in fact an even closer parallel to the activity of Jesus when Xenophon defends Socrates against the charge of 'rejecting the gods acknowledged by the state': 'Socrates

And when this is interpreted as insolence to the high priest he replies (18.23):

> If I spoke amiss, state it in evidence; if I spoke well, why strike me?

In other words he is denying any secret or subversive activity and demanding that they produce witnesses prepared to testify on oath in open court. This is a clear indication, as Luke says, that these had not yet been called nor the charges specified. The earlier resolution that he should be put to death (11.53) still required to be backed by a hearing of the prisoner in person (cf. 7.51) and the evidence of at least two witnesses (8.17) which would stand up to the strict procedures of a Jewish court (cf. M. *Sanh.* 3.6; 4.5; 5.1–4) before formal conviction could be passed – quite apart from the presentation of a charge which would carry with the Romans.

John's particular contribution at this stage is that he gives us the fullest account of this private interrogation (Matthew and Mark merge it with the subsequent trial and Luke passes it over altogether). This is explained by the fact that he claims through the 'other disciple' (whether it is himself or not) to have had entrée to the high priest's household, at any rate below stairs (18.10, 15f., 26), and it is not at all impossible that he could subsequently have learnt the drift of the proceedings from these sources,[119] if, as the details of names and relationships may suggest, they found their way into the Johannine community. In contrast, Luke's independent material is to be trusted for the time and place of the formal meeting of the Sanhedrin in the morning, while the Markan tradition, followed by Matthew, for all its confusion gives us additional information on what went on in the witness box and on the final verdict.

But why does John pass over what was brought up at the trial before the Council? In an important sense he does not. Brown[120] and Dodd[121]

---

lived ever in the open; for early in the morning (πρωΐ) he went to the public promenades and training-grounds; in the forenoon he was seen in the market; and the rest of the day he passed just where most people were to be met: he was generally talking, and anyone might listen. Yet none ever knew him to offend against piety and religion in deed or word' (*Mem.* 1.1.10; tr. E. C. Marchant, LCL 1923).

[119] Benoit, *Jesus and the Gospel* I, 161, makes the point that if the Markan tradition does go back to Peter it is not surprising that it is confused about precisely what was going on inside the palace. He had plenty on his mind down below. The other disciple, whoever he was, would be a more reliable informant.

[120] *John* II, 833f.; cf. his 'John and the Synoptic Gospels: A Comparison', *NT Essays*, 198–203.

[121] *Historical Tradition*, 89–92.

both make the point that much of the matter occurs at different points in the Johannine narrative. Thus there are echoes of the trial scene in:

1.51, 'In truth, in very truth I tell you all, you shall see heaven wide open, and God's angels ascending and descending upon the Son of Man'.[122]
6.62, 'Does this shock you? What if you see the Son of Man ascending to the place where he was before?'
8.28, 'When you have lifted up the Son of Man you will know that I am what I am' (cf. Mark 14.61f. and pars.).
2.19, 'Destroy this temple', Jesus replied, 'and in three days I will raise it again' (cf. Mark 14.58 and par.).
7.12, 'No', said others, 'he is leading the people astray' (cf. b. *Sanh*. 43a: 'He has practised sorcery and enticed Israel to apostasy').
10.24f., 'If you are the Messiah say so plainly.' 'I have told you', said Jesus, 'but you do not believe' (cf. Luke 22.67).
10.36, 'Why do you charge me with blasphemy because I . . . said, "I am God's son"?' (cf. Mark 14.61–64 and par.; Luke 22.70f.).

John does not give the evidence in court, so much as the basis for it in the teaching ministry of Jesus.[123] But the basic reason why he can pass over the session of the Sanhedrin to confirm Jesus' guilt and ratify the which took the fundamental decision that he must be put to death (11.47–53).[124]

[122]For the interpretation of this difficult saying I would refer to my *Jesus and His Coming*, 168 n. 1. I still incline to take it, like Mark 14.62, as a prophecy of *vindication*, with the angelic powers from heights and depths converging in homage upon the exalted Son of Man, the basis perhaps in the words of Jesus for the church's expectation in Phil. 2.10; I Peter 3.18–22; Eph. 1.20f.; I Tim. 3.16.

[123]Yet conversely the reply in John 18.20, 'I have spoken openly to all the world; I have always taught in the synagogue and in the temple where all Jews congregate; I have said nothing in secret', is placed by John in the interrogation by Annas, while the setting of the Synoptic parallel ('Day after day I was with you in the temple teaching, and you did not seize me', Mark 14.49 par. Matt. 26.55; Luke 22.53) is the Garden of Gethsemane. Luke, improbably, supposes that 'the chief priests, the *στρατηγοί* of the temple and the elders' (22.52) were there to hear it. Benoit, *Jesus and the Gospel* I, 161, believes that the Synoptic tradition at this point betrays traces of the later interrogation which John has in the correct place.

[124]The passing over of the significance of this meeting is the only major point at which I should wish to differ from Benoit's reconstruction of events in *Jesus and the Gospel* I, 147–66.

At this point we may introduce the evidence from the Mishnah, which is usually used to demonstrate how illegal the Jewish proceedings against Jesus were. Whether its regulations applied at the time must remain extremely doubtful. Earlier scepticism[125] has been reinforced by recent work by Jacob Neusner[126] who maintains that most of the Mishnah can be shown to be evidence only for its final period of redaction in the last part of the second century AD, and that that applies *par excellence* to the whole of the fourth division *Nezikin* or 'Damages', containing the crucial tractate *Sanhedrin* which describes court-procedures. He argues that the editors of the Mishnah were producing an ideal 'tableau' of how things ought to be, based on their judgment that 'nothing of worth had happened from the time of Moses to their own day'.[127] Where possible the rules were developed out of Scripture by a sort of halakhic mathematics. But, as he says, 'Most of Sanhedrin derives from some source of information independent of Scripture and prior to the Mishnah's work on that subject. Since the work of Sanhedrin as a tractate appears to be mainly that of second-century philosophers and legislators, there is no way to know how long before the time of the framing of the tractate, let alone where, the facts were *made up*.'[128] But there would seem to be an *a priori* probability that these were *not* simply 'made up' but go back to earlier traditions of how things were done.[129] To prescind from the question of historical origin or development because the writers of the Mishnah were not themselves interested in it does not dispose of it. One gets the impression that as with so many redaction critics of the New Testament the history behind the material is simply being reduced to

[125]Cf. e.g., H. Danby, 'The Bearing of the Rabbinical Criminal Code on the Jewish Trial Narratives in the Gospels', *JTS* 21, 1920, 51–76; Blinzler, *Trial*, 149–57; *Prozess*[4], 216–29.

[126]Brilliantly summarized in his book *Judaism: the Evidence of the Mishnah*, Chicago and London 1981.

[127]Ibid., 171. He goes on: 'That explains why they could ignore whatever was available in their own day and leap back to what was not. So from Scripture to their own day whatever custom or practice had come into general usage was treated as if it did not exist.' Yet that hardly justifies him in doing the same!

[128]Ibid., 201. Italics mine.

[129]Cf. the long review-article by Yaakov Elman, 'The Judaism of the Mishnah: What Evidence?', *Judaica Book News* 12.2, 1982, 17–25, who says 'It may just be in the anonymous material which Neusner grudgingly includes as late that we find the most demonstrably early stratum of the Mishnah's laws – the civil and criminal laws of Damages. It is only in the last generation or so . . . that we have begun to see just how much of the Mishnah's law is the common heritage of the ancient Near East. This traditional law of truly hoary antiquity is the background against which the Mishnah must be viewed' (22).

the history of the community that shaped it.

It is perfectly true that one cannot take the regulations of *Sanhedrin* on capital trials or *Pesaḥim* on the Passover ritual as primary evidence of how things were ordered in the first century. But starting from the first century evidence of the Gospels or of Qumran (especially the Temple Scroll),[130] Philo or Josephus, if one finds correlations with the Mishnaic rules, then this helps to bear out that these were not simply being made up.[131] Nothing in the reconstruction that follows turns on the trustworthiness of the evidence of the Mishnah. But equally that evidence cannot be used, as it has often been used, not least from the Jewish side,[132] to discredit the reliability of the Gospel accounts. What I wish to argue is that *if* the later regulations applied in the first century (and some, e.g., on the rules of evidence, are inherently more likely to have done so than others,[133] e.g., the details of unenforceable death penalties), then they are more compatible with the Gospel accounts of the trial of Jesus, not least that of the Fourth, than is often asserted. Indeed while they would clearly show some aspects of the Synoptic presentation to be irregular, this does not I believe apply to the Johannine.

The crucial passage from the Mishnah runs as follows:

> In non-capital cases they hold the trial during the daytime and the verdict may be reached during the night; in capital cases they hold the trial during the daytime and the verdict must also be reached during the daytime. In non-capital cases the verdict, whether of acquittal or of conviction, may be reached the same day; in capital cases a verdict of acquittal may be reached on the same day, but a verdict of conviction not until the following day. Therefore trials may not be held on the eve of a Sabbath or on the eve of a Festival-day (*Sanh*. 4.1).[134]

[130]Pending an English translation of Y. Yadin's edition, cf. J. Milgrom in *BA* 41, 1978, 105–20.

[131]This was essentially the approach of Abrahams, 'The Tannaite Tradition and the Trial Narratives', *Pharisaism and the Gospels* II, 129–37, who concluded: 'On the whole, when every allowance is made for the theoretical and academic tendencies in the Mishnaic account of legal procedure, there seems no adequate reason why that account should not be utilized, cautiously and critically, in discussing and illustrating the Trial Narratives of the Gospels' (137).

[132]A recent popular example is Raymond Apple, 'The Trial of Jesus', *Common Ground* (Journal of the Council of Christians and Jews, London), 1979.4, 4–7.

[133]But account has to be taken of the greater bias in the prisoner's favour in a code dominated by the Pharisees than could have been expected in courts ruled by the Sadducees. Cf. Josephus, *Ant*. 13.294; 20.199.

[134]Tr. Danby, *The Mishnah*, 387. D. R. Catchpole, 'Trial of Jesus', *IDB* Supplementary Vol., 919, says that the Tosefta, *Sanh*. 10.11, 'shows no awareness' of the rule for a

This passage is usually held to show that John's chronology, just as much as the Synoptists', would make the trial of Jesus irregular because it could not legally have been held on the eve of a festival any more than on the day itself. But a clear distinction is here drawn between a 'trial' and a 'verdict'. Capital trials ending in conviction could not be held on the eve of a festival because the verdict would have to be given the next day. But there would be nothing to stop the verdict being passed on the eve of a festival[135] if the trial had been held earlier. And this is what a combination of the Johannine and the most reliable Synoptic evidence asserts. The trial had been held earlier (John 11.47–53). No doubt it would have been followed by the verdict on the morrow (M. *Sanh.* 5.5) – *if* the prisoner could have been produced. For the law required that he be heard in person (John 7.51). As it was, there was an unavoidable delay between the two meetings – according to b. *Sanh.* 43a of forty days. Yet when the verdict was passed (κατέκριναν, Mark 14.64),[136] it was at a properly constituted meeting of the Sanhedrin in the Council chamber by daylight (Luke 22.66) and, according to John, on the eve of the festival (18.28). John does not record the verdict in the Jewish court, though, as we shall see, he is aware of it, as of the cross-examination

---

second session to ratify a capital sentence, which may therefore be later. On the contrary, it is clear that the case it refers to of the 'beguiler' to idolatry (Deut. 13.6–11) is seen as the *exception* to the customary rules for capital cases (cf. 3.3; 7.2).

[135]As long as the proceedings were over on the eve of a sabbath by 3 p.m. (Josephus, *Ant.* 16.163).

[136]*Pace* Bickermann, 'Utilitas Crucis', 180–4, the word must in the context have a juridical and not merely a moral meaning. Mark is the only evangelist actually to use it at the trial, though it is referred to in the prophecy (reflecting the event?) of Mark 10.33 = Matt. 20.18 and also in Judas' remorse that Jesus had been 'condemned' (κατεκρίθη) in Matt. 27.3, showing that it was presupposed by Matthew. Luke, surprisingly, never uses κατακρίνειν judicially in his Gospel or Acts, but the summary of Acts 13.27 says that 'the people of Jerusalem and their rulers' fulfilled the prophets by 'condemning' Jesus (κρίναντες), which Winter, *Trial of Jesus*, 28, simply ignores when he merely quotes 13.28: 'though they failed to find grounds for the sentence of death'. Catchpole, *Trial of Jesus*, 184f., finds Winter demonstrably wrong at this point. Harvey, *Constraints of History*, 174f., is constrained to reduce the meaning of κρίναντες to 'they fulfilled the prophets by their decision', but 'the tension between the clauses' ('condemned even though they found no ground for doing so') would not appear to be nearly strong enough to render impossible the regular translation and interpretation. He admits (29) that Paul's description of the crucifixion in Gal. 3.13 as the penalty imposed by Deut. 21.23 implies that *he* believed him to have been condemned under the Jewish law. Far too much seems to be being built on Luke's silence at 22.71. Josephus is quite clear that 'our law . . . forbids us to slay a man, even an evil-doer, unless he has first been condemned (κατεκρίθη) by the Sanhedrin' (*Ant.* 14.167), even though this is prior to Roman direct rule.

with both its political (18.33) and religious (19.7) aspects which led up to it. But it was largely a formality in any case. For 'finding'[137] (Luke 23.2) the prisoner guilty of death (ἔνοχος θανάτου, Mark 14.64 = Matt. 26.66) and declaring that under Jewish law he 'ought (ὀφείλει) to die' (John 19.7) was one thing. Putting it into effect was another.

But before proceeding further, it will be useful to sum up the probable sequence of events so far. The evidence may be tabulated as follows:

	Matthew	*Mark*	*Luke*	*John*
1. Jesus is taken to the high priest's house	26.57	14.53	22.54a	18.13f.
2. Peter follows into the courtyard	26.58	14.54	22.54b–55	18.15f.
3. Jesus is interrogated by night				18.19–21
4. Jesus is abused by his captors	26.67f.	14.65	22.63–5	18.22f.
5. Peter denies Jesus	[26.69–75	14.66–72	22.56–62	18.17f., 25–27]
6. Jesus is taken before the Sanhedrin at dawn	27.1	15.1a	22.66	18.24
7. Jesus is tried before the Sanhedrin	[26.59–66	14.55–64]	22.67–71	
8. Jesus is led off to Pilate	27.2	15.1b	23.1	18.28

3, 4 and 5 must be understood as going on simultaneously. 5 is introduced at different points by the different evangelists. But if this and the Sanhedrin trial in Matthew/Mark (the bracketed passages) are taken out, there is a continuous sequence in all the Gospels. Luke and John preserve the correct order, though each has his omissions. The placing of the Sanhedrin trial in Matthew and Mark stands out as the erratic block.[138]

6. *The Roman Trial*

But now we must move to the hinge on which the rest of the proceedings turns, for it is absolutely clear that the trial did not end with Jesus being sentenced to death by the Jewish court. Why? The

[137]In the technical judicial sense used also in John 18.38; 19.4, 6; Acts 13.28; 23.9, 29; 24.20.

[138]Cf. D. R. Catchpole, 'The Historicity of the Sanhedrin Trial' in Bammel, ed., *The Trial of Jesus*, 64f., who strongly emphasizes the priority to be accorded to the (independent) Lukan and Johannine traditions. For the historical preference to be given to Luke over Mark, cf. his *Trial of Jesus*, ch. 3.

presupposition behind all the narratives is that recourse to the Government was necessary. The Synoptists do not think to give a reason for this: they take it for granted.[139] John alone gives the explanation that, from the point of view of the Jewish authorities, 'We are not allowed to put any man to death' (18.31).

It is remarkable that there should have been such reluctance to accept this basic statement. Again it is largely a matter of presumption. If it is presumed incorrect until proved otherwise, it is impossible to show that this was always the case, for exceptions can be quoted, though they turn out to be examples where the rule of law has broken down.[140] On the other hand, if the statement is accepted until proved otherwise, then there is almost everything to be said in its favour and little positively against. For there is no doubt that in Judaea as in other provinces the Roman governor had the final authority to order execution. Josephus tells us that Coponius, the first governor, was sent out by Augustus 'with full powers, including the infliction of capital punishment' (*BJ* 2.117). Did this imply that the authority was reserved to him? Sherwin-White is clear that it did:

> Though much use was made of the local municipal governments in managing the administration and jurisdiction of the Roman provinces, the power of capital jurisdiction was more carefully and deliberately withheld from them, and not only from them but from all the Roman personnel in the provinces except the supreme governors themselves.[141]

[139]Cf. Winter, *Trial of Jesus*, 10: 'As it stands, the Markan account is wanting in coherence; it remains unexplained why the prisoner was handed over to Pilate if sentence had already been passed.' His response is to deny the historicity of the Sanhedrin trial *in toto*. It is a less violent treatment of the evidence to suppose that Mark is simply presuming what John makes explicit.

[140]Thus the stoning of Stephen is evidently a case of lynch-law. After hearing the witnesses (Acts 6.11–14) the Council never reached the point of hearing out the case for the defence, let alone of passing a legal verdict (Acts 7.57f.). What Paul was fearing from the Sanhedrin was not legal execution but a miscarriage of justice and plain, not even judicial, murder (Acts 23.20f., 30; 25.7–11). It is made clear that if a capital charge had been pressed the Romans would have been involved (23.29; cf. Luke 23.15). Again James the Lord's brother was condemned to be stoned by an irregularly convened meeting of the Sanhedrin in an interregnum between two procurators, Ananus the high priest being subsequently deposed for his action (Josephus, *Ant.* 20.200–3). For other apparent exceptions, cf. Jeremias, 'Zur Geschichtlichkeit des Verhörs Jesu vor dem hohen Rat', *ZNW* 43, 1950–1, 145–50.

[141]'The Trial of Christ', in D. E. Nineham et al., *Historicity and Chronology in the New Testament*, SPCK Theological Collections 6, London 1965, 108.

Special permission was indeed given to the Jews to punish by death a Gentile entering the temple precincts, even if he were a Roman citizen (Josephus, *BJ* 5.193f.; 6.124–6; *Ant.* 15.417). But this did not involve a judicial trial, nor was it merely lynch-law, but what Bickermann[142] calls the exercise of the people's 'right of self-protection against infection', which the Romans continued to respect. The warning notices would have been put up at the time of Herod the Great's dedication of the temple and not removed. As Sherwin-White says, 'If the Sanhedrin already had the general power of capital jurisdiction, this special power would not have been necessary.'[143] Certainly in AD 62 the Jewish authorities in their desperation to get rid of another Jesus, the son of Ananias, who kept on speaking against Jerusalem and the sanctuary, had to refer him when other sanctions failed to the Roman governor Albinus, who however, after flaying him to the bone, let him off as a madman (Josephus, *BJ* 6.300–5). It is doubtful whether the regulations in the Mishnah about the various death penalties under the Jewish law correspond to more than reconstructions of the ideal, and there is a *baraita* in the Jerusalem Talmud (j. *Sanh.* 1.1; 7.2)[144] which says that the right of pronouncing sentences of life and death was taken from Israel forty years before the destruction of the temple, a round figure for a state of affairs which many would argue applied from the beginning of direct Roman rule in AD 6.

The question will doubtless continue to divide scholars,[145] but the

[142]'The Warning Inscriptions of Herod's Temple' in his *Studies in Jewish and Christian History* II, Leiden 1980, 210–24.

[143]'The Trial of Christ', 109.

[144]Tr. M. Schwab, *Le Talmud de Jérusalem* X, Paris 1888, 228; XI, 1889, 3.

[145]For a recent survey, cf. Schürer, *History* II, 219–23 and the full bibliography on 199f. Against the historicity of John's statement: from the Jewish point of view, J. Juster, *Les Juifs dans l'Empire Romain*, Paris 1914, II, 127–49; Winter, *Trial of Jesus*, 11–15, 75–90; Cohn, *Trial and Death*, 31–4; 345–50; and from the Christian: H. Lietzmann, 'Der Prozess Jesu', reprinted in his *Kleine Schriften* II, TU 68, Berlin 1958, 251–63 and with replies 264–76; T. A. Burkill, 'The Competence of the Sanhedrin', *VC* 10, 1956, 80–96; 'The Trial of Jesus', *VC* 12, 1958, 1–18; 'The Condemnation of Jesus: A Critique of Sherwin-White's Thesis', *NovT* 12, 1970, 321–42; S. G. F. Brandon, *The Trial of Jesus of Nazareth*, 90–2; Barrett, *John*, 533–5.

For the historicity of John's statement from the Jewish point of view: E. Bickermann, 'Utilitas Crucis', 188–93; M. Stern, 'The Province of Judaea', *Compendia* I. 1, 336f.; while S. Safrai, 'Jewish Self-Government', *Compendia* I. 1, 398–400, agrees that, whatever the *de jure* situation, 'in all instances involving violations of public order or movements of revolt, the Roman authorities intervened.' From the Christian side: R. W. Husband, *The Prosecution of Jesus*, Princeton 1916; Bernard, *John* II, 607f.; F. Büchsel, 'Die Blutgerichtsbarkeit des Synedrions', *ZNW* 30, 1931, 202–10; V. Holzmeister, 'Zur Frage der Blutgerichtsbarkeit des Synhedriums', *Bibl* 19, 1938, 43–59; Jeremias, 'Geschichtlichkeit des Verhörs Jesu' (see n. 140 above); Blinzler,

upshot would seem to be that while the Jews possessed the right to pass sentences of death they could not carry them out. If John's statement had appeared in the Synoptists there would surely have been little argument about it. For it is a presupposition of the story in all the Gospels. Otherwise the transference of the case after a death sentence in the Jewish court is inexplicable.[146] Yet all the accounts record, without explanation, that Jesus is forthwith led away to Pilate (Matt. 27.2; Mark 15.1; Luke 23.1; John 18.28). And the same transition is implied in b. *Sanh.* 43a: Jesus is indicted on a charge carrying the penalty of stoning but is in fact 'hanged'.[147]

Trial, 157–63 (*Prozess*[4], 229–44); G. D. Kilpatrick, *The Trial of Jesus*, London 1953; E. Lohse, *συνέδριον*, *TDNT* 7.865f.; Sherwin-White, *Roman Law*, 36–43; Dodd, *Historical Tradition*, 105f.; Brown, *John* II, 849f.; Catchpole, 'The Problem of the Historicity of the Sanhedrin Trial' in Bammel, ed., *Trial*, 59–63; and his book *The Trial of Jesus*, 1971, 238–54; Lindars, *John*, 556f.; Benoit, *Jesus and the Gospel* I, 134–6, 164; A. Dauer, *Die Passionsgeschichte im Johannesevangelium*, Munich 1972, 143–5; Harvey, *Jesus on Trial*, 54f.; Bammel, 'Die Blutgerichtsbarkeit in der römischen Provinz Judäa', *JJS* 25, 1974, 35–49.

[146]Brown, *John* II, 850, rightly observes that John does not introduce the statement to explain the history (though it may do this for us) but to make the theologically significant point that Jesus is 'lifted up' by the Roman penalty of crucifixion rather than stoned (18.32); so too Harvey, *Constraints of History*, 19f. But this of course does not again mean that the theology created the history.

[147]It is important to recognize that hanging was not one of the statutory Jewish ways of putting to death (in contrast at times with earlier practice). According to the Mishnah, 'The court had power to inflict four kinds of death-penalty: stoning, burning, beheading, and strangling' (*Sanh.* 7.1). Hanging was imposed *after* the victim was dead from stoning (though cf. the Qumran Temple Scroll (54.8): 'you shall hang him upon a tree *that he may die*'), as an exhibition to others till nightfall (cf. Josephus, *Ant.* 4.202, 264), and is contrasted with what 'the State does' (b. *Sanh.* 46b). It was not done on a cross but on a beam in the ground with a piece of wood jutting from it, the two hands being tied together. Yet under the Roman occupation 'hanging' and 'crucifixion' came to be equated. Thus Josephus writes, 'Even malefactors who have been sentenced to crucifixion are taken down and buried before sunset' (*BJ* 4.317), clearly applying to it the regulation in Deut. 21.23 which relates to those who are 'hanged', exactly as in John 19.31. The same is true of T. *Sanh.* 9.7 where the story of twin brothers one of whom was hung (b. *Sanh.* 46b) is told in terms of crucifixion and cited to explain the meaning of Deut. 21.23. Indeed Paul would not have felt the need to disarm the force of this text in Gal. 3.13 unless the equation had been made. The equivalence of the punishments is also presupposed in Luke 23.39; Acts 5.30 and 10.39 (cf. Josephus, *BJ* 7.202). So Horbury is I believe correct, against other interpreters, in saying that b. *Sanh.* 43a 'may be counted among the passages where hanging is mentioned as though it were an independent mode of execution, crucifixion' ('The "Benediction of the *Minim*"', *JTS*, n.s. 33, 1982, 56). Indeed he thinks the hanging (= crucifixion) is likely to be the historical core of the tradition which was then brought into line with the Jewish regulation requiring this as the sequel of stoning. D. J. Halperin, 'Crucifixion, the Nahum Pesher and the Penalty of Strangulation', *JJS* 32, 1981, 32–46, argues that the Mishnaic penalty, strangulation, unknown to the Bible, *replaced* crucifixion as a more

But the Gospels are clear that it is not simply a question of the governor ratifying the verdict of the Jewish court. The case has to be tried again. The judges now have to turn counsel for the prosecution, and the first thing they must do is to present the charge or charges. It is still *their* case which the Romans have to try. There is no suggestion in any of the records that the Romans initiated proceedings against Jesus, as they would have, for instance, against Barabbas. This must count decisively against any reconstruction like that of Brandon's that Jesus was really a political rebel. If he could be presented as one – which was necessary if he was to be executed by the Romans – it had to be by the Jews.

So the first question of the governor in the Johannine account is, naturally: 'What charge do you bring against this man?' (18.29). The exchange that follows is full of irony and deeper meaning, yet historically again quite credible.

> 'If he were not a criminal,' they replied, 'we should not have brought him before you.' Pilate said, 'Take him away and try him by your own law.' The Jews answered, 'We are not allowed to put any man to death' (18.30f.).

It is not stated whether collusion is to be assumed, with the Jews thinking they had it all 'arranged', or whether they were trying it on in the hope that Pilate would be content to rubber-stamp their verdict. Unless the governor was being particularly sarcastic, it is probably best to assume that, before being informed that it was a capital charge, he was seeking to evade jurisdiction, as he did later, according to Luke (23.6–12), on learning that the prisoner was a Galilean. There is no reason to suppose that as governor he was personally involved in ordering the arrest,[148] at which John says that the party specifically names the wanted man as Jesus *of Nazareth* (18.7), let alone that he was working in collaboration with the Jews, which would scarcely have been in character (cf. Josephus, *BJ* 2.169–77; *Ant.* 18.55–62).

Their initial ploy having failed, the Jews are forced to specify the charge. John does not say what it is, any more than do Matthew and Mark. Luke is here more informative, supplying the full charge-sheet: 'We found this man subverting our nation, opposing the payment of

---

humane penalty. But both these last judgments are very hypothetical.

[148] That would have been within the province of the commander at the Antonia. Cf. above, p. 242 n. 92, and Ruckstuhl, *Chronology of the Last Days of Jesus*, 33 n. 35.

taxes to Caesar and claiming to be Messiah, a king' (23.2). All are, naturally in this context, political crimes. But it is more than likely that the charge of subversion, or stirring up (ἀνασείειν) the people (23.5), started life as a Jewish count against him, namely, that of 'enticing Israel and leading them astray'. For διαστρέφειν (23.2) and ἀποστρέφειν (23.14) mean primarily to mislead and alienate. And this is the charge, along with that of practising sorcery, which is recorded as Yeshu's crime in b. *Sanh.* 43a, and for which he was condemned to die by stoning. It is the offence, as is recognized in the same passage, of the enticer to idolatry in Deut. 13.6–11 who must be put to death by stoning, the punishment prescribed also in the Mishnah for 'the common man' (*Sanh.* 7.10; cf. John 10.33?) who 'beguiles [others to idolatry] and . . . leads [a whole town] astray, and the sorcerer' (*Sanh.* 7.4).[149] Within the Gospel tradition John alone provides evidence of this accusation against Jesus: 'He is leading the people astray (πλανᾷ . . . τὸν ὄχλον)' (7.12; cf. 7.47); and this is borne out by the description of him as a sorcerer and misleader of the people (μάγος . . . καὶ λαοπλάνος) in Justin, *Dial.* 69; cf. 108.[150] In the other Gospels the charge has been lost (though cf. Matt. 27.63: 'that deceiver', ὁ πλάνος) or 'politicized'.

Of the charges presented to Pilate, the only one he bothers to take up, that of high treason or claiming to be 'king', is presupposed in the identical question put to the prisoner in all the Gospels: 'Are you the king of the Jews?' (Matt. 27.11; Mark 15.2; Luke 23.3; John 18.33). And the same reply comes back in each case: 'The words are yours (σὺ λέγεις)'. But John greatly elaborates the implications of this qualified acceptance (18.34–38). The conversation between Pilate and Jesus, though full of delicate touches,[151] is, of course, to be read as interpretation rather than reportage – though that not because no

[149]The penalty imposed on 'the false prophet' for doing the same (Deut. 13.1–5) is strangling, as it is for the rebellious elder (*Sanh.* 11.1). There is, I believe, no real evidence (despite W. A. Meeks, *The Prophet-King*, 47–57) of Jesus being charged or condemned specifically as a 'false prophet'. Mark 14.65 and pars. can hardly count, let alone supply 'unassailable witness' (Jeremias, *Eucharistic Words*, 79). Only so, according to the Mishnah, would the greater Sanhedrin of 71 persons have been required to judge him (*Sanh.* 1.5); 23 were enough for other capital charges (1.4; 4.1).

[150]The charge of sorcery could be reflected in the accusation that he 'has a demon' and heals by the power of evil spirits (John 10.20f.; cf. Mark 3.22f. and pars.), though cf. exactly the same charge against John the Baptist (Matt. 11.18 = Luke 7.33) who 'did no signs' (John 10.41). For a defence of the tradition in Justin and b. *Sanh.* 43a, cf. Horbury, 'Benediction of the *Minim*', 55.

[151]Lightfoot, *Biblical Essays*, 188, draws attention to the withering scorn, which cannot be brought out in the English, behind the μήτι ἐγὼ Ἰουδαῖός εἰμι? of 18.35 and

witness could have been present:[152] it is made clear that the priests could have entered the Praetorium had they been willing.[153] But, whatever the actual wording, the distinction between the kind of kingship for which Jesus stood and the kind which he repudiated (illustrated earlier by his responses in 6.15 and 12.14f.) could not be driven home better than by the unanswerable logic of 18.36: 'My kingdom is not ἐκ τοῦ κόσμου τούτου: it does not find its source or resources in this world-order. If it did, my henchmen (ὑπηρέται) would be fighting to save me from arrest by the Jews.' Indeed, Cullmann in his study *Jesus and the Revolutionaries*,[154] based largely on the Synoptic evidence, says that he could have used this reply as 'the motto' for his whole presentation. In other words, he believes that John's interpretation provides the clue to the correct understanding of what was at stake.[155]

In any case there is no ground for doubting the historicity of the basic situation, common to all the Gospels, that Jesus accepted the title king 'with a difference', nor for dismissing Pilate's subsequent statement, shared by the traditions of Luke and John: 'I find no case for this man to answer' (Luke 23.4; John 18.38).[156] It only makes explicit what is implicit in the subsequent course of the story. Otherwise it would have ended there with a verdict of 'guilty', whereas all the traditions agree that resort had to be had to other pressures.

In Luke the Jews continue to press the politically dangerous nature of Jesus' teaching, as spreading disaffection throughout the country, beginning from Galilee (23.5); and this gives Pilate, who was evidently ignorant of his origin, the excuse to refer the case to Herod Antipas (23.6–12). But Herod sends him back without finding any support for their charges, and Pilate again affirms that there is no case to answer, even in respect of the lesser charge of subversion (23.13–15). He proposes therefore to 'let him off with a beating' (23.16) – or it could mean 'Having beaten him, I will therefore release him.'

At this (23.18) there follows a general outcry: 'Away with him! Give

---

the word order of οὐκοῦν βασιλεὺς εἶ σύ? in 18.37. It certainly does not add to the notion that John is portraying Pilate as sympathetic in contrast with 'the Jews'.

[152]So Dodd, *Interpretation*, 450.

[153]Cf. Bernard, *John* II, 608f.; Morris, *Studies in the Fourth Gospel*, 195.

[154]ET New York 1970, 42.

[155]So too Blinzler, *Trial*, 192; *Prozess*[4], 282. For an expansion of this, cf. again my 'His Witness is True', *Twelve More NTS*, esp. 128–37.

[156]Cf. Benoit, *Jesus and the Gospel* I, 140: 'This establishment of the political innocence of Jesus by Pilate is a historical truth we must stoutly uphold. It agrees with everything we know of Jesus from the Gospels.'

us Barabbas.' Luke tells us what sort of person Barabbas was (23.19), but according to the best texts (for 23.17 is evidently a gloss) gives no explanation, as do all the other evangelists, of the custom involved of an amnesty at the festival – though John alone makes it specific to the Passover (Matt. 27.15; Mark 15.6; John 18.39). There is no support in Josephus or in Roman sources for the existence of such a custom. But it is possible – one cannot say more – that there could, as we have seen, be an allusion to it in M. *Pes.* 8.6: 'They may slaughter the Passover ... for one whom they have promised to bring out of prison.' On this Barrett comments,

> The Mishnah continues in such a way as to suggest that doubt remained about the release, and this would hardly have been so if a Jewish court had been involved. A special promise of release, at Passover time, by the foreign authority, may therefore be in mind; and unless this happened with some regularity it would be unlikely to become the subject of legislation.[157]

According to John Pilate says '*You* have a custom, that I release to you', and Origen[158] suggests that the Romans had allowed them to retain this ancestral custom. But it is to be understood as a concession to the Jews rather than a Jewish custom. The lack of documentary evidence for it is scarcely decisive. Like most things dictated by reasons of state it was doubtless not put down in black and white. It would in any case have lapsed after 70 and may well not have survived Pilate's recall to Rome. But there is equally no good reason for doubting it. It features in all the three apparently independent passion traditions of Mark/Matthew, Luke and John (as well as in the early preaching summary of Acts 3.14). And of the three accounts John's says it all in quite the most succinct space of 32 words – his terse comment 'Now Barabbas was a λῃστής' (18.40) presupposing full familiarity with what *that* meant. Mark (15.7) and Luke (23.19) spell it out for their readers, while Matthew (27.16) strangely suppresses it altogether, calling him simply 'a prisoner of some notoriety'.

In the Synoptists (Mark 15.12–14 and pars.) this scene is followed by a general clamour for the crucifixion of Jesus. Again Pilate says 'Why, what wrong has he done?' According to Luke he adds once more

[157] *John*, 538; cf. especially Blinzler, *Trial*, 218–21; *Prozess*[4], 317–20. But Jeremias, *Eucharistic Words*, 73, dismisses this passage as referring to parole from a Jewish prison for the evening, citing the Jerusalem Talmud (j. *Pes*. 8.36a, 45f.).

[158] *In Matt.* 120 (on 27.15, PG 13.1771); quoted by Horbury, 'The Passion Narratives and Historical Criticism', *Theology* 75, 1972, 58–71, specif. 67 (cf. 66–9).

that he has not found him guilty of any capital offence and proposes, in the same words as before, to let him off with a beating (παιδεύσας), or, having beaten him, to release him (23.22). John says definitely at this point that 'Pilate now took Jesus and had him flogged (ἐμαστίγωσεν)' (19.1). This has been held against the historicity of his account, on the grounds that Mark (15.15) and Matthew (27.26) have a flogging, quite correctly, as an immediate antecedent of crucifixion and as part of the preliminaries to this barbaric punishment.[159] In fact in Mark and Matthew this also follows directly upon the Barabbas incident, since, unlike John, they have nothing further to relate. Yet a preliminary flogging as an accompaniment to the process of examination is also ordered by the commandant (before he discovers Paul is a Roman citizen) in Acts 22.24f. (cf. 16.22) and it is described by the same term (μάστιξι) used by John at this point. There is an interesting parallel too in the trial of Jesus the son of Ananias referred to earlier in Josephus, *BJ* 6.300–5. The Governor also has him 'flayed to the bone with scourges (μάστιξι)' before he is released as a madman. So there is no ground for saying that John has deliberately or ignorantly distorted the Markan/Matthaean order.[160] Whether in fact Jesus was scourged once or twice must remain a matter of doubt.

In both the Synoptic and Johannine traditions mockery by the soldiers follows the scourging (Matt. 27.27–31; Mark 15.16–20; John 19.2f.). But in John the trial goes on, and twice more (as in the Lukan tradition) Pilate repeats that he finds no case against the prisoner (19.4, 6). In response to the cries of 'Cruficy! Crucify!' he taunts the chief priests with the words: 'Take him and crucify him yourselves.' This provokes them to say: 'We have a law; and by that law he ought to die, because he has claimed to be Son of God' (19.7).

John at this point thus reveals knowledge of the proceedings of the session of the Sanhedrin which he has not cared to relate. This had been dominated, like the earlier one which he did describe in 11.47–53, by Caiaphas. With things again seemingly getting nowhere (Mark 14.55–9; cf. John 11.47f.), the high priest intervened from the chair, and with great shrewdness framed the crucial question: 'Are you the Messiah, the Son of God?' (Matt. 26.63; Mark 14.61; cf. Luke 22.67, 70). Dodd has well summed up the situation which confronted the

[159]Cf. Josephus, *BJ* 2.306–8; 5.449; Livy, *Hist.* 33.36.

[160]E.g., Mastin in Sanders, *John*, 399f.; Lindars, *John*, 363f. Cf. Gardner-Smith, *St John and the Synoptic Gospels*, 65: 'Once more we note that the Fourth Evangelist, untrammeled by knowledge of the Marcan story, is able to give a better historical account, even though "history" was not the main purpose of his work.'

Jewish authorities:

> Jesus must be removed by death; he must also be discredited. The death sentence therefore must be legally and formally pronounced by the governor. The surest way to secure such a sentence would be to cite the Defendant on a charge of political disaffection. But such a charge would by no means discredit him in the eyes of the Jewish public; quite the contrary. It was for the Sanhedrin to show that he was guilty of an offense against religion.[161]

The one charge which met both these requirements was that of claiming to be Messiah, which could be interpreted politically as the seditious one of a bid for the throne and religiously as the blasphemous one of making himself Son of God. Wherein precisely the βλασφημία consisted has been much disputed. According to the Mishnah (*Sanh.* 7.5), '"The blasphemer" is not culpable unless he pronounces the Name itself' (cf. Lev. 24.10–16). But this may well represent a later codification to limit the mandatory imposition of the death penalty. For in the first century Philo (*Vit. Mos.* 2.204–6) and Josephus (*Ant.* 4.202) do not seem to know of any such restriction.[162] In the New Testament blasphemy is a wide and imprecise term (cf. e.g. Mark 3.28).[163] According to John it seems to have attached to the implication that in calling himself Son of God Jesus was claiming equality with God (cf. 5.18; 10.33–36), and this appears to be borne out by the charge in Mark 2.7 and pars. that Jesus was usurping the place of God, 'This is blasphemy! Who but God can forgive sins?', and by the transition in Luke 22.67–71:

> 'Tell us,' they said, 'are you the Messiah?' 'If I tell you,' he replied, 'you will not believe me; and if I ask questions, you will not answer. But from now on, the Son of Man will be seated at the right hand of Almighty God.' 'You are the Son of God, then?' they all said, and he replied, 'It is you who say I am.' They said, 'Need we call further witnesses? We have heard it ourselves from his own lips.'

At any rate the religious offence attached to the term 'Son of God'

[161] *Founder of Christianity*, 156. For a good assessment of the interrelation of the religious and political charges, cf. also Brown, *John* II, 798–802.

[162] Cf. Harvey, *Jesus on Trial*, 77–81; cf. also Blinzler, *Trial*, 105f., 127–33; *Prozess*[4], 152–4, 188–96; O. Linton, 'The Trial of Jesus and the Interpretation of Psalm 110', *NTS* 7, 1960–1, 258–62; J. C. O'Neill, 'The Charge of Blasphemy' in Bammel, ed., *Trial*, 72–7.

[163] This is heavily emphasized by Bickermann, 'Utilitas Crucis', 175–80.

rather than 'Messiah', as in John 19.7, though the beauty of the situation, from the priests' point of view, was the ease with which the three categories 'Christ', 'Son of God' and 'King' could slide, or be slid, into one another (Matt. 26.63; 27.42f.; Mark 14.61; 15.32; Luke 22.67–70; 23.2, 35–37; John 1.41, 49;[164] 18.33; 19.7; cf. Acts 17.37).

So now in the trial before Pilate, with the political charge apparently making no headway, the priests subtly switch to the other track, drawing upon the ambiguity of the confession that clinched the matter for the Sanhedrin: 'He has claimed to be Son of God.' What matter if all he had done was not to deny it? And what matter if by John's deliberate omission of the definite article (*υἱὸν θεοῦ*)[165] the implication is given to Pilate that he is one of the sons of the gods, a *θεῖος ἄνθρωπος* or divine man?[166] The play upon his pagan superstitions is nicely calculated: 'When Pilate heard that, he was more afraid than ever' (19.8).

The conversation within the Praetorium that follows (19.9–11) must again be seen as interpretative – there could surely have been no Christian eyewitness. Pilate's question 'Where have you come from?' followed by Jesus' refusal to give him any answer is fascinatingly echoed in Josephus' account of the trial of the other Jesus: 'When Albinus, the governor, asked him who and whence he was and why he uttered these cries, he answered him never a word' (*BJ* 6.305). The silence of Christ which was imprinted on the memory of the church (I Peter 2.23; cf. Acts 8.32) – as well as his defence before Pilate (I Tim. 6.13), of which John alone speaks – is attested in each of the three trial traditions: in Mark (15.4f.) and Matthew (27.12–14) before Pilate in public, in Luke (23.9) before Herod, and in John (19.9f.) before Pilate in private. The circumstances differ, and there is clearly no case for dependence, but the substance remains the same.

The result of the exchange is that the religious charge equally falls to the ground. 'From that moment Pilate tried hard to release him' (19.12). But the clamour prevails, as in the Synoptists. Yet they never

[164]On this verse, 'You are the Son of God; you are king of Israel', Scott Holland wrote, 'By the date at which the Gospel is written such an order in the titles would be an impossible anti-climax' (*Fourth Gospel*, 213). Similarly, Nolloth, *Fourth Gospel*, 209, 'It is Messianic – not metaphysical – Sonship which is acknowledged.' Here 'king of Israel' is epexegetic of 'Son of God' as 'Son of God' is of 'the Christ' in 20.31.

[165]That John's usage in this respect is not accidental is, I believe, borne out by the absence of the articles in 1.14; 5.27; 10.36; 19.21 (cf. also Mark 15.39 = Matt. 27.54).

[166]Cf. Dodd, *Historical Tradition*, 114: 'The whole episode . . . is entirely in character, and to all appearances it owes nothing to theological motives. Thus in the one place where the course of the narrative invites theological exploitation, it remains on a strictly matter-of-fact level. This is surely a very remarkable feature in a work so dominated by theological interests.'

explain why Pilate's better judgment was overruled. John however goes on to fill in the picture in a way that makes sense of the dynamics of the situation.

The Jewish leaders, having failed to secure a legal conviction on either the political or the religious aspect of their double-edged charge, return to the political tack, but at the populist rather than the judicial level. They blatantly trade on Pilate's insecurities: 'If you let this man go, you are not "Caesar's friend"; anyone who makes himself a king is defying Caesar' (19.12). Not only the quasi-technical ring of the term φίλος τοῦ Καίσαρος[167] (a title seldom conferred on men like Pilate of equestrian rather than senatorial rank) but his susceptibility to the very accusation that brought his recall to Rome a few years later reveals accurate knowledge of the local political scene. Brown's comment at this point is apposite:

> The Synoptic Gospels never adequately explain why Pilate yielded to the importunings of the crowd and the priests. Mark 15.15 says that Pilate wished to satisfy the crowd; Matt. 27.24 says that Pilate saw he was gaining nothing and that a riot was breaking out; Luke 23.23 simply underlines the urgency of the demand for crucifixion. But these descriptions scarcely fit the Pilate familiar to us in Josephus' accounts: a Pilate who broke up riots and was stubborn in face of Jewish demands.[168] John's picture of a Pilate worried about what might be said at Rome has a very good chance of being historical. According to Philo, *Leg. ad Gaium* 301f., Pilate was naturally inflexible and stubbornly resisted when the Jews clamoured against him until they mentioned that the Emperor Tiberius would not approve his violating their customs. 'It was this final point that particularly struck home, for he feared that if they actually sent an embassy, they would also expose the rest of his conduct as governor.'[169] Moreover, at the very moment when Jesus stood before Pilate, the governor may have been vulnerable in Rome as

[167]Cf. Bammel, 'Φίλος τοῦ Καίσαρος', *TLZ* 77, 1952, 205–10; J. Crook, *Consilium Principis*, Cambridge and New York 1955, 21–30; Stauffer, *Jesus and His Story*, 109; Sherwin-White, *Roman Society*, 47, who quotes, e.g., Philo, *Flacc*. 40. For further references, see G. Stählin, in *TDNT* IX, 167 n. 171. It is probable that Herod the Great already enjoyed this title (M. Stern, 'The Reign of Herod and the Herodian Dynasty', *Compendia* I.1, 237 n. 4).

[168]Nevertheless according to Josephus he backed down in face of sustained Jewish resistance by removing the standards from Jerusalem (*BJ* 2.172–4; *Ant*. 18.55–9).

[169]He adds: 'Note however that the historicity of Philo's report has been questioned by P. L. Maier, ["The Episode of the Golden Roman Shields at Jerusalem",] *HTR* 62, 1969, 109–21.' This episode evidently occurred between AD 31 and 36.

> never before. Many theorize that Pilate owed his appointment in Palestine to Aelius Sejanus; and it was in the year 31 that Sejanus lost favour with Tiberius. Perhaps the tremors that presaged the fall of Sejanus were already felt by sensitive political observers, and Pilate feared that soon he would have no protector at court. A shrewd ecclesiastical politician like Caiaphas would have been quite aware of the prefect's vulnerability and prompt to probe it.[170]

Brown quotes earlier Tacitus' comment in *Ann.* 6.8: 'Whoever was close to Sejanus had claim on *the friendship of Caesar*.'[171] None of these connections are certain but are more plausible than the dismissive comment of Haenchen, quoted by Barrett, that 'John would not have been aware of these political entanglements'.[172] One may ask why not, in view of his otherwise keen sense of the political background. It is also to be observed that the final cynical thrust that won Pilate's acquiescence, 'We have no king but Caesar' (19.15f.), reveals a Jewish obsequiousness to Rome that is scarcely credible in a document written after the Jewish revolt of 66–70. If indeed it does come from a later period, then it is a masterly piece of historical reconstruction.

At this point John proceeds to fix the scene with a note of place, date and hour, which has something of the precision of a police report. It is the sort of statement that marks him off most sharply from Luke, whose tradition on the trial and passion of Jesus appears in other respects the most reliable and stands closest to John's. In contrast with the 'we' passages in Acts, where Luke supplies very exact topographical and chronological detail where he really knows it, his Gospel is often remarkably vague. Indeed it gives us confidence in Luke as a historian that when he does not know he does not invent: he generalizes. But John does know, or gives every appearance of knowing. For the setting of what follows is carefully drawn:

[170]*John* II, 890f. There are some, e.g., Stauffer, *Jesus and His Story*, 108–10, and Maier, 'Sejanus, Pilate and the Date of the Crucifixion', *Church History* 37, 1968, 3–13, who actually use the fall of Sejanus to date the crucifixion to 32 or 33. But this is without foundation. Cf. E. M. Smallwood, 'Some Notes on the Jews under Tiberius', *Latomus* 15, 1956, 322–9, who points out that Eusebius, *HE* 2.5.6, quoting Philo, presupposes that the crucifixion must have been before 31, since he regards Sejanus' attack on the Jews as retribution for it (though this is only Eusebius' construction); and H. E. W. Turner, 'The Chronological Framework of the Ministry' in Nineham et al., *Historicity and Chronology* (n. 141 above), 68–74.

[171]*John* II, 880; italics Brown's. Cf. Philo, *Leg. ad Gaium* 37. Sejanus was notoriously anti-Semitic: Philo, *Flacc.* 1; *Leg. ad Gaium* 159–61.

[172]*John*, 543.

When Pilate heard what they were saying, he brought Jesus out and took his seat[173] on the tribunal at the place known as 'The Pavement' ('Gabbatha' in the language of the Jews). It was the eve of Passover, about noon (19.13f.).

The reference to the tribunal (βῆμα) is fully borne out by similar scenes in Josephus.[174] The Λιθόστρωτον (Gabbatha) is unfortunately not now identifiable, on the assumption, which I am convinced is overwhelmingly probable, that the Praetorium was in Herod's Palace and not in the Antonia.[175] It appears from archaeological evidence that the palace was built, like the temple, to whose esplanade the word λιθόστρωτον was also applied,[176] on a very large raised platform,[177] which has long since been destroyed. Yet the kind of Roman paving which is still to be found beneath the Ecce Homo Convent, and which was probably a street or courtyard from Hadrian's time,[178] though not

[173]It is most unlikely that John intended to suggest that Pilate literally set Jesus on the judgment seat (for ἐκάθισεν could be transitive), even if there may be theological overtones of this. Cf. Bultmann, *John*, 664; Barrett, *John*, 544; Brown, *John* II, 880f.; and my 'His Witness is True', *Twelve More NTS*, 129.

[174]E.g., *BJ* 2. 172, 'On the following day Pilate took his seat on the tribunal in the great stadium' (cf. 2.175); and 2.301, 'Florus lodged at the palace (ἐν τοῖς βασιλείοις) and on the following day had a tribunal placed in front of the building and took his seat; the chief priests, the nobles, and the most eminent citizens then presented themselves before the tribunal.' Cf. also Matt. 27.19; Acts 25.6f., 17.

[175]The crucial passages are Josephus, *BJ* 1.402; 2.301, 328, 430f.; 5.176–83; Philo, *Leg. ad Gaium* 299–306. Cf. decisively, in my judgment, Benoit, 'Prétoire, Lithostroton et Gabbatha', *RB* 59, 1952, 531–50; *Jesus and the Gospels* I, 167–88. For the literature cf. Blinzler, *Trial*, 173–6; *Prozess*[4], 256–9. Mackowski, *Jerusalem*, 102–11, supports the identification of the Praetorium with Herod's palace but identifies the λιθόστρωτον with 'the upper agora' mentioned in *BJ* 2.305, 315. But this is *distinguished* from where Florus set up his βῆμα in front of the palace (*BJ* 2.301). Earlier Pilate had set up his βῆμα in 'the great stadium' (*BJ* 2.172) and not, as Mackowski says (108), 'in front of the Praetorium'. To say that this 'was somehow adjacent, though not continguous, to the Praetorium' is to blur the evidence.

[176]II Chron. 7.3; Ep. Aristeas, 88, Josephus, *BJ* 6.85, 189.

[177]Cf. D. Bahat and M. Broshi in Yadin, ed., *Jerusalem Revealed*, 55: 'The platform extended over an area of about 300–350 metres from north to south and some 60 metres, at least, from west to east.' Indeed it seems to have been about 130 metres wide if a street which has been uncovered (58f.) was its eastern boundary. The platform appears to have been similar to that of Herod's temple enclosure, raising the area and levelling it off by means of a huge podium. Of the palace itself no signs remain, Titus having razed everything but the towers (Josephus, *BJ* 7.1–3), some of whose stonework survives.

[178]Cf. Benoit, 'L'Antonia d'Hérode le Grand et le forum oriental d'Aelia Capitolina', *HTR* 64, 1971, 135–67.

the *Λιθόστρωτον* that L.-H. Vincent[179] so imaginatively reconstructed, nevertheless gives a vivid impression of what it must have been like.

The date John gives, on the *παρασκευή*, or eve of Passover, we have already argued is to be accepted as a statement of high probability, and there is no ground for resorting to the translation in the NEB margin (to try to make it harmonize with the Synoptists), 'It was Friday in Passover.' This indeed it was (cf. 19.42), but John makes it quite clear that that Friday was also the eve of the festival (18.28; 19.31). The time of day too, I believe, is to be trusted. That Jesus was still before Pilate 'about the sixth hour' (or noon) is clearly incompatible with Mark's statement (15.25) that 'the hour of the crucifixion was nine in the morning' (the third hour). Yet this last is not to be found in either Matthew or Luke and I am persuaded that it belongs to the class of material that Mark added to the triple tradition, rather than that Matthew and Luke agreed, independently, to leave it out.[180] For there is no reason why they should. It is perfectly compatible with the later statement, shared by all the Synoptists, that 'at midday darkness fell over the whole land which lasted till three in the afternoon (the ninth hour)' (Mark 15.33 and pars.), since Jesus could well have been on the cross for three hours before that. Yet the probability of the statement must be assessed on its own merits, especially if it is a Markan editorial addition.

If the interrogation before Annas occurred in the period of cock-crow, the third watch of the night (cf. Mark 13.35), that is between 12 a.m. and 3 a.m., then Jesus could have been escorted to Caiaphas (Luke 22.66; John 18.24) and come before the Sanhedrin in the course of the fourth watch (*πρωΐ*), that is between 3 a.m. and 6 a.m., as Mark 15.1 = Matt. 27.1 may be asserting. But Luke insists that day had already started (23.1), which would have been necessary for the legality of the session. In fact *πρωΐ* (early) is probably not to be taken too technically, any more than when John uses it in 18.28 for Jesus' transfer to Pilate. Though the working day of a Roman official may indeed have begun at

[179]'L'Antonia et le Prétoire', *RB* 42, 1933, 83–113; 'Autour du Prétoire', *RB* 46, 1937, 563–70; 'Le Lithostrotos évangélique', *RB* 59, 1952, 513–30; 'L'Antonia, palais primitif d'Hérode', *RB* 61, 1954, 87–107.

[180]Blinzler, *Trial*, 267–9; *Prozess*^{4}, 418–21, argues quite persuasively that it is an interpolation. The triple tradition has already recorded the crucifixion in Mark 15.24, and Mark 15.25, literally, 'It was the third hour *and* they crucified him', placed *after* the division of the prisoner's clothes, has all the appearance of a clumsy insertion. The passage reads much more smoothly without it, as in Matthew and Luke. The attempt by A. Mahoney ('A New Look at "the Third Hour" of Mark 15.25', *CBQ* 28, 1966,

first light, it is surely arbitrary to say with Sherwin-White that 'if the Sanhedrin had spent the early hours of daylight examining Christ they would have been too late for Pilate's tribunal'[181] and therefore to rule out the former examination as unhistorical:[182] indeed, according to John, he was still at work at noon. But if the statutory daytime trial before the Council, with its calling of witnesses, could not start till after 6 a.m., it is surely unlikely that the prisoner would have been brought before the Governor, across the other side of the city, until at least eight or nine. Moreover, the hearing before Pilate was no formality, involving, according to John, a series of scenes in and out of the Praetorium and if, as is probable, Luke is to be trusted (23.6–12)[183] it was interrupted by yet a further journey to Herod Antipas and back, almost certainly at the old Hasmonaean palace near the Xystos to the west of the temple area (Josephus, *BJ* 2.344; *Ant.* 20.189f.). That Jesus could also have been scourged, subjected to horseplay by the soldiers, led out of the city dragging his cross, and be nailed up by 9 a.m. is surely incredible. Perhaps the Markan time-reference retains a confused memory of when the process which led to crucifixion (i.e. the Roman trial) started, or the moment when he was put under guard (Mark 15.1; for cf. the reading of D and the Old Latin ἐφύλασσον in 15.25). The probability that it was still about noon, as John says, before Pilate had finished with him is inherently far greater, though it leaves little margin for the Synoptic statement that he hung on the cross between 12 and 3 p.m. At any rate there is really no case for supposing that the Johannine timing has been altered, unhistorically, for theological reasons. Whatever symbolism may be seen in the hour (and there is singularly little evidence that John intended any), there is no reason to think that the chronology has been created to fit it.[184]

292–9) to make it refer backwards to the division of the clothes (after an earlier scourging) is an unconvincing piece of harmonization.

[181]'The Trial of Christ' in Nineham et al., *Historicity and Chronology*, 114; cf. *Roman Society*, 45. Others, ironically, argue that for Pilate to have been available to hear the case so early there must have been prior collusion. It simply shows how arbitrary such judgments are at this distance.

[182]Burkill, 'The Condemnation of Jesus' (see n. 145 above), 341, has some valid criticism of Sherwin-White at this point.

[183]Bickermann, 'Utilitas Crucis', 204–8; cf. Blinzler, *Trial*, 203f., *Prozess*[4], 291–300; H. W. Hoehner, 'Why did Pilate hand Jesus over to Antipas?' in Bammel, ed., *Trial*, 84–90; Benoit, *Jesus and the Gospel* I, 136f.

[184]N. Walker, 'The Reckoning of Hours in the Fourth Gospel', *NovT* 4, 1960, 69–73, argues that 'the sixth hour' means 6 a.m. and that this would fit with Jesus being on the cross at 9 a.m. as Mark says; but the improbabilities are enormous. Ruckstuhl, *Chronology*, 47f., argues that 'the third hour' is actually the right reading in John 19.14.

With this the trial is over. What assessment is to be made in retrospect of the Johannine picture? It has evoked the most diverse judgments. Thus Barrett uses such phrases as 'quite incoherent' and 'incomprehensible' and says that 'no reliance can be placed on his version of the story (although probably numerous historical details remain in it)',[185] while Winter says: 'From John 18.29 onward the Fourth Gospel contains nothing of any value for the assessment of historical facts. . . . Such a series of happenings defies any attempt at being fitted in to the actualities of space and time.'[186] On the other hand Brown writes, 'With all its drama and its theology, John's account of the trial is the most consistent and intelligible we have',[187] concurring with Sherwin-White's judgment that 'after the survey of the legal and administrative background it is apparent that there is no historical improbability in the Johannine variations from the synoptic version';[188] and Dodd concludes his long section on the trial with an assessment which merits reproducing at some length:

> Here we have for the first time an account which, although it leaves some gaps, is coherent and consistent, with a high degree of verisimilitude. Verisimilitude, no doubt, is not the same thing as historical accuracy. . . . But I doubt very much whether a writer whose work we must place late in the first century[189] and in a Hellenistic environment, could have invented such a persuasive account of a trial conducted under conditions which had long passed away. It is pervaded with a lively sense for the situation as it was in the last half-century before the extinction of Judaean local autonomy. It is aware of the delicate relations between the native and the imperial authorities. It reflects a time when the dream of an independent Judaea under its own king had not yet sunk to the level of a chimaera, and when the messianic idea was not a theologumenon but impinged on practical politics, and the bare mention of a 'king of the Jews' stirred violent emotions; a time, moreover, when the constant preoccupation of the priestly holders of power under

---

But the manuscript evidence is suspiciously secondary and this looks to be an attempt at harmonization with Mark. He can only maintain such an early hour for the final stage of the trial because he believes, with Jaubert, that it was spread over three days.

[185] *John*, 525, 530.

[186] *Trial of Jesus*, 89f.

[187] *John* II, 861; similarly F. F. Bruce, 'The Trial of Jesus in the Fourth Gospel' in France and Wenham, edd., *Gospel Perspectives* I, Sheffield 1980, 7–20.

[188] *Roman Society*, 47.

[189] This is of course Dodd's dating, for which I see no necessity.

Rome was to damp down any first symptoms of such emotions. These conditions were present in Judaea before AD 70, and not later, and not elsewhere. This, I submit, is the true *Sitz im Leben* of the essential elements in the Johannine trial narrative . . . in substance it represents an independent strain of tradition, which must have been formed in a period much nearer the events than the period when the Fourth Gospel was written, and in some respect seems to be better informed than the tradition behind the Synoptics, whose confused account it clarifies.[190]

Nevertheless John is regularly accused of having distorted the story by theological bias. Above all he is seen as being the end of the line in a progressively loaded account of the trial of Jesus in an anti-Jewish and pro-Roman direction. Yet it has constantly to be conceded that features in the Johannine story palpably go against this tendency. Thus Winter, who strongly propounds this thesis, admits, as we have seen, that it is contradicted by the Roman participation in the arrest of Jesus[191] and is 'the more remarkable seeing that in the Fourth Gospel *no trial of Jesus is being conducted by a Jewish tribunal*'.[192] He also makes the point that in this Gospel, 'which reveals the most pro-Roman and most anti-Jewish attitude of the four, there is only one description of Jesus' mockery, and that takes place at the hands of Roman soldiers – not at the hands either of the Sanhedrin members, as in Mark and Matthew, or of the Jewish police as in Luke.'[193] He tries to insist that John 19.16–18 must mean that Pilate handed Jesus over for crucifixion to the Jews and that it was *they* who took him off and crucified him[194] – while agreeing that this is 'immediately contradicted by the ensuing narrative'[195] which puts it beyond doubt that this was the work of the Roman soldiers (19.23f.). Similarly Cohn says that 'the fourth evangelist was determined to outvie his predecessors in blaming and branding the Jews. . . . All the same, he gave up the Markan tradition of their tirades against Jesus on the cross, though Matthew

[190] *Historical Tradition*, 120.
[191] *Trial of Jesus*, 47.
[192] Ibid., 57; italics his. Bickermann, 'Utilitas Crucis', 219, also makes the same point from the Jewish point of view.
[193] *Trial of Jesus*, 105f.
[194] The phrasing is admittedly careless but it clearly means, as in the NEB, 'Then at last, to satisfy them, he handed Jesus over to be crucified', as in the Synoptic Gospels. The various phrases are, as Sherwin-White says, *Roman Law* 26f., the equivalent of the Latin *duci jussit*.
[195] *Trial of Jesus*, 57.

and, to a less extent, Luke had adopted it. To be faithful to his tendentious purpose, he should have been quick to take it up and exploit it to the hilt.'[196] It begins to look as if the 'tendentious purpose' is more in the eye of the interpreter, and it is remarkable how often these writers make use of the Johannine evidence when it suits them.

The further inference is often drawn that John is racially anti-Semitic and responsible, wittingly or unwittingly, for the pinning of the charge of deicide on the Jewish race that has been such a blot on the history of the Christian church. That he says anything which implies that every succeeding generation of Jews is guilty of the death of the Son of God is of course absurd. If there is a text that could be twisted in that direction it is Matt. 27.25, 'His blood be on us, and on our children,'[197] where the emphasis is on *Pilate's* evasion of the responsibility that so clearly belongs to him. What John does is indeed to make Jesus say to Pilate: 'The deeper guilt lies with the man who handed me over to you' (19.11), i.e. Caiaphas, acting as the representative of the Jewish nation (18.35). And that on any reading of the story is surely unquestionable. The initiative and direction of the proceedings lie with him and his colleagues (not even the Jerusalem crowds are involved in John), and in retrospect Luke makes a Jewish Christian say 'our chief priests and rulers handed him over to be sentenced to death, and crucified him' (24.20; cf. Acts 5.28–30).

The responsibility of the Jews is fully accepted in b. *Sanh*. 43a[198] and significantly is never contested in early Jewish apologetic,[199] which is concerned to show that he was *rightly* condemned. Moreover the reason given in the aforementioned passage for the unusual delay in his sentence, which is not that his guilt was in doubt but that 'he was close

[196] *Trial and Death of Jesus*, 224f.

[197] But this is simply stating the implication of their own law, that 'in capital cases the witness is answerable for the blood of him [that is wrongfully condemned] and the blood of his posterity' (M. *Sanh*. 4.5).

[198] Cohn, who discusses this passage fully and fairly, in the end simply discards it, without any evidence, as not referring to Jesus of Nazareth – along with two others which indeed almost certainly do not (*Trial and Death of Jesus*, 298–308). This is a very weak reply to what he recognizes as 'the most compelling argument that can be advanced against the theory propounded in this book', namely, 'that it finds no support in the Jewish, that is, in the talmudic, sources' (297) – nor, one might add, in *any* sources, for it certainly stands the Gospel evidence on its head. A similar contention in J. Maier, *Jesus von Nazareth in der talmudischen Überlieferung*, Darmstadt 1978, 219–37, that b. *Sanh*. 43a did not originally refer to Jesus is answered by Horbury, 'Benediction of the *Minim*', 56f.

[199] Cf. Bammel, 'Christian Origins in Jewish Tradition', *NTS* 13, 1966–7, 328; Horbury, 'The Trial of Jesus in Jewish Tradition', in Bammel, ed., *Trial*, 113–15.

to the government' indicates that Jewish tradition also thought that the Romans took his side. So the picture of the Governor's desire to acquit, common to John and the Synoptists, may not be a purely Christian construction. Likewise, in Josephus' famous reference to Jesus, he is indicted before Pilate by 'the leading men (πρῶτοι ἄνδρες) among us',[200] and there is no reason at this point in the text to suspect Christian influence.[201] Nor is there any ground for playing off, as some modern Jewish scholars seem to wish to do,[202] the Sadducees, as 'baddies', against the Pharisees, as 'goodies'. In all the Gospels, and John here merely observes more carefully a distinction which is not of his creation, the Pharisees are, as we noted earlier (pp. 226f. above), the main constituency of the *religious* opposition; the chief priests (John does not call them Sadducees, any more than do any of the other evangelists during the trial, since it is not in their party role that they are acting) are the leading, but by no means the sole, instrument of the *judicial* process, since it was they who controlled the Sanhedrin. Hence in the Synoptists as in John the Pharisees dominate the opposition in the early chapters and fall into the background once the trial starts.[203]

Nor is John especially virulent against the Jews. He does not even go so far as Mark (15.10 = Matt. 27.18) in attributing to them the motive of 'spite' in arraigning Jesus. Nor is he ever quite so vehement about them as Paul in I Thess. 2.14f., who says outright that 'the Jews killed the Lord Jesus', which is the consistent picture also of the early Acts summaries which from the beginning attribute the initiative and main responsibility for Jesus' death to the Jews (2.23, 36; 3.13–15, 17–19; 4.10f., 26; 5.30; 7.52f.; 10.39 and 13.27f.). These are all statements made by Jews and, except in the last two instances, to Jews. Similarly John, writing as a Jew for other Jews, is concerned from beginning to end to present the condemnation of Jesus, the *true* king of Israel, as the

[200] *Ant.* 18.64. The phrase is reflected in the description of the Sanhedrin in Acts 25.2, 'the chief priests and the πρῶτοι of the Jews'; cf. 13.50; 28.17; and Josephus, *Vit.* 21, 'the chief priests and the πρῶτοι of the Pharisees'. Cf. Thackeray, *Josephus, the Man and the Historian*, 147: '"The principal men" is common form in Josephus, though I am not sure that the "our" can be paralleled.'

[201] 'The passage appears to be genuine', Winter, *Trial of Jesus*, 27.

[202] E.g., Winter, *Trial of Jesus*, 111–35.

[203] Winter notes this of Mark (*Trial of Jesus*, 119–26) but without any warrant attributes chs. 2–12 to later tradition than chs. 14 and 15. But then he believes that '*all the Marcan* [and *a fortiori* the Matthean and Johannine] "*controversy stories*", *without exception, reflect disputes between the "Apostolic Church" and its social environment, and are devoid of roots in the circumstances of the life of Jesus* (125, italics his). For a critique of Winter at this point, cf. Catchpole, 'Historicity of the Sanhedrin Trial', in Bammel, ed., *Trial*, 48–51.

great betrayal of the nation by its own leadership. Their motivation is exposed as unashamedly collaborationist, and it could be said that the most un-Jewish remark in the Gospel, indeed in the Bible, is one which is placed on the lips not of the evangelist but of the chief priests: 'We have no king but Caesar' (John 19.15). The contrast with authentic Judaism, where Yahweh alone is Israel's king (Judges 8.23; I Sam. 8.7; Isa. 26.13), could hardly be more stark.

Dodd concludes that 'the statement, which is often made, that the Johannine account is influenced by the motive of incriminating the Jews cannot be substantiated, when it is compared with the other gospels.'[204] And Horbury, after noting 'the suggestive rapports of the Jewish trial tradition with peculiarities of the Fourth Gospel', observes:

> One result of attention to Jewish tradition might be the placing of further emphasis on the precariousness of *Tendenzkritik*. Many passages from Jewish texts would, if found in Christian sources, certainly be ascribed to anti-Jewish sentiment.[205]

Moreover, the Romans, far from being exculpated by John, are deeply involved – from the arrest onwards. Pilate's threefold assertion of Jesus' legal innocence is precisely what we find in Luke – our only serious alternative account of the Roman trial, for Mark's (followed by Matthew with but two extra-judicial insertions) is so sketchy as to be quite inadequate for comparison.[206] And this assertion is recorded not to excuse him but to show him as morally weak and despicable. There is a greater sense in John than in any of the other Gospels that *he* is the one who is on trial, and the playing upon his religious fears and political insecurities reveals him in the end to be as fully discredited as his Jewish opponents. If the Pilate of the Synoptists is 'a poor stick',[207]

[204] *Historical Tradition*, 107. Since it is not publicly available, it may be of interest to add the pencilled note he wrote in his copy of D. E. Nineham's commentary on *Mark* (Harmondsworth, Penguin Books 1964), 404, where Nineham says 'The early church . . . exhibited a steadily growing tendency to transfer the responsibility for Jesus' death from the Romans to the Jews': 'The only "steady growth" is between Mark and Matthew. Luke and John go no further than Mark, John perhaps not so far, and none of them goes any further than the most primitive form of the *kērygma* – or than Paul.'

[205] 'Trial of Jesus in Jewish Tradition' in Bammel, ed., *Trial*, 115; cf. his 'The Passion Narratives and Historical Criticism', *Theology* 75, 1972, 64–6.

[206] As Dodd points out, *Historical Tradition*, 116, 'Of the twenty-five lines [in Nestle] devoted to the proceedings before Pilate eighteen are occupied with the episode of Barabbas, which is not a judicial affair at all.'

[207] Dodd, *Historical Tradition*, 119.

then in John he is a pathetic and quasi-tragic figure. As Brown well puts it,

> He thinks he can persuade the Jews to accept a solution that will make it unnecessary for him to decide in favor of Jesus. . . . Having failed to listen to the truth and decide in its favor, he and all who would imitate him inevitably finish in the service of the world.[208]

Far from being a distortion of the primitive record there is, I believe, nothing in the Johannine story that is palpably unhistorical and a great deal that makes the other accounts *when taken alongside it* intelligible. No one is arguing for it in isolation: it has its gaps like any of the others. But as far as its overall interpretation is concerned, its balance is exactly that of the earliest Christian assessment of the matter, put into the mouth of Peter in his speech to the citizens of Jerusalem on the day of Pentecost: 'When he had been given up to you, by the deliberate will and plan of God, you used heathen men to crucify and kill him' (Acts 2.23; cf. 13.28). Nowhere more than in the Fourth Gospel do we get the impression of the Romans being 'used' – from Judas and the Jewish authorities 'taking' the cohort to arrest Jesus through to the final manipulation of Pilate, whose exasperation breaks through in his sarcastic comment 'What! am I a Jew?' (18.35) and his petulant refusal to be told what to write on the *titulus* (19.21f.). Yet all, Jews and Romans alike, are seen supremely in this Gospel, as in the earliest Acts accounts, as fulfilling 'the deliberate will and plan of God' (11.51f.; 19.11), which nevertheless excuses them not a whit.

Once again in his account of the trial John emerges as both the alpha and omega of the New Testament witness. Alike of the history and of the interpretation we may say that 'his testimony is true' (21.24), and that if we really want to know what was going on and why, at depth and not merely at documentary level, we cannot do better than turn to him.[209]

7. *The Crucifixion*

With the trial over the Johannine narrative moves swiftly, basically following the same course of events as the Synoptists but adding a

[208] *John* II, 864.

[209] Cf. the comments quoted from C. H. Turner and Fergus G. B. Millar, editor of the *Journal of Roman Studies*, at the end of my 'His Witness is True', *Twelve More NTS*, 136 n. 72.

number of characteristic details, none of which there is good reason historically to doubt. Like Mark (15.22 = Matt. 27.33) but not Luke, John gives us the local name *Golgotha*, or skull, for the place of the crucifixion, though the Greek and Aramaic are in reverse order and no literary dependence can be considered likely. He alone introduces the journey to the cross with the word 'went out', implying, as was certainly the case, that the site lay outside the city (Heb. 13.12; cf. Matt. 21.39; Luke 20.15). For executions would have taken place there (Lev. 24.14, 23; Num. 15.35; Deut. 17.5; 21.19; I Kings 21.10, 13; Acts 7.58; M. *Sanh.* 6.1), and of course burials too.[210] John specifically tells us that 'the place where Jesus was crucified was not far from the city' (19.20), close enough for the *titulus* to be read perhaps from the walls.[211] This would fit the well-supported traditional site of Golgotha and the Holy Sepulchre. For again John says that 'the tomb was near at hand' (19.42), indeed '*at* the place where he had been crucified' (19.41). This would have lain then just outside what Josephus calls 'the second wall' on the north-west side of the city (*BJ* 5.146).[212] It would comport too with the tradition that Simon of Cyrene was press-ganged (by the Romans) to carry the *patibulum* or transverse beam of the cross as he came into the city (no doubt through the Jaffa gate) from the fields (Mark 15.21 and pars.). This Synoptic feature would incidentally support the Johannine timing, since in Judaea work stopped at midday on Passover-eve (M. *Pes.* 4.5). John omits this incident. For Simon and his sons Alexander and Rufus may simply have been as locally familiar to the Markan community[213] (Mark 15.21) in Rome (cf. the Rufus in Rom. 16.13?) as Malchus and his relative were to the Johannine in Jerusalem (John 18.10, 26). John says that Jesus carried his own cross (19.17). But it is not impossible, nor indeed improbable, that the two accounts can be harmonized, as subsequent tradition has done. As Dodd says, 'That Jesus ἐξῆλθεν (*scil.* from the Lithostroton) carrying his own cross, but later had to be relieved of it, is a perfectly reasonable interpretation of the evidence.'[214]

[210] Cf. the ἐξῆλθεν of John 20.3, on which Bengel comments: 'ex urbe'.

[211] So Jeremias, *Golgotha*, Leipzig 1926, 3. Josephus (*BJ* 5.449) describes Titus later as crucifying victims 'opposite the wall' specifically as a spectacle for those in the city.

[212] For all the disagreement about the line of the walls and the literature it has provoked this at any rate is generally agreed.

[213] This is another feature of the second Gospel that I believe is best explained as an addition by Mark to the triple tradition rather than something independently omitted by both Matthew and Luke.

[214] *Historical Tradition*, 125. Brown, *John* II, 899, concurs.

John also notes the fact that Jesus was not crucified alone but between others, though the expression he uses for 'one on either side (ἐντεῦθεν καὶ ἐντεῦθεν) with Jesus in the midst' (19.18) is quite different from that of the Synoptists and has often been noted as a Semitism (cf. Num. 22.24; and ἔνθεν καὶ ἔνθεν in Dan. 12.5; I Macc. 6.38; 9.45).[215] He does not specify that they are λῃσταί (Mark and Matthew) or even criminals (Luke), but from the mode of their execution this could be taken for granted, and in all likelihood they were fellow-insurgents with Barabbas (Mark 15.7), who himself escaped punishment.

John goes on to speak of the public exhibition of the *titulus*, a technical term which he alone uses, recording the *causa poenae*.[216] All the Gospels agree on the wording 'the king of the Jews' (Mark 15.26 and pars.), Luke adding 'this man' (23.38), Matthew 'Jesus' (27.37); while John has 'Jesus of Nazareth' (Ναζωραῖος) (19.19), as at the identification of the prisoner at his arrest (18.7), which could well reflect the official charge-sheet. Its tri-lingual character (19.20) in Hebrew (or Aramaic), Latin and Greek, representing native usage, the official record and the *lingua franca*, is entirely credible.[217] Pilate's responsibility for it is stressed, and the understandable attempt by the Jews to get the wording changed to 'He said, "I am King of the Jews"' is resisted not only on grounds of exasperation but of accuracy (19.21f.). For in Mark too (15.12) Pilate makes it clear to the Jews that it was *they* who said it, in their accusation, and not Jesus. Westcott[218] also draws attention to the absence of the article in 19.21, 'Do not write "the king of the Jews" but "This man said, I am king (or, a king) of the Jews".' For them Jesus is simply one of many: 'everyone who (πᾶς ὁ) makes himself a king' (19.12), exactly as in Josephus, *Ant.* 17.285: 'Anyone might make himself a king'. The Johannine presentation of the Jews' position is therefore also fully in line with Luke's (23.2): 'We found this man . . . saying that he was Messiah, a king.'

The division of the prisoner's clothes by lot between the soldiers, which is simply mentioned by the Synoptists (Mark 15.24 and pars.), is narrated by John in much greater detail (19.23f.). He distinguishes

[215]Barrett rightly comments: 'The expression indicates a Semitic mind, but not a translation from a Semitic original' (*John*, 548).

[216]Cf. Suetonius, *Calig.* 32.2; *Domit.* 10.1: Dio Cassius, *Hist.* 54.3.7. Yet all these, as Harvey, *Constraints of History*, 13, points out, refer to placards being carried in front of the criminal on the way to execution, rather than affixed to a cross.

[217]Cf. Josephus, *Ant.* 14.191; *BJ* 5.194; 6.125.

[218]*John*, ad loc.

between the seamless tunic (χιτών)[219] for which they tossed and the rest of the clothes which they divided into four, thus incidentally revealing that the job was done, as regularly in such assignments,[220] by a *quaternion* (cf. the four quarternions in Acts 12.4). This is a point to which J. B. Lightfoot long ago drew attention as significant of John's knowledge: 'The information is not paraded in any way; it is involved in the narrative.'[221] John alone makes explicit the quotation (in full) of Psalm 22 (LXX 21).19, while Mark and the others allow it to control the story. As Dodd says, this reflects two ways of using Scripture:

> The language of the Old Testament might be absorbed into the narrative, or the story might be told without any Old Testament colouring, and the passage associated with it in Christian teaching might then be adduced as a *testimonium*. Mark (14.18), as we have seen, has adopted the former method with Ps. 40 [Heb. 41].10, while John (13.18) has adopted the latter.[222]

John prefers to separate fact and comment, Mark to merge them (one might perhaps have expected it to be the other way round); but there is no reason in either case to think that the *testimonium* created the happening.[223] If so, as Brown says, the actual wording of the narrative would have been more closely controlled by it.[224]

There then follows the scene of the women at the cross (19.25–7). We have already discussed the names in comparison with the Markan (15.40) and Matthaean (27.55f.) accounts – Luke (23.49) again is entirely vague at this point – and seen reason to believe that an intimate knowledge of the relationships is involved.[225] The Synoptists simply

[219]There is no reason to suppose that John here intends the reader to see a reference to the seamless χιτών of the high priest (Josephus, *Ant.* 3.161) and therefore to Jesus in this role. Cf. Bernard, *John* II, 630.

[220]Cf. Vegetius, *De re milit.* 3.8; Philo, *Flacc.* 13; Polybius, *Hist.* 6.33.

[221]*Biblical Essays*, 161.

[222]*Historical Tradition*, 40.

[223]'Legal texts confirm that it was the accepted right of the executioner's squad to share out the minor possessions of their victim' (Sherwin-White, *Roman Law*, 46, citing Mommsen).

[224]*John* II, 920.

[225]Cf. ch. II, pp. 119f. above. By way of contrast one may compare Bultmann's comment at this point. After saying that the scene 'in face of the Synoptic tradition (*sic*) can have no claim to historicity', he proceeds to give it a purely symbolic meaning. 'The mother of Jesus, who tarries by the cross, represents Jewish Christianity that overcomes the offence of the cross. The beloved disciple represents Gentile Christianity, which is charged to honour the former as its mother from which it has come, even as Jewish Christianity is charged to recognize itself as "at home" within Gentile Christianity, i.e. included in the membership of the one great fellowship of the Church' (*John*, 673). If

record the 'distant scene' (ἀπὸ μακρόθεν), John, rightly or wrongly, giving a close-up.[226] This is in line with the fact that in the Synoptists the crucifixion is viewed entirely from the point of view of outsiders (Mark 15.27–39 and pars.; Luke 23.39–43, 48), in John from the point of view of insiders and particularly from the closest insider of all, 'the disciple whom Jesus loved'.

This leads to the most specific claim to eyewitness veracity in the entire Gospel (19.35). Of the details, the provision of a sponge of sour wine is common to all the accounts (Mark 15.36 and pars.; John 19.28f.), though in the Synoptists it is associated with the taunting of Jesus, in John with the fulfilment of Scripture (apparently of Ps. 69.21). In Mark it is handed up by 'someone', in Matthew by one of the bystanders, on a cane. Luke is unspecific about the means but attributes it to the soldiers, whom he and John alone mention at the cross. According to the best texts, John says it was put on, or rather around (περιθέντες), hyssop, but this small bushy plant is so totally inapposite that I am persuaded that the NEB is right in following the reading ὑσσῷ, a javelin.[227] No doubt this is a scribal amendment in the single Greek manuscript (476) in which it is found, but I suspect this is one of a number of cases where the writer would have been the first to correct what, maybe, the autograph itself had: for nothing of any length is ever written, let alone dictated, without error. In this case the action, as in Luke, would certainly have been that of the soldiers, and this is explicitly the case in the two further incidents which John alone records (19.31–7).

The breaking of the victim's legs, the *crurifragium*, in order to hasten death[228] has recently been visibly confirmed by the skeleton of a crucified man of the first century AD, Johanan, dug up in Jerusalem in

---

taking the relationships literally may seem fanciful, nothing surely can be quite as fanciful as this. There is no hint in the text, here or elsewhere, that such symbolism was in the evangelist's mind.

[226]Jewish parallels representing friends of the victim standing near enough to converse with him are adduced by Barrett, *John*, 551. But he does not think that these could outweigh the military restrictions – though why is not clear.

[227]So Dodd, *Historical Tradition*, 124: 'Palaeographically it is a perfect example of corruption by dittography, υσσωπωπερι for υσσωπερι, and a copyist seeing the letters υσσωπ might easily suppose that he had before him the word "hyssop" with its ritual associations.' Against the emendation however cf. G. D. Kilpatrick, quoted in Metzger, *Textual Commentary*, 253f.

[228]Cf. T. Keim, *History of Jesus of Nazara*, ET London and Edinburgh 1873–83, VI, 253 n. 3; and Lactantius, *Institutes* 4.26. The Gospel of Peter, 4.14, has 'They were angry with him and commanded that his legs should not be broken in order that he

1968, both of whose legs were smashed.[229] This skeleton also confirms the use of nails in crucifixion (which John alone explicitly attests [20.25], though Luke 24.39 presupposes it) through the ankles and base of the forearm.[230] They could not in any case have gone through the palms, which would not have supported the weight of the body;[231] but χείρ, hand, which both Luke and John use, would include the wrist, a position which is attested, if it is genuinely ancient, by the Shroud of Turin. This latter would also confirm that the legs of Jesus, as John says, were not broken. Dramatically, too, it would bear out the other wound of which he alone speaks, the lance-stab through the rib-cage, with an apparent effluence of blood and colourless fluid, which the evangelist goes on to describe with an emphatic claim to veracity: 'This is vouched for by an eyewitness, whose evidence is to be trusted. He (ἐκεῖνος) knows that he speaks the truth, so that you too may believe.' Who the witness is is not stated, but I would agree with Brown that 'There can be little doubt that in the writer's mind this witness was the Beloved Disciple mentioned in verses 26–7.'[232] He is the only male recorded as present at the crucifixion (apart from the soldiers), and the truthfulness of his testimony is again referred to in 21.24, where indeed he is specifically stated to be the writer of the Gospel.[233] That the ἐκεῖνος ('that man') introduces a third person or even, as some have argued, Christ or God, would seem quite unnatural and improbable.[234]

---

might die in agony.' It is probably dependent on the Johannine tradition, though the Greek is quite different.

[229]Cf. J. H. Charlesworth, 'Jesus and Jehoḥanan: An Archaeological Note on Crucifixion', *ExpT* 84, 1972–3, 147–50; and the literature there cited.

[230]Cf. Josephus, *BJ* 5.451, for the use of nails and the variety of methods: 'The soldiers out of rage and hatred amused themselves by nailing their prisoners in different postures.' M. *Shab*. 6.10 refers to 'a nail of one that was crucified'.

[231]Cf. P. Barbet, *A Doctor at Calvary*, ET New York 1953 (= *The Passion of Our Lord Jesus Christ*, London and Dublin 1954), ch. 5.

[232]*John* II, 936f. The objection that this disciple had just left the scene with the mother of Jesus would seem to interpret 'from that hour' (19.27) unnecessarily woodenly. Dodd, who raises this objection, believes that the evangelist is referring not to himself but to a third party for whose veracity he can implicitly vouch. But he takes the claim to eyewitness attestation very seriously and believes it incredible that the effusion of blood and water can be intended to be merely symbolic: 'You cannot "see" a theologumenon; you can see only sensible facts' (*Historical Tradition*, 133–5).

[233]The point has been made (Askwith, *Historical Value*, 16) that the first half of the testimony, 'This is vouched for by an eyewitness, whose evidence is to be trusted', might represent external attestation (as in 21.24), but that the internal witness of 'he knows that he speaks the truth, that you too may believe' (cf. 20.31) points to the evangelist himself.

[234]Cf. Dodd, *Historical Tradition*, 134 n. 1: 'Certainly ἐκεῖνος can refer to God the Father (as in 6.29; 8.42) or to Christ (as in 1.18; 5.11), or to the Holy Spirit (as in 14.26;

Of this last incident we have no external attestation (*unless* the Shroud of Turin turns out to be authentic), but the solemn claim to historical accuracy as the basis of faith – neither being a substitute for the other – is not lightly to be dismissed in this author. Nor can the *testimonia* that follow, from Ps. 34.20 and Zech. 12.10, be plausibly understood to have generated the events. Indeed the reflection of the latter in Rev. 1.7 points to a wider (and probably independent)[235] acceptance of Jesus' 'piercing' as one of the received facts of the tradition, of which, unlike blood and water in I John 5.6, 8 (and perhaps John 7.38f.) nothing is made theologically.

8. *The Burial*

In the account of the burial that follows John is uncharacteristically imprecise in introducing it with his vaguest temporal connection, μετὰ ταῦτα (19.38). In Mark (15.42) and Matthew (27.57) it was already 'getting late' (ὀψίας γενομένης) when Jesus was taken down from the cross, Luke once more having no indication of time. But John clearly implies the lateness of the hour when he says later: 'There, because the tomb was near at hand and it was the eve of the Jewish sabbath, they laid Jesus' (19.42). Yet in substituting spatial for temporal proximity he tells us what we should not otherwise know, namely that 'the garden' in which Jesus was buried was 'at the place where he had been crucified' (19.41). That it was in a garden is distinctive to John, though the presence of gardens outside the north wall of the city is borne out by Josephus (*BJ* 5.57, 410) and by the location of 'the garden gate' in this wall (*BJ* 5.146).[236] The request to Pilate for the body of Jesus by Joseph of Arimathea is of course something John shares with the Synoptists, each of the evangelists adding something to the profile of him – none of them improbably. Matthew (27.57) tells us that he was 'a man of means, and had himself become a disciple of Jesus'; Mark (15.43) that he was 'a respected member of the Council, a man who was eagerly

---

15.26; 16.8); but in every such case the pronoun either stands in apposition or resumes one of the terms of a previous sentence. But here the only term in the previous sentence to which it could possibly refer is ὁ ἑωρακώς.' So N. Turner, *Grammatical Insights into the New Testament*, 137f., who argues that the ἐκεῖνος is simply used in an 'anaphoric' sense, 'referring back to a subject already mentioned and taking it up again with no strong emphasis (merely "he"). Decidedly it does not introduce a new subject'; similarly Westcott, *John* I, liii–lvii, citing Johannine usage.

[235]So Dodd, *According to the Scriptures*, 65.

[236]For burial in one's own garden, cf. Josephus, *Ant.* 9.227.

awaiting the kingdom of God'; Luke (23.50f.) that he was 'a member of the Council, a good, upright man, who had dissented from their policy and the action they had taken. He came from the Jewish [or rather Judaean][237] town of Arimathea, and he was one who looked forward to the kingdom of God'; John (19.38) that he was 'a disciple of Jesus, but a secret disciple for fear of the Jews'. John's account of his action is the least developed of all (for those who regard this as a sign of primitiveness). He 'asked to be allowed to remove the body of Jesus. Pilate gave permission; so Joseph came and took the body away' (19.30). One could hardly say it more baldly.

But John's distinctive contribution to the scene is the participation of a second man:

> He was joined by Nicodemus (the man who had first visited Jesus by night), who brought with him a mixture of myrrh and aloes, more than half a hundredweight. They took the body of Jesus and wrapped it, with the spices, in ὀθόνια [for the moment deliberately left untranslated] according to Jewish burial-customs (19.39f.).

This has been dismissed as unhistorical not least because of the quantity of spices involved – 'about a hundred pounds' – though this time, ironically, it is because the figure is taken, and is evidently intended to be taken, literally and not symbolically.

The first thing to be said is that the Roman *libra* was only three-quarters of our pound – hence it is seventy-five pounds, or what the NEB seeks to get by 'more than half a hundredweight'. Then it is important to distinguish between these ἀρώματα and those which the women had bought when the sabbath ended at nightfall (Mark 16.1),[238] precisely as the Mishnah prescribes (*Shab.* 23.4), with which they were going to 'anoint' the body of Jesus. The latter were clearly oils, in liquid form, such as that which the woman 'poured' (Matt. 26.7; Mark 14.3) when 'anointing' the feet or head of Jesus (Luke 7.38, 46; John 11.2; 12.3). They were the equivalent of our scented soap and were to be used in conjunction with the obligatory washing of the

[237] Πόλις τῶν Ἰουδαίων, a good example of the geographical use of Ἰουδαῖος. Arimathea was a small hill village in north-west Judaea between Lydda and Antipatris. But Luke's use of Ἰουδαία is not so consistent as John's. For as well as Luke 2.4; 3.1; 5.17, cf. 4.44; 7.17; 23.5.

[238] Luke (23.56) has them prepare spices and perfumes early on the Friday evening before resting on the sabbath. But the preparations could doubtless have occupied both evenings.

corpse,[239] for which it is clear from the silence of all the canonical Gospels (in contrast with the later Gospel of Peter, 24) that there had been no time on the Friday. At most one *libra* was here involved (John 12.3) and this was regarded as a waste (ἀπώλεια) (Matt. 26.8; Mark 14.4), mainly because of the quality of the oil, though the suggestion is that the whole flask was broken and therefore exhausted (Mark 14.3). There is no hint that Joseph and Nicodemus used their vast quantity of mixed spices to *anoint* the corpse.[240] The function of these appears to have been very different – namely to preserve the body as far as possible from putrefaction and to keep it sweet-smelling over the sabbath. Palestinian custom, which John insists was being followed (and τοῖς Ἰουδαίοις here has primarily a geographical reference), unlike Egyptian,[241] did not include embalming.[242] But the Mishnah (*Shab.* 23.5) makes specific provision for the corpse to be laid on sand over the sabbath 'that it may be the longer preserved' until it could be attended to. The spices, in powdered or granule form,[243] were doubtless a more effective (if much more costly) preservative, and if the corpse was to be underlaid with them and perhaps packed around, as their binding in *with* the ὀθόνια suggests, then a considerable amount would have been required. Moreover what evidence we have from royal or rich burials (and the implication is that expense was not spared at the burial any more than at the anointing of Jesus) points to large quantities being used. At the funeral of Herod the Great there were 500 servants carrying spices (ἀρωματοφόροι)![244] The Johannine figure, even were it to be exaggerated to bring out the generosity of the gesture, is quite within the bounds of credibility as a rich man's last tribute.[245]

But if John's material about Nicodemus is not inherently improbable, is there any reason to believe that he was a real-life character? The

[239]Acts 9.37; cf. M. *Shab.* 23.5, 'anoint and wash it'; and more generally Matt. 6.17; Luke 7.46.

[240]*Contra* D. Daube's otherwise valuable discussion in *The New Testament and Rabbinic Judaism*, London and New York 1956, 312–24, there is no more suggestion in John that Jesus' dead body was anointed than in the Synoptists.

[241]Even for Jews. Cf. Gen. 50.26 of Joseph, 'He was embalmed and laid in a coffin.'

[242]Or even a coffin. Cf. II Kings 13.21.

[243]Cf. Proverbs 7.17: 'I have sprinkled my bed with myrrh, my clothes with aloes and cassia' – hardly liquid!

[244]Josephus, *Ant.* 17.199; cf. also 15.61; II Chron. 16.14 and b. *Sem.* 47a (quoted by Brown, *John* II, 960), where it is said that more than 80 pounds of spices were burnt at the funeral of Rabbi Gamaliel the Elder (AD 40–50).

[245]Contrast the itself rather ludicrous symbolic interpretation placed on Nicodemus' contribution by Meeks, 'Man from Heaven', 55: 'His ludicrous "one hundred pounds"

situation is in fact rather remarkable. Joseph of Arimathea is remembered for one incident only, occupying at most four verses in any of the Gospels. We never hear of him before or after – except of course in apocrypha and legend.[246] Yet no one seriously doubts that he was a historical character.[247] But that is because he is mentioned in the Synoptists as well as in John. Nicodemus, on the other hand, appears only in John. Yet he enters the story of Jesus at three points, in 3.1–12 when he first comes to him by night, in 7.50–52 when he intervenes to demand that he be given a fair hearing, and in 19.39–42 when he helps Joseph to bury him. From this we learn that he was a Pharisee and, like Joseph, a member of the Sanhedrin (3.1; 7.50); he is characterized as 'this famous teacher of Israel' (ὁ διδάσκαλος τοῦ Ἰσραήλ, 3.10); and clearly, like Joseph too, he was a wealthy man (19.39) as well as a courageous one (7.50f.; cf. Mark 15.43, τολμήσας, of Joseph). Of course it could be said that he is introduced into the Gospels purely as a representative figure and a foil; and if he disappeared after ch. 3, as quickly as Joseph disappears, that might be plausible. Yet his re-emergence as a defender and evidently, like Joseph again, a secret disciple of Jesus is not what we should expect from the upshot of the earlier dialogue. But above all there are some interesting parallels in Jewish tradition which indicate that the name Nicodemus was a well-known one in Jerusalem at the time and attached to persons of considerable eminence and affluence. Whether there was any connection with our Nicodemus, and if so what, cannot be proved, but it does look as if John is not merely inventing. At the expense of a little diversion it is worth trying to set out and sort out the evidence.

There are two sources of information, Josephus and the Babylonian Talmud.

1. In Josephus, *Ant.* 14.37 a Nicodemus is sent as an envoy on behalf of Aristobulus from Jerusalem to Pompey in Syria in 64 BC. He is of course chronologically irrelevant, except for the incidence of the name even then as belonging to a leading personage in the city.

2. Later, in *BJ* 2.451, a Gorion, son of Nikomēdes (Latin, Nicodemi), accepts the surrender of the Roman garrison in Herod's

---

of embalming spices indicate clearly enough that he has not understood the "lifting up" of the Son of Man'!

[246]He is mentioned in the Gospel of Peter 2.3, as 'the friend of Pilate and of the Lord', and there follows an extraordinary exchange in which Pilate asks *Herod* for the body of Jesus. It is clearly historically worthless.

[247]Cf., e.g., Benoit, *The Passion and Resurrection of Jesus Christ*, ET New York and London 1969, 229: 'He is certainly historical.' Similarly from the Jewish side Cohn, *Trial and Death*, 237–9.

palace, in August 66 AD, as a representative of the citizens of Jerusalem.

3. In *BJ* 2.563, in November 66, a Joseph, son of Gorion, with Ananus the high priest is appointed to supreme military command of Jerusalem.

4. In *BJ* 4.159 a Gorion, son of Joseph, among the 'leaders of outstanding reputation' rallies the opposition of the citizens to the Zealots. He is almost certainly the son of the previous Joseph. He is also in all probability to be identified with the Gurion in *BJ* 4.358, 'a person of exalted rank and birth, and yet a democrat and filled with liberal principles, if ever Jew was', whose outspokenness 'added to the privileges of his position' led to his murder by the Zealots in 67–8. The last two Gorions (3 and 4) have nothing whatever to do with Nicodemus, and they are mentioned here only because Jeremias confuses them with the other Gorion (2), and those yet to be mentioned, in his discussion of the New Testament figure,[248] and also because this family bears out the well-established custom, which we shall observe in the other of similar name, of a man taking his grandfather's name (Gorion, Joseph, Gorion). The only relevant figure thus far is therefore the Gorion, son of Nicodemus (2), who was a prominent Jerusalem citizen at the beginning of the Jewish revolt.

We now pass to the Talmudic evidence. The first is an undated story, yet coming clearly from before the war of 66–70:

> Once it happened when all Israel came up on pilgrimage to Jerusalem that there was no water available for drinking. Thereupon Nakdimon ben Gurion approached a certain [heathen] lord and said to him: Loan me twelve wells of water for the pilgrims and I will repay you twelve wells of water; and if I do not, I will give you instead twelve talents of silver, and he fixed a time limit [for repayment].

When the time came no rain had fallen and still as the day passed none fell. But finally Nakdimon entered the temple and prayed and 'rain fell until the twelve wells were filled with water and there was much over'. But the man claimed that Nakdimon still owed him the money because the sun had by then already set and the time-limit was exceeded. Nakdimon entered the temple again and prayed; immediately the clouds dispersed, the sun broke through and the claim lapsed.

He was called Nakdimon because the sun had broken through

[248] *Jerusalem in the Time of Jesus*, 96 n. 27. There is some coalescence too in D. Flusser's *Jesus*, ET New York 1969, 120.

(*nikdera*) on his behalf. The rabbis have taught: For the sake of three [men] the sun broke through, Moses, Joshua and Nakdimon ben Gurion (b. *Taan*. 19b–20a).

Then, again during the siege of Jerusalem, we read:

There were in it three men of great wealth, Nakdimon ben Gurion, Ben Kalba Shabua' and Ben Zizith Hakeseth. Nakdimon ben Gurion[249] was so called because the sun continued shining for his sake. . . . One of these [Nakdimon] said to the people of Jerusalem, 'I will keep them in wheat and barley.' A second said, 'I will keep them in wine, oil and salt.' The third said, 'I will keep them in wood.' . . . These men were in a position to keep the city for twenty-one years (b. *Git*. 56a).

We are told that 'the *biryoni* [the reference is obviously to the Zealots] were then in the city.' The rabbis were for treating with the Romans, the Zealots for fighting them. When the rabbis said 'You will not succeed', the Zealots 'rose up and burnt the stores of wheat and barley so that a famine ensued', and this is followed by a description of the flight and death of Martha, the daughter of Boethius, one of the richest women in Jerusalem. The scene is fully confirmed by Josephus' description of internecine fighting between the Ẓealots which involved setting light to buildings stocked with corn and all kinds of provisions (*BJ* 5.24).

So Nakdimon lost his fortune, and his daughter Miriam, whose marriage settlement included 'a million gold denarii from her father's house besides the amount from her father-in-law's house', and who had been used to every extravagance, was reduced to abject poverty, picking barley-grains from the dung of Arab cattle (b. *Keth*. 66b). Nakdimon's obituary reads ambiguously:

Did not Nakdimon ben Gurion, however, practice charity? Surely it

[249]According to the Midrash Rabbah on Lamentations (I.5.31) 'In Jerusalem there were four councillors, viz., Ben Ẓiẓit, Ben Gurion, Ben Nakdimon, and Ben Kalba-Shabua'. Each of them was capable of supplying food for the city for ten years' (ET, Soncino ed., London 1951, 101). But it looks as if Ben Gurion and Ben Nakdimon are a duplication, unless indeed they are father and son. (In the Midrash on Ecclesiastes VII.12.1 the same tradition appears with three councillors, specifying Nakdimon ben Gurion). John Lightfoot, who cites this (*Horae Hebraicae et Talmudicae* III, 262) also observes that Nicodemus' proper name was Boni (b. *Taan*. 20a) and that a Buni is among the disciples of Jesus in *Sanh*. 43a. But he confuses the generations by equating the two – though, as we shall see, it is not impossible that we may be dealing with grandfather and grandson bearing the same name.

was taught: It was said of Nakdimon ben Gurion that, when he walked from his house to the house of study, woollen clothes were spread beneath his feet and the poor followed behind him and rolled them up [to take the stuff away with them]! If you wish I might reply: He did it for his own glorification. And if you prefer I might reply: He did not act as he should have done, as people say, 'In accordance with the camel is the burden' [that is, he did not give in accordance with his means] (*Keth.* 66b–67a).

What correlations may be drawn from this material? The Nicodemus of John's Gospel asks 'How is it possible for a man to be born when he is old?' (3.4), on which Barrett reasonably comments: 'The most natural conclusion to draw is that Nicodemus himself was an old man; this would agree with his being an ἄρχων.'[250] If Nicodemus speaking in AD 28 was, let us say, about 50 or 60, then the Gorion son of Nicodemus mentioned by Josephus (*BJ* 2.451) who was a senior citizen of Jerusalem 38 years later in AD 66 could well have been his (now elderly) son, and Nakdimon ben Gurion, the millionaire whose family fortune collapsed in the siege, his grandson.[251] At any rate the connection alike of office, affluence and genuine, if ostentatious, piety is not at all impossible; and there could not have been that number of top people in Jerusalem with the name of Nicodemus – although we know of one other such family, the ben-Josephs, as well as the ben-Gurions. At any rate John would appear to be talking of a real person with far better connections than Joseph, the *nouveau riche* country cousin with his brand-new tomb,[252] which may suggest the lack of an established family mausoleum in the city. If there is no good reason for doubting the historicity of the latter, then it is surely captious to dismiss the former.[253]

[250]*John*, 208.

[251]Bowman *identifies* Nicodemus with Nakdimon ben Gurion. But then for him the characters in this Gospel are simply interchangeable with later personages, for example, Martha with Martha the wife of Jesus ben Gamala, one of the last of the high priests, Annas with Ananus, Lazarus with Eleazar the hero of Masada, Joseph of Arimathea with Joseph ben Gurion (who is equated with Nicodemus ben Gurion, so that Joseph and Nicodemus are really the same person!). With such methods any serious historical criticism goes out of the window.

[252]A detail common in different vocabulary to Matthew (27.60), Luke (23.53) and John (19.41), though not, interestingly, to Mark.

[253]Cf. Dodd, *Historical Tradition*, 139: 'Nor is it certain that Nicodemus is a less historical character than Joseph.' But he does not go into the question.

9. *The Resurrection*

After this excursus we may return to the tomb which Joseph and Nicodemus left on the Friday evening. The next time-reference is precise but varies slightly in all the Gospels. It was 'on the first day of the week', 'about daybreak' (τῇ ἐπιφωσκούσῃ εἰς μίαν σαββάτων) (Matt. 28.1),[254] 'very early' (λίαν πρωΐ) . . . just after sunrise' (Mark 16.2), 'very early' (ὄρθρου βαθέως) (Luke 24.1), 'early (πρωΐ) . . . while it was still dark' (John 20.1). But the differences are insignificant, especially since even in John it is evidently light enough for Mary Magdalene to see that the stone had been moved from the entrance. John, like Luke, has not previously mentioned the rolling in place of the stone (Matt. 27.60; Mark 15.46), but they clearly presuppose it (John 20.1; Luke 24.2). Nor in contrast with the others has he mentioned the women; and now he only specifies Mary Magdalene, the one name common to all four evangelists, though in the following verse (20.2) she uses the plural 'we', thereby implying the presence of others. Indeed, as Bernard says,[255] 'It is unlikely that a woman would have ventured by herself outside the city walls before daylight.' Like Matthew (28.1), John does not say that they have come to anoint the body (Mark 16.1; Luke 24.1), though this should certainly not be ruled out by the provision of spices that Nicodemus had made; and commentators who see this as one of the 'contradictions' between John and the Synoptists misunderstand the situation. Nor at this stage does he mention any angelic figures at the tomb. Mary Magdalene and her associates merely run off to report to Peter and to the beloved disciple[256] (in Matthew to 'his disciples', in Luke to 'the eleven and all the rest') that 'they have taken

[254]Matthew confusingly precedes this phrase with ὀψὲ δὲ σαββάτων which has led some (e.g. M. Black, *An Aramaic Approach to the Gospels and Acts*, 136–8) to think that he means lighting-up time, or the first appearance of the stars, on the Saturday *evening* (cf. the same expression in Luke 23.54 and the Gospel of Peter 2.5, of the previous evening). But this seems most improbable in the face of all the other evidence.

[255]*John* II, 656.

[256]Bernard, ad loc., quotes Bengel for the observation that the repetition of the πρός indicates that Peter and 'the other disciple' were not living in the same house. The πρὸς ἑαυτούς of 20.10 could of course be interpreted either way (though the description in Luke 24.12 of Peter 'going away πρὸς ἑαυτόν' and 'wondering what had happened' suggests that he was on his own). It is best rendered with Bernard 'to their lodgings'. He cites Josephus, *Ant.* 8.124, where it means 'each to his own home'. We may compare John 16.32: 'The hour is coming . . . when you are all to be scattered each to his own home (εἰς τὰ ἴδια).' This is the same phrase as in 19.27, where the beloved disciple is described as taking Mary to his own home. For the later Christian tradition about this house (which located it in the same quarter as the high priest's establishment), see above, ch. II, pp. 64–7.

the Lord out of the tomb and we do not know where they have laid him.' This is the only explanation offered in any of the Gospels for the absence of the corpse. It hints merely at the action of persons unknown, possibly grave-robbers[257] or, as Jeremias suggests,[258] religious or political fanatics concerned to rectify the decision of the pagan governor to allow the body burial in other than one of the two cemeteries reserved for criminals (M. *Sanh.* 6.5). Later on Mary Magdalene says to the stranger whom she takes to be the gardener, 'If it is you, sir, who removed him, tell me where you have laid him, and I will take him away' (20.15), indicating perhaps removal from a temporary resting place where the body had been deposited 'because the tomb was near at hand and it was the eve of the Jewish sabbath' (19.42). At any rate the explanations, however inadequate, are entirely natural and reasonable. Faith is not presented as compelled simply by the lack of any other option. Even, indeed especially, in this most theological of the Gospels believing in the risen Christ is presented as the supremely, superly natural response to the emptily natural alternative.

There follows in 20.3–8 the vivid description of the race to the sepulchre, which until recently would hardly have been taken seriously as containing the most primitive account of the empty tomb story. But Jeremias showed himself open to this,[259] following what he calls the 'pioneering article' by P. Benoit in his own *Festschrift.*[260] Admittedly Benoit thinks that in the original version only one disciple, Peter, was involved, as in Luke 24.12: 'Peter, however, got up and ran to the tomb, and, peering in, saw the *ὀθόνια* and nothing more; and he went home amazed at what had happened.' The authenticity of this verse has been the subject of much doubt, since it is omitted by D, the Old Latin version, and Marcion. It is part of the problem of what Westcott and Hort[261] called the 'Western non-interpolations' in Luke 24. But recent

[257]Cf. the edict against grave-robbers issued at Nazareth under Claudius (M. P. Charlesworth, ed., *Documents Illustrating the Reigns of Claudius and Nero*, Cambridge [2]1951, 15, 'which may well be in some way connected with Christian origins' (Barrett, *John*, 562f.).

[258]*New Testament Theology* I, 305.

[259]Ibid., 304.

[260]'Marie-Madeleine et les Disciples au Tombeau selon Joh 20.1–18' in W. Eltester, ed., *Judentum—Urchristentum—Kirche, Festschrift für Joachim Jeremias*, BZNW 26, Berlin 1960, 141–52; cf. more popularly, Benoit, *The Passion and Resurrection of Jesus Christ*, ch. 10.

[261]B. F. Westcott and F. J. A. Hort, *The New Testament in the Original Greek: Introduction and Appendix*, Cambridge and London 1881, 175–9.

scholarship has been increasingly sceptical of this category[262] and a consensus seems to be growing in favour of regarding Luke 24.12 as an integral part of the text.[263] (It is after all present in every Greek manuscript but one, now including P^{75}.) If so, then its dependence on John or John's on it becomes an open question. The differences of detail here and in the other instances in the chapter (especially 'hands and feet' as opposed to 'hands and side' in 24.40) suggest parallel traditions rather than literary dependence. If so then John's story is not without independent support. The excising of the part of the beloved disciple as secondary rests of course on no textual or literary basis,[264] merely on the presumption of Synoptic (in this case Lukan) priority,[265] though it is obviously more likely that a story that did not have anyone believing would be expanded into one that did, rather than the other way round (as on the view, commonly held, that Luke 24.12, where no faith was involved, was added to the text *from* the Johannine tradition).

But let us consider the story as it stands in John, which an older generation would have seen as resting *par excellence* on eyewitness testimony.[266] Thus Bernard wrote:

> That the first disciple to note the presence of the grave-clothes in the tomb did not actually go into it first is not a matter that would seem

[262]Cf. Metzger, *Textual Commentary* 191–3; and K. Snodgrass, 'Western Non-Interpolations', *JBL* 91, 1972, 369–72, who argues that this tendentious category should be 'relegated to history'.

[263]It is included in the United Bible Societies' text and Nestle-Aland, *Novum Testamentum Graece*, Stuttgart [26]1979. Cf. K. Aland, 'Neuetestamentliche Papyri II', *NTS* 12, 1965–6, 206f.; Jeremias, *New Testament Theology* I, 305; F. Neirynck, 'John and the Synoptics' in *Évangile*, 98–106; R. Schnackenburg, 'Der Jünger den Jesus liebte', *EKK* 2, 1970, 103f., who argues that it may have been removed by a scribe because Peter only wonders and John is omitted.

[264]For a defence of the historicity of the part of the beloved disciple, cf. W. L. Craig, 'The Empty Tomb of Jesus', in France and Wenham, edd., *Gospel Perspectives* II, 187–9, 198f.

[265]The passage has provided the occasion for the most diverse analyses, sparked off by what Brown calls 'an extraordinary number of inconsistencies that betray the hand of an editor who has achieved organization by combining disparate material' (*John* II, 995). Yet they are in fact mostly infelicities or repetitions in the telling, and the great majority of people have always read the narrative without being aware of them. The various theories of composition (pp. 996–1004) are dominated by the assumption that 'Synoptic-like' and 'non-Synoptic' elements are being combined, as if this difference were the criterion for establishing the original strands of the Johannine tradition.

[266]Cf. still L. Morris, 'Was the Author of the Fourth Gospel an Eyewitness?' in his *Studies in the Fourth Gospel*, 201–5.

worth noting, to anyone except the man who refrained from entering.[267]

Similarly towards the end of his life Dodd desired to reiterate some words he had written earlier: 'This story never came out of any common stock of tradition; it has an arresting individuality.' He did not of course accept that the evangelist himself was an eyewitness.

Yet I cannot for long rid myself of the feeling (it can be no more than a feeling) that this *pericopé* has something indefinably first-hand about it. It stands in any case alone. There is nothing quite like it in the gospels. Is there anything quite like it in all ancient literature?[268]

But the credibility of the description must turn on the authenticity of the detail. The description of the structure of the tomb presents little problem.[269] But what of the grave-clothes? The account appears to be very different from that of the Synoptists (Mark 15.46 and pars.), who mention simply a single linen cloth (*σινδών*) in which Joseph of Arimathea 'wrapped' (*ἐνείλησεν*, Mark) or 'folded' (*ἐνετύλιξεν*, Matthew and Luke) the body of Jesus. According to John (19.40), Joseph and Nicodemus 'bound (*ἔδησαν*)[270] it with the spices', according to the NEB translation 'in strips of linen' (*ὀθονίοις*). But this is interpretation, and I believe a false (as well as a relatively recent) interpretation. Investigation[271] has shown that *ὀθόνια* is almost certainly to be understood not as a diminutive but as a generic term meaning linen cloths or clothes, here, grave-clothes. And this is borne out by Luke 24.12 (if a genuine part of Luke's text), where the term *ὀθόνια* is used to cover, or to include, what he has previously described as the *σινδών* (23.53). In John 20.5f. the beloved disciple peers in, without entering, and sees 'the *ὀθόνια* lying there'. But Simon Peter goes in and sees 'the *ὀθόνια* lying and the *σουδάριον* which had been over his head not lying with the *ὀθόνια* but folded (*ἐντετυλιγμένον*: the same

[267] *John* II, 660. [268] *Historical Tradition*, 148.

[269] Cf. Finegan, *Archaeology of the NT*, 166–9, 181–202.

[270] *Θ* and Theodoret have *ἐνείλησεν*, which the NEB's 'wrapped' appears to render. It may be an assimilation to the text of Mark, but Wuenschel (see next note) defends it as original on the basis of the old Syriac tradition.

[271] Cf. the studies of E. A. Wuenschel, 'The Shroud of Turin and the Burial of Christ', *CBQ* 7, 1945, 405–37; and especially 8, 1946, 135–78; P. A. Vaccari, '*Ἔδησαν αὐτὸ ὀθονίοις*, Joh. 19.40' in *Miscellanea biblica B. Ubach*, Montisserati, 1953, 375–86; and C. Lavergne, 'La preuve de la resurrection de Jésus d'après Jean 20.7', a reprint from *Sindon* 3, 1961, 8–10. Brown, who has no interest in defending the Shroud of Turin, concurs. I have here drawn on and expanded material from my essay 'The Shroud and the New Testament' in *Twelve More NTS*, 81–94.

word as Matthew and Luke used of the σινδών at the burial) apart in (εἰς) a place by itself'.

Σουδάριον is by derivation a sweat-cloth or handkerchief (as in Acts 19.12; cf. Luke 19.20) and is also used in the account of the raising of Lazarus (John 11.44). There 'his face was bound round' with it. In the case of Jesus it was 'over his head (ἐπὶ τῆς κεφαλῆς αὐτοῦ)' (not 'round' it as in the AV). The only thing that could be described as going round the face and over the head is a jaw-band and this is almost certainly what it was, the Mishnah testifying to its use in Jewish burial custom, permitting the chin to be bound even on a sabbath, though 'not in order to raise it [that was work] but that it may not sink lower' (*Shab.* 23.5). Such a band would appear to have been constructed by folding, or rolling, a large handkerchief or neckerchief in the manner of a triangular bandage. John observes that the cloth was still in this state when found on Easter morning, 'rolled up in an oval loop', as Brown, I believe correctly, interprets it,[272] as it would have been had it been slipped off the jaw – by whatever means.[273] It lay separately from the ὀθόνια, which, as in Luke 24.12, seem to refer to the main grave-clothes, consisting of, or at least including, the σινδών or shroud.

In addition Lazarus had been bound hand and foot with κειρίαι (11.44). These again are not 'linen bands' (NEB) but thongs or cords. There is nothing to say what they were made of, but our only ancient evidence (the scholiast on Aristophanes' *Birds*, 816) tells us that a κειρία was 'a kind of binder made of twisted rushes, somewhat like a thong, with which bedsteads were strung'. All we know is that they restricted, though evidently not totally, the movement of Lazarus' hands and feet. Their function was probably to tie the shroud (too obvious evidently to mention in this case) in place, in lieu of a coffin, until the body decomposed and the bones could be gathered into an ossuary (cf. M. *Sanh.* 6.6). In Jesus' case no κειρίαι are mentioned, because they would not have been required until the women had finished their work. But the body would clearly have been covered (cf. Acts 5.6) and the sort of σινδών claimed to be the burial cloth of Jesus in the Shroud of Turin, folded under and over the body lengthwise, would perfectly well fit the evidence, whether it turns out to be genuinely

[272]*John* II, 987. He agrees that it served as a jaw-band (986), as does Mastin in Sanders, *John*, 276.

[273]There is no suggestion in the text of what Lightfoot, *Biblical Essays*, 183, with many others calls 'the orderly folding of the napkin'. The orderliness of the scene which so impressed commentators like Chrysostom, Bengel, Godet and Westcott as an argument against grave-robbers is entirely in the eye of the beholder. The clothes might have been lying about (κείμενα) all over the place as far as John's description goes.

ancient or not. There is no suggestion in any of the language used in the Gospels of a cloth wound *round* the body, like a mummy or mediaeval winding-sheet: no compound of περί is used, except to describe the σουδάριον tied round the face. But if so in such an arrangement the σινδών would have passed right over the body with the σουδάριον in position inside it. In that case, if the σουδάριον was subsequently found separated 'in a place by itself' and *not* between the layers of the σινδών, the grave-clothes must have been moved (as indeed the preposition εἰς could suggest, though need not in *koinē* Greek require).[274] Yet this is no objection. For John never actually suggests that the body had simply passed through the clothes leaving them undisturbed. In fact this is a typically twentieth-century picture of the relation of spirit to matter.[275] If we ask how he or any first-century Jew would naturally have imagined resurrection (which of course is quite different from saying what happened), it would be rather in terms of an awakening from death (John 11.11; cf. Matt. 27.52f.; Mark 5. 38–43 and pars.; Acts 9.40) and a walking out of the tomb, except that Jesus, not being restored like Lazarus simply to the weakness of the flesh-body, would himself have cast off the trappings of death and not have to have had the stone removed by others. Something like this seems to have been imagined by the Gospel according to the Hebrews[276] where Jesus hands the σινδών to the servant of the (high?) priest, an account which,

[274]Blass-Debrunner, *Greek Grammar of the New Testament* § 205, p. 110. Cf. e.g. John 1.18; 19.13.

[275]Brown (*John* II, 1007) traces it back to Ammonius of Alexandria in the fifth century, and no doubt it recurs, but it is notably absent from the classical commentators. Thus Chrysostom makes the point that the arrangement of the grave-clothes argues not that they had not been moved but that it could not have been the work of robbers, who would either have taken them with the body or left them in disarray. Bengel in the eighteenth century says that it means that they were not 'thrown off in a disorderly manner: the angels doubtless ministered to the rising man, one of them composing the linen cloths, the other the napkin'! But the neatness of the arrangement entirely depends on ἐντετυλιγμένον meaning 'folded up', which it almost certainly does not. F. Godet at the end of the nineteenth century says, 'The napkin especially, wrapped together and carefully put aside, attested not a precipitate removal, but a calm and holy awakening' (*The Gospel of St John* III, ET Edinburgh 1893, 311). Westcott too comments: 'There were no traces of haste. The deserted tomb bore the marks of perfect calm. . . . It was clear, therefore, that the body had not been stolen by enemies.' But it is interesting that between the sentences his son and editor added in brackets: 'The grave-clothes lay as the body had withdrawn from them', thus introducing Bishop Westcott's later conviction derived from H. Latham's book *The Risen Master*, Cambridge 1901, of dematerialization through the undisturbed clothes (*John* II, 339f.). The influence of this book seems to have been decisive in changing popular presumptions.

[276]Jerome, *Vir. ill.* 2; fragment 7 in *NTApoc* I, 165.

however legendary, reflects the presuppositions of the ancient world.

But John no more describes the resurrection than any of the other canonical evangelists (contrast the Gospel of Peter 10.39f.); and precisely what the beloved disciple saw to make him believe is not spelt out. Yet nothing in the account can be shown to be incompatible with Jewish burial customs, nor, accepting that, as in Luke, the ὀθόνια are to be equated with the σινδών, is there anything that cannot be harmonized with the evidence of the Synoptists or, if it is genuine, with the Turin Shroud. Once again the effect of the Johannine story is to take us *into* the history, both literally and spiritually, in a way that none of the other Gospels do.

When we come to the appearances, the Gospel traditions notoriously diverge in where they locate them. But John backs Matthew, after Mark deserts us,[277] in having appearances both to Mary Magdalene at the tomb (Matt. 28.9f.; John 20.14–18) and to a group of the Twelve in Galilee (Matt. 28.16–20; John 21.1–13), though these could hardly be more different and clearly there is no literary dependence. The one common point is the charge to Mary to tell 'my brothers', which I would agree with Dodd[278] means what it says (despite the fact that she goes off and tells 'the disciples') and is connected with the early tradition of an appearance to James (I Cor. 15.7). John also concurs with Luke in having an appearance of Jesus to the disciples on Easter Sunday evening (Luke 24.36–43; John 20.19–23). Once again they are independent,[279] even if, as I believe, the Johannine 'echoes' in Luke 24.36 ('And he said to them "Peace be with you!"') and 24.40 ('After saying this he showed them his hands and his feet'), form a true part of the Lukan text (again they are omitted by only one Greek manuscript (D)). Yet clearly the two accounts represent the same story differently told.

John's distinctive contribution to the record of the resurrection appearances lies in (1) the conversation with Mary Magdalene (20.1–

[277]I have long been inclined to think that the ending of Matthew incorporates material from the triple tradition which has been lost in our authentic texts of Mark, embodying as it does the Galilean parousia-scene in terms of exaltation to which Mark points (9.1–9; 16.7). Cf. my *Jesus and His Coming*, 130–2; *Redating the New Testament*, 102. Independently also Stanton, *Gospels as Historical Documents* II, 202; E. J. Goodspeed, *An Introduction to the New Testament*, Chicago and Cambridge 1937, 156; Dodd, *Interpretation*, 440.

[278]*Historical Tradition*, 324.

[279]Cf. Dodd, ibid., 145: 'If we were to postulate borrowing on the one side or the other, Luke must be the borrower. But there is in fact so little coincidence in verbal expression that there is no sufficient ground for the hypothesis of literary dependence.'

18), where many again have heard the *ipsissima vox* in the 'Mary' and the Aramaic '*Rabbuni*'; (2) the two scenes with Thomas (20.24–29), the latter providing the only datable appearance subsequent to Easter Day; and most notably (3) the 'third' and final appearance of the epilogue (21.1–14), which is as vivid in its details of name and place and number[280] as anything in this or any other Gospel. To Gardner-Smith it was 'more primitive than the traditions embodied in the First and Third Gospels': 'This is just the kind of conclusion to which all may judge that Mark was leading,[281] and there is every reason to suppose that it represents a very early form of the tradition of the resurrection. It appears also in the Gospel of Peter.'[282] Nothing can prove that it is authentic – or inauthentic. Its credibility will stand or fall by whether we judge *in toto* that John is writing symbolic history or symbolic fiction.[283]

[280]Bernard again shows his good judgment, as it seems to me, in refusing to see purely allegorical significance in them (*John* I, lxxxviif. and II, 699f.). Moreover, the 'third' appearance no more argues a separate source-collection, than the 'second' sign in 4.54. Fortna, *Gospel of Signs*, 96, sees it as the third *sign* (misplaced from the ministry) and judges (94) that originally the number had no symbolic significance.

[281]Though I should say Matthew's ending was the better candidate: see n. 277 above.

[282]*St John and the Synoptic Gospels*, 85; Gospel of Peter, 14.59: 'But I, Simon Peter, and my brother Andrew took our nets and went to the sea.' The fact that Levi, the son of Alphaeus, is also included in the party suggests that it is not simply drawing on John 21.

[283]For a recent defence of its essential historicity, cf. G. R. Osborne, 'John 21: Test Case for History and Redaction in the Resurrection Narratives', in France and Wenham, edd., *Gospel Perspectives* II, 293–328.

VII

The Teaching of Jesus

While there has been growing receptivity to the idea that the Gospel of John may well incorporate surprisingly good historical material in its narrative sections, little credence has been accorded to any similar claim for the teaching of Jesus embodied in its discourses. Even so open-minded a scholar as Geoffrey Lampe, with whom I should find myself as sympathetic in theological outlook as with any other contemporary scholar, said in his Bampton Lectures: 'It is likely . . . that the historical link between the Jesus who speaks in the Fourth Gospel and the actual Jesus of Nazareth is at best extremely tenuous.'[1] At worst, presumably, it is nil, as indeed Bultmann said categorically in his *Jesus and the Word*: 'The Gospel of John cannot be taken into account at all as a source for the teaching of Jesus, and it is not referred to in this book.'[2] Less categorically, but equally firmly, it is simply ignored in the most recent assessment of his teaching by Geza Vermes, *The Gospel of Jesus the Jew*.[3]

1. *The Difference in Technique*

Let us admit at the outset that the situation is at this point different. In the story of Jesus John's technique of telling it is remarkably straight. He allows the events to speak for themselves. This is especially true of the passion narrative. As Dodd pointed out in his earlier book, *The Interpretation of the Fourth Gospel*, by the time the passion narrative starts the reader has already been apprised of the significance of Jesus'

[1] *God as Spirit*, Oxford 1977, 63.
[2] ET, Fontana ed., London 1968, 17.
[3] The Riddell Lectures, Newcastle-upon-Tyne 1981.

death as the lifting up and glorification of the Son of Man and the finishing of the Father's work. The theological interpretation has been given in the last discourses and final prayer in which Jesus is already speaking from the other side of what, historically, has yet to be accomplished.

> It is as though the evangelist, having sufficiently set forth the meaning of the death and resurrection of Christ, turned to the reader and said, 'And now I will tell you what actually happened, and you will see that the facts themselves bear out my interpretation.'[4]

The story itself can therefore be told with the minimum of comment, though that does not mean to say that every detail may not be instinct with symbolic significance and resonant with overtones for those with the ear to hear them. And the effect is conveyed with the starkest of statements: 'That is what the soldiers did' (19.25). There is little need for interpretation by the evangelist – only the occasional explanation or back-reference or testimony from Scripture (18.2, 9, 13f., 32, 40; 19.24, 28, 35–7, 39; 20.9). For the rest it all comes out in the narrative and conversation. One gets the strong impression that fact is sacred, comment free – but unnecessary. The theology is drawing out the history rather than creating it or even moulding it. It is an exercise in 'remembering', in the pregnant Johannine sense of reliving the events 'from the end', through the mind of the interpreter Spirit, presenting what they 'really' meant, in spirit and in truth.[5] It is a meta-history: not any the less historical the more theologically it is understood, but the depth and truth *of* the history.

This is true both of what happened to Jesus – and there is as terrible an objectivity in John as there is in Mark – and still more of what he did. For supremely in this Gospel the events of the passion are seen as actions, whose meaning he controlled even when he suffered them (cf., above all, 10.18). And John is concerned to convey their inner

[4] 431f.

[5] Cf. F. Mussner, *The Historical Jesus in the Gospel of John*, ET London 1966, esp. 40–54. But in Mussner's treatment the distance from the historical Jesus is so great that in the Johannine vision 'the Jesus of history and the glorified Christ are essentially identical' (90) and the one becomes swallowed up and transmuted into the other. 'The Johannine Christ speaks John's language, and to such an extent that the question of the *ipsissima vox Jesu*, which in regard to the synoptic tradition is an entirely meaningful one, becomes almost without object, if not meaningless, in regard to the fourth gospel' (81). I shall hope to show that such a 'monophysite' merger does not do justice to John's perspective.

significance, what was really happening on the inside of the events, what everyone involved was meaning and intending, and above all what the Father's purpose was meaning and intending through them. John's narrative is at the furthest remove from mere documentary, yet at the furthest remove also from fiction.

Yet when we come to the teaching of Jesus we see him using a different technique to the same end, though the difference is one of degree rather than of kind, for the works and words of Jesus are not sharply distinguished. John is still concerned with what Jesus is really saying and meaning, and the words, like the actions, can be understood at very different levels. Yet he does not simply set them down straight, and then comment upon them – allowing the sayings and their interpretation to stand side by side, with the raw material presented in its untreated state. Rather, it is worked up; the interpretation is thoroughly assimilated and integrated.

But the same is after all true in different degree with the Synoptists. For they too are interpreting the words and works of Jesus in the light of the one whom they have discovered him to be within the life-setting of their communities. One may freely grant that how they represent Jesus as speaking may be *more* like how he would have been heard if one had had a tape-recorder around. That is to say, by the criterion of verisimilitude, as he was to be encountered 'in the flesh', their record may be truer to life. But in terms of what he was really saying, perhaps this may not be the case.

The analogy of the material about Socrates is again relevant. The stories and sayings recorded by Xenophon, like the stories and sayings recorded by Boswell about Johnson, may bring us closer to what the company he kept would have recalled of the man. 'How like him!' they might have said. But they tell as much about Xenophon, as Boswell's *Life of Johnson* does about Boswell, as they do about the master – or rather they tell us what Xenophon saw, and was able to see, in Socrates. And such is of course the case with every creative artist. 'I see five archbishops', said Opie of Cosmo Gordon Lang; 'which do you want me to paint?' The Socrates that Xenophon saw, or that Aristophanes saw, was not the same as the one, or the ones, that Plato saw. And they all could have been true. Yet who is to say that Plato did not know him best, both in the flesh and in the spirit? Indeed through the mouth of Alcibiades in the *Symposium* Plato says, 'Let me tell you that none of you know Socrates; but I shall reveal him to you.'[6] By the

[6]*Symp.* 215c; quoted by Culpepper, *Johannine School*, 68, who says that 'the similarity to passages like Matt. 11.27 and John 17.25 is merely superficial and

criterion of verisimilitude we may judge Plato's words put into Socrates' mouth to be less 'like' him and to reflect more of Plato than Xenophon's do of Xenophon (as surely there was more to reflect).[7] In fact in the *Dialogues* Socrates and Plato are so assimilated that both in style and thinking they are now inseparable. There is a deliberate recasting to bring out the teaching, and great freedom of treatment. Yet the process may be one of deepening truth rather than of falsification or fiction.

The Johannine Christ is the Jesus John saw. No one else may have seen him thus. It is a highly personal portrait. The vocabulary, the perspective, the interpretation are distinctively and recognizably his. Yet the colouration may not be purely subjective. As Dodd put it at the conclusion of an article which used the same metaphor, 'The Portrait of Jesus in John and in the Synoptists',

> John's rendering of the portrait of Jesus will be neither his own invention nor the re-colouring of another artist's sketch. He will have had, through memories or traditions available to him, access to the sitter, and the similarities we have noted will go far to assure us that behind the two renderings of the portrait there stands a real historical person.[8]

Both the Synoptic portrait – or rather portraits: for Matthew's and Mark's and Luke's are very different – and the Johannine may be true; and the Johannine, as at points the others, may be truer, in the sense that one may enable us to make deeper sense of the others. None is self-sufficient. But what happens if the Johannine is allowed priority, instead of being dismissed as purely secondary and interpretative, significant for the Christ of faith but insignificant for the Jesus of history? That is the question that remains to be pursued first of the teaching of Jesus and then of his person. The two for John are of course inseparable – as are his words and works. So much of the teaching of this Gospel is focused on his person. But we shall postpone discussion of the content of this and concentrate as far as it is possible on the form

---

coincidental'. Yet the similarity in relation to their masters between Plato and the beloved disciple is I believe more than superficial.

[7]The conventionality of Xenophon's portrait of Socrates comes out in his concluding presentation of him as a man 'so religious . . . , so just . . . , so self-controlled . . . so wise . . .' that 'to me he seemed to be all that that a truly good and happy man must be' (*Mem.* 4.8.11).

[8]*Christian History and Interpretation: Essays Presented to John Knox*, edd. W. R. Farmer, C. F. D. Moule and R. R. Niebuhr, Cambridge 1967, 183–98 (195).

of the teaching and the distinctive context, of ethics and eschatology, in which it is presented.

2. *The Common Ground*

First it is proper to show that this is not simply a bizarre exercise, since, especially with the teaching of Jesus, it is regularly assumed that John presents a tradition so eccentric and remote from source that it cannot be taken seriously as a contribution to history. Alike in form, vocabulary and perspective any connection with how Jesus actually spoke must at best be regarded as 'extremely tenuous'.

To begin with, the division between narrative (where an element of historicity is now increasingly, if often reluctantly, allowed) and discourse is much less sharp than is often presumed, not least by those who would trace separate 'signs' and 'discourse' *sources*. In fact the line between works and words, miracles and sayings, eschatology and ethics, *kerygma* and *didache*, event and interpretation, is less marked in John than in any of the other Gospels, and especially that of Matthew. As I sought to show in my book *Jesus and His Coming*,[9] the 'separation' of the milk of the gospel into ethics and eschatology, the one set of teaching providing a guide to the present, the other to the future, has gone much further in Matthew than in Luke, where the eschatology is presented more as an accent of finality laid upon the present, as, I believe, was true of the original message of Jesus. In John there are separate discourses on neither subject. Of course the construction of the Gospel, carefully and selectively planned round certain festivals, signs and debates, is the literary work of the evangelist. But then so is that of Matthew's Gospel, whose five blocks of teaching on different subjects each closing with a similar formula, 'when Jesus had finished this discourse' (7.28; 11.1; 13.53; 19.1; 26.1), are just as artificial: no one believes that Jesus delivered this material in five extended sessions. In fact the Matthaean discourses are a good deal more artificial, for they are for the most part simply *collections* of sayings on common themes[10] strung together without narrative or interruption, apart from occasional questions for clarifica-

[9] 94–100.

[10] This was a point that Schleiermacher already made in his *Einleitung ins neue Testament, Sämtliche Werke*, I viii, 324: The Matthaean discourses are summaries of general teaching whereas the Johannine are accounts of speeches which Jesus gave on individual occasions to those who stood in an intimate relation to him.

tion (13.10, 36; 18.21; 24.3) which merely serve to get the monologue started again.

But in John things are very different. If discourse is to be defined as uninterrupted teaching of Jesus, then there is actually surprisingly little of it in the Gospel. One gets the impression that the Gospel is studded with soliloquies, rather like *Hamlet*. But this is not in fact the case. Apart from the last discourses and ch. 17, where Jesus is talking to the Father (not himself), there are only three continuous passages of discourse, all early in the Gospel, in 3.11–21 (after the conversation with Nicodemus) 3.27–36 (where John the Baptist is speaking, in any case until v.30, and thereafter perhaps the evangelist) and 5.19–47 (in reply to the Jews). Moreover the last discourses themselves are uninterrupted only from 14.25 to 16.16 (if we ignore the evident break in continuity at 14.31).[11] For the rest they are interspersed with genuine questions and perplexities (14.5, 8, 22; 16.17–19, 29–30), which do more than serve as foils. In the conversations and debates which make up the heart of the Gospel in chs. 3–12 we are dealing with anything but collections of sayings strung together (as for instance in the Gospel of Thomas). There is real and often acrimonious dialogue – far more than in the Socratic dialogues of Plato.

Moreover there is not the isolation of discourse from narrative, and therefore from details of chronology and topography, which the usual classification might suggest. In fact much of the evidence on which our earlier reconstruction of the story rests comes from the discourse material. For, as Dodd observed, in marked contrast with the dialogue form in the Synoptists and the *Hermetica*,[12] and he might have added Plato, there is in John's discourses a wealth of local colour and setting from life. His summary could not be bettered:

> Particulars of time and place are frequent: a dialogue takes place at Jerusalem, in the temple, in the treasury, in Solomon's cloister; or in

[11]I owe these observations to a paper of R. T. Fortna, 'The Relation of Narrative and Discourse in the Fourth Gospel: An Approach to the Question', presented to the Fourth Gospel Seminar of the Society for New Testament Studies at Durham in August 1979.

[12]There is I believe, no solid evidence for his remark that 'the evangelist, it seems, has moulded his material in forms based upon current Hellenistic models of philosophical and religious teaching' (*Historical Tradition*, 321). Cf. the refutation of this thesis, which was set forth in an earlier article of Dodd's, 'The Dialogue Form in the Gospels', *BJRL* 37, 1954, 54–70, by E. E. Lemcio, 'External Evidence for the Structure and Function of Mark 4.1–20, 7.14–23 and 8.14–21', *JTS*, n.s. 29, 1978, 323–38, where he shows that both Mark and John reflect forms already thoroughly familiar in the Old Testament and Jewish tradition.

the synagogue at Capernaum; or at a city of Samaria called Sychar, near the property which Jacob gave to his son Joseph, where Jacob's well was. One dialogue takes place in the middle of the Feast of Tabernacles, another on the last day of the same festival, another at the Encaenia in winter. Individual characterization, again, which is slight in the Synoptics, sometimes emerges strikingly in John: the Samaritan Woman at the well, and Pontius Pilate, are full-length character studies like nothing that the Synoptics offer, and even characters more lightly sketched, such as those of Caiaphas the High Priest (11.49–50), the blind beggar badgered by the court (9.14–34), the apostle Thomas, with his odd but entirely convincing combination of pessimism and impulsiveness (11.16; 20.24–5, 28), and others, go beyond almost anything in the Synoptic dialogues except, perhaps, the Lucan picture (10.38–42) of Martha and Mary (whose characters emerge also in the Fourth Gospel).[13]

This 'earthing' of the discourses in real time and space, which, as Fortna says of the signs, are each 'inseparably attached to a specific locale',[14] has led to the question whether some of them at least may not reflect actual, and datable, occasions within the ministry of Jesus, in a way again that it would be impossible to derive from the Synoptic material. Even, or especially, such a highly theological and 'Johannine' discourse as that of ch. 6 on the bread of life turns out to reflect synagogue preaching patterns[15] and perhaps seasonal lections[16] in a way which convinces Hunter after observing all due caution (and much is here in place)[17] that 'John 6.25–50, for all its Johannine style, may well preserve the substance of what Jesus said as "he was teaching in

[13] *Historical Tradition*, 317. This point was also drawn out long ago by Lightfoot in his lectures on St John in *Biblical Essays*, 36–9, 183–90.

[14] *Gospel of Signs*, 99.

[15] P. Borgen, 'Observations on the Midrashic Character of John 6', *ZNW* 54, 1963, 232–40; subsequently expanded in his *Bread from Heaven*.

[16] Cf. A. Guilding, *The Fourth Gospel and Jewish Worship*, 58–68; Brown, *John* I, 278–80; B. Gärtner, *John 6 and the Jewish Passover*, Coniectanea Neotestamentica XVII, Lund 1959.

[17] Cf. the stringent and to my mind convincing critique of Guilding's book by L. Morris, *The New Testament and the Jewish Lectionaries*; also the reviews by Brown, *CBQ* 22, 1960, 459–61; Haenchen, *TLZ* 86, 1961, cols. 670–2; and the bibliography in Schürer, *History* II, 451. That Jesus' teaching reflected readings at the synagogue, if we could establish them (and the evidence is both late and uncertain), is entirely credible. But that the structure and chronology of John's Gospel is determined by its being a Christian commentary on these Jewish lections or that it was composed itself for lectionary use seems to be entirely incredible.

synagogue in Capernaum".'[18] Peder Borgen says dogmatically: 'John 6.31–58 reflects this use of the homiletic pattern, *since* the passage represents the Church's understanding of Jesus' teaching rather than it being a homily directly from Jesus himself.'[19] I am not so persuaded that these are either-ors. Clearly, not least in strong eucharistic overtones, it reflects the teaching of the church, but I see no reason why the homiletic structure, which he agrees fits precisely the *Sitz im Leben* of teaching 'in synagogue' (6.59)[20] should not represent how Jesus himself spoke in these circumstances. At any rate he has demonstrated that it is the work of an evangelist who was himself deeply soaked in this pattern of teaching. The same I believe may be said, *mutatis mutandis*, for the teaching in the temple at Tabernacles in 7.37–8.20 and at Dedication in 10.22–40 with its very specific framing both of time and place. I would think that there is at least as much evidence in the Fourth Gospel for what, in essence, Jesus said on these occasions as there is for his sermon at Nazareth in Luke 4.16–30 or for Paul's address to the elders at Miletus in Acts 20.17–38.

Not only is the teaching material much more integrated with the narrative of the Gospel than is often supposed, but there is not the isolation of 'signs' and 'discourses' which their attribution to separate sources would indicate or the balancing of the two in Dodd's structural analysis of 'the Book of Signs'[21] might suggest. Thus, in 3.1–21 there is conversation but no sign, as also in 4.4–42. In 4.46–54 there is sign but no discourse. In 5.1–47 a sign is followed by a discourse, as in 6.1–58, though here the two are interrupted by narrative (6.14–25). In chs. 7 and 8 there is prolonged argumentation but no sign. In ch. 9 a sign is followed by narrative and conversation, with only four verses on the lips of Jesus (35, 37, 39, 41). In 10.1–36 a parable leads into a discourse and dispute; while finally in ch. 11 narrative, sign, teaching, and their consequences are completely intertwined. The closest formal parallels to these Johannine passages are the conflict stories of Mark 2.1–3.6 and 11.27–12.44, or the mixture of teaching and miracle, say, in the Q passage of the healing of the centurion's servant (Matt. 8.5–13 = Luke 7.1–10) which in form is indistinguishable from John 4.46–53, except that the Synoptic version contains more conversation.

Yet clearly there are obvious differences in the form of Jesus'

[18] *According to John*, 96–8.

[19] *Bread from Heaven*, 57. Italics mine.

[20] Ibid., 55f. It is interesting that at this one point alone he allows there may be strength in Guilding's thesis.

[21] *Interpretation*, 289–389.

teaching in the Synoptists and in John, so much so that doubt is often cast on whether one man could have given both. In the Synoptists the teaching is contained in separate poetic oracles, parables and apophthegms, in John in connected argument and dialogue. The difference is partly due to the recognizable techniques of the evangelists, Mark's being more that of the cinema with its rapidly flashing scenes, John's that of the theatre with its slowly building drama in carefully staged acts. Moreover both the isolated pericope and the set piece are evidently the work of the church, the former being no less than the latter shaped and smoothed, as the form critics have taught us, by the evangelistic, apologetic, catechetical and liturgical uses of the Christian community. It is hardly to be supposed that Jesus went round peppering his auditors with pellets of disconnected apophthegms. To the crowd indeed he may well have taught in easily memorized poetic utterances, stories and images, but with individuals and groups there is every reason to suppose that he engaged in connected conversation and sustained argument, like Paul after him. This appears to have been Paul's regular habit, whether in synagogue or church or personal discourse (Acts 17.2, 17; 18.4, 19; 19.8f.; 20.7, 9; 24.12, 25). Yet the word for such activity, *διαλέγεσθαι*, is not used by him, or for that matter of Jesus. They simply did it.

There would seem also no good reason to doubt that Jesus should, like other spiritual teachers and gurus, have conducted meditations with his disciples (including question and answer) on the major themes of his teaching. Indeed Harald Riesenfeld specifically envisages this as necessary to explain how the Gospel material came to be.

> I should incline to the view that the Gospel of John rests on an independent line of tradition, which had its original starting point in the activity of Jesus, and which then ran parallel with the Synoptic line of tradition. And here the starting point is to be found in the discourses and 'meditations' of Jesus in the circle of his disciples, such as certainly took place side by side with the instruction of the disciples proper, with its more rigid forms. Such a view is not incompatible with this line of tradition having also undergone a long and complex development.[22]

[22]*The Gospel Tradition and its Beginnings*, London 1957, 28; cf. also B. Gerhardsson, *Origins of the Gospel Traditions*, 72, who, alas, only refers peripherally to John (44, 82–8). But he says, 'John seems in certain essential respects to have built upon a different branch of the tradition than the synoptics, and to have treated the tradition material much more freely than the men behind the Synoptics felt free to do. At the same time, however, the clues given in John's Gospel seem to be of help as we seek

The evangelists represent Jesus as giving his teaching to three very different audiences: the crowds, the Jewish leadership and the disciples. The balance in the different Gospels varies according to the milieux and purposes in and for which they were composed, the Synoptists concentrating more on the first, John on the second (since this was the setting of his more specifically metropolitan mission),[23] though, surprisingly perhaps, no more on the third than the others.[24] But *within* the different genres of teaching the differences of form are not all that great. We may compare, for instance, Matthew's diatribe against the scribes and Pharisees (21.23–23.39) with 'the great controversy', as the NEB calls it, of John 7–10. There is a remarkable parallelism too between the eschatological discourse in the Synoptists and the last discourses in John, each of which are given privately to the disciples and occupy the same place between the ending of the public ministry of Jesus and the opening of the passion story. They speak of 'the things that are to come' (John 16.13) and practically all the themes of the Synoptic apocalypse are to be found in John:[25] the injunction against alarm, the forewarning against apostasy, the prediction of travail and tribulation for the sake of the name, the need for witness, the promise of the Spirit as the disciples' advocate, the reference to 'that day', when, in an imminent coming, Christ will be seen and manifested, the elect will be gathered to him, and the world will be judged.[26] The idiom indeed is different and the point of reference to *when* all shall be 'accomplished' (Mark 13.4; cf. John 19.28) different too (though compare Luke 13.32 and 24.26). To this we shall return. But for the moment we may note the formal similarities.

There are other respects too in which the differences between the Synoptic and Johannine teaching material have been much exaggerated, alike in form, vocabulary and content. If the two streams of

---

to clarify the history of the Synoptic tradition as well' (84). Much of this present book could be said to be an expansion of this last sentence.

[23]Thus Israel Abrahams was ready to recognize that his Gospel 'enshrines a genuine tradition of an aspect of Jesus' teaching which has not found a place in the Synoptics', *Studies in Pharisaism and the Gospels* I, 12.

[24]Thus, on a rough count, John contains 193 verses of teaching given to the disciples or in their presence (4.31–3; 6.61–70; 13–17; 20.19–29; 21.15–23), while Matthew has 287 (9.37–10.42; 11.25–7; 13.10–23, 36–52; 16.5–18.35; 19.10–12, 23–30; 20.17–28; 24–25; 28.18–20).

[25]For the detailed references, see my *Jesus and His Coming*, 172f.

[26]As I subsequently noted in my *Redating*, 277, the only topics *absent* are significantly the prophecies of the siege and fall of Jerusalem, which I believe John shows evidence of presupposing as a past event even less than the Synoptists; and any reference to the Gentile mission, with which his community was not involved.

tradition are indeed independent, then the correspondences between them suggest that John is by no means creating *ex nihilo* or that the distinctively Johannine material *merely* represents his own style, theology and thought-forms set on the lips of Jesus. Rather, it would point to the fact that both go back directly or indirectly to the same common original.

First, we may observe, as has often been pointed out, that for all their differences the form and rhythm of much of Jesus' teaching alike in John and in the Synoptists fall into the same cadences of Semitic poetry. Evidence for what C. F. Burney called *The Poetry of our Lord*[27] is to be seen as powerfully in the Fourth Gospel as in the others, with its characteristic examples of synonymous (6.35) antithetical (9.39) and climactic parallelism (14.2f.).[28] In fact in 7.38 the poetic parallelism of the passage provides a criterion (apart from the greater probability that the source of living water is Christ rather than the believer) for preferring (with the NEB) the punctuation:

> If anyone is thirsty let him come to me;
> whoever believes in me let him drink.[29]

The words, 'As Scripture says, "Streams of living water shall flow out from within him"', will then stand as the evangelist's comment, rather than as in the traditional rendering: 'If any one thirst, let him come to me and drink. He who believes in me, as the scripture has said, "Out of his heart shall flow rivers of living water"' (RSV).[30] There are plenty of other examples which could be quoted. As Hunter observes,

> Their poetic form does not automatically prove them words of the Lord. We may, if we will, credit the poetic form of the sayings to the fourth evangelist. The trouble about this suggestion is that we do not

[27]Oxford and New York 1925.

[28]Other examples are conveniently set out in Howard, *Fourth Gospel in Recent Criticism*, [4]1955, 307–9. Jeremias, *New Testament Theology* I, 14–16, notes that antithetical parallelism (which he regards as particularly distinctive of Jesus) occurs more than 30 times in the sayings of Jesus in John. But unfortunately he offers no detailed analysis or comparison. His figures for the Synoptists are Mark 30, Q34, special Matthew 44, special Luke 30. Thus John is fairly typical.

[29]Cf. the parallel in 6.35:

> Whoever comes to me shall never be hungry,
> and whoever believes in me shall never be thirsty.

[30]So too Brown, *John* I, 320; Bultmann, *John*, 303 and Dodd, *Interpretation*, 349. Barrett inclines on balance to the opposite view (*John*, 326f.).

know that the evangelist had this poetic gift. We do know, from the synoptic gospels, that Jesus had.[31]

Then it is necessary to insist that the vocabulary and manner of speaking set on Jesus' lips are not as divergent in the different traditions as may initially appear. At first hearing everything in John is characteristically 'Johannine' in ring. It is impossible to mistake the provenance of even the shortest passage. Everyone in the Gospel appears to be talking in the same way: Jesus, John the Baptist, Jews and Samaritans, Pilate and the evangelist. Indeed the uniformity of style is what makes it so difficult to analyse out sources or even strata. No one today would claim that we have in John the literal words of Jesus. But few would make such a claim for the Synoptists either. The Gospels are recognized as in the first place church documents embodying the *kerygma* and *didache* of the Christian mission. That is after all the purpose for which they were written, as Luke's preface most explicitly shows. But, as that preface also claims, they presented the church's *kerygma* and *didache* by deliberate reference to what Jesus himself preached and taught and did from the time that he came into Galilee until the time that he was taken up. And, as New Testament study has shown, they did not merely place *their* preaching and teaching on *his* lips, making use of him as the mouthpiece of their message. The categories in which they proclaimed him after the resurrection, pre-eminently as Lord and Christ (Acts 2.36; etc.), are seldom unequivocally in his mouth, whereas others, notably the Son of Man, which apparently played little or no part in the church's mission and teaching, are constantly on his lips and on those of no others. All this is well known; and Jeremias has contended further[32] that it is possible to designate certain characteristic and distinctive features of what he called the *ipsissima vox* of the Master. What is important from our present point of view is that these features are equally represented in

[31]*According to John*, 91. He also cites Matthew Black's judgment: 'An inspired "targumizing" of an Aramaic sayings tradition, early committed to a Greek form, is the most likely explanation of the Johannine speeches. . . . The rabbinical character of the discourses and their predominantly poetical form do not discourage the belief that much more of the *ipsissima verba* may have been preserved in the fourth gospel – with John as inspired "author" – than we have dared believe possible for many years' (*Aramaic Approach to the Gospels and Acts*, 151.) The same conclusion emerges from the important Manson Memorial Lecture by A. J. B. Higgins, 'The Words of Jesus according to St John', *BJRL* 49, 1967, 363–86; cf. his earlier book, *The Historicity of the Fourth Gospel*, 72–5.

[32]Cf. especially, *The Prayers of Jesus*, SBT 2.6, London and Nashville 1967, 108–15, and *New Testament Theology* I, 29–37.

John. That does not mean that they are not elaborated and developed in his own manner – as they are by the other evangelists. But the point of departure is recognizably the same.

The first and most obvious example is the one already mentioned, the use of the term 'the Son of Man'. Again in John we find its use *always and only* on the lips of Jesus himself, except in 12.34, when the crowd asks, 'Who is this Son of Man that you are always talking about?', which confirms its strangeness and distinctiveness. It is significant that, for all the accumulation of christological titles in ch. 1, which introduces the themes to be explored in the rest of the Gospel (Logos, Son of God, Lamb of God, Elect One, Rabbi or Teacher, Messiah or Christ, son of Joseph, King of Israel), only the Son of Man, in 1.51, is set on Jesus' own lips. Just as in Mark 8.30f. and 14.61f. 'the Christ' on the lips of others is immediately countered by 'the Son of Man' on Jesus' own, so the same transition is reflected in John 12.34: 'Our law teaches that the Messiah continues for ever. What do you mean by saying that the Son of Man must be lifted up?' In this case as elsewhere John draws out the significance of the title in his distinctive way (notably in the Son of Man's 'coming down from heaven' at the beginning rather than the end), but he has certainly not invented it. It was a mode of speaking remembered as characteristic of Jesus.

Still more is this true of two other turns of phrase on which Jeremias concentrated as authentically original to the voice of the Master.

One is his bald use of *abba*, Father, in prayer to God. Surprisingly, perhaps, only Mark among the evangelists retains it in the Aramaic: we could have expected John to do so, as he does with ῥαββί and ῥαββουνί and, uniquely, with ὁ μεσσίας. But the memory of its association with Jesus in his native speech is confirmed and preserved very early by Paul (Gal. 4.6; Rom. 8.15). Moreover its retention as the way in which Jesus, again *alone and always* (except when quoting Ps. 22.1 on the cross), addressed God in prayer, and taught others to do so, has left its mark on all our sources, not only the Synoptic (Mark 14.36 and pars.; Matt. 11.25f. = Luke 10.21; Luke 11.2) but also John (12.28; 17.1, 5, 11, 21, 24f.).[33] That it was also Jesus' most distinctive way of talking

[33]There are other echoes in John of the language of the Lord's Prayer. Indeed C. F. Evans, *The Lord's Prayer*, London 1963, 76f., has seen John 17 as written round the themes of this prayer. 'Father, hallowed be thy name' is echoed not only in 17.11, 'Holy Father, keep them in thy name', but even more directly in 12.28, 'Father, glorify thy name', especially if the 'divine passive' of ἁγιασθήτω is to be interpreted as Brown suggests ('The Pater Noster as an Eschatological Prayer', *Theological Studies* 22, 1961, 175–208; reprinted in his *NT Essays*, 217–33) as a prayer to *God* to vindicate his holiness. There is good reason to think that δοξάζω is here being used in the Septuagintal

about God is further drawn out by the characteristic use of 'Father' for God on his lips (Mark 3, Q 4, special Luke 4, special Matthew 31, John 100) and even more when he speaks absolutely of 'the Father' (Mark 1, special Matthew 1, special Luke 2, John 73).[34] John clearly develops this usage much more than the others. Yet the Johannine fruiting does not deny the dominical rooting, but rather reinforces it.

The other distinctive usage of Jesus to which Jeremias drew attention was that of ἀμήν followed by 'I say to you' to introduce his utterances. 'Whereas the Jew [like Paul and the other New Testament writers, and Christians ever since] concluded his prayer to God with Amen, thus expressing his faith that God would act, Jesus *prefaces* his words with an "Amen"', thus identifying God in advance with what he would say.[35] Indeed, it has been said that this distinctive form of address expresses 'the whole of Christology *in nuce*':[36] and to this we must return. But for now we note it as a mark of the teaching style of Jesus which again is common to the Synoptists and the Fourth Gospel, and this time more evenly distributed (Matthew 30, Mark 13, Luke 6,[37]

---

sense of 'vindicate by open display' (cf. G. B. Caird, 'The Glory of God in the Fourth Gospel: An Exercise in Biblical Semantics', *NTS* 15, 1968–9, 265–77, especially 271–3). Note particularly Ezek. 38.23, where it is combined with ἁγιάζω, and Isa. 5.16 and 33.10, where it is linked with ὑψόω. The correlation of δοξάζω, ἁγιάζω and ὑψόω is of course very close in John (cf. 10.36; 17.17, 19 with 17.1–5, 10, 22, 24; and 12.27f. and 13.31f. with 3.14; 8.28 and 12.32), as already in Isa. 52.13 and Acts 2.33; 3.15; 5.31. Other overtones of the Lord's Prayer may be heard in John 6.32, 'My Father *gives* you the real *bread* from heaven'; and 17.15, 'Keep them from the evil one.' It is significant that Jeremias never even discusses the question of how far John 17, by far the most substantial piece of evidence for 'the prayers of Jesus', might actually correspond to how Jesus prayed on this or any other occasion. No one is saying that here above all one does not have the relationship between Jesus and the Father seen through the reflection and spirituality of the church. The *lex orandi* is ever the matrix and norm of the *lex credendi.* Yet to say that it is *simply* the product of the church's devotion or liturgy or school of prayer is to beg the question of what *Sitz im Leben* such a prayer on the lips of Jesus would have. One can visualize a setting for the material, say, in I Peter, Ephesians and Revelation, but what liturgical or devotional occasion would lead the praying community to *create* a prayer which Jesus alone could utter? Of course there are overtones to be heard of the living Christ interceding for the unity of his church, though I believe that on Jesus' lips the prayer that 'they may all be one' (17.11, 20–3) is to be interpreted against the background of 10.16 and 11.52 as a prayer for scattered and disrupted Judaism. At any rate it is perhaps significant that John 17 is never quoted in the chapter on 'the church at worship' (or any other) in Moule's *The Birth of the New Testament.* Is it in any way evidence for how Christians prayed?

[34]Statistics from Jeremias, *Prayers of Jesus*, 30, 36.

[35]R. H. Fuller, *The New Testament in Current Study*, New York and London 1962, 43.

[36]H. Schlier, art. ἀμήν, *TDNT* I, 338.

[37]Luke often seems to avoid it for his Gentile readership (as Matthew piles it on for his Jewish), but on three of the six occasions he introduces it himself.

John 25), though John, perhaps characteristically, always has it in the reduplicated form ἀμὴν ἀμήν. It has been held, e.g., by Lindars, that this formula is 'a recurring sign that John is making use of a saying of Jesus from his stock of traditional material'[38] – even though 'traditional' is typically defined as non-Johannine and tested by its approximation to Synoptic material. But at least it is recognized that it is not of John's creation.

In fact it embraces and cuts across any recognizable classification including:

(*a*) Sayings having a Synoptic parallel with ἀμήν, like 'Unless you become as little children' (Matt. 18.3; Mark 10.15; Luke 18.17; John 3.3, 5), 'One of you shall betray me' (Matt. 26.21; Mark 14.18; John 13.21, where the wording is identical), and 'Before the cock crows you will betray me three times' (Matt. 26.34; Mark 14.30; John 13.38).

(*b*) Sayings having a Synoptic parallel without ἀμήν, such as 'A servant is not greater than his master' (John 13.16; cf. Matt. 10.24; Luke 6.40), 'He who receives any messenger of mine receives me; receiving me, he receives the One who sent me' (13.20; cf. Matt. 10.40; 18.5; Mark 9.37; Luke 9.48; 10.16), and 'If you ask the Father for anything in my name, he will give it you' (16.23; cf. 14.12–14; Matt. 7.7f.; 18.19f.; 21.22; Mark 11.24; Luke 11.9f.).

(*c*) 'Synoptic-type' sayings, like 'You shall see heaven wide open, and God's angels ascending and descending upon the Son of Man' (1.51; cf. Matt. 26.64; Mark 14.62).

(*d*) Parables (the Shepherd in 10.1, and the Grain of Wheat in 12.24) and proverbial statements ('Everyone who commits sin is a slave to sin' in 8.34; cf. Rom. 6.16, 20; II Peter 2.19).

(*e*) Characteristically 'Johannine' utterances like 'We speak of what we know, and testify to what we have seen' (3.11), 'The Son can do nothing by himself; he does only what he sees the Father doing' (5.19),[39] and 'Unless you eat the flesh of the Son of Man and drink his blood you can have no life in you' (6.53).

(*f*) 'I am' sayings in 6.32–35, 47f. (the bread of life); 8.58 (before Abraham was); and 10.7 (the door of the sheepfold).

'Αμήν appears thus to represent in all the traditions a remembered asseveration of Jesus, which no doubt was also added to sayings by the evangelists (as 'the Son of Man' replaces 'I', and *vice versa*), but which yet is clearly not created by any of them.

[38]*Behind the Fourth Gospel*, 44; cf. 'Traditions behind the Fourth Gospel' in *Évangile*, 115.

[39]Or perhaps this should be classed as a parable; cf. p. 319 below.

Finally, among the marks of the *ipsissima vox*, I would add one which I have argued[40] to be characteristic if not distinctive of Jesus' teaching, a use of Scripture which as far as I can see is attributed to him and no one else. Apart from the allusive, confirmatory and argumentative uses of Scripture which occur on everybody's lips in the New Testament and out of it, there is a challenging use, to pose rather than to prove, somewhat in the manner of a parable, beginning with a question like 'Have you not read?' or 'What do you make of this text?' This again is found across the Gospel sources and is reflected also in John 10.34: 'Is it not written in your own law, "I said: You are gods"?' Indeed this whole passage (10.31–38) with its very rabbinic argument, its functional Hebraic understanding of sonship in terms of moral affinity, and Jesus' claim not to be blaspheming because he is truly being a son of God such as every one ought to be, has a very primitive ring. We shall return to it in considering John's christology. But in the form of the argument it looks again as if we may have something that the evangelist did not create and which goes back to source.[41]

But what still of the very distinctive Johannine idiom? No one is disputing the imprint of the evangelist's style – any more than that of Plato on the speech of Socrates. The question is whether his vocabulary and thought-forms are so foreign to those of Jesus or first-century Palestine that nothing which has passed through this medium can tell us any longer what lay behind it. Is the light so stained with Johannine colouration that it is evidence merely for the composition of his own windows? What of what he calls Jesus' λαλιά, his language or manner of speaking?

'Why do you not understand my language?', Jesus asks the Jews in 8.43. 'It is', he says in reply to his own question, 'because my revelation is beyond your grasp', or literally, 'you cannot hear my word.' It is not because of its linguistic peculiarity or alien thought-forms. The only category that confessedly mystifies them is 'this Son of Man' (12.34), and that is certainly not distinctively Johannine or non-Jewish. Again in 7.45f. the chief priests and Pharisees ask 'Why have you not brought him?' 'No man', the constables answer, 'ever spoke as this man speaks.' But this is not because he uses strange language but because he

[40]'Did Jesus Have a Distinctive Use of Scripture?' in *Twelve More NTS*, 25–43.

[41]Cf. Bernard, *John*, ad loc: 'The argument is one which would never have occurred to a Greek Christian, and its presence here reveals behind the narrative a genuine reminiscence of one who remembered how Jesus argued with the Rabbis on their own principles.' Similarly, Hunter, *According to John*, 94: 'Such an argument, which does not clearly set Jesus apart from other men, would hardly have been invented by the early Church.'

speaks with such authority. It is the same reaction as in Mark: 'This is a new kind of teaching! He speaks with authority' (1.27; cf. 2.12). The impact of Jesus' manner of speaking has indeed left a stronger mark on the Johannine narrative than on any other. There are more occurrences of λαλεῖν than in any other Gospel, almost all of him or about him. But again it is the origin, not the vocabulary, of his utterance that is so distinctive. He does not speak 'of himself' (7.17f.; etc.), but from source. 'We speak of what we know' (3.11), he says. Nevertheless it is nothing esoteric. He speaks ἐπίγεια, down to earth things (3.12), yet not ἐκ τῆς γῆς (3.31), with merely earthly authority. As he insists at the culmination of his ministry, 'I have always taught in synagogue and in the temple, where all Jews congregate; I have said nothing in secret. . . . Ask my hearers what I told them; they know what I said' (18.20f.). 'Who are you?', they ask: 'What I have told you all along' (8.25; NEB margin). Yet for all this 'they did not understand what he meant' (10.6), even though the language, of a shepherd and his sheep, could not have been more everyday or familiar to his listeners. And the same applies equally to the disciples. To them too Jesus had been seeming to speak in figures of speech or riddles (ἐν παροιμίαις); and when they say 'Why, this is plain speaking; this is no figure of speech. . . . Because of this we believe that you have come from God', he replies 'Do you now believe?' and proceeds to predict their desertion of him (16.25–32). For John there is no 'messianic secret' in the sense that he forbids open speech but privately tells all to the inner group. He discloses himself freely – even to the half-believer (4.26; 9.37). Yet not even the disciples can understand – until the Spirit shall make everything clear (14.26). John is the last to present Jesus as a mystagogue, purveying arcane instruction of another world to a closed circle of initiates. The restriction of the disclosure to the disciples and not to the world in 14.22–24 is imposed by lack of love, not by lack of knowledge. Significantly it is the so-called 'Secret Gospel of Mark' which, in Gnostic circles, takes this further step from the contrast between 'insiders' and 'outsiders', with which the Second Gospel works but not the Fourth.

Yet has not John emphasized the mystical teaching of Jesus, the inner spiritual message as opposed to the outward bodily facts, to which Clement and the Christian Gnostics were to warm? Obviously in one sense yes, in so far as he is concerned more than any other New Testament writer to penetrate to the inwardness of Jesus' meaning, beneath the surface level of the flesh (8.15), of what the eyes see (7.24), to that of spirit and of truth (4.23). We shall be returning to the question of how he does this and examine his relation to the Gnostic quest. Yet no one could say that this was not the point to which Jesus himself was equally concerned to press his hearers, alike in his parables and in his moral teaching – to the inside, the heart, the root, the ἀρχή or principle (cf. Mark 10.6; etc.). And now that the Qumran literature has shown that the categories in which John represents him as speaking are not nearly so strange to the Palestinian world of first-century Judaism as was previously supposed, we are bound to ask whether the Johannine 'tinting' is any further from the original style of Jesus than, say, the apocalyptic and programmatic tone increasingly given to it by Mark and Matthew.[42] Albert Schweitzer's assumption that if Jesus was genuinely a Jew of the first century then he must have spoken predominantly in the idiom of apocalyptic is only an assumption. For this was socially conditioned language, as much as adventist language has been in the Christian church, flourishing in bad times and in oppressed circles. There is no reason to suppose that the Sadducees would have found it natural, or indeed many of the Pharisees or the 'quiet of the land'. And Qumran has shown us how both the mystical, pre-gnostic vocabulary and the more militant and apocalyptic could co-exist within the same stream of piety. And if so, why not in the same person, as was certainly true later of Paul? W. H. Brownlee, the Qumran scholar, has written,

> The really serious question posed by the Scrolls is whether the two types of vocabulary belonged authentically to Jesus, with a polarization of the two elements taking place in different Gospel traditions: the Synoptics preserving and emphasizing Jesus' ethical teaching in an apocalyptic context. Palestinian Judaism contained both elements, not simply in different communities but also in the same community. More than this, apocalypticism and light-darkness dualism were blended together in the same passages![43]

[42]Cf. my *Jesus and His Coming*, 94–102; also 'The Place of the Fourth Gospel' in P. Gardner-Smith, ed., *The Roads Converge*, 63–7, and 'The Use of the Fourth Gospel for Christology Today' in *Twelve More NTS*, 150, where I have discussed this question previously.

[43]'Jesus and Qumran' in F. T. Trotter, ed., *Jesus and the Historian*, 76. Cf. Higgins, 'Words of Jesus' (n. 31 above), 384: 'The upshot is, I venture to suggest, . . . that there is a certain amount of evidence that Jesus did not only speak as the Synoptists report him to have done, but also used "Johannine" phraseology and ideas.' He quotes Brown, *John* I, lxiv: 'It is time to liberate ourselves from the assumption that Jesus' own thought and expression were always simple and always in one style, and that anything that smacks of theological sophistication must come from the (implicitly more intelligent) evangelists.'

Indeed we are coming to recognize that apocalypticism and mysticism were not polar opposites: the function of both was to provide 'a door into heaven' (Rev. 4.1), an entry into the throne-room of the Most High, the mysteries of God. Jewish mysticism and apocalyptic Gnosticism had common roots in the Wisdom speculation which was also the seed-bed of John's theology.[44] As Hugo Odeberg recognized in his uncompleted commentary on the Gospel from these sources (though well before the more recent discoveries),[45] John stands in the stream of Jewish 'salvation-mysticism' and 'uses an idiom most nearly related to the Rabbinic style and terminology'.[46] Or as Schillebeeckx has said subsequently, 'We must look for the background of the models used in the Gospel of John to *Jewish* circles in which wisdom traditions were fused with Jewish angelology.'[47] If Nicodemus could not believe if Jesus used the language of ἐπουράνια and of ascent and descent (John 3.12–14; cf. 1.51), it was not because such talk would have been unfamiliar to his tradition.[48] The contrast between τὰ ἐπίγεια and τὰ ἐπουράνια is already to be found in Wisd. 9.16 (cf. II Esd. 4.10f., 21), and Prov. 30.4 had asked the question 'Who has ever gone up to heaven and come down again?' (cf. John 3.13).[49] 'What?', says Jesus, 'is this famous teacher of Israel ignorant of such things?' (3.10). Of course not. We are not outside the ambit of first-century Palestinian Judaism. The only astonishment expressed by the Jews is 'How is it that this untrained man has such learning?' (7.15). But the reason given

[44]Cf. G. G. Scholem, *Major Trends in Jewish Mysticism*, London 1935, especially ch. 2 ('Merkabah Mysticism and Jewish Gnosticism'), and a growing body of subsequent literature, including: G. MacRae, *Some Elements of Jewish Apocalyptic and Mystical Tradition and their Relation to Gnostic Literature*, Dissertation, Cambridge 1966; A. F. Segal, *Two Powers in Heaven*, Leiden 1978; I. Grünwald, *Apocalyptic and Merkavah Mysticism*, Leiden 1980; C. Rowland, *The Open Heaven: A Study of Apocalyptic in Judaism and Early Christianity*, London and New York 1982.

[45]He was accordingly led to go further afield both in space and time, particularly to Mandaean mysticism, than now looks necessary.

[46]*The Fourth Gospel*, 215.

[47]*Christ*, 327; cf. 327–31. He observes that the Odes of Solomon (cf. esp. 12.6; 22.1) like John reject an angel christology but retain the *katabasis-anabasis* model.

[48]Cf. Meeks, 'Man from Heaven', *JBL* 91, 1972, 44–72, especially 52–7; Borgen, 'Some Jewish Exegetical Traditions as Background for Son of Man Sayings in John's Gospel (John 3.13–14 and context)', in *Évangile* 243–58; A. F. Segal, 'Heavenly Ascent in Hellenistic Judaism, Early Christianity and their Environment', in W. Haase, ed., *Aufstieg und Niedergang der Römischen Welt*, II.23.2, Berlin 1980, 1333–94, with his extensive bibliography.

[49]Cf. from slightly later Baruch 3.29: 'Has any man gone up to heaven to gain wisdom and brought her down from the clouds?'; and 3.37: 'Thereupon wisdom appeared on earth and lived among men' (cf. earlier Ecclus. 24.3–9).

for that is that he did not derive it from men (7.16), not because it was imported from an alien thought-world. John's world was Jesus' world as much as Plato's was Socrates', even if both were to draw out their master's teaching in their own direction.

But it is not only the difference in the form of Jesus' teaching between John and the Synoptists which can be exaggerated, but also its content. For there is a good deal more common material than has often been acknowledged. John Marsh simply sums up a growing recognition when he writes, 'The synoptic gospels are far more Johannine than is commonly supposed. But likewise the fourth gospel is far more "synoptic" than is usually perceived.'[50]

The example that most obviously sticks out is of course the so-called 'bolt from the Johannine sky' in Matt. 11.27 (= Luke 10.22):

> Everything is entrusted to me by my Father; and no one knows the Son but the Father, and no one knows the Father but the Son and those to whom the Son may choose to reveal him (cf. John 3.35; 7.29; 10.15; 13.3; 17.2, 25).

The substance of this famous *logion* must engage us when we come to consider the person of Christ, but purely formally I would agree with Dodd when he concludes:

> The saying we are now considering belongs to the earliest strain of tradition to which we can hope to penetrate, since it can be traced to the period before the formation of the common source (whether oral or written) of Matthew and Luke (Q), and the evidence suggests that before any written record of it appeared it had developed variant forms, three of which appear independently in Matthew, Luke and John, while others appear in ancient versions and patristic citations.[51]

It lies close to the common source from which both the Synoptic and Johannine traditions derive. As Jeremias puts it:

> Matt. 11.27 is not a Johannine verse amidst the synoptic material, but rather one of those sayings from which Johannine theology developed. Without such points of departure within the synoptic tradition it would be an eternal puzzle how Johannine theology could have originated at all.[52]

[50] *John*, 75.
[51] *Historical Tradition*, 361.
[52] *The Central Message of the New Testament*, London and New York 1965, 25.

It is interesting to observe that the one word in the saying which is non-Johannine is the word 'reveal', despite the fact that the Johannine Christ is *par excellence* 'the Revealer', as Bultmann calls him throughout. Still closer in fact to the Johannine vocabulary is Mark 13.32 (despite its highly apocalyptic context): 'But about that day or that hour no one knows, not even the angels in heaven, nor even the Son; only the Father.'

But more significant are the sayings, common to John and the Synoptists, which use different vocabulary (so that literary dependence is inherently improbable) but which are clearly the same teaching going back to a single source. Dodd has analysed these common sayings in detail[53] and there is no need to repeat his demonstration that it is most unlikely that John has simply derived them from the Synoptists. Indeed the variants he thinks may at times point back to different attempts to render the *ipsissima verba* of the original Aramaic.

These are sayings such as:[54]

12.25 : 'He who loves his life loses it, and he who hates his life in this world will keep it for eternal life' (cf. Matt. 10.39; 16.25; Mark 8.35; Luke 9.24: 17.33).[55]

13.20 : 'Truly, truly, I say to you, he who receives any one whom I send receives me; and he who receives me receives him who sent me' (cf. Matt. 10.40; Mark 9.37; Luke 9.48; 10.16; John 20.21).

16.23f.: 'Truly, truly, I say to you, if you ask anything of the Father, he will give it to you in my name . . . ask, and you will receive' (cf. Matt. 7.7; 18.19f.; 21.22; Mark 11.24; Luke 11.9; John 14.13f.).

[53] *Historical Tradition*, 335–65, listing 14, together with two earlier on pp. 88–91 and 239f., as well as 18.11, 'Sheathe your sword. This is the cup my Father has given me; shall I not drink it?' both parts of which have parallels in the Synoptic tradition (Matt. 26.52; Mark 10.39; 14.36) (78, 68). Hunter, *According to John*, 91f., would uncover 'more than two dozen', as well as others that 'have undoubtedly a synoptic ring about them' but no parallels (e.g. 4.34, 48). Cf. also Higgins, *Historicity of the Fourth Gospel*, 67–72, who lists others.

[54] I have deliberately quoted them in the RSV in order to preserve the literalness for purposes of comparison.

[55] E. E. Lemcio has drawn my attention to the striking parallels between the whole of John 12.23–6 and Mark 8.34–8 (cf. the echoes of *διακονεῖν, διάκονος* also in Mark 10.43–5). The saying occurs in precisely the same setting though the occasion is quite different and there is no case for any literary connection. The same applies to the words that follow in John 12.27–30 with their echoes of the Gethsemane story in Mark 14.33–6 and pars. (cf. John 18.11).

20.23 : 'If you forgive the sins of any, they are forgiven; if you retain the sins of any, they are retained' (cf. Matt. 18.18).

There is also at the heart of the typically Johannine dialogue with Nicodemus the double saying of 3.3 and 5:

> Truly, truly, I say to you, unless one is born anew, he cannot see the kingdom of God.
> Truly, truly, I say to you, unless one is born of water and the Spirit, he cannot enter the kingdom of God.

This is closely paralleled in Matt. 18.3:

> Truly, I say to you, unless you turn and become like children, you will never enter the kingdom of heaven.

When Justin quotes this saying in the form 'Unless you are born again, you will never enter the kingdom of heaven' (*Apol.* 1.61. 4), it is rightly in my judgment taken as evidence that Justin knew the Fourth Gospel, for he goes on to echo it in commenting 'for that it is quite impossible for those that are once born to enter into their mother's womb is manifest to all.'[56] Yet, as Jeremias points out,[57] except for the influence of one word, ἀναγεννηθῆτε, which in fact is not Johannine so much as Petrine (I Peter 1.3, 23; John has γεννηθῇ ἄνωθεν), it is an exact reproduction of Matthew. In fact Justin is most probably quoting from memory; but the very fact that the saying comes out as a mixture of both styles shows that they cannot be as different as chalk and cheese.[58]

The same merger of 'Synoptic' and 'Johannine' vocabulary is to be found on a larger scale in the fragments of an unknown Gospel in Egerton Papyrus 2[59] which interestingly combines Synoptic-*type* material evidently derived from oral tradition with matter very much

[56] As Lightfoot points out (*Biblical Essays*, 87), he has just made a fairly clear allusion in the previous chapter (1.60) to the 'brazen serpent' in the same discourse (John 3.14f.), 'If you look on this image, and believe, you will be saved in him'.

[57] *Infant Baptism in the First Four Centuries*, ET London and Philadelphia 1960, 51f.

[58] Even more likely to show acquaintance with John is Hermas, *Sim.* 9.16.2: 'It was necessary for them to rise up through water, that they might be made alive, for otherwise they could not enter the kingdom of God', where δι᾽ ὕδατος, ἠδύνατο and εἰσελθεῖν εἰς τὴν βασιλείαν τοῦ θεοῦ (rather than τῶν οὐρανῶν) all suggest echoes of the Johannine version. Cf. *Sim.* 9.12.5: 'A man (ἄνθρωπος; cf. John 3.4) cannot enter into the kingdom of God except by the name of his Son that is beloved by him.' If, as I have argued (*Redating*, 319–22), the Shepherd of Hermas is to be dated before 85, then this represents much earlier knowledge of the Fourth Gospel than is usually quoted.

[59] H. Idris Bell and T. C. Skeat, edd., *Fragments of an Unknown Gospel and Other Early Christian Papyri*, London and New York 1935.

closer to the actual text of John and almost certainly dependent on it. While the *recto* and *verso* of the first fragment are described by Dodd as 'characteristically Johannine in language', his overall analysis yields the conclusion that 'the new text has in respect of vocabulary a much closer affinity with the Lukan writings than with the Gospels according to Matthew, Mark and John.'[60] That both of these statements can be true reveals again that the differences can be exaggerated.[61] We are not dealing with oil and water, and the early church was evidently happy in mixing the two,[62] as later were the Gnostics. Thus the Gospel of Thomas is primarily 'Synoptic' in tradition but with Johannine elements,[63] the Gospel of Truth 'Johannine' in its concepts (the Word, the Father, the Son, the Truth, the Name) though probably making no direct literary use of John.[64] But in 31–2 it mixes clear allusions to Synoptic material, 'He is the Shepherd who left the ninety and nine sheep which had not gone astray; he sought the one that had gone astray; he rejoiced when he found it' (Matt. 18.12–14 = Luke 15.4–6) with a conflation of Matthaean and Johannine themes: 'This Man himself laboured on the Sabbath for the sheep when it was discovered that it had fallen into a pit. He gave life to the sheep which He brought aloft from the pit, so that you may know in your hearts what the Sabbath is, whereon it is not permitted that redemption should rest' (Matt. 12.11; John 10.28; 5.17).[65]

One of the great differences between the teaching of Jesus in the

[60]'A New Gospel', reprinted in his *New Testament Studies*, Manchester 1953, New York 1954, 12–52; quotations, 25 and 19f.

[61]One might cite too *Did.* 10.2: 'We give thanks to thee, *holy Father*, for thy holy *name*, which thou didst make to *tabernacle* in our hearts.' The language is almost purely 'Johannine', yet there is no other demonstrable sign of the *Didache* being influenced by the Fourth Gospel (I would discount 9.4 as an echo of John 6.13). I would see it as a sign not of dependence on John but of the rootage of John's vocabulary in primitive Jewish Christianity.

[62]Cf. too the 'experiment' which Dodd tries (*Historical Tradition*, 404) of conflating the Synoptic and Johannine sayings about mission and harvest.

[63]See Brown's valuable study, 'The Gospel of Thomas and St John's Gospel', *NTS* 9, 1962–3, 155–77. He points to a number of sayings where the traditions are blended, even if somewhat superficially (e.g., 19, 43, 69a, 78, 79, 91, 100, 101). R. M. Wilson, *Studies in the Gospel of Thomas*, London 1960, 87f., regards the influence of the Gospel of John as remote.

[64]So F.-M. Braun, *Jean le Théologien* I, 112–33; G. Quispel, *L'Évangile de Jean*, Recherches Bibliques III, Louvain 1958, 197f. But cf. W. C. van Unnik, 'The "Gospel of Truth" and the New Testament' in F. L. Cross, ed., *The Jung Codex*, London 1955, 81–129, specif. 122; and Barrett 'The Theological Vocabulary of the Fourth Gospel and the Gospel of Truth', *Essays on John*, 50–64, who however shows how slight any deeper affinities are.

[65]Tr. van Unnik, 'Gospel of Truth', 96, 113.

Synoptists and John was held to be that the latter had no parables,[66] and since these were so central and distinctive to Jesus' message John clearly must be judged to belong to another, remoter world, in which symbolism and allegory had taken the place of the vivid likenesses which the historical Jesus drew from the immediacies of everyday life.[67] It is now being realized how superficial this judgment is. Dodd listed seven Johannine parables: the Grain of Wheat (12.24), the Pains of Childbirth (16.21), the Benighted Traveller (11.9f.), the Slave and Son (8.35), the Shepherd, the Thief and the Doorkeeper (10.1–5),[68] the Bridegroom and the Bridegroom's Friend (3.29), and the 'hidden parable' of the Apprenticed Son (5.19f.),[69] as well as the parabolic saying, or *Bildwort*, of the Night Wind (3.8).[70] Subsequently Hunter[71] brought the total up to thirteen, adding the Harvest (4.35–38), the Journeyer at Sunset (12.35f.) and, more tentatively, the Father's House (14.21f.), the Vine (15.1f.), and the acted parable of the footwashing (13.1–15).[72] For, as he rightly reminds us, the Hebrew *mashal* and Aramaic *matla*, which lie behind the Greek both of the Synoptists' παραβολή and of John's παροιμία (10.6)[73] apply to far more than stories – for example, to the picturesque saying, 'Nothing that goes into a man from the outside can defile him', or the proverb, 'Physician, heal yourself', both of which are called 'parables' in Mark 7.15, 17 and Luke 4.23.[74]

[66]'Parables are altogether absent' (Schmithals in the Introduction to Bultmann, *John*, 4).

[67]Cf. E. Renan, *The Life of Jesus*, ET Everyman's Library, 1927, 15; G. H. C. Macgregor, *The Gospel of John*, London 1928, xvii.

[68]He follows me in regarding this as a fusion of two parables.

[69]'Une parabole cachée dans le quatrième Évangile', *Revue d'Histoire et de Philosophie Religieuses* 42, 1962, 107–15; ET, 'A Hidden Parable in the Fourth Gospel' in his *More New Testament Studies*, Manchester and Grand Rapids, Mich. 1968, 30–40. In it he observes, 39: 'It is a significant detail that the apprentice *watches* his father at work. . . . This detail is not made use of in the theological exposition which follows; it is not a feature dictated by the requirements of the deeper meaning which is to be conveyed. It is integral to the scene as realistically conceived. It is precisely at this point that the difference between the parable and the allegory reveals itself most clearly.'

[70]*Historical Tradition*, 366–87.

[71]*According to John*, 78–89.

[72]This again is a highly datable piece of teaching, to the same context as Luke 22.24–27. I have not discussed it here because I have written on it in 'The Significance of the Footwashing', *Twelve More NTS*, 77–80.

[73]For the two in synonymous parallelism, cf. Ecclus. 47.17 (LXX). Cf. also the ἐν παροιμίαις of John 16.25–29 with the ἐν παραβολαῖς of Mark 4.11, in both cases meaning probably 'in riddles'.

[74]Cf. T. W. Manson, *The Teaching of Jesus*, 57–81; Gerhardsson, *Origins of the Gospel Traditions*, 69–72. Bultmann, *John*, 713, makes the interesting suggestion that

To this list I should wish to add the maxim 'A servant is not greater than his master nor an agent than the one that sent him' (13.16; cf. 15.20). The first half of this double analogy John shares with Matthew (10.24f.), who combines it with that of the similar relation between pupil and teacher, found (by itself) in Luke 6.40. John alone has the image of the agent, which, as we shall see, serves as an important model for his christology.[75]

I should also now like to expand what I said in 'The Parable of the Shepherd (John 10.1–5)', where I had already detected the fusion of two parables.[76] I believe that John 10 contains three parables to do with sheep, for only one of which is the shepherd the central figure:

1. Verses 1–3a, focusing on the door-keeper (as in the parable of Mark 13.34), which is concerned with the sheep-stealer coming by night (cf. Matt. 24.43; I Thess. 5.1) when the sheep are herded in the croft.

2. Verses 3b–5, where the shepherd leads his sheep out to pasture in the morning

3. Verses 12f., where the central figure is the hired man (the word used in Mark 1.20 of Zebedee's servants in contrast with his sons) confronted by the wolf (cf. Matt. 10.16 = Luke 10.3; Acts 20.29) scattering and ravaging the flock by day (cf. the 'sees' of v. 12). His reaction is compared with that of the shepherd to whom the sheep are ἴδια – not literally his own, but the family's. For the shepherd is evidently the sheep-owner's son, since the sheep are 'given' into his charge (v. 29) and he is acting simply on his father's instructions (v. 18). The model of the true shepherd is David (cf. Ezek. 34.23), the farmer's son. The implicit contrast in this parable (as explicitly in that of John 8.35; cf. 15.15) is between the status and behaviour of servant and son.[77]

All these I believe are genuine and vivid scenes from Palestinian life which are built by the evangelist into the allegory.[78] Indeed we may

---

behind the words of 21.18 lies a proverb about the young man being able to dress himself and go where his fancy takes him while the old man has to feel for support and for someone to lead him. He may be right, but the evangelist clearly interprets the stretching out of the hands to refer to crucifixion (21.19).

[75]See below, ch. VIII, pp. 350, 371f.

[76]*Twelve NTS*, 67–75. I will not repeat the many indications that 'we have here material in a state which the most searching tests suggest is early and authentic' (75).

[77]Cf. also the parable of Mark 12.1–12, which I have suggested poses the same challenge to the Jewish leadership (ibid., 71f.).

[78]Cf. my analysis of Matthew's construction in 'The "Parable" of the Sheep and the Goats', *Twelve NTS*, 76–93.

surmise that they reflect the winter conditions when, according to v. 22, the teaching was first given. The shepherd and his sheep are in at night, in contrast with Luke 2.8 (which as has been pointed out scarcely fits the traditional dating of Christmas!). The wolf is more likely to venture down by day to attack the flock when food is scarce; and in Galilee at any rate sheep-farming was predominantly a winter activity. 'In summer I caught fish, in winter I kept sheep' (Test. Zeb. 6.8).

There is also the simile used by the evangelist in 1.14 – though again derived I believe from Jesus' own parabolic use of the father-son relationship[79] – of the only son who, as we should say, is the spitting image of his father.[80] For there are no articles in the Greek (δόξαν ὡς μονογενοῦς παρὰ πατρός) and δόξα is here I believe the equivalent of εἰκών, and means reflection, as regularly in late Judaism[81] and elsewhere in the New Testament, especially I Cor. 11.7: 'Man is the image and glory of God; but the woman is the glory of man.'[82] For the sense but not the language of the simile one could cite Ecclus. 30.4, where it is said of a son, 'When the father dies it is as if he were still alive, for he has left a copy of himself (ὅμοιον γὰρ αὐτῷ κατέλιπε) behind him.' John's meaning is succinctly represented in Hugh Montefiore's comment on Heb. 1.3, where the context is also full of this language: 'As a son may be said to reflect his father's character, so the Son is the refulgence of his Father's glory, and the exact representation of God's being.'[83]

Instead of seeking to demonstrate again that the parables ascribed to Jesus in John reflect the same mind as in the other Gospels (though in this Dodd was preoccupied with distinguishing Johannine colouring from supposedly non-Johannine tradition), it may be more useful to

[79]Cf. further below ch. VIII, pp. 373–6.

[80]In a letter to me shortly before he died Dodd agreed that this was the meaning of John 1.14.

[81]Cf. L. H. Brockington, 'The Septuagintal Background to the New Testament use of δόξα' in D. E. Nineham, ed., *Studies in the Gospels*, 7f.; J. Jervell, *Imago Dei*, FRLANT 76, Göttingen 1960, especially 17f.; 299f.; 326f., who takes this to be the meaning in John 1.14 but does not notice it as a simile; and the extensive literature cited by R. P. Martin, *Carmen Christi: Philippians 2.5–11 in Recent Interpretation in the Setting of Early Christian Worship*, Cambridge and New York 1967, 102–19.

[82]Cf. also II Cor. 3.18, 'We all reflect as in a mirror the glory of the Lord; thus we are transfigured into his image, from glory to glory' and 8.23 (NEB margin), 'They are delegates of our congregations: they reflect Christ (δόξα Χριστοῦ).' See further my 'Use of the Fourth Gospel for Christology Today', *Twelve More NTS*, 147f.

[83]*The Epistle to the Hebrews* (Black's New Testament Commentaries), London 1964, ad loc.

trace the function which they fulfil in John compared with the Synoptists. For it provides a clue to his handling also of the non-parabolic teaching and to the perspective in which everything in this Gospel is viewed and recast.

3. The Process of Transposition

The Synoptic Gospels are controlled by the method, which was assuredly Jesus' method, of *para-bolē*, or throwing alongside, images, similes, paradoxes, situations from life – and saying the kingdom of God is 'like' or 'as if' this, that or the other. They demand lateral thinking or action, often depending on shock-effect, like the Zen *koan*. Everyone has to take away his own truth, to see where the cap fits. It is the same with the 'shocking' injunctions of the Sermon on the Mount. As Dodd said,[84] they are not general rules of conduct but more like parables of the moral life, disclosing the kind of thing that at any moment the claims of the kingdom or of love may require of one. Their function is to jerk into recognition or action, often by use of the exaggerated or the unexpected, not supplying an answer so much as turning the question (as in Luke 10.29, 36), or asking another: 'What do you think?' (Matt. 17.25; 18.12; 21.28; 22.17; Luke 10.36).

In John the invitation is to the journey inwards rather than sideways, to believe into (πιστεύειν εἰς), to penetrate behind and beyond the visible and the superficial. The challenge is to enter at depth into the significance of Jesus' words and works and person, which are seen as 'signs', pointers to the interior. Their meaning is to be grasped not so much by putting two situations side by side as by challenging the reader to a different level of seeing and hearing and understanding, which the Spirit alone can disclose. Hence the deliberate *doubles entendres* of the Gospel, using the same word at different levels or with different nuances.

In the Synoptists, especially in Matthew, the typical term of comparison is ὅμοιος, ὁμοιόω. The kingdom of heaven is like or to be likened to a vineyard and its owner, a flock and its shepherd, etc. In John ὅμοιος and ὁμοιόω never occur in a theological context. Rather, Jesus says, 'I *am* the true vine, the good shepherd.'[85] He pushes beyond

[84]*Gospel and Law*, Cambridge 1951.

[85]Cf. Headlam, *The Fourth Gospel as History*, 78. Of the Johannine instances of 'I am' he writes, 'They state explicitly what is implicit in words and parables as quoted in other Gospels:

Jesus said: "Follow me" which is interpreted, "I am the Way."

the simile to the symbol, through the parable to the metaphor or allegory, from 'like a son to his father' (1.14), to the relationship of the Son to the Father (in 1.18). Of course this process is also true of the Synoptists – parable becomes allegory, a son the Son, and so on – and we shall return to it when examining the christology of the Gospel. It is a matter of degree, of relative insight. But John is allowing, indeed inviting, the reader to catch overtones and harmonics only subsequently to be heard in and through the Spirit. It is as if Jesus is saying through this Gospel, in a deep sense, 'Do you hear me?' – and 'hearing his voice' in that sense is the clue to discipleship (10.27), distinguishing those who are 'his own', or in Markan terms 'those within'. For there is nothing radically different or new here. It is the same distinction as in the Synoptists between seeing and not seeing, hearing and not hearing, and the same quotation from Isa. 6.9f. is used in John 12.40 as in Matt. 13.14f., Mark 4.12 and Acts 28.26f. At this point John stands in the mainstream of early Christian interpretation. Yet there is a subtle difference. His Jesus is not just demanding that his would-be followers should have 'cars to hear'. His Jesus is as he *has been* 'heard', as he has been understood in the Spirit. The reader is intended to be conscious throughout of a 'second language', of what he is *really* saying at depth. Hence there is a deliberate process of transposition, of arrangement in the musical sensc, going on, to permit new things to be heard in the old themes. We are listening to interpretation by a great composer, with skilful development and variations. The style is Johannine, much as the style of a Beethoven or a Mozart or a Brahms. Yet John is not simply devising new melodies of his own. In the Spirit he is taking the things of Jesus and showing them to us, not speaking 'of himself'. He is controlled by the historical Jesus.

What he is giving us is of course a portrait, not a photograph; yet there is a real sitter. He is taking up, not making up; seeing stars for

---

Jesus said: "Enter ye in at the strait gate"; "I am the door."
Jesus said: "I have compassion on the multitude as sheep without a shepherd;" "I am the good Shepherd."
Jesus said: "Ye shall receive in the world to come eternal life;" "I am the resurrection and the Life."'

He could have added: 'This is my body'; 'I am the bread of life.' Cf. too A. Feuillet, 'Les *Ego Eimi* christologiques du quatrième Évangile', *RSR* 54, 1966, 1–22, 213–40, (233), who points out also that Matt. 7.13f. speaks of 'the gate' and 'the way' that leads to 'life', all of which become in John predicates for Jesus; while 'the seed' of the kingdom of God sown in the ground in Mark 4.26–32 becomes in John 12.23f. the grain of wheat that symbolizes the death and glorification of the Son of Man.

points, not putting up new stars. That there is 'development' in John cannot be doubted: there is in all the Gospels. But it is not enough, with J. D. G. Dunn,[86] to point to the difference and distance. It is a question, here as elsewhere, of whether his development, his witness, is 'true', and that not in terms so much of ἀκρίβεια, accuracy, which is Luke's aim,[87] as of ἀλήθεια, verity. He is concerned with the relation of all of which he speaks to the ἀρχή, the root and ground, rather than to trace its αἰτία, or cause; with fidelity of transposition rather than simply of transmission.

This difference of perspective controls all that he does and affects what we may call the 'laws of transformation' which determine his presentation of the teaching of Jesus in comparison with that of the Synoptists.

In Mark the dominant contrast in Jesus' teaching ministry is between the crowds and those 'in the house'. The Gospel is written for those within, yet always in relation to those without. In the case of John too the Gospel is written for 'his own', so that through them the others may come to faith. Yet the primary focus is upon how this inner group stands not to the edges but to the centre, not to the kingdom they are to inherit and rule (Luke 12.32; 22.29f.), but the king,[88] the αὐτοβασιλεία as Origen was to call him. The overriding issue is the relationship of 'the sons of the kingdom' not to the many from east and west (Matt. 8.11f.) but to the Son; of the Shepherd not to the lost scattered sheep (though they *will* be gathered in: John 10.16) but to his own sheep, who are not to be sent into the midst of wolves (Matt. 10.16 = Luke 10.3) so much as guarded from the wolf (John 10.12). It is not, again, the relationship of the vineyard to others (Mark 12.9 and pars.) but of the vine to the branches (John 15.1–6) that concerns John. In the Synoptists the manifestation will be to the world (Matt. 24.30, etc.) and the disciples when they have done all are still unprofitable servants (Luke 17.10); in John the manifestation is to be to the disciples (14.22), who are called not servants but friends (15.14f.); and the place of intimacy and disclosure is not ἐν τῇ οἰκίᾳ (Mark 9.33; 10.10; etc.) but ἐν τῷ κόλπῳ (13.23; cf. 1.18). The promise of Jesus is not 'I shall be with you' (in the world) (Matt. 28.20) but 'You shall be with me' (in

[86]*Christology in the Making*, 29–32. He is discussing at this point the self-consciousness of Jesus, and to the content of this we shall return in the next chapter.

[87]Luke 1.3. There are five further occurrences of ἀκριβῶς in Acts, and only one other in the Gospels (Matt. 2.8).

[88]*Βασιλεύς*, king, is used of Jesus in John 15 times, compared with 8 in Matthew, 6 in Mark and 5 in Luke.

the Father) (14.3; 17.21–3), and the 'going' is not of the apostles to the ends of the earth (Acts 1.8) but of the Apostle, the One sent (9.7; 10.36; etc.), to the Father (14.12, 28; 16.5; etc.) and of his taking them to him (14.3). Here the most obvious contrast is with Luke, who uses 'going' 50 times and 'abiding' 7 times, while John uses 'going' 13 times (and 8 of these of Jesus going to the Father, or in misunderstanding) and 'abiding' 41 times. And yet in both each relationship presupposes the other; John insists as strongly as any that as the Father has sent Jesus into the world, so he sends his disciples (13.20; 20.21; etc.), that the purpose of abiding is to bear fruit (15.4–8), and that the ultimate point of it all is that the world may believe through them (17.20f.) and that all men shall be drawn to him (12.32). It is a difference of emphasis, not an antithesis. Yet it governs the selection and slant of the material, of what is heard and how it is heard.

This transposition affects the perspective in which the teaching of Jesus is presented throughout the Gospel and Epistles of John. It can easily be misunderstood, so that it appears to be set at several removes from source, with little claim to take us back to the original or to interpret his own mind. This misunderstanding comes out in two charges which in particular have been laid against the distinctive perspective of the Johannine writings. The first is the one-sided individualistic twist which the Gospel seems to give to the message of Jesus, resulting in its esoteric appeal to Gnostics of all ages; and the second is the introspective exclusivism, especially of the Epistles, that appears to narrow down the universal ethic of Jesus to the in-group of believers.

4. *The Charge of Individualism*[89]

This first is I believe an understandable, but mistaken, inference from the distinctive purpose with which the Gospel is written. The Gospel of Mark is written to present 'the gospel of Jesus Christ, the Son of God' (1.1). The purpose of John's is defined in remarkably similar terms: 'that you may believe that Jesus is the Christ, the Son of God'. But it

[89]Cf. C. F. D. Moule, 'The Individualism of the Fourth Gospel', *NovT* 5, 1962, 171–90, reprinted in his *Essays in New Testament Interpretation*, Cambridge 1982, 91–109; and *The Birth of the New Testament*, ³London 1981, San Francisco 1982, 136, where he describes the message of the Gospel as 'extremely individualistic'. See also E. Schweizer, 'The Concept of the Church in the Gospel and Epistles of St John' in A. J. B. Higgins, ed., *New Testament Essays*, 230–45; and, to the contrary, R. Schnackenburg, *The Moral Teaching of the Early Church*, ET London and New York 1965, 330f.

goes on significantly to add: 'and that believing you may have life in his name' (20.31). His particular care is the *appropriation* of the Christ, the *entering into* the life that was the light of men. It is not so much individualizing as existentializing and personalizing. This comes out not only in the replacement of the language of the kingdom by that of the king, but in the replacement of 'the kingdom of God' by 'life' or 'eternal life'. This is a phrase which is not part of a process of Hellenization but just as firmly rooted in Judaism (Dan. 12.2; Ps. Sol. 3.16; 1QS 4.7). And again it is not something that John has simply put onto the lips of Jesus. 'Entering into the kingdom' and 'entering into life' stand as parallels in Mark 9.43–7, and Matthew (18.9) can at this point substitute 'life' for Mark's 'kingdom of God'. Similarly in Mark 10.17–30 and pars. 'inheriting' or 'receiving' 'eternal life' alternates with 'entering into the kingdom of God' (or 'life'); while in Luke 10.28 'Do this and you shall *live*' replaces Mark's 'You are not far from the kingdom of God' (12.34). Conversely in John his much rarer 'seeing the kingdom of God' (3.3; cf. Mark 9.1) and 'entering the kingdom of God' are clearly the same as 'having eternal life' (3.15f., 36) and 'seeing life' (3.36).[90] Similarly in one of Paul's infrequent uses of 'the kingdom of God' he internalizes it, as the rabbis did, to mean 'living by God's rule', which for him means not observing food-laws but 'justice, peace and joy, inspired by the Holy Spirit' (Rom. 14.17). Again, being 'translated into the kingdom of his Son' (Col. 1.13) is evidently the equivalent of John's 'crossing from death to life' (John 5.24; I John

[90]There is a comparable equivalence between language of the 'kingdom' of God and 'glory'. In the Synoptists the mighty works of Jesus are the signs of the kingdom of God in action (e.g., Matt. 12.28 = Luke 11.20). In John the works of Jesus are the 'signs' that manifest the 'glory' of the Father in the Son (2.11; 11.4, 40). Yet this transposition is again not peculiar to John but part of a much older Jewish parallelism. In Matt. 16.27f. the Son of Man coming in the glory of his Father is followed in the next verse by the Son of Man coming in his kingdom. In Mark 10.37 sitting at the right hand and the left 'in your glory' is paralleled in Matt. 20.21 by 'in your kingdom'. In Luke Jesus' entering upon his kingdom (23.42) is the same as entering upon his glory (24.26), while the promise of 'seeing the kingdom of God' (9.27) is apparently reflected in anticipation five verses later by the fact that the disciples 'saw his glory' (9.32), the very phrase which John makes his own (1.14; 11.40; 12.41; 17.24). John here as elsewhere is giving the inner spiritual content of the language of traditional eschatology (cf. the combination 'throne of glory' in Matt. 25.31). Meeks makes the interesting observation ('Man from Heaven', 52 n. 33) that in Wisd. 10.10 Jacob's dream is interpreted in terms of Wisdom 'showing him the kingdom of God (*βασιλείαν θεοῦ* – anarthrous) and giving him knowledge of holy things', thus already linking such revelations with the heavenly journeys of Jewish apocalyptic mysticism. Cf. John 1.51, this time in terms of seeing the Son of Man.

3.14). The kingdom is life with God at its centre, living at the level of the things that are not seen but 'eternal' (II Cor. 4.18). The translation of this into 'eternal life' is simply taken further in John than in the rest of the New Testament. There is no need to suppose that John has done something peculiar, or that he has distorted rather than deepened or internalized.

Nor can he credibly be seen as gnosticizing the teaching of Jesus into an individualized, esoteric, eclectic, unhistorical or purely 'spiritual' life-style. In fact John's relation to Gnosticism (though as an 'ism', as a system of salvation or world-view, I believe it to be an anachronism in the first century) is subtle. There is no doubt that his Gospel was seized on by the Gnostics, and has been ever since by gnosticizers ancient and modern, Eastern and Western, as 'their' Gospel. Moreover he seems to have been well aware of this danger, of being so near and yet so far, in the words that he apparently quite consciously avoids. His approach in this regard is notably different from Paul's. Paul, like Clement of Alexandria later, was evidently concerned to present Christ as the true wisdom and Christianity as the true *gnosis*. He deliberately takes the gnosticizers' words and turns them against themselves, especially in I Corinthians and Colossians. Among these would appear to be πίστις, σοφία, γνῶσις, φύσις, πνευματικός, μυστήριον, ἀποκάλυψις, πλήρωμα, and εἰκών. It cannot simply be an accident that John has none of these words (not even πίστις!), except on one occasion (in 1.16) πλήρωμα in a purely non-technical sense. Of course he has the *verbs* for believing and knowing *passim*, though, as I said earlier, he surprisingly avoids even the verb 'to reveal', except once in quoting from Isa. 53.1, 'to whom has the arm of the Lord been revealed?' (12.38). But he seems to wish to give his opponents no handle by using the nouns.[91]

When, despite this, he is appropriated by the 'advanced' (II John 9), gnosticizing teachers attacked in the Epistles,[92] he reacts in horror. If that is what you think I meant, he says, then this is very Antichrist (I John 2.22; 4.3; II John 7) – if you think you can negate the importance

[91]Sidebottom, *The Christ of the Fourth Gospel*, 65, 105f., makes the valid point that John's use of λόγος, in the absence of all the other terms, suggests that for him it did not have Gnostic associations but was 'safe'.

[92]It is a measure of how subjective judgments on the Johannine literature have been that Schwartz in his classic article 'Aporien im vierten Evangelium' (*Nachrichten der Göttinger Gesellschaft der Wissenschaften* 1907, 342–72; 1908, 115–88, 487–560) denied any anti-gnostic tendency in the Epistles in contrast with the Gospel. Most have concluded the exact opposite. He also thought that the view that Jesus was the Paschal Lamb was the only trait that could with certainty be traced to the Johannine narrative of

of Christ come in the flesh (I John 4.2f.; II John 7; cf. the stress in I John 1.1f. and John 1.14), or have the Father without the Son in an unmediated God-mysticism (I John 2.22f.; 5.11f.; II John 9),[93] or deny the reality of sin and therefore the necessity for Christ's sacrificial and atoning death (I John 1.5–10; 2.1f.; 3.4–9; 4.10; 5.6–8, 18), or ignore the material needs of your brother (I John 3.17; 4.20f.), or say that everything 'spiritual' is as such good (I John 4.1–3). These errors could easily be derived from the Johannine teaching, as Brown demonstrates,[94] once a 'gnostic' metaphysical dualism between spirit and matter is substituted for the moral and eschatological dualism[95] which John shares with the men of Qumran, with whose language there are no closer parallels than in I John.[96] Both of them stood in what Bo Reicke well designated[97] the 'pre-gnostic' tradition, but both would have been equally horrified to have been called 'gnostic'. In fact when John does, apparently, confront his opponents' teaching full on he insists that the 'anointing' (I John 2.20, 27), the 'seed' (3.9) and the 'understanding' (5.20) which Christians have is a knowledge shared by *all* (2.20; cf. I Cor. 8.1, 'we all have knowledge', though Paul significantly alone uses the noun).[98] It is nothing esoteric or individualistic. Moreover, his sense of community, of *κοινωνία* (cf. especially I John 1.3, 6f.), is stronger than that of any other New Testament writer,

---

the crucifixion; the rest was the work of interpolators! Cf. Stanton, *Gospels as Historical Documents* III, 40f.

[93] I am inclined to think that the clause 'and Jesus Christ whom thou hast sent' in John 17.3, which is a crude, and for John unique, anachronism on the lips of Jesus and, with 1.17 in the Prologue, the only occurrence in the Gospel of 'Christ' as a proper name (it is normative in the Epistles), represents an addition from the time of the writing of the Epistles and Prologue to guard against the inference which without it had been drawn, that eternal life *is* simply direct knowledge of the Father, the one true God. On the contrary, he insists, 'This is eternal life': dwelling in the Son and *thus* also in the Father (I John 2.24f.; 5.20). Westcott makes the observation that 'it is most worthy of notice that no use is made in the Epistle of the language of the discourses in John 3 and 6' (*John* I, clxxviii). This is particularly interesting since the supposedly anti-docetic sacramentalism of 6.52–58 is often attributed to editorial addition.

[94] *Community*, 109–44; *Epistles*, 71–86.

[95] Hence the need for him also to re-emphasize the moral implications of eschatology (I John 2.18f.; 2.28–3.3; 4.17), which many in modern as well as ancient times have deemed to be merely residual in the Fourth Gospel.

[96] Cf. especially 1QS 3.13–4.26 and M.-É. Boismard, 'The First Epistle of John and the Writings of Qumran' in J. H. Charlesworth, ed., *John and Qumran*, 156–65.

[97] 'Traces of Gnosticism in the Dead Sea Scrolls?', *NTS* 1, 1954–5, 137–41.

[98] Bultmann, *Johannine Epistles*, 37, simply says it is 'curious' that John here does not use *γνῶσις*; but then he believes that the Johannine literature expressed the Christian faith 'in the conceptual apparatus of Gnostic thought' (101), which it clearly does not.

except again Paul. I should therefore prefer to talk of the personalism rather than the individualism of John.

5. *The Charge of Introversion*

But what of the second accusation commonly levelled against John that this very stress on Christian fellowship leads him to an introverted and exclusivist ethic; that whereas Jesus said 'Love your enemies', the Johannine community restricted this love to love of one's fellow Christians?

This case was argued with particular cogency some years ago by Hugh Montefiore in an article in *Novum Testamentum*, 'Thou Shalt Love thy Neighbour as Thyself'.[99] In it he specifically challenges the contention of my 'New Look on the Fourth Gospel',[100] that John must be regarded as a serious witness not only to the Christ of faith but to the Jesus of history. For, he concludes, 'Concerning "the central and governing idea of Christianity" the Fourth Evangelist gives a distorted account of Jesus' teaching.' Here at any rate he believes the evidence to show that John is simply 'the end-term of theological development in first-century Christianity', and he adds: 'While it is necessary for scholars critically to examine their presuppositions, it is equally necessary for them to cut their suits according to their cloth.'[101]

His central thesis is that the Jesus of the Synoptic Gospels preached love of the loveless and enemies, whereas the Jesus of John teaches only love of friends and fellow-Christians, and this represents a disastrous diminution of his original message. This narrowing down and introversion is reflected also, he contends, in the Epistles generally compared with the Synoptic Gospels; but John has gone further down that road than any.

Now there is no disputing that there is a real difference of emphasis, though I shall argue again that it can be exaggerated. The real question is how it is to be interpreted. Is it a distortion, with the implication that the larger view has simply been denied and replaced by the narrower,

[99]*NovT* 5, 1962, 157–70. A similar line has been adopted by many others; e.g., C. R. Bowen, 'Love in the Fourth Gospel', *JR* 13, 1933, 39–49; C. H. Ratschow, 'Agape, Nächstenliebe und Bruderliebe', *ZST* 21, 1950, 162–82 (especially 171–6); J. Knox, *The Ethic of Jesus in the Teaching of the Church*, Nashville 1961, 95f.; E. Käsemann, *The Testament of Jesus*, 61–5; H.-D. Wendland, *Ethik des Neuen Testaments*, Göttingen 1970, 112, 115; J. L. Houlden, *Ethics and the New Testament*, London and Oxford 1973; ²London 1975, 35–41; and Brown, *Community*, 131–5.

[100]Reprinted in *Twelve NTS*, 94–106.

[101]'Love thy Neighbour', 167f.

with the result that the historical Jesus, truly reflected in the Synoptic Gospels, has been overlaid in the Epistles and lost to sight in John?

Before turning to the specifically Johannine evidence it is proper to set it in the wider context in which Montefiore rightly places it. For we must recognize and allow for the shift of perspective represented by the concerns of the Epistles. These are written to Christians and are primarily concerned with the life of the church. If we wish to know what Paul preached to Jewish or pagan audiences, they afford us only very indirect evidence. Yet this preaching is clearly presupposed and assumed rather than gone back on in his letters. And what goes for the *kerygma* applies to the *didache*. The primary concern of the Epistles is with fostering or correcting attitudes within the body of Christ. Yet they take for granted what was in the first instance presented to converts as the distinctively Christian rather than Jewish or pagan ethic. Moreover, for all that the foreground is occupied by the quality of life within the fellowship of believers, the background of their witness in and to the world is never lost sight of.

A crucial point of interpretation turns on how foreground and background are seen to be related. Montefiore quotes a number of texts which mention both and says:

> Paul even instructs his readers to show love to non-Christians, but only as it were as an overflow: a Christian's first duty is to love his fellow-Christians. He prays on behalf of the Thessalonians that the Lord may 'make your love mount and overflow towards one another and towards all' (I Thess. 3.12). He instructs them 'always to aim at doing the best you can for each other and for all men' (I Thess. 5.15). He exhorts his Galatian readers: 'As opportunity offers, let us work for the good of all, especially members of the household of the faith' (Gal. 6.10).

And from that he draws the conclusion that 'Paul did not regard it as a Christian duty to go out of his way to love a non-Christian.'[102]

But is this really fair? Would Paul have accepted this construction placed upon his words? Would it not be just as true to say that the primacy he gives to attitudes within the church (e.g., the emphasis he lays on avoiding strife) is because unless the love commandment is seen to be operative there nothing that Christians do or say to their pagan neighbours will carry any credibility? Unless it can genuinely be said, in the words reported by Tertullian,[103] 'See how they love one another',

[102]Ibid., 162.
[103]*Apol.* 39.7.

and unless they show themselves to be 'guileless and above reproach, faultless children of God in a warped and crooked generation' (Phil. 2.15), then they will never by their good conduct be able to 'put ignorance and stupidity to silence' (I Peter 2.15). Consequently, says Peter, 'Let all your behaviour be such as even pagans can recognize as good' (I Peter 2.12), or Paul, 'Let your aims be such as all men count honourable' (Rom. 12.17; cf. also 14.18; Phil. 4.5). This last injunction comes from the major passage in which Paul relates the love-command both to life within the body of Christ and to the attitudes of Christians towards the institutions of the world (Rom. 12 and 13). For while 'love for our brotherhood' (12.10) is the precondition of all else, it does not begin to exhaust Christian love: 'Discharge your obligations to all men. . . . Leave no claim outstanding against you, except that of mutual love. He who loves his neighbour has satisfied every claim of the law. . . . Love cannot wrong a neighbour; therefore the whole law is summed up in love' (13.7–10). The context in which that is set makes it quite clear that Paul is not restricting love of neighbour to love of fellow-Christians or regarding love for the non-Christian as a weak left-over. Far from confining love to friends, he specifically echoes Jesus' words in the Synoptic tradition (Matt. 5.44; Luke 6.28): 'Call down blessings on your persecutors – blessings not curses' (12.14),[104] and he backs them with the text from Proverbs (25.21f.): 'If your enemy is hungry, feed him; if he is thirsty, give him a drink; by doing this you will heap live coals on his head' (12.20). Again it is surely unfair to comment that while 'Jesus taught that we should help the hungry and the thirsty out of compassion' Paul taught it simply to pile on compunction.[105] For this is not presented as the *motive* for love of the enemy. In the context he is counselling *against* retribution: 'Never pay back evil for evil.' Rather, *this* is the way to heap live coals on his head: 'use good to defeat evil' (12.17–21; cf. I Peter 3.9). There is little here to suggest that Paul thought the duty to love one's neighbour 'is restricted to fellow-members of the Christian community' and 'gave no instructions . . . about loving those outside the Church'.[106]

It is against this background that one must turn to the Johannine evidence. For the context of the Johannine Epistles is again important

[104]Cf. V. P. Furnish, *The Love Command in the New Testament*, Nashville 1972, London 1973, 106: 'This is perhaps the earliest version of Jesus' commandment to love one's enemies.'

[105]'Love thy Neighbour', 161.

[106]Ibid.

to their interpretation. They are written to counter self-consuming divisions within the Christian fellowship. Consequently this more than ever is the primary point of reference of the teaching given. Yet because the love-command is focused on the brotherhood this does not mean that it is restricted to it.[107] I John regularly uses the term ἀδελφός, brother, and in the setting the primary *application* of it is evidently to believers. Yet it is begging the question simply to translate it, as Monetefiore does (departing at this point from his usual following of the NEB), 'fellow-Christian'. For that is not the only, or often even the primary, aspect in question. For instance, in the argument of I John 4.20, 'If a man says, "I love God", while hating his brother, he is a liar. If he does not love the brother whom he has seen, it cannot be that he loves God whom he has not seen', the contrast is clearly between the visibility of the human object of love and the invisibility of the divine. The point is that the neighbour is seen; whether or not he is a believer is irrelevant. Again, in I John 3.16f., 'It is by this that we know what love is: that Christ laid down his life for us. And we in turn are bound to lay down our lives for our brothers. But if a man has enough to live on, and yet when he sees his brother in need shuts up his heart against him, how can it be said that the divine love dwells in him?', it is improper to say that the brother here *means* 'fellow-Christian' – however often in John it may *refer to* him. For it is his sheer humanity that is at issue. 'Brother' here simply means fellow-man, as frequently in the Old Testament (e.g., in Gen. 9.5, where the NEB properly renders 'from a man will I require satisfaction for the death of his fellow-man') and indeed in the New Testament (e.g., Matt. 5.22–24; 18.15, 21, 35). When John says: 'This command comes to us from Christ himself: that he who loves God must also love his brother' (I John 4.21), he is evidently referring to Jesus' remembered command[108] to love both God and one's neighbour (ὁ πλησίον), a term he never uses. That both 'neighbour' and 'brother' were interpreted as 'fellow-Israelite'[109] or as 'fellow

[107]Cf. R. F. Collins, '"A New Commandment I give to you, that you love one another" (John 13.34)' *Laval Théologique et Philosophique* 35, 1979, 235–61, who says of the Johannine formulation: 'It is sectarian in the sense that it is a reflection on the Johannine church against a dualistic background, but it is not sectarian if that means that hatred for those outside of the brotherhood is the necessary concomitant of those who belong to the brotherhood' (259).

[108]Cf. Furnish, *Love Command*, 151: 'This is the only New Testament passage outside the Synoptic Gospels where we can be fairly sure of a direct reference to the Great Commandment with equal stress on each of its parts.'

[109]For the extensive literature, cf. Furnish, *Love Command*, 65; also J. Piper, '*Love your Enemies': Jesus' Love Command in the Synoptic Gospels and in the Early*

Christian' does not mean that this is what either word signifies.

In fact by careful exegesis Schnackenburg,[110] who is followed by Furnish,[111] demonstrates that in context 'brother' here must mean 'fellow-man'. For in I John 2.9–11 the man who loves his brother is contrasted with the gnosticizer who says 'I am in the light' but hates his brother – clearly not a fellow-Christian (or even a fellow-Gnostic) but his fellow-man. Similarly, in 3.13f., John says '*we* love our brothers', as opposed to those who hate, not each other, but us. 'If he is reproaching the "world" for its hatred towards Christians, it would be unintelligible of him to limit the Christian's love to the circle of the community of the Church.'[112] Again in 4.20, in attacking the person who says 'I love God' but hates his brother, he evidently has in mind the same opponent as in 2.9–11:[113] he cannot love the human being in front of his very eyes. 'Consequently', says Furnish, 'when the double commandment of the Synoptic tradition is invoked in verse 21, but using the word "brother" instead of "neighbour", the conclusion to be drawn is not that this writer is thereby limiting love's scope. The more accurate conclusion is that, for this writer, the term "brother" can be used as a synonym for "neighbour".'[114]

It is true that there is nothing in the Johannine Epistles about loving one's enemy, but there is nothing about hating him either, as in the otherwise closely parallel dualism of Qumran, where the members of the community are told to 'love all the sons of light each according to his lot among the council of God, but hate all the sons of darkness, each according to his guilt in the vengeance of God' (1QS 1.9f.; cf. 2.7f.; 9.21f.,[115] though contrast 5.24–6; 10.18; 11.1). The furthest that John goes is to say: 'If anyone comes to you who does not bring this doctrine, do not welcome him into your house or give him a greeting; for anyone who gives him a greeting is an accomplice in his wicked deeds' (II John 10f.). But this is fully in line with the injunctions of the Synoptic Jesus

---

Christian Paraenesis, SNTSMS 38, Cambridge and New York 1979, 30f. Unfortunately this study lacks even an incidental discussion of the Johannine literature.

[110] *Die Johannesbriefe*, 117–21.

[111] *Love Command*, 153f.

[112] Schnackenburg, *The Moral Teaching of the New Testament*, 328.

[113] Cf. the common designation ψεύστης in 2.4, 22; 4.20.

[114] *Love Command*, 154. Similarly (perhaps surprisingly) Bultmann, *Johannine Epistles*, 28, on I John 2.9f.: '"Brother" means, as in 3.15 and 4.20, not specially the Christian comrade in the faith, but one's fellow man, the "neighbour".' He says the same thing of 'love one another' in 3.11: 'The meaning is everywhere the same: love of neighbour is demanded' (54).

[115] Cf. Brownlee, 'Jesus and Qumran' in Trotter, ed., *Jesus and the Historian*, 73–5; O. J. F. Seitz, 'Love Your Enemies', *NTS* 16, 1969–70, 39–54, especially 50.

(Matt. 10.13f. and pars.; Luke 10.10f.), not to mention the common practice of the early church (Acts 13.51; 18.6; II Thess. 3.6; Rom. 16.17f.; Eph. 5.11).

The only text that Montefiore can adduce to suggest that the love-command in John positively excludes non-Christians is I John 2.15: 'Love not the world'. But it is clear that this means 'the world with all its allurements' – 'all that panders to the appetites or entices the eyes, all the glamour of its life' (2.15–17). This is what Paul refers to by 'the flesh', and to say with John that 'anyone who loves the world is a stranger to the Father's love' is the same as saying with Paul that 'the outlook of the flesh' is 'enmity with God' (Rom. 8.5–8): it has nothing to do with loving or not loving non-Christians.[116]

The contrast between I John 2.15, 'Love not the world', and John 3.16, 'God so loved the world', is indeed striking. But it merely demonstrates how rich a concept *κόσμος* is for John, varying (in much the same way that *σάρξ* does for Paul) from 'the world' that God made and yearns to save to 'the world' that epitomizes the devil's opposition to him. What it cannot be interpreted to show is that 'God alone loves the world' – and that no one else does or should, not even Jesus. If in his last prayer Jesus says 'I am not praying for the world' (John 17.9) it is not, as Montefiore asserts, 'to be presumed that he does not love the world, only his disciples', any more than when he says he will not disclose himself to the world but only to them (14.22): for that depends on their love for him, not his for them (14.21). 'The full extent' of the love which he shows to 'his own' (13.1) is a matter of concentration rather than exclusion.[117] It has to be thus, not because he rejects the world but because the world rejects him. His mission is all-embracing. He has come to be the saviour of the world (3.17; 4.42; 12.47), the light of the world (8.12; 9.5; 12.46; cf. 1.9), to remove the sin of the world (1.29); and the bread which is himself he gives for the life of the world (6.33, 51). The Son of Man when he is lifted up from the earth

[116] Cf. Bultmann, *John*, 528: 'The ἀγαπᾶν . . . is limited not because it has to do with a group that is orientated on the *world*, but because it has to do with the *eschatological* community, and this means that the world always has the possibility of being included within the circle of the ἀγαπᾶν.'

[117] Cf. again Bultmann, *John*, 488, on the ἴδιοι: 'Although *they* are the object of his love, whereas in 3.16 it was the *κόσμος* that was the object of the Father's love, this distinction between the two involves no contradiction, but is quite appropriate. Of course the love of the Son, like that of the Father, is directed towards the whole world, to win everyone to itself; but this love becomes a reality only where men open themselves to it. And the subject of this section is the circle of those who have so opened themselves.' (The second half of this is also quoted with approval by Barrett, *John*, 438.)

will draw all men to himself (3.14; 8.28; 12.32). To say that there is here a 'strong contrast' with the saying of Mark 10.45, 'The Son of Man did not come to be served but to serve and to surrender his life as a ransom for many', is simply not true. 'The universalism of Mark is' *not* 'here very different from the particularism of John'.[118]

Nevertheless is it not true that Jesus' 'new commandment' of love is in John restricted to Christians loving one another (13.34)? Once again I think we must say, no.[119] For the same logic obtains as in Paul: 'If there is this love among you, then all will know that you are my disciples' (13.35). The love is not to be confined to Christians, but it is to be defined in Christians: for if it is not seen here it will not be seen anywhere. But again, when later the commandment is repeated, 'Love one another, as I have loved you', is there not a subtle shift reflected in the words: 'There is no greater love than this, that a man should lay down his life for his *friends*' (15.12f.)? Has not the extroverted love for enemies become the introverted love for friends? Yet once more this is not a fair interpretation. For the contrast in the context is not between 'friends' and 'enemies' but between 'friends' and 'servants'. It is intimacy, not inversion, that is at issue, the intimacy which alone makes possible mutual love and self-disclosure (15.14–17; cf. 8.31–36). And that Jesus called his disciples 'my friends' is not a peculiar mark of Johannine exclusivism: it is common to Luke (12.4).

Yet for all this there does remain a real and undeniable difference of emphasis between the Fourth Gospel and the Synoptists. How then are we to explain it, if it is *not* a question of narrowing down and distortion?

In the Gospels, as we observed earlier, Jesus' teaching is given in three main settings: (1) to the crowds, chiefly in Galilee; (2) to the Jewish leadership, chiefly in Jerusalem; and (3) to the disciples, chiefly in the last year of the ministry. In the Synoptists the teaching material is mainly concentrated upon (1), with less on (2) and (3). In the Fourth Gospel it is mainly concentrated upon (2) and (3), with much less on (1). Now within the Synoptists the teaching about loving the unloving is almost entirely to be found in (1).[120] In the Fourth Gospel, with the absence of detailed teaching to the crowds goes the absence of teaching on love of the loveless. The tone of address to the Jewish leadership

[118] 'Love thy Neighbour', 165.

[119] Cf. Barrett, *John*, 96, 452, 476.

[120] As C. G. Montefiore observed, there is not much about Jesus loving his rabbinic antagonists (*Rabbinic Literature and Gospel Teachings*, London and New York 1930, 104).

remains much the same. But the emphasis on love between disciples, as an example to the world, is much stronger. In other words, the Synoptists give us a good deal more about the one kind of teaching, John a good deal more about the other. Yet who is to say that there is an either-or here? On the contrary, the probability is surely that Jesus taught both, and what evidence we have bears this out. Though there may not in John be specific moral teaching on attitudes to the unloving (there is remarkably little specific moral teaching at all, and no one imagines that Jesus gave none), yet there is 'love to the loveless *shown*'.[121] The encounter with the adulterous Samaritan woman depicts Jesus giving himself in one person to three classes of rejects with which the Synoptists associate his bad repute.[122] In fact in this Gospel he is even *called* a 'Samaritan' (8.48). And in the healing of a man born blind he is seen as a friend of 'the people of the land' (cf. 7.49; 9.34), who, as Vermes concedes, are more accurately depicted in John than in any other first-century literature.[123] On the other side, the lesson of the foot-washing, of mutual service between disciples (John 13.12–16), is precisely that spoken, rather than acted, in the same context in Luke 22.24–27. It is surely inconceivable that Jesus should not have told his followers to love one another and based his words on the example of his own love to them. As Dodd put it, 'Though the synoptics do not say

[121]This is in line with the Johannine emphasis on loving as Jesus *lived* and not merely as he taught: 13.34, 'As I have loved you, so you are to love one another'; I John 2.6, 'Whoever claims to be dwelling in him, binds himself to live as Christ himself lived'; 3.16, 'It is by this that we know what love is: that Christ laid down his life for us'; cf. also 3.3 The new commandment is 'true in you' because it is first true 'in him' (2.8).

[122]Perhaps it is not reading in too much to detect in this incident, followed by the healing of the son of the βασιλικός, part of the transition we noted earlier between Jesus' early image of his mission accepted from one who came neither eating or drinking to his subsequent role as the companion of prostitutes and sinners. In fact there are interesting parallels to the conversation with the Syrophoenician woman (Mark 7.24–30; Matt. 15.21–29) which occupied the second period of transition and reappraisal. In both cases Jesus is where he is only under constraint (John 4.4; Mark 7.24; Matt. 15.21) and finds himself having to talk with a non-Israelite woman to his disciples' dismay (John 4.27; Matt. 15.23). He is compelled by human need to drink from the Samaritan's cup (John 4.9) and to help the other woman's daughter (Matt. 15.25). In both he stands on his Jewishness (John 4.22; Matt. 15.24) to be subsequently transcended (John 4.21, 23; Matt. 15.28) and in both under pressure appears to betray his suppressed resentment (John 4.48; Mark 7.27). In each case we watch the barriers of sex and race which his formation would dictate being broken through. The conclusions to the two Johannine stories (4.39–42, 53) lend no more countenance to exclusiveness in the mission of Jesus than does the Synoptic tradition.

[123]*Jesus the Jew*, 55f. Martyn, *History and Theology in the Fourth Gospel*, 93, says the same, despite seeing the Gospel as anything but a source-book for the Jesus of history.

so, the implicit background of it all is the mutual love of Jesus and his disciples. John makes it explicit.'[124] The centrality of the command to love of one another in the earliest Christian communities of every tradition is inexplicable if it was self-generated, or even Spirit-generated or derived from sectarian or scriptural models or sociological pressures.[125] Nor surely is it intelligible as a secondary (and false) development from a larger love. John is much more credible in asserting that it is no new command, 'We have had it before us from the beginning' (II John 5f.; I John 3.11), and indeed that it 'comes to us from Christ himself: that he who loves God must also love his brother' (I John 4.20f.) – whether he be Christian or not. The one love is not a perversion or narrowing down of the other.

If in fact the apostolic church was as introverted as Montefiore suggests, it is a mystery why it went out of its way to preserve and reproduce the teaching of the Synoptic Gospels on love of enemies. Presumably it fitted its catechetical needs. Indeed the *Didache*, which I believe to be a very early Christian manual of instruction for Gentile converts,[126] gives it pride of place. After announcing 'the two ways' of life and death, it goes straight in:

> The *didache* is this. Bless them that curse you, and pray for your enemies and fast for them that persecute you. For what credit is it, if you love those that love you? Do not even the Gentiles the same? But you must love those that hate you, and you will not have an enemy (1.3).

The blessing and forgiving of its persecutors seems to have been one of the most distinctive and noteworthy features of the whole Christian movement (Acts 7.60; I Thess. 5.15; I Cor. 4.12; Rom. 12.14; I Peter 3.9) and it went on into the post-apostolic age (*Ep. Polyc.* 12.3). Indeed in its famous profile of Christians in the world the *Epistle to Diognetus* says that they are marked out because 'they love all men, and they are persecuted by all' (5.11) and 'as the soul loves the flesh which hates it . . ., so Christians love those who hate them' (6.6). It is interesting too that the anonymous *Second Epistle of Clement* specifically draws out the connection (rather than the antithesis) to which we referred earlier between the external and the internal loves. Speaking to the Gentiles, this writer says:

[124] 'The Portrait of Jesus in John and the Synoptics' (see n. 8 above), 197.
[125] As Montefiore says, 'Love thy Neighbour', 168–70.
[126] *Redating*, 322–7.

For when they hear from us that God says 'It is no credit to you if you love those that love you, but it is credit to you if you love your enemies and those that hate you'; when they hear these things, I say, they marvel at their exceeding goodness; but when they see that we not only do not love those that hate us, but not even those that love us, they laugh us to scorn, and the Name is blasphemed (13.4).[127]

This is not to say that under the pressures of persecution, heresy and schism the church did not become introverted and sub-Christian in teaching as well as in practice. It would have been astonishing if it had not. For within the old Israel there had been a strong particularist as well as a universalist streak. And both come out in the Johannine as in the Pauline tradition. That cannot be denied. But what I do not believe one can substantiate is that there was in the church as a whole 'a sea-change in outlook'[128] from a wider love to a narrower, or that the Johannine tradition simply reflects its end-term.[129] Nor can we conclude that its presentation of the moral teaching of Jesus is unhistorical or stands 'in sharp and violent contrast to the bidding of the Synoptic Jesus'.[130] On the contrary, the two are complementary and John is I believe indispensable testimony at this as at other points to the alpha as well as to the omega of the New Testament message. His representation of what he calls love being brought to its τέλος, its full term or perfection (John 13.1; I John 2.5; 4.12, 17f.), is most truly faithful to what was there from 'the beginning' (2.7, 24; 3.11). In fact without him our understanding of what Jesus called the love with which *he* loved (John 13.34) would be impoverished both in its

[127]Furnish overlooks this passage in his discussion of the Apostolic Fathers, but in his conclusion makes the same point: 'In certain places, and on the part of some writers more than others, there is an apparent preoccupation with love's task within the church. But it is important to remember that even when this is or appears to be the case, there is an operative presumption that the life of love *interior* to the Christian community has at the same time an *exterior* visibility and effect' (*Love Command*, 212).

[128]Montefiore, 'Love thy Neighbour', 167.

[129]Indeed I believe that the designation of the Johannine community as a sect, let alone the implication that they made an 'ism' of it, as in Meeks's title 'The Man from Heaven in Johannine Sectarianism', *JBL* 91, 1972, especially 69–72, is much exaggerated. On the contrary there would seem to be a straight way through to the 'early catholicism' of Ignatius and Irenaeus. Cf. Hoskyns and Davey, *Fourth Gospel*, 105–18, 122. Dodd, *Johannine Epistles*, xlii, similarly speaks of the 'universal, catholic significance' of I John.

[130]C. G. Montefiore, 'Notes on the Religious Value of the Fourth Gospel', *JQR* 7, 1894, 54.

'newness' and in its profundity. We need the Synoptists in order to appreciate its breadth, John in order to penetrate its depth.

6. *The Johannine Eschatology*

But, finally, what of the overall context within which the ethical and all the other teaching of Jesus is set? What of the teaching about the τέλος itself? Has not the whole once again been given a setting in John far removed from the eschatology of Jesus himself as represented in the Synoptic Gospels? Is not this a prime example of the 'posteriority' of John, of his doing a 'rewrite' of the primitive message alike of Jesus and of the early church?

On this subject there was a marked swing of the pendulum even within the writing of Dodd himself. In his epoch-making book *The Apostolic Preaching and its Developments*[131] he depicted the Johannine eschatology as the last term in the development of the original apostolic message. When the primitive apocalyptic expectation reached a point at which no literal fulfilment could be looked for, John presented a reinterpretation in terms of a timeless, quasi-Platonic mysticism. True, there were occasional references to a resurrection and judgment at the last day (5.25–29; 6.39f., 44, 54; 11.24; 12.48),[132] but these could be put down to the relics of a cruder stage of thought not wholly 'refined away' or, with Bultmann, to the subsequent work of a redactor.

Yet it is difficult to point to any passages in the body of the Gospel where such a corrective or revaluation of unfulfilled hopes looks like being offered (as for instance in II Peter 3.8f.). There is no polemic or dissuasive directed at Christian circles, such as has been detected in the case of Baptist groups – only a revision of traditional *Jewish* eschatology, that resurrection need not await the last day (11.23–5). Moreover, if this was the direction of development within the Johannine community, how is one to explain away the *greater* use of 'traditional' eschatological language in the Epistles (which Dodd agreed were later), including such terms as 'his parousia', 'the day of judgment' and 'the Antichrist' (I 2.18, 22, 28–3.3; 4.3, 17; II John 7), and in the Epilogue (John 21.22f., though this usage of course could

[131]London 1936, 65–9.

[132]These are part of the fundamental Jewish framework in which John stands and does not dream of denying. But he never associates the distinctively Christian message of the coming or presence of Christ simply with the last day.

always be attributed to a different author)? But in fact the purpose of these references is apparently to counter the subsequent exposure of the community to such language ('you have heard'),[133] to seek to enter into its truth by 'demythologization' (especially in I John 2.18f., 22f.; 4.3; II John 7), and to rescue it from misunderstanding (John 21.23). Subsequently Dodd came round to the view, to which I found myself driven by the study of the emergence of the parousia hope, namely, that the Johannine eschatology represents a tradition that had never seriously undergone the process of increasing apocalypticization visible in the Synoptic tradition.[134] In the concluding chapter of my *Jesus and His Coming* (where I find that over twenty-five years ago I was saying that 'there seems to me now very little to *rule out* the view that the Gospel was in substance composed relatively early'), I argued that 'it does not set forth a view of the End with a balance, or lack of it, all of its own, but, rather, an inaugurated eschatology in all essentials identical with that of the primitive preaching, and indeed also with that of Jesus himself as we have sought to reconstruct it from the earliest strands of the Synoptic tradition.'[135] I need not repeat the detailed argument, that it is John who does best justice to unities which tend to get broken up in other presentations – between the different moments of the coming of Christ to his own (cross, resurrection, ascension, parousia and the gift of the Spirit), between the now and the not yet,[136] between the twin aspects of vindication and visitation and between eschatology and ethics. All is focused for John in the great 'from now on' inaugurated, but only inaugurated, by the passion (which I believe faithfully reflects the meaning of Jesus' reply to the high priest in Matt. 26.64 = Luke 22.69). One cannot derive a purely 'realized

[133]Cf. the similar motif in II Thess. 2.1f.: 'About the coming of our Lord Jesus Christ and his gathering of us to himself: I beg you, do not suddenly lose your heads or alarm yourselves, whether at some oracular utterance, or pronouncement. . . . ' The difference is that at that time Paul was happy himself to use that way of putting it, as he used the Gnostic terms while John avoids them. Later he stood much nearer to the teleology of John.

[134]His later position was foreshadowed in the appendix to *The Interpretation of the Fourth Gospel* on 'the historical aspect of the Fourth Gospel'.

[135]*Jesus and His Coming*, 162. Cf. the whole section, 165–80, and, subsequently, Hunter, *According to John*, 113f.

[136]Cf. Dodd, *Interpretation*, 447: 'His formula ἔρχεται ὥρα καὶ νῦν ἐστιν, with the emphasis on the νῦν ἐστιν, without excluding the element of futurity, is, I believe, not merely an acute theological definition, but is essentially historical, and probably represents the authentic teaching of Jesus as veraciously as any formula could. If that is so, it follows that a picture of the ministry of Jesus largely controlled by that maxim cannot be without historical value.'

eschatology' from the Fourth Gospel. For all his stress on the τετέλεσται (19.30) and the completing of the work given to Jesus to do (17.4), this is but penultimate to the work of the Spirit (7.39; 14.25f.; 16.7–15), quite apart from what must still happen at the last day. Barrett is I believe quite correct in saying that for John 'the historical figure was central for his understanding of God; central but not final. . . . The theme of futurist eschatology runs deeper into Johannine thought than is often supposed.'[137]

Of course the Johannine presentation represents a massively mature construction, closely corresponding, as I said,[138] to that of the later Paul. But I ventured even then to suggest that it also takes us back as far to source as we can hope to get. I argued that if there is foundation in the words of Jesus for the promise of his return it may well be *more like* such sayings as John 14.28, 'I am going away, and coming back to you', and 16.16, 'A little while, and you will see me no more; again a little while, and you will see me' (cf. also 14.3,[139] 18f.; 16.22), which are remarkably similar to the assurance given by Jesus to the disciples in Mark that 'after he is raised' they will 'sce' him 'as he said' (14.28; 16.7).[140] In fact the laboured fourfold repetition in 16.16–19 of the saying about 'the little while' and 'because I go to the Father' seems extraordinary if the church had simply created these words. Why should it have invented them only to make such a meal of them? It looks much more as if it was wrestling with a remembered 'word of the Lord', whose interpretation had been subject to debate and misunderstanding. The same applies to the λόγος whose meaning gave rise to such puzzlement, 'For a little longer I shall be with you; but then I am going away to him who sent me. You will look for me, but you will not find me. Where I am you cannot come' (7.33–36; taken up again in 13.33); to the 'hard saying' in 14.21–23 that he would not manifest

[137] *Essays on John*, 4f.

[138] *Jesus and His Coming*, 183–5.

[139] I suggested (*Jesus and His Coming*, 25, 178) that 14.3, 'I shall come again and receive you to myself, so that where I am you may be also', could even be the 'word of the Lord' claimed by Paul in I Thess. 4.15–17, where he writes that 'The Lord himself will descend from heaven; first the Christian dead will rise, then we who are left alive shall join them, caught up in clouds to meet the Lord in the air. Thus we shall always be with the Lord.' This is precisely what John says in non-apocalyptic terms: cf. 17.24, 'that these . . . may be with me where I am, so that they may look upon my glory', in which he refers, as I argue was primitively the case, to *the resurrection as inaugurating the parousia*. Cf. also H. E. Edwards, *The Disciple Who Wrote These Things*, 136–9.

[140] Compare also John 14.23, 'We will come to him and make our dwelling with him', with Matt. 28.20, 'I am with you always, to the end of time.'

himself to the world; and to the misinterpreted word about 'waiting till I come' in 21.22f.

Subsequently Dodd was to examine these predictions in detail and make the point that they antedate the development already found in Mark of such sayings into predictions of *either* resurrection *or* parousia:

> I suggest that John is here reaching back to a very early form of tradition indeed, and making it the point of departure for his profound theological reinterpretation; and further, that the oracular sayings which he reports have good claim to represent authentically, in substance if not verbally, what Jesus actually said to his disciples – a better claim than the more elaborate and detailed predictions which the Synoptics offer.[141]

Short of asserting the presence of *ipsissima verba* one could scarcely make higher claims for any piece of Gospel tradition.

Hunter uses a similar argument for what he calls 'the three *hypsoun* sayings', noting that the *double entendre* 'crucify' and 'raise up' goes back behind the Greek to the Aramaic;[142] 3.14, 'As Moses lifted up the serpent in the wilderness, so *must the Son of man* be lifted up'; 8.28, 'When you have lifted up *the Son of man*, then you will know that I am he'; and 12.34, 'How can you say that *the Son of man must* be lifted up?'.[143] He comments: 'These correspond to the three synoptic predictions of the Passion (Mark 8.31; 9.31; 10.32f.). They seem to echo Isa. 52.13 ('My servant . . . shall be *lifted up*'); and since they are less detailed than their synoptic equivalents, are conceivably more ancient than they.'[144] Again, it is significant that they do not distinguish (any more than does the same language in the early speeches in Acts 2.33; 5.31) between resurrection and ascension, which later came to be regarded as separate events.

So our testing of the teaching material has again suggested that there is no necessary absurdity or contradiction in asserting that the Johannine presentation could be *both* the most mature *and* the most faithful to the original truth about Jesus.

But what, finally, of its portraiture of the person himself?

[141] *Historical Tradition*, 420. Cf. the whole discussion, 413–20.

[142] But this cannot be used as an argument for the Gospel being originally written in Aramaic. Cf. Meeks, 'Man from Heaven', 62, who draws attention to the wider provenance.

[143] Italics his, to draw out the common wording with Mark.

[144] *According to John*, 92.

VIII

The Person of Christ

So we come to the final and decisive question about the Gospel of John: *Whom* does he show us? *What* Jesus does he give us? Is it one that bears any but a remote relation to history? Here above all John has been seen as standing at the end of the line. In other respects his witness may be usable for historical reconstruction – in the outlines of the ministry, in details of place and time and political and social background, even at points in the teaching of Jesus. But for the understanding of his person we are thrown back on the Synoptic record. Even that may tell us more – some would say, much more – about the Christ of the church's faith than about the Jesus of history. But in the case of John the former is at a maximum, the latter at a minimum. His picture, it is said,[1] is so different that it must be set aside as evidence either for the historical Jesus or for a viable reconstruction for today. It provides no *foundations* for New Testament or for contemporary christology, however crucial it may be for understanding the transition in doctrinal superstructure from the apostolic to the Nicene church.

1. *The Making Explicit of the Implicit*

The thesis of this chapter will be that, on the contrary, what John gives us is basically the same Jesus of history who is the Christ of the church's faith, the Christ of the church's faith who is also the Jesus of history. For all the manifold differences of presentation, it is the one 'man

[1]Cf. the quotations I cited as typical from such moderate scholars as W. R. Matthews, H. W. Montefiore, G. Bornkamm and P. Tillich in my essay 'The Use of the Fourth Gospel for Christology Today' in *Twelve More NTS*, 139f. I shall be drawing on this study at different points in this chapter.

Christ Jesus' whom the Gospels portray. That does not of course mean that there is any simple equivalent or fundamentalist identity between the Jesus of history and the Christ of the church's faith. Prolonged and varied reflection has taken place upon the significance of this man, and the portraits come out very differently. Nor could anyone doubt that the Johannine portrait embodies greater and deeper reflection than that of any of the other Gospel writers and indeed than any other New Testament writer, with the possible exception of Paul. Of all the evangelists John is also the clearest that his object is to present the Christ of faith: 'These (signs, or things) are written that you may *believe* that Jesus is the Christ, the Son of God, and that believing you may have life in his name' (20.31). Yet of all the evangelists he is the most concerned with the Word becoming *flesh* (1.14) and with affirming 'Jesus Christ come in the flesh' (I John 4.2; II John 7).

Clement of Alexandria long ago made the distinction that while the other three Gospel writers presented the bodily facts (τὰ σωματικά) John wrote 'a spiritual Gospel'.[2] This, as we have argued, is untrue if it means that he wrote in deliberate reaction to the Synoptists, whether to complement or correct them. It is also untrue if John is seen as presenting the spiritual truth *as opposed to* the bodily facts. For that was evidently the way his gnosticizing opponents understood him, and against them he was devastating. But if the phrase is interpreted to mean that he was concerned with the inwardness *of* the outer events, the truth *of* the history *really* entered into, in the Spirit from the end, then it may stand as a fine description of his purpose. For his Gospel is presenting the history 'remembered', internalized, seen and understood in the light of Scripture and the Spirit. Typical of his perspective are his comments in 2.22,

> After his resurrection his disciples recalled what he had said [about the temple of his body], and they believed the Scripture and the words that Jesus had spoken.

and 12.16,

> At the time his disciples did not understand this [his entry as king upon a donkey], but after Jesus had been glorified they remembered that this had been written about him, and that his had happened to him [i.e., both event and interpretation].

This is not just a neutral exercise in historical reminiscence – what

[2]Quoted, Eusebius, *HE* 6.14.7.

Justin called the ἀπομνημονεύματα, or memoirs, of the apostles (*Dial.* 106.2f.). It is ἀνάμνησις in the deep Hebraic sense of a recalling of the past that does not leave it in the dead past but recreates it as present experience at a deeper level. The interpreter Spirit, always for the New Testament that element of the last days in the present, can alone reveal the truth about Christ. Yet he does it not by inventing or creating *ex nihilo*, speaking 'of himself' through the church, itself seen as the present voice of the living Lord.[3] Rather, insists the Johannine Jesus, 'Everything that he makes known to you he will draw from what is mine' (John 16.13f.). He will show the things of Jesus by holding them to the true light, so that *in* the flesh one may see the glory, not destroying the flesh as flesh,[4] but allowing it to become diaphanous to spirit.

Hence for this writer the relation between flesh and spirit, seeing and believing, theology and history, is always a dialectical one, never a simple either-or. He is operating at several levels at once. Indeed one could say that there were three ways of 'seeing' Christ which are represented in the Gospel, with a fourth hovering on the brink which is addressed in the Epistles.

1. *On the outside*, as the eyes see, at the level of flesh. This is the level of the unbelieving or merely the uncomprehending Jews, of seeing without believing (6.36) or indeed without *really* seeing (6.26). At this level the 'whence?' of Jesus is viewed purely in terms of his earthly origins and he will appear to be mad or bad, a deceiver of the people. This is the level, to use our earlier comparison, of Socrates' judges or of the caricature of him in Aristophanes' *Clouds*.

2. *From the outside in*. This is a necessary first approach for everyone, of believing through seeing. It is the way in for the first disciples (cf. especially 1.38, 46, 50), 'the Jews who believe' (cf. especially 2.23), the Samaritan woman and her villagers (cf. 4.39–42), the man in the royal service (4.53), Thomas (20.29), and even the beloved disciple himself (20.8f.: 'he saw and believed, for as yet they did not understand . . . '; cf. 12.16). It is believing for the works' sake, though this is not because they are miracles but because the Father is to

[3]Cf. Gerhardsson, *Origins of the Gospel Traditions*, 35: 'These passages [I Cor. 7.10, 12, 25] are embarrassing evidence against the common opinion that in the early church no distinction was made between what was said "by the Lord (himself)" and what was said by someone else "in the Lord", that words of Jesus were freely constructed, or that sayings of some early Christian prophet were freely placed in the mouth of Jesus.'

[4]This is the charge of Käsemann against John, leading to the accusation of 'naive docetism', that his insistence that 'the Word was made flesh' is 'totally overshadowed by the confession "we beheld his glory"' (*Testament of Jesus*, 9, 26).

be seen in them (10.37f.; 14.10f.). And this must still go on into the age of the church. Others will have to come in through the word of those who have seen and heard (17.20): hence the continuing need of witness. This is the predominant perspective of the Synoptic Gospels and Acts, and *mutatis mutandis* of Xenophon's *Memorabilia*: through the σωματικά to bring men from being on the outside to being on the inside.

3. *From the inside out*. This is the perspective of those who have made this transition, who see Christ from within from the end, in the Spirit, for whom the flesh has now become shot through with the glory and the truth. The σωματικά are not in consequence the less significant but the more, as they are entered into in their true depth. This is the vision of those who have been 'there and back again'. It is no longer a position of pointing and saying 'This is the Christ' but of seeing the Logos *as* this man, the Father *in* the Son. It involves being prepared to treat the history and the teaching freely, drawing out meaning from it not perceived at the time. This is the perspective, which though certainly not alien to the purpose of the Synoptists, is the distinctive contribution of the Fourth Gospel – and again *mutatis mutandis* of Plato's Dialogues.

4. Yet John is aware of a further stage into which this can easily tip over, of seeing simply *on the inside*. This is the esoteric vision of the initiate, of believing without seeing, of kicking away the ladder of history, dispensing with the incarnation and having the Father without the Son. This is the way of the Gnostics (and later of the Neo-Platonists) which John so vehemently attacks in the Epistles, because, as we have seen, it is so near and yet so far.

Hence it is important to insist that for this Gospel above all there is no *antithesis* between the history and the theology, so that the more theological it is (which no one would dispute), the less historical it is (as many would conclude). John is concerned throughout with the drawing out – or the lighting up from within – of the history, the indispensable locus of the Word made flesh. The flesh by itself, mere historicizing, 'gets one nowhere' (6.33; as in the same phrase in 12.19); but equally to think that one can get beyond, or leave behind, Christ come in the flesh is very Antichrist (I John 4.2f.; II John 7–9). In fact it is characteristic of this Gospel to be at its most theological when it is laying its greatest stress on history. Thus in 19.35f. we get the evangelist's note,

> This is vouched for by an eyewitness, whose evidence is to be trusted.

He knows that he speaks the truth, so that you too may believe – for this happened in fulfilment of the text of Scripture.

It is the truth of *faith* that he is concerned for; yet he grounds it in the most specific claim to veracity for the physical details of Jesus' death – the emission of blood and water. But the blood and water are *also* of profound symbolic and theological significance for this writer – and can never be separated from the interpreter Spirit; for there is no antithesis between them (I John 5.6–8; cf. John 3.5). Typical too, as we have seen, is his account of the desert feeding and its significance in ch. 6 – supplying us with the most penetrating insight into *both* the political *and* the spiritual levels at the same time. And this incident is no exception but characteristic of his whole theology of 'signs'–uncovering the depth of significance in what is there to be seen at very different levels (cf. especially 4.48; 6.26, 30). Here above all is Browning's dictum true of John, that 'what first were guessed as points, I now knew stars'. His claim is to be making explicit what was implicit from 'the beginning', drawing out what was *there* all along; making out, not making up.

In this John is not of course alone. The making explicit of what was implicit is the process behind all the Gospels – and indeed the Epistles. As Westcott put it succinctly long before the advent of form criticism, 'The Synoptic narratives are implicit dogmas, no less truly than St John's dogmas are concrete facts.'[5] The titles used by the church, 'the titles of glory'[6] – Messiah, Lord, Son of God – draw out and light up what was implicit in the works and words of Jesus. But a notable feature of all the Gospels is the reserve with which these are put back upon his own lips.[7] And this is as true of John as of the Synoptists.

As we have seen, of all the christological titles in ch. 1 only Son of Man occurs in Jesus' own mouth. While he acknowledges, when it is introduced by others, that he is the Messiah (4.26), this is no more than he does in Mark (14.62), though it comes earlier and less publicly.[8] Otherwise such confessions are always on the lips of other people (1.41, 49; 6.69; 11.27; as in Mark 8.29).

'Lord' is applied to him, as in Luke, with the greatest reserve – except

[5] *John* I, lxxxv.

[6] Cf. F. Hahn, *The Titles of Jesus in Christology*, ET London and New York 1969.

[7] Cf. Lemcio, 'The Intention of the Evangelist Mark', forthcoming in *New Testament Studies*.

[8] The name 'Jesus Christ' on Jesus' lips in 17.3 is, as we have argued above (p. 328 n. 93), as likely to be secondary as 'because you are Christ's' in Mark 9.41 (contrast Matt. 10.42).

after the resurrection. In 4.1 the correct reading is almost certainly 'Jesus'[9] and in 6.23 the phrase 'where the Lord had given thanks' is in all probability a scribal gloss.[10] 11.2, describing Mary as 'the woman who anointed the Lord with ointment', is an evangelist's comment from the other side of Easter, and 13.14 is Jesus' reaction to the address 'Teacher' and 'Lord' which in the vocative is equally common in the Synoptists.[11] The contrast in usage from the resurrection onwards is very marked: 20.2, 13, 18, 20, 25, 28; 21.7, 12.

Equally, 'Son of God' as a title occurs but once on the lips of Jesus during the ministry, in 11.4, where the purpose of Lazarus' illness is seen as being not death but the glorification, i.e. the manifest vindication, of the Son of God.[12] Father–Son language is of course constantly on the lips of Jesus in John, but this again is an elaboration of the intimacy of the *abba* relationship familiar to us from the Synoptists. We have seen that it is originally parabolic language, and the process of its allegorization into 'the Father' and 'the Son' already occurs both in the material common to Matthew and Luke (Matt. 11.27 = Luke 10.22) and in Mark (13.32). A high christology of sonship is, as we know from Paul, extremely early (cf. Gal. 1.16; Acts 9.20, tracing it back to his conversion). What John affords is more insight into the process by which the points became stars in the church's usage. For the parabolic base lies very close beneath the surface in 1.14; 5.19f.; and 8.35, as does the functional rather than the titular understanding of sonship in 10.31–8.

John also allows us to catch a glimpse of points that never became stars: 'the prophet' (like Moses) (1.21, 25; 6.14; 7.40, 52;[13] cf. Acts 3.22f.; 7.37); 'the elect of God' (1.34, NEB text; cf. Luke 23.35); 'the Christ' as a title (*passim*, cf. Acts 2.31; 3.20; 4.26; 5.42; etc.) especially in the Aramaic in 1.42 and 4.25; 'king' (1.45; 6.15; 18.37; cf. Luke 23.2; Acts 17.7); and of course 'the Son of Man' (uniquely without the

[9]'Had κύριος been present in the original text, it is unlikely that a scribe would have displaced it with Ἰησοῦς, which occurs twice in the following clauses' (Metzger, *Textual Commentary*, 205).

[10]See above, ch. V, p. 201 n. 24.

[11]In 13.16 and 15.15, 20, 'lord' in contrast with 'servant' is parabolic, as again constantly in the Synoptists.

[12]3.18 must be regarded as evangelist's comment and 5.25 refers to the Son of God's activity at the last day. In 1.49; 10.36; 11.27; and 19.7 the title is addressed or attributed to Jesus by others; and in 1.34; 6.69; and 9.35 other readings are to be preferred on textual grounds.

[13]Ὁ προφήτης conjectured by Owen in the eighteenth century is now supported by the original hand of P^{66}, and apparently by P^{75} (though this latter is disputed in Nestle-Aland, *NT Graece*[26], 1979).

articles in 5.27; cf. Dan. 7.13; Rev. 1.13; 14.14), which failed to establish itself in the Gentile mission. All the other contacts of these titles are with the earlier rather than later strands of the Christian preaching. That they should have survived in John is an indication of his links with 'the beginning' and suggests that his tradition is not simply a creation of the mature flowering of the church's theology.

Nor is there any sign of the building up of Jesus into a 'divine man' of contemporary Hellenistic religion who could work wonders by his own powers.[14] The miracles are entirely and solely the works of the Father (5.36; 9.3f.; 10.25, 32, 37f.; 14.10; 17.4), and this is in close agreement with the Synoptic picture where all things are possible not to Jesus but to God (Mark 10.27) and power is available to everyone who has faith (Mark 9.23). 'The people', we read, 'praised God for granting such authority to *men*' (Matt. 9.8), and in John too the Son has authority and power only because it is given him (5.19–30; 8.28f.; 17.2). The furthest that even Matthew with his heightening of the supernatural makes Jesus go is to say in Gethsemane, 'Do you suppose that I cannot appeal to my father, *who* would at once send to my aid more than twelve legions of angels?' (26.53). There is no suggestion that he could lay them on because he was God. He is a man of power because he is a man of prayer. But because he is a man of prayer, he knows that it is not the Father's will to win that way. The Johannine picture is no different. All his power comes from prayerful dependence on the Father (11.22; 17.7f.). He can act because he is heard (11.41f.), and he is 'always' heard because it is ever his meat and drink to do the Father's will and to be pleasing to him (4.34; 8.29).

The impression so often formed that whereas in the Synoptists it is God and his rule which are central, in John it is Christ and his claims, is quite misleading. In the final summary of his public teaching Jesus is made to 'shout' so that all can hear, 'When a man believes in me, he believes in him who sent me rather than in me' (12.44; as if to correct the balance of his 'cry' in 7.37f.?). Indeed, as E. M. Sidebottom says,

[14]For this category, cf. H. D. Betz, 'Jesus as Divine Man' in. F. T. Trotter, ed., *Jesus and the Historian*, 114–33; Robinson and Koester, *Trajectories*, 187–93; 216–9, and the bibliography there given (216f.). How flimsy is the evidence for this entire concept in the New Testament has been shown by C. H. Holladay, *Theios Anēr in Hellenistic Judaism: A Critique of the Use of this Category in New Testament Christology*, Missoula, Mont., 1977, esp. 236–42. When scholars argue that a hypothetical signs-source presents an understanding of Jesus in this hypothetical role, one may be reasonably sure that they are building castles in the air. Cf. Schillebeeckx, *Christ*, 374f.; and Barrett, *Essays on John*, 13 n. 22, who quotes an unpublished Durham Ph.D. thesis

> An essential point about the theology of the Fourth Gospel is that the centre of the picture is not Jesus but the Father. The Fourth Gospel and the First Epistle are the great theocentric tracts of the New Testament. The Johannine Christ takes every opportunity to point to the Father as the source of all his signficance and effectiveness.[15]

This conclusion has been more recently followed up and borne out by C. K. Barrett.[16] The picture which John presents is of Jesus as the Father's agent, drawn in contemporary Jewish terms[17] of the *shaliaḥ*, or ἀπόστολος, the one sent (cf. the parable of 13.16, 'an agent is not greater than he who sent him'). The agent is wholly there to represent his principal, speaking for him, acting for him, doing nothing 'on his own account' but everything with the accreditation (5.43), seal (6.27) and authorization (12.49) of him who sent him.[18] There is no sense in which the agent has chosen his master, but always the other way round (cf. 15.16). Yet according to the halakhic rules the sender 'had to authorize the agent by transferring his own rights and property concerned to the agent'[19] (cf. John 6.37; 17.7). Under the commission the two parties were completely *ad idem*[20] (cf. John 10.30–38), so that whether the agent acted or negotiated in his own name or in that of his principal was a matter of indifference.[21]

This combination of Jesus having been *given everything*, with equal stress on each word, wholly dependent and wholly free, is again but drawing out what comes through the Synoptists. 'For', it has truly been said, 'what strikes us about the Gospel story is that, as a man among men, Jesus claims nothing for himself as a man, but everything for the

---

of 1973 by Edwin Jones, *The Concept of the Theios Anēr in the Graeco-Roman World with special reference to the first two centuries* AD.

[15] *The Christ of the Fourth Gospel*, 194; cf. Scott Holland, *Fourth Gospel*, 218.

[16] 'Christocentric or Theocentric? Observations on the Theological Method of the Fourth Gospel', *Essays on John*, 1–18; cf. earlier *John*, 97.

[17] Cf. Harvey, *Jesus on Trial*, 88–92; *Constraints of History*, 161–3; Borgen, *Bread from Heaven*, 158–64 and 'God's Agent in the Fourth Gospel' in Neusner, ed., *Religions in Antiquity*, Leiden 1968, 137–48; J. A. Bühner, *Der Gesandte und sein Weg*, Tübingen 1977, esp. 196–8; and earlier Strack-Billerbeck, *Kommentar* I, 590; II, 558; H. Vogelstein, 'The Development of the Apostolate in Judaism and its Transformation in Christianity', *HUCA* 2, 1925, 99–123; K. H. Rengstorf, ἀπόστολος in *TDNT* I, 413–20.

[18] Cf. Num. 16.28 of Moses: 'Hereby you shall know that the Lord has sent me to do all these works (LXX ἔργα) and that it has not been of my own accord (οὐκ ἀπ' ἐμαυτοῦ).'

[19] Borgen, *Bread from Heaven*, 160.

[20] Z. W. Falk, 'Jewish Private Law', *Compendia*, I. 1, 512f.

[21] Cf. b. *B.K.* 70a: 'Go forth and take legal action so that you may acquire title to it and secure the claim for yourself', quoted, Borgen, *Bread from Heaven*, 160.

God and Father to whom he is utterly obedient and on whom he is utterly dependent.'[22] That could have been a summary of John; yet it was written of the Synoptists. For there too Jesus makes no claims for himself, but everything for what God is doing through him. His authority is expressed not so much in nouns or titles (apart from the mysterious Son of Man) as in verbs and adverbs. He does not go around saying he is God. Yet all our sources agree that he was condemned for blasphemy (Mark 14.63f. and pars.; John 19.7), for 'making himself God' (John 10.33–6) or 'equal with God' (5.18) – not, however, as far as any of our evidence goes, for arrogating to himself the name of God,[23] but precisely for speaking without so much as a 'Thus saith the Lord'. In the 'Amen, I tell you', common to the Synoptists and John, he associates God, as we have seen, with his own utterance. In overruling and re-editing the Law with his astonishing contrast, 'You have heard that it was said to the men of old time [i.e. by God] 'but I say to you' (Matt. 5.21–48), and in many other ways in the eyes of his contemporaries he steps into the space reserved for God (Mark 1.27; 2.7; 4.41). He refuses to 'make room' for God. He says that men's attitude to himself will decide God's attitude to them (Mark 8.38 and pars.; Matt. 10.33; Luke 12.9). It is impossible to escape the conclusion that he went round not just talking *about* God (this would not have provoked the reaction he did) but standing in God's place, acting and speaking for him. This is what really riled the Pharisees. 'Take away every hint of this', it has been said, 'and you are left with a blank.'[24]

This is the Synoptic picture. But it is basically the same in John. Here too there is no question of Jesus usurping the position of God. The essential difference between representation and replacement[25] comes out in Acts 12.22f.: '"It is a god speaking, not a man!" Instantly an angel of the Lord struck him down, because he had usurped the honour (δόξα) due to God.' Despite the Jews' failure to distinguish (John 10.33), Jesus for John is never 'the voice of God and *not* a man'. He resolutely refuses to seek his own δόξα (7.18; 8.50, 54), and his utter dependence, as we shall draw out later, is never more stressed than in this Gospel. His vocation is simply to represent the one who sent him, to let himself be nothing in order that the Father and his glory may be

[22] H. Anderson, *Jesus and Christian Origins: A Commentary on Modern Viewpoints*, New York and London 1964, 171.

[23] See below, pp. 385–7, for the interpretation to be given to 'I am'.

[24] F. G. Downing, *A Man for Us and a God for Us*, London and Philadelphia 1968, 45. Cf. more fully my *Human Face of God*, 190–4.

[25] Cf. D. Sölle, *Christ the Representative*, ET London and Philadelphia 1967.

everything, to *be* God to men. Hence there is no need to look beyond him: anyone who has seen him has seen the Father (12.45; 14.9).

Yet there has appeared to be an immense difference between the Jesus of the Synoptists and of John. For does not the latter talk of his relationship with the Father in a way that suggests he is really not human at all? The 'I' of the Johannine Christ seems to lift him out of the discourse of ordinary mortals and to suggest, to say the least, that he has a 'hot line' to heaven. Indeed it often sounds as if he is on the other end of it. How can a man who talks like that be a genuine human being?

2. *The Self-Consciousness of Jesus*

There are at least two issues here. The most important is, obviously, the substance of what John is saying about Jesus. *Is* he presenting him as superhuman, a visitor to this planet from another realm of being, who does not start where we start? That is the main point which requires elucidation and to which we must come back. But, first, I believe there is a question to be brought out into the open which this generation of Johannine study needs to face afresh, the question, namely, of whether we can speak of the self-consciousness of Jesus at all. And the credibility of John's evidence and the use that may legitimately be made of Johannine texts has been central to the whole debate. Giving *uncritical* priority to John has produced the picture just alluded to. Rejecting that and swinging over to refuse any kind of place to the Johannine evidence has had the effect in scholarly circles of dismissing not only the answer but also the question. Together with the wider doubts about whether any of the Gospels provides material for settling the quest of the historical Jesus, the self-consciousness of Jesus in particular has become a sort of 'no go area' for New Testament theology. It has been sealed off as a minefield into which none but fools would dare to venture. The 'new quest' for the historical Jesus has given it a wide berth. In fact after sex and death it could be called the last taboo. Since the Johannine material is so heavily affected, not to say infected, by this 'history', it cannot be approached freely or dispassionately.

In the classical debates of the Christian church it was taken for granted that texts from this Gospel were primary data of the problem to be solved.[26] No christology which did not do justice to both the

[26] Cf. M. Wiles, *The Spiritual Gospel*, Cambridge and New York 1960, 112–47; T. E. Pollard, *Johannine Christology and the Early Church*, SNTSMS 13, Cambridge 1970.

sayings 'I and the Father are one' (10.30) and 'my Father is greater than I' (14.28), or which failed to posit in Jesus both genuine limitations, like tiredness, tears and thirst (4.6; 11.35; 19.28), and also a memory of pre-existent glory (8.58; 17.5), could satisfy the 'facts'. It was material from the Gospel of John which more than any other compelled, and tested, the doctrine of the Two Natures in its different presentations, and most of the patristic examples of what it meant for Christ to do some things as God and some things as man were drawn from this Gospel. Still as late as the nineteenth century so liberal a theologian as Schleiermacher used as an argument for the priority of John the authority of its eyewitness to the person of Christ. 'It is, according to him', wrote Schweitzer, 'only in this Gospel that the consciousness of Jesus is truly reflected.' 'The contradictions', Schleiermacher maintained, between this and the others 'could not be explained if all our Gospels stood equally close to Jesus.'[27] But if John stands closer than the others, as he believed, then the problem could be resolved. Even up to the First World War it was possible for Bishop Frank Weston to write his great book *The One Christ* as though the data for the self-consciousness of Jesus were still basically set, largely by the Fourth Gospel, in the way they had been for Cyril of Alexandria. What Weston claimed to do, not without some success, was to produce a more adequate hypothesis to account for the same data: he did not question, let alone set aside, the Johannine material. 'The most important evidence', he wrote, 'to the divine nature of Christ is that . . . based upon the revelation of His self-consciousness, His knowledge of His pre-existence, and His memory of the state of eternal glory.'[28]

The swing away from this position, which of course had set in in liberal circles long before Weston, has been almost total. Yet nothing has been put in its place. In respect of what Clement of Alexandria called 'the bodily facts', John's evidence has again come back into serious contention. But what lay at the centre of Jesus' life has been left a blank, and indeed been regarded as forbidden territory. We can say what the church said about him, but we cannot say – or apparently be allowed to care – what he thought about himself. He could have meant something entirely different, or been a deluded megalomaniac. But what if he did not understand himself as anything like what the church proclaimed him to be? Is it possible to be content with – let alone to believe – a Christ *malgré lui*? 'Do you think you're what they say you

[27] *The Quest of the Historical Jesus*, ET London [3]1954, 66f., quoting Schleiermacher, *Über die Schriften des Lucas*, Berlin 1817.

[28] *The One Christ*, London [2]1914, 38.

are?' asks the chorus in *Jesus Christ Superstar*, representing, as choruses are supposed to, the ordinary man. And if he did not, then it is difficult to persuade the ordinary man or 'the simple believer' that it is a matter of complete indifference.

Yet the scholars, particularly those grasping the relief afforded by Kähler's book, which seemed to offer indemnity from what Tillich called 'historical risk' and to secure churchmen from being at the mercy of the latest deliverances of the Herr Professor, have thought it possible to ring off for faith what Kähler called an 'invulnerable area' from 'the papacy of scholarship'.[29] Bultmann's statement of this position in his *Theology of the New Testament* could stand for many:

> The acknowledgment of Jesus as the one in whom God's word decisively encounters man, whatever title be given him – 'Messiah (Christ)', 'Son of Man', 'Lord' – is a pure act of faith independent of the answer to the historical question of whether Jesus considered himself to be the Messiah. Only the historian can answer this question – as far as it can be answered at all – and faith, being personal decision, cannot be dependent on a historian's labour.[30]

One may agree that only the historian can answer this question, and grant too that the historian's labour cannot give faith, but still question whether it may not take it away, by rendering what lay at the heart of the truth about Jesus so uncertain, so vacuous or so culturally conditioned that men and women cease in fact to find it worth believing. I am not persuaded that it is possible to remain indifferent to the findings of the historian on how Jesus understood himself, nor that an ultimate scepticism is either tolerable or necessary. Yet are we in a position to give any answer? Have we the materials? Is it not inaccessible, even if not invulnerable?

At this point a distinction needs to be made. The materials clearly fail for reconstructing Jesus' self-consciousness in psychological terms, for analysing his psyche, its history or its type. The Gospels are no more in the business of supplying answers to psychological questions than they

[29] M. Kähler, *The So-called Historical Jesus and the Historic Biblical Christ* ([2]1896), ET Philadelphia 1964; P. Tillich, *Systematic Theology* II, Chicago and London 1957, 134. See my *Human Face of God*, 125–7, and the literature there cited; *Roots of a Radical*, 68–70; and the fascinating appendix to F. W. Dillistone's *C. H. Dodd: Interpreter of the New Testament*, London and Grand Rapids, Mich., 1977, 242f., where Langdon Gilkey recounts a classic conversation on this issue (at Union Theological Seminary, New York, in 1950) between Tillich and Dodd.

[30] *Theology of the New Testament* I, 26.

are to sociological or economic questions – though this does not mean that it is illegitimate *for us* to ask them. They do not even tell us what he looked like. Nor do they concern themselves with the dawning or development of his self-awareness. They are not bio-graphy, in the sense of writing about his life as *βιός*, let alone providing fragments of autobiography from the lips of Jesus. But this does not mean that they presuppose there *was* no development in his apprehension of God or himself, or that his was a static perfection. They would surely have agreed with Cullmann that 'the life of Jesus would not be fully human if its course did not manifest a development.'[31] Indeed the writer to the Hebrews is quite clear that he learned obedience through the things that he suffered, that he had to become what he was, to be made perfect, to go through the process of individuation and maturation like every other human being (2.10, 17f.; 4.15; 5.5, 8f.; 6.20; 7.28). Luke certainly recognized its beginning in the boy Jesus (2.52) in words that deliberately echo the growth of the child Samuel (I Sam. 2.26) and which Barth delighted to observe is described by the word *προκόπτειν*, meaning 'to extend by blows, as a smith stretches metal by hammers'.[32] But the Gospels are not interested in continuing to trace this process. One only gets glimpses of it, for example, in the story of the Syrophoenician woman, where under pressure Jesus comes through to a position he has apparently no intention of adopting at the outset (Matt. 15.21–28; Mark 7.24–30), or in Gethsemane, where he struggles to align his will with that of his Father (Mark 14.32–42 and pars.; Heb. 5.7). But even here of course the accounts are not written with an interest in tracing the psychological processes involved.

In John, for all the concentration on Jesus' inner life and relationship to the Father, there is even less attention to questions of psychic development or to the human factors that obedience involved. Yet they can be read between the lines of a number of passages, such as 7.1–10 (his prevarication about going up to Jerusalem for Tabernacles: life is easy for those for whom 'any time is right', he must abide his 'hour'; cf. 2.4; 12.23; 13.1); or 11.1–16 (where again in the conflict brought to a head by Lazarus' illness the reluctance to face a return to Judaea comes through); or 12.27–31 (the Johannine equivalent of Gethsemane, with its turmoil of soul and inner dialogue). Indeed the marks of emotional strain and psychic disturbance in Jesus are quite as evident in John as they are in Mark. There is the scarcely-suppressed exasperation in the questions of 4.48, 'Will none of you ever believe without seeing signs

[31] *Christology of the New Testament*, 97.
[32] *Church Dogmatics*, ET Edinburgh and Grand Rapids, Mich., 1936–69, I.2, 158.

and portents?'; of 8.25, 'Why should I speak to you at all?'; of 14.9, 'Have I been all this time with you, Philip, and you still do not know me?' There is the agitation of 11.33; 12.27 and 13.21, especially in the ἐτάραξεν of the first passage (almost 'he worked himself up'),[33] where it is combined with the obscure ἐμβριμᾶσθαι (repeated in 11.38), which appears to mean to 'shake with anger' (cf. Dan. 11.30; Lam. 2.6; Mark 1.43; 14.5; Matt. 9.30). Barrett's comment here is apposite (and he is as far from 'psychologizing' as anyone):

> Jesus perceives that the presence and grief of the sisters and of the Jews are almost forcing a miracle upon him, and as in 2.4 the request for miraculous activity evokes a firm, almost rough, answer, here, in circumstances of increased tension, it arouses his wrath. This miracle it will be impossible to hide (cf. vv. 28, 30); and this miracle, Jesus perceives, will be the immediate occasion of his death (vv. 49–53).[34]

The reference back to 2.4 is a reminder that this passage too cannot be glossed over as smoothly as expositors have often desired. There may be nothing harsh in the address *γύναι*, 'woman' (cf. 19.26), yet Jesus' retort to his mother, *Τί ἐμοὶ καὶ σοί;*', must mean 'What do you want with me?' with overtones of 'What have you against me?' The formula, frequent in the Old and New Testaments (Judg. 11.12; II Sam. 16.10; 19.22; I Kings 17.18; II Kings 3.13; II Chron. 35.21; Mark 1.24; 5.7; Matt. 8.29; Luke 4.34; 8.28), 'is invariably addressed to someone who represents a threat or danger to the speaker'.[35] Jesus evidently senses he is being put under unfair pressure to show his hand too soon.

Thus it would, I believe, be quite false to conclude that John supposed there *was* no development in his subject, or that the static effect and the semblance of effortless superiority which his Gospel has conveyed *when read from the viewpoint of modern psychology* was his intention.

Nevertheless a distinction needs to be made in the case of Jesus as of every other human being between his ego and his self, his *ego-consciousness* and his *self-knowledge*. Unhappily the Greek ἐγώ like

[33]In contrast with what is quoted immediately below, Barrett's comment seems singularly inappropriate: 'it must be intended to underline the contention that Jesus was always master of himself and his circumstances' (*John*, 399).

[34]*John*, 399. It is the need for suppressing publicity that also leads to this word being used of Jesus in Mark 1.43 and Matt. 9.30.

[35]J. Miranda, *Being and the Messiah: The Message of John*, ET New York 1973, 104f., where he spells this out forcefully. Cf. Brown, *John*, 99: 'There is always some refusal of an inopportune involvement.'

the English 'I' has to stand for both. Who, deep down, was the person who said ἐγὼ εἰμί or ἀμὴν λέγω ὑμῖν? How we are to understand such words, and with what aim are they recorded? There is an important difference to be drawn at this point between psychological verisimilitude and theological verity. None of the Gospels is primarily interested in the former; all are deeply concerned with the latter. And particularly of course is this true of John. If the distinction is not grasped, then the misunderstanding in his case will be the greater. If the Jesus of John and his words are taken at the level of psychological verisimilitude, then the impression is indeed left that never did any true man speak as he spoke, or, as those openly say in this Gospel who *do* take him at this level, that he was mad (2.17; 6.42; 7.20; 8.48, 52; 10.20) or bad (7.12; 9.16, 24; 10.21, 33; 18.30). And to many since the Johannine Christ has come through as intolerable or repellent.[36]

Yet at the level of theological verity John is simply deepening the question posed by all the Gospels, Who is this man? (Mark 4.41 and pars.; cf. 1.27; 2.7). Where is he *from*, that he speaks and acts with such authority, direct 'from source' (ἐξ-ουσία)? '*Quis et unde*?': so Krister Stendahl has brilliantly elucidated the two questions behind the opening chapters of Matthew's Gospel.[37] And these two questions, τίς καὶ πόθεν;, are those round which the whole of John's Gospel may be said to be written. 'Where do you come from?', asks Pilate in desperation and not a little apprehension (19.8f.). At one level Jesus' contemporaries claim to know this well enough (7.27f.) – they are perfectly familiar with his parentage and his home (6.42) – and in irony they are represented as saying that if he *were* the Messiah they would *not* know: for 'no one is to know where *he* comes from' (7.27). Yet at a deeper level they do not and cannot know (8.14; 9.29f.). *But he knows* (7.29; 8.14; 13.3). This last is a presupposition of the whole Gospel, which is written to draw it out for its readers. In this sense the *self-knowledge* of Jesus is the indispensable heart of the mystery: to regard it as a matter of indifference or as a 'no go' area is to leave a blank at the centre of Christian theology. Rather, John's concern is to take the reader into the very heart of this relationship, to disclose the inside story, what was really going on and who he really was, ἀληθινῶς, at the level of πνεῦμα rather than ψυχή.

[36]F. C. Burkitt was not alone in sensing a quality in 'the utterances of the Johannine Christ which, taken as the report of actual words spoken, is positively repellent' (*The Gospel History and its Transmission*, 227).

[37]'Quis et Unde? An Analysis of Matt. 1–2' in W. Eltester, ed., *Judentum—Urchristentum—Kirche*, BZNW 26, 1960, 94–105.

In the Synoptists the relation of Jesus to God, the distinctive relationship which allows him to speak of 'my Father' and to know himself called in a unique manner to the vocation of sonship, is everywhere presupposed. It is declared by the heavenly voice at his baptism, tested in the wilderness temptations, reiterated at the Transfiguration, and summed up at the close of his public teaching in the distinction between the servants and the son in the parable of the Wicked Husbandmen. The relation to source, the freedom and the authority with which Jesus speaks and acts, the intimacy of his union with God as Father: all these are presupposed and taken for granted. Yet, apart from hints from supernatural powers 'in the know' (Mark 1.24, 34; 3.11; 5.7 and pars.), there is really only one point at which we are permitted a glimpse into the inside of that reality. That is when a door is opened into the relationship between Jesus and his Father which forms the centre and core of his being:

> At that time Jesus spoke these words: I thank thee, Father, Lord of heaven and earth, for hiding these things from the learned and wise, and revealing them to the simple. Yes, Father, such was thy choice. Everything is entrusted to me by my Father; and no one knows the Son but the Father, and no one knows the Father but the Son and those to whom the Son may choose to reveal him (Matt. 11.25–27).

This mutual 'knowledge' is of course that of *connaître*, not *savoir*, even in the Lukan version, 'no one knows who the Son is but the Father, or who the Father is but the Son' (10.21f.). It is the knowledge of personal intimacy, and has been shown to have its closest parallel not in Hellenistic 'gnosis' but in the 'knowledge' of the Dead Sea Scrolls.[38] Indeed the precedence given to the Father knowing the Son, in contrast to what we should instinctively think of or quote, shows that it is grounded in the Hebraic understanding of God's prevenient knowledge and covenant-love (as the presence of the word εὐδοκία, or choice, in the context clearly indicates): 'You only have I known of all the families of the earth' is the presupposition of Yahweh's judgment of Israel (Amos 3.2). Similarly in Isaiah the charge that 'Israel does not know' rests on the divine premise, 'Sons have I reared and brought up' (1.2f.). And within the new covenant the same order still holds: 'I shall know even as also I have been known' (I Cor. 13.12). So in John, the order is 'the Father knows me and I know the Father' (10.15); and the

[38]Cf. W. D. Davies, 'Knowledge in the Dead Sea Scrolls and Matt. 11.25–30' in *Christian Origins and Judaism*, London and Philadelphia 1962, 119–44, esp. 141–4.

good shepherd knows his sheep before they know him (10.14).

That Jesus is thus known or loved (for the two are practical equivalents) by the Father, that he is 'the son of his love' (Paul's equivalent in Col. 1.13 of υἱὸς ἀγαπητός or ἐκλεκτός), that he finds his entire life and being in responding to this relationship, is, as Jeremias contended,[39] his secret, his revelation, the clue to his whole mission, which, as he tells Peter, flesh and blood cannot reveal, but only his Father in heaven (Matt. 16.17).[40] Without this clue we should miss everything. The Synoptic Gospels, as we have said, presuppose it, but they do not expose it. And in this, we may judge, they are true to Jesus. It is not, as Bornkamm states,[41] because they are 'extremely indifferent and evasive' to the consciousness of Jesus. It is because they respect the privacy and intimacy of the relationship with the one he called 'my Father'.[42] Like Socrates of his δαιμόνιον, he evidently did not talk of it freely. Yet that Socrates had this inner conviction of a reality that was always with him is deeply embedded in our sources, in Xenophon (*Mem.* 1.1.2; 4.8.1, 5; *Apol.* 4, 12f.) as well as Plato (*Apol.* 40a; *Theaet.* 151a; *Euthyd.* 272e; *Euthyphr.* 3b), and has to be regarded as one of the most certainly remembered facts about him. Equally, with Jesus, this inner relationship as the umbilical cord of his life must be accepted as irreducibly necessary to the understanding of who and what he was, and, Riesenfeld has insisted,[43] to the authority of his teaching. Though the passage which brings it to the surface may appear in the Synoptic Gospels to stick out like a sore thumb and 'gives the impression of a thunderbolt fallen from the Johannine sky',[44] recent critical study has shown that there is less and less ground for doubting its genuineness as a saying of Jesus.[45] This is especially true if, with Jeremias again, we recognize that on Jesus' own lips the 'the' of 'the

[39]*NT Theology* I, 59–61.

[40]For the setting of this cf. ch. V, p. 194 n. 8 above.

[41]*Jesus of Nazareth*, ET London 1960, New York 1961, 169.

[42]Cullmann similarly recognizes this distinctive sonship, which he does not hesitate to say 'expresses the very essence of Jesus' self-consciousness', as spoken with 'reserve'; for it is 'the profound secret that Jesus has been aware of since his baptism and constantly experiences in executing his obedience, the secret that he is related to God as no other man is' (*Christology of the NT*, 282f.).

[43]*The Gospel Tradition and its Beginnings*, 28f.

[44]K. von Hase, *Die Geschichte Jesu*, ²Leipzig 1876, 422.

[45]Cf. Jeremias, *NT Theology* I, 56–9, and the literature there cited; also Hunter, *The Work and Words of Jesus*, London and Philadelphia ²1973, 84; 'Crux Criticorum – Matt. 11.25–30 – A Re-Appraisal', *NTS* 8, 1961–2, 241–9; Cullmann, *Christology of the NT*, 286–8; J. D. G. Dunn, *Jesus and the Spirit*, 26–34; *Christology in the Making*,

father' and 'the son' is the generic 'the' constantly to be found in parables, like 'the sower' that went out to sow (Mark 4.3) or 'the grain of wheat' that falls into the ground (John 12.24). In these cases we should use the indefinite article, so Jeremias renders: 'Just as only a father (really) knows his son, so only a son (really) knows his father'.[46] It is still indeed a parable of Jesus' unique relationship to God, like 'the son' in the story of the Wicked Husbandmen. But, as James Dunn has rightly said, it does not by itself commit us to any particular interpretation of 'divinity': 'Schweitzer's claim that Matt. 11.27 "may be spoken from the consciousness of pre-existence"[47] is never more than a possibility, neither finally excluded nor positively indicated by careful exegesis.'[48] To the content of what is or is not here being claimed I shall come back. At this point we are simply concerned with whether such insight into the self-knowledge of Jesus is a legitimate or important quest. And on this Dunn is unequivocal:

> Can the historian hope to penetrate into the self-consciousness (or self-understanding) of a historical individual? The answer must be in the affirmative, otherwise history would be nothing more than a dreary catalogue of dates and documentation.[49]

He goes on to illustrate from Louis XIV and Winston Churchill how particular utterances or revealing comments, especially at crucial moments, may 'provide as it were a key which unlocks the mystery of the historical personality, a clue into his or her character, a window into his or her soul'. He asks whether there are any statements of Jesus which provide similar windows into his inner feelings and consciousness, and he replies: 'In my judgment the answer is almost certainly Yes.' He cites[50] 'those sayings of Jesus which express what Bultmann himself called "the immediacy of eschatological consciousness"' (Matt. 11.5f. = Luke 7.22f.; Matt. 13.16f. = Luke 10.23f.; Matt. 12.41f. = Luke 11.31f.; Luke 12.54–56; and he adds Matt. 12.28 =

1980, 29, 198–200; I. H. Marshall, *The Origins of New Testament Christology*, Leicester and Downers Grove, Ill., 1976, 115.

[46]*NT Theology* I, 59. So earlier G. Dalman, *Words of Jesus*, ET Edinburgh and New York 1902, 193f., 283.

[47]*Geschichte der Leben-Jesu-Forschung*, ²1913, 310. The passage does not appear in the ET. It is quoted, with favour, by Cullmann, *Christology of the NT*, 288, and *Johannine Circle*, 81.

[48]*Christology in the Making* 29; so Cullmann, *Christology of the NT*, 288.

[49]*Christology in the Making*, 25.

[50]Ibid., 26.

Luke 11.20).[51] But none of these begins to take one inside his relationship to God in the manner of Matt. 11.27 = Luke 10.22. Yet remarkably this saying is never cited anywhere in Bultmann's *Theology of the New Testament*;[52] and it is significant that he always speaks of Jesus' 'messianic self-consciousness', asking whether he saw himself as Messiah or Son of Man or Lord. His relationship to the Father as Son, which Jeremias rightly saw as central, is not even discussed.

But what is so rare as to be almost unique in the Synoptists is normative in John. And if, as I am convinced, there is no literary interdependence it is surely very significant that the one Synoptic window should be thoroughly Johannine in colouring. It suggests strongly that the Johannine picture of Jesus' self-understanding as 'the unique Son of God who has a unique knowledge of the Father, and a unique function as Mediator of that knowledge'[53] is not simply of his creation but a taking up and drawing out of what surfaces so sketchily elsewhere. Cullmann very properly has raised the question,

> Might we not have a special kind of teaching here? It would not be secret, or systematically withheld from the majority of disciples, but it would have been more intimate teaching which not all the disciples knew (and which they may barely have understood). The author of the Gospel of John may have developed it *freely*, in the way that we know, but still keeping Jesus' teaching as a foundation.[54]

This would presuppose an interpreter very close to source, even if not, in Cullmann's judgment, one of the Twelve.

This aspect of 'St John's Contribution to the Picture of the Historical Jesus' was stressed in an inaugural lecture of that title given by T. E. Pollard at Knox Theological Hall, Dunedin, in 1964. Since it has appeared only in a privately circulated journal for ministers of the Presbyterian Church in New Zealand,[55] I should like to give it wider circulation by some more extended citation than would otherwise be

[51] *The History of the Synoptic Tradition*, ²1968, 126.

[52] In his *History of the Synoptic Tradition*, 159f., it is called 'a Hellenistic revelation saying'. Similarly, as Anderson notes in a balanced discussion in his *Jesus and Christian Origins*; 159: 'The reader of Bornkamm's *Jesus of Nazareth* will search in vain for discussion of such a logion as this. It is excluded as a community confession, and every effort to define the self-consciousness of Jesus as an *a priori*, authenticating his message and mission, is here avoided.'

[53] I take the phrase from the lecture of T. E. Pollard quoted below.

[54] *Johannine Circle*, 82.

[55] *Forum* 16.6, August 1964, 2–9.

appropriate.

He believes that the paucity of Synoptic reference to the self-consciousness of Jesus represents a faithful reflection of his own reticence.

If he avoids using Messianic categories, it is not because he did not believe himself to be Messiah; but because, as the sequel to Peter's confession of him as the Messiah shows so clearly, there was a vast difference between what Peter and the rest understood by the title and the meaning it had for Jesus himself. Luke testifies to the failure of the disciples to understand the significance of Jesus and his words in the disillusionment and perplexity of the two disciples on the road to Emmaus. The Synoptics give an accurate picture of this failure on the part of the disciples to understand the personality and the words and deeds of Jesus. They are recording the consciousness and personality of Jesus as they dimly apprehended it in the days of his ministry.

On the other hand, John writes in order to bring out the real personality of Jesus and the real nature of his ministry, which had been there all the time, but which, during Jesus' sojourning with them, they had failed to see clearly. . . . It is not that John is reading back into the earthly life something that was not there; rather, with the penetrating insight born of reflection and faith, he sees the personality of Jesus as it really was, and as the disciples would have seen it had their eyes not been blinded by preconceptions and misunderstanding. As he writes his Gospel John is saying in effect, 'This is what Jesus was really like; we did not realize it then, but now we know it.'

Pollard goes on to use R. G. Collingwood's distinction between the 'outside' and the 'inside' of the same event, between 'everything belonging to it that can be described in terms of bodies and their movements' and 'that in it which can only be described in terms of thought'.[56]

Applying this distinction I would say that the Synoptists are more concerned with the 'outside' of the events they record, even though they record them because they believe that they have a theological or soteriological significance. John, on the other hand, is concerned with the 'inside' of the events; to use Collingwood's words, he

[56] *The Idea of History*, Oxford and Toronto 1959, 174.

> 'remembers that the events were actions, and that his main task is to think himself into these actions, to discern the thoughts of the agent'.[57] In other words, the Synoptists see Jesus and his words and actions from the outside through the eyes of the disciples: John 'enters sympathetically into the mind' of Jesus, or 'puts himself into the shoes' of Jesus.

He draws the conclusion that

> On Collingwood's definition of the real task of the historian, it could well be argued that John is a better historian than the Synoptists.[58] John portrays Jesus as the one who at every point is conscious of his Messianic function as Son of God, whose every action, thought and word are governed by this consciousness. There is no need to interpret this portrait as an invention by John or a falsification of what Jesus really was. Rather it is an attempt to portray Jesus as he was, in his earthly life, in and for himself. It is not that this Jesus of St John is any less human than the Jesus of the Synoptics; it is rather that John penetrates with deeper insight into the inner springs of the personality of Jesus. Nor was John's portrait a more highly developed theological interpretation; rather because of his deeper insight he makes explicit what is implicit, and, for the most part, veiled in the Synoptics.[59]

This is in remarkable harmony with what we have been trying to say throughout. And he ends by predicting:

> As the New Quest progresses, the Gospel of John must come into its

[57]*The Idea of History*, 174. Pollard refers here to P. van Buren, *The Secular Meaning of the Gospel*, London and New York 1963, 114, who also quotes Collingwood. But van Buren goes on to say: 'The evangelists were not doing history in Collingwood's sense. . . . They did not try to "enter sympathetically" into the mind of Jesus, and they have left us little to go on if we take that as the historical task. . . . They wrote as believers, even as worshippers' (115f.). Yet why should these two perspectives be mutually incompatible?

[58]Cf. Dodd, *Interpretation*, 445f. and the quotation he gives from Hugh Last, *JRS* 39, 1949, 4, presenting the case 'that the primary concern of history is with the various elements – ideas, sentiments, emotions and passions – which together make up the conscious life of men; that events produced by human agency are of very little interest except as clues to the motives and purposes of the agents; that such motives and purposes are the essence of the experiences which the historian has to recreate.'

[59]Cf. Cullmann's very similar conclusion: 'Though John openly proclaimed what the historical Jesus only referred to with veiled allusion, he very impressively expressed, in their very solidarity, the two sides of Jesus' Son-consciousness: obedience and oneness with the Father' (*Christology of the NT*, 303).

own again as a primary source. To quote E. M. Sidebottom,[60] 'The Fourth Gospel is . . . best understood as a complement to the others not in the sense that it interprets them but that it shows us how to interpret them.'

Though he uses very different categories and appears to have a diametrically opposed estimate of the historicity of the Fourth Gospel, John Knox tells me that he was trying to make much the same point when he spoke of the 'memory' of the church telling us a good deal more about the inner life of Jesus than 'the Gospels'. But he confesses that by the latter he did not make it clear that he meant 'the Synoptic Gospels'.

These are, generally speaking, strangely silent about Jesus' own inner attitudes, states of mind and heart. They tell us where he went, what he did or said, what happened to him, but rarely give us any hint of what he was feeling. One may infer from his teaching about God how he himself felt toward God, but we are not explicitly told. One may draw conclusions from his ethical teaching, not only how he *thought* about one's duty towards others, but also as to what his actual feelings toward others were; but these are never described and are seldom referred to. Sometimes in his most passionate (and more characteristic) teachings, his inner feelings break through what may appear to be the determined objectivity of the Gospel record, and one seems for a moment to hear his very voice.[61] But these occasions are rare indeed; and I wonder just what impression of the inner personal life of Jesus we should have if we needed to depend on the Gospels alone, or whether we should be able to hear his voice in his recorded words if we were not also hearing it in the common life of the Church. . . . Undoubtedly one reason why the Church has always cherished the Fourth Gospel and has been unable to believe that it does not contain authentic historical truth about Jesus is that one can read there, and there only, such words as 'Having loved his own . . . he loved them to the end' and 'This is my commandment, that you love one another as I have loved you' (John 13.1; 15.12) – words which express a love of Jesus for his own which has a deep, sure place in the memory of the Church.[62]

[60] *The Christ of the Fourth Gospel*, 187.
[61] Cf. Jeremias' *ipsissima vox*.
[62] *The Church and the Reality of Christ*, New York 1962, London 1963, 55f.

But I question whether he has not set up a false division between 'the Gospels' and his elusive and much debated category 'the memory of the Church' because he confines the former to the Synoptists and does not treat John (whom he firmly classes with 'the Epistles') as just as authentic a source of knowledge about Jesus, if not a more penetrating one, than the other three.

3. *The Invader from Another World?*

But, to return to Pollard, is it really true that the Jesus of St John is 'not . . . any less human than the Jesus of the Synoptics'? This is not how it has seemed to most, and the main issue must now be faced, Is not John actually giving us a very different Christ, one who is not *in origin* a man at all but a heavenly being come to earth?

This common assessment of Johannine christology has recently been reinforced by Dunn's impressive study, *Christology in the Making*. He believes that John presents, perhaps alone among the writers of the New Testament but certainly the most explicitly, a picture of the Incarnation which was to become the received doctrine of the church at Nicaea and Chalcedon. This is of a pre-existent divine being, subsequently confessed as the second Person of the Trinity, who descended from heaven and became man by assuming a human as well as his own divine nature. The working out of this doctrine was to occupy the intervening centuries, but John supplied the material and the impetus for it by his presentation of Jesus as the Word and Son of God, who came from God and went to God, and who, while a totally genuine human being as a man among men, nevertheless 'belonged' essentially to a different order. Metaphysically if not physically (for John says nothing about the manner of his birth)[63] he did not begin where we are. He came from the divine side of the line. He was part of the life of God, unique *because* of his origin and nature, and marked off by an absolute difference of kind and not simply of degree from every other human being. Whereas we are 'from below' he was 'from above', 'out of God', pre-existing eternally 'in the bosom of the Father' from 'before the foundation of the world'. The line of separation and the point of difference are apparently clear and distinct.

Yet there is an obvious danger of reading John through the spectacles of later understandings of pre-existence and incarnation. What his own presuppositions were and whether, as Dunn believes, he

[63]Clearly the plural in 1.13 is the preferable reading.

operated with and introduced into Christian theology this notion of a heavenly Person who took on flesh cannot be decided *a priori*, for John never states them explicitly. They can only be inferred from his use of language and from the conclusions to which it leads either him or others.

One of these conclusions, with which he has been charged from the beginning, is that, however unintentionally, he is inescapably presenting a quasi-docetic picture of the humanity of Jesus. For even if this heavenly being genuinely touches ground on the path of his parabola and does not, as many in both ancient and modern times have interpreted him as doing, pass through this world some inches off the earth, there can be no doubt that he is *not* in the fullest sense 'one of us'. He does not start where we start, even if he comes to take us where he is. He is a cuckoo in the human nest. And if this *is* the picture of Jesus which John presents, it is hardly surprising that the first heresy in the Johannine community should be the denial of 'Jesus Christ come in the flesh'. That his language is patient of this interpretation is obvious.[64] That it is a misinterpretation is equally obvious from his horrified reaction that this is nothing less than Antichrist.

But is it simply that he does not realize the implications and the tendency of his presentation? Or is it that this picture of Christ as a divine visitant is not what he meant at all, however unsuccessful he has been in guarding against its being so understood? I shall argue that it is the latter. This is not simply because this notion of a fully individuated heavenly person, as distinct from personifications of God's attributes and agencies, cannot be demonstrated, as Dunn agrees, in pre-Christian Judaism or in the rest of the New Testament. It had to start somewhere; and it could have started as well as anywhere with John's reflections on the significance of the Christ-event: he was a creative enough theologian. Rather it is because careful study of his language does not, I believe, bear out that this is the real point of difference between Jesus and the rest of mankind. That he *is* unique – in Johannine terms, the only Son of the Father – is not in dispute. It is a question whether this way of expressing it puts the distinctiveness in the right place, for him or for us.

On the face of it, there is for John a clear line of demarcation, and

[64]So supremely and simplistically, Käsemann, *Testament of Jesus*, who accuses the Gospel of 'naive docetism' (26, 45, 70) and says that its admission to the canon was 'through man's error and God's providence' (75). For an effective answer cf. L. Morris, 'The Jesus of Saint John' in R. A. Guelich, ed., *Unity and Diversity in New Testament Theology: Essays in Honor of George E. Ladd*, Grand Rapids, Mich. 1978, 37–53.

Jesus is on the one side of it and everyone else on the other. Yet the line is a good deal more blurred than at first sight appears. John's phrases are by no means univocal; they are not applied to Jesus alone; and it is often a question of how much is to be read into them. This is not to say that the phrases mean the same in every context or on everyone's lips, nor that there is not a real difference between Jesus and all other men. It is simply that the point of difference is not to be located on so decisive or absolute a line as the Johannine evidence has usually been assumed to presuppose.

Let us begin with a sample passage which is characteristically and typically Johannine, from John 6.42–46. 'The Jews' are speaking:

> They said, 'Surely this is Jesus son of Joseph; we know his father and mother. How can he now say, "I have come down from heaven"?' Jesus answered, 'Stop murmuring among yourselves. No man can come to me unless he is drawn by the Father who sent me; and I will raise him up on the last day. It is written in the prophets: "And they shall all be taught by God." Everyone who has listened to the Father and learned from him comes to me. I do not mean that anyone has seen the Father. He who has come from God has seen the Father, and he alone.'

In the course of these few verses three apparently equivalent phrases are used of Jesus: that he has

> come down from heaven
> been sent by the Father
> come (or, literally, is) from God.

Moreover all of them are compatible with his being the son of Joseph and with his father and mother being known. For it is quite clear that John does not intend to *deny* the facts of his paternity and human origin. Elsewhere he is described as 'the son of Joseph, the man from Nazareth' (1.45), and the offence of his coming out of Nazareth (1.46) and out of Galilee (7.41, 52) is not in the least played down (rather the contrary) – though John may by his silent irony also convey an awareness of his birth at Bethlehem (7.42) and of the doubts about its legitimacy (8.41). In fact the *doubles entendres* of this Gospel, clustering around the 'whence?' of this man, clearly presuppose that the question can be answered at two levels, neither of which is to be denied. He is from or out of Nazareth *and* he is from or out of the Father, and not one at the expense of the other. It is a premiss of any interpretation of Johannine thought that it is not to stand self-condemned. There can be no question of Jesus not being of human origin like everyone else or of his not being 'a man'. Indeed ἄνθρωπος is used of him more often in this Gospel than in all the others put together. The figures are: Matthew 3; Mark 2; Luke 6 (plus ἀνήρ 1); John 15 (plus ἀνήρ 1).[65] It has been observed too that John uses the human name Jesus, in a manner reminiscent of the Epistle to the Hebrews, more often than any of the other evangelists (Matt. 150; Mark 81; Luke 89; John 237).[66]

Of the indications in this passage of his divine origin by far the commonest is his being 'sent' by God or the Father.[67] It is clearly not of John's creation since it occurs in one of the sayings common to him and the Synoptists (Matt. 10.40; Mark 9.37; Luke 9.48; 10.16; John 13.20; 20.21). In one form or other (and the two words πέμπω and ἀποστέλλω are evidently stylistic variants without significant difference of meaning),[68] this phrase is used of Jesus by John some 42 times. It evidently of itself does not presuppose pre-existence, since it is regularly used elsewhere in the Bible of the prophets[69] and indeed of Jesus as God's 'son' (Mark 12.2–6 and pars.) without any such implication (cf. Luke 4.43 with Mark 1.38; also Matt. 15.24); and in John of John the Baptist (1.6, 33; 3.28) and human agents generally (7.18; 13.16). In fact its emphasis is regularly to bring out dependence and subordination – that the agent is entirely responsible to the principal whom he represents and in whose name he acts. He can say or do nothing 'of himself' – only what he is 'given' or 'told'. Typical are such expressions as:

[65]The figures I gave in *The Human Face of God*, 171, and 'The Use of the Fourth Gospel for Christology Today', 68 n. 39, were slightly inaccurate. I have corrected them in the version of the latter reprinted in *Twelve More NTS*, 145 n. 26.

[66]I owe this, and the figures, to L. Morris, 'The Jesus of Saint John', 48.

[67]Cf. J. Comblin, *Sent from the Father: Meditations on the Fourth Gospel*, ET New York 1979.

[68]Cf. especially 5.36–38 and 20.21 (despite J. Seynaeve, 'Les verbes ἀποστέλλω et πέμπω dans le vocabulaire théologique de saint Jean', in *Évangile*, 385–9). For some reason πέμπω is preferred for the participle and ἀποστέλλω for the indicative (cf. the more detailed analysis in Howard, *Fourth Gospel in Recent Criticism*, 291). To that extent the words of the departing angel in Tobit 12.20, ἀναβαίνω πρὸς τὸν ἀποστείλαντά με, which, says Sidebottom, *Christ of the Fourth Gospel*, 141 'is what we should expect John to put into Jesus' mouth', is unJohannine. What John makes him say is ὑπάγω πρὸς τὸν πέμψαντά με (7.33; 16.5).

[69]Cf. e.g., Jer. 1.5–7, where Jeremiah is both consecrated and sent, like Jesus in John 10.36 and the disciples in 17.17–19; and Isa. 61.1, applied to Jesus by himself in Luke 4.18, where the prophet is anointed and sent (χρίω is not used by John, but cf. I John 2.20, 27, where believers have a χρῖσμα from 'the Holy One').

I cannot do anything of myself; as I hear I judge (5.30).
I do nothing on my own authority, but in all that I say I have been taught by my Father (8.28).
Me, a man who told you the truth, as I heard it from God (8.40; cf. 8.26).
I do not speak on my own authority, but the Father who sent me has himself commanded me what to say and how to speak (12.49; cf. also 15.15; 17.8).

And this relationship of obedient listening[70] to the teaching of God is not peculiar to Jesus. Indeed in the passage from which we started he refers his hearers to a passage in their own scriptures, referring to all the sons of Israel (Isa. 54.13):

It is written in the prophets: 'And they shall all be taught by God.' Everyone who has listened to the Father and learned from him comes to me (6.45).

Jesus stands in solidarity with all other men in pupillage to the Father. In fact J. E. Davey,[71] who has made a special study of this dependence of Jesus on God for everything he is and does as 'the ruling element in John's portrait of Christ', stresses that in this respect 'the Christ of John is actually more "human" than in almost any of the other New Testament writings.'[72]

But in this passage it is not simply that Jesus is 'a man who has heard the truth from God' (8.40): he himself 'is from God (παρὰ τοῦ θεοῦ)' (6.46). Is not this a way of saying that he is not human but divine? May be, but if so it is not by reason of this phrase alone. For John the Baptist too was a man sent παρὰ θεοῦ (1.6), and when Nicodemus acknowledged Jesus as a teacher come from God, ἀπὸ θεοῦ (3.2), he certainly implied no divinity thereby, any more than those who were debating whether the healer of the blind man was 'a man from God' (παρὰ θεοῦ) (9.16, 33). For this phrase is equated with being 'a prophet' (9.17) and indeed 'anyone who is devout and obeys his will' (9.31).

[70]It is perhaps surprising that the words ὑπακοή and ὑπακούω (as opposed to ἀκούω) are not applied by John to Jesus, in contrast with Paul and the author to the Hebrews. But the thought is clearly there. Indeed Hoskyns calls Jesus' obedience to the will of God 'the central theme of the Gospel' (*Fourth Gospel*, 78). The situation is rather the same as with the absence of the words 'reveal' and 'revelation'.

[71]*The Jesus of St John*, London 1958, especially 90–157. Cf. Barrett, '"The Father is Greater than I" (John 14.28): Subordinationist Christology in the New Testament', in *Essays on John*, 19–36. He commends and extends Davey's thesis (22–5).

[72]*The Jesus of John*, 89.

Nor is it possible, with Dodd,[73] to differentiate between, on the one hand, ἀπὸ τοῦ θεοῦ and παρὰ τοῦ θεοῦ, which he urges could be used of any prophet or messenger, and on the other ἐκ τοῦ θεοῦ signifying unique origination in the being of God.[74] For it is very doubtful if the alternation of παρά in 16.27, ἐκ in 16.28 (if it *is* the right reading) and ἀπό in 16.30 represents more than stylistic variation: in any case they are all combined with the verb ἐξέρχομαι. Above all, being ἐκ τοῦ θεοῦ, which is applied to Jesus in 8.42, is in 8.47 applied to any man, and should apply even to the Jews: 'He who is ἐκ τοῦ θεοῦ listens to the words of God. You are not ἐκ τοῦ θεοῦ; that is why you do not listen.' Indeed to be, or be born, ἐκ (τοῦ) θεοῦ is John's regular way of describing believers as children of God (1.13; I John 2.29; 3.9f.; 4.4, 6f.; 5.1, 4, 18f.; III John 11).[75]

Similarly, to 'come into the world', which might suggest some special kind of supernatural entry, is used identically of Jesus (9.39; 12.46; 16.28; 18.37), of 'the prophet' (6.14), of the Messiah (11.27; cf. 4.25; 7.27, 31, 41f.) and indeed, if this is the right punctuation, of 'every man' (1.9). It is the equivalent in 18.37 of being 'born' or 'born into the world' (16.21) which is applied to Jesus and to any woman's child. Similarly the disciples are 'sent into the world' exactly as (καθώς) Jesus has been sent into the world (17.18). In fact they are not 'of this world' any more than he is of this world (17.14, 16; 15.19). For believers too are 'from above' (ἄνωθεν; 3.3, 7) as he is 'from above' (3.31). And when Jesus says to the Jews in 8.23, 'You are ἐκ τῶν κάτω, but I am ἐκ τῶν ἄνω,' it is not because they are human and he is divine but because they are 'worldly' and judge simply at the level of 'flesh' (8.15). As Comblin says, 'The reference is not to separate places of origin but to antithetical ways of being.'[76]

Yet this same contrast, in terms this time of being ἐκ τῆς γῆς, earthy, is made in 3.31 with 'the one who comes from heaven'. And this brings us to the last of the three phrases from which we began, in 6.42, 'coming down from heaven'. This may strike *us* as being in a different category from being 'sent' by the Father or even being 'from God' and putting Jesus in the class of a supernatural being or visitor from outer

[73] *Interpretation*, 259f. Cullmann, *Christology of the NT*, 298, takes this over uncritically.

[74] Surprisingly Pollard, 'The Father–Son and God–Believer Relationships according to St John: a Brief Study of John's Use of Prepositions' in *Évangile*, 363–9, tries to claim the same unique reference for παρά rather than ἐκ (365f.). But this, as we are about to show, is impossible.

[75] Cf. below, p. 376.

[76] *Sent from the Father*, 35.

space. But of course 'heaven' is simply a periphrasis for 'God'. In 3.27, 'A man can only have what is given him from heaven' is properly rendered by the NEB, 'what God gives him' (cf. the similar periphrasis 'from above' in 19.11). When John the Baptist sees the Spirit 'coming down from heaven' and resting on Jesus he recognizes him as the one marked out by *God* (1.32–4); and the bread or the Son of Man that comes down from heaven (3.13; 6.33, 41, 50f., 58) means God's bread, God's man. When therefore Jesus says 'I have come down from heaven to do the will of him who sent me' (6.38) and that he will 'ascend where he was before' (6.62), it is but another way of saying that he has 'come from God and is going to God' (13.3) and must 'leave this world and go to the Father' (13.1). Heaven is where he belongs, his home; his life is in 'the realms above', 'hidden with God', as Paul might have put it (Col. 3.1–3). His being is essentially 'in the bosom of the Father' (1.18) – though the phrase 'who is in heaven' (that is, even during the Incarnation) is almost certainly no part of the text of 3.13. That verse is indeed asserting uniqueness of Christ: 'No one ever went up to heaven except the one who came down from heaven'; and I would agree with Borgen's persuasive discussion of it[77] that it implies that the Son of Man has previously gone up to heaven,[78] as in Dan. 7.13f., for his installation, to receive his seal of office (6.27) and be 'given' his universal ἐξουσία over men (5.27; 17.2; exactly as in Dan. 7.14 LXX) and the Father's commission and instructions (cf. 3.34; 7.16; 8.26; 12.49; 14.24; 17.4, 6). But this does not imply, as Borgen presupposes, that the Son of Man is previously or pre-existently a divine or heavenly being. On the contrary the Son of Man in Dan. 7, who represents 'the saints of the most high', or Moses, who goes up into the mountain to receive the 'commandments' (Exod. 19; 24; 34) or Enoch who ascends to heaven to be identified with the Son of Man, that is, God's man or messianic agent (I Enoch 70.2–4; 71.14–17), are earthly, human figures. In the context of first-century gnosticizing

[77]'Some Jewish Exegetical Traditions as Background for Son of Man Sayings in John's Gospel (John 3.13–14 and context)' in *Évangile*, 243–58.

[78]Sidebottom, *Christ of the Fourth Gospel*, 120 (cf. Lindars, *John*, 156), tries to make it mean 'No one has ascended, *but one has* descended'. But as Moule says, 'The Individualism of the Fourth Gospel', *NovT* 5, 1962, 176 n. 1 (*Essays in New Testament Interpretation*, 96 n. 6), 'I cannot see how ὁ καταβάς can thus be turned into an indicative clause.' So Barrett, *Essays on John*, 110 on a similar attempt in F. J. Moloney, *The Johannine Son of Man*, Rome ²1978. The parallels Borgen quotes from John 6.46 and 17.12 for the implied conclusion 'except . . . the Son of man, he has ascended into heaven' are compelling. The only alternative is to refer it to the future ascension of Jesus and to see it as 'a post-resurrection formulation of the Church's faith' (Moule) set anachronously on the lips of Jesus (so Barrett, Brown and Schnackenburg, ad loc.).

Judaism the assertion of the uniqueness of Christ is very likely being set against similar claims for Moses[79] or directed at those, whether Jewish[80] or Christian, who take their stand upon visions and revelations of God on the basis of mystical 'trips' (cf. II Cor. 12.1–4; Col. 2.18). It is God's accredited agent who alone can give first-hand reports of what he has seen and heard (1.18; 3.32; 6.46) to those who 'never heard his voice or saw his form' (5.37), though it is implied that 'hearing his voice' at any rate should have been open to them, had his word found a home in them (5.38).[81] But this is because he speaks what he has seen in his Father's presence, whereas they do what they have heard from their father the Devil (8.38). It is not because he is not human.

4. *The True Son*

But this raises the question of *why* Jesus alone is thus privileged. It is too easy to close the discussion by saying simply 'because he was God'. That for this Gospel he is the revelation and embodiment of God for man is of course never to be denied, and to this God-language we shall return. It would however be precarious to rest any answer on the quotation of John 1.18, that 'the only one, himself God, the nearest to the Father's heart, has made him known' (NEB margin). For there is a notorious textual crux at this point. From the manuscript evidence there is every reason to believe that *μονογενὴς θεός* is the reading that reaches furthest back to source,[82] and every modern edition of the Greek Testament properly gives it precedence. It is equally noticeable however that both the RSV and the NEB still prefer *ὁ μονογενὴς υἱός* in

[79]Cf. Philo, *Vit. Mos.* 1.158, 'For he was named god and king of the whole nation, and entered, we are told, into the darkness where God was, that is into the unseen, invisible, incorporeal and archetypal essence of existing things. Thus he beheld what is hidden from the sight of mortal nature, and, in himself and his life displayed for all to see, he has set before us, like some well-wrought picture, a piece of work beautiful and godlike, a model for those who are willing to copy it' (tr. F. H. Colson, LCL). Borgen also quotes (244) 'the same kind of polemic as in John 3.13 . . . in the old tannaitic midrash *Mek.* Exod. 19.20 ("Moses and Elijah did not go up, nor did the glory come down")' and the view of which Josephus will have nothing, that Moses on the mountain 'had been taken back to the divinity' (*Ant.* 3.96).

[80]Cf. Odeberg, *Fourth Gospel*, 72f., 89. He quotes I Enoch, II Enoch, the Testament of Levi, II Baruch and the Ascension of Isaiah, as well as later mystical and rabbinic literature.

[81]In III John 11 it appears to be implied that it is evil-doing that also prevents a man seeing God (cf. I John 3.6).

[82]For the classic statement of this case cf. F. J. A. Hort, *Two Dissertations: I, On μονογενὴς θεός in Scripture and Tradition*, Cambridge 1876, 1–72.

their text, as opposed to the margin, and I am inclined to judge that they are right. For the contrast with 'the Father' appears overwhelmingly to demand 'the only Son' (as in 1.14), and *μονογενὴς θεός* is literally untranslatable ('the only one, himself God' is a paraphrase to make the best of it) and out of line with Johannine usage (contrast 5.44 and 17.3 of the Father). In other words, I believe that *θεός* may indeed be the best attested reading, and even go back to the autograph, but that it was a slip for *υἱός* (there is only the difference between *YC* and *ΘC*) and the author would have been the first to correct it.[83] But nothing should be made to turn or rest on this, one way or the other.

For the overwhelming Johannine answer to why Jesus alone is privy to the Father's secrets and has been given his 'glory' and his 'name' to reveal to others is not that he is 'God' but that he is 'the Son'. But what does that mean for John?

We should begin again with the recognition that for him, as for the Synoptists and Jesus himself, this is primarily parabolic language, as when he first introduces it in 1.14:[84] Jesus is as close to God as a son to his father. But what does being son to father, and hence 'the Son' to 'the Father', mean?

First of all it means everything, and more, that being an 'agent' means. In fact as Harvey says,[85] a man's best agent is his son, as in the classic instance of Tobit 5.1–3 or in the parable of Mark 12.6 and pars.:[86] for no one else could better be guaranteed to represent him and his interests. Everything the father was and had was his. And John makes explicit even more than the Synoptists this Hebraic understanding of sonship.[87] To 'be son of' means to 'do the works of', to reflect the nature of ('like father, like son'), whether this be of God or Abraham or the Devil (8.31–47; cf. I John 3.7–12). And this functional understanding is, as we saw, brought home in 10.31–38, where the Jews charge Jesus with blasphemy: 'You, a mere man, claim to be a god.' He replies that their own scriptures (Ps. 82.6) call those to whom the word of God came 'gods' – referring probably either to Moses, who is described as being 'as God' to Pharaoh (Exod. 4.16; 7.1) and who is

[83]As I believe that in Rom. 5.1 Paul would have corrected ἔχωμεν, if that is what Tertius heard, to ἔχομεν. We always assume that the autograph was without slip, but that is not true of anything of any length that I or anyone else has written.

[84]See above, ch. VII, p. 321.

[85]*Jesus on Trial*, 89–91; *Constraints of History*, 161–3.

[86]Cf. J. D. M. Derrett, *Law in the New Testament*, London 1970, 302f.

[87]Cf. again Harvey, *Constraints of History*, ch. 7, who argues for very much the same position as I am doing here; also E. Schillebeeckx, *Christ*, 431.

boldly called 'God' by Philo,[88] or (as the thrust of the psalm would suggest) to the judges of the Old Testament, to whom men were to go 'as to God' (Exod. 21.6; 22.8f., 28):[89] they represented God, acted in his place, just as Jesus is claiming to do. The only surprise is that he does not continue the quotation: 'and you shall all be called sons of the Most High' (probably because John avoids calling anyone else 'son' except Jesus).[90] As Dodd says,[91] the conclusion is assumed (in the rabbinic manner), for it forms the presupposition of what follows: 'Then why do you charge me with blasphemy because I . . . said "I am God's son" (υἱὸς θεοῦ εἰμι), again without the article. For to be a son of God is what all men ought to be.[92] And the test and meaning of sonship is moral correspondence: 'If I am not acting as my Father would, do not believe me.' That is what would discredit his claim.[93] But 'if I am . . .

[88] *Vit. Mos.* 1.158; *Prob.* 42–4; *Som.* 2.189; *Mut.* 19; *Sacr.* 8–10; though he explains that it is only by analogy (*Det.* 160f.). Cf. W. A. Meeks, 'Moses as God and King' in J. Neusner, ed., *Religions in Antiquity*, Leiden 1968, 354–71; 'The Divine Agent and his Counterfeit in Philo and the Fourth Gospel' in E. S. Fiorenza, ed., *Aspects of Religious Propaganda in Judaism and Early Christianity*, Notre Dame, Ind., 1976, 43–67; C. H. Holladay, *Theios Anēr in Hellenistic Judaism*, 108–55. If this is the reference, then it is part of the pervasive Moses-typology in the Fourth Gospel: if even Moses is called 'God', then *a fortiori*. . . . Cf. also T. F. Glasson, *Moses in the Fourth Gospel*, SBT 40, London and Naperville 1963; Meeks, *The Prophet-King: Moses Traditions and the Johannine Christology*; Schillebeeckx, *Christ*, esp. 306–21.

[89] So Brown, *John* I, 409. The interpretation of 'gods' to mean angels by J. A. Emerton, *JTS*, n.s. 11, 1960, 329–32; 17, 1966, 399–401, though evidenced in late Judaism, fits the context neither of the psalm (cf. vv. 2–4) nor of John (cf. v. 33, 'a mere man'). Meeks, 'Divine Agent', 65, agrees.

[90] So Sidebottom, *Christ of the Fourth Gospel*, 55.

[91] *Interpretation*, 271; *According to the Scriptures*, 47.

[92] Of John 10.33–36 J. E. Davey, *The Jesus of John*, 37, wrote: 'This form of argument was such as no early Christian, whether Jew or Gentile, was likely to formulate; it gives a moral and functional meaning to divinity in men, and does not set Christ clearly apart from other men, as the Church tended more and more to do; therefore I think we may claim the argument here as in nucleus historical and a foundation pillar of *John*.'

[93] Cf. R. A. Culpepper, 'The Pivot of John's Prologue', *NTS* 27, 1981, esp. 17–31, for the Jewish background which John shared to this language of sons/children of God. He quotes (21) this striking passage from Philo: 'But they who live in the knowledge of the One are rightly called "sons of God" (υἱοὶ θεοῦ), as Moses also acknowledges when he says, "Ye are sons (υἱοί) of the Lord God" (Deut. 14.1), and "God who begat thee" (32.18), and "Is not He Himself thy father?" (32.6). . . . But if there be any as yet unfit to be called a Son of God (υἱὸς θεοῦ), let him press to take his place under God's First-born, the Word (λόγον), who holds the eldership among the angels, their ruler as it were. And many names are his, for he is called "the Beginning", and the Name of God, and His Word, and the Man after His image, and "he that sees", that is Israel. And therefore I was moved a few pages above to praise the virtues of those who say that "We are all

you may recognize and know that the Father is in me, and I in the Father.' And this is what is meant by his earlier statement that started the controversy: 'My Father and I are one' (10.30). It is not a distinctive metaphysical identity,[94] which would be exclusive to Christ, but moral and spiritual unity, potentially open to all. For believers are to be one (ἕν) 'just as (καθώς) we are one' (17.21–23): the Johannine καθώς[95] links Father, Son and believers in a great analogy of being.

This stress on the functional and ethical understanding of sonship is *not* just 'mere' functionalism, making an 'ism' of the functional and repudiating the metaphysical. Indeed John's language is not merely functional any more than it is merely symbolic. But it is symbolic, and profoundly symbolic. Similarly it is functional because sonship is *most really*, at the level of spirit and of truth, to do with relationship rather than status, with verbs rather than substantives (let alone substances). Yet it is not anti-metaphysical, and later theology was not wrong to draw it out in this direction. For John is profoundly concerned with how things really are, with τὸ ἀληθινόν. What was distortive was to subject his language to an ontology which opposed being and doing and sought to postulate another ground for Jesus' union with the Father than that of pure ἀγάπη, and one therefore which set an unbridgeable metaphysical divide between the Son of God and the children of God.

Any attempt to establish an ontological *as distinct from* a moral basis for the unique sonship of Jesus in this Gospel is I believe wrong-headed and purely on linguistic grounds doomed to failure.[96] Jesus' sonship for John is one of its kind (μονογενής) *because of* his *total*

sons (υἱοί) of one man" (Gen. 42.11). For if we have not yet become fit to be thought sons of God (θεοῦ παῖδες) yet we may be sons of His invisible image, the most holy Word. For the Word (λόγος) is the eldest-born image of God' (*Conf. ling.* 145–7; tr. F. H. Colson and G. H. Whitaker, LCL). Culpepper acknowledges his debt here to M. Hengel, *The Son of God*, ET London and Philadelphia 1976, 51–6. But he fails here or elsewhere to mention John 10.33–8, presumably because the clause from Ps. 82.6 on which the argument ultimately hangs, 'and you shall all be called sons of the Most High', is not explicitly quoted.

[94]As Bultmann insists, *John*, 387 n. 2, it is a statement of revelation, not of cosmological theory.

[95]Twenty-one times in the Gospel with theological significance, plus ὥσπερ twice.

[96]Pollard begins his article 'The Father–Son and God–Believer Relationships' (*Évangile*, 363): 'Some years ago in a far too brief discussion of the Father–Son relationship within the context of St John's Gospel [*Johannine Christology and the Early Church*, 1970, 17], I ventured to criticize C. K. Barrett's assertion that the sonship of Jesus has both an ontological and a moral sense for John' (though for Barrett's position cf. his note on 10.30; *John*, 382). I venture to think that he would have done better not to have had second thoughts!

moral unity, and the moral unity *is* for John that which is most really real. The later (Greek) distinction and debate about whether he is one with the Father by 'nature' or by 'will' is not only anachronistic but distortive for the interpretation of John. Just as this Gospel is most historical when it is most theological, so it is most metaphysical when it is most moral, and *vice versa*. The personal union of Son with Father is the ultimate reality; and the basis of that is drawn out in the first Epistle with the statement that 'God *is* love', with its corollary that '*anyone* who dwells in love dwells in God, and God in him' (I John 4.16).

For John there is no division, however paper-thin, between metaphysics and morals, knowing and loving. For disciple as for master the designation and definition of what it means to be ἐκ θεοῦ (and the same preposition of origin, as we have seen, applies to both) is in terms of 'doing the will'. There is ultimately no distinction between 'abiding in him' (whether it be Father or Son; cf. I John 2.24) and 'abiding in love'. That is why the process of being 'born of God' or of 'passing from death to life' can be expressed, and had to be expressed, indifferently in terms of believing and of loving:

> Anyone who gives heed to what I say and believes in him who sent me has hold of eternal life, and does not come up for judgment, but has already crossed over from death to life (John 5.24).
>
> We for our part have crossed over from death to life; this we know, because we love our brothers. The man who does not love is still in the realm of death (I John 3.14).

The verification and therefore the meaning of being from (ἐκ) or in (ἐν) God is the life of love. And this has to be reiterated time and again:

> Everyone who does justice is born of him (I John 2.29). This is the distinction between the children of God and the children of the devil. No one who does not do justice is of God, nor is anyone who does not love his brother (3.10; cf. 3.17f.; 4.20).
>
> Everyone who loves is born of God and knows God. But he who does not love does not know God, because God is love (4.7f.).
>
> The one who does good is of God (III John 11).

Yet this is no substitute for faith (as if John were teaching justification by works) or even its corollary or consequence. It is the meaning of faith. For

> Everyone who believes that Jesus is the Christ is born of God; and

everyone who loves the parent loves the child. By this we know that we love the children of God when we love God and do his commandments (I John 5.1f.).

The indicative and imperative are but two sides of the same coin. Hence only he who 'does the will' can 'know the doctrine', whether it be 'of God' (John 7.17). There is no 'pure' theology: all Christian theology is moral theology, political theology. That is why, at first sight surprisingly, this most 'spiritual' of the Gospels has been recognized and seized upon not only by the Gnostics but (I believe more truly to itself) by the liberation theologians. For much of the above I owe to a book by the remarkable Mexican scholar José Miranda, who in the course of a short career has been a professor of mathematics, of economic theory, of philosophy, of the philosophy of law, and of biblical exegesis: *Being and the Messiah: The Message of St John*.[97]

Cullmann too makes the interesting observation that even if the ancient version of the singular 'who was born' in John 1.13 were original it would not prove that John had in mind a distinctively virginal conception of Jesus. He renders it, 'He gave the power to become the children of God to those who believe in the name of him who was born not of blood, nor of the will of the flesh, nor of the will of man, but of God', and comments: 'This is a typical Johannine idea, expressed also by Paul: *our* sonship is grounded in the sonship of *the* Son and becomes a reality through him.'[98] There may also be in I John 5.18 an interesting equivalent of Paul's insistence that Christ is 'the first-born among many brothers' (Rom. 8.29; cf. Heb. 2.10), where 'everyone who *has been* born of God' is kept from sin by 'him who *was* born of God'.[99] Unless the singular is original in John 1.13, this is the only time that John uses 'born of God' of Jesus as he does frequently of believers. But if it is the correct interpretation it designates him *the* son of God '*par excellence*',[100] not by exception or exclusion.

[97]Esp. 73–100. He also makes the valid point that this 'linkage' is not just the creation of John but goes back, as far as we can be sure of anything, to Jesus himself (and indeed behind him to the whole Hebraic tradition, as in Jer. 22.15: 'Did not your father . . . do justice and righteousness? . . . Is not this to know me, says the Lord?'). For according to the Synoptic tradition also Jesus defined sonship in terms of being 'true' to the character of the Father: 'You will be sons of the Most High, because he himself is kind to the ungrateful and the wicked' (Luke 6.35; cf. Matt. 5.9, 44f.).

[98]*Christology of the NT*, 296f.

[99]The interpretation of the verse is disputed, though that given here is that of the majority of commentators and both the RSV and the NEB (which paraphrases). Cf. Brown, *Epistles of John*, 619–22, who comes down against but also paraphrases.

[100]So Dodd, *Johannine Epistles*, 138.

For to be son is not to have a unique ontological or biological status: it is to allow God wholly and utterly to be the Father. But in the case of only one man can that truly be said to have been done. That is why the designation 'son' is reserved by John (unlike Paul) for Jesus alone: others, however close, are only 'children' of God, and that through him. Yet this is not because he is divine and they are not, but because only he 'always does what is acceptable to him' (8.29). He is unique because he alone is truly normal, standing where every son of Adam should stand, not because he is abnormal. This does not mean that he was an ordinary man. Indeed, as W. F. Lofthouse put it (in another largely forgotten book), 'If we could tolerate the paradox, we might say that he was man because he was what no man had ever been before . . . Christ did not become what men were; he became what they were meant to be, and what they too, through accepting him, actually became.'[101] And for this very reason, and not because he is more than man, but because he allows the Father to be everything, all that the Father has is his and all he has is the Father's (16.15; 17.10). As a truly and totally human being he is utterly transparent to and therefore of the Father, so that to see the Son is to see the Father (8.19; 12.45; 14.9). And the nature of this moral and spiritual union is mutual love (3.35; 10.17; 14.31; 15.9f.; 17.23f., 26), the fully personal relationship of reciprocal indwelling – exactly analogous to that which is to be shared by believers (17.21). 'What is true of one relation must be true of the other.'[102] Jesus, in Whitehead's language, is not the metaphysical exception, but the supreme exemplification – unique, but representative not exclusive. And this is what is implied by the climax of the Prologue, that the Logos, the self-expressive activity of God in all nature, history and humanity, finally comes to expression, not simply in a people, that refused (except partially) to receive him, but fully and utterly in a person, who perfectly reflected him as his very mirror-image.

So what finally is John's understanding of incarnation, and is it so different?

[101] *The Father and the Son: A Study in Johannine Thought*, London 1934, 115, 118; quoted by Pollard, *Fullness of Humanity: Christ's Humanness and Ours*, Sheffield 1982, 86. It is a merit of this book that he commends the work of both Lofthouse and Davey (83–6).

[102] Lofthouse, *The Father and the Son*, 120. He goes on to make the point that this does not mean that John has a low, or 'merely' moral, understanding of personal union. 'The real objection (if objection it be) is not that the Johannine doctrine is meagre or thin. It is, if anything, so rich and audacious as to frighten us by its refusal to stop short till it has placed us where Christ is' (121).

5. *Pre-existence and Incarnation*

At this point I should like to return to the restatement of Johannine christology by James Dunn which I mentioned earlier.[103] In his masterly survey, from whose scope and strength particular criticisms must not be allowed to detract, John is presented as the odd man out in the company of the New Testament writers. Neither Paul nor the author to the Hebrews nor any of the rest, he thinks, presents Christ as a personal pre-existent heavenly being; but John does. John represents the decisive step towards the christology of Nicaea, of the eternal divine Son of God who took on human nature. 'Only with the Fourth Evangelist', he believes, 'is the implication of a sonship of degrees or stages left behind', and 'only in the Fourth Gospel can we speak of a doctrine of the incarnation.'[104] Yet I am not convinced that he has put his finger on the right place in identifying the difference or describing the distinctiveness of John.

There is no doubt whatever that for John there is a decisively new situation introduced with Jesus. As Dunn puts it elsewhere, with him the boundary is crossed between inspiration and incarnation: Jesus is 'the man Wisdom became – not merely inspired, but became.'[105] But this is said – and well said – of Paul and the Epistle to the Hebrews. Similarly Dunn recognizes the decisive step introduced at John 1.14 as the transition from 'impersonal personification to actual person',[106] for which only the language of incarnation is appropriate. In Jesus the Logos is '*identified* with a particular person'. This is the great new thing. But is it the great new thing of Christianity or of John?

I suggest it is the former – and that it is precisely what Paul is saying, e.g., in Col. 1.19, that 'in him the complete being of God, by God's own choice, came to dwell.' The subject in each case is the self-expressive activity and being of God. Dunn recognizes that up to John 1.14 there is nothing in the Prologue that would have been strange to a Hellenistic Jew. The Word is 'the utterance of God personified' and it is incidental that in Greek the word λόγος is masculine, rather than feminine like σοφία (wisdom) or neuter like πνεῦμα (spirit); ῥῆμα (as in Isa. 55.11 and Acts 10.37), also neuter, might equally have established itself. But in v. 14 the Logos becomes personalized and not just personified, comes into being as a particular person: 'The Word of God is identified with a

[103]In what follows I have expanded material from an article 'Dunn on John' which appeared in *Theology* 85, 1982, 332–8.

[104]*Christology in the Making*, 256, 259.

[105]Ibid., 212.

[106]Ibid., 243.

particular historical person.' But he goes on: 'whose pre-existence as a person with God is asserted throughout'.[107] It is this latter clause that I would question – of John as much as of any other New Testament writer.

On the contrary I would say that John's position is essentially contained in a series of statements Dunn makes to sum up the earliest understanding of the church:

> Initially at least Christ was not thought of as a divine being who had pre-existed with God but as *the climactic embodiment of God's power and purpose . . . God's clearest self-expression, God's last word.*
>
> *The Christ-event defined God more clearly than anything else had ever done.*
>
> 'Incarnation' means initially that *God's* love and power had been experienced in fullest measure in, through and as this man Jesus, that Christ had been experienced as God's self-expression.[108]

This I believe is precisely what John sums up in 1.18 when he says that Jesus Christ as Son of God has given an 'exegesis' of the Father.

Where I would differ from Dunn is in my conviction that John gives us the richest and most mature interpretation of this 'initial' doctrine of incarnation, not that he changes it into something else – which Dunn claims[109] can for the first time properly be described as a 'myth', that of a heavenly divine figure who becomes man. Yet the personification of Wisdom as God's companion and agent in creation is surely just as 'mythical'; it is merely a different myth.

What I believe John is saying is that the Word, which was *θεός* (1.1), God in his self-revelation and expression, *σὰρξ ἐγένετο* (1.14), was embodied totally in and as a human being, became a person, was personalized not just personified. But that the Logos came into existence or expression as a person does not mean that it was a person before. In terms of the later distinction, it was not that the Logos was hypostatic (a person or hypostasis) and then assumed an impersonal human nature, but that the Logos was anhypostatic until the Word of God finally came to self-expression not merely in nature and in a people but in an individual historical person, and thus *became*

107 *Christology*, 250.
108 Ibid., 262. Italics his.
109 Ibid., 262.

hypostatic.[110]

This distinction, I believe, is vital in order to guard John's christology, and our own, from the charge of docetism to which it has so often been subjected. For John, I am convinced, as for all the other New Testament writers, Jesus is genuinely and utterly a man who so completely incarnates God that the one is the human face of the other.[111] This is precisely what John Bowker seems to be saying in the restatement in modern terms, considerably less pellucid, one may say, than John's, which Dunn commends, of Jesus as 'the wholly God-informed person'. 'It is possible on this basis', concludes Bowker, 'to talk about a wholly human figure, without loss or compromise, and to talk also of a wholly real presence of God so far as that nature . . . can be mediated to and through the process' of a human life.[112]

This quotation, of which I have merely given an extract, occurs in a footnote to a statement of Dunn's that

> We honour [John] most highly when we follow his example and mould the language and conceptualizations in transition today into a gospel which conveys the divine, revelatory and saving significance of Christ to our day as effectively as he did to his.

For prior to this Dunn shows himself uneasily conscious that the way John put it (as he interprets it) cannot really be ours today, and indeed that he was perhaps being taken for something of a ride by the 'cultural evolution' of the late first century:

> It could be said that the Fourth Evangelist was as much a prisoner of his language as its creator. . . . That is to say, perhaps we see in the Fourth Gospel what started as an elaboration of the Logos-Son imagery applied to Jesus inevitably in the transition of conceptualizations coming to express a conception of Christ's personal pre-existence which early Gnosticism found more congenial than early orthodoxy.[113]

I agree that this happened, but I believe it happened to John rather than in John, and that he was 'taken over' by the gnosticizers. In evidence I would cite again the Johannine Epistles, which are saying in

[110]So P. Schoonenberg, *The Christ*, ET London 1972, 54–66, 80–91.

[111]Cf. Schillebeeckx, *Christ*, 431: 'For John, Jesus is really man, but in a unique, all-surpassing relationship with God. Anyone who knows him knows the Father (8.19).'

[112]J. Bowker, *The Religious Imagination and the Sense of God*, Oxford 1978, 187f.; quoted by Dunn, *Christology*, 352.•

[113]*Christology*, 264.

effect: 'If *that's* what you think I meant, that I was teaching a docetic-type christology – denying Christ come in the flesh and trying to have the Father without the Son – then this is the very opposite: it is Antichrist.'

Yet John is so near as well as so far. It is entirely explicable that he should have been taken in this way. For the 'retrojective' process, which Geoffrey Lampe so well described in his Bampton Lectures,[114] of reading back the revelation of the Logos as 'a son', as a human being, that is, who at last perfectly imaged God as an only son his father, on to the revelation of 'the Son', a pre-existent heavenly being, later the Second Person of the Trinity, who became a man, was probably inevitable. The content of the Christian revelation of God in Jesus, in and as an individual person, was combined with the cultural transition in Judaism and Gnosticism to the notion of fully hypostatized celestial figures such as Son of Man and Son of God, to produce this result.[115]

Now the parable or simile 'as in a son', to use Theodore of Mopsuestia's language which is John's too (1.14), is, as we have seen, allegorized as 'the Son' in relation to 'the Father' not only in John (1.18) but in Mark (13.32) and Q (Matt. 11.27 = Luke 10.22). Yet, as Dunn rightly argues, that does not imply the personal pre-existence of a heavenly being in the theology of the Synoptists, let alone in the consciousness of Jesus. But when he comes to John he contends that the *combination* of the wisdom christology of the Logos-hymn (which he

[114] *God as Spirit*, 39f.

[115] Dunn agrees with me (cf. *The Human Face of God*, ch. 5, esp. 149–54) that this shift began, though I would stress only began, about the end of the first century AD. John, on my reckoning, antedates this development. Yet nothing turns on this dating. For still in the mid-second century Justin Martyr presupposes the older non-hypostatized way of thought, personifying activities or agencies of God: 'I shall give you another testimony . . . from the Scriptures, that God begat before all creatures a Beginning (or, in the beginning, before all creatures), a certain rational power (or, spiritual force, λογικὴ δύναμις) from himself, who is called by the Holy Spirit, now the Glory of the Lord, now the Son, again Wisdom, again an Angel, then God, then Lord and Logos' (*Dial.* 61). 'The Son' is here still seen as a variant name of 'the power of God'; and equally in the Spirit-christology of Hermas (*Sim.* 5.5f.) 'the πνεῦμα which God makes to dwell in the flesh of Jesus is regarded not as a divine person, but as a divine power' (A. Grillmeier, *Christ in Christian Tradition*, ET London and New York 1965, 92). So too in the Odes of Solomon, which are clearly later than John (though perhaps not much), the presuppositions of Jewish Wisdom literature remain determinative: e.g., 'There is nothing outside the Lord, because he was before anything that came to be. And the words were made by his Word, and by the thought of his heart' (16.18f.). Whether here or elsewhere the Odist is actually presupposing the Gospel of John, this is evidence of how his Logos teaching would have been understood in early Christian circles.

thinks, I believe improbably, is pre-Johannine but agrees does not in itself require to be read as speaking of a pre-existent Person) with John's dominant Son of God christology produces an entirely different situation. And in fact it is this latter Son of God language rather than the Logos language as such which compels him to this conclusion.

Yet is John really so divergent at this point from the rest of the New Testament? Dunn fully accepts that initially this language 'had no overtones of pre-existence',[116] and that even when Paul speaks of God 'sending his own Son' (Gal. 4.4) or of 'the second man from heaven' (I Cor. 15.47) this does not necessarily imply *personal* pre-existence. I would agree with him. Moreover I have long interpreted Philippians 2 along the same lines as he does,[117] as telling not of a divine being who became man but of a man whose entire being was 'shaped' by God (ἐν μορφῇ θεοῦ), perfectly reflecting his nature and glory, who yet chose to live the poverty-stricken, humiliating form of existence common to all other men. The deepest veriest significance of Jesus Christ, what at bottom he really was (ὑπάρχων), is phrased not so much in terms of pre-existence (there is no such explicit language in Philippians 2) as of true existence. So it is with the Johannine Son of Man, whose whole life, as the authentic man, has its source, centre and goal in God. This true existence is of course given expression in terms of eternal existence, of above rather than below, of the heavenly rather than the earthly. But it is important to recognize what is happening here. Otherwise the impression will quickly be given that Jesus is *not* truly an earthly, historical human being at all. And John more than anyone else can be quoted for statements of pre-existence which appear to throw radical doubt on the genuineness of his humanity – such as his being before Abraham (8.58) or sharing the Father's glory before the world began (17.5; cf. 17.24). How could such a man be normally human, let alone normative of humanity?

It is important in the first place to understand the logic which led to such assertions of pre-existence.[118] The Samaritan woman asks of Jesus 'Are you greater than our father Jacob?' (4.12) and the Jews 'Are you greater than our father Abraham?', with the rider 'What do you claim to be?' (8.53). It is the same claim made by Jesus in the Synoptists that 'a greater than Solomon is here' (Matt. 12.42 = Luke 11.31), or 'a

[116] *Christology*, 244. Cf. Schillebeeckx, *Christ*, 317, '"To be sent from God" does not mean pre-existence in itself; as such it has a different content.'

[117] Cf. my *Human Face of God*, 162–6, and *The Roots of a Radical*, 68.

[118] I am grateful at this point for a communication by Professor Morna Hooker to the New Testament seminar at Cambridge in April 1982.

greater than the temple' (Matt. 12.6), and which is focused in his challenging question about the Messiah, 'David himself calls him "Lord"; how can he also be David's son?' (Mark 12.37 and pars.). If he is superior, then he cannot simply be posterior. *Precedence implies priority*. And this logic is made explicit in John's Gospel from the beginning, when the Baptist says of Jesus (as Dodd translates 1.15 and 30): 'There is a man in my following who has taken precedence of me, because he is and always has been essentially my superior.' That he ranks above me must mean that he is before me. In the same way the fact that Abraham (8.56), Moses (5.46) and Isaiah (12.41) point to Jesus as their fulfilment means that he is their superior and therefore before them. And this primacy finds expression not only as priority, being 'before' all, but as superiority, being 'above all' (3.31), and as ultimacy, being there at 'the last day' (5.21–9; 6.54). Yet these are all statements about *this man*, this son of man (cf. especially 5.27: he has authority to judge because he is 'son of man' or 'a son of man').[119] They are made not to question his humanity but to enhance it. In fact when the Baptist reiterates the assertion of Jesus' priority in 1.30 he adds the word ἀνήρ: to say that Jesus is 'before' him is not to lift him out of the ranks of humanity but to assert his unconditional precedence. To take such statements at the level of 'flesh' so as to infer, as 'the Jews' do that, at less than fifty, Jesus is claiming to have lived on this earth before Abraham (8.52, 57), is to be as crass as Nicodemus who understands rebirth as an old man entering his mother's womb a second time (3.4). These are not assertions about the ego of the human Jesus, which is no more pre-existent than that of any other human being. Nor are statements about the glory that he enjoyed with the Father before the world was to be taken at the level of psychological reminiscence. As such they would clearly be destructive of any genuine humanness, whereas for the Johannine Jesus the revelation of 'what I saw in my Father's presence' (8.38) is described unequivocally only two verses later as the work of '*a man* who told you the truth as I heard it from God' (8.40). Again, to confuse theological verity with psychological verisimilitude is to confound everything. Yet at the level of spirit and truth (4.23; 3.6), of ζωή (6.63) rather than *βίος*, the voice with which Jesus speaks and the authority with which he acts and claims allegiance is that of the Word which transcends time and space.

There are two ways in which Jesus' way of speaking (λαλιά) is

[119]Sidebottom, *Christ of the Fourth Gospel*, 93–7, argues strongly that the absence of the article here (as with 'son of God' in 10.36 and 19.7) is not accidental, and is meant to indicate that 'Jesus judges by virtue of his manhood'.

misunderstood and his word therefore cannot be 'heard' (8.43) that are reflected in the Fourth Gospel and its subsequent interpretation. The first is to take the 'I' of such utterances at the level of the ego of Western empiricism, and so make nonsense of his humanity. The other is to go in the opposite direction and see him as usurping the divine name, as for instance Stauffer[120] does when he interprets the 'I am' of this Gospel as claiming identification with the 'I am he' (*ani hu*) of Yahweh in the Old Testament. But this I believe to be an equal misreading which can be shown to be such by careful attention to the text.

Of the 'I am' sayings in this Gospel, those with a predicate ('I am the bread of life', 'the door', 'the way', 'the good shepherd', etc.) certainly do not imply that the subject is God. As Barrett rightly says, 'ἐγώ εἰμι does not identify Jesus with God, but it does draw attention to him in the strongest possible terms. "I am the one – the one you must look at, and listen to, if you would know God".'[121] If there is a proto-Gnostic style to this formula (which must remain doubtful, since all the evidence, especially the Mandaean on which Bultmann relied so heavily, is later), it is that of the mystagogue, the initiator into and revealer of the divine secrets, not of God himself.[122] Borgen detects here 'a midrashic formula for identifying Old Testament words with a person in first person singular, a formula which can . . . be used to refer to John the Baptist and Trajan as well as to Jesus Christ' and argues that 'in the homily of John 6.31–58 the "Ego eimi" sayings can definitely be explained on the background of Old Testament and Judaism.'[123] I believe he is too definite, but there is so far nothing to suggest any claim to divinity.

Of the 'absolute' uses of ἐγώ εἰμι, the majority are simply establishing identification: 'I am he.'[124] This is so of 4.26 (the Messiah you speak of); 6.20 (confirming Jesus' identity on the lake at night, exactly

[120] *Jesus and His Story*, 142–9; cf. Bernard, *John* I, cxvi–cxxi.

[121] *John*, 342; cf. 98.

[122] Cf. G. W. MacRae, 'The *Ego*-Proclamation in Gnostic Sources' in Bammel, ed., *Trial of Jesus*, 122–34: 'There is no positive indication . . . that the Gnostics were aware of the absolute use of ἐγώ εἰμι as a claim to divinity, nor is there any reason to suggest that this Gnostic usage [by the Demiurge of the text of Isa. 45.18, 'I am God and there is no other'], is indebted to the Christian use of Deutero-Isaiah or to the claims of Jesus' (129). He opposes the interpretation of Stauffer.

[123] *Bread from Heaven*, 72, 158. He admits that the '*I am* the voice of one crying in the wilderness' on the lips of the Baptist in John 1.23 lacks the copula.

[124] There is not even a clear division between the two classes. Thus 8.18, 'I am the one who witnesses about myself', is rightly rendered by the NEB, 'Here I am, a witness in my own cause.' It is a reminder too of how precarious it is to count up *seven* 'I ams' (cf. also 8.23). For differentiation into further classes, cf. Bultmann, *John*, 225 n. 3.

as in Mark 6.50; Matt. 14.27); 9.9 (on the lips not of Jesus but of the blind man); and 18.5–8, the 'I am your man' at the arrest (cf. Acts 10.21), even though it evokes awe (though *not* the reaction to blasphemy)[125] in the arresting party. There is the same usage in the resurrection scene of Luke 24.39, 'It is I myself', where John does *not* have it just where we might expect it, any more than he has an equivalent to the 'I am' of Mark 14.62 at the climax of the Jewish trial. Three other occurrences (8.24, 28; 13.19) are I believe correctly rendered by the NEB 'I am what I am', namely, the truth of what I really am. They do not carry with them the implication that he is Yahweh (indeed in the latter two especially there is *contrast* with the Father who sent him) but, in Johannine terms, 'the Christ, the Son of God'.[126] Barrett is unusually emphatic at this point. Referring to 8.28 he writes, 'It is simply intolerable that Jesus should be made to say, "I am God, the supreme God of the Old Testament, and being God I do as I am told"'; and to 13.19, 'I am God, and I am here because someone sent me.'[127] The sole remaining instance is 8.58, 'Before Abraham was born, I am'. This certainly asserts pre-existence,[128] as in the Baptist's statement of 1.15 and 30, but there, as we saw, the subject is specifically designated 'a man'. That Jesus is arrogating to himself the divine name is nowhere stated or implied in this Gospel.[129] Even 'the Jews' do not accuse him of this – only of calling God 'his own Father', and thereby implying

[125]Bernard, *John* II, 587, who believes there is an echo of the divine name elsewhere denies it here. The Old Testament background suggests to him that 'ἔπεσαν χαμαί might be rendered in colloquial English "were floored".'

[126]Cf. E. D. Freed, '*EGŌ EIMI* in John 8.24 in the Light of its Context and Jewish Messianic Belief', *JTS*, n.s. 33, 1982, 163–7, who argues that the phrase is specifically Messianic.

[127]*Essays on John*, 12f.; cf. 69–71.

[128]Barrett perhaps is too dismissive: '8.58 soon falls out of the discussion, for the main sense is here that of the continuous being of the Son' (*Essays on John*, 12). But I agree with his conclusion: 'Jesus' EGŌ EIMI is not a claim to divinity; John has other ways, both more explicit and more guarded, of making this claim' (71).

[129]So Schweizer, *Ego Eimi*, 44 n. 241; Bultmann, *John*, 327f.; Barrett and Lindars on John 8.58. Brown (*John*, Appendix IV, I, 533–8) and Dodd (*Interpretation*, 95f.) argue that Jesus can thus speak because he has been 'given' the divine 'name' (17.11f.). But this is in order to reveal and pass it on to the disciples (17.6, 26), and the fact that he comes (5.43) and does everything in the Father's name (10.25) does not mean that he is being identified with Yahweh but that he has been accredited by him, exactly as in Exod. 23.21, 'my name is in him', which the NEB rightly renders 'my authority rests in him'. If there are 'overtones' of the divine name in ἐγώ εἰμι it is certainly not its primary meaning for John; and his christology, with its strong subordination of Jesus to the Father, would not suggest that they were intended to be heard. Indeed I believe that they would have been as blasphemous to him as to 'the Jews'.

equality with God (or as H. Odeberg[130] interprets this from rabbinic parallels, rebellious independence, being 'as good as God') (5.18). What they take to be the blasphemy of making himself 'a god' in 10.33 is again made clear to be a misunderstanding of Jesus calling himself 'God's son' (10.36). It is inconceivable, if Stauffer's interpretation were the correct one, either in the evangelist's intention or in the mind of Jesus' opponents, that it should not come out in the charges against him at the trial, where again the worst that can be said about him is that he claimed to be 'God's son' (19.7, again without the article).

If then the 'I' with which Jesus speaks is neither that simply of the individual ego nor of the divine name, what is it? I suggest that it is to be understood as the totality of the self, of which Jung spoke in contrast with the ego. As he saw it,[131] the Christ-figure is an archetypal image of the self, the God-image in us, 'consubstantial' alike with the ground of our being and with our own deepest existence. It is the 'I' of the mystics, who make the most astonishing claims to be one with God, without of course claiming to *be* God,[132] the 'I' of Meister Eckhart and Angelus Silesius, of the Sufis and the Upanishads, where *atman* and *Brahman* are completely 'one', as in John 10.30. Such is Bede Griffiths' interpretation, born of long exposure to this tradition. In his latest book he says of Jesus,

> In the depths of his being, like every human being, he was present to himself, aware of himself, in relation to the eternal ground of his being. In most people this intuitive awareness is inchoate or imperfect, but in the great prophet and mystic, in the seer like Gautama Buddha or the seers of the Upanishads, this intuitive knowledge of the ground of being becomes a pure intuition, a total awareness. Such according to the tradition of St John's Gospel (which in its origin is now considered to be as old as that of the other gospels) was the nature of the knowledge of Jesus. He knew himself in the depth of his spirit as one with the eternal ground of his being.[133]

[130] *The Fourth Gospel*, 203.

[131] C. J. Jung, *Aion, Collected Works* IX.2, ET London 1959, 37–9. As he is always careful to insist, *he* is writing at the level of psychology not theology, but these categories can usefully be applied in a theological context to what is true at the level of πνεῦμα and not simply of σάρξ.

[132] E.g., Catherine of Genoa: 'My "I" is God, and I know no other "I" but this is my God.' For other examples cf. my *Truth is Two-Eyed*, 1979, 10f.

[133] *The Marriage of East and West*, London 1982, 189. This is true without prejudice to the question *how* others may enter this relationship potentially open to all, on which the Upanishads and John would differ. For John the right to become the children of

Westcott indeed believed that the great commentary on St John waited to be written by an Indian – though I doubt if this will happen until Indian theology has risen above its tendency to depreciate the historical or to absorb the 'thou' of personal union to the 'that' of impersonal identity.[134] But it is Buber the Jew – shall we say 'the Israelite without guile' of this Gospel? – who perhaps gets nearest to what John is indicating by his *ἐγώ εἰμι*:

> How powerful, even to being overpowering, and how legitimate, even to being self-evident, is the saying of *I* by Jesus! For it is the *I* of unconditional relation in which the man calls his *Thou* Father in such a way that he is simply Son, and nothing else but Son. Whenever he says *I* he can only mean the *I* of the holy primary word that has been raised for him into unconditional being.[135]

There is nothing here that is not utterly and 'superly' human, as well as being totally transparent of God. To have seen the one is to have seen the other, without either being dissolved in the other. The 'I' that says 'I and the Father are one' is as unequivocally human as the 'I' that says 'I thirst'. There can be no residue or trace of a christology that says that Jesus said or did some things as God and some things as man. That is wholly alien to the interpretation of John. He did everything as the integral human being who was totally one with his Father and with all other men, so that in him the fullness of deity as well as the fullness of humanity becomes visible. The distinctive thing about that 'I' is not that it was *not* human but that it was *wholly* one with the self-expressive activity of God, and thus *uniquely* human. What he was the Logos was and what the Logos was God was, so that in his 'I' God is speaking and acting. Bultmann in his commentary on John gets it succinctly by making a careful distinction: 'In Jesus' words God speaks the *ἐγώ εἰμι*. We should, however, reject the view that *ἐγώ εἰμι* means "I (Jesus) am God".'[136]

What John is doing, here as elsewhere, is, I am convinced, drawing

---

God, to stand to God as Father exactly as (*καθώς*) Jesus does, comes only *through* him (1.12). But the norm and the goal are the same for all humanity: being totally 'one' with the Father and in him with all being.

[134]The best study I know so far is C. Duraisingh and C. Hargreaves, edd., *India's Search for Reality and the Relevance of the Gospel of John*, Delhi 1975.

[135]*I and Thou*, ET R. Gregor Smith, Edinburgh and New York 1937, 66f. Cf. my reference in 'The Use of the Fourth Gospel for Christology Today', *Twelve More NTS*, 152f., to Greville Norburn's picture of the 'charismatic man'.

[136]*John*, 327 n. 5.

out what is already there in the rest of the Christian tradition. for the 'I' of this Gospel is already in principle that of the Synoptics.[137] It is the 'I' of the great 'I have come' (ἦλθον, ἐλήλυθα) which declare the purpose of his mission and are common to all the Gospels (Mark 2.17 and pars.; 10.45 and pars. (where Luke substitutes 'I am' for 'the Son of Man came'); Matt. 5.17; 10.34f.; Luke 12.49; 19.10; John 5.43; 9.39; 10.10; 12.46f.; 16.28; 18.37; etc.);[138] the 'I' to whom everything is given by his Father in the most intimate personal union (Matt. 11.25 = Luke 10.21f.); in whose person God's rule is made present (Matt. 12.28 = Luke 11.20); who in the name of the divine Wisdom speaks the invitation of God (Matt. 11.28–30; cf. Ecclus. 51.23–7) and sends his emissaries (Matt. 23.34; cf. Luke 11.49); the 'I' of the Sermon on the Mount, who goes behind what was said not merely by them of old time (AV) but to them by God on Sinai (Matt. 5.21–48); the 'I' who says '*Amen*, I say to you' (nearly twice as often in the Synoptists as in John); who as the Son of Man on earth is Lord of the sabbath (Mark 2.28), enjoying the same superiority, as John is to bring out (5.16f.), to the sabbath-rest as the Creator himself; who pronounces the forgiveness of sins (Mark 2.1–12, cf. Luke 7.48f.), thereby stepping into the space reserved in the minds of his contemporaries for God (cf. John 5.18); who quells the powers of demons and of nature (Mark 1.23–27; 4.35–41; cf. the ἐγώ of 9.25), and exercises before the time the prerogatives of the last judgment, saying that men's attitude to him will decide God's attitude to them (Mark 8.38 and par.; Matt. 10.33 = Luke 12.9; cf. John 14.21; 15.23); the 'I' too, as in John, who will dispense the Father's Spirit (Luke 21.15, in conjunction with Matt. 10.19f.; 24.49; Acts 2.33; John 15.26) and promises his abiding presence (Matt. 18.20; 28.20; John 14.3, 18–20, 23, 28; etc.).

In John this 'I' is portrayed and projected, backwards and forwards, in terms of the pre-existence and post-existence of a heavenly person. But that is the language of myth, picturing the other-side, as Bultmann would put it, in terms of this side. It is pushing the truth of the sonship that Jesus embodied back to the very beginning of God's purpose – as well as, with the Synoptists, forward to its end. For John, as for the author to the Hebrews, it is through the Son and on account of the Son

[137]Cf. E. K. Lee, *The Religious Thought of St John*, London 1950, 60f.: 'The difference between the Synoptists and John is not a difference between a human Jesus and a divine Christ. We can discern in Mark and the document called Q a Christology as profound as that found in John. . . . If the Fourth Gospel displays a more mature reflexion of the Person of Christ, the author only makes explicit what is implicit in the earlier records.'

[138]Cf. Noack, *Zur johanneischen Tradition*, 50f.

and the bringing of many sons to glory that all things are done that are done. But all this is but drawing out to recognition the full cosmic significance of what was disclosed in the 'glory' of this utterly human life. John, again, differs only in the maturity with which he elicits and elaborates the 'initial' understanding of incarnation, common in principle to all the New Testament writers. He has not, I think, as Dunn suggests (even if only in the form of a question expecting the answer 'yes'), 'left behind the earlier idea of God acting in and through the Christ-event' by presenting 'Christ . . . conceived as a heavenly being distinct from God'.[139]

When writing of Paul, Dunn says perceptively:

> Did he think of Christ as a man, a created being, chosen by God for this purpose, perhaps even appointed to this cosmic role as from his resurrection? or alternatively, as a heavenly being who had pre-existed with God from the beginning? Texts in Paul could readily be interpreted either way. The more plausible interpretation however is that such alternatives had not yet occurred to him: his overwhelming conviction was that God himself had acted in and through Christ, that what happened in the whole Christ-event was God himself opening the way for man for righteousness and redemption, and that this had been the same power and purpose through which and for which God had created the world.[140]

I believe that with little modification of phraseology the same statement could be made about John. The alternative Dunn poses is, I suggest, a false one for both John and Paul. Each has statements which, as he says, could be pushed in either direction, and I am persuaded that he sets up a misleading polarization between John and the rest of the New Testament by taking the statements of Paul, Hebrews and the Synoptists one way and those of John the other. The issue is not for either camp a choice between a 'mere man' christology and a 'divine being' christology. Hebrews and John are I believe much closer than he allows in presenting a real, and not merely an 'ideal', pre-existence and a genuinely incarnational theology, though *not* of a heavenly being who came to earth in the form of a man, but of a man shaping and embodying in its fullness the self-expressive activity of God from the beginning.

To sum up the Johannine presentation of the incarnation I should be

[139] *Christology in the Making*, 263.
[140] Ibid., 255.

perfectly happy to take over the wise words of T. W. Manson, whose judgment was always so sound. He wrote of John in material published posthumously:

> I very much doubt whether he thought of the Logos as a personality. The only personality on the scene is 'Jesus the son of Joseph from Nazareth'. That personality embodies the Logos so completely that Jesus becomes a complete revelation of God. But in what sense are we using the word 'embodies'? I think in the old prophetic sense, but with the limitations that attached to the prophets removed. The word that Isaiah speaks is the word of the Lord, but it is also Isaiah's – it has become part of him. Not every word of Isaiah is a word of the Lord. For John every word of Jesus is a word of the Lord.[141]

Having drawn the line between John and the other New Testament writers at what seems to me the wrong place, Dunn fails, I believe, to do justice to the real difference (or at any rate a real difference) between their presentations, which is again not one of kind but of degree. Let me put it like this.

Both Paul and still more the writer to the Hebrews *combine* pre-existence language with what might be called 'designatory' language, taken over from the early formulations of Christ's significance as 'a man approved, or singled out, by God' (Acts 2.22; etc.). This is the kind of language which by later standards can appear so adoptionist. Thus, in Paul Jesus is 'appointed' (as Dunn says ὁρισθέντος should be rendered)[142] 'Son of God from the resurrection' (Rom. 1.3f.) and after being raised to the heights has bestowed on him the 'name above all names' (Phil. 2.9). Again, in Hebrews he is 'made heir' (1.2), 'becomes superior to the angels' (1.4), is 'anointed (or, made Christ) above his fellows' (1.9), 'perfected' (2.10; 5.9; 7.28); and most explicitly perhaps there is 5.5f.: 'He did not confer upon himself the glory of becoming high priest: it was granted by God, who said to him, "Thou art my son; today I have begotten thee."'

As has often been observed, this 'today' is pushed back in the reflection of the early church from the resurrection (it may even have begun, if I am correct in my interpretation of Acts 3.12–26, as a messianic appointment still to be confirmed at the Parousia)[143] to the

[141] *On Paul and John*, 156f.
[142] *Christology in the Making*, 34.
[143] Cf. my 'The Most Primitive Christology of All?', *Twelve NTS*, 139–53.

baptism, to the birth of Jesus, and indeed, in Hebrews and Colossians at least, to the beginning. In John the process is complete: there is no moment when he 'becomes' Son of God. The role which he occupies, his designation by the Father as 'the son of his love',[144] antedates the birth of this historical individual, or the call of Israel, or the creation of Adam as 'son of God' (cf. Luke 3.38): the relationship is from before the world was, from the ἀρχή, whether it is expressed in terms of υἱός or εἰκών or λόγος.

But it must also be recognized, as I am not sure that it is by Dunn, that the 'designatory' language has not simply disappeared in John (thus suggesting the transition of which he speaks from degree to kind). What has happened is that it too has been set at the beginning, so pre-empting any impression, properly repudiated in later doctrine, of God lighting upon Jesus as an afterthought. As the predestinarian terms that accompany it in Hebrews or Paul or I Peter make clear, that is a false inference even in the rest of the New Testament. But John is careful to give it no handle. As we have seen, in this Gospel also Jesus is 'sealed' (6.27) and 'consecrated' (10.36) by God, in language not dissimilar from that of Hebrews, where the Son is a 'priest appointed by the words of an oath' (7.28). Yet in Hebrews this happens only *after* he is 'made perfect'. In John it takes place from the start.[145] True, its 'finishing', as in Hebrews, has to await the moment of his 'glorification' and 'exaltation' (for there *is* a moment when Jesus is 'not yet glorified' [7.39], 'not yet ascended to the Father' [20.17]). Yet both of these are viewed by John as a *return* to what obtained before (3.13f.; 6.62; 17.5) – to his true state, as in Phil. 2.5–11, of being always at home with God (8.29, 35; cf. Luke 2.49), 'nearest to the Father's heart' (1.18). And it is this that gives the counter-impression, which I believe to be equally false, that for John, in contrast with the author to the Hebrews, Jesus was not a real man. He was just as real. But if this *man*, as Hebrews also insists, was 'the reflection of God's glory and the stamp of his very being' (Heb. 1.2f.), then, as John comes to see it, the glory, or the 'name', must have been 'given' him not merely after his exaltation (as in Philippians) but from the beginning (17.11f.,[146] 22, 24; cf. 5.22, 26f.; 13.3; 17.2).

[144]As is well recognized, ἀγαπητός and John's μονογενής are virtual synonyms. Cf. e.g. Th. C. de Kruijf, 'The Glory of The Only Son (John 1.14)' in *Studies in John: Presented to Dr J. N. Sevenster*, *NovT* Suppl 24, Leiden 1970, 111–23.

[145]Cf. p. 371 above.

[146]According to what is clearly the more original and difficult text it is 'the name' (rather than the disciples) which has been given to Jesus.

Finally one must ask how the language of 'God' applies to Jesus.[147] That 'the Logos is God' (1.1), God expressing himself, is not in doubt, nor that the Logos is uniquely and fully embodied in and as this human person. He is God 'as in a son', God 'uniquely begotten', if that is the true reading and interpretation of 1.18. Yet Jesus has God for his Father as much as any other human being: he speaks of him as 'my God and your God' (20.17). Nevertheless a few verses further on Thomas uses exactly the same expression, 'my God', of *him* (20.28). For in this human friend and companion (cf. 11.16, 'let us go that we may die *with* him') he recognizes the one in whom the lordship of God meets him and claims him, though not as a heavenly being but as a wounded yet transfigured man of flesh and blood, whose glorification lay in making himself nothing so that in him God might be everything. This is the language, not of ontological identity nor simply of functional equivalence, but of existential embodiment.

Perhaps Brown, as so often, gets the balance right when he comments on an earlier passage (10.32–39):

> Such a description of Jesus is *not* divorced from the fact that Jesus was sent by God and acted in God's name and in God's place. Therefore, although the Johannine description and acceptance of the divinity of Jesus has ontological implications (as Nicaea recognized in confessing that Jesus Christ, the Son of God, is himself true God), in itself this description remains primarily functional and not too far removed from the Pauline formulation that 'God was in Christ reconciling the world to Himself' (II Cor. 5.19).[148]

For John, Jesus is not God *simpliciter*. Jesus is a man who incarnates in everything he is and does the Logos who is God. He is the Son, the mirror-image of God, who is God for man and in man. The 'I' of Jesus speaks God, acts God. He utters the things of God, he does the works of God. He is his plenipotentiary, totally commissioned to represent him – *as* a human being. He speaks and acts with the 'I' that is one with God, utterly identified and yet not identical, his representative but not his replacement – and certainly not his replica, as if he were God dressed up as a human being. He is not a divine being who came to

[147]On this cf. G. H. Boobyer, 'Jesus as "Theos" in the New Testament', *BJRL* 50, 1967–8, 247–61, specif. 259f.; Brown, *Jesus God and Man*, Milwaukee, London and Dublin 1968, 1–38; B. Mastin, 'A Neglected Feature of the Christology of the Fourth Gospel', *NTS* 22, 1975–6, 32–51.

[148]*John* I, 408.

earth, in the manner of Ovid's *Metamorphoses*, in the form of a man, but the uniquely normal human being in whom the Logos or self-expressive activity of God was totally embodied. As Cullmann sums it up, '*Jesus Christ is God in his self-revelation.*'[149] But, to use the later distinction, he was *totus deus*, everything that God himself is, not *totum dei*, the whole of God. For there are greater things to come and to be revealed (14.12; 16.12f.). As well as being the only Son (μονογενής), he is, in New Testament terms, also the first-born (πρωτότοκος), not the exclusive or terminal embodiment of God, but the beginning, the ἀρχή, of a new mutual indwelling of God with men. For 'of his fullness have *we all* received' (1.16). It is only as 'they are in us' 'just as thou, Father, art in me and I in thee' (17.21), and not *simply* as God is glorified (or vindicated) in the Son (12.28), that the divine love comes to its 'perfection' (I John 2.5; 4.12, 17f.). This is but another way of saying that the locus of the incarnation or the 'Christ-event' is not simply the one man Christ Jesus but, as John Knox has put it, 'the human community in which that event culminated and in which, in the measure of the Church's fidelity, it is perpetuated. . . . "God was in Christ" but "Christ" is a broader term than "Jesus".'[150]

6. *John's Contribution to Christology Today*

So in closing we may come back to the question of how the Gospel of John may be used for our christology, of what doctrine, both of the doctrine of Christ's person and of the Trinity, can properly be built upon his foundation and what difference giving priority to his portrait should make.

The Fourth Gospel has traditionally served as the foundation for the 'Alexandrian' model of christology that came out on top at Nicaea and Chalcedon, epitomized in the work of Athanasius and Cyril. This does not mean to say that the christology of these Councils which defined Christian 'orthodoxy' was simply that of Alexandria – the Antiochenes had their concerns safeguarded too, and they of course also used John, as did the Arians earlier. But the *interpretation* of Chalcedon that was

[149] *Christology of the NT*, 325. Italics his.

[150] In a long private letter of 18 February 1982, chiding me for the absence of this emphasis (so long one of his great contributions: cf. especially, *The Church and the Reality of Christ*) from the chapter 'Honest to Christ Today' in my *Roots of a Radical*, 59–77. As he acknowledges, I bring it out in other ways; but I am grateful to have this opportunity of paying tribute to all that I have received from him as a scholar and very dear friend.

sanctioned in the Letters of Cyril which the Council endorsed clearly gave the edge to those who wished to understand Christian orthodoxy, as the dominant theology of the Middle Ages did, in a quasi-docetic, monophysite *direction*. And for this model the Gospel of John was *par excellence* the tool. It supplied the key texts for the christology of the heavenly Person, God the Son, who came down from heaven to take human nature and become man.

We have argued that in this John was 'used', and that this was not his christology. It is only by the retrojection of the personhood of the human Jesus on to the divine Logos to make him a heavenly being prior to the incarnation that this schema can be read into or read out of John. How then can he properly be used?

Let me start from a quotation from a book which though only just over twenty years old is now largely forgotten, though its author still lives in retirement a few miles from me in the Yorkshire Dales. It seems older, since it antedates the 'new look' and, to all intents and purposes, the difference which the Dead Sea Scrolls and the new Gnostic texts have made to the perspective in which John is now viewed. But in the direction in which it pleads, for a reconsideration of the historicity of John and not least in its assessment of his christology, it comes close to the position for which I have been arguing. It is a work which I have had occasion to refer to in passing from time to time, *The Christ of the Fourth Gospel* by E. M. Sidebottom. In it he writes:

> We may thus see how near and how far from the Chalcedonian theology is the Fourth Gospel. Jesus is Man as God intended him; he lives the life God intended and as such is Son of God: because he thus lives, signs appear which reveal his glory, his relation to God. The Son then is son in the only true sense – the sense in which John uses the word 'true':[151] he shares his Father's character. This is no more than to say that he is true Son of Man.[152]

He does not in fact offer to say how near or how far in his judgment this christology is from Chalcedon. It is certainly a long way from the doctrine of the one divine Person in two natures and from that of *anhypostasia*, that the Logos was hypostatic (a person) but the

[151]He refers at this point to his earlier discussion, on p. 129, of the 'good' shepherd, who is good at his job, the 'true' vine, the stock which fruits true, like the ἄμπελος ἀληθινός of Jer. 2.21 or the goodly vine of Ezek. 17.8.

[152]162f. Cf. his *Good News of God*, London 1982, 26: 'Jesus' sonship itself depends on his shared character with God.'

humanity not, though this latter doctrine was only implicit in Chalcedon and was repudiated by the Antiochenes. Yet, if one is going to use the language of substance, John is not at all far from the central and essential affirmation of Jesus' 'consubstantiality', both with us and with God, or, as John Hick was to retranslate it,[153] *homoagapē*, or oneness of love with the Father and with all men. Later on Sidebottom puts it thus of the Johannine Christ:

> The sonship to God is not in contrast to the manhood. It consists in the relationship which exists between Jesus and God. . . . That the eternal Son of Man is the Word of God is expressed in terms of his sonship to God, because in this aspect he embodies and so reveals the divine character. . . . John does not think in terms of person and substance. He merely thinks of the Man who embodies the will or kingdom of God, who is still a man but so related to God as to be his son. . . . but for John the Man *is* the divine Word, and this involves his obedience and likeness to the Father.[154]

What is the meaning of this 'is'? I suggest it is the same as when John says 'the Word *was* God' (1.1), which the NEB I believe gets fairly precisely with its 'what God was the Word was'. It is a statement of equivalence rather than of identification. It is not reversible, so that one could say that God *was* the Word, simply and without remainder. In the same way, for John the man Jesus was the Word of God, or as Sidebottom suggests,[155] 'the word for God', God spelt out in human terms. Everything about him bespoke God; to have seen him was to have seen the Father. Yet he was not simply God, nor God he. The same care has to be exercised, as Vatican II observed, over the uncritical assertion that the Holy Catholic Church *is* the Roman Catholic Church. They are not merely interchangeable. Rather one must say that the Holy Catholic Church *subsists in*, rather than consists of, the Roman Catholic Church. So, to be true to John, we should say that the Word of God subsisted in the man Jesus, *utterly and completely*, that he was *totus deus*, God all through, his perfect reflection and image, but not that he was *totum dei*, all there is of God. Yet this last is not what catholic Christianity has ever meant, but rather that God was fully incarnate in him. And in this I believe John is wholly in line with

[153]'Christology at the Cross-Roads' in F. G. Healey, ed., *Prospect for Theology: Essays in Honour of H. H. Farmer*, London 1966, 137–66.

[154]*Christ of the Fourth Gospel*, 194f.

[155]Ibid., 48.

catholic Christianity and catholic Christianity with him.[156] To allow the Johannine Christ to stand forth, from under what churchmen and scholars alike have often made of him, fully a man of our history and uniquely his Father's son, is, I believe and hope, both a service to that faith and a fulfilment, in less triumphalist language than that to which the eighteenth century accustomed him, of the will of the Reverend John Bampton.

[156]Of course this has far-reaching implications for a corresponding doctrine of the Trinity. It is clear that patristic and mediaeval theology misused the Fourth Gospel by taking its christological statements out of context and giving them a meaning which John never intended. Functional language about the Son and the Spirit being sent into the world by the Father was transposed into that of eternal and internal relationships between Persons of the Godhead and words like 'generation' and 'procession' given technical meanings which New Testament usage simply will not substantiate. One small example may suffice for this note. Under the influence of the Arian controversy Jerome translated *μονογενής* of Jesus as *unigenitus* (John 1.14, 18; 3.16, 18; I John 4.9; of all others, except Isaac in Heb. 11.17, he preserves the *unicus* of the Old Latin [Luke 7.12; 8.42; 9.38], as well as in the texts from the Apocrypha); and this became perpetuated in the AV as 'only begotten'. Yet the word does not derive from γεννᾶν but γένος; it means 'one of its kind' (cf. p. 375 above). And this means, as Edward Schillebeeckx says outright (*Christ*, 875 n. 57), that 'there is no basis in Johannine theology for the later scholastic theology of the procession of the Son from the Father within the Trinity *per modum generationis* (birth).'

Such transpositions from the Johannine vocabulary have been the traditional foundation of the doctrine of the Trinity. But if they are removed, it remains to be seen what will be left from the wreckage. In my article 'The Fourth Gospel and the Church's Doctrine of the Trinity', *Twelve More NTS*, 171–180, I have discussed this problem more fully and attempted to contribute to the reconstruction that lies ahead.

Select Bibliography

Abrahams, I., *Studies in Pharisaism and the Gospels*, 2 vols., Cambridge 1917, 1924.

Askwith, E. H., *The Historical Value of the Fourth Gospel*, London 1910.

Bammel, E., ed., *The Trial of Jesus: Cambridge Studies in Honour of C. F. D. Moule*, SBT 2.13, London and Naperville 1970.

Barrett, C. K., *The Gospel according to St John* (1955), London and Philadelphia [2]1978.

— *The Gospel of John and Judaism*, London and Philadelphia 1975.

— *Essays on John*, London and Philadelphia 1982.

Benoit, P., *Jesus and the Gospel* I, ET London and New York 1973.

Bernard, J. H., *A critical and exegetical Commentary on the Gospel according to St John*, ICC, 2 vols., Edinburgh and New York 1928.

Bickermann, E., 'Utilitas Crucis: Observations sur les récits du procés de Jésus dans les Évangiles canoniques', *RHR* 112, 1935, 169–241.

Black, M., *An Aramaic Approach to the Gospels and Acts*, [3]Oxford 1967, New York 1968.

Blinzler, J., *The Trial of Jesus*, ET of 2nd ed., Westminster, Md. 1959; *Der Prozess Jesu*, revised and enlarged, Regensburg [4]1969.

Boismard, M.-É., *Synopse des Quatre Évangiles en français* III: *L'Évangile de Jean*, Paris 1977.

Borgen, P., *Bread from Heaven: An Exegetical Study of the Concept of Manna in the Gospel of John and the Writings of Philo*, *NovT*Suppl 10, Leiden 1965.

Braun, F.–M., *Jean le Théologien*: I, *Jean le Théologien et son Évangile dans l'église ancienne*; II, *Les grands traditions d'Israël et l'accord des Écritures selon la Quatrième Évangile*, Paris 1959, 1964.

Brown, R. E., *New Testament Essays*, Milwaukee 1965.

— *The Gospel according to John*, 2 vols., Anchor Bible 29–29A, New York 1966, 1971, London 1971.

— *The Community of the Beloved Disciple*, New York and London 1979.

— *The Johannine Epistles*, Anchor Bible 30, New York 1982.

Bultmann, R., *The Gospel of John: a Commentary* (1941), ET Oxford and Philadelphia 1971.
— *Theology of the New Testament*, 2 vols., ET New York and London 1952, 1955.
— *The History of the Synoptic Tradition*, ET Oxford and New York [2]1968.
— *The Johannine Epistles*, ET Hermeneia, Philadelphia 1973.
Catchpole, D. R., *The Trial of Jesus: a Study in the Gospels and Jewish Historiography from 1770 to the Present Day*, Leiden 1971.
Charlesworth, J. H., ed., *John and Qumran*, London 1972.
Cullmann, O., *The Christology of the New Testament*, ET London and Philadelphia [2]1963.
— *The Johannine Circle: Its Place in Judaism, among the Disciples of Jesus and in Early Christianity*, ET London and Philadelphia 1976.
Culpepper, R. A., *The Johannine School*, SBLDS 26, Missoula, Mont. 1975.
Danby, H., tr., *The Mishnah*, Oxford 1933.
Davies, W. D., *The Gospel and the Land*, Berkeley, Calif. and London 1974.
Dodd, C. H., *The Johannine Epistles*, Moffatt NT Commentary, London and New York 1946.
— *According to the Scriptures*, London 1952, New York 1953.
— *The Interpretation of the Fourth Gospel*, Cambridge and New York 1953.
— *Historical Tradition in the Fourth Gospel*, Cambridge and New York 1963.
— *The Founder of Christianity*, New York 1970, London 1971.
Dunn, J. D. G., *Christology in the Making*, London and Philadelphia 1980.
Edwards, H. E., *The Disciple Who Wrote These Things*, London 1953.
Edwards, R. A., *The Gospel according to John*, London and Toronto 1954.
Fortna, R. T., *The Gospel of Signs: A Reconstruction of the Narrative Source underlying the Fourth Gospel*, SNTSMS 11, Cambridge 1970.
France, R. T., and Wenham, D., edd., *Gospel Perspectives*, 2 vols., Sheffield 1980–81.
Gardner-Smith, P., *Saint John and the Synoptic Gospels*, Cambridge 1938.
Gerhardsson, B., *The Origins of the Gospel Traditions*, ET Philadelphia and London 1979.

Harvey, A. E., *Jesus on Trial: A Study in the Fourth Gospel*, London 1976, Atlanta, Ga. 1977.

— *Jesus and the Constraints of History* (Bampton Lectures), London and Philadelphia 1982.

Headlam, A. C., *The Fourth Gospel as History*, Oxford and New York 1948.

Higgins, A. J. B., ed., *New Testament Essays: Studies in memory of T. W. Manson*, Manchester 1959.

— *The Historicity of the Fourth Gospel*, London 1960.

Holland, H. Scott, *The Fourth Gospel*, Part Two of *The Philosophy of Faith and the Fourth Gospel*, London and New York 1920, published separately 1923.

Hoskyns, E. C., *The Fourth Gospel*, ed. F. N. Davey, 2 vols., London and Chicago 1940.

Howard, W. F., *The Fourth Gospel in Recent Criticism*, London 1931; 4th ed., rev. C. K. Barrett, London and Naperville 1955.

Hunter, A. M., *According to John*, London and Philadelphia 1968.

Jeremias, J., *Jerusalem in the Time of Jesus*, ET London and Philadelphia 1969.

— *New Testament Theology* I: *The Proclamation of Jesus*, ET London and New York 1971.

Jonge, M. de, ed., *L'Évangile de Jean*, BETL 44, Louvain 1977 (cited as *Évangile*).

Käsemann, E., *The Testament of Jesus: A Study of the Gospel of John in the Light of Chapter 17*, ET London and Philadelphia 1968.

Kümmel, W. G., *Introduction to the New Testament*, ET London and Nashville ²1975.

Kysar, R., *The Fourth Evangelist and His Gospel: an Examination of Contemporary Scholarship*, Minneapolis 1975.

Lightfoot, John, *Horae Hebraicae et Talmudicae: Hebrew and Talmudical Exercitations upon the Gospels, the Acts . . .*, rev. ed. by R. Gandell, Oxford 1859.

Lightfoot, Joseph Barber, *Biblical Essays*, London and New York 1893.

Lindars, B., *Behind the Fourth Gospel*, London 1971.

— *The Gospel of John*, New Century Bible, London 1972.

Mackowski, R. M., *Jerusalem, City of Jesus*, Grand Rapids, Mich. 1980.

Manson, T. W., *Studies in the Gospels and Epistles*, ed. M. Black, Manchester and Philadelphia 1962.

— *On Paul and John*, ed. M. Black, SBT 38, London and Naperville 1963.

Martyn, J. L., *History and Theology in the Fourth Gospel*, New York and Evanston 1968.
— *The Gospel of John in Christian History*, New York 1979.
Meeks, W. A., *The Prophet-King: Moses Traditions and the Johannine Christology*, *NovT*Suppl 14, Leiden 1967.
— 'The Man from Heaven in Johannine Sectarianism', *JBL* 91, 1972, 44–72.
— '"Am I a Jew?" Johannine Christianity and Judaism' in J. Neusner, ed., *Christianity, Judaism and Other Greco-Roman Cults: Studies for Morton Smith* I, Leiden 1975, 163–86.
Metzger, B. M., *A Textual Commentary on the Greek New Testament*, London and New York 1971.
Morris, L. L., *Studies in the Fourth Gospel*, Exeter and Grand Rapids, Mich. 1969.
Odeberg, H., *The Fourth Gospel Interpreted in its Relation to Contemporary Religious Currents in Palestine and the Hellenistic-Oriental World*, Chicago 1928, Uppsala 1929.
Robinson, J. Armitage, *The Historical Character of St John's Gospel*, London and New York [2]1929.
Robinson, J. A. T., 'The Temptations', *Theology* 50, 1947, 43–8, reprinted in *Twelve NTS*, 53–60.
— 'The Parable of the Shepherd (John 10.1–5)', *ZNW* 46, 1955, 233–40, reprinted in *Twelve NTS*, 67–75.
— 'The "Parable" of the Sheep and the Goats', *NTS* 2, 1955–6, 225–37, reprinted in *Twelve NTS*, 76–93.
— 'The Most Primitive Christology of All', *JTS*, n.s. 7, 1956, 177–89, reprinted in *Twelve NTS*, 139–53.
— *Jesus and His Coming*, London and New York 1957.
— 'The Baptism of John and the Qumran Community', *HTR* 50, 1957, 175–91, reprinted in *Twelve NTS*, 11–27.
— 'Elijah, John and Jesus: An Essay in Detection', *NTS* 4, 1957–8, 263–81, reprinted in *Twelve NTS*, 28–52.
— 'The "Others" of John 4.38', *StEv*, TU 73, 1959, 510–15, reprinted in *Twelve NTS*, 61–6.
— 'The New Look on the Fourth Gospel' (a paper delivered to the Oxford Conference on 'The Four Gospels in 1957'), *StEv*, TU 73, 1959, 338–50, reprinted in *Twelve NTS*, 94–106.
— 'The Destination and Purpose of St John's Gospel', *NTS* 6, 1959–60, 117–31, reprinted in *Twelve NTS*, 107–25.
— 'The Destination and Purpose of the Johannine Epistles', *NTS* 7, 1960–61, 56–65, reprinted in *Twelve NTS*, 126–38.

Robinson, J. A. T., *cont.*

— 'The Significance of the Foot-Washing' in *Neotestamentica et Patristica: Eine Freundesgabe Herrn Professor Dr Oscar Cullmann zu seinem 60. Geburtstag überreicht*, Leiden 1962, 144–7, reprinted in *Twelve More NTS*, 77–80.

— *Twelve New Testament Studies*, SBT 34, London and Naperville 1962, cited as *Twelve NTS*.

— 'The Relation of the Prologue to the Gospel of St John', *NTS* 9, 1962–3, 120–29, reprinted in *Twelve More NTS*, 65–76.

— 'The Place of the Fourth Gospel' in P. Gardner-Smith, ed., *The Roads Converge: A Contribution to the Question of Christian Reunion . . .*, London and New York 1963, 49–74.

— *Exploration into God*, Stanford, Calif. and London 1967, reissued London and Oxford 1977.

— *The Human Face of God*, London and Philadelphia 1973.

— 'The Use of the Fourth Gospel for Christology Today', in B. Lindars and S. S. Smalley, edd., *Christ and Spirit in the New Testament: Studies in Honour of C. F. D. Moule*, Cambridge 1973, 61–78, reprinted in *Twelve More NTS*, 138–54.

— 'The Parable of the Wicked Husbandmen', *NTS* 21, 1974–5, 443–61, reprinted in *Twelve More NTS*, 12–34.

— *Redating the New Testament*, London and Philadelphia 1976.

— 'The Shroud and the New Testament' in P. Jennings, ed., *Face to Face with the Turin Shroud*, Great Wakering, Essex, and Oxford 1978, 69–80, reprinted in *Twelve More NTS*, 81–94.

— *Truth is Two-Eyed*, London and Philadelphia 1979.

— *The Roots of a Radical*, London and New York 1980.

— 'Did Jesus Have a Distinctive Use of Scripture?', in R. F. Berkey and S. A. Edwards, edd., *Christological Perspectives: Essays in Honor of H. Harvey K. McArthur*, New York 1982, reprinted in *Twelve More NTS*, 35–43.

— 'Dunn on John', *Theology* 85, 1982, 332–8.

— '"His Witness is True": A test of the Johannine claim', in C. F. D. Moule and E. Bammel, edd., *Jesus and the Politics of his Day*, Cambridge and New York 1984, 453–76, reprinted in *Twelve More NTS*, 112–37.

— *Twelve More New Testament Studies*, London and Philadelphia 1984, cited as *Twelve More NTS*.

— 'The Fourth Gospel and the Church's Doctrine of the Trinity', *Twelve More NTS*, 171–80.

Robinson, J. M., and Koester, H., edd., *Trajectories through Early*

Christianity, Philadelphia 1971.

Ruckstuhl, E., *The Chronology of the Last Days of Jesus*, ET New York 1965.

Sanday, W., *The Authorship and Historical Character of the Fourth Gospel*, London 1872.

— *The Criticism of the Fourth Gospel*, Oxford and New York 1905.

Sanders, E. P., Baumgarten, A. I., and Mendelson, A., edd., *Jewish and Christian Self-Definition* II. *Aspects of Judaism in the Graeco–Roman Period*, London and Philadelphia 1981 (cited as *Self-Definition* II.)

Sanders, J. N., *The Fourth Gospel and the Early Church*, Cambridge and New York 1943.

— *A Commentary on the Gospel according to St John*, ed. B. A. Mastin, London and New York 1968.

Schillebeeckx, E., *Christ: the Christian Experience in the Modern World*, ET London and New York 1980.

Schnackenburg, R., *The Gospel according to St John*, 2 vols., ET London and New York 1968, 1982.

— *Die Johannesbriefe*, Theologischer Kommentar zum Neuen Testament, Freiburg ^{2}1963, ^{4}1970.

Schürer, E., *The History of the Jewish People in the Age of Jesus Christ*, new ET, rev. G. Vermes, F. Millar and M. Black, 2 vols., Edinburgh 1973, 1979 (cited as *History*).

Schweizer, E., *Ego Eimi. Die religionsgeschichtliche Herkunft und theologische Bedeutung des johanneischen Bildreden*, FRLANT 56, Göttingen 1939, ^{2}1965.

Sherwin-White, A. N., *Roman Law and Roman Society in the New Testament*, Oxford and New York 1963.

Sidebottom, E. M., *The Christ of the Fourth Gospel in the Light of First-century Thought*, London 1961.

Smith, D. M., *The Composition and Order of the Fourth Gospel: Bultmann's Literary Theory*, New Haven, Conn. and London 1965.

Stanton, V. H., *The Gospels as Historical Documents:* III. *The Fourth Gospel*, Cambridge 1920.

Stendahl, K., ed., *The Scrolls and the New Testament*, New York 1957, London 1958.

Westcott, B. F., *The Gospel according to St John: the Greek Text with Introduction and Notes*, 2 vols., London 1908.

Wilkinson, J., *Jerusalem as Jesus Knew It*, London and New York 1978.

Winter, P., *On the Trial of Jesus*, Berlin 1961.

Index of Modern Authors

* = editor
‡ = major references only (Barrett, Brown, Bultmann, Dodd)
+ = translator
Footnote numbers in brackets indicate that the author is discussed in the text and the footnote adds the reference only.

Index of References

'Cf.' preceding a page number indicates that 'cf.' precedes the reference in the text.

OLD TESTAMENT

APOCRYPHA AND PSEUDEPIGRAPHA

TESTAMENTS OF THE TWELVE PATRIARCHS

DEAD SEA SCROLLS

NEW TESTAMENT

PHILO

JOSEPHUS

RABBINICAL LITERATURE

MISHNAH

TOSEFTA

MEKILTA

BABYLONIAN TALMUD

JERUSALEM TALMUD

MIDRASH RABBAH

EARLY CHRISTIAN WRITINGS

OTHER ANCIENT AUTHORS